Handbook of Research on Economic and Political Implications of Green Trading and Energy Use

Ramesh Chandra Das
Vidyasagar University, India

IGI Global
DISSEMINATOR OF KNOWLEDGE

A volume in the Advances in Finance, Accounting, and Economics (AFAE) Book Series

Published in the United States of America by
IGI Global
Business Science Reference (an imprint of IGI Global)
701 E. Chocolate Avenue
Hershey PA, USA 17033
Tel: 717-533-8845
Fax: 717-533-8661
E-mail: cust@igi-global.com
Web site: http://www.igi-global.com

Library of Congress Cataloging-in-Publication Data

Names: Das, Ramesh Chandra, 1973- editor.
Title: Handbook of research on economic and political implications of green trading and energy use / Ramesh Chandra Das, editor.
Description: Hershey, PA : Business Science Reference, [2020]
Identifiers: LCCN 2018055813| ISBN 9781522585473 (hardcover) | ISBN 9781522585497 (ebook)
Subjects: LCSH: Environmental policy--Economic aspects. | Energy policy--Economic aspects. | Emissions trading.
Classification: LCC HC79.E5 E2655 2020 | DDC 363.738/747--dc23 LC record available at https://lccn.loc.gov/2018055813

This book is published in the IGI Global book series Advances in Finance, Accounting, and Economics (AFAE) (ISSN: 2327-5677; eISSN: 2327-5685)

British Cataloguing in Publication Data
A Cataloguing in Publication record for this book is available from the British Library.

Advances in Finance, Accounting, and Economics (AFAE) Book Series

Ahmed Driouchi
Al Akhawayn University, Morocco

ISSN:2327-5677
EISSN:2327-5685

Mission

In our changing economic and business environment, it is important to consider the financial changes occurring internationally as well as within individual organizations and business environments. Understanding these changes as well as the factors that influence them is crucial in preparing for our financial future and ensuring economic sustainability and growth.

The **Advances in Finance, Accounting, and Economics (AFAE)** book series aims to publish comprehensive and informative titles in all areas of economics and economic theory, finance, and accounting to assist in advancing the available knowledge and providing for further research development in these dynamic fields.

Coverage

- Managerial Accounting
- Stock Market
- Wages and Employment
- E-Accounting
- Macroeconomics
- Economics of Agriculture and Biotechnology
- Economic Downturn
- Theoretical Issues in Economics, Finance, and Accounting
- Economic Policy
- Internet Banking

IGI Global is currently accepting manuscripts for publication within this series. To submit a proposal for a volume in this series, please contact our Acquisition Editors at Acquisitions@igi-global.com or visit: http://www.igi-global.com/publish/.

The Advances in Finance, Accounting, and Economics (AFAE) Book Series (ISSN 2327-5677) is published by IGI Global, 701 E. Chocolate Avenue, Hershey, PA 17033-1240, USA, www.igi-global.com. This series is composed of titles available for purchase individually; each title is edited to be contextually exclusive from any other title within the series. For pricing and ordering information please visit http://www.igi-global.com/book-series/advances-finance-accounting-economics/73685. Postmaster: Send all address changes to above address.

Titles in this Series

For a list of additional titles in this series, please visit: www.igi-global.com/book-series

Foreign Business in China and Opportunities for Technological Innovation and Sustainable Economics
Anna Visvizi (Deree – The American College of Greece, Greece) Miltiadis Lytras (Deree – The American College of Greece, Greece) Xi Zhang (Tianjin University, China) and Jie Zhao (Anhui University, China)
Business Science Reference • copyright 2019 • 284pp • H/C (ISBN: 9781522589808) • US $195.00 (our price)

Handbook of Research on Global Issues in Financial Communication and Investment Decision Making
Hasan Dinçer (Istanbul Medipol University, Turkey) and Serhat Yüksel (Istanbul Medipol University, Turkey)
Business Science Reference • copyright 2019 • 540pp • H/C (ISBN: 9781522592655) • US $365.00 (our price)

Behavioral Finance and Decision-Making Models
Tripti Tripathi (Jiwaji University, India) Manoj Kumar Dash (Khallikote University, India) and Gaurav Agrawal (Indian Institute of Information Technology and Management Gwalior, India)
Business Science Reference • copyright 2019 • 333pp • H/C (ISBN: 9781522573999) • US $215.00 (our price)

Global Challenges in Public Finance and International Relations
Deniz Şahin Duran (Tokat Gaziosmanpaşa University, Turkey) Yusuf Temür (Tokat Gaziosmanpaşa University, Turkey) and Doğan Bozdoğan (Tokat Gaziosmanpaşa University, Turkey)
Business Science Reference • copyright 2019 • 304pp • H/C (ISBN: 9781522575641) • US $225.00 (our price)

International Financial Reporting Standards and New Directions in Earnings Management
Jonas da Silva Oliveira (Instituto Universitário de Lisboa (ISCTE-IUL), Portugal) Graça Maria do Carmo Azevedo (University of Aveiro, Portugal) and Augusta da Conceição Santos Ferreira (University of Aveiro, Portugal)
Business Science Reference • copyright 2019 • 342pp • H/C (ISBN: 9781522578178) • US $225.00 (our price)

Throughput Accounting in a Hyperconnected World
Ionica Oncioiu (European Academy of the Regions, Belgium)
Business Science Reference • copyright 2019 • 362pp • H/C (ISBN: 9781522577126) • US $195.00 (our price)

Organizational Auditing and Assurance in the Digital Age
Rui Pedro Marques (University of Aveiro, Portugal) Carlos Santos (University of Aveiro, Portugal) and Helena Inácio (University of Aveiro, Portugal)
Business Science Reference • copyright 2019 • 404pp • H/C (ISBN: 9781522573562) • US $225.00 (our price)

IGI Global
DISSEMINATOR OF KNOWLEDGE

701 East Chocolate Avenue, Hershey, PA 17033, USA
Tel: 717-533-8845 x100 • Fax: 717-533-8661
E-Mail: cust@igi-global.com • www.igi-global.com

Editorial Advisory Board

List of Contributors

Table of Contents

Detailed Table of Contents

One major concern that has emerged in the post-globalization period is climate change. Given that pollution and environmental degradation is a public bad, the adverse change in the climate of one region will have ubiquitous effect and therefore will hamper the process of sustainable development across the globe. There are substantial links between international trade and environmental issues – one being that of the perverted comparative advantage which evolves mainly out of the neglect of environmental damage caused by productive activities. In this chapter, an attempt has been made to build a theoretical framework related to intra-industry trade with production differentiation based on the environmental quality of the goods and price to address how liberalization of trade happens to affect the environment of the trading nations. The study shows a steep decline in the environmental quality of the good that was relatively cleaner under autarky while a meagre improvement in the environmental quality of the relatively dirtier good. Hence, it is revealed hereby how trade alters the nature of international inequality in the environmental quality of the productive activities.

Higher technological developments, product diversity, international trade, and population growth have greatly increased the energy demand of countries. It is very significant that this growing demand should

This chapter deals with some contemporary issues related to trade and environment, which are mainly faced by the developing nations of the world. In this context, the present study has considered some facts and figures of Indian tannery industry for realization of the above-mentioned objective. In this chapter, an attempt has been made to analyze theoretically the effect of both environmental regulation and trade liberalization on the output of different sectors and also on the national welfare in a small open economy. To categorize this, the authors have presented a theoretical model based on the general equilibrium framework that mainly highlights a paradoxical result. Apart from this, the present research shows that the capital used specifically in advanced export sector is likely to affect the welfare positively, and the capital used by the rest of the economy is likely to affect the welfare adversely when usual export sector of the economy vanishes, and the opposite will occur when the pollution-intensive informal sector of the economy vanishes.

The chapter investigates the role of FDI on growth, the role of FDI on environmental quality, and the role of environmental quality on FDI in 23 emerging market economies over the period of 1993-2014 by panel VAR analysis. It observes that FDI contributes to economic growth and environmental degradation in emerging market economies. In addition, environmental degradation attracts FDI inflows into host emerging market economies. The results support pollution haven hypothesis and contradict pollution halo hypothesis.

In order to understand the role of sustainability in the era of development, the broader purpose of the chapter is to examine the quantitative linkages between HDI and environmental performance for the selected developed and developing nations from 2002 to 2017. To test if the degree of economic expansion and standard of living has a systematic relationship with the level of environmental deterioration (existence of Kuznets curve hypotheses) in a country, the study employs fixed effects panel modeling on the selected country set. Several other macroeconomic and capital flow variables are considered in the extended empirical model development in order to supplement the holistic review of the situation. In addition, the study finds its novelty by considering relevant governance indicators in order to map the umbrella view. The findings of the panel analysis discover HDI to be positively associated with EPI, depicting higher human capital accumulation leading to lower environmental damage and better environmental performance. Additionally, the results confirm the deviation from EKC hypotheses in the context of developing nations while the same is established in case of developed nations.

This chapter is on the use of the Sustainable Development Goals (SDGs) for the achievement of green economy in Nigeria with the specific aim of assessing the performance of key issues in the SDGs. Five goals SDGs 6, 7, 11, 12, and 15 for water and sanitation, safe human settlements, renewable energy, sustainable consumption and production, and ecosystem, respectively, are selected for assessment for the green initiatives and the economy. Budgets on economic and social services follows the pattern theory: that government allocates and reallocates at will without cognizance of the population's interests. The assessment holds the fact that only two of these goals are being met somehow—renewable energy and clean water—and not necessarily because of the need to achieve the goals but as part of private sector and dynamic market initiatives, clearly indicating failures for the others. For the most part, Nigeria failed in the areas of ecosystem, good human settlement, and responsible consumption. The chapter suggests the encouragement of entrepreneurial initiatives, the initiation of new policies on green economy, and the enforcement of regulations already in place to power the economy.

Over the last decade there has been a gradual change in the global energy landscape, with fast-growing emerging markets overtaking the traditional centers in terms of energy demand. International Energy Outlook 2017 forecasts that energy consumption in non-OECD countries would increase by 41% between 2015 and 2040 in contrast to a 9% increase in OECD countries. The chapter focuses on two major areas: (1) examining the changing pattern of the composition of energy use in the two selected countries of Asia (India and China) and (2) examining the short-run and long-run relationship among energy use, GDP per capita, energy intensity, use of electricity power, extent of urbanization. Using ARDL bound test for the period 1990 to 2014 for the World Development Indicator data 2017-18, it reveals that the powerhouses of global energy demand growth are led by the developing economies of Asia (i.e., China, India, Indonesia, Morocco, Brazil, Singapore, and Thailand). In the case of India, a long-run association has been found between energy use and GDP per capita, energy intensity, use of electricity power, and extent of urbanization, but no instances are for China.

Recently, the climate regulations and stop-loss regulations have become a central policy parameter globally. In market-oriented economies, insurers as the biggest stakeholder-industry of natural disaster risk are facing the issue related to industry sustainability. Thus, the policy implications of natural disasters regulation on the insurance industry are enormous. Therefore, this chapter has made an effort to analyze the disaster management in the integrated framework. This integrated framework is based upon the analysis of the role of regulatory actions taken by three actors, namely, disaster regulation, insurance regulations, and firms' actions across the three stages of disaster management, namely, pre-disaster, underwriting, and post-disaster stages in G-7 economies. Based on the outcomes of the current analysis, the chapter found that there are two polar opposite integrated models (i.e., isolated best policy model in the case of Japan and spiral policy model in the case of Italy). Five models fall in between the two.

The objective of the chapter is to analyze the role of the institutions in the biodiesel industry in order to know if there is a relationship with the quality and maturity of the same with the ventures. Starting from a literary review, the framework of the current situation is identified, covering aspects related to formal institutions, laws, rules, regulatory bodies, and the theory that supports the relationship between institutions and entrepreneurship. It is thus concluded that the institutions in Mexico have increased their maturity and incentive to increase the number of producers and distributors of biodiesel, thus taking advantage of the growing market.

After the Kyoto Protocol, the new concept of carbon trading emerged. The carbon emission can be controlled by cap and tax system. Cap and trade is the permit that determines the maximum amounts of carbon emission. Carbon tax is imposed on amount of carbon emission. Other instruments of carbon emission are border adjustment and cash payment. Carbon permit is determined by market mechanism through demand and supply. Generally, there are two types of markets: regulated and voluntary. The chapter analyzes mechanisms and discusses the mitigating policies like Kyoto Protocol and tries to examine all aspects related to carbon leakage. The developed countries import carbon-intensive goods. Underdeveloped countries produce and export carbon-intensive goods. In this study, the authors show the prospect of carbon trading and various effects of carbon emission reduction policies on a theoretical framework.

Renewable energy is energy that is collected from renewable resources that are essentially inexhaustible like sunlight, wind, hydropower, and various forms of biomass. India has a huge renewable energy potential, and the availability of renewable energy sources is widely dispersed. The key objectives of the chapter are to assess the state development of renewable energy in India. It is seen that the average

Foreword

Natural resource endowments on this planet earth are finite, sources of energy inputs in to the system in the shape of solar radiation are restricted, and waste absorption capacities of our ecosystems are limited. It is true that technology can address some of these limitations. But that too to an extent, since physical laws like conservation of mass and energy act as constraint on what can be done.

Gradual realization of these facts culminated into our current global concerns with the environment. These concerns rest on the common notion that natural resource exploitation and concomitant environmental modification has gone too far and has gone to the point where wellbeing of current and future generations are threatened. As a consequence, a global consensus has been gaining shape in the form of concrete policy making around the areas of environmental protection. One manifestation of such efforts is the serious query involving economic and political implications of green trading and green energy use. The present book, titled *Handbook of Research on Economic and Political Implications of Green Trading and Energy Use*, I hope, will serve the purpose of extending the extant knowledge base of such queries and help academic researchers of various disciplines and motivate environment related policy makers and executers.

Rabindra N. Bhattacharya
Jadavpur University, India

Rabindra N. Bhattacharya *is presently Honorary Adjunct Professor of Economics in the School of Oceanographic Studies, Jadavpur University, India. He has almost fifty years of teaching and research experience in various institutes in India & abroad (including SANDEE). His areas of interest are Natural Resource & Environmental Economics and Development Economics. Professor Bhattacharya has published around 50 papers in almost all the leading national and international journals on Environmental Economics including Journal of Environmental Economics and Management as well as in reputed edited volumes. He personally edited a book on Environmental Economics with Oxford University Press, India.*

Preface

Starting from the Kyoto Protocol, the world policy makers have been framing different guidelines and control mechanisms in the areas of environmental protection. Besides scientific inventions and innovations in controlling environmental pollution, the economists prescribe for indirect or market-based policies and direct control policies. Emission permit trading is one of the effective policies so far and widely applied in many economies. Industrial houses are now tending towards green products and the financial institutional are forwarding investible funds to the environmentally friendly industries on the priority basis. Hence, the term, 'green financing' or 'green trading', has come into global perspectives for about two decades. Implementation of green policy requires economics as well as political supports from different income earning countries in the world. Success of the greening policy will inevitably make the entire biodiversity better off.

Again, starting from the same protocol, an international agreement framed in 1997 linked to the United Nations Framework Convention on Climate Change which commits its Parties by setting internationally binding emission reduction targets, the world policy makers have been framing different guidelines and control mechanisms in the areas of environmental protection. The environmental summits in different years and in different locations of the globe have been also following the concerned guidelines and trying hard to achieve the environmental standards in terms of emissions of different pollutants. The initiatives in overall phenomenon are known as greening the global environment so that the countries can have sustainable developments. There is always a debate between economic growth and environmental pollution, in particular the appearance of Environmental Kuznets Curve (EKC) to speak of, to present the scenario of the debate. As economy grows, energy uses increases, environment gets polluted in one hand and natural resources get eroded, and pressure on the ambient environment increases which in turn puts costs on the human society in particular and biodiversity in general. To control environmental pollution, particularly off Green House Gases (GHGs), economists usually moves for market based solutions and institutional based solutions. Under the market based solutions, indirect pollution tax and tradable pollution permits are considered as the front runners in the field. Emission permit trading, or the Green Trading, has been widely applied in the EU Zones and US state levels that have their history of good performance as well as difficulties. Besides, there is huge debate at the diplomatic level with regard to implementation and structurizations of the emission standards in different countries. There is a list of studies and observations that the authorities and stake holders often involved in corruption while dealing with carbon financing, permit issues, etc. It thus calls for good governance to tackle the issue and foster towards sustainable development. Therefore, it is now required to have a fresh look on the studying of the economic and political implications of green trading and energy use for different types of countries in the world.

Based upon the above background the proposed book had tried to investigate the economic and political aspects of green trading and energy use in global perspectives. It tried to highlight the issues related to carbon trading, carbon credit, energy use and energy efficiency, impact of these factors on economic outputs, diplomatic conflicts in implementing the environmental policies, etc.

Upon the above milieu I wrote an edited book proposal to IGI Global, the USA based premier publisher at Pennsylvania. Thereafter the proposal faced different phases of reviews and scrutiny and finally it was accepted and the title of the book was short listed to *Handbook of Research on Economic and Political Implications of Green Trading and Energy Use*. Starting the journey from the writing of book proposal to assemblage of chapters of different authors round the globe, it is now an impassable gratification that the ongoing edited book project has finally been unearthed.

After invitation to the potential authors through the official website of the IGI Global and my personal networks for contributions to the said mission by chapter submission on the recommended topics, a number of chapters have been singled out after a double-blind peer review process. All the chapters have attempted to justify their positions in terms of standard quantitative analysis at per their capabilities. After the double-blind review and additional review by me, as editor, the number of chapters in revised form ultimately turned out to be twenty-two forming a standard volume. The entire book has been arranged by two different sections in the content to cover the basic themes as addressed in the title.

Entire coverage of the book comprises two broad sections. Section 1 captures the series of studies discussing on the economic implications of green trading and energy use for countries and groups. It contains 14 chapters covering the above broad topic. The chapters in this section confine the theoretical and empirical studies belonging to the emerging economies and developed economies in general and countries like India, China, Mexico and Nigeria in particular. There are the chapters that model international trade and environmental effects in general equilibrium system and chapters covering poverty-environment jinx, FDI-environment trade off and use of renewable energies to establish the economic effects of green trading and energy use. In another part, Section 2 covers eight chapters on green innovations, green urbanization and political aspects for environmental protection (Chapters 15-22). The issues of discussion in this section cover perceptions towards green products, green financing, green urbanizations and political aspects of growth and environmental degradations. Most of the chapters have dependent heavily on empirical foundations with modern tools of quantitative economics to generate concrete research outputs. Brief outcomes of the chapter contributions under Section 1 are addressed below consecutively.

Chapter 1 has attempted to build a theoretical framework related to intra-industry trade with production differentiation based on the environmental quality of the goods and price to address how liberalization of trade happens to affect the environment of the trading nations. The study shows a steep decline in the environmental quality of the good that was relatively cleaner under autarky while a scanty improvement in the environmental quality of the relatively dirtier good.

Chapter 2 aims to identify the causal relationship between the use of renewable energy and energy imports for E7 countries (Brazil, China, Indonesia, India, Mexico, Russia and Turkey) for the period 1990-2015 by using the Pedroni panel cointegration method and the Dumitrescu Hurlin panel causality analysis. Results reveal a long-term relationship between energy imports and renewable energy usage but there is no causal relationship between energy imports and renewable energy usage.

Chapter 3 explores the nexus among FDI, trade, carbon dioxide emission level and the renewable energy use for 18 emerging economies over the period of 1990-2014 using panel VAR econometric methodology. Granger causality test results indicate that FDI, carbon emission and renewable energy use make a cause to trade. Carbon emission and renewable energy use Granger cause FDI, FDI Granger causes carbon emission, and FDI granger causes renewable energy use. Moreover, carbon emission decreases trade, and increases FDI whereas it is decreased by renewable energy use. Results indicate that the Pollution Haven and the Pollution Halo hypothesis are valid for the FDI; however, the Pollution Haven hypothesis is not valid for trade.

Chapter 4 makes comparison of India with China and U.S. and world as a whole in respect of composition, pattern of primary energy use, fuel access to clean cooking energy and access to electricity for the households. It further looks at the issue of energy poverty, in particular, rural-urban magnitude of energy poverty by estimating the specific concentration curve using National Sample Survey (NSSO) household unit level data from the 68th round (July 2011 – June 2012). The study comments on how the optimum fuel mix design should look like and talks about sustainable strategies involving the use of new renewable for breaking India's energy poverty jinx.

Chapter 5 analyzes theoretically the effect of both environmental regulation and trade liberalization on the output of different sectors and also on the national welfare in a small open economy. To categorize this it has presented a theoretical model based on the general equilibrium framework which mainly highlights on a paradoxical result. Apart from this the study shows that the capital used specifically in advanced export sector is likely to affect the welfare positively and that the capital used by rest of the economy is likely to affect the welfare adversely when usual export sector of the economy vanishes and the opposite will occur when the pollution intensive informal sector of the economy vanishes.

Chapter 6 investigates the role of FDI on growth, the role of FDI on environmental quality, and the role of environmental quality on FDI in 23 emerging market economies over the period of 1993-2014 by using panel VAR analysis. It observes that FDI contributes to economic growth and environmental degradation in emerging market economies. In addition, environmental degradation attracts FDI inflows into host emerging market economies. The results support pollution haven hypothesis and contradict pollution halo hypothesis.

Chapter 7 aims to examine the quantitative linkages between HDI and Environmental Performance for the selected developed and developing nations from 2002 to 2017 employing fixed effects panel modeling on the selected country set. Several other macroeconomic and capital flow variables are considered in the extended empirical model development in order to supplement the holistic review of the situation. The findings of the study discover HDI to be positively associated with EPI, depicting higher human capital accumulation leading to lower environmental damage and better environmental performance. Additionally, the results confirm the deviation from EKC hypotheses in the context of developing nations while the same is established in case of developed nations.

Chapter 8 focuses on the use of the Sustainable Development Goals (SDGs) for the achievement of green economy in Nigeria with the specific aim of assessing the performance of key issues in the SDGs. Five goals SDGs 6. 7, 11, 12, and 15 for water and sanitation, safe human settlements renewable energy, sustainable consumption and production and ecosystem respectively are selected for assessment for the green initiatives and the economy. The assessment holds that only two of these goals are being met somehow: renewable energy and clean water, and not necessarily because of the need to achieve the goals but as part of private sector and dynamic market initiatives, clearly indicating failures for the others. For the most part Nigeria failed in the areas of ecosystem, good human settlement and responsible consumption.

Chapter 9 emphasizes on two major areas- (a) examining the changing pattern of the composition of energy use in the two selected countries of Asia (India and China) and (b) examining the short run and long run relationship among energy use, GDP per capita, energy intensity, use of electricity power, extent of urbanization. Using ARDL bound test for the period 1990 to 2014 for the World Development indicator data 2017-18 it reveals that the powerhouses of global energy demand growth are led by the developing economies of Asia viz. China, India, Indonesia, Morocco, Brazil, Singapore and Thailand. In case of India a long run association has been found between energy use and GDP per capita, energy intensity, use of electricity power and extent of urbanization but no instances are for China.

Chapter 10 has made an effort to analyze the disaster management in the integrated framework where the integrated framework is based upon the analysis of the role of regulatory actions taken by three actors namely, disaster regulation, insurance regulations, and firms actions across the three stages of disaster management namely, pre-disaster, underwriting, and post-disaster stages in G-7 economies. Based on the outcomes of the current analysis, the study found two polar opposite integrated models, i.e., Isolated Best Policy Model in the case of Japan and Spiral Policy Model in the case of Italy. Rest five models fall in between the two.

Chapter 11 focuses on analyzing the role of the institutions in the biodiesel industry in Mexico in order to know if there is a relationship with the quality and maturity of the same with the ventures. Starting from a literary review, the framework of the current situation is identified, covering aspects related to formal institutions, laws, rules, regulatory bodies and the theory that supports the relationship between institutions and entrepreneurship. It is thus revealed that the institutions in Mexico have increased their maturity and incentive to increase the number of producers and distributors of biodiesel thus taking advantage of the growing market.

Chapter 12 analyses mechanism and discuss the mitigating policies like Kyoto protocol and tries to examine all aspects related to Carbon Leakage. The developed countries import carbon intensive goods. Under developed countries produce and export carbon intensive goods. In this study we show the prospect of carbon trading and various effects of carbon emission reduction policies on a theoretical framework.

Chapter 13 tries to assess the state-wise development of renewable energy in India. It is seen that the average percentage users of solar power in India has increased from 0.27% in 2001 to 0.44% in 2011. ANOVA results indicate there is significant difference among the states of India in renewable energy development in comparison to their potential capacities and there is enough scope for the development of renewable energy like solar energy in India.

Chapter 14 analyzes the trend and pattern of energy use, energy challenges of India and the sustainability through green growth strategy. It observes that energy security and sustainable development are critical issues to ensure India's economic growth and its human development. Transport sector energy demand witnesses a noticeable increase in emission and it has one of the largest programs in the world for deploying renewable energy products and systems. There is thus urgent need to have proper integrated energy policy in India with emphasis more on renewable sources of energy.

Now a brief outcome of the chapter contributions under Section II are addressed below consecutively.

Chapter 15 addresses the issue that both consumers as well as corporate houses are paying attention on environmental issues today and green products are also gaining momentum as a result. This chapter studies the concept of green marketing along with its important aspects influencing the buying decision of consumers in south Kolkata only for a sample of 266 respondents consisting of 103 males and 163 females with the help of structured open and close ended questionnaires. A mixed result is observed regarding perceptions towards green products. Thus based on such findings no such generalization can be made and have to consider heterogeneity among culture, demographic, geographical variables-which varies from place to place.

Chapter 16 focuses on Corporate Social Responsibility (CSR) activities of companies registered under BSE SENSEX and evaluating their current status in CSR activities from the perspective of the broad heading of planet and people. A detailed analysis is done to highlight the current situation of the companies towards sustainable development through Corporate Sustainability Index and statistical tools like Kruskal-Wallis test and Mann-Whitney U test to represent the contributions of these companies towards the environmental responsibilities. The study reveals the endeavors of surveyed companies towards the holistic development covering the noteworthy issue of environmental protection and sustainability, however a continuous vigil from the regulatory bodies is the need of the hour to ensure that adherence to CSR practices should not only be in mere form but in true spirits.

Chapter 17 discusses different aspects of marketing of greener products with some secondary source information. The theoretical analysis and the data reveal that there have been increasing implications of different generations towards greener or ecological products. More specifically the younger generations prefer the greener products more as compared to the older population.

Chapter 18 focuses on the aspects of green urbanization in some cities and towns in West Bengal, India. Though urbanization of an area is tried to be measured by some academicians through applying the method of indexing with available indicators and their data-driven weights, environmental issues are not incorporated there for any kind of factor analysis to identify their individual relative importance. This article intervenes at this juncture and focuses on construction of an Urbanization Index for some selected 'town area units' belonging to some selected districts of West Bengal and run a factor analysis of it on some identified environmental factors. It observes negative relationship between QVSE and IGU; positive association between IGU and PR, and positive relation between IWDS and IGU.

Chapter 19 presents a review of the vehicular population in urban Indian cities with its pattern and determinants. The transport system is shared by two parts such as public transport as well as private transport system. In an underdeveloped country it is very tough to use public transport. Due to lack of government fund, new technology, proper checking etc. private cars, buses and tracks are increased rapidly. This causes huge pollution.

Chapter 20 aims to introduce and investigate the political economy of the green innovations in the construction industry. This chapter emphasizes that the effectiveness of the green innovations in the construction industry can be fostered by effective political economy and strategies.

Chapter 21 addresses that environmental degradation and concern for environmental protection and maintaining ecological balance, in the last few decades has become the subject of serious political contention and public outcry. Eco-development demands structural and moral transformation of the current social, political and value system. It presupposes a participatory political structure that allows maximum devolution of power to the local communities. And such a coordination and cooperation between development discourse and survival of nature can be found in the works and ideas of Mahatma Gandhi.

Chapter 22, the final chapter of the book, speaks of the energy security and economic growths are interrelated and South Asia is at a critical juncture today. Development is the overriding priority for the region because of the high incidence of poverty but energy is proving to be a critical constraint. The entire region is suffering from an acute energy crisis. The chapter explores new alternatives of energy sources of South Asian States, searching for relationship between energy security and economic growth, and re-thinking about an alternative policy options regarding energy security in South Asia.

The summary results of the chapters in Section I show that opening up of the economies in different trade sectors and foreign direct investments have no doubt improved the economic growths of the trading partners but have been equally damaging in terms of environmental degradation. Pollution Heaven

Hypothesis has been seen as the dominating exposition compared to the Pollution Hallo Hypothesis. The studies included in Section II indicate that there have been growing consumers' perceptions towards green and environmentally friendly products particularly the population of the millennial age groups. It is also observed how green urbanization can be promoted by the help of selected indicators to get a sustainable urban planning and habitat. Hence, it is prescribed through this book project that the over-emphasis upon free flow of goods and capitals across the borders should be made screening and the developing or backward trading zones can be allowed to protect their own environment to produce a good global environment to comply with the millennium sustainable developmental goals as proposed by the United Nations.

It is now the information that the proposed book project has drawn closer to reality. I look forward that the said research outcome will help out to the academicians, environmentalists and policy makers all around the world to have a better understanding of the sustainability issues from the global perspectives.

Ramesh Chandra Das
Vidyasagar University, India

Acknowledgment

It was an elongated journey from planning to execution of the proposed title of the book, *Handbook of Research on Economic and Political Implications of Green Trading and Energy Use*. It is now a profound delight to proclaim from my part as editor that the proposed book on the said title has been in due course unearthed. The ultimate success in mounting such a huge volume of the edited book could not be talented if the offerings of the concerned overabundance of academicians all around the planet were assembled particularly when the entire work was controlled and managed from a rural belt of Indian subcontinent. Hence, it would be chargeable if I do not acknowledge the offerings of the concerned academicians and other members of the society connected to the project.

First, I must acknowledge the IGI Global Team for approving the proposal and continuously guiding me at all stages of impediments by means of their cordial suggestions. I did not face any kind of non co operations from their part and so their sincere efforts were always commendable. Secondly, I should be grateful to my research guides Professor Soumyen Sikdar of Indian Institute of Management, Calcutta, India and formerly Professor Sarmila Banerjee of Calcutta University, India for persistently encouraging me to undergo such a project and circulating the message to the budding chapter contributors of the said fields. Thirdly, I must express gratitude to Dr. Amaresh Das and Dr. Frank Martin of College of Business, Southern University at New Orleans, USA, and Professor Rabindranath Bhattacharya, Jadavpur University and Professor Soumyananda Dinda The University of Burdwan, India, for their continual efforts in guiding me throughout the entire duration of the project besides added encouragements to me. Fourthly, I should acknowledge the efforts of the editorial advisory board members for reviewing the chapters with greater sincerity and providing me suggestions continuously even though their busy academic schedules. Fifthly, I must be grateful to Dr. Hasan Dincer of Istanbul Medipol University, Turkey for his sincere participation in editing a major part of the book with bubbles of good suggestions and recommendations. Sixthly, I honor to all the contributing authors for their valuable chapter contributions and showing their patience for such a long duration project coming into reality.

Last but not the least I must be grateful to my parents, wife and daughter and other members of the family for their continuous persuading, supports and sacrifice in carrying out the long lasting project. Of course, no one other than me, as the editor, discloses to remain entirely responsible for any errors still appear in the book.

Ramesh Chandra Das
Vidyasagar University, India

Section 1

Economic Implications of Green Trading and Energy Use for Countries and Groups

Chapter 1
Trade and Environment Nexus: A Theoretical Appraisal

Debashis Mazumdar
The Heritage College, India

Mainak Bhattacharjee
Loreto College, India

Jayeeta Roy Chowdhury
Jadavpur University, India

ABSTRACT

One major concern that has emerged in the post-globalization period is climate change. Given that pollution and environmental degradation is a public bad, the adverse change in the climate of one region will have ubiquitous effect and therefore will hamper the process of sustainable development across the globe. There are substantial links between international trade and environmental issues – one being that of the perverted comparative advantage which evolves mainly out of the neglect of environmental damage caused by productive activities. In this chapter, an attempt has been made to build a theoretical framework related to intra-industry trade with production differentiation based on the environmental quality of the goods and price to address how liberalization of trade happens to affect the environment of the trading nations. The study shows a steep decline in the environmental quality of the good that was relatively cleaner under autarky while a meagre improvement in the environmental quality of the relatively dirtier good. Hence, it is revealed hereby how trade alters the nature of international inequality in the environmental quality of the productive activities.

INTRODUCTION

The growth of world economy over the last century has been unprecedented. Particularly over the second half of the twentieth century, the global economy has consolidated into a more integrated entity than ever before. This has been made possible by advancements in communication and information technologies and reduced barriers to trade and foreign investment. The increasing scale of production

DOI: 10.4018/978-1-5225-8547-3.ch001

and manufacturing to sustain a world population that has expanded at a staggering rate is bound to have multiple long-lasting consequences. The major brunt of gigantic scale of economic activities has been borne by the world environment. Problems range from deforestation, loss of bio-diversity, natural resource depletion, and air pollution to ozone layer depletion, global warming, discharge of plastics in oceans and more. Slow progress in introduction of adequate measures to protect the environment on the part of various national and international players has been blamed for the persistent environmental degradation that has been crippling our planet. The environmental community is fearful that international trade will magnify the effects of poor environmental policies around the world. Regardless to say, the very existence of the ecological deterioration is welfare reducing for every individual, irrespective of the source of the problem.

After the end of the Second World War, the priority was reconstruction of the world trading system and global environment and its potential degradation was largely ignored. In fact, prior to the initiation of the North American Free Trade Agreement (NAFTA) and the Uruguay Round of GATT, environmental issues had not been an important factor in trade negotiations. The environmental issues took centre stage in the 1990s with the tuna-dolphin dispute between the US and Mexico. Since then, provisions for environment have been included in the subsequent agreements and negotiations concerning international trade, but they have hardly been controversy free. Some argue that the two issues – trade and environment – are interrelated while others believe that they should be kept separated. The former are of the view that the interrelations will assure that free trade will triumph and environment will suffer while the latter endorse the idea that trade promotes development which in turn can implement better methodology to improve the environment. It is therefore important to understand why and for what reasons trade enters the sustainable development discourse. To what extent international trade has harmful effects on environment and what possible benefits of trade exist to counter that is still under debate. In this backdrop the current chapter is intended for examining the consequence of trade liberalization for environment and thereby its implication for attainment of sustainable development.

LITERATURE REVIEW

With increased integration of the global economy, it has now become difficult to ignore the consequences of domestic environmental policy on the global environment. Research on trade and environment is nothing new. Since 1970s, several issues relating to trade and its impact on environment have been debated. These researches, which became more intense during 1990s, have suggested that commitment to free trade may create incentive to distort environment.

Two contradictory views emerged around that time namely, pollution haven hypothesis and Porter hypothesis. The *pollution haven hypothesis* postulated by Copeland and Taylor (1994) illustrates between two countries, the higher income country with stronger environmental protection will specialize in relatively clean goods while the lower income country with lax environmental laws will become a safe haven for pollution intensive industries. In this context, Copeland and Taylor (1994, 2004) have isolated three broad effects of trade on environment, viz. scale, technique and composition effects. Scale effect refers to increased pollution and environmental deterioration due to increased economic activity. Technique effect is due to the move towards cleaner production methods which is made possible by greater wealth arising out of expanded trade and better access to advanced technology. Composition effect captures the change in the share of dirty goods in national income due to trade. Among various works trying to give empirical support to pollution haven hypothesis, Jaffe et. al (1995) examining the effects of environmental regulations on net exports and plant-location decisions have produced estimates that are small, statistically insignificant and not robust. Similarly, Tobey (1990) found that world distribution of dirty industries has not been affected by differing country levels of environmental stringency.

Lucas, Wheeler and Hettige (1992) examined and found that toxic releases per unit of GDP fall as countries become richer. This only occurs because the composition of output in richer countries becomes cleaner. This led the authors to conclude that more strict regulation of pollution-intensive production in the OECD countries has led to significant locational displacement making industrial pollution more intensive in developing countries.

Cole (2004) also found pollution intensive industries grew at a rapid speed in developing countries in periods when environmental regulations had been very stringent in the OECD countries. On the contrary, Van Beers and van den Bergh (1997) did not find any significant impact of environmental regulation stringency on the trade of dirty goods in 21 OECD countries. Similarly, Xu (2000) found that countries with more stringent environmental regulations (case for 25 OECD countries) neither reduced their exports of environmentally sensitive goods nor put trade barriers emerge in any statistically significant way.

Among more recent works, Cole et. al (2010) used disaggregated firm level data from Japan and showed that the effects of environmental regulation on trade are dependent on mobility of the industry. Milimet and Roy (2015) used state level data of US for the period 1977-1994 and found that pollution intensive industries like chemicals, chemical products tend to move to states that have weaker environmental regulations. Riti (2016) investigated the relationship between FDI inflows, manufacturing export and environment in Nigeria over the period 1980-2013. The findings support the existence of pollution haven hypothesis through the positive impact of foreign direct investment on CO_2 emissions while a positive relationship was also found to exist between manufacturing exports and emissions.

The mixed results in the context of pollution haven hypothesis suggest that there can indeed be arguments against it. One such argument that has been developed is the *Porter hypothesis* which postulates that foreign direct investment (FDI) in home country can lead to induction of cleaner and efficient technologies. In other words, the costs of compliance with environmental standards may be offset by adoption of innovations they trigger. Based on data on trade, FDI, economic development and environmental conditions of 30 provinces of China between 1990-2002, Haisheng et. al (2005) found that trade has contributed significantly to economic growth and has played a positive role in introducing advanced pollution-preventing technology and environmental management methodology in China.

Tan et. al (2013) focuses on CO_2 emissions embodied in the China-Australia bilateral trade, i.e. the CO_2 emissions due to the production of goods traded between the two countries. They analyse the difference between the actual CO_2 embodiment and those in a hypothetical no-trade scenario and observe that the net CO_2 emissions due to bilateral trade declined over the period 2002-2010; that is the bilateral trade contributed to a reduction of the global carbon emissions in the recent years. Thus this analysis gives a strong, robust support against the pollution haven hypothesis.

Economic growth has harmful consequences on the environment as well as beneficial effects. Several studies have found that increased trade, which typically means higher income, can have both positive and negative impact on various environmental factors. An inverted-U shaped relationship is observed for some environmental measures, i.e. at lower levels of income per capita growth brings about environmental deterioration until an intermediate income level is reached, after which environmental quality improves with further rise in income. Grossman and Krueger (1995) illustrated this by investigating the relationship between the scale of economic activity and environmental quality for a broad set of environmental indicators of urban air pollution (sulphur dioxide, smoke) and several measures of water pollution for a cross section of countries. They find no evidence that economic growth does unavoidable harm to the environment. Instead, they assert an inverted-U shaped relationship between increases in GDP and environmental damage. However, the turning points in these inverted-U shaped relationships vary for the different pollutants, but in almost every case, they occur at an income of less than $8000 (1985 $). The findings are very much consistent with those of the World development Report (1992) which particularly explores the relationship between development and environment. The latter also assert an inverted-U shaped relationship between per capita income and concentrations of sulphur dioxide and suspended particulate matters in city air. This inverted-U shaped relationship has since come to be known as the *Environmental Kuznets Curve.*

A small departure from the above category of findings is that by Holtz-Eakin and Selden (1992). This study uses global panel data to estimate the relationship between per capita income and carbon-dioxide emissions and then uses the estimated trajectories to forecast global emissions of CO_2. Despite diminishing marginal propensity to emit CO_2 as the economy develops, their forecasts indicate that environmental conditions appear to be still worsening with growth at income levels of even the most prosperous economies.

Frankel and Rose (2005) arrive at mixed results. On one hand, they observe that the effects of trade and growth on air pollution, as measured by concentrations of SO_2, NO_2 and particulate matter are generally good and that there is little or no evidence of race to bottom hypothesis. But on the other hand, the Kuznets' curve in the case of CO_2 does not seem to turn down on its own and trade openness is found to have a detrimental effect for a given level of income.

Various studies over the decades have already established the economic and ecological interdependence. This interdependence requires coordinated national policies and international collective action. Esty and Ivanova (2003) propose a global bargaining forum that could act as a catalyst between countries or private entities negotiating over resource management. Designing a new global environmental regime, comparable in size and quality to WTO to facilitate greater developing country participation in the international policymaking process is imperative in bringing gains which will go beyond the environmental domain. Similar thoughts are echoed in Esty (2001). He says environmental rules cannot be seen as simply pollution control or natural resource management standards but that the real task lies in building environmental sensitivity into the trade regime in a thoughtful and systematic way that could be of interest to both the trade community and environmental advocates.

Of recent actions, the adoption of Paris Agreement is definitely a milestone in international climate politics as it seeks to establish a *'global warming goal of well below 2° C on pre-industrial averages'* and defines a universal, legal framework to *'strengthen the global response to the threat of climate change'* (Art. 2). However, as Streck et. al (2016) notes, nevertheless, there remains a risk that individual country contribution may fall short of the overall global goal and that the agreement remains a shell without sufficient action and support, thus unable to address the problem of climate change.

Le *et al* (2016) examine the relationship between trade openness and the environment using a sample of 98 countries, with emission of particulate matter as the basic indicator of environment quality. The test results show a long run relationship between particulate matter emissions, trade openness and economic growth. They find that increased trade openness leads to environmental degradation for the global sample. However, the results differ according to the income of the countries. Trade openness has a benign effect on the environment in the high income countries but a harmful effect in the middle and low income countries.

Shen *et al* (2017) analyses the location and relocation patterns of pollution-intensive industries in Guangdong province, China from 2000 to 2013 to evaluate the role of environmental regulation and test the pollution-haven hypothesis. Their study confirms the existence of pollution-haven hypothesis in the Chinese province as the investigation reveals that hundreds of polluting industries relocated from the more developed areas to the peripheral ones. This study is an affirmation that suitable environmental regulation policies control and prevent the growth and expansion of pollution-havens in the developed areas.

Cherniwchan (2017) reveals that trade played a key role in the clean-up of the U.S. manufacturing sector. He estimates the effects of NAFTA on the emissions of particulate matter and sulphur dioxide from manufacturing plants in the U.S. The findings suggest that trade liberalization led to significant reduction of these pollutants at affected plants. On average, nearly two-thirds of the reductions in the two types of emissions considered, from the U.S. manufacturing sector between 1994 and 1998 can be attributed to trade liberalization following NAFTA.

Shahbaz *et al* (2017) explores the relationship between trade openness and carbon dioxide emissions by incorporating economic growth as an additional and potential determinant of this relationship for three groups of high, middle and low income countries. They find that the three variables are cointegrated in the long run. Trade openness impedes environmental quality for the global, high income, middle and low income panels but the impact varies in these diverse groups of countries.

OBJECTIVE

The Chapter develops a theoretical model in alignment with the reciprocal dumping premise on strategic trade (Brander, 1981) to examine the implication of international trade for the environmental condition of the countries involved in trade. Moreover, attempt has been made to empirically overhaul such implication.

THE MODEL

The theoretical framework constructed in this chapter is essentially based on reciprocal dumping model on intra-industry strategic trade with some modifications necessary for explaining the environmental consequences of international trade.

The model is based on a 2-country hypothetic world, where in each country a single good is being produced whose environmental consequence is indicated by the pollution emitted out of its production as epitomised by environmental quality index denoted as E spread over the interval $[0, \bar{E}]$, the higher is the value of E cleanlier the good is. Now the environmental quality of the good being produced in each country depends the standard of pollution abatement technology, the installation cost of which in one country is different from that of the other. In particular, the installation cost in country j is given by:

$$C_j = \frac{E_j^2}{j}, \text{ j} = 1,2$$

which means that country 2 has low cost technology compared to country 1.

Moreover, each country has continuum of buyers with α being the taste parameter distributed uniformly over [0, 1].

Given the above, at first it can be shown that under autarky, the environmental standard of the good produced in one country differs from that of the other as illustrated in the following subsection.

Situation Under Autarky

In the situation of autarky market in each country is monopolistic in nature where the monopolist at the first determines the price and quantity for a given the environmental standard and thereafter the firm decides optimal environmental standard with view maximising the profit net of the cost of abating pollution. Hence we have: (a) demand side and (b) supply side as what follows.

Demand Side

In each country under autarky, given that every one consumes only 1 unit of the good with preference over the environmental quality of the good as indicated by the taste parameter α, the aggregate demand is determined by the number the consumers for whom net utility from consumption is positive. Thus a consumer will consider buying the good if and only if:

$$U = \alpha E - P \geq 0 , \tag{1}$$

where, P is the price being charged by the monopolist

Thus, the aggregate demand is: $D = 1 - \hat{\alpha}$, where $\hat{\alpha} = \frac{P}{E}$

Thus, for country j, the aggregate demand is: $D_j = 1 - \frac{P_j}{E_j}$ for j = 1, 2.

Supply Side

Now the gross profit of the monopolist in country j is:

$$\pi_j = P_j \left(1 - \frac{P_j}{E_j} \right)$$

Now the optimum P_j is determined from maximisation of gross profit and from the first order condition of such maximisation we have

$$\frac{\partial \pi_j}{\partial P_j} = 1 - 2\frac{P_j}{E_j} = 0 \Rightarrow P_j = 0.5E_j = P_j^* \tag{2}$$

Equation (2) shows the optimum price that the monopolist considers charging given the environmental quality E_j and thereof the optimum quantity of output is, as determined by substituting (2) in the demand function, $q_j^* = 0.5$. Thus the net profit of the firm in country j in this case is:

$$\Pi_j = \pi_j - {E_j^2}/{j} = 0.25E_j - {E_j^2}/{j} \quad \text{for j =1,2} \tag{3}$$

Now the firm in country j will decide on optimum E_j by maximising net profit that the following condition:

$$\frac{\partial \Pi_j}{\partial E_j} = 0 \Rightarrow 0.25 - 2\left({E_j}/{j}\right) = 0 \Rightarrow E_j = 0.125j = E_j^*, \text{ for j =1,2} \tag{4}$$

Hence the environment standard in,

country 1, is $E_1^* = 0.125$

country 2, is $E_2^* = 0.25$

Thus, we have the following proposition:

Proposition 1: Under autarky the country 2 which incurs lower abatement cost relative country1 registers better environmental standard compared to country 1. Hence the environmental quality of production in each country under autarky depends on solely on nature of technology (in terms of cost) being used by the country for abating pollution.

Situation Under Free Trade

After the countries open up to trade, in each country the market structure resembles that of duopoly market with the firm producing differentiated goods with the differentiation arising in terms of environmental quality. Moreover, in each country a consumer faces the choice between consuming the good produced by firm 1 having the environmental quality E_1 and the one produced by firm 2 having the environmental quality E_2. Hence after the opening up of trade, the demand condition in each country will get changed in the manner that the entire market will now split into buyers consuming E_1 type good and those consuming E_2 type good.

Thus, a consumer in country j will prefer consuming E_1 type good to E_2 type good if and only if:

$$\theta E_1 - P_1 \geq \theta E_2 - P_2 \Rightarrow \theta \geq \frac{P_1 - P_2}{E_1 - E_2} = \hat{\theta}.$$

Hence the demand faced by firm 1 in country j is given as

$$D_{1j} = 1 - \hat{\theta} = 1 - \frac{P_1 - P_2}{E_1 - E_2} \quad (5)$$

On the other hand, a consumer will prefer E_2 type good to E_1 type good if and only if:

$$\tilde{\theta} \le \theta \le \hat{\theta}$$

where, $\tilde{\theta} = \frac{P_2}{E_2}$. Hence the demand faced by firm 1 in country j is given as:

$$D_{2j} = \hat{\theta} - \tilde{\theta} = \frac{P_1 - P_2}{E_1 - E_2} - \frac{P_2}{E_2} \quad (6)$$

Now, each firm in country j determines optimum price, quantity in the first stage and environment quality thereafter in the way illustrated earlier, since the decision making by each firm in one market is independent of that in the other. Moreover, limiting the analysis to one market will suffice to encompass the other since one is analogical to the other post trade.

Thus in market j, firm 1 and firm 2 decide on the respective prices and quantity by maximising the gross profit. Thus the first order conditions are:

$$\frac{\partial \pi_{1j}}{\partial P_{1j}} = 0 \Rightarrow P_{1j} = 0.5(E_1 - E_2 + P_{2j}) \quad (7)$$

$$\frac{\partial \pi_{2j}}{\partial P_{2j}} = 0 \Rightarrow P_{2j} = \frac{0.5 P_{1j} E_2}{E_1} \quad (8)$$

Solving (7) and (8) optimum P_{1j} and P_{2j} for the given E_1 and E_2 as:

$$P_{1j}^{**} = \frac{2(E_1 - E_2)E_1}{4E_1 - E_2}, P_{2j}^{**} = \frac{(E_1 - E_2)E_2}{4E_1 - E_2}$$

Now given the above, the net profits of firm 1 and firm 2 in country j (j= 1,2) in terms E_1 and E_2 of are:

$$\Pi_{1j} = \frac{4(E_1 - E_2)E_1^2}{(4E_1 - E_2)^2} - E_1^2, \Pi_{2j} = \frac{(E_1 - E_2)E_1 E_2}{(4E_1 - E_2)^2} - \frac{E_1^2}{2}$$

Thereafter each firm will determine the optimal environmental quality of its good by maximising the net profit. Hence we have the following conditions:

Now the equations (9) and (10) can be interpreted as the reaction functions of the respective firms in terms of choice of environmental quality in response each other's decision on the same. However, the reaction functions are nonlinear they cannot be solved in conventional method and henceforth we have taken an alternative way to determining the optimal environmental standard for each firm by supposing:

$$E_1 = \delta E_2, \quad (11)$$

where $\delta > 0$. Thus after the substitution of (11) into (9) and (10) we have the following:

$$\frac{2(4\delta - 1)(3\delta - 2) - 16\delta(\delta - 1)}{(4\delta - 1)^3} = E_2 \quad (12)$$

$$\frac{(4\delta - 1)(\delta^2 - 2\delta) - 8\delta(\delta - 1)}{(4\delta - 1)^3} = E_2 \quad (13)$$

Now, δ, E_1 and E_2 can be determined by solving (11), (12) and (13) simultaneously . In this regard it has to be mentioned that at first (12) has been equated with (13) which produces the following equation:

$$4\delta^3 - 25\delta^2 + 16\delta - 4 = 0 \quad (15)$$

[Note: Thereafter δ has been determined numerically where the solution for δ found to be lying at the interval [0.563313, 0.563314] since the values of the polynomial in δ (as depicted by the left-hand side of (15)) at δ =0.563313 and δ =0.563314 being 0.0000263 and (–) 0.0000828. Thu s the value of δ where the polynomial becomes approximately zero is $\delta = 5.5633135$]

Thus, we have the required solutions which are true for country j (j =1, 2) as:

$$\delta = 5.5633135$$
$$E_1^{**} = 0.126$$
$$E_2^{**} = 0.0277$$

Hence we have the following proposition:

Proposition 2: *After the liberalization of trade, the environmental quality of production improves in country 1; while that of country 2 worsens. However the improvement noticed in the environmental quality for country 1 is meagre compared to the degree of deterioration in the environmental quality in country 2. This in turn hints at the implication of opening up of trade for the international inequality in environmental health.*

EMPIRICAL ANALYSIS

This section contains the empirical analysis of the plausible link between the degree of trade openness and level of environmental damage. The key elements of this analysis has been framing Environmental Impairment Index (EII) based on some primordial indicator of environmental pollution namely, CO2 emission, Methane emission, Nitrous Oxide emission, Other green house gases and PM 2.5 (Particulate matter 2.5 microgram) using relative distance methodology for 101 countries with respect to the year 2012 . After obtaining index for each indicator the, the overall index has been determined from taking geometric mean of the component indices. This apart, the degree of trade openness has been measured in terms of Trade-GDP ratio. Thereafter, Pearsonian Chi-square Test has been used to determine the existence of link between trade openness and environmental damage over 101 middle and low income countries classified with degree of trade openness and EII. Moreover, the classification of the selected countries has been performed with respect to trade openness and exposure to environmental damage using Cluster Analysis. Besides, to indicate potentially adverse influence of trade openness on environment, regression has been employed.

The findings in Table 1 broadly indicate the existence of significant association between the degree of trade openness and the level of environmental damage, since the Pearsonian Chi-square test statistic comes significant at level of one per cent. Moreover, quite worth noting is the case that the countries in the medium level of trade openness are mostly associated with the highest order of EII and hence are subject to more environmental detriment relative to those in the '*High*' and '*Low*' echelons of trade openness. However, the countries classified with low degree of trade openness are majorly associated with the medium level of environmental damage and so is the case for the countries classified with the high level.

The issue of potential causal effect of trade openness on the environmental degradation has been addressed in Table 2. Herein it is evident at the outset that the said causal relation is captured by the model specified non-linearly in Trade Openness Index without intercept, so far the yardsticks of adequacy (indicated by R^2 and Adjusted R^2) and goodness of fit (as indicated by p-value of F-statistic). Now the best model chosen henceforth indicates that the Trade Openness Index (the dependent variable of the regression model) at first rise with the degree of trade openness and then decline after as certain point, as evident from the positive coefficient of Trade Openness Index and negative coefficient of Trade Openness Index ^{2} (both being significant as indicated at the footnote of Table 2). The implication of this finding is that the it is the countries in the middle order of openness to international trade that are at

Table 1. Association between Trade Openness and Environmental Degradation

	Environmental Impairment Index		
Trade Openness	***High***	***Medium***	***Low***
High	6	25	1
Medium	18	12	1
Low	4	27	0
Pearsonian Chi-square statistic	70.68 (0.0001)		

Note: Figure in parenthesis indicates p-value
Source: Authors' computation based on World Bank data

Table 2. Impact of trade openness on environment

Model Type	Explanatory Variable	Coefficient	R^2	Adjusted R^2	F-Statistic
Linear Trade Openness Index with intercept	Intercept	2.4667 (0.6800)	0.0398	0.0294	3.81 (0.0539)
	Trade Openness Index	0.0141** (0.0072)			
Linear Trade Openness Index without intercept	Intercept	-	0.1258	0.1164	13.38 (0.0004)
	Trade Openness Index	0.0103* (0.0028)			
Non-linear Trade Openness Index with intercept	Intercept	3.4940 (1.6244)	0.0449	0.0239	2.14 (0.1237)
	Trade Openness Index	0.0403** (0.0382)			
	Trade Openness Index ^{2}	– 0.0014** (0.0002)			
Non-linear Trade Openness Index without intercept	Trade Openness Index	0.0391*** (0. .0101)	0.7832	0.7006	11.54 (0.0000)
	Trade Openness Index ^{2}	– 0.0025*** (0.0008)			

Note: Figure in parenthesis indicates standard error, *(**)(***)significant at 10%(5%)(1%)
Source: Authors' computation based on World Bank data

large associated with worsening environmental quality on an average as opposed to those in the relatively lower and higher orders . This in turn confirms the inequality of environmental quality resulting in free trade as conjectured in the theoretical model described before.

CONCLUSION

The study at the outset brings forth that under autarky the environmental standard of the production in each country is solely determined by the cost of installing the pollution abatement mechanism and in turn the environmental calibrates the domestic price. Moreover, the international difference in pollution abatement cost has been found to be instrumental in causing international price differential. Now after the inception of trade the market structure in each country become that of duopoly with two firm selling differentiated goods in term of the environmental quality. In this regard, the current study shows a steep decline in the environmental quality of the good that was relatively cleaner under autarky while a meagre improvement in the environmental quality of the relatively dirtier good. Hence, it is revealed hereby how trade alters the nature of international inequality in the environmental quality of the productive activities. The study also provides the empirical testimony to the complicity of trade openness with adverse change in the environment.

REFERENCES

Cherniwchan, J. (2017). Trade liberalization and the environment: Evidence from NAFTA and U.S. manufacturing. *Journal of International Economics*, *105*, 130–149. doi:10.1016/j.jinteco.2017.01.005

Cole, M. A. (2004). Trade, the pollution haven hypothesis and the environmental Kuznets curve: Examining the linkages. *Ecological Economics*, *48*(1), 71–81. doi:10.1016/j.ecolecon.2003.09.007

Cole, M. A., Elliott, R. J., & Okubo, T. (2010). Trade, environmental regulations and industrial mobility: An industry-level study of Japan. *Ecological Economics*, *69*(10), 1995–2002. doi:10.1016/j.ecolecon.2010.05.015

Copeland, B. R., & Taylor, M. S. (1994). North-South Trade and the Environment. *The Quarterly Journal of Economics*, *109*(3), 755–787. doi:10.2307/2118421

Copeland, B. R., & Taylor, M. S. (2004). Trade, Growth, and the Environment. *Journal of Economic Literature*, *42*(1), 7–71. doi:10.1257/.42.1.7

Esty, D. C. (2001). Bridging the trade-environment divide. *The Journal of Economic Perspectives*, *15*(3), 113–130. doi:10.1257/jep.15.3.113

Esty, D. C., & Ivanova, M. (2003). Globalization and environmental protection: a global governance perspective. *Global Environmental Governance: the Post- Johannesburg Agenda.* Yale Center for Environmental Law and Policy. Retrieved from www.unpan.org

Frankel, J. A., & Rose, A. K. (2005). Is Trade Good or Bad for the Environment? Sorting Out the Causality. *The Review of Economics and Statistics*, *87*(1), 85–91. doi:10.1162/0034653053327577

Grossman, G. M., & Krueger, A. B. (1995). Economic Growth and the Environment. *The Quarterly Journal of Economics*, *110*(2), 353–377. doi:10.2307/2118443

Haisheng, Y., Jia, J., Yongzhang, Z., & Shugong, W. (2005). The impact on environmental kuznets curve by trade and foreign direct investment in China. *Chinese Journal of Population Resources and Environment*, *3*(2), 14–19. doi:10.1080/10042857.2005.10677410

Holtz-Eakin, D., & Selden, T. M. (1995). Stoking the Fires? CO2 Emissions and Economic Growth. *Journal of Public Economics*, *57*(1), 85–101. doi:10.1016/0047-2727(94)01449-X

Jaffe, A. B., Peterson, S. R., Portney, P. R., & Stavins, R. N. (1995). Environmental regulation and the competitiveness of US manufacturing: What does the evidence tell us? *Journal of Economic Literature*, *50*, 132–163.

Le, T., Chang, Y., & Park, D. (2016). Trade openness and environmental quality: International evidence. *Energy Policy*, *92*, 45–55. doi:10.1016/j.enpol.2016.01.030

Lucas, R., Wheeler, D., & Hettige, H. (1992). Economic Development, Environmental Regulation and the International Migration of Toxic Industrial Pollution: 1960–1988. In International Trade and the Environment. Washington, DC: World Bank.

Millimet, D. L., & Roy, J. (2015). Empirical tests of the pollution haven hypothesis when environmental regulation is endogenous. *Journal of Applied Econometrics*, *31*(1), 652–677.

Riti, J. S. (2016). Foreign direct investment, manufacturing export and the environment in Nigeria: A test of pollution haven hypothesis. *NIDA Development Journal*, *56*(2), 73–98.

Shahbaz, M., Nasreen, S., Ahmed, K., & Hammoudeh, S. (2017). Trade openness - carbon emissions nexus: The importance of turning points of trade openness for country panels. *Energy Economics*, *61*, 221–232. doi:10.1016/j.eneco.2016.11.008

Shen, J., Dennis Wei, Y., & Yang, Z. (2017). The impact of environmental regulations on the location of pollution-intensive industries in China. *Journal of Cleaner Production*, *148*, 785–794. doi:10.1016/j.jclepro.2017.02.050

Streck, C., Keenlyside, P., & von Unger, M. (2016). The Paris Agreement: A New Beginning. *Journal for European Environmental & Planning Law*, *13*(1), 3–29. doi:10.1163/18760104-01301002

Tan, H., Sun, A., & Lau, H. (2013). CO2 embodiment in China–Australia trade: The drivers and implications. *Energy Policy*, *61*, 1212–1220. doi:10.1016/j.enpol.2013.06.048

Tobey, J. A. (1990). The effects of domestic environmental policies on patterns of world trade: An empirical test. *Kyklos*, *43*(2), 191–209. doi:10.1111/j.1467-6435.1990.tb00207.x

Van Beers, C., & Van Den Bergh, J. C. (1997). An empirical multi-country analysis of the impact of environmental regulations on foreign trade flows. *Kyklos*, *50*(1), 29–46. doi:10.1111/1467-6435.00002

World Bank. (1992). *World Development Report 1992: Development and the Environment*. Washington, DC: The World Bank.

Xu, X. (2000). International trade and environmental regulation: Time series evidence and cross section test. *Environmental and Resource Economics*, *17*(3), 233–257. doi:10.1023/A:1026428806818

KEY TERMS AND DEFINITIONS

Environment: The sum total of all surroundings of a living organism, including physical, chemical and other natural forces and other living things, which provide conditions for development and growth.

Globalization: The process of integration and interaction among different nations (through trade agreements), companies (through investment in other countries) and people is called globalization. It influences the environment, political systems, as well as economic development of societies around the world.

Intra-Industry Trade: Intra-industry trade (IIT) is export and import of identical or similar products. Similar products may be products of different varieties or different qualities.

Perverse Comparative Advantage: It is comparative advantage generated by environmental factors and rests on the weakness rather than the strength of the economy. It is a perverse, rather than genuine comparative advantage because it is based on an under-estimation of social cost.

Product Differentiation: It is the process of distinguishing a good or a service from others. Firms use product differentiation to showcase their product's attributes and uniqueness to the buyers.

Sustainable Development: It is the development that meets the needs of the present, without compromising the ability of the future generations to meet their own needs. It is the delicate balance between the human need to improve lifestyles on one hand and preserving natural resources and ecosystems on which both present and future generations depend.

Trade Openness: Trade openness refers to the orientation of a country's economy in the context of international trade. The degree of openness is measured by the actual size of registered imports and exports of an economy.

APPENDIX

Table 3. Indices for trade openness and environmental impairment of the year 2012

Country Name	Trade Openness Index (Trade-GDP Ratio)	Environmental Impairment Index
Afghanistan	81.59	0.42
Angola	91.80	0.37
Armenia	75.97	0.00
Azerbaijan	78.26	0.57
Burundi	43.70	0.13
Benin	54.75	0.78
Burkina Faso	62.68	0.54
Bangladesh	48.11	1.37
Bulgaria	124.78	0.60
Bosnia and Herzegovina	87.94	0.26
Belarus	153.09	0.61
Belize	124.90	0.00
Bolivia	84.95	2.62
Brazil	24.77	0.00
Bhutan	101.76	0.27
Botswana	110.65	1.01
Central African Republic	33.43	1.55
China	48.11	0.03
Cote d'Ivoire	93.67	1.58
Cameroon	56.39	2.33
Congo, Dem. Rep.	68.35	1.80
Congo, Rep.	144.10	0.35
Colombia	38.87	0.43
Cabo Verde	100.28	0.04
Costa Rica	68.14	0.21
Djibouti	–	0.00
Dominica	84.00	0.02
Dominican Republic	58.39	0.42
Algeria	65.40	4.78
Ecuador	61.75	1.10
Egypt, Arab Rep.	40.71	3.51
Eritrea	–	0.21
Ethiopia	45.40	2.25
Fiji	124.65	0.16
Micronesia, Fed. Sts.	110.69	0.04
Gabon	92.34	0.33

continued on following page

Table 3. Continued

Country Name	Trade Openness Index (Trade-GDP Ratio)	Environmental Impairment Index
Georgia	95.95	0.77
Guinea	86.67	0.74
Gambia, The	75.13	0.14
Guinea-Bissau	41.17	0.00
Equatorial Guinea	116.68	0.11
Guatemala	60.98	0.00
Guyana	148.13	0.76
Honduras	121.19	2.02
Haiti	70.07	0.24
Indonesia	49.58	19.81
Iran, Islamic Rep.	47.37	2.49
Iraq	73.55	0.56
Jamaica	82.04	0.14
Jordan	120.51	0.52
Kazakhstan	73.72	1.59
Kenya	57.77	0.36
Kyrgyz Republic	139.68	0.71
Lebanon	94.64	0.14
Liberia	122.17	0.11
Libya	114.37	0.00
St. Lucia	94.35	0.13
Sri Lanka	51.49	2.34
Lesotho	138.98	0.73
Moldova	127.42	0.48
Maldives	160.50	0.07
Marshall Islands	155.51	0.03
Macedonia, FYR	112.22	0.48
Mozambique	110.83	0.41
Mauritius	119.50	0.16
Malawi	67.88	0.27
Malaysia	147.84	3.99
Niger	61.23	0.69
Nigeria	44.53	1.71
Nicaragua	115.18	0.40
Nauru	121.24	0.00
Pakistan	32.81	1.09
Peru	52.62	1.03
Papua New Guinea		0.26
Korea, Dem. People's Rep.		0.75
Romania	79.94	2.69
Russian Federation	47.11	5.70

continued on following page

Table 3. Continued

Country Name	Trade Openness Index (Trade-GDP Ratio)	Environmental Impairment Index
Rwanda	44.57	0.56
Sudan	24.72	2.81
Senegal	61.26	0.53
Solomon Islands	120.88	0.18
Sierra Leone	93.27	0.13
Sao Tome and Principe	-	0.01
Suriname	-	0.11
Chad	80.58	1.60
Togo	106.99	0.57
Thailand	138.48	1.90
Tajikistan	83.18	0.23
Turkmenistan	109.33	3.40
Timor-Leste	133.68	0.12
Tonga	77.77	0.07
Tunisia	106.53	0.74
Tuvalu		0.01
Tanzania	54.40	1.68
Uganda	53.34	0.58
Ukraine	104.09	9.42
St. Vincent and the Grenadines	85.44	0.04
Vietnam	156.55	0.00
Vanuatu	99.93	0.27
South Africa	60.90	5.95
Zambia	79.10	0.79

Source: Authors' computation based on World Bank data

Chapter 2
A Strategic Approach to Reduce Energy Imports of E7 Countries:
Use of Renewable Energy

Hasan Dinçer
Istanbul Medipol University, Turkey

Serhat Yüksel
Istanbul Medipol University, Turkey

Zehra Nur Canbolat
Istanbul Medipol University, Turkey

ABSTRACT

Higher technological developments, product diversity, international trade, and population growth have greatly increased the energy demand of countries. It is very significant that this growing demand should be satisfied with a safe and accessible energy source. Because of this issue, it is thought that countries should be directed towards renewable energy sources so that these countries can meet their rising energy demand without increasing their energy imports. This chapter aims to identify the causal relationship between the use of renewable energy and energy imports. Within this framework, the data between 1990 and 2015 of E7 countries (Brazil, China, Indonesia, India, Mexico, Russia, and Turkey) is taken into the consideration by using the Pedroni panel cointegration method and the Dumitrescu Hurlin panel causality analysis. Results show that there is a long-term relationship between energy imports and renewable energy usage, but there is no causal relationship between energy imports and renewable energy usage. This situation gives information that the use of renewable energy is important and effective in order to reduce imports, but using only this method is not sufficient to remove the import problem for these countries.

DOI: 10.4018/978-1-5225-8547-3.ch002

INTRODUCTION

Energy is a major component of economic activity in the global world. Therefore, it is accepted as a major force playing a role in competition and growth for countries. In addition to this situation, it is also thought that there is a significant relationship between energy and the development of the countries (Huang et al., 2008). In other words, when energy is abundant, it has a significant influence on the welfare of the countries. On the other side, in case of scarce energy, economic expansion is limited. Moreover, this situation has also negative effects on the consumption amount in the countries. In summary, it can be said that the presence of energy thus determines the path of development of a society (Dinçer et al., 2018b; Blum & Legey, 2012).

The scarcity problem in the energy caused significant financial crisis in the past, such as oil crisis in 1973 and 1979 (Dinçer, Yüksel & Şenel, 2018; Yüksel, 2017a,c). In these crisis period, it is seen that there is an important increase in the inflation rates (Dinçer, Hacıoğlu & Yüksel, 2017; Yüksel, Canöz & Özsarı, 2017). Additionally, the production levels in these countries went down at a significant level. This situation led to great recession in the world economy (Kettell, 2016; Yüksel, Dinçer & Emir, 2017). The governments of different countries aimed to take necessary actions in order to minimize the negative effects of these crisis (Yüksel et al., 2018 a, b; Dinçer & Yüksel, 2018a,c). After these issues, energy supply and security has become a crucial concept that is emphasized in national and international energy policies. It is thought that so as to achieve this objective, the gap between energy demand and supply should be reduced. Hence, it can be possible to provide efficiency regarding energy usage (Yüksel & Zengin, 2017).

Alternative energy sources also play a significant role with respect to the aim of energy efficiency. Within this framework, renewable energy is an outstanding concept that refers to the energy which is provided from renewable resources, such as solar energy, wind energy, geothermal energy, hydraulic energy. Additionally, renewable energy usage has many different benefits. For instance, the usage of solar and wind energy does not have any harmful effects on the environment. Furthermore, it can be said that renewable energy usage has also economic advantages. As an example, because it is provided from renewable sources, it has a positive effect on the efficiency (Dinçer et al., 2019d). Moreover, it is believed that this situation makes a contribution to the sustainable development of the countries (Chontanawat et al., 2006).

Renewable energy also plays a very significant role for emerging economies. Because these economies have not been developed yet, they try to take different actions in order to be developed economies (Dinçer, Yüksel & Çetiner, 2019). Within this context, they mainly focus on the way of increasing economic growth. Nonetheless, high amount of import has a negative influence on economic growth for these countries (Yüksel, 2016a,b). Thus, if they have to make energy import, it means that this situation becomes a barrier to reach economic growth. Owing to this issue, the governments of these countries aim to develop a policy in order to prevent this problem. Therefore, it can be understood that renewable energy is an appropriate policy for these countries so ass to minimize the amount of energy import.

Parallel to the issues emphasized above, the aim of this study is to identify the causal relationship between the use of renewable energy and energy imports. Within this framework, the data between 1990 and 2015 of E7 countries (Brazil, China, Indonesia, India, Mexico, Russia and Turkey) is taken into the consideration. In addition to this situation, Pedroni panel cointegration method and the Dumitrescu Hurlin panel causality analysis are used in order to reach this objective. As a result of this analysis, it can be understood whether renewable energy usage affects the energy imports for these countries. Therefore, it will be possible to present recommendations to reduce energy imports so that higher economic growth can be achieved.

This study consists of 5 different parts. After this introduction part, renewable energy policies in E7 economies are detailed in the second part. In addition to them, similar studies in the literature are explained on the third part. Within this scope, the missing part in the literature regarding the subject of renewable energy is underlined. Moreover, an application on E7 economies is taken place on the fourth part. For this purpose, first of all, the methods used in this study are explained. After that, analysis results of these approaches are given. In the final part, necessary recommendations are presented by considering these analysis results.

RENEWABLE ENERGY POLICIES IN E7 ECONOMIES

What Is Renewable Energy?

The term renewable energy refers to energy that emerges naturally in the environment and is basically inexhaustible (Hogg & O'Regan, 2010). The International Energy Agency (2017) defines renewable energy as "energy that is renewed faster and consumes natural processes than consumed". In another word, renewable energy is the energy obtained from the energy flow that exists in natural processes, such as solar light, wind, rain, tide, wave, geothermal heat and biomass energy (Dinçer, Yüksel & Bozaykut-Buk, 2018; Ellabban et al., 2014).

- **Solar Energy:** Solar energy provides a clean, abundant, climate-friendly and inexhaustible source of energy for mankind (IEA, 2011). Solar energy can be used for lighting, heating, cooling, electric power, transportation and even environmental cleaning. Solar energy will play an important role in the future, in reducing carbon emission rates and in ensuring sustainable energy. At the end of 2015, globally installed capacity for solar-powered power plants reached approximately 227 GW and 1% of the world's used electricity was produced (Solar Energy, 2016). According to BP's latest report, until the end of 2016 total solar energy production capacity reached 301 GW. In 2016, a total of 75 GW new plants were added to the global solar energy capacity. China (78.07 GW) ranked first in the solar energy production capacity while Japan (42.75 GW) and Germany (41.22 GW) followed China as the leading countries (Table 1).

Table 1. Top 5 largest solar energy producing countries in the world

Rank	Country	Total Capacity GW, 2016
1	China	78.07
2	Japan	42.75
3	Germany	41.22
4	United States	40.3
5	Italy	19.28

Source: International Energy Agency (IEA)

- **Wind Energy:** Wind energy is used to generate wind turbines to provide electrical power to turn electrical generators. As an alternative to burning fossil fuels, it has advantages such as wind energy, renewable, clean, no greenhouse gas emissions and water consumption during processing, and low land use (Fthenakis and Kim, 2009). World wind energy production capacity reached 435 GW, about 7% of the total global energy production capacity at the end of 2015. China has produced more wind energy in 2016 than the European Union can produce. China holds 33.6% of world production in wind energy. Considering the long coastline and wide geography of the country, the advantage of wind energy can be seen. The United States is second to China in wind energy (Table 2.), ("Wind Energy," 2016). After China and the US, Germany holds 10% of world production. India is one of the most promising countries for the development of wind energy in the World (Thapar et al., 1999).

- **Hydropower Energy:** Hydropower is derived from the energy of moving water. Flowing water is poured into the turbine blades installed in the hydroelectric power plants and the water energy is released during this spill. Commonly used hydroelectricity forms dams. However, waves and tidal power and different forms are becoming widespread (Ellabban et al., 2014).Hydroelectric energy is an energy source that constitutes 71% of renewable energy sources and is the world leader in electricity generation. By 2016, with an installed power supply of 1.064 GW, it accounted for 16.4% of the world's electricity in all renewable sources("Hydropower," 2016). Leading countries were listed as China, Canada, Brazil, USA and Russia, respectively, according to hydroelectric power generation statistics in the world in 2017 ("Hydropower generation globally," 2017) (Table 3).

- **Geothermal Energy:** Geothermal energy is the thermal energy generated from the hot water and the boiler, which is generated by the heat that accumulates underground (Barbier, 2002). Geothermal energy capacity in the world has increased by 4.3% in 2017 to 14.3 GW. Turkey (243 MW) and Indonesia (220 MW) are the countries with largest contribution to this increase in capacity. The US has the largest share in geothermal energy capacity, with 3.7 GW (26% of the world's total), followed by the Philippines (1.9 GW) and Indonesia (1.9 GW). Geothermal energy works with a much higher load factor than the wind or sun, and therefore generates more electricity per MW capacity. In 2017, geothermal capacity increased by 4.3% (600 MW) to reach 14.3

Table 2. Top 5 largest wind power producing countries in the world

Rank	Country	Total Capacity MW, 2016
1	China	168,69
2	European Union	153,73
3	United States	82,18
4	Germany	50,01
5	India	28,66

Source: International Energy Agency (IEA)

Table 3. Top 5 largest hydropower producing countries in the world

Rank	Country	Total Capacity TW, 2017
1	China	1194
2	Canada	403.35
3	Brazil	401.06
4	United States	322.39
5	Russia	178.09

Source: https://www.statista.com/statistics/474799/global-hydropower-generation-by-major-country/

GW. Largest contribution to geothermal capacity is provided by Turkey (243 MW) and Indonesia (220 MW). The US has the largest geothermal capacity with 3.7 GW (26% of the world total), followed by Indonesia (1.9 GW), the Philippines (1.9 GW) and New Zealand (1 GW) ("Geothermal Power," 2017).

- **Bioenergy:** Bioenergy is the energy obtained from organic matter (biomass), in other words, from all biological sources that are not buried in geological formations("Biomass," 2016).Biomass is a biologically original material, such as wood, fertilizer or charcoal, and does not contain materials that have been buried in geological formations and converted to fossils. In the United States alone, there are 500 biomass-operated power plants with a power of 7 GW installed (IEA, 2010).In the Global Bioenergy Statistics 2017 report, Bioenergy has a growth rate of 2.3% and is globally the largest source of renewable energy (Kummamuru, 2017).

General Information About Renewable Energy

According to REN21's 2017 report, renewable energy sources contribute 19.3% to global energy consumption in 2015 and 2016, contributing 24.5% to electricity generation. Worldwide investments in renewable energy technologies (particularly those in countries such as China and the US) exceeded US $ 286 billion in 2015(Ren21, 2016; Tunay et al., 2019; Pınarbaşı and Canbolat, 2018). According to the US International Energy Outlook Report (IEO2017), energy demand is expected to increase by about 30% by 2040, with the largest share expected to come from India, which is 11% to E7. According to the IEO2017 report, it is predicted that all the energy resources consumed in the world market will rise except for the coal demand which is expected to remain stable until 2040. Renewable energy sources are expected to be the fastest growing energy source. Renewable energy consumption is projected to increase by an average of 2.3% between 2015 and 2040 (IEA, 2017).

Why Renewable Energy?

The energy crisis in 70's, led developed countries to taking measure about energy because they were aware of the running out of fossil fuels. Therefore, alternative energy sources had been focused on by both government and energy companies (Tunay & Yüksel, 2017; Yüksel & Zengin, 2016 a, b, c). Renewable resources had important role in this focus(Chynoweth et al, 2000). Renewable energy sources were also considered as alternative energy sources. Renewable energy sources have a wide range of offers; including energy security, reducing the health and environmental effects and prevention of climate change and lastly economic and social development. The critical role of renewable energy resources on economic and social development is not enough for development alone. But renewable energy resources are essential part of sustainable development (Owusu & Asumadu-Sarkodie, 2016).

One functions of a sustainable economy is related to energy security which was referring to a constant supplying role (Chynoweth et al., 2000). Given the energy consumption and the interdependence of economic growth, accessing to a stable energy source is important for both developed and developing countries (Edenhofer et al., 2011).Renewable energy sources are evenly distributed across the world compared to fossil sources, while they are traded less in markets. Other benefits of renewable energy are;

- Reducing energy imports,
- Reducing vulnerability of economy to price volatility (Dinçer, Hacıoğlu & Yüksel, 2018b)
- Increasing energy security worldwide
- Reducing energy imports

Today, renewable energy technologies are not only tools for ensuring energy security and preventing climate change, they have also economic advantages (direct or indirect) by reducing economic dependence on imported fuels (Ren21, 2017; Dinçer, Hacıoğlu & Yüksel, 2016). The other issue about renewable energy refers to geographic scope. Renewable energy investments are usually made in the country and often in the same city as energy users. As a result of this situation, energy costs do not go out of the country, jobs are created within the country and economic development in local economies is ensured. Major economies such as China, Japan, India and the EU are spending up to 7% of GDP in energy imports. These rates are in close proximity to public health in many countries (3% in China, 8% in Japan) and education (4% in most countries in the world) (Ferroukhi et al., 2016).

The trend about renewable energy sources in these large economies may reduce imports. This impact could refer to an important economic benefit for developing countries, especially those with large current account deficits. In addition to these, more than 24 million jobs could be supported in 2030 by renewable energy. Other projection refers that creating new markets and export opportunities could lead to up to 180 billion dollars import (Ferroukhi et al., 2016). Beyond the financial effects of renewable energy, environmental effect also matters. Renewable energy sources are attracting countries in terms of being clean, accessible and affordable. Renewable energy sources used in energy production are contributing to the environment due to climate change mitigation, carbon dioxide (CO2) emission reduction and low water hazards (Akella et al., 2009).

Renewable Energy in E7 Countries

In our dynamic world, the geography of capitalism has begun to change with recent developments in the world, and the difference between the average economic growth rates between the developing countries and the developed countries has become remarkably consistent (Marrmolejo, 2012). Hawksworth economist at PricewaterhouseCoopers John and Cookson (2006), due to the emerging economies of China, Brazil, Russia, Mexico, India, Indonesia and Turkey, the countries where the E7 group ("Emerging 7") as they define. E7 countries have become the fastest growing economies in the world and have experienced significant economic developments in these countries over the last 20 years.

Table 4. Emerging markets will dominate the world's top 10 economies in 2050 (GDP at PPPs)

Country	2016	2050	Country
China	1**	1**	China
US	2*	2**	India
India	3**	3*	US
Japan	4*	4**	Indonesia
Germany	5*	5**	Brazil
Russia	6**	6**	Russia
Brazil	7**	7**	Mexico
Indonesia	8**	8*	Japan
UK	9*	9*	Germany
France	10*	10*	UK

*G7 Economies
**E7 Economies
Source: IMF for 2016 estimates, PwCanalysisforprojectionsto 2050

In the main economic indicators updated throughout the global economy, emerging economies, called E7, are predicted to be 50% larger by 2050 than the existing G7 (US, Germany, UK, Japan, Italy, France and Canada). According to this situation, China is expected to be the biggest economy in 2025 before the United States, but India has a potential to grow to the US by 2050 (Table 4) (John & Cookson, 2006).

According to the PWC Report, the economies of E7 countries are predicted to be ahead of the GDP order of 2016 and the GDP order of 2050.The failure of most of the G7 countries to successfully overcome long-term structural problems has slowed their growth. On the other hand, E7 countries are continuing their economic growth in a healthier and higher way. E7 countries now have low debt levels and manageable budget deficits("The World in 2050," 2016). As a result, E7 countries are generally moving on a fast and consistent economic growth path.

LITERATURE REVIEW

Renewable energy is a very popular subject in the literature. Therefore, it can be seen that it attracted the attention of many different researchers. It is defined that these studies focused on different topic related to the renewable energy. Some selected studies are demonstrated on Table 5.

Table 5 shows that a number of empirical studies have been conducted showing the importance of renewable energy in relation to the global economy. While some of the work is country-based, some work for country groups. Studies of renewable energy consumption and economic growth have examined the one-way and two-way causality relationships. For example; Fang (2011) and Saidi (2016) indicate that there is a two-way causality between renewable energy consumption and real per capita GDP. On the other side, Sadorsky (2009) argued that the economy grew with an increase in renewable energy consumption. In parallel with these studies, Apergis and Payne (2010), who examined the same relation

Table 5. Literature review

Authors	Subject	Method	Sample/Data	Result
Dinçer (2000)	A study to examine the relationship between renewable energy and sustainable development	Case Study	Saarbrucken city with a population of 180,000 in Germany	Renewable energy sources and their use are closely linked to sustainable development.
Asif and Muneer(2007)	An overview of the existing and envisioned energy scenarios for the countries which depend heavily on fuel imports to sustain energy demands	Descriptive Statistics	China, India, Russia, United Kingdom	Concerns about climate change, depletion of fossil fuel reserves and search for clean energy are possible by switching to renewable energy sources
Zhao and Wu (2007)	A study to investigate China's determinants of energy import demand	VECM Analysis	China's quarterly data from 1995 to 2006	International oil prices are not an important determinant of China's oil imports.
Chien and Hu (2008)	Impact of renewable energy on GDP	Structural Equation Model	116 OECD and non-OECD economies' indicators for 2003	Contrary to the prediction that renewable energy production will reduce energy imports, there is a small positive correlation between renewable energy production and energy imports.
Sözen(2009)	Estimation of energy dependence of Turkey by considering main indicators	Artificial Neural Networks	Indicators used to estimate the energy dependence on a sectoral basis in Turkey	It is identified that energy dependence of Turkey rose to 60% in 2006, but it is expected that this ratio will exceed 82% in 2020.
Sadorsky(2009)	Research on the relationship between per capita income and per capita renewable energy consumption in developing countries	Panel Cointegration Analysis	Annual data on renewable energy consumption and income for 18 developing countries	It has been determined that the real increase per capita has a positive effect on per capita renewable energy consumption and that 1% increase in per capita real income has increased renewable energy consumption per capita by about 3.5%.
Apergisand Payne(2010)	The causal relationship between renewable energy consumption and economic growth	Pedronicointegration analysis	In the period of 1992-2007, 13 countries in Eurasia	Both short-term and long-term bi-directional causality between renewable energy consumption and economic growth have been identified.
Fang(2011)	A study to assess the amount and share of renewable energy consumption in the economic welfare	Regression	1978- 2008, China	As renewable energy consumption increases, real GDP and per capita real GDP have also increased.
Menegaki(2011)	The causal relationship between economic growth and renewable energy	One-way random effects model	Between 1997 and 2007, 27 European countries	Short and long-term causality between renewable energy consumption and economic growth has not been identified.
BilginoğluandDumrul(2012)	A study to examine determinants of energy dependence in Turkey's economy	Johansen-JuseliusCointegrationAnalizi	Annual data for the years 1960-2008	The result was that the energy intensity, the gross national product, and the energy consumption in the houses affected the energy dependency positively.
Demir(2013)	Turkey's industrial production and the relationship between energy imports and the current account deficit	Granger Causality Analysis	Turkey's data between the years of 1987-2012	It has been seen that the increase in production led to current account deficits by increasing energy demand.

continued on following page

Table 5. Continued

Authors	Subject	Method	Sample/Data	Result
Pehlivanoğluet al.(2013)	A study on the relationship between energy consumption and economic growth in E7 countries	Holtz-Eakin Panel Causality Test	Between 1990 and 2009, E7 countries	There is a bi-directional relationship between economic growth and energy consumption.
Rosenberg et al. (2013)	Examine long term variables of energy demand	Regression	Annual data of Norway	Increasing energy demand is increasing the production of renewable energy. The most profitable solution to meet increasing demand is to increase the use of bioenergy and to implement energy efficiency measures.
Sözen et al. (2014)	Assessing Turkey's energy growth reports	Data envelopment analysis	Between 1998 and 2006, 25member states of the European Union	It is emphasized that the most important purpose of Turkey is to reduce energy dependence.
Aslaniet al.(2014)	A study on Finland's energy dependence	Causal cyclic diagram system dynamics model	Finland scenarios of renewable energy policies	Despite 7% electricity consumption by 2020 in Finland, the dependence on imported resources will be reduced by 1% to 7% depending on the scenario selected.
Jebliand Youssef(2015)	Renewable and non-renewable energy consumption and causality related to international commercialization	Kao panel cointegration analysis	A sample group of 69 countries between 1980 and 2010	In the short run there is a causal link between renewable energy and trade.
York (2015)	To examine the relationship between domestic production and fossil fuel imports in the United States	Prais-WinstenRegression	US data from 1960 to 2011	It is understood that domestic energy production does not reduce net energy imports.
BüyükyılmazandMert(2015)	Modeling the relationship between per capita CO2 emissions, renewable energy consumption and gross domestic product	Granger Causality Analysis	Annual data between 1960-2010	It has been determined that the growth of the economy is as important as CO2 emissions as well as renewable energy consumption.
Gondaet al.(2015)	A study demonstrating and analyzing countries' development strategies due to increased energy dependence of countries	Descriptive Statistics	Qatar, Hungary and Lithuania Strategic Plans for 2010-2015	In countries' sustainable development strategies, fragility caused by uncontrollable restructuring of the energy market is seen as a threat.
Vaona(2016)	A study examining the link between renewable energy production and import dynamics	Regression	26 different countries	It is defined that renewable energy production reduces the increase in energy imports.
Bhattacharya et al.(2016)	The effects of countries' economic growth on increased renewable energy consumption	DumitrescuHurlin panel causality analysis	The data of 38 different countries between 1991 and 2012	Renewable energy consumption has a significant positive effect on economic output in 57% of the selected countries.
Inglesi-Lotz(2016)	A study to estimate the effect of renewable energy consumption on economic welfare level	Pedroni panel cointegration analysis	Between 1990 and 2010, 34 OECD countries	The effect of renewable energy consumption on economic growth is positive and statistically significant.

continued on following page

Table 5. Continued

Authors	Subject	Method	Sample/Data	Result
Jebli et al.(2016)	The relationship between renewable and non-renewable energy consumption and international trade data	Pedroni panel cointegration analysis	Data set for 25 OECD countries between 1980 and 2010	It is defined that renewable energy and trade have a negative impact on per capita CO2 emissions.
Saidiand Mbarek(2016)	The causal relationship between renewable energy and per capita real GDP	Pedroni panel cointegration analysis	9 developed countries between 1990-2013	Two-way causality was found between renewable energy consumption and per capita real GDP.
Unbehaun(2017)	The relationship between renewable energy production and non-renewable energy imports	Regression	A panel covering countries from the European Economic Area and Norway for 1990-2014	The increase in renewable energy production was found to be associated with an increase in non-renewable energy imports.
Afonso et al.(2017)	The relationship between economic actions and renewable and non-renewable energy consumption	Pedroni panel cointegration analysis	28 different countries using annual data for the period 1995-2013	While renewable energy does not contribute to economic growth, it has been learned that renewable energies contribute to the economy.
Fotourehchi(2017)	Long-term causality relationship between renewable energy consumption and economic growth	Pedroni panel cointegration analysis	Developing countries in the period of 1990-2011	A one-way causality relationship has been identified from the renewable energy consumption to the economic growth.
Doğan and Değer (2018)	The relationship between total energy consumption and economic growth	Pedroni panel cointegration analysis	E7 countries for the period 1990-2016	A 1% increase in energy consumption leads to an increase of 0.123% in economic growth.

for OECD countries in panel data, reached similar result. Bhattacharya *et al* (2016) found that renewable energy consumption has a significant positive effect on economic output in 57% of the selected countries in their study with 38 countries with the highest renewable energy consumption.

On the other hand, some studies identify the different results in comparison with the previous examples. For instance, Menegaki (2011), in his study of 27 European countries, emphasized that a short-term and long-term causality relationship between renewable energy consumption and economic growth cannot be established. Afonso et al. (2017) have reached a similar conclusion that the renewable energy contributes to the economic growth, whereas the non-renewable energy contributes to the economy. In addition, Apergis and Payne (2009), Jebli and Youssef (2015), Büyükyılmaz and Mert (2015), Inglesi-Lotz (2016), Jebli et al. (2016), Fotourehchi (2017) investigated the bi-directional causality between renewable energy consumption and economic growth and achieved different results for various country and country groups.

When studies on energy dependency are examined, it is emphasized that there is a general consensus in the world economy that both the energy demand and the increase in the energy consumption rate and the decrease in the oil reserves increase the dependency of the countries on energy imports. Also, this dependency should be directed towards alternative energy sources. For example, Aslani (2014) focuses on the role of renewable energy resources on energy dependence in Finland and has determined that the implementation of energy actions saves more than $ 4 billion in natural gas imports through the installation of new renewable energy capacities. Bilginoğlu and Dumrul (2012) determined that energy intensity, energy consumption in the houses and energy dependency of the gross national product are positively influenced in their studies, which analyze the determinants of energy dependency in the Turkish economy. Sözen (2009) emphasized that the energy dependence of the country when in 2020 will rise to 82%. Therefore, incentives for the use of their existing primary and renewable energy resources should be developed to reduce this problem.

In addition to these studies, some of them underlined the importance that renewable energies pave the way for solutions to environmental problems, sustainable development and growth, as well as efforts to reduce energy dependence by keeping energy imports under control. For example, Rosenberg et al. (2013) emphasizes that increased energy demand is an important driving force for the development of energy systems. Therefore, they concluded that the most profitable solution to meet this growing demand is to increase the use of bioenergetics and implement energy efficiency measures. Asif (2007), Afonso et al. (2017),Dinçer (2000) and Unbehaun (2017) also underlined the same aspect with the help of different approaches. On the other hand, Iron (2013) indicated that rising energy demand due to increases in production led to current account deficits by increasing imports.

Additionally, Vaona (2015) has reached the conclusion that renewable energy production is reducing the increase in energy imports in its study of the relationship between renewable energy production and import dynamics in terms of 26 different countries. On the other hand, in their study of energy imports as a control variable, Chien and Hu (2008), studying the relationship between renewable energy and gross domestic product (GDP) in 116 countries in 2003, found that there was a small positive correlation between these two variables. Unbehaun (2017), on the other hand, noted that there is a positive relationship between renewable energy production and energy imports. This result refuted the expectation of European Union that renewable energy produced within the country will reduce the country's fossil fuel import needs.

While analyzing the studies in Table 1, it is concluded that the studies that cover E7 countries regarding renewable energy are very limited. For example, Pehlivanoğlu et al (2007) and Doğan and Değer (2018) observed a bi-directional relationship between economic growth and energy consumption in their studies based on E7 countries. However, there is not a study in the literature that will contribute to economic growth by decreasing the dependence of E7 countries on energy imports, which are known as the fastest growing economies in the world economy. Owing to this aspect, it is believed that this study makes a contribution to the literature by providing a strategic solution for these countries to reduce energy import.

AN APPLICATION ON E7 ECONOMIES

Data and Scope

In this study, E7 economies are taken into the considerations which are the largest emerging economies, such as Brazil, China, India, Indonesia, Mexico, Russia and Turkey. The study aims to identify the causality relationship between energy import and renewable energy usage. Therefore, annual data on the import and renewable energy use of E7 countries between 1990 and 2015 are obtained from the World Bank website. The percentage of both variables to the GDP is taken into the consideration.

Pedroni Panel Cointegration Analysis

Cointegration analysis tries to evaluate whether there is a long-term relationship between the variables. The difference of Pedroni panel cointegration in comparison with the other methods is that this approach can be used for panel data. In the analysis process of Pedroni panel cointegration tests, 7 different test results are presented which are Panel v-statistic, Panel rho-statistic, Panel PP-statistic, Panel ADF-statistic, Group rho-statistic, Group PP-statistic and Group ADF-statistic. As it can be seen that 4 of these tests are related to panel statistics that make analysis within the dimensions. On the other side, 3 of them are related to the group statistics. These tests make analysis between the dimensions. If the probability values of at least 4 of these 7 tests are lower than 0.05, it means that there is a long run relationship between the variables (Pedroni, 2004).

Dumitrescu Hurlin Panel Causality Analysis

Dumitrescu Hurlin panel causality analysis is accepted as the advanced form of Granger causality test. The main difference of this methodology is that it can be used for panel data. The main purpose of this method is to understand if there is a causal relationship between the variables (Dumitrescu & Hurlin, 2012). It is possible to make causality analysis in both ways. If the purpose is to see whether there is a causality relationship between X and Y, in this analysis, it is possible to learn whether X is the cause of Y or Y is the cause of X. When these two different types of causality analysis are found at the same time, it is called as "bidirectional causality". This methodology was preferred in many different studies in the literature, such asAdalı and Yüksel (2017), Dinçer et al. (2017), Dinçer et al. (2018a), Dinçer et al. (2019a,b,c), Dinçer and Yüksel (2018b), Dinçer, Hacıoğlu and Yüksel (2018b), Yüksel (2017b), Yüksel and Canöz (2017), and Yüksel and Oktar (2017).

ANALYSIS OF RESULTS

Before panel cointegration analysis is applied, panel unit root test is performed to see whether the variables are stationary or not. For this purpose, Im, Pasaran and Shin panel unit root test is used (Im et al., 2003). The details of this analysis are given on Table 6.

Table 6 gives information that the variable important is stationary on its level value. The main reason is that its probability value is lower than 0.05. In addition to this aspect, it is also concluded that the variable renewable energy usage has a unit root since the probability value is greater than 0.05. Thus, in the analysis process, the first different of renewable energy usage is considered. After panel unit root test, Pedroni panel cointegration analysis is performed to understand if there is a long-term relationship

Table 6. Im, Pesaran and Shin panel unit root test results

Variables	Level Value (Probability)	First Difference (Probability)
Import	0.0000	-
Renewable Energy Usage	0.7820	0.0000

between renewable energy consumption and import of the countries. The details of these results are demonstrated on Table 7.

Table 7 explains that there is cointegration between the variables because the probability values of 6 tests are lower than 0.1. This means that it is possible to reject the null hypothesis at 10% significance level. In other words, the existence of a long-run relationship (at a 10% confidence interval) between the two variables is determined. This situation shows that there is a long run relationship between renewable energy usage and import values in E7 economies. Asif and Muneer (2007) and Vaona (2015) underlined the same issues in their studies. According to these results, it can be said that E7 economies should focus on renewable energy production in order to minimize energy import. Therefore, it can be much easier to solve the problem of current account deficit. After Pedroni panel cointegration analysis, Dumitrescu Hurlin panel causality analysis is also performed in this study to understand whether there is causal relationship or not. The details of this analysis are demonstrated on Table 8.

Table 8 shows that all probability values are greater than 0.1. This condition explains that the null hypotheses of "renewable energy usage does not cause import" or "import does not cause renewable energy usage" cannot be rejected. In other words, it is understood that there is not a causal relationship between renewable energy usage and import for E7 economies. Zhao and Wu (2007), Chien and Hu (2008), York (2015) and Unbehaun (2017) also underlined that there is not a causal relationship between renewable energy usage and import level of the countries.

While considering the results of Pedroni panel cointegration and Dumitrescu Hurlin panel causality analyses, it can be seen that there is a long-term relationship between renewable energy usage and import. However, it is also identified that this relationship cannot be defined at causality level. It refers that energy dependence is not the only reason of import for these countries. Therefore, in addition to the renewable energy production, the governments of these countries should also focus on other factors in order to solve current account deficit problem.

Table 7. Pedroni panel cointegration test results

Within-Dimension		
	Probability	**Probability**
Panel v-statistic	0.858	0.830
Panel rho-statistic	0.003	0.022
Panel PP-statistic	0.000	0.002
Panel ADF-statistic	0.175	0.257
Between-Dimension		
Group rho-statistic	0.220	
Group PP-statistic	0.032	
Group ADF-statistic	0.089	

Table 8. DumitrescuHurlin panel causality test results

The Way of Relationship	Lag	Probability Value
Renewable Energy Usage → Import	1	0.969
	2	0.600
	3	0.547
Import → Renewable Energy Usage	1	0.781
	2	0.490
	3	0.822

SOLUTIONS AND RECOMMENDATIONS

In this study, it is found that there is a long run relationship between renewable energy usage and import values in E7 economies. On the other side, it is also determined that there is not a causal relationship between these variables. While looking at these results, it can be understood that renewable energy is not the only factor that affects the import amount of E7 countries. Therefore, it is recommended that the governments of these countries should also spotlight on some other factors in addition to the renewable energy in order to minimize current account deficit.

FUTURE RESEARCH DIRECTIONS

This study aims to understand the relationship between renewable energy consumption and import amount of E7 countries. Because current account deficit is a significant problem for emerging economies, it is believed that this study makes a contribution to the literature by focusing on this important aspect. However, for future studies, it is thought that a new study which aims to find the indicators of import or current account deficit is also very beneficial. By considering many different indicators at the same time, it can be possible to understand the main reasons of current account deficit problem in emerging economies.

DISCUSSION AND CONCLUSION

Energy plays a key role in the economic performance of the countries. Thus, it is accepted that there is a positive relationship between energy consumption and economic growth. However, because of the scarcity in energy sources, the economies of the countries may be affected in a negative manner. This situation is especially important for emerging countries because most of these countries have to import energy from outside. This situation has a strong effect on the import amount of these countries. Hence, this situation leads to a structural current account deficit problem.

Owing to this condition, the popularity of alternative energy sources increased very much. Within this context, countries give importance to the renewable energy because it provides energy from renewable sources, such as solar energy, wind energy, geothermal energy, hydraulic energy. According to some researchers, it is thought that renewable energy can be a solution for these problems. Therefore, countries make investments in renewable energy resources. In this circumstance, some of these countries aim to decrease import to solve current account deficit problem.

Parallel to the aspects emphasized above, this study aims to evaluate the causal relationship between the use of renewable energy and energy imports. For this purpose, E7 countries (Brazil, China, Indonesia, India, Mexico, Russia and Turkey) are taken into the consideration. Annual data of these variables for the periods between 1990 and 2015 are used to achieve this objective. In addition to these issues, Pedroni panel cointegration method and the Dumitrescu Hurlin panel causality approach are considered in the analysis process.

According to the results of Pedroni panel cointegration analysis, it is defined that there is a long run relationship between renewable energy usage and import values in E7 economies. This demonstrates that in order to minimize energy import E7 economies should focus on renewable energy production. Hence, current account deficit problem can be minimized. Additionally, as a result of DumitrescuHurlin panel causality analysis, it is concluded that there is not a causal relationship between renewable energy usage and import for E7 economies. This condition gives information that energy dependence is not the only reason of import for these countries.

REFERENCES

Adalı, Z., & Yüksel, S. (2017). Gelışmekte Olan Ekonomılerde Doğrudan Yabancı Yatırım Ve Ekonom ıkGelışmeArasındakıNedensellıkİlışkısı. *Marmara İktisat Dergisi*, *1*(2), 109–118.

Afonso, T. L., Marques, A. C., & Fuinhas, J. A. (2017). Strategies to make renewable energy sources compatible with economic growth. *Energy Strategy Reviews*, *18*, 121–126. doi:10.1016/j.esr.2017.09.014

Akella, A. K., Saini, R. P., & Sharma, M. P. (2009). Social, economical and environmental impacts of renewable energy systems. *Renewable Energy*, *34*(2), 390–396. doi:10.1016/j.renene.2008.05.002

Apergis, N., & Payne, J. E. (2010). Renewable energy consumption and economic growth: Evidence from a panel of OECD countries. *Energy Policy*, *38*(1), 656–660. doi:10.1016/j.enpol.2009.09.002

Asif, M., & Muneer, T. (2007). Energy supply, its demand and security issues for developed and emerging economies. *Renewable & Sustainable Energy Reviews*, *11*(7), 1388–1413. doi:10.1016/j.rser.2005.12.004

Aslani, A., Helo, P., & Naaranoja, M. (2014). Role of renewable energy policies in energy dependency in Finland: System dynamics approach. *Applied Energy*, *113*, 758–765. doi:10.1016/j.apenergy.2013.08.015

Barbier, E. (2002). Geothermal energy technology and current status: An overview. *Renewable & Sustainable Energy Reviews*, *6*(1–2), 3–65. doi:10.1016/S1364-0321(02)00002-3

Bhattacharya, M., Paramati, S. R., Ozturk, I., & Bhattacharya, S. (2016). The effect of renewable energy consumption on economic growth: Evidence from top 38 countries. *Applied Energy*, *162*, 733–741. doi:10.1016/j.apenergy.2015.10.104

Bilginoğlu, M. A., & Dumrul, C. (2012). Türk Ekonomisinin Enerji Bağımlılığı Üzerine Bir Eş-Bütünleşme Analizi. *Journal of Yasar University*, *7*(26), 4392–4414.

Biomass. (2016). Retrieved July 20, 2018, from https://www.worldenergy.org/data/resources/resource/biomass/

Blum, H., & Legey, F. L. L. (2012). The challenging economics of energy security: Ensuring energy benefits in support to sustainable development. *Energy Economics*, *34*(6), 1982–1989. doi:10.1016/j.eneco.2012.08.013

Büyükyılmaz, A., & Mert, M. (2015). CO2 Emisyonu, Yenilenebilir Enerji Tüketimi ve Ekonomik Büyüme Arasındaki İlişkinin MS-VAR Yaklaşımı ile Modellenmesi: Türkiye Örneği. *ZeitschriftfürdieWelt der Türken/Journal of World of Turks*, *7*(3), 103-117.

Chien, T., & Hu, J. L. (2008). Renewable energy: An efficient mechanism to improve GDP. *Energy Policy*, *36*(8), 3035–3042. doi:10.1016/j.enpol.2008.04.012

Chontanawat, J., Hunt, L. C., & Pierse, R. (2006). Causality between Energy Consumption and GDP: Evidence from 30 OECD and 78 Non-OECD Countries. *Surrey Energy Economics Discussion Paper Series*, *113*, 1–58.

Chynoweth, D. P., Owens, J. M., & Legrand, R. (2000). Renewable methane from anaerobic digestion of biomass. *Renewable Energy*, *22*(1–3), 1–8.

Demir, M. (2013). The Relationship Between Energy Import and Current Account Deficit: The Case Of Turkey With Var Analysis. *Journal of AcademicResearchesandStudies*, *5*(9), 2–27.

Dinçer, H., Hacıoğlu, Ü., & Yüksel, S. (2016). Managerial and Market-Based Appraisal of Agriculture Banking Using ANP and ELECTRE Method. *Management and Organizational Studies*, *3*(3), 29. doi:10.5430/mos.v3n3p29

Dinçer, H., Hacıoğlu, Ü., & Yüksel, S. (2017). A Strategic Approach to Global Financial Crisis in Banking Sector: A Critical Appraisal of Banking Strategies Using Fuzzy ANP and Fuzzy Topsis Methods. *International Journal of Sustainable Economies Management*, *6*(1), 1–21. doi:10.4018/ijsem.2017010101

Dinçer, H., Hacıoğlu, Ü., & Yüksel, S. (2018a). Determining Influencing Factors of Currency Exchange Rate for Decision Making in Global Economy Using MARS Method. In *Geopolitics and Strategic Management in the Global Economy* (pp. 261–273). IGI Global. doi:10.4018/978-1-5225-2673-5.ch013

Dinçer, H., Hacıoğlu, Ü., & Yüksel, S. (2018b). Conflict Risk and Defense Expenses and Their Impact on the Economic Growth. In R. C. Das (Ed.), *Handbook of Research on Military Expenditure on Economic and Political Resources* (pp. 1–23). IGI Global. doi:10.4018/978-1-5225-4778-5.ch001

Dinçer, H., & Yüksel, S. (2018a). Comparative Evaluation of BSC-Based New Service Development Competencies in TurkishBankingSectorwiththeIntegratedFuzzyHybrid MCDM Using Content Analysis. *International Journal of Fuzzy Systems*, *20*(8), 2497–2516. doi:10.100740815-018-0519-y

Dinçer, H., & Yüksel, S. (2018b). Identifying the Causality Relationship between Health Expenditure and EconomicGrowth: An Application on E7 Countries. *Journal of Health Systems and Policies*, *1*(1), 10–38.

Dinçer, H., & Yüksel, S. (2018c). Financial Sector-Based Analysis of the G20 Economies Using theIntegratedDecision-MakingApproachwith DEMATEL and TOPSIS. In *EmergingTrends in Banking and Finance* (pp. 210–223). Cham: Springer. doi:10.1007/978-3-030-01784-2_13

Dinçer, H., Yüksel, S., & Adalı, Z. (2017). Identifying Causality Relationship between Energy Consumption and Economic Growth in Developed Countries. *International Business and Accounting Research Journal, 1*(2), 71–81.

Dinçer, H., Yuksel, S., & Adalı, Z. (2018a). Relationship Between Non-Performing Loans, Industry, and Economic Growth of the African Economies and Policy Recommendations for Global Growth. In *Globalization and Trade Integration in Developing Countries* (pp. 203–228). IGI Global.

Dinçer, H., Yüksel, S., Adalı, Z., & Aydın, R. (2019a). Evaluating the Role of Research and Development and Technology Investments on Economic Development of E7 Countries. In *Organizational Transformation and Managing Innovation in the Fourth Industrial Revolution* (pp. 245–263). IGI Global. doi:10.4018/978-1-5225-7074-5.ch013

Dinçer, H., Yuksel, S., & Bozaykut-Buk, T. (2018). Evaluation of Financial and Economic Effects on Green Supply Chain Management With Multi-Criteria Decision-Making Approach: Evidence From Companies Listed in BIST. In *Handbook of Research on SupplyChain Management forSustainable Development* (pp. 144–175). IGI Global.

Dinçer, H., Yüksel, S., & Çetiner, İ. T. (2019). Strategy Selection for Organizational Performance of Turkish Banking Sector With the Integrated Multi-Dimensional Decision-Making Approach. In *Handbook of Research on Contemporary Approaches in Management and Organizational Strategy* (pp. 273–291). IGI Global. doi:10.4018/978-1-5225-6301-3.ch014

Dinçer, H., Yüksel, S., Eti, S., & Tula, A. (2019c). Effects of Demographic Characteristics on Business Success: An Evidence From Turkish Banking Sector. In *Handbook of Research on Business Models in Modern Competitive Scenarios* (pp. 304–324). IGI Global. doi:10.4018/978-1-5225-7265-7.ch016

Dinçer, H., Yüksel, S., Korsakienė, R., Raišienė, A. G., & Bilan, Y. (2019d). IT2 Hybrid Decision-Making Approach to Performance Measurement of Internationalized Firms in the Baltic States. *Sustainability, 11*(1), 296. doi:10.3390u11010296

Dinçer, H., Yüksel, S., & Martínez, L. (2018b). Balanced scorecard-based Analysis about European Energy Investment Policies: A hybrid hesitant fuzzy decision-making approach with Quality Function Deployment. *Expert Systems with Applications.*

Dinçer, H., Yüksel, S., Pınarbaşı, F., & Çetiner, İ. T. (2019b). Measurement of Economic and Banking Stability in Emerging Markets by Considering Income Inequality and Non performing Loans. In *Maintaining Financial Stability in Times of Risk andUncertainty* (pp. 49–68). IGI Global. doi:10.4018/978-1-5225-7208-4.ch003

Dinçer, H., Yüksel, S., & Şenel, S. (2018). Analyzing the Global Risks for the Financial Crisis after the Great Depression Using Comparative Hybrid Hesitant Fuzzy Decision-Making Models: Policy Recommendations for Sustainable Economic Growth. *Sustainability, 10*(9), 3126.

Dincer, I. (2000). Renewable energy and sustainable development: A crucial review. *Renewable & Sustainable Energy Reviews, 4*(2), 157–175. doi:10.1016/S1364-0321(99)00011-8

Doğan, B., & Değer, O. (2018). The Energy Consumption and Economic Growth in the E7 Countries: Cointegration in Panel Data with Structural Breaks. *Journal for Economic Forecasting, 1*, 63–75.

Dumitrescu, E. I., & Hurlin, C. (2012). Testing for Granger non-causality in heterogeneous panels. *Economic Modelling*, *29*(4), 1450–1460. doi:10.1016/j.econmod.2012.02.014

Edenhofer, O., Pichs-Madruga, R., Sokona, Y., Seyboth, K., Matschoss, P., Kadner, S., & von Stechow, C. (2011). *IPCC special report on renewable energy sources and climate change mitigation. Prepared By Working Group III of the Intergovernmental Panel on Climate Change*. Cambridge, UK: Cambridge UniversityPress.

Ellabban, O., Abu-Rub, H., & Blaabjerg, F. (2014). Renewable energy resources: Current status, future prospects and their enabling technology. *Renewable & Sustainable Energy Reviews*, *39*, 748–764. doi:10.1016/j.rser.2014.07.113

Fang, Y. (2011). Economic welfare impacts from renewable energy consumption: The China experience. *Renewable & Sustainable Energy Reviews*, *15*(9), 5120–5128. doi:10.1016/j.rser.2011.07.044

Ferroukhi, R., Lopez-Peña, A., Kieffer, G., Nagpal, D., Hawila, D., Khalid, A., … Fernandez, A. (2016). Renewable Energy Benefits: Measuring the Economics. IRENA International Renewable Energy Agency.

Fotourehchi, Z. (2017). *Renewable Energy Consumption and Economic Growth: A Case Study for Developing Countries*. Academic Press.

Fthenakis, V., & Kim, H. C. (2009). Land use and electricity generation: A life-cycle analysis. *Renewable & Sustainable Energy Reviews*, *13*(6–7), 1465–1474. doi:10.1016/j.rser.2008.09.017

Geothermal Power. (n.d.). Retrieved July 18, 2018, from https://www.bp.com/en/global/corporate/energy-economics/statistical-review-of-world-energy/renewable-energy/geothermal-power.html

Gonda, G., Noor Mubaral, A., & Navickas, V. (2015). Article. *Vadyba*, *1*(1), 1–120.

Hogg, K., & O'Regan, R. (2010). Renewable energy support mechanisms: an overview. *Global Law and Business*, 1–7.

Huang, B.-N., Hwang, M. J. J., & Yang, C. W. W. (2008). Causal relationship between energy consumption and {GDP} growth revisited: A dynamic panel data approach. *Ecological Economics*, *67*(1), 41–54. doi:10.1016/j.ecolecon.2007.11.006

Hydropower. (2016). Retrieved July 11, 2018, from https://www.worldenergy.org/data/resources/resource/hydropower/

Hydropower generation globally. (2017). Retrieved July 11, 2018, from https://www.statista.com/statistics/474799/global-hydropower-generation-by-major-country/

IEA. (2011). *Solar energy perspectives* (Vol. 9789264124). Solar Energy Perspectives. doi:10.1787/9789264124585-

IEA. (2017). International Energy Outlook 2017 Overview. *U.S. Energy Information Administration*, *IEO2017*, 143.

Inglesi-Lotz, R. (2016). The impact of renewable energy consumption to economic growth: A panel data application. *Energy Economics*, *53*, 58–63. doi:10.1016/j.eneco.2015.01.003

Jebli, M. B., & Youssef, S. B. (2015). The environmental Kuznets curve, economic growth, renewable and non-renewable energy, and trade in Tunisia. *Renewable & Sustainable Energy Reviews*, *47*, 173–185. doi:10.1016/j.rser.2015.02.049

Jebli, M. B., Youssef, S. B., & Ozturk, I. (2016). Testing environmental Kuznets curve hypothesis: The role of renewable and non-renewable energy consumption and trade in OECD countries. *Ecological Indicators*, *60*, 824–831. doi:10.1016/j.ecolind.2015.08.031

Kettell, S. (2016). *Oil Crisis*. Retrieved from https://www.britannica.com/topic/oil-crisis

Kummamuru, B. (2017). *Wba Global Bioenergy Statistics 2017*. Retrieved from https://worldbioenergy.org/

Marrmolejo, M. (2012). *The New World Order: G7 and E7 Nations*. Retrieved July 18, 2018, from http://www.understandglobalization.com/2012/02/26/the-new-world-order-g7-and-e7-nations/

Menegaki, A. N. (2011). Growth and renewable energy in Europe: A random effect model with evidence for neutrality hypothesis. *Energy Economics*, *33*(2), 257–263. doi:10.1016/j.eneco.2010.10.004

Owusu, P. A., & Asumadu-Sarkodie, S. (2016). A review of renewable energy sources, sustainability issues and climate change mitigation. *Cogent Engineering*, *3*(1), 1–14. doi:10.1080/23311916.2016.1167990

Pedroni, P. (2004). Panel cointegration: Asymptotic and finite sample properties of pooled time series tests with an application to the PPP hypothesis. *Econometric Theory*, *20*(3), 597–625. doi:10.1017/S0266466604203073

Pınarbaşı, F., &Canbolat, Z. N. (2018). Evaluation Of Augmented Reality Mobile Applications In Turkey Market: A Data Mining Approach To Consumer Reviews. *Changing Organizations*, 187.

Ren21. (2016). *Renewables 2016 global status report 2016*. Author.

Rosenberg, E., Lind, A., & Espegren, K. A. (2013). The impact of future energy demand on renewable energy production–Case of Norway. *Energy*, *61*, 419–431. doi:10.1016/j.energy.2013.08.044

Sadorsky, P. (2009). Renewable energy consumption and income in emerging economies. *Energy Policy*, *37*(10), 4021–4028. doi:10.1016/j.enpol.2009.05.003

Saidi, K., & Mbarek, M. B. (2016). Nuclear energy, renewable energy, CO2 emissions, and economic growth for nine developed countries: Evidence from panel Granger causality tests. *Progress in Nuclear Energy*, *88*, 364–374. doi:10.1016/j.pnucene.2016.01.018

Solar Energy. (2016). Retrieved from https://www.worldenergy.org/data/resources/resource/solar/

Sözen, A. (2009). Future projection of the energy dependency of Turkey using artificial neural network. *Energy Policy*, *37*(11), 4827–4833. doi:10.1016/j.enpol.2009.06.040

Sözen, A., Alp, I., & Iskender, Ü. (2014). An evaluation of Turkey's energy dependency. *Energy Sources. Part B, Economics, Planning, and Policy*, *9*(4), 398–412. doi:10.1080/15567249.2010.509080

Thapar, V., Agnihotri, G., & Sharma, A. (1999). Wind farm development- Government incentives. In *Proceedings of the National Conference on Wind Energy Commercialisation* (pp. 152–5). Academic Press.

Tunay, K. B., & Yüksel, S. (2017). The relationship between corporate governance and foreign ownership of the banks in developing countries. *Contaduría y Administración*, *62*(5), 25–26. doi:10.1016/j.cya.2017.05.007

Tunay, N., Yüksel, S., & Tunay, K. B. (2019). The Effects of Technology on Bank Performance in Advanced and Emerging Economies: An Empirical Analysis. In *Handbook of Research on Managerial Thinking in Global Business Economics* (pp. 263–280). IGI Global. doi:10.4018/978-1-5225-7180-3.ch015

Unbehaun, S. (2017). *The Relationship Between Renewable Energy Production and Energy Imports Among Countries in the European Economic Area* (Doctoral dissertation). Georgetown University.

Vaona, A. (2016). The effect of renewable energy generation on import demand. *Renewable Energy*, *86*, 354–359. doi:10.1016/j.renene.2015.07.062

Wind Energy. (2016). Retrieved July 10, 2018, from https://www.worldenergy.org/data/resources/resource/wind/

York, R. (2015). How Much Can We Expect the Rise in US Domestic Energy Production to Suppress Net Energy Imports? *Social Currents*, *2*(3), 222–230. doi:10.1177/2329496515589850

Yüksel, S. (2016a). Türkiye'de Cari İşlemler Açığının Belirleyicileri: Mars Yöntemi ile Bir İnceleme. *Bankacılar Dergisi*, *96*(27), 102–121.

Yüksel, S. (2016b). Bank aların Takipteki Krediler Oranını Belirleyen Faktörler: Türkiye İçin Bir Model Önerisi. *Bankacılar Dergisi*, *98*, 41–56.

Yüksel, S. (2017). The impacts of research and development expenses on export and economic growth. *International Business and Accounting Research Journal*, *1*(1), 1–8. doi:10.15294/ibarj.v1i1.1

Yüksel, S. (2017b). Determinants of the credit risk in developing countries after economic crisis: A case of Turkish banking sector. In *Global financial crisis and its ramifications on capital markets* (pp. 401–415). Cham: Springer. doi:10.1007/978-3-319-47021-4_28

Yüksel, S. (2017c). Strategies Out of Global Recession in EmergingMarkets: An Application for 2008 Global Crisis. In *Global Business Strategies in Crisis* (pp. 57–75). Cham: Springer. doi:10.1007/978-3-319-44591-5_5

Yüksel, S., & Canöz, İ. (2017). Does Islamic Banking Contribute to Economic Growth and Industrial Development in Turkey? *IKONOMIKA*, *2*(1), 93–102. doi:10.24042/febi.v2i1.945

Yüksel, S., Canöz, İ., & Özsarı, M. (2017). Causality Relationship between Interest Rate of Deposit Banks and Profit Share Rate of Islamic Banks in Turkey. *IKONOMIKA*, *2*(2), 131–148. doi:10.24042/febi.v2i2.1894

Yüksel, S., Dinçer, H., & Emir, Ş. (2017). Comparing the performance of Turkish deposit banks by using DEMATEL, Grey Relational Analysis (GRA) and MOORA approaches. *World Journal of Applied Economics*, *3*(2), 26–47. doi:10.22440/wjae.3.2.2

Yüksel, S., Mukhtarov, S., Mahmudlu, C., Mikayilov, J. I., & Iskandarov, A. (2018a). Measuring International Migration in Azerbaijan. *Sustainability*, *10*(1), 132. doi:10.3390u10010132

Yüksel, S., Mukhtarov, S., Mammadov, E., & Özsarı, M. (2018b). Determinants of Profitability in the Banking Sector: An Analysis of Post-Soviet Countries. *Economies*, *6*(3), 41. doi:10.3390/economies6030041

Yüksel, S., & Oktar, S. (2017). Okun yasasının farklı gelişme düzeyindeki ülkelere ilişkin ekonometrik analizi. *Marmara Üniversitesi İktisadi ve İdari Bilimler Dergisi*, *39*(1), 323–332. doi:10.14780/muiibd.329945

Yüksel, S., & Zengin, S. (2016a). Leading Indicators of 2008 Global Crisis: An Analysis with Logit and Mars Methods. *Finansal Araştırmalar ve Çalışmalar Dergisi*, *8*(15), 495–518.

Yüksel, S., & Zengin, S. (2016b). Causalityrelationshipbetweenimport, exportandgrowth rate in developingcountries. *International Journal of Commerce and Finance*, *2*(1), 147–156.

Yüksel, S., & Zengin, S. (2016c). Identifying the Determinants of Interest Rate Risk of the Banks: A Case of Turkish Banking Sector. *International Journal of Research in Business and Social Science*, *5*(6), 12-28.

Yüksel, S., & Zengin, S. (2017). Influencing Factors of Net Interest Margin in Turkish Banking Sector. *International Journal of Economicsand Financial Issues*, *7*(1), 178–191.

Zengin, S., Yüksel, S., & Kartal, M. T. (2018). Understanding the Factors that affect Foreign direct investment in Turkey by Using Mars method. *Finansal Araştırmalar ve Çalışmalar Dergisi*, *10*(18), 1309–1123.

Zhao, X., & Wu, Y. (2007). Determinants of China's energy imports: An empirical analysis. *Energy Policy*, *35*(8), 4235–4246. doi:10.1016/j.enpol.2007.02.034

KEY TERMS AND DEFINITIONS

E7 Countries: They explain seven biggest emerging countries in terms of economic growth.

Emerging Economy: It refers to the country which has a strong potential to become a developed economy in a short time.

Energy Import: It is the amount of money spent from the country's earnings for purchasing different energy from other countries.

G7 Countries: They contain seven developed countries that have highest economic growth.

GDP: It refers to the gross domestic product.

Chapter 3
The Benefits and Costs of Foreign Direct Investment for Sustainability in Emerging Market Economies

Deniz Güvercin
Istanbul Arel Üniversitesi, Turkey

ABSTRACT

The chapter contributes to the growing body of empirical researches by exploring the nexus among FDI, trade, carbon dioxide emission level, and the renewable energy use. Panel VAR econometric methodology upon the data for 18 emerging economies over the period of 1990-2014 is applied to uncover the interactive and simultenous relations among variables. Granger causality test results indicate that FDI, carbon emission, and renewable energy use Granger cause trade. Carbon emission and renewable energy use Granger cause FDI, FDI Granger causes carbon emission, and FDI granger causes renewable energy use. Impulse response analysis results indicate that FDI decreases trade, carbon emission, and renewable energy use. Moreover, carbonemission decreases trade, and increases FDI whereas it is decreased by renewable energy use. Results indicate that the Pollution Haven and the Pollution Halo hypothesis are valid for the FDI, however, the Pollution Haven hypothesis is not valid for trade. Additionally, results indicate that FDI decreases trade implying the presence of substitution relation between FDI and trade.

INTRODUCTION

The nexus between the pollution and the economic variables, in particular the nexus between the carbon emission and the GDP per capita has been studied by many scholars. The Environmental Kuznets Curve (EKC) is the diagram representing the inverse U-shaped relation between the carbon emission level and the GDP per capita. There are empirical studies in the literature providing evidences that pollutants, such as nitrogen oxide (Cole, Rayner & Bates; 1997), sulfur oxide (Shafik & Bandyopadhyay, 1992),

DOI: 10.4018/978-1-5225-8547-3.ch003

carbon monoxide (Carson, Jeon & Mc Cubbin, 1997) has inverse U-shaped relation with GDP per capita. However, although several studies in the literature providing evidences on the presence of the inverse U-shaped relation between GDP per capita and the greenhouse gas emission, there are also numerous studies providing evidences against the validity of the EKC hypothesis.

The affordability of the abatement technology, and the stringency ofenvironmental regulationsgenerate more environmental friendly conditions for economic activies in the developed economies relative to the developing economies. Moreover, feasibility of renewable energy sources and the energy efficient production processes decrease the demand for energy (Mielnik & Goldemberg, 2002). Additional to change in production technology and processes towards clean technology and energy efficient production, the people would be more prone to environmental goods rather than carbon dioxide intensive goods affecting the average pollution in the country.

Hassler et al. (2012) using data for U.S. show that R&D activity on inputs are scarce, or expensive, thus, consumption and particularly production activities at the lower GDP per capita levels might lead to the destruction of environment. Therefore, clean environment (and non-renewable energy reserves) becomes more scarce in the process of economic development. However, at high GDP levels, R&D activities on energy saving and renewable energy technologies increase.

The literature that has been developing in recent years focus on external sources of carbon emission. In particular, these studies examine empirically the impact of trade and the FDI on the carbon emission level in the country. There are two main hypothesis in the literature that are most of the empirical studies are referring to regarding the nexus between the carbon emission level and the trade and the FDI.

The Pollution Haven hypothesis argue that firms would prefer to produce in countries where the enforcement of environmental laws and regulations are less stringent. In other words, it argues that multinational companies would produce at and trade from the countries where the environmental laws are less stringent (Jensen, 1996; Hoffman et al., 2005; Dietzenbacher & Mukhopadhyay, 2007).Therefore, the multinationals through trade and FDI would raise the carbon emission level in the countries where the environmental rules are weak (and weakly applied). The Pollution Halo hypothesis argues (Birdsall & Wheeler, 1993; Görg and Strobl, 2004) that FDI transfers the environment friendly technologies to the host country contributing to the carbon emissiondecline in the country. In other words, the pollution halohypothesis claims that the introduction of low carbon intensive and clean production technologies by FDI would result in lower pressures on the non-renewable energy sources, and would lead tosustainable economic growth in the host country.

Trade and FDI might contribute to the production and consumption of carbon intensive goods in the country. Therefore, trade, FDI might contribute to the environmental degradation although they contribute significantly to the economic development. Developing countries and developed countries specialize on the production of commodities at the different ends of the value added distribution. Developed countries produce mostly high value added, environment friendly commodities whereas developing countries produce most of the industrial intermediate commodities containing highly mechanical andchemical componentsused in the production of high value added commodities. Therefore, lowering the trade barriers might lead to the rise of importof carbon intensive (intermediate) goods from countries where the enforcement of environmental laws are less stringent (Copeland & Taylor, 2004). Countries where the environmental laws are strictly enforced are mostly developed whereas countries where environmental laws are weakly enforced are mostly developing.

Therefore, liberalization of the trade would lead to the relocation of the production of carbon intensive goods from developed to the developing countries. In other words, relocation of production of commoditiesby trade and FDI would lead to more skewedcross country distribution of greenhouse gas emissions. Moreover, weakening of the environmental laws and regulations bydeveloped countries through trading with countries where the environmental laws are less stringently applied would increase the demand for carbon intensive goods globally that would generate upward pressures on the global greenhouse gas emissions.

An increase in the production and consumption of carbon intensive goods due to international and domestic economic activities would exert significant upward pressure on the energy cost which in turn increases the financial fragility (i.e. against the energy prices, exchange rates), in particular for oil importing economies. On the other hand, countries allocating resources for energy efficiency and the renewable energy such as biomass, hydropower and solar energy would have lower greenhouse gas emission, lower pressure on the conventional energy sources, and the lower financial fragility.

Renewable energy technologies such as solar thermal power, biodiesel and biomass gasifier would reduce the greenhouse gas emission and global warming via substituting conventional energy sources. Hassler *et al* (2012) argue that following 1970 oil price increases there was R&D efforts in the form of directed technological change to reduce the dependency of production to the non-renewable energy sources. Therefore, increasing pressure on the non-renewables leading to the rise in pricesof non-renewables relative to the renewable energy sources would stimulate thesubstitution of the non-renewables with the renewables in production processes due to profit considerations. Moreover, the usage of renewable energy technologiesfollowing the lowering of trade barriers would depend on several factors, in particular for developing countries, such as the nexus between the FDI and the renewable energy usage in the country, enforcement of environmental laws and regulations in the country, and the energy costs in the country.

The study contributes to the literature by examining empirically the impact of trade and FDI on the carbon emission level and the renewable energy use in the country. Because these variables interact and are endogenously determined, the Panel VAR methodology is preffered. We use data for 18 emerging economies over the period of 1990-2014. The emerging economies are selected as these economies face rising carbon emission costsfollowing the integration to the global economy.

The study contributes to the literature by examining empirically the interactions among the variables of carbon emission, trade openness, foreign direct investment and renewable energy use in the context of the emerging market economies. Because there are very few studies accounting the rising carbon emission cost in the emerging market economies, and the studying empirically of the carbon emission determinants in these economies, the study makes significant contribution to the literature. The paper identifies the impact of globalization on the carbon emission and renewable energy use in the context of emerging economies by referring to the pollution haven and the pollution halo hypothesis.

The structure of the paper is as follows; in the next section we refer about studies on the nexus among the carbon dioxide emission, the trade openness, the foreign direct investment and the renewable energy use. The following section would be on the data and the empirical methodology where we discuss the suitablity of the empirical model for the purpose of the study. Inthe fourth section we report panel granger causality test results, Panel VAR econometric model results, variance decomposition results and the impulse response analyze results.The discussion and conclusion is the final section where we discuss the results and implications of the empirical model.

REVIEW OF RELEVANT LITERATURE

In their seminal work, Holtz-Eakin and Selden (1992) describe the greenhouse gas emission cost of economic development. They state that "..their reading of the evidence suggests that there has been substantial and on-going change in the composition of the earth's atmosphere since the start of the Industrial Revolution, and that economic growth in countries at all levels of development appears to likely to exacerbate the flow of emissions into the atmosphere". In the following studies (Grossman and Krueger,1991; Selden and Song, 1994) the inverted-U shape relation between the GDP and the greenhouse gas emissions is more clearly described.The implication of the inverted U-shape relation between the GDP and the greenhouse gas emissions would be that developed countries and developing countries are located at the different ends of the global greenhouse gas emissions, and the direction of change inthe greenhouse gas emission by the GDP per capita is not same across countries.

Inverted U-shape relation imply that growing economies would have lower carbon emission cost of economic development suggestingthat global carbon emission cost of economic development would decline as world GDP per capita grows. Contrarily, Jorgensen (2014) report that the effect of economic development on the carbon intensity in Asia and South and Central America has been positive for 40 year, and switched in recent years from negative to positive in Africa and has been positive and stable around 0.126 for combined regions of North America, Europe and Oceania.

There are several empirical researches testing the validity of the EKC hypothesis. Apergis and Payne (2010), Lee and Chang (2008), Narayan and Smyth (2008) show the unidirectional causality running from energy consumption to economic growth. Ozturk and Acaravci (2010) confirms the presence of the EKC in Turkey whereas Özcan et al. (2018) and Katırcıoğlu and Katırcıoğlu (2018) provide evidences against the validity of EKC in Turkey. Bilgili et al. (2016) show the validity of EKC in OECD countries, Dinda (2009) shows that bidirectional causality between economic growth and carbon emission in OECD countries. Jaunky (2011) could not provide evidence supporting the EKC by using 36 high income countries, Atasoy (2017) provides weak empirical support for the EKC hypothesis by using data for 50 U.S. states. Therefore, although there are several studies providing empirical evidences supporting EKC, there are studies providing evidences negating the hypothesis.

The EKC is based on the fact that the demand for health and environment would increase with the income which might lead to change in social conventions, laws and regulations on the pollution. However, the income rise might be the induced by economic activities containing the production/consumption of the carbon intensive goods without installment of technology required to switch from environment hostile production to environment friendly production which would not generate results as predicted by EKC. Countries that are linked to global value chain by exporting carbon intensive goods and providing their land for production of carbon intensive goods would face significant challenges in tackling with the carbon cost of the economic development. In particular, countries securing their place in global value chain by exporting carbon intensive commodities would have difficulty in reducing costs of economic development.

The nexus between trade liberalization and the environmental degradation has received great interest by scholars. Grossman and Krueger (1991)focusing on the nexus between trade and the carbon emission argue that different channels might be present through which trade impact the environment. They argue about three channels through which trade liberalization might affect the environment. The scale effect channel is introduced to explain the increase in domestic consumption, production and carbon dioxide emission due to trade liberalization. The technique channel is introduced to explain the transfer of advanced technology reducing the environmental degradation in the host country. The composition channel is introduced to explain the change in economic structure of the host country by trade openness. Grossman and Krueger (1991), Bhagwati (1993), Panayotou (1993) and Selden and Song (1994) show that composition and technique channel together outweighs the scale effect. Tsurumi and Managi (2010) using semiparametric method of generalized additive modelsexamine the impact of technique, scale and composition channel on the sulfur dioxide emission and carbon dioxide emission. They find that the technique effect is sufficient to reduce sulfur dioxide emissions, but is not enough to reduce carbon dioxide emissions and energy use unless the country isdeveloped.

Birdsall and Wheeler (1992) argue that trade liberalization leads to transfer of higher environmental standards of developed countries to developing countries resulting in reduction in environmental degradation in developing countries. Contrarily, Hakimi and Hamdi (2016) using data for Tunisia and Morocco for the period of 1971-2013 show that trade openness damages environmental quality. Managi et al. (2009) using data for 88 countries where some of these countries from the OECD for the period of 1973-2000 show that trade liberalization reduces CO_2 (carbon dioxide) and SO_2 (sulfur dioxide) emission in OECD countries whereas trade liberalization increases CO_2 and SO_2 emission in non-OECD countries.

There are studies in the literature emphasizing theinstitutions in the country as the determining factor at the nexus between trade liberalization and the carbon emission. Rehman, Ali and Nasir (2007) using data for Pakistan, India, Bangladesh, and Sri Lanka for the period of 1984-2003 show that trade liberalization reduces the environmental degradation if the corruption is not common in the country. Cole et al. (2006) show that FDI contributes to the local pollution level if the local government is corrupted.Pellegrini and Gerlagh (2006) show that democracy improves environmental quality, but corruption decreases it.

As it is emphasized previously, countries might adopt renewable energy technologies as their rapid industrialization lead to the exhaustion of conventional energy sources. Sadorsky (2009) by using data for G7 countries show that main drivers of adoption of renewable energy is the increase in real GDP per capita, and inCO_2 per capita. Other than domestic reasons, adaptation of renewables in production might occur due to FDI spillover.

FDI spillover might lead to the adaptation of the renewable energy technologies in the production processes in the host country decreasing the carbon emission which is also emphasized by Pollution Halo hypothesis.Zarsky (1999) argue that multinationals from OECD countries utilize cleaner production technology as it is required to have qualified environmental management systems and advanced pollution abatement technologies by law. Wallace (1996) argue that environment friendly technologies including renewable energy technologies might spill over to indigenous firms through backward and forward linkages. Kim and Adilov (2011) argue that multinationals through FDI might transfer greener environmental standards to host countries to please local governments or due to uncertainty about local regulations.

Pollution Haven hypothesis argue that multinational companies would produce where the environmental laws and regulations are lax. Markusen (1993; 1997) Descroches (2007), Albornoz et al. (2009), Wagner and Timmins (2009), Manderson and Kneler (2012), Chung (2014) Doytch and Uctum (2015) provide theoretical and empirical evidences supporting the Pollution Haven hypothesis. Hanna (2015) using a panel of firm-level data over the period 1966-1999 to measure the effect of Clean Air Act Amendments (CAAA) on the multinational companies' production decision. They report that by implementation of CAAA, multinational companies increase their assets in other countries by 5.3% and output by 9%.

Pollution Haven hypothesis can also be present ininternational trade in the form that countries where environmental policies are stringent import carbon intensive goods from countries where environmental policies are lax. Peters et al. (2011) using data for the period of 1990-2008 show that from carbon emissions in developed countries fluctuated around some certain value however it increased dramatically in developing countries. They report that international trade was the main driver of carbon emission rise in developing countries, in particular from 0.4 Gt to 1.6 Gt from 1990 to 2008. Levinson (2009) argues that due to rise in import of carbon intensive goods, carbon emission incurred by U.S. manufacturers declined. He particularly reports that trade causeddecline in pollution by 10 percent in U.S. Therefore, it can be argue that through trade multinational contribute to the greenhouse gas emission rise in developing countries, and greenhouse gas emission decline in developed countries. On the other hand, Cole and Eliott (2005), Chung (2014), Antweiler et al. (2001) could not provide empirical evidences supporting the pollution haven hypothesis. However, they report that after controlling for the capital level in the country, the empirical results supports the pollution haven hypothesis.

It might be argued that the presence of strictenvironmental laws, and enforcement of environmental laws detoriates the competitiveness in the international market.Damania et al. (2003) emphasize the endogeneity of the environmental laws, and regulations by arguing that policymakers in host country might use environmental laws to attract FDI particularly to the polluting industries. Cole et al. (2006) argue in the related context that polluting firms might lobby to the host country policy makers to lower the environmental legal restrictions. Contarirly,Dechezlepretre and Sato (2017, p.3)states that "there is little evidence to suggest that strengthening environmental regulations reduces international competitiveness. The effect of current environmental regulations on where trade and investment take place has been shown to be negligible compared to other factors such as market conditions and the quality of the local workforce."

FDI might prompt innovation in the host country that promotes energy efficiency. Eskeland and Harrison (2003), Doytch and Uctum (2011) report that multinationals use renewable energy sources in the host country. Doytch and Narayan (2016) argue that FDI to underdeveloped sectors might lead to transfer of advanced technologies resulting in transition from conventional energy sources to renewable energy sources. Doytch and Uctum (2011)using data for 76 countries from different income groups show that FDI affects positively renewable energy use and reduces non-renewable energy sources in high, low and lower middle income countries.

The Porter hypothesis (Porter and van der Linde, 1995; Eliste and Frederiksson, 1998) argues that tight environmental rules and regulations stimulates technological and managerial innovation and renewable energy technologies. Therefore, FDI flowing into developing countries might not find it attractive to invest in green technology to enable cost efficiency which would affect negatively both innovation in renewable technology in home and host country. On the other hand, the multinational companies that produce under strict environmental laws might invest in renewable energy technologies and undertake innovations to enable energy saving which would affect their outflow decision. Therefore, the Porter hypothesis would contradict with, and restrict the realization of the Pollution Halo hypothesis.

Trade and FDI both contributes to the stock of technology in the host economy by providing monetary and material resources such as foreign exchanges for the (risky) technological investments, and intangible resources such as know-how transfers including operation and maintenance or after-sale services affecting both the carbon emission and the use of renewables. Chuang and Hsu (2004) argue that the FDI inflows to the China increased the technology import that increase the technology use in domestic industries and widened the international market for the China. Chuang (1998) argues that countries traded and characteristics of traded goods learned play a significant role in the advancement of technology in the home country.

There are several studies in the literature arguing that FDI and trade are inter-related. Tadesse and Ryan (2011) using data for the period 1989-1999 show that after controlling for the host's market maturity, host's export platform affects significantly the FDI flows, and the nexus between FDI and trade. FDI, thus, might choose to inflow to the countries from where it is less costly to export to nearby countries. Japanese multinational companies invest in Mexico (which is in NAFTA) to have easy access to U.S. and Canadian markets(Tadesse and Ryan, 2011). Nishitateno (2012) using data for Japanese origin FDI covering 37 products and 49 host countries over the period 1999 to 2008, report that increase in FDI outflows in upstream firms do not pass through down stream firms in the form of decreasing demand for intermediate goods. Therefore, they report that increase in FDI outflow do not lead to decrease in intermediate exports from home country.

Additionally, being the horizontal FDI or vertical FDI affects the nexus between the FDI and trade. Horizontal FDI is undertaken to produce final goods to serve for the host market, and vertical FDI is undertaken to produce intermediate goods in the host country to benefit from local comparative advantages such as low labor costs. Literature on the nexus between horizontal FDI and the trade argue that FDI and trade relation is substitution rather than complementary (Brainard, 1997; Aizenman and Noy, 2005).

The identification of interaction between FDI and trade plays a significant role in identifying the indirect paths through which these variables might exert an influence on the carbon emission. FDI inflow might increase the export of the carbon intensive goods from the host country. In particular, multinationals through FDI might use host country as an export platform to produce carbon intensive goods for large markets nearby. Thus, FDI might stimulate export where the combined effect leads to superior environmental degradation

Therefore, since FDI and trade might interact, and be endogenously determined, the impact of these variables on the carbon emission and renewable energy use should be formulated by the econometric technique taking account the interactive and simultaneity among variables. Panel VAR econometric technique is well-suited for this purpose. Moreover, using Panel VAR econometric analysis would reveal the systematic dynamic relationships, which would not be uncovered due to idiosyncratic effects on the country level (Gavin and Theodorou, 2005). Panel VAR econometric technique also allows for Granger causality, Cholesky decomposition and Impulse Response function that displays the causal relations among variables in the short, medium and long-run.

Emerging market economies drive the global economic growth by attracting significant size of capital investments. Emerging market economies due to their high integration to the global economy face with carbon emission costs of production and high energy costs. IEO2005 midterm outlook report that emerging economies account for approximately 70% of the increase in world energy use. It is reported that emerging market economies' energy use would surpass the energy use in the developed market economies in 2020, and it is expected that the energy use in emerging market economies would surpass the developed market economies' energy use by % 9 in 2025. There are several studies examining the impact of various variables on the carbon dioxide emission in the emerging market economies.

Sadorsky (2010) using a panel data set on 22 emerging countries over the period 1990- 2006 show that financial development measured by stock market indicators increases the energy consumption increasing the carbon dioxide emission level in these countries. Sadorsky (2014)using a panel of emerging economies show that urbanization has ambigous effect on the carbon dioxide emission. Paramati et al (2016) using a panel of 20 emerging market economies over the period 1991-2012 show that FDI and stock market developments have positive significant impact on the clean energy consumption.

Apergis and Payne (2011) using a panel of 16 emerging market economies over the period 1990-2007 show that there is a long run equilibrium relationship between real GDP, renewable electricity consumption, non-renewable electricity consumption, real gross fixed capital formation and the labor foce. The panel error correction model shows that there is a unidirectional causality from economic growth to renewable electricity consumption in the short run and a bidirectional causality in the long run. Sadorsky (2009) by using the panel of emerging market economies confirms that increase in real GDP per capita increases renewable energy consumptionper capita. He shows that in long term, a 1% increase in real income per cappita increases the consumption of renewable energy per capita by approximately 3.5% . Salim and Rafiq (2012) using a panel of 6 emerging market economies, show that in the long run renewable energy consumption is significantly determined by income and pollutant emission. These results show the significance of the renewable energy sources in substituting the conventional energy sources used up in the economic growth in the emerging market economies.

DATA AND METHODOLOGY

We used data for 18 Emerging Economies over the period of 1990-2014. The countries that are included are; Brazil, China, Chile, Colombia, Czech Republic, Hungary, Kore Republic, Indonesia, India, Mexico, Malaysia, Peru, Phillipines, Poland, South Africa, Russian Federation, Thailand, Turkey. The sample period is selected according to availability of the data, and the purpose of the study. The variables are Foreign Direct Investment, Trade Openness, CO_2Emission and Renewable Energy Use. The Table 1 displays the variables, and the sources of data. Table 2 displays the summary statistics for these variables.

The variables in the study are interrelated and are endogenously determined, thus, we employed the Panel VAR model to unravel the dynamic relations among variables where we use the panel data to avoid the spurious relations imposed by country specific structures. Panel VAR model is based on

Table 1. Variables and source

Variable	Source
Foreign Direct Investment (% of GDP) – (FDI)	World Development Indicators
Renewable Energy Consumption (% of total final energy consumption) – (Renewable)	World Development Indicators
Trade (% of GDP) - (Trade)	World Development Indicators
Carbon Dioxide Emissions (Metric Tons Per Capita) - (CO_2)	World Development Indicators

Table 2. Descriptive statistics

Variable	Observation	Mean	Std. Dev.	Minimum	Maximum
D.FDI	431	1.18	8.05	-41.88	84.3
D.Renewable	409	.081	3.5	-49.5	32.9
D.Trade	428	.041	.32	-1.6	1.2
D.CO_2	432	-.3	1.27	-7.97	5.05

"Helmert procedure" which is priorily introduced by Arellano and Bover (1995). The procudure helps to lower the biased caused by the country fixed structures. The mean - differencing generate bias since the country fixed effects are correlated with the regressors due to lags of the dependent varaibles. The "Helmert procedure" by removing the forward mean render orthogonal transformed variables and lagged regressors. These transformed variables and lagged regressors are used as instruments for estimations through System GMM (Love and Zicchino, 2006). Panel VAR econometric technique allows for Granger causality, Cholesky decomposition and Impulse Response function used to uncover the interrelations among variables in the short, medium and long-run.

The table 3 shows the unit root tests for these variables. Because the Panel VAR methodology requires the stability of the system, the series should be tested whether they are stationary by unit root tests. We used Im, Peseran and Shin unit root test for the purpose.

Unit root tests results indicate that all series are stationary at first differences. Therefore, we use the first difference levelseries for these variables.

$$x_{it} = \mu_i + T(l) X_{it-1} + e_{it} \quad (1)$$

i =1,..., 21 ; t =1,...,19

x is dependent variable; **X** is vector of (lagged) regressors ; **T** is the vector of coefficients including own and cross-effects of the *l*th lag of the regressors (including the dependent variable). The country-specific effects are correlated with the error term and estimating it by the OLS would lead tobiased coefficients. The model is transformed in terms of forward orthogonal deviations (Arellano and Bover, 1995) and estimated with GMM methodology using lagged values as instruments. (Amorim and Alves de Silva, 2016). The model results displayed at table 6. Abrigo & Love (2016)'s Stata code of Panel VAR is used for estimation purposes.

Table 3. Im, Peseran and Shin panel unit root test result

Variable	Statistic	P-Value	Order of Integration
FDI	-14.62	.00	I(1)
Renewable	-11.4	.00	I(1)
Trade	-12.93	.00	I(1)
CO_2	-13.81	.00	I(1)

Table 4. Optimal lag selection criteria

LAG	CD	J	J pvalue	MBIC	MAIC	MQIC
1	-.44	56.3	.19	-219.1	-39.61	-111.36
2	.63	26.3	.75	-157.4	-37.74	-85.57
3	.66	17.3	.36	-74.51	-14.68	-38.6

Note: MBIC: Value of modified BIC; MAIC: Value of modified AIC; MQIC: Value of modified HQ; J: Value of Hansen's J statistics.

The optimal lag selection criteria[1] indicate that (the lowest values of MBIC, MAIC, MQIC) the optimal number of lag is one. Table 5 shows the Panel Granger Causality test results. The Null hypothesis is that the excluded variable granger causes the variable of interest in the column.

RESULTS AND DISCUSSION

Granger causality test results indicate that FDI, co_2emission, renewable energy use granger cause to trade openness. CO_2 emission and renewable energy use granger cause FDI. FDI granger causes co_2emission, and FDI granger causes to renewable energy use.

The ordering of the variables in the VAR model should be made according to endogeneity of the variables in the sense that the most exogenous of the variable is ordered before other variables. The granger causality test results as well as economic theory are used for the determination of the ordering of the variables. Panel VAR estimation results are displayed at the table 6.

Panel VAR stability analysis is used to show whether the VAR model is stable. Lutkepohl (2005) and Hamilton (1994) show that if all moduli displayed at table 7 is less than one, then the VAR model is stable.

Figure 1 represents show that the eigenvalues lie inside the unit circle, thus, the Panel VAR is stable. Stability ensures the known interpretation of estimated impulse-response functions and forecast error variance decompositions (Abrigo & Love, 2016).

Forecast error variance decomposition which is sensitive to the ordering of the variables is displayed below at the Table 8. The decomposition measures the forecast error variance of an endogenous variable that can be attributed to orthogonalized shocks to itself or to another endogenous variable.

Table 8 shows that the greatest portion of variances of all variables are explained by the variables themselves. On the other hand, significant portion of (first difference of) FDI (14%) is explained by the CO_2 emission indicating the presence of pollution haven hypothesis.

Impulse response functions (which are simply derived from the model displayed at table 6) show the response of the variable to a one time, one standard deviation innovation in another (endogenous) variable.

Figure 2 displays the graphs for impulse response functions. Response of trade to a one time, one standard deviation in FDI is negative significant. Response of co_2emission to a one time, one standard

Table 5. Panel VAR granger causality test results

Equation/Excluded	D.Trade	D.FDI	D.Carbon	D.Renewable
D.Trade		**21.9** **(.000)**	**4.57** **(.032)**	**3.3** **(.069)**
D.FDI	1.47 (.225)		**8.841** **(.003)**	**15.45** **(.019)**
D.Carbon	1.559 (.212)	**14.55** **(.000)**		2.431 (.119)
D.Renewable	.677 (.411)	**6.155** **(.013)**	0.975 (.323)	

Note: The Ch-Square values are in the cells and the probability values are in the parenthesis. The bold characters represent the presence of granger causality from the excluded variable in the column to the equation variable in the row. The bold characters show the presence of Granger causality.

Table 6. Panel VAR estimates

	Coefficient	Standard Errors	Z-Value	P- Value	95% Confidence Interval
D.Renewable (t)					
D.Renewable (t-1)	.27	.081	3.34	.001	.11-.43
D.Carbon (t-1)	.15	.15	.99	.323	-.15 - .46
D.FDI (t-1)	-.04	.017	-2.48	.013	-.07 - -.009
D.Trade (t-1)	-.005	.006	-.82	.411	-.018 -.007
DCarbon (t)					
D.Renewable (t-1)	-.014	.009	-1.56	.119	-.03 - .003
D.Carbon(t-1)	-.015	.076	-.2	.843	-.16 - .13
D.FDI (t-1)	-.005	.0015	-3.82	.000	-.0087 - -.002
D.Trade (t-1)	.003	.002	1.25	.212	-.0019 - .0086
D.FDI (t)					
D.Renewable (t-1)	.72	.31	2.34	.019	.11 – 1.33
D.Carbon (t-1)	5.14	1.73	2.97	.003	1.75 – 8.53
D.FDI (t-1)	.076	.075	1.01	.313	-.0717 -.224
D.Trade (t-1)	.05	.04	1.21	.225	-.032- .13
D.Trade (t)					
D.Renewable (t-1)	-.48	.27	-1.82	.069	-1.01- .038
D.Carbon (t-1)	-5.39	2.52	-2.14	.032	-10.34- -.45
D.FDI (t-1)	-.2	.04	-4.68	.00	-.28- -.11
D.Trade (t-1)	.07	.07	1.1	.271	-.06-.21
Number of Observation			37118		
Number of Panels			12.84		
Average Number of T			20.6		
Final GMM Criterion Q(b)			.137		
Instruments			l(1/4).(D.Renewable D.Carbon D.FDI D.Trade)		

Source: Author's own calculation

Table 7. Panel VAR stability conditions

Eigenvalue		
Real	**Imaginary**	**Modulus**
.06	-.27	.28
.06	.27	.28
.22	0	.21
.06	0	.062

Figure 1. Eigenvalues

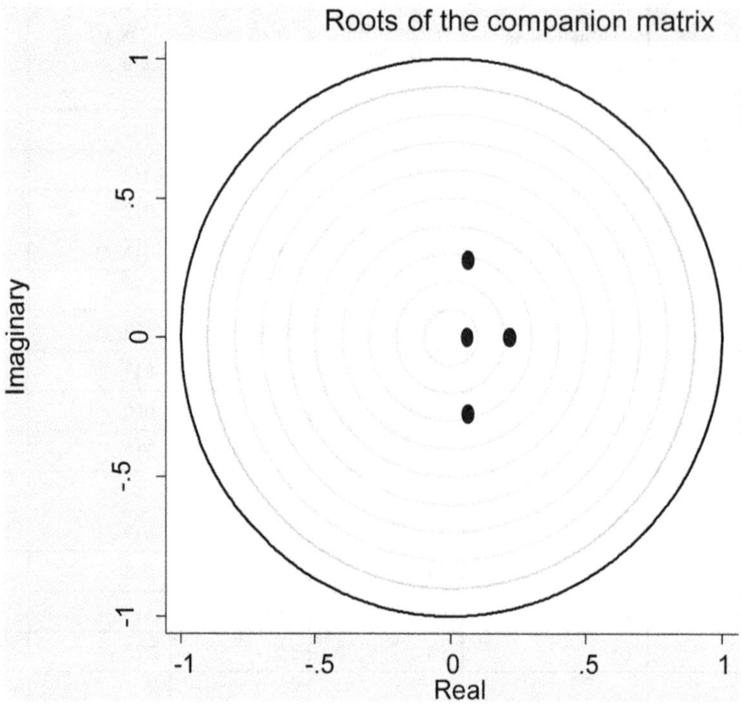

Table 8. Forecast error variance decomposition

Response Variable	Forecast Horizon	Impulse Variable			
		D. Renewable	D.Carbon	D.FDI	D.Trade
D.Renewable	3 7 10	.975 .975 .975	.002 .002 .002	.021 .021 .021	.001 .001 .001
D.Carbon	3 7 10	.029 .029 .029	.96 .96 .96	.0048 .0049 .0049	.0048 .0048 .0048
D.FDI	3 7 10	.02 .02 .02	.14 .14 .14	.83 .83 .83	.007 .007 .007
D.Trade	3 7 10	.007 .007 .007	.068 .068 .068	.015 .015 .015	.9 .9 .9

deviation in FDI is negative significant, and response of renewable energy use to a one time, one standard deviation in FDI variable is negative significant.

Response ofTradeto a one time, one standard deviation in co_2emissionvariable is negative significant, whereas the response of FDI variable to a one time, one standard deviation in co_2emission variable is positivesignificant.Additionally, response of co_2 emission to a one time, one standard deviation in the renewable energy use is negative significant.

Figure 2. Impulse responses

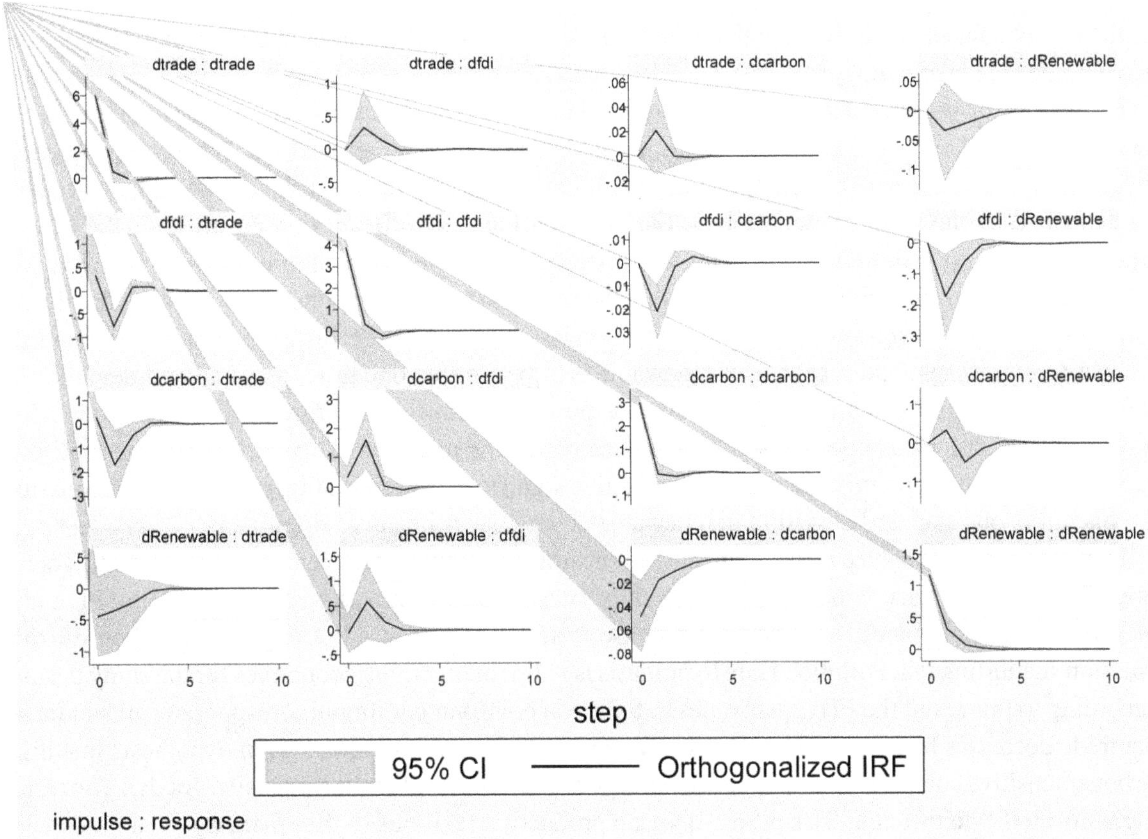

CONCLUSION AND POLICY SUGGESTIONS

This section aims to discuss the direct and indirect pathes that FDI and trade might exert on the renewable use and the carbon emission that are suggested by the empirical model results. Because the variables are endogenously determined the Panel VAR methodology is used. We used data for 18 Emerging Economies over the period of 1990-2014.

Econometric model, the Panel-VAR methodology accounts the dynamic, interactive and simultanous relations among variables. Becuase the data include the time dimension, to avoid the spurious relations the non-stationary processes are determined beforehand, and differenced forms of the non-stationary variables are used. Granger causality test results indicate that FDI, co_2 emission, renewable energy use granger causes trade openness. CO_2emission, and renewable energy use granger cause FDI. FDI granger causes co_2emission, and FDI granger causes renewable energy use. Granger causality results suggest that there is a path that FDI would affect the co_2emission and renewable energy use which is emphasized by the Pollution Halo and the Pollution Haven hypothesis. CO_2 emission and the renewable energy use affect trade and the FDI, indicating the significance of host country's energy sources and how it is linked to the trade flows which opens the avenue for the validity of the Pollution Haven and the Pollution Halo hypothesis. On the other hand, althoughFDI granger causes trade, the econometric results do not suggest the indirect path through (trade) which the FDI might affect the carbon emission or the renewable energy use.

Forecast error variance decompositions are used to explore the determinants of the variations in the variables in the short, medium and the long terms by the variables included into the system. According to forecast error variance decomposition; the greatest portions of the variances of all the variables are explained by the variables themselves. On the other hand, significant portion of the FDI (%14) is explained by the co_2emission which would indicate the presence of the pollution haven hypothesis.

Impulse response functions results show that the response of trade to a one time, one standard deviation in FDI is negative significant, response of co_2emission to a one time, one standard deviation in FDI is negative significant, and response of renewable energy use to a one time, one standard deviation in FDI variable is negative significant. Moreover, response of trade to a one time, one standard deviation in co_2emission variable is negative significant, whereas the response of FDI variable to a one time, one standard deviation in co_2emission variable is positive significant. Additionally, response of co_2emission to a one time, one standard deviation in renewable energy use is negative significant.

Impulse response analyze results indicate the substitution relation between trade and the FDI. Therefore, FDI decreases trade which might be result of substitution of import with production by FDI, and the presence of horizontal FDI.Impulse response results indicate that FDI decreases carbon dioxide emission suggesting that Pollution Halo hypothesis is valid for emerging economies for the study period. According to this result the FDI contributes to the clean environment. Impulse response results indicate that trade decreases by co_2emission. The result conflicts with the Pollution Haven hypothesis that high carbon intensive countries would not be selected to make import (of carbon intensive goods). The result might also indicate that countries prefer to set up production facilities in the emerging economies with high carbon emission level rather than import from them due to possibility of satisfying demand in both country of the origin and in the host country. Moreover, FDI inflows would decrease trade directly, but increases indirectly through decrease in co_2emission.

On the other hand, carbon dioxide emission increases FDI suggesting that domestic pollution level stimulates FDI entrances as claimed by the Pollution Haven hypothesis. Therefore, impulse response analysis results indicate that there are evidences providing support for both the Pollution Haven and the Pollution Halo hypothesisin the emerging economies over the study period.The results would indicate that even FDI inflows rise by pollution level, FDI through its advanced green technology, and lower energy demand contributes to the clean environment in the host country. It can also be argued that if the FDI absorb the domestic demand and crowd out some of the domestic firms, it would lead to lower total energy demand, and lower carbon emission levels in the country.

Impulse response results indicate that renewable energy use decreases by FDI. Moreover, impulse response results indicate that renewable energy use decreasesco_2emission. The result might be led by the energy efficiency in production together with market stealing effect. In other words, as more of the domesticdemand is absorbed by FDI, the total demand for conventional energy sources as well as renewable energy sources would decrase. Neverthless, FDI reduces renewable energy use which decreases co_2emission, FDI decreases co_2emission.

FDI might exert a positive impact on the carbon emission due to reduced renewable energy use. Eventhough it can be claimed that the multinationals would subtitute domestic firms in production reducing the energy and carbon emission costs of production, in the long run domestic firms would not have sufficiently long history of using renewables in production processes. FDI,thus, might lead to lower effort by domestic firms in making innovations in renewable energy sector resulting in exponentially increased cost of installment of complex renewable energy technologies in the presence of crisis in conventional energy sources.

The domestic policy makers to preserve the conventional energy sources in the long run should promote the renewable energy use in the presence of FDI inflows. On the other hand, FDI inflows should be promoted as it leads to lower carbon emission cost. Because the results indicate that FDI would substitute away the trade it would decrease the heavy dependence on import and significance of the foreign currencies reducing the financail fragility of these economies. Policy makers, thus, must be selective in policies favoring foreign companies by abstaining the false trade-offs between economic growth and environment.

Eventhough there are significant resuls played through the FDI over other variables in the system, results display that trade does not affect neither carbon emission level nor the renewable energy use in the country. Therefore, economic policies should be formulated to promote FDI to reduce carbon emission level in the long run while spillover mechanisms generate incentives for domestic firms to follow the energy efficient production techniques adapted by multinations.

Because there are very few studies accounting the rising carbon cost in the emerging market economies and the determinants of carbon dioxide emission in these economies, the study makes substantial contribution to the literature by contributing to the body of empirical researches. The paper in particular identify the impact of globalization on the carbon emission and renewable energy use by examining the presence of several hypothesis including the Pollution Haven and the Pollution Halo hypothesis.

Moreover, the paper by showing the validity of both the Pollution Haven and Pollution Halo hypothesis at the nexus between FDI and carbon emission provide significant empirical evidence in the growing body of empirical researhces on the nexus between FDI and carbon emission. Moreover, the paper identifies the indirect path through which FDI might exert positive influence on the carbon emission which is also significant contribution to the literature on the nexus among the varialbles of FDI, renewable energy use and carbon emission. The paper also shows that the Pollution Haven hypothesis is not valid for trade in emerging economies. We argue that the result indicates that multinationals preffer FDI over import if the emerging economy has high carbon emission level.

REFERENCES

Adilov, N., Dilts, D. A., Kim, M. H., & Samavati, H. (2011). *Climatology and Finance: Is There a Relation Between Stock Market and Climate Change?* Academic Press.

Aizenman, J., & Noy, I. (2006). FDI and trade—Two-way linkages? *The Quarterly Review of Economics and Finance*, *46*(3), 317–337. doi:10.1016/j.qref.2006.02.004

Albornoz, F., Cole, M. A., Elliott, R. J., & Ercolani, M. G. (2009). In search of environmental spillovers. *World Economy*, *32*(1), 136–163. doi:10.1111/j.1467-9701.2009.01160.x

Amorim, G., & Da Silva, M. E. A. (2016). *Governance and Growth: A Panel VAR Approach*. Academic Press.

Antweiler, W., Copeland, B. R., & Taylor, M. S. (2001). Is free trade good for the environment? *The American Economic Review*, *91*(4), 877–908. doi:10.1257/aer.91.4.877

Apergis, N., & Payne, J. E. (2010). The Emissions, Energy Consumption, and Growth Nexus: Evidence from the Commonwealth of Independent States. *Energy Policy*, *38*(1), 650–655. doi:10.1016/j.enpol.2009.08.029

Apergis, N., & Payne, J. E. (2011). Renewable and non-renewable electricity consumption–growth nexus: Evidence from emerging market economies. *Applied Energy*, *88*(12), 5226–5230. doi:10.1016/j.apenergy.2011.06.041

Arellano, M., & Bover, O. (1995). Another look at the instrumental variable estimation of error-components models. *Journal of Econometrics*, *68*(1), 29–51. doi:10.1016/0304-4076(94)01642-D

Atasoy, B. S. (2017). Testing the environmental Kuznets curve hypothesis across the US: Evidence from panel mean group estimators. *Renewable & Sustainable Energy Reviews*, *77*, 731–747. doi:10.1016/j.rser.2017.04.050

Bhagwati, J. (1993). The case for free trade. *Scientific American*, *269*(5), 42–49. doi:10.1038cientificamerican1193-42 PMID:8337597

Bilgili, F., Koçak, E., & Bulut, Ü. (2016). The dynamic impact of renewable energy consumption on CO2 emissions: A revisited Environmental Kuznets Curve approach. *Renewable & Sustainable Energy Reviews*, *54*, 838–845. doi:10.1016/j.rser.2015.10.080

Birdsall, N., & Wheeler, D. (1993). Trade policy and industrial pollution in Latin America: Where are the pollution havens? *Journal of Environment & Development*, *2*(1), 137–149. doi:10.1177/107049659300200107

Brainard, S. L. (1997). An Empirical Assessment of the Proximity-Concentration Trade-off Between Multinational Sales and Trade. *The American Economic Review*, *87*(4).

Carson, R. T., Jeon, Y., & McCubbin, D. R. (1997). The relationship between air pollution emissions and income: US data. *Environment and Development Economics*, *2*(4), 433–450. doi:10.1017/S1355770X97000235

Chuang, Y. C., & Hsu, P. F. (2004). FDI, trade, and spillover efficiency: Evidence from China's manufacturing sector. *Applied Economics*, *36*(10), 1103–1115. doi:10.1080/0003684042000246812

Chung, S. (2014). Environmental regulation and foreign direct investment: Evidence from South Korea. *Journal of Development Economics*, *108*, 222–236. doi:10.1016/j.jdeveco.2014.01.003

Cole, M. A., & Elliott, R. J. (2005). FDI and the capital intensity of "dirty" sectors: A missing piece of the pollution haven puzzle. *Review of Development Economics*, *9*(4), 530–548. doi:10.1111/j.1467-9361.2005.00292.x

Cole, M. A., Elliott, R. J., & Fredriksson, P. G. (2006). Endogenous pollution havens: Does FDI influence environmental regulations? *The Scandinavian Journal of Economics*, *108*(1), 157–178. doi:10.1111/j.1467-9442.2006.00439.x

Cole, M. A., Rayner, A. J., & Bates, J. M. (1997). The environmental Kuznets curve: An empirical analysis. *Environment and Development Economics*, *2*(4), 401–416. doi:10.1017/S1355770X97000211

Copeland, B. R., & Taylor, M. S. (2004). Trade, growth, and the environment. *Journal of Economic Literature*, *42*(1), 7–71. doi:10.1257/.42.1.7

Damania, R., Fredriksson, P. G., & List, J. A. (2003). Trade liberalization, corruption, and environmental policy formation: Theory and evidence. *Journal of Environmental Economics and Management*, *46*(3), 490–512. doi:10.1016/S0095-0696(03)00025-1

Dechezleprêtre, A., & Sato, M. (2017). The impacts of environmental regulations on competitiveness. *Review of Environmental Economics and Policy*, *11*(2), 183–206. doi:10.1093/reep/rex013

Dietzenbacher, E., & Mukhopadhyay, K. (2007). An empirical examination of the pollution haven hypothesis for India: Towards a green Leontief paradox? *Environmental and Resource Economics*, *36*(4), 427–449. doi:10.100710640-006-9036-9

Dinda, S. (2009). Climate change and human insecurity. *International Journal of Global Environmental Issues*, *9*(1/2), 103–109. doi:10.1504/IJGENVI.2009.022088

Doytch, N., & Narayan, S. (2016). Does FDI influence renewable energy consumption? An analysis of sectoral FDI impact on renewable and non-renewable industrial energy consumption. *Energy Economics*, *54*, 291–301. doi:10.1016/j.eneco.2015.12.010

Doytch, N., & Uctum, M. (2011). *Globalization and the Environmental Spillovers of sectoral FDI.* Unpublished manuscript.

Eliste, P., & Fredriksson, P. G. (1998). *Does open trade result in a race to the bottom? Cross country evidence.* World Bank.

Eskeland, G. S., & Harrison, A. (2003). *Moving to greener pasture.* Multinationals and the Pollution Haven.

Faiz-Ur-Rehman, A., & Nasir, M. (2007). Corruption, trade openness, and environmental quality: A panel data analysis of selected South Asian countries. *Pakistan Development Review*, 673–688.

Gavin, W. T., & Theodorou, A. T. (2005). A common model approach to macroeconomics: Using panel data to reduce sampling error. *Journal of Forecasting*, *24*(3), 203–219. doi:10.1002/for.954

Görg, H., & Strobl, E. (2004). Spillovers from Foreign Firms through Worker Mobility: An Empirical Investigation. *The Scandinavian Journal of Economics*, *107*(4), 693–709. doi:10.1111/j.1467-9442.2005.00427.x

Grossman, G. M., & Krueger, A. B. (1991). *Environmental impacts of a North American free trade agreement.* National Bureau of Economic Research. doi:10.3386/w3914

Hakimi, A., & Hamdi, H. (2016). Trade liberalization, FDI inflows, environmental quality and economic growth: A comparative analysis between Tunisia and Morocco. *Renewable & Sustainable Energy Reviews*, *58*, 1445–1456. doi:10.1016/j.rser.2015.12.280

Hamilton, J. D. (1994). *Time series analysis* (Vol. 2). Princeton, NJ: Princeton university press.

Hanna, R. (2010). US environmental regulation and FDI: Evidence from a panel of US-based multinational firms. *American Economic Journal. Applied Economics*, *2*(3), 158–189. doi:10.1257/app.2.3.158

Hassler, J., Krusell, P., & Olovsson, C. (2012). *Energy-saving technical change (No. w18456)*. National Bureau of Economic Research. doi:10.3386/w18456

Hoffmann, R., Lee, C. G., Ramasamy, B., & Yeung, M. (2005). FDI and pollution: A granger causality test using panel data. *Journal of International Development: The Journal of the Development Studies Association*, *17*(3), 311–317. doi:10.1002/jid.1196

Jaunky, V. C. (2011). The CO2 emissions-income nexus: Evidence from rich countries. *Energy Policy*, *39*(3), 1228–1240. doi:10.1016/j.enpol.2010.11.050

Jensen, V. M. (1996). *Trade and environment: the pollution haven hypothesis and the industrial flight hypothesis; some perspectives on theory and empirics*. University of Oslo, Centre for Development and the Environment.

Jungmittag, A. (2004). Innovations, technological specialisation and economic growth in the EU. *International Economics and Economic Policy*, *1*(2-3), 247–273. doi:10.100710368-004-0018-5

Katircioğlu, S., & Katircioğlu, S. (2018). Testing the role of urban development in the conventional environmental Kuznets curve: Evidence from Turkey. *Applied Economics Letters*, *25*(11), 741–746. doi:10.1080/13504851.2017.1361004

Lee, C. C., & Chang, C.-P. (2008). Energy Consumption and Economic Growth in Asian Economies: A More Comprehensive Analysis Using Panel Data. *Resource and Energy Economics*, *30*(1), 50–65. doi:10.1016/j.reseneeco.2007.03.003

Levinson, A. (2009). Technology, international trade, and pollution from US manufacturing. *The American Economic Review*, *99*(5), 2177–2192. doi:10.1257/aer.99.5.2177

Lütkepohl, H. (2005). *New introduction to multiple time series analysis*. Springer Science & Business Media. doi:10.1007/978-3-540-27752-1

Managi, S., Hibiki, A., & Tsurumi, T. (2009). Does trade openness improve environmental quality? *Journal of Environmental Economics and Management*, *58*(3), 346–363. doi:10.1016/j.jeem.2009.04.008

Manderson, E., & Kneller, R. (2012). Environmental regulations, outward FDI and heterogeneous firms: Are countries used as pollution havens? *Environmental and Resource Economics*, *51*(3), 317–352. doi:10.100710640-011-9500-z

Markusen, J. R. (1997). Costly pollution abatement, competitiveness and plant location decisions. *Resource and Energy Economics*, *19*(4), 299–320. doi:10.1016/S0928-7655(97)00014-6

Markusen, J. R., Morey, E. R., & Olewiler, N. D. (1993). Environmental policy when market structure and plant locations are endogenous. *Journal of Environmental Economics and Management*, *24*(1), 69–86. doi:10.1006/jeem.1993.1005

Mielnik, O., & Goldemberg, J. (2002). Foreign direct investment and decoupling between energy and gross domestic product in developing countries. *Energy Policy*, *30*(2), 87–89. doi:10.1016/S0301-4215(01)00080-5

Narayan, P. K., & Smyth, R. (2008). Energy Consumption and Real GDP in G7 Countries: New Evidence from Panel Cointegration with Structural Breaks. *Energy Economics*, *30*(5), 2331–2341. doi:10.1016/j.eneco.2007.10.006

Nishitateno, S. (2012). *Global Production Sharing in the Japanese Automobile Industry: A Comparative Analysis* (No. 2012-02). Academic Press.

Ozcan, B., Apergis, N., & Shahbaz, M. (2018). A revisit of the environmental Kuznets curve hypothesis for Turkey: New evidence from bootstrap rolling window causality. *Environmental Science and Pollution Research International*, *25*(32), 32381–32394. doi:10.100711356-018-3165-x PMID:30229495

Ozturk, I., & Acaravci, A. (2010). CO_2 Emissions, Energy Consumption and Economic Growth in Turkey. *Renewable & Sustainable Energy Reviews*, *14*(9), 3220–3225. doi:10.1016/j.rser.2010.07.005

Panayotou, T. (1993). *Empirical tests and policy analysis of environmental degradation at different stages of economic development (No. 992927783402676).* International Labour Organization.

Paramati, S. R., Ummalla, M., & Apergis, N. (2016). The effect of foreign direct investment and stock market growth on clean energy use across a panel of emerging market economies. *Energy Economics*, *56*, 29–41. doi:10.1016/j.eneco.2016.02.008

Pellegrini, L., & Gerlagh, R. (2006). Corruption, democracy, and environmental policy: An empirical contribution to the debate. *Journal of Environment & Development*, *15*(3), 332–354. doi:10.1177/1070496506290960

Peters, G. P., Minx, J. C., Weber, C. L., & Edenhofer, O. (2011). Growth in emission transfers via international trade from 1990 to 2008. *Proceedings of the national academy of sciences*. 10.1073/pnas.1006388108

Porter, M. E. (1991). Towards a dynamic theory of strategy. *Strategic Management Journal*, *12*(S2), 95–117. doi:10.1002mj.4250121008

Porter, M. E., & Van der Linde, C. (1995). Toward a new conception of the environment-competitiveness relationship. *The Journal of Economic Perspectives*, *9*(4), 97–118. doi:10.1257/jep.9.4.97

Sadorsky, P. (2009). Renewable energy consumption and income in emerging economies. *Energy Policy*, *37*(10), 4021–4028. doi:10.1016/j.enpol.2009.05.003

Sadorsky, P. (2011). Financial development and energy consumption in Central and Eastern European frontier economies. *Energy Policy*, *39*(2), 999–1006. doi:10.1016/j.enpol.2010.11.034

Sadorsky, P. (2014). The effect of urbanization on CO2 emissions in emerging economies. *Energy Economics*, *41*, 147–153. doi:10.1016/j.eneco.2013.11.007

Salim, R. A., & Rafiq, S. (2012). Why do some emerging economies proactively accelerate the adoption of renewable energy? *Energy Economics*, *34*(4), 1051–1057. doi:10.1016/j.eneco.2011.08.015

Selden, T. M., & Holtz-Eakin, D. (1992). *Stoking the Fires? Co2 Emissions and Economic Growth.* National Bureau of Economic Research.

Selden, T. M., & Song, D. (1994). Environmental quality and development: Is there a Kuznets curve for air pollution emissions? *Journal of Environmental Economics and Management, 27*(2), 147–162. doi:10.1006/jeem.1994.1031

Shafik, N., & Bandyopadhyay, S. (1992). *Economic growth and environmental quality: time-series and cross-country evidence* (Vol. 904). World Bank Publications.

Solomon, S., Plattner, G. K., Knutti, R., & Friedlingstein, P. (2009). Irreversible climate change due to carbon dioxide emissions. *Proceedings of the National Academy of Sciences of the United States of America, 106*(6), 1704–1709. doi:10.1073/pnas.0812721106 PMID:19179281

Tadesse, B., & Ryan, M. (2004). Host market characteristics, FDI, and the FDI–trade relationship. *The Journal of International Trade & Economic Development, 13*(2), 199–229. doi:10.1080/0963819042000218683

Tsurumi, T., & Managi, S. (2010). Decomposition of the environmental Kuznets curve: Scale, technique, and composition effects. *Environmental Economics and Policy Studies, 11*(1-4), 19–36. doi:10.100710018-009-0159-4

Wagner, U. J., & Timmins, C. D. (2009). Agglomeration effects in foreign direct investment and the pollution haven hypothesis. *Environmental and Resource Economics, 43*(2), 231–256. doi:10.100710640-008-9236-6

Wallace, D. (1996). Sustainable industrialisation. London: Royal Institute of International Affairs.

Zarsky, L. (1999). Havens, halos and spaghetti: untangling the evidence about foreign direct investment and the environment. *Foreign Direct Investment and the Environment, 13*(8), 47-74.

KEY TERMS AND DEFINITIONS

Pollution Halo Hypothesis: Pollution halo hypothesis argue that multinational companies through FDI transfer their greener technology to host country. Technology transfer might involve green technologies such as pollution abatement technologies, renewable energy using technologies, and it might involve advanced energy efficient technologies reducing the demand for conventional energy sources.

Pollution Haven Hypothesis: Contrary to the pollution halo hypothesis, the pollution haven hypothesis argue that multinationals contribute pollution in the host country. The hypothesis is centered around the idea that multinationals use lands of developing countries to produce for the country of origin or for the world since in the country of origin the environmental laws and regulations restrict the use of cheap technologies that are hostile to the environment. Therefore, while multinationalgain substantial competitive edge by producing in countries with less stringent environmental laws, these countries would experience adverse environmental consequenceswith increase in their GDP per capita.

Renewable Energy Use: World economicdevelopment and rising world population put substantial pressure on the conventional energy sources such as coal, oil, natural gas, electricity. Countries use increased technological knowledge and infrastructure for innovations in renewable energy such as solar, thermal, photovoltaics, bioenergy, hydro energy that would enable sustainable economic growth. Renewable energy use decreases the demand for non-renewable energy sources, increases the long run sustainable economic growth, and mitigates the irrevocable adverse climate consequences.

ENDNOTE

1 According to lag selection criteria; the lag with lowest values of MBIC, MAIC, MQIC is selected.

Chapter 4
Energy Poverty Jinx:
Can India Overcome?

Sovik Mukherjee
St. Xavier's University, India

ABSTRACT

The chapter starts by comparing India with China, U.S. and world as a whole in respect of composition, pattern of primary energy use, fuel access to clean cooking energy, and access to electricity for the households. Moving on, this relationship between energy and poverty has preoccupied development economists for decades and begs for a policy dialogue on whether the lack of energy in terms of the 3E's—energy security, energy accessibility, and energy use—makes a nation energy poor or not. This moves the focus on the state of equity in the distribution of energy in India. The chapter, then, looks at the issue of energy poverty, in particular, rural-urban magnitude of energy poverty by estimating the specific concentration curve using National Sample Survey (NSSO) household unit level data from the 68th round (July 2011 – June 2012). To conclude, the study comments on how the optimum fuel mix design should look and talks about sustainable strategies involving the use of new renewables for breaking India's energy poverty jinx.

INTRODUCTION

If conservation of natural resources goes wrong, nothing else will go right. —M.S Swaminathan (Quoted in saying as a part of a interview in News 18 Network, June 7, 2017)

In the last 500 years, the human civilization has been continuously expanding their technological limits manifold, increasingly drawing in huge amounts of energy resources from Mother Nature. The per capita energy that man has drawn is almost 100 times more than what his predecessors extracted in the neolithic age. To the extent, humans have overdrawn; the un-sustainability issue became prominent bringing with itself its two off-springs, *viz.*, climate change, consequentially global warming and energy poverty to which India is no exception. As the starting point, firstly, this chapter will traverse the different ages

DOI: 10.4018/978-1-5225-8547-3.ch004

or epochs, right from Stone Age to fossil fuel age, to review the position of the energy demand-supply balance that existed and even existent in the human society at the present point of time. Moving on, this chapter will discuss more about the recent anthropocentric interference that has given rise to this menace called "energy poverty" in our society, in general.

Given the existing notions of the concept of sustainable development, redefining it, the author states that economic growth can be sustained when it socially, economically and environmentally non-disruptive. While economic sustainability requires the economic growth process to be cost effective (i.e. minimize the real source cost of production) to generate surplus and savings of a society, the social sustainability would require the process to be socially inclusive as well, so as to generate adequate gainful employment and thereby ensure equitable distribution of the benefit of growth among the people. Moving on, environmental sustainability requires on the other hand conservation of natural resources and control of generation of wastes arising from the entropic process of conversion of resources into products that there is no environmental risk of collapse of the ecosystems. The latter is of critical importance from the view point of control of the negative externalities of economic production on both human health and health of the ecosystems (i.e., their ability of regeneration) in the different regions of our planet. As this paper will discuss, these requirements of multidimensional sustainability has obvious implications in respect of the energy policy for sustainable development of the energy sector of India (Sengupta, 2015).

Energy poverty comes next. Energy is the most crucial infrastructural sector in determining the pace of economic development and impact of stress created by an economy on the ecosystem as measured by the carbon foot print component of the ecological foot print. The notion of energy poverty in India entails two conflicting issues, i.e., one of ensuring equity and the other of energy development given the dualistic nature of the society. This brings us to the specific context of energy policy for India, the sustainability of growth and the social sustainability of development process requires the following, — a) energy security at the macro level so that there is always a adequate supply and accessibility of such energy either in primary or final forms; b) the energy use should also meet the efficiency and cleanliness criteria before ensuring that there is no energy poverty resulting from the demand-supply mismatch of electrical energy. The process of economic growth thus gets conditioned on this. After looking into the rural-urban energy poverty scenario using NSSO data from the latest available rounds data in a set-up where the estimation of the specific concentration curve of energy (refer to key words definition section) is carried out, this chapter intervenes into this aspect that what should be the optimum choice of fuel mix if the long run growth has to be made sustainable. The paper further comments on strategies for breaking this energy poverty jinx based on a time series projection analysis.

Given the role energy plays in how a nation progresses, the long term prospects of energy policy needs to be sustained for India in terms of energy security, energy accessibility and energy use. While the considerations of the first two components are likely to raise the kind of use of fossil fuel, those of the third one are targeted to reduce it. In the Indian context, the sustainability of energy production and use in India in fact depends both on the consideration of energy security, accessibility (which includes affordability) and efficiency along with cleanliness of the fuel.

Thus, the question is then how an economy ends up in a situation of energy poverty? Figure 1 illustrates this diagrammatically. Since the author discusses the case of India, the focus will be on the nexus among energy security, energy use and energy accessibility (includes affordability) in the context of India. In India, since the proportion of people lying below the poverty line is comparatively higher than the developed ones, affordability issue arises. The income distribution of the households and fuel prices have to be such that there is universal access to cleaner cooking fuel (like, LPG) and lighting fuel (like,

Figure 1. The energy poverty nexus
Source: Adapted from Pye et al. (2015)

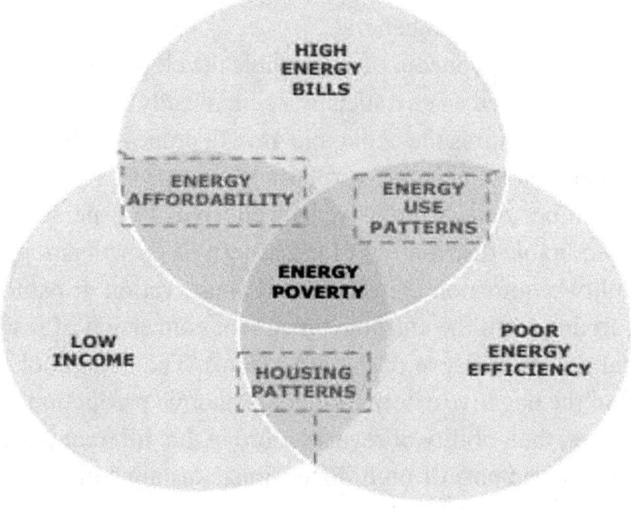

electricity) at the household level. The income position puts a hindrance in terms of accessing such a clean energy fuel which in turn pushes the poor households to go in for an alternative fuel (may be poor in terms of energy efficiency) resulting in high energy bills and further sucking these households into the trap of energy poverty.

The focus objective of the chapter has been summarized as follows. At the outset, it starts by comparing India with China, U.S. and world as a whole in respect of composition, pattern of primary energy use, fuel access to clean cooking energy and access to electricity for households. Next, this chapter highlights the importance of both energy conservation and subsequently, the choice of a clean fuel, specifically for the generation of electrical energy. Moving on, the relation between energy and poverty has preoccupied development economists for decades and begs for a policy dialogue on whether the lack of energy in terms of the 3E's — energy security, energy accessibility and energy use makes a nation energy poor or not. This moves the focus on the state of equity in the distribution of energy in India. The paper, then, looks at the issue of energy poverty, in particular, the rural-urban magnitude of energy poverty by estimating the specific concentration curve using National Sample Survey (NSSO) household unit level data from the 68th round (July 2011 – June 2012). To conclude, the paper comments on how the optimum fuel mix design should look like and talks about sustainable strategies involving the use of using new renewables for breaking India's energy poverty jinx.

ANTHROPOCENTRISM AND ENERGY GENERATION

Anthropocentrism is the belief that humans are the most important species on earth and the rest of nature is for their use and enjoyment. As put forward in *Book of Genesis*,

And God said; Let us make man in our image, after our likeness: and let them have dominion over the fish of the sea ...and over every creeping thing that creepeth upon the earth.

Anthropocentrism legitimizes uncontrolled exploitation of nature for human use. As an ideology, anthropocentrism drives the creation of increasing amounts of surplus energy by overdrawing energy from nature. Going back in time, eight thousand years ago, forests covered 40 per cent of the world's landmass, i.e., 60 million km^2, since then, one-third of which has been colonized by humans, that is, over six times India's land area, to make way for agricultural lands. The energy used to cut forests is estimated to be greater than the energy contained in 160 million Hiroshima-sized nuclear bombs (Dhara, 2017). A consequence of anthropocentrism is not only associated with loss of human and civilization but also environmental degradation in different perspectives. As we have seen in real life examples in countries across the globe, humans have exploited the environment for their benefit to such an extent that its life-support systems — air, water and land have been badly degraded (Minamata disaster, Bhopal Gas Tragedy to name a few). Quite frankly, anthropocentric behaviour devastates both nature and humanity when it is practiced. Incidentally, the question is, to what extent are such forms of anthropocentric activities a cause for energy poverty?

Perhaps, the biggest anthropocentric issue relating to sustainable development and use of energy resources is concerned with climate change largely due to open Green House Gas emissions from mostly the fossil fuel use in energy. In spite of the recognizing that fossil fuels constitute more than 50 per cent of the share in the total ecological footprint of the human race, the consumerist society of ours continues its indefinite accumulation of wealth in view of some material gain. As a result we are not only depleting our fossil fuels and other non-renewable resources, but also exhausting our renewable resources by over exploiting them at rates exceeding their respective rates of regeneration as driven by the dynamics of the ecosystems. The biggest challenge that the modern human economy ever faced in respect of sustainability in all its dimensionalities has in fact been the climate change which is going to be the case of greatest market failure in human history (Das & Sengupta, 2015). As already discussed, fossil fuel based sources provide one of the cheapest and energy efficient means of energy generation. What is needed is the conversion of the fossil fuel assets into clean energy assets but not by withdrawing altogether extraction of fossil fuels rather by using the resource rent arising from their extraction. The question is how one can transit from a fossil fuel based regime to one based on renewables at the least possible cost. There should of course every effort of converting the existing fossil fuels through some technical measures into cleaner ones, particularly, for the generation of electrical energy. This is the motivation for the introduction of the concept of "enlightened anthropocentrism" — i.e. implementing policies for the human race in real world situations recognizing our obligations to contemporary generations but not at the cost of sacrificing environmental health (Keulartz,2012). The fossil fuel production and use and development of new renewables and alternative energy should occur simultaneously, and in a planned co-ordinated manner making the two tracks of the energy sector development processes as complementary one.

ENERGY SCENARIO OF INDIA VIS-À-VIS ECONOMIC GROWTH

Energy Scenario

Since the introduction of economic reforms in 1991, the Indian economy grew at annual average rate of 6 per cent till 2000 followed by a period of accelerated growth of 7.5 per cent during the period 2000 till 2016 with slight hiccups in between during 2008-13 on account of the financial crises (Mukherjee & Karmakar, 2018). Against this average growth rate of 6.56 per cent of the entire period 1990 to 2016, the energy use of all kinds of fuel together grew at an annual average rate of 4.1 per cent during the period 1990 to 2016. This yields an estimate of GDP elasticity energy use of 0.625 in India which is lower than the world average value of such elasticity 0.734, but higher than those of China and USA. In view of the value being lower than unity, the overall energy intensity of GDP has been declining over this period, although the per capita energy use of India was only 637 oil equivalent kg (oeq.kg.) in 2014 which has been less than one third of the global per capita energy use value of 1921 oil equivalent kg (oeq.kg.). India is, in fact, a relatively energy poor country vis-a-vis the major economies of China, USA, and the world as a whole (See Table 1 for the comparative estimates of per capita energy consumption and growth of energy use).

So far as the composition of primary energy supply is concerned, Table 1 shows that for India share of fossils fuels in per capita energy use is 73.5 per cent while that of renewables and waste as having 23.5 per cent which is much higher than the world average in 2014. So far as the final energy use is concerned the cleanest fuel is electricity. In this regard, it is to be noted that India's low per capita electricity production and use at the level of 996 kwh in 2014 is less than one third of world average, one fourth of China and less than that of USA. Coming to the accessibility issue, in 2014 where only 79.2 per cent of India's population had access to electricity, it was 85.3 per cent at the global level, and 100 per cent for the people of USA and China that sums up the energy poverty story (see Table 2). Besides, an issue of major concern has been that most of the CO_2 emission in the energy sector takes place from the fuel combustion in the electricity and the transport sector both of which are heavily dependent on fossil fuels in India. Table 2 provides the fuel-wise comparative composition of gross generation of power in India for 2014 as compared to those of China, USA and world as a whole. It may be noted that the share of fossil fuel based power generation has been as high as 81.8 per cent for India in 2014, while those of hydro, nuclear and new renewables (i.e. wind, solar, etc.) in percentage terms have been 10.2, 2.8 and

Table 1. Primary energy use

Countries	Per Capita Primary Energy Use (All Fuels) 2014 in kgoe	Annual Average Growth Rate Of Energy Use 1990 to 2014 (%)	Rate of Growth of GDP (1990 to 2016 (%)	Share of Fossil Fuel (%)	Share of Renewables, Combustible Biomass and Waste (%)
India	637	4.1	6.56	73.5	23.5
China	2237	6.1	10.1	87.5	7.1
USA	6956	0.6	2.4	82.8	4.6
World	1921	2.1	2.83	80.0	5.8

Source: Compiled from the World Bank database as per availability of data

Table 2. Generation of electricity

Countries	Per Capita Gross Generation Kwh in 2014	Share of fossil Fuel in Gross Generation in 2014	Share of Renewables in Electricity in 2014 (%) **	$C0_2$ Emission per Capita_2014
India	996	81.8	15.4	1.7
China	4154	74.8	22.6	7.5
USA	13548	67.5	13.0	16.5
World	3287.5	66.4	22.3	5.0

**Storage hydro and new renewables
Source: Compiled from the World Bank database as per availability of data

5.2 respectively in the same year. Although, India's power generation has been more dependent on fossil fuels but CO_2 emission has been comparatively less compared to other large economies like China, USA and the global average - something commendable in terms of energy efficiency.

The other major problem that holds back India on the energy security front is her high level of dependence on imports for energy supply. Going by World Bank's database, net import of energy in India had a share of 34 per cent of total energy use in India in 2013-14 which has grown over time from a relative low level of 8 per cent in 1990. The growth of net imports of all fossil fuels taken together in oil equivalent terms has been 8.79 per cent per annum over the period under reference (i.e. from 1990 to 2014) and the unit price (in nominal dollar terms) of the fossil fuel in oil equivalent units increased. In this backdrop, India's net import bill started rising at very high unsustainable rates of 19.2 per cent per annum, leading to almost 55 times increase in 2010-11 over the base of 1990-91 (Sengupta, 2015). The scenario started changing from 2014-15 when the international price of oil crashed in 2014-15 and the share of import bill of oil went down. However, the price volatility of energy as experienced in recent years in the global market does not necessarily lead to any exceptional condition of stable low prices in the coming years, but add to the uncertainty regarding prices induced specially by the imperfect competitive nature of the oil market. Such price volatility exposes countries like India to the conditions of energy insecurity and macroeconomic non-sustainability of development as may arise from its pressure on the balance of payments situation. This becomes an added reason for India's special thrust on switching to new renewable energy resources replacing fossil fuels.

Energy Poverty and Social Sustainability: The Basic Motivation

Before starting off with energy poverty, one should be clear with a few definitions at the outset. As NSSO defines it,

- **Primary Source of Energy for Cooking:** For a household, this is the major source of energy used for cooking in the 30 day period preceding the date of enquiry. This happens in terms of various sub-classifications, — (a) coke, coal; (b) firewood and chips; (c) LPG (d) gobar gas; (e) dung cake; (f) charcoal; (g) kerosene; (h) electricity; (i) others
- **Primary Source of Energy for Lighting**: For a household, this is the major source of energy used for lighting during the 30 day period preceding the date of enquiry. The classification of sources is given below: *(a) kerosene; (b) other oil; (c) gas; (d) candle; (e) electricity; (f) others.*

International Energy Agency (IEA) defines energy poverty as, — "a lack of access to modern energy services. These services are defined as household access to electricity and clean cooking facilities (e.g. fuels and stoves that do not cause air pollution in houses.)". In this section, the author talks about the lack of energy access in terms of energy security, energy accessibility and affordability and efficiency through energy use. To ensure sustainable development of energy supply, two things are essential. First, analyzing household level data on the proportion of people having access to electricity and clean cooking fuel and second share of electricity generated out of renewable resources, particularly the new renewable like — wind, solar and microhydel or biomass. Again comparing with USA, China and the global average, Table 3 shows that India's attainment of values of these indicators falls substantially short of the achievements of China and at global level due to higher energy poverty of India.

An analysis of the 68th round NSSO micro data on household consumption for the year of 2011-12 shows that the rural Indian households (irrespective of the state concerned) uses firewood & chips and L.P.G as the main cooking fuels while electricity and kerosene are used mainly for lighting (see Table 4, 5 and 6) irrespective of the state concerned.

To sum up the major findings from Table 4, 5 and 6, we have, dung cake was one of the major fuels for cooking for 33.4 per cent of rural households in Uttar Pradesh, 30.3 per cent in Punjab, 24.4 per cent in Haryana, 20.8 per cent in Bihar and 10.6 per cent in Madhya Pradesh. Compared to other states, incidence of use of LPG for cooking in households was much higher for Tamil Nadu (37.2 per cent), Kerala (30.8 per cent) and Punjab (30.5 per cent) . However, Punjab's use of LPG was at par with that of dung cake and firewood & chips. Use of LPG in households was least in Chhattisgarh (1.5 per cent) preceded by Odisha (3.9 per cent). Rural Jharkhand (14.3 per cent) and Rural West Bengal (6.5 per cent) evidently reported coke & coal as primary source of energy for cooking.

Nearly 40 per cent or more of the urban households used LPG as principal fuel for cooking in all the major States. Haryana (86.5 per cent households) tops the list, followed by Andhra Pradesh (77.3 per cent) and Punjab (75.4 per cent). It is lowest in Chhattisgarh (39.8 per cent). Compared to rural areas, interestingly, use of kerosene as primary source of energy for cooking was more prevalent in urban areas of Gujarat (10.5 per cent), Maharashtra (10.1 per cent) and that of Punjab (10.0%). Urban Jharkhand and West Bengal continue their dependence on coke & coal as primary source of energy for cooking. Coming to lighting, in urban India, use of kerosene as primary energy source for lighting was 3.2 per cent or less in ten out of seventeen major states. The remaining seven states having higher percentages are Bihar, Uttar Pradesh, Assam, Gujarat, West Bengal, Chhattisgarh and Odisha. The proportion of urban households dependent on electricity for lighting was more than 90 per cent in all major States except Assam,

Table 3. Access to clean energy

Countries	Per Capita Primary Energy Use (All Fuels) 2013 in kgoe	Renewable Electricity Share (%) 2014	Access to Electricity (% Share of Population) 2014		
			Rural	Urban	Overall
India	34.2	15.4	70.00	98.3	79.2
China	57.2	22.6	100	100	100
USA	100	13.0	100	100	100
World	57.4	22.3	73.00	96.4	85.3

Source: Compiled from the World Bank database as per availability of data

Table 4. Per 1000 distribution of rural households in each major State by primary source of energy used for cooking (per 1000 number of households using)

State	Coke, Coal	Firewood & Chips	LPG	Dung Cake	Kerosene	Other Sources	No Cooking Arrangement	All
Andhra Pradesh	2	675	289	2	2	3	27	1000
Assam	1	810	172	0	3	5	9	1000
Bihar	6	564	59	208	5	157	1	1000
Chattisgarh	9	932	15	31	2	5	6	1000
Gujarat	0	797	139	9	35	7	12	1000
Haryana	0	417	267	244	12	58	3	1000
Jharkhand	143	777	29	29	3	2	16	1000
Karnataka	0	805	147	0	20	7	21	1000
Kerala	1	663	308	0	1	7	20	1000
Madhya Pradesh	2	808	62	106	5	7	8	1000
Maharashtra	0	621	231	2	10	97	38	1000
Odisha	9	870	39	18	2	56	6	1000
Punjab	0	305	305	303	27	42	19	1000
Rajasthan	0	893	89	6	7	4	1	1000
Tamil Nadu	0	583	372	0	25	2	18	1000
Uttar Pradesh	2	561	67	334	1	28	6	1000
West Bengal	65	629	66	53	5	175	6	1000
All-India	**11**	**673**	**150**	**96**	**9**	**49**	**13**	**1000**

Source: NSS Report No.567: Energy Sources of Indian Households for Cooking and Lighting, 68th Round
#: Other sources include gobar gas, charcoal, electricity, others

Uttar Pradesh and Bihar. In rural India, where nearly three-fourth of all households used electricity and slightly more than one-fourth used kerosene, inter-state variation of the use of primary source of energy for lighting was much greater as compared to that of cooking. Use of kerosene by households was as high as 73.5 per cent in Bihar, 58.5 per cent in Uttar Pradesh, 43.3 per cent in Assam, 36.8 per cent in Jharkhand. Contrary to this, states like Andhra Pradesh (97.6 per cent), Punjab (97.4 per cent being the highest for Punjab), Tamil Nadu, Kerala, etc. had a very high proportion using electricity

In the Indian context, the author defines energy poverty in a slightly different way. We consider a household to be cooking energy poor in the following analysis if its principal fuel of use for cooking is biomass while the other households have been considered as non-poor in terms of cooking energy. Similarly, any household which declares electricity to be its primary lighting fuel would be considered as non-poor and the other households would be treated as poor. The household's consumption data of 68th round of NSSO for 2011-12 shows the cooking poverty ratio to be around 79 per cent in rural India and 19 per cent in urban India as per such definition. Similarly, it was found that in rural area the lighting poverty ratio is 29 per cent while the same is only 6 per cent in urban area. The details are given in Table 7 and 8.

Table 5. Per 1000 distribution of urban households in each major State by primary source of energy used for cooking (per 1000 number of households using)

State	Coke, Coal	Firewood & Chips	LPG	Dung Cake	Kerosene	Other Sources	No Cooking Arrangement	All
Andhra Pradesh	1	101	773	0	27	7	91	1000
Assam	1	168	710	1	57	23	40	1000
Bihar	40	249	605	55	5	33	13	1000
Chhattisgarh	113	347	398	33	27	21	59	1000
Gujarat	9	159	620	3	105	57	47	1000
Haryana	0	60	865	31	14	5	25	1000
Jharkhand	311	56	539	5	12	9	68	1000
Karnataka	0	148	640	0	68	4	139	1000
Kerala	0	363	554	0	6	5	72	1000
Madhya Pradesh	8	257	652	18	36	2	27	1000
Maharashtra	2	57	745	0	101	15	80	1000
Odisha	38	365	435	2	48	27	85	1000
Punjab	1	67	754	32	100	7	38	1000
Rajasthan	5	187	716	2	20	0	70	1000
Tamil Nadu	0	112	709	0	85	2	92	1000
Uttar Pradesh	6	210	668	75	10	8	23	1000
West Bengal	135	107	565	6	87	15	84	1000
All-India	**21**	**140**	**684**	**13**	**57**	**15**	**69**	**1000**

Source: NSS Report No.567: Energy Sources of Indian Households for Cooking and Lighting, 68th Round
#: Other sources include gobar gas, charcoal, electricity, others

However, this simple definition does not consider any standard level of lighting or cooking fuel requirement in quantitative terms to define poverty line and derive accordingly the poverty ratio. To make things clear for the readers, the variation in the efficiency levels of such a diverse range of fuels, both for lighting or cooking services makes it extremely difficult to define composite energy poverty lines for the rural and urban areas separately. Although, our definition of poverty is based on qualitative category of fuel use in terms of cleanliness, the non-poor for cooking energy would be using anything other than biomass which is mostly inefficient and unclean fuel. The consumption of non-poor would include kerosene as well as LPG although the two differ in terms of both efficiency as well as cleanliness. Since LPG is the most efficient cooking fuel as mostly used among others excluding electricity (whose share in cooking fuel used would be very limited due to the relative higher costs of use) we find the share of population using LPG as the principal cooking fuel has been 13 per cent in the rural areas while it is a mammoth 88 per cent in urban areas as observed using the data given in the survey under reference. If one considers alternatively a household to be cooking energy poor if its principal cooking fuel is anything other than LPG, then the cooking poverty ratio would become as high as 87 per cent in rural areas, while there would be practically no such poverty in terms of deprivation of principal clean fuel use in urban areas — the gap between the rural and urban areas is thus huge.

Table 6. Per 1000 distribution of rural-urban households in each major State by primary source of energy used for lighting (per 1000 number of households using)

State	Rural (per 1000 No. of Households Using)				Urban (per 1000 No. of Households Using)			
	Kerosene	Electricity	Other Sources#	All	Kerosene	Electricity	Other Sources#	All
Andhra Pradesh	21	976	3	1000	11	985	2	1000
Assam	433	553	4	1000	79	897	19	1000
Bihar	735	258	3	1000	172	812	4	1000
Chhattisgarh	138	850	7	1000	36	931	28	1000
Gujarat	64	932	0	1000	52	940	7	1000
Haryana	15	951	28	1000	1	979	20	1000
Jharkhand	368	621	10	1000	26	964	2	1000
Karnataka	45	952	3	1000	12	986	1	1000
Kerala	33	962	4	1000	14	973	5	1000
Madhya Pradesh	152	845	2	1000	17	980	0	1000
Maharashtra	99	888	5	1000	8	989	1	1000
Odisha	323	676	1	1000	35	962	1	1000
Punjab	15	974	11	1000	5	984	8	1000
Rajasthan	216	777	7	1000	17	977	5	1000
Tamil Nadu	31	969	0	1000	10	988	0	1000
Uttar Pradesh	585	404	10	1000	108	881	9	1000
West Bengal	293	702	4	1000	50	945	2	1000
All-India	**265**	**727**	**5**	**1000**	**32**	**961**	**5**	**1000**

Source: NSS Report No.567: Energy Sources of Indian Households for Cooking and Lighting, 68th Round
#: Other sources include includes other oil, gas, candles

Introduction to Specific Concentration Curve: The Econometric Methodology

In order to get a more precise idea about inequality in the distribution of the major cooking and lighting fuels, the author derives the specific concentration curve for each of the major fuel used and juxtaposed it to the Lorenz curve corresponding to the overall consumption distribution. The specific concentration curve, thus, plots the cumulative share of the total use of a given cooking or lighting fuel against the cumulative share population from the lower end of the scale of per head or per household income or consumption expenditure. Its position vis-a-vis the 45° line is indicative of inequality in sharing the fuel for cooking and lighting vis-a-vis inequality of similar distribution of total consumption expenditure on all items together.

The comparative position of the Lorenz curve and the specific concentration curve indicates if the concerned fuel may be considered as a necessity or luxury item by the concerned segments of the households. If the specific concentration curve lies between 45° line and the Lorenz curve it is considered by households in the concerned range of income or per capita expenditure variation as a necessity, while it would be considered as a luxury item if it lies outside the Lorenz curve but above the axes (Refer to Figure 1 and Figure 2). Using Figures 1 and 2, the author shows the inequalities or concentration in the total consumption and in those of the fuels for the rural and urban segments of the Indian economy. This would provide useful policy insights for abating any social tension arising from inequality or poverty resulting from absolute or relative deprivation of clean fuels.

Formally, the Concentration Index (CI) the author uses in this context is actually derived from the standard health inequality concentration index (see for details, Kakwani et al., 1997; Clarke et al., 2002; Wagstaff, 2005, Das & Das, 2013, etc.) can be computed in a number of ways. The different formulae for the computation of the CI are given below,

Firstly, when the energy variable in question is continuous, the CI can be expressed as follows,

$$CI = 1 - \int_0^1 L_h(p)dp \tag{1}$$

where, Concentration Index is the CI and $L_h(p)$ is the area between the Concentration Curve and the line of equality. This formula defines the CI as follows — 1 minus twice the area above the Concentration Curve. Second, when the energy variable is discrete, the CI can be expressed as follows,

$$CI = \frac{2}{n\mu}\sum_{i=1}^{n} e_i r_i - 1 - \frac{1}{n} \tag{2}$$

where e_i is the energy variable, μ is its mean, and $r_i = i/n$ is the fractional rank of deciles class i in the living standards distribution, with $i = 1$ for the poorest class and $i = n$ for the richest. This formula makes it clearer that the CI reflects the relation between the energy variable and rank in the income distribution. Here for large n, the final term approaches zero and is often omitted. In relation to these formulae for the computation of CI, one needs to keep in mind that CI depends only on the relationship between the energy variable and the rank of the living standards variable and not on the variation in the living standards variable itself. Therefore, a change in the degree of income inequality need not always affect the CI measure of income-related energy inequality.

Estimation of Energy Poverty using the Concentration Index

Estimations shown in Table 9 according to the data extracted from the NSSO 68th Round 2011-12 shows how the prices of the different fuels have varied across the rural and urban areas of India. The Total Fuel price Column for both rural and urban segment shows the combined fuel prices derived through the weighted geometric mean of prices of electricity, biomass, LPG and kerosene with weights being the share of these fuels in the consumption basket. Figures 1 and 2 (India taken as a whole) shows the degree of inequality in how these fuels are distributed. If one observes closely, the concentration curve for biomass fuel lies entirely above the 45 degree line, indicating the inferior nature of this good for the urban section of the population. While the relative position of specific concentration curves for LPG for cooking and electricity for lighting vis-a-vis the Lorenz curve show these to be luxury goods and those of kerosene for rural lighting and electricity required for urban lighting to be necessities. These characterizations depend upon the preference structure of the households in different income-expenditure classes as revealed through their behaviour.

Table 7. Rural household energy poverty

Deciles Class of MPCE	Cumulative Share of Population	Share of Total Population Falling in the Respective Deciles Group and Primary Cooking Fuel as Biomass	Cumulative Share	Share of Total Population Falling in the Respective Deciles Group and Primary Cooking Fuel as LPG	Cumulative Share	Share of Total Population Falling in the Respective Deciles Group and Principal Fuel for Lighting as Electricity	Cumulative Share
1	10	0.092	0.092	0.000	0.000	0.045	0.045
2	20	0.089	0.181	0.001	0.002	0.051	0.096
3	30	0.088	0.269	0.003	0.004	0.056	0.151
4	40	0.089	0.359	0.004	0.008	0.065	0.216
5	50	0.084	0.442	0.006	0.014	0.068	0.284
6	60	0.082	0.525	0.009	0.023	0.073	0.357
7	70	0.079	0.604	0.014	0.038	0.080	0.437
8	80	0.075	0.679	0.018	0.056	0.085	0.522
9	90	0.066	0.744	0.029	0.085	0.087	0.609
10	100	0.046	0.790	0.045	0.130	0.093	0.703
Households with principal fuel as biomass for cooking are poor for cooking energy							
Households with principal fuel as other than electricity for lighting are poor in terms of lighting energy							
Poverty ratio for cooking energy (rural) **0.79**							
Poverty ratio for lighting energy (rural) **0.30**							

Source: Author's derivations

However, we have also to remember that the pattern of fuel consumption is mostly dependent on its availability and therefore has been often constrained by the supply side situation. The absolute and relative deprivation of fuels for the households have been forced more by the conditions of availability of fuels rather than those of their income effects inducing the choice. This leads to the importance of policy thrusts in respect of making fuels particularly electricity for lighting and LPG for cooking available to the households irrespective of their ability to pay. Besides, the greater consumption of electricity for lighting and LPG/kerosene for cooking as facilitated by the greater availability of these respective fuels would thus reduce the lighting and the cooking fuel poverty arising from the deprivation of such clean fuels for these purposes. Table 9 further shows how the price actually paid by the people of different expenditure classes are different in terms of price per unit of oil equivalent kg across the fuels and also how they are different between urban and rural areas. Next, the question which needs to be answered is how should the optimum fuel-mix be like and the role of new renewables in this regard.

Table 8. Urban household energy poverty

Deciles Class of MPCE	Cumulative Share of Population	Share of Total Population Falling in the Respective Deciles Group and Primary Cooking Fuel as Biomass	Cumulative Share	Share of Total Population Falling in the Respective Deciles Group and Primary Cooking Fuel as LPG	Cumulative Share	Share of Total Population Falling in the Respective Deciles Group and Principal Fuel for Lighting as Electricity	Cumulative Share
1	10	0.060	0.060	0.036	0.036	0.081	0.081
2	20	0.043	0.103	0.067	0.103	0.092	0.173
3	30	0.029	0.131	0.086	0.189	0.096	0.269
4	40	0.023	0.154	0.098	0.288	0.096	0.365
5	50	0.015	0.169	0.111	0.399	0.098	0.462
6	60	0.010	0.179	0.118	0.517	0.097	0.560
7	70	0.006	0.185	0.120	0.637	0.097	0.657
8	80	0.004	0.189	0.121	0.758	0.099	0.756
9	90	0.002	0.191	0.122	0.880	0.099	0.855
10	100	0.001	0.192	0.120	1.000	0.099	0.954
Households with principal fuel as biomass for cooking are poor for cooking energy							
Households with principal fuel as other than electricity for lighting are poor in terms of lighting energy							
Poverty ratio for cooking energy (rural) **0.19**							
Poverty ratio for lighting energy (rural) **0.05**							

Source: Author's derivations

CAN NEW RENEWABLES SOLVE THE PROBLEM?

In order to appreciate the economy - energy - sustainability connection and explore the options to get out of the current state of energy poverty state, it is important to look back very briefly at the period when industrial revolution was happening in Western Europe. While the first revolution revolved around coal and steam power and the second one around hydrocarbons – oil and gas – and electricity, the latter as a converted clean highly efficient energy for final use as fuel came up. The two together brought out the automobile revolution and the use of clean electric power replacing the steam power in the industry, commerce and transport. This further led further to the emergence of power grid, telecommunication networks of telegraph, telephone, radio, television etc. having a vast impact on the organization and efficiency of society and economy in delivering human welfare.

Both the first and second industrial revolution have however been driven by the development of fossil fuels which are non-renewable in human time scale and are involved with a high intensity of pollution. In view of the implication of climate change, desertification, degradation of soil and water bodies and air and atmospheric pollution, the concern has developed for saving the world by creating an ecologically sustainable economic order. With the world still grappling with the problems of the second industrial

Table 9. Price variation (rural & urban) in Rupees per kgoe units

Deciles Class of MPCE	Rural (Prices per kgoe Units)					Urban (Prices per kgoe Units)					Rural-Urban Differential in Price
	Electricity	Biomass (Firewood and Dungcake)	LPG	Keros-ene	Total Fuel_ Price/Kgoe (Rural)	Electricity	Biomass (Firewood and Dungcake)	LPG	Keros-ene	Total Fuel_ Price/Kgoe (Urban)	
1	3.03	6.61	30.7	213.1	6.64	3.58	7.93	26.8	220.1	7.12	0.48
2	3.07	7.37	26.6	218.3	6.98	3.62	8.35	26.2	234.1	7.22	0.24
3	3.13	7.25	26.2	215.5	6.83	3.61	8.15	26.7	258.9	7.21	0.37
4	3.17	7.23	27.1	214.1	6.62	3.74	7.99	26.4	256.8	7.09	0.47
5	3.23	7.02	27.1	213.2	6.44	3.72	7.41	26.1	276.4	6.80	0.36
6	3.24	6.81	26.8	212.6	6.24	3.76	7.24	26.0	277.7	6.62	0.38
7	3.25	6.79	26.5	209.1	6.12	3.78	7.25	26.1	317.0	6.49	0.37
8	3.36	6.82	26.1	210.5	6.18	3.93	7.51	26.1	341.9	6.38	0.20
9	3.37	6.91	26.3	211.5	6.25	4.01	6.01	26.1	423.6	6.10	-0.14
10	3.38	6.64	26.2	222.0	5.96	4.35	6.07	25.8	298.7	5.60	-0.37
Total	**0.3**	**6.94**	**26.4**	**213.9**	**6.33**					**6.40**	**0.07**

Source: Author's derivations

revolution, the search and thrust of research in science and technology are now for the discovery and development of a carbon free renewable resource. This calls for a Third Industrial Revolution which would essentially focus on shifting from fossil fuels to renewable energy resources, including, solar,

Figure 2. Specific concentration curve for fuels & Lorenz curve for income (rural)

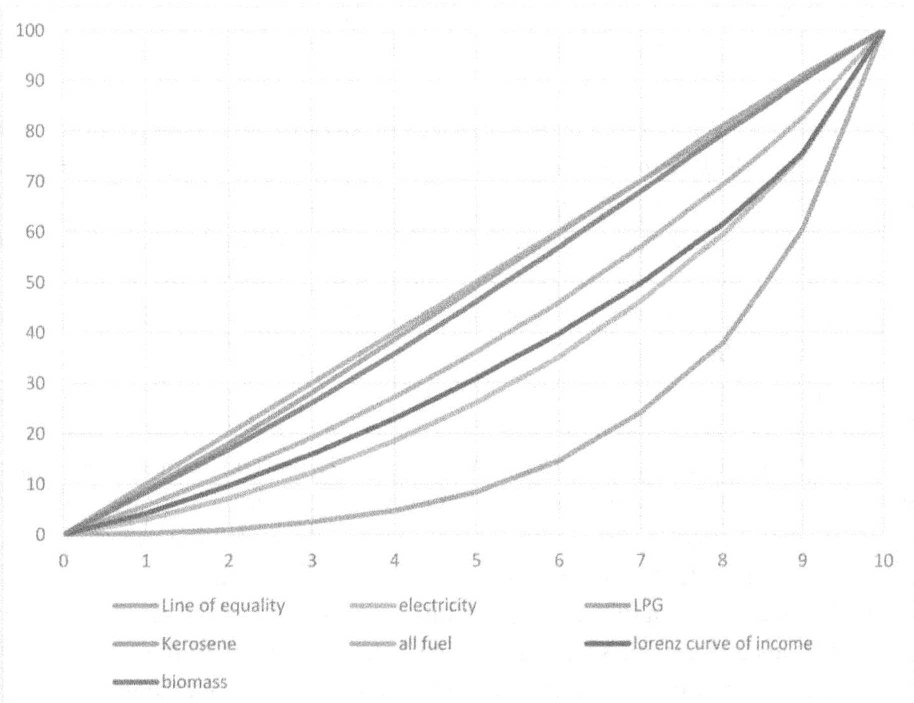

Figure 3. Specific concentration curve for Fuels & Lorenz curve for income (urban)

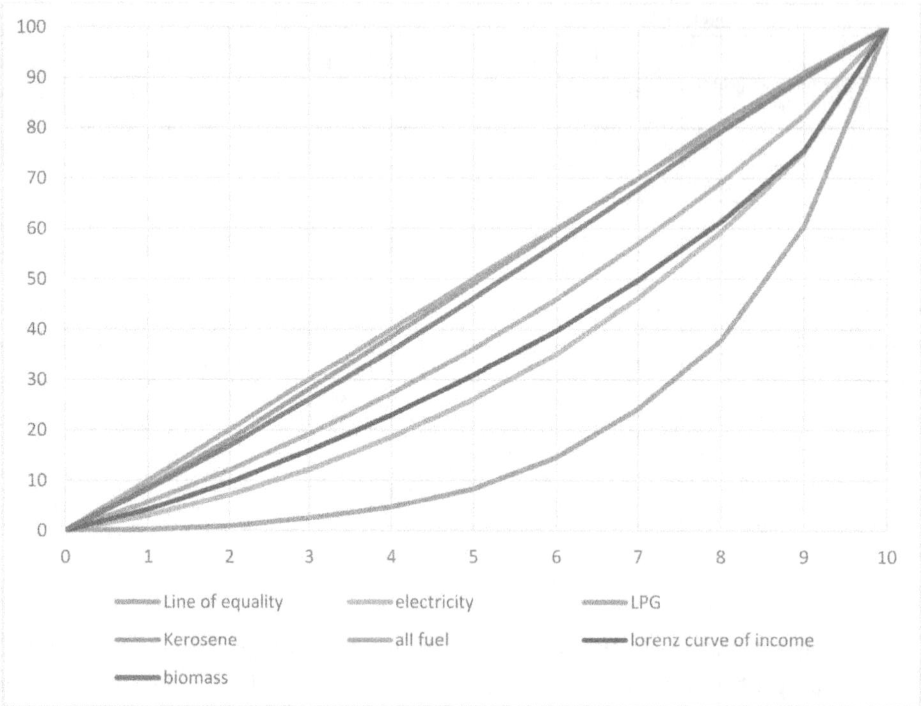

wind, geo-thermal, biomass, water, etc. (Rifkin, 2011). While clean energy production and use have been growing fast in the recent years them mainly through focusing on the issue of energy efficiency both in its end use in the non-energy sectors (energy conservation) and in the supply of primarily electrical energy by reducing conversion loss, auxiliary loss and T&D losses. The other way by which the countries are trying to get out of the current problem of pollution and unsustainable fossil fuel use has been by reducing the share of fossil fuel (coal an oil) in the gross electricity generation, and by raising that of natural gas or coal bed methane (cleanest among the fossil fuels), nuclear, biomass and wastes and other abiotic renewables like wind, solar, geo-thermal, tidal, etc.

In this backdrop, this section tries to project an optimal fuel-mix in the years to come based on a simple projection analysis using an accelerated share of renewables share in gross electricity generation. Such scenarios of the Accelerated Share of Renewables (ASR) vis-à-vis the Business As Usual (BAU) is taken to be the same as that of the NITI AAYOG in its document of Energy Policy Draft 2017. To begin with, this projection model assumes the planning horizon to be the terminal years of 2021-22 and 2031-32 with 2014-15 (actual) as the base. The scenario assumes 8 per cent overall GDP growth and accelerated rates of introduction of carbon free new renewable fuels. The comparative scenarios will be ASR and BAU ones. The level of aggregate electricity generated after taking care of the auxiliary and transmission & distribution losses (as reported in Table 10) have been derived from the Energy Balance data over the years from the International Energy Agency's (IEA's) database.

These are the shares with which the projected estimates in table 11 have been derived. The main essence of carrying out this entire exercise, results of which are reported in Table 12 is to predict to what extent electricity generation is possible using new renewables and to what extent it can be sustained.

Table 10. Phasing of auxiliary and T&D losses

Time Horizon	Auxiliary Loss as % of Gross Generation	T&D Loss as % Gross Generations	Auxiliary + T&D Loss as % Gross Generations
2011-12 (actual)	6.1	22.16	28.26
2021-22 (projected)*	6	20	26
2031-32 (projected)*	5.5	17	22.5

Source: Compiled from the Government Of India, Ministry of Power, Central Electricity Authority Report (March 2013) and Annual Report on The Working of State Power Utilities and Electricity Departments, Power & Energy Division, Government of India (Retrieved: http://planningcommission.gov.in/reports/genrep/rep_arpower1305.pdf).

* denotes simple linear projection based on historical data from 2010 onwards.

Table 11. Business as Usual_(BAU) vs. accelerated share of renewables (ASR) share comparison

Energy Fuels	2021-22*	2031-32#	2041-42*	2021-22*	2031-32#	2041-42*
	(ASR)	(ASR)	(ASR)	(BAU)	(BAU)	(BAU)
coal	62.600	51.76176	42.800	64.909	60.750	56.500
gas	6.500	6.5	6.500	5.444	7.500	4.000
nuclear	3.700	4.343961	5.100	3.488	3.000	3.500
hydro storage	9.000	7.937254	7.000	9.103	9.350	5.400
Solar PV	4.200	6.640783	10.500	4.211	4.643	9.100
Solar CSP	0.600	1.549193	4.000	0.468	1.150	2.300
Distributed Solar PV	2.300	3.108054	4.200	2.339	1.800	3.600
Total Solar	7.100	11.52259	18.700	7.018	7.593	15.000
Onshore Wind	5.500	7.074602	9.100	5.487	5.750	8.500
Offshore Wind	0.300	0.774597	2.000	0.255	0.650	1.300
Total Wind	5.800	8.023715	11.100	5.742	6.400	9.800
Other Renewables	5.350	6.861487	8.800	3.658	5.313	5.900
Imports	-	-	-	-	-	-
Total	100.050	100.025	100.000	100.000	99.906	100.100

Source: Compiled by the Author

*: The estimates are taken from NITI Aayog's Energy Policy draft (2017)

#: For 2031-32, both the BAU estimates and the ASR have been taken as the geometric mean of the 2021-22 and 2041-42 estimates.

Electricity generation is the cornerstone to solve the energy poverty problem given the energy security, accessibility and cleanliness issue. If electricity generation is made possible at larger magnitudes from these new renewables then accessibility problem (which is the prime force behind energy poverty) gets solved. The results in Table 12 show that temporally India can definitely switch over from the fossil fuel based sources to the new renewable based ones (as reported) of electricity generation**. However, as mentioned in the outset, in the Indian context, fossil fuels are not a substitute for new renewables but rather the fuel mix has to be designed optimally so as to ensure that the transition from fossil fuel based regimes to the new renewables one happens smoothly.

Table 12. Business as usual_(BAU) vs. accelerated share of renewables_(ASR) electricity generation comparison

Energy Fuels	2011-12 (actual)	2021-22* (ASR)	2031-32* (ASR)	2021-22* (BAU)	2031-32* (BAU)
coal	729.403036	1449.531859	2590.998945	1504.921046	2984.441629
gas	118.4764818	150.5104965	319.5729249	254.6789462	368.4495838
nuclear	27.81621747	85.67520572	216.3262876	57.88157867	147.3798335
hydro storage	148.3531599	208.399149	393.3205229	307.9299985	459.3338145
Solar PV	2.060460554	97.25293622	358.9049772	4.283236822	228.0702924
Solar CSP	-	13.8932766	113.0796503	-	56.49560286
Distributed Solar PV	-	53.25756031	162.2447157	-	88.42790012
Total Solar	2.060460554	-	-	4.283236822	372.9937954
Onshore Wind	32.96736886	127.3550355	358.9049772	69.45789441	282.4780143
Offshore Wind	-	6.946638301	54.0815719	-	31.93229727
Total Wind	32.96736886	-	-	69.45789441	314.4103116
Other Renewables	47.39059273	123.8817164	349.0719641	109.4193363	261.0096852
Imports	5.151151384	-	-	-	-
Total	1111.618469	2316.703874	4916.506536	2308.572036	4908.018653

Source: Author's calculations

*: The estimates are derived from a linear projection of the aggregate electricity generation based on actual levels in Twh units from 2011-12 to 2016-17. The linear projection model used is: $y = a + bt$ where y is aggregate energy generation and t is time.

**: This question can be answered in greater details and more aptly if one can estimate the resource rent (using a sophisticated time series energy demand model) arising out of such fossil fuel extraction and using that rent fund to finance the new renewable sources based generation.

CONCLUSION

The growth of deployment of clean technologies in the first decade of the new millennium shows the decadal growth rate to be varying across countries mostly in the range of 27 per cent to 56 per cent as per the Global Carbon Capture and Storage Institute (GCCSI) data base 2011, the world is still largely dependent on fossil fuels to satisfy the growing energy demand. In the last decade fossil fuel has supplied 50 per cent of the new energy demand, oil has supplied 94 per cent of the total fuel requirement of the transport sector and non-hydro power from renewables has supplied only 6 per cent of total gross electrical energy produced in 2014 at the global level (Sengupta, 2015).

To sum up, the author reiterates the 3E's yet again. In the context of electricity and LPG, energy security implies that there should be wide access to and use of electricity and LPG. Second, the distribution of income or purchasing power of the households and fuel prices have to be such that there is universal access of households to clean cooking fuel (like LPG) and lighting fuel (like electricity) at the household level. Social sustainability should require that there is no energy poverty in terms of life line supply of electricity for lighting and gas or petroleum fuel like kerosene as defining the poverty benchmarks. Third, the energy use and conversion of primary energy (fuels) into final forms should be as efficient and clean as possible. Here, both electricity and LPG (although LPG is not that clean when compared to biomass but is very efficient) scores well comparatively. The paper further shows how the prices paid by the people of different expenditure classes are different in terms of price per unit of oil equivalent kg across the fuels and also how they are different between urban and rural areas — bringing the focus on energy poverty through the CI index. This was so far missing from the literature in the Indian context. Also, another major contribution of this paper is to point out the extent to which the household energy prices of fuels are regressive in the Indian case. Therefore, putting emphasis on the role of new renewables as a part of the design of the optimal fuel-mix should be the priority.

From the deliberations, it is clear that the removal of energy poverty requires the provision of electrical power to all and at the same time replacing the hydrocarbons (especially, LPG) for cooking. In spite of the enforcement of the programme of electrification of all homes to provide the lifeline requirement of electrical energy to all by 2010-11, nearly 48 per cent of the Indian households going by the 68th round NSSO data still depend on biomass as a means of household energy. It becomes important to have in place cooking appliances and other devices for the wide-scale implementation of biomass. Thus, extensive effort needs to go into R & D i.e. research and development. But on the other hand, if the nation is willing to accept a certain basic level of CO_2 emissions, then LPG will give biomass a run for its money. Therefore, optimally designing the policy mix becomes crucial and herein lies the novelty of the paper. The paper not only gives us an estimate of energy poverty quantitatively, contrary to other recent studies like Bhide and Monroy (2011) which only highlight the problems and the methods to eradicate energy poverty but also emphasizes on the role new renewable can play in this regard. In view of this, the ushering of a third industrial revolution (based on new renewables based sources of energy) has to be conceptualized much ahead of time, induced by purposeful policy resourcefulness and international energy co-operation at its forefront. This can be achieved mainly through energy conservation and accelerated introduction of non-hydro renewable among others. It is important to review at this stage and remains one of the future endeavors that how a large developing country like India is trying to incorporate new energy technologies in power industry in order to transit to a Green Regime of Energy Technology.

REFERENCES

Bhide, A., & Monroy, C. R. (2011). Energy poverty: A special focus on energy poverty in India and renewable energy technologies. *Renewable & Sustainable Energy Reviews, 15*(2), 1057–1066. doi:10.1016/j.rser.2010.11.044

Clarke, P. M., Gerdtham, U. G., Johannesson, M., Bingefors, K., & Smith, L. (2002). On the measurement of relative and absolute income-related health inequality. *Social Science & Medicine, 55*(11), 1923–1928. doi:10.1016/S0277-9536(01)00321-5 PMID:12406461

Das, R. C., & Das, U. (2013). Industrial Credit and Economic Inequality: A descriptive study of the major Indian states before and after economic reforms. *Sumedha Journal of Management, Hyderabad, 2*(2), 58–80.

Das, S., & Sengupta, R. P. (2015). *From the Fossil Fuel Present to a Low Carbon Future*. Edmonton, Canada: Cambridge Strategies.

Dhara, S. (2017). The Central Role of Surplus Energy in Human Development and a Class- divided Unsustainable Society. In P. Mukhopadhyay, N. Nawn, & K. Das (Eds.), *Global Change, Ecosystems, Sustainability: Theory, Methods, Practice* (pp. 82–97). New Delhi, India: Sage. doi:10.4135/9789353280284.n9

If Agriculture Goes Wrong, Nothing Will Go Right: Father of Green Revolution. (2017). Retrieved from https://www.news18.com/news/india/if-agriculture-goes-wrong-nothing- will-go-right-warns-father-of-green-revolution-1425659.html

Kakwani, N., Wagstaff, A., & Van Doorslaer, E. (1997). Socioeconomic inequalities in health: Measurement, computation, and statistical inference. *Journal of Econometrics*, *77*(1), 87–103. doi:10.1016/S0304-4076(96)01807-6

Keulartz, J. (2012). The emergence of enlightened anthropocentrism in ecological restoration. *Nature and Culture*, *7*(1), 48–71. doi:10.3167/nc.2012.070104

Mukherjee, S., & Karmakar, A. K. (2018). A Hardheaded Look: How Did India Feel the Tremors of Recent Financial Crises? In H. Dincer, Ü. Hacioglu, & S. Yüksel (Eds.), *Global Approaches in Financial Economics, Banking, and Finance* (pp. 25–51). Cham, Switzerland: Springer. doi:10.1007/978-3-319-78494-6_2

Pye, S., Dobbins, A., Baffert, C., Brajković, J., Grgurev, I., Miglio, R. D., & Deane, P. (2015). *Energy poverty and vulnerable consumers in the energy sector across the EU: analysis of policies and measures*. London: INSIGHT_E. Retrieved from https://ec.europa.eu/energy/sites/ener/files/documents/INSIGHT_E_Energy%20Poverty %20-%20Main%20Report_FINAL.pdf

Rifkin, J. (2011). *The third industrial revolution: how lateral power is transforming energy, the economy, and the world*. London: Macmillan.

Sengupta, R. P. (2015). Role of New Renewables in the Sustainable Energy Development of India: Environmental Aspects and Other Drivers. In R. Tongia (Ed.), *Blowing Hard or Shining Bright? Making Renewable Power Sustainable in India*. New Delhi, India: Brookings India Publications.

Wagstaff, A. (2005). The bounds of the concentration index when the variable of interest is binary, with an application to immunization inequality. *Health Economics*, *14*(4), 429–432. doi:10.1002/hec.953 PMID:15495147

ADDITIONAL READING

Birol, F. (2007). Energy economics: A place for energy poverty in the agenda? *Energy Journal*, *28*(3), 1–7. doi:10.5547/ISSN0195-6574-EJ-Vol28-No3-1

Casillas, C. E., & Kammen, D. M. (2010). The energy-poverty-climate nexus. *Science*, *330*(6008), 1181–1182. doi:10.1126cience.1197412 PMID:21109654

Cherni, J. A., & Kentish, J. (2007). Renewable energy policy and electricity market reforms in China. *Energy Policy*, *35*(7), 3616–3629. doi:10.1016/j.enpol.2006.12.024

Ellabban, O., Abu-Rub, H., & Blaabjerg, F. (2014). Renewable energy resources: Current status, future prospects and their enabling technology. *Renewable & Sustainable Energy Reviews*, *39*(C), 748–764. doi:10.1016/j.rser.2014.07.113

Kumar, A., Kumar, K., Kaushik, N., Sharma, S., & Mishra, S. (2010). Renewable energy in India: Current status and future potentials. *Renewable & Sustainable Energy Reviews*, *14*(8), 2434–2442. doi:10.1016/j.rser.2010.04.003

Nussbaumer, P., Bazilian, M., & Modi, V. (2012). Measuring energy poverty: Focusing on what matters. *Renewable & Sustainable Energy Reviews*, *16*(1), 231–243. doi:10.1016/j.rser.2011.07.150

Pachauri, S., Mueller, A., Kemmler, A., & Spreng, D. (2004). On measuring energy poverty in Indian households. *World Development*, *32*(12), 2083–2104. doi:10.1016/j.worlddev.2004.08.005

Sagar, A. D. (2005). Alleviating energy poverty for the world's poor. *Energy Policy*, *33*(11), 1367–1372. doi:10.1016/j.enpol.2004.01.001

Sims, R. E., Rogner, H. H., & Gregory, K. (2003). Carbon emission and mitigation cost comparisons between fossil fuel, nuclear and renewable energy resources for electricity generation. *Energy Policy*, *31*(13), 1315–1326. doi:10.1016/S0301-4215(02)00192-1

KEY TERMS DEFINITIONS

Anthropocentrism: Anthropocentrism refers to a human-centered or "anthropocentric" point of view. Philosophically, anthropocentrism means humans are the only, or primarily the most important entity in the universe. Anthropocentric value systems thus see nature in terms of its value to humans; but many see it clearly going the sustainable use of natural resources.

Carbon Footprint: A carbon footprint is historically defined as the total emissions caused by an individual, event, organization, or product, expressed as carbon dioxide equivalent.

Energy Conservation: Energy conservation is the effort made to reduce the consumption of energy by using less of an energy service. This can be achieved either by using energy more efficiently (using less energy for a constant service) or by reducing the amount of service used (for example, by driving less).

Energy Intensity: Energy intensity measures how efficient a nation is in terms of energy. It is calculated as units of energy per unit of GDP.

Energy Security: Energy security is a measure of the availability of natural resources for energy consumption. Also, access to (relatively) cheap energy has become essential to the functioning of modern economies is also one of the parameters of energy security.

Renewable Energy: Renewable energy is a form of energy that is collected from naturally replenished renewable resources, including, sunlight, wind, rain, tides, waves, and geothermal heat.

Specific Concentration Curve: The specific concentration curve plots the cumulative share of the total use of a given cooking or lighting or biomass-based fuel against the cumulative share population from the lower end of the income distribution, very similar to the concept of a Lorenz curve.

Chapter 5
Environmental Regulation, International Trade, and Informal Sector:
Theory, Policy, and Indian Experience

Tonmoy Chatterjee
Ananda Chandra College, India

ABSTRACT

This chapter deals with some contemporary issues related to trade and environment, which are mainly faced by the developing nations of the world. In this context, the present study has considered some facts and figures of Indian tannery industry for realization of the above-mentioned objective. In this chapter, an attempt has been made to analyze theoretically the effect of both environmental regulation and trade liberalization on the output of different sectors and also on the national welfare in a small open economy. To categorize this, the authors have presented a theoretical model based on the general equilibrium framework that mainly highlights a paradoxical result. Apart from this, the present research shows that the capital used specifically in advanced export sector is likely to affect the welfare positively, and the capital used by the rest of the economy is likely to affect the welfare adversely when usual export sector of the economy vanishes, and the opposite will occur when the pollution-intensive informal sector of the economy vanishes.

INTRODUCTION

The relationship between trade and environment is a complex and highly debated issue. Addressing this relationship is fundamental in order to achieve sustainable development. As a result of increasing global economic interdependence and further trade liberalization as well as growing pressure on the environment and the use of natural resources, there is an ever growing interface between trade and environment. It is widely recognized that trade and environment can be mutually supportive, but, differences remain on effective implementation. The Commission Communication on Trade and Environment, adopted in

DOI: 10.4018/978-1-5225-8547-3.ch005

1996, underlined that a mutually supportive relationship between trade and environment can occur but is in no way automatic. In fact, trade liberalization and trade policy have positive and negative impacts on the environment (Mukhopadhyay, 2004; Chatterjee, Gupta & Chatterjee, 2017). However, a number of conditions should be met to ensure that the net gains deriving from trade liberalization will support and reinforce the protection of the environment.

One essential condition for making sure that trade and environment are mutually supportive is to ensure that the trade liberalization process is paralleled with the development and strengthening of effective and non-protectionist environmental legislation, at national, regional and international levels. Environmental policies could, in turn, provide an incentive for technological innovations, promote economic efficiency and, consequently, improve productivity. Having recognized the need for such policies, one should also ensure that trade rules do not unnecessarily constrain but rather support and promote the ability of countries to develop and implement adequate and non-protectionist environmental measures, at both national and international levels.

Trade policy has also a role to play in actively supporting sustainable trade flows and, in particular, environmentally friendly trade. Trade policy and trade related instruments should be further encouraged to act as a sustainable driver by providing incentives for more sustainable trade flows. This is valid at the multilateral level but even more so at the regional and bilateral levels where the identification of positive synergies among trading partners as well as convergence and co-operation should be easier than is the case at the international level. Trade tools could, for instance, be instrumental in making tangible progress towards more sustainable consumption and production patterns. Economic instruments also need to be more actively developed, notably with a view to allow for the necessary internalization of external environmental costs. In addition, positive synergies between trade, environment and development should be further considered, particularly regarding the elimination of environmentally damaging subsidies and the promotion of environmentally friendly goods and services, with a special focus on those originating in Developing Countries (DCs).

International trade contributes to economic growth, benefits all participating countries, while growth, in turn, increases the demand for environmental quality and provides the financial resource for environmental protection. It is commonly assumed by economists and environmentalists alike that greater economic openness will lead to increase pollution in developing countries, as free trade will increase environmental degradation in developing countries. Thus there are points at which trade and environmental objectives are in potential conflict. If left unattended, these conflicts can weaken the trade system and become an obstacle to sustainable development (Wright, 1974; Hayami & Nakamura, 2002; Mukhopadhyay & Chakraborty, 2004; Jha & Rabindran, 2004).

But what is the impact of trade liberalization on the environment is a matter of debate. Two conflicting hypotheses have emerged from the debate. First one is pollution haven hypothesis (hereafter PHH). This hypothesis suggests that the developed countries impose tougher environmental policies than do the developing countries, which results in distortion of existing patterns of comparative advantage. So the polluting industries shift operations from the developed to the developing countries; developing countries thus become "pollution havens." The second hypothesis, the factor endowment hypothesis (hereafter FEH), states that trade liberalization will result in trade patterns consistent with the Heckscher-Ohlin-Samuelson-Vanek (hereafter HOSV) theory of comparative advantage based on factor endowment differentials. Rich countries are typically well endowed with capital. Since capital-intensive goods are often also pollution-intensive, factor-endowment theories of international trade predict that rich countries specialize in polluting goods. Thus the manifestation of the PHH is in direct conflict with the FEH. This debate is of great concern among economists, environmentalists and world bodies like World Trade Organization (WTO hereafter).

The issues associated with the link between trade and the environment is very complex and evolves in a dynamic manner, involving various states and other actors in the process. The development of this linkage often focuses on the North–South dynamics of international debates on trade and the environment. Renewed interest in trade and the environment has generated new concerns about the effects of environmental regulations/regimes upon trade-induced economic development, particularly in developing countries. This phenomenon has assumed and will continue to assume paramount significance in international trade negotiations. The magnitude of the debate arising from trade and environment policy tensions indicates that trade and environmental issues will play an increasingly large role both within and beyond the WTO.

The fundamental conflict of interests between the North and the South lies at the center of these issues. In fact, in the North, environmental protection issues are seen as matters to be addressed in order to protect the global environment, while in the South, environmental protection issues are considered to be linked with the economic development of the nations concerned.

While developing countries initially resisted the linkage between trade and environment, they later accepted the reality that economic development cannot be separated from its environmental consequences. Economic development, in order to be sustainable, needs to take into account environmental concerns arising from the developmental process.

Developing countries oppose inclusion of trade and environment issues in the WTO as not favorable to their economic interests. The inclusion of trade-and-environment-related issues in the WTO also means that developing countries could be forced to engage in negotiations on trade and environment issues without an explicit inclusion of environment in the negotiating mandate. Unless resolved in a satisfactory way, these issues have the potential to dictate the terms of trade negotiations in the multilateral trade regime and may further exacerbate the North–South tensions that exist at the trade–environment interface.

Pollution haven hypothesis argues that the industries that are highly pollution intensive i.e. dirty industries have been migrating from developed economies to the developing world. It is argued that the environmental concerns of the developed economies caused them to enact strict environmental regulations, which have increased the cost of production of the dirty industries at home. On the other hand, the developing countries with their low wages and lax environmental regulations have been attractive alternative producers in these sectors. At the same time this migration is also beneficial for developing countries that are in need of financial resources for industrial development. Consequently, developing countries provide pollution havens for dirty industries. In this process while the dirty industries have been migrating to the developing countries, the developed countries also have become net importers of these sectors.

The maintenance of the sustainability of environmental functions constitutes a community interest, so that it demands responsibility, openness and a role for members of the community, which can be channeled by people individually, environmental organizations, such as non-government organizations, traditional community groups and others, for maintaining and increasing environmental supportive and carrying capacity which becomes a mainstay of sustainable development. Development which incorporates the environment, including natural resources, is a medium for attaining sustainable development which is a guarantee of prosperity and quality of life of present and future generations.

This work mainly focuses on the Leather Tannery Sector of India and through this sector; the linkages between trade and environment have been established. There are many empirical and few theoretical models on the "Issues related to Trade and Environment". Unlike others[1] here we have attempted to built a theoretical model that focuses on the effects of environmental legislation or regulation and international trade (in the presence of environmental pollution) on the output of different sectors in a small open economy and which also entails a paradoxical result, that strict environmental control accentuates the total level of pollution. Thus the present work will help us to provide answer for the questions- Is the informal sector mainly responsible for the increase in total level of pollution? Does strict environmental control leads to more pollution? Does trade policy adversely affect the economy by enhancing the potentiality of informal sector? Apart from these the welfare implications in the presence of environmental related issue both at autarky and in the presence of trade has also been discussed in this present study.

The paper is organized in the following manner: Second section deals with a brief review of the literature. Third section considers some facts and figures about environmental pollution in the context of the Indian leather industry. Fourth section deals with an analytical framework of the problem. Section Five considers the effects of environmental regulation on the output and welfare of a small open economy. Sections Six and seven examine the effects of trade liberalization on the output and welfare of our stylized small open economy. Finally, the concluding remarks are made in section eight.

LITERATURE REVIEW

Trade enables a country to consume a good without incurring the pollution externality created during its production. So a country importing a good effectively displaces the implicit pollution load to the exporting country. Low and Yeats (1992) find that the share of "dirty" industries in exports from developed countries fell from 20% to 16% over the 1965-1988 period, while the share of dirty goods in exports from poor countries rose. The last numbers are different by regions: in West Asia the percent rises from 9% to 13%, in Eastern Europe from 21% to 28%, in Latin America from 17% to 21%, and in South-East Asia the share of dirty goods exports in total exports is flat at 11%. Lucas et al. (1992) empirically examine how the structure of manufacturing production varies, both across countries and over time, in relation to the toxic emission of component industries. They find evidence for an inverse U-shape relationship between industrial pollution intensity and income. On the other hand Mani and Wheeler (1998) examine the Pollution Haven Hypothesis (PHH) using international data on industrial production, trade and environmental regulation for the period 1960-1995. Their cross country analysis gives a result that is consistent with the PHH. They find that pollution intensive output as a percentage of manufacturing has fallen consistently in the OECD economies and risen steadily in the developing world. Besides, it is revealed that periods of rapid increase in net exports of pollution-intensive product coincide with periods of rapid increase in the costs of pollution abatement in the OECD countries. The tanning industry wastes have been extensively examined for their environmental impact, consequently they are branded as one of the worst anthropogenic polluters (Eye & Lawrence, 1971). Davis et al. (1994) have shown that the reducing environment created due to these wastes can result in the precipitation of amorphous iron sulphide and subsequent increased Cr(III) solubility leading to an increased Cr(III) mobility.

Two conflicting hypotheses emerge from the debate. The first competing hypothesis, known as the pollution haven hypothesis (PHH), argues that changes in environmental legislation can distort existing patterns of comparative advantage. In the developed world the costs of complying with environmental regulations appear to be increasing steadily. Since the stringency of environmental regulations increases with income and economic development (Dasgupta, et al., 2002) the PHH assumes that developing countries possess a comparative advantage in pollution intensive production. Thus "pollution havens" arise.

There has been a tremendous change in the trade policy of the Indian economy since July 1991 which has been motivated by a full recognition of the important role that trade can play in promoting sustained economic growth in the context of sustainable development. This section will briefly review some of this literature. Grossman and Krueger (1992), Lucas et al. (1992), Antweiler et al. (2001) and Eskeland and Harrison (2003) have made significant contributions on this issue. The role of international trade in determining the environmental damage has been addressed by specialists using input-output techniques such as in Wright (1974), Hayami and Nakamura, (2002), Lange G-M and R. Hassan (2002), Gerilla, Kagawa and Inamura (2002), Hann (2002) and Wadeskog (2002). Unfortunately very little work has been done in India. Recently, preliminary attempts have been made by Mukhopadhyay (2004), Mukhopadhyay and Chakraborty (2004), Dietzenbacher and Mukhopadhyay (2004), Mukhopadyhay, Chakravorty and Dietzenbacher (2005) and Jha and Rabindran (2004), Chatterjee, Gupta and Chatterjee (2016).

Chaudhuri and Gupta (2004) have considered a three sector general equilibrium model with an informal manufacturing sector. They have shown that, under some reasonable conditions, an inflow of foreign capital raises total domestic pollution, raises national income and also raises national welfare. These results are true both in the presence and in the absence of transfer of environmentally sound technology (EST).

Mukhopadhyay and Chakraborty (2005) work aims at testing both hypotheses, PHH and FEH, for India's trade with the rest of the world and the European Union during the 1990s when radical economic reforms were introduced. The input-output method is used and suitably modified to test both the hypotheses considering three pollutants, carbon dioxide, sulphur dioxide and nitrogen dioxide (CO2, SO2 and NOx). It is clear from the results that import-related pollution is much greater than the export-related pollution for India. The findings of the present work challenge the pollution haven hypothesis, arguing that liberalization of trade policy in India has not been associated with pollution-intensive industrial development and attempts to contribute to the environment and trade debate by examining the impacts of international trade with the rest of the world and also with the EU on emissions of CO_2, SO_2 and NOx in the Indian economy during the 1990s using input-output techniques. Testing both hypotheses, PHH and FEH for India's trade with the rest of the world and the European Union were done during the 1990s when radical economic reforms were introduced. The input-output method is used and suitably modified to test both the hypotheses considering three pollutants, carbon dioxide, sulphur dioxide and nitrogen dioxide (CO_2, SO_2 and NOx). It is clear from the results that import-related pollution is much greater than the export-related pollution for India. The findings of the present work challenge the pollution haven hypothesis, arguing that liberalization of trade policy in India has not been associated with pollution-intensive industrial development.

In spite of the existence of vast literature on this subject, the significance of this study originates from the fact that, in none of the works, the focus has been given on the different trade and environmental issues with reference to a particular informal sector, say the tannery sector .The present paper tries to cover the effect of environmental pollution on the output of different sectors in a small open economy and which also entails a paradoxical result, that strict environmental control accentuates the total level of pollution. Thus, this paper can be considered as a new contribution in this arena.

PROFILE OF ENVIRONMENTAL POLLUTION IN LEATHER TANNERY SECTOR IN INDIA

The leather industry is India's fourth largest export industry, employing 2.5 million people and having a target value of about A$10 billion in 2002. The preparation of leather requires the use of large amounts of salt. Tannery discharges are causing loss of agricultural production due to making more salinity of rivers and groundwater. It is also adding to the salinity of drinking water. In the past few years, Indian authorities have set stringent regulations for tannery discharges. Regulations for biochemical oxygen demand, chemical oxygen demand and chromium levels are now being met, though at considerable cost. However, levels of total dissolved solids (TDS) remain too high. If the tanning industry does not deal with this problem, it will face legal action and closures, leading to social and economic hardship. The leather industry has been identified as a thrust sector for export promotion in India but it is also perceived to be highly polluting as well. The leather industry has both some sustainable aspects as well as some unsustainable aspects. Until 2002, the leather sector was reserved for small scale sector and this may have prevented Foreign Direct Investment (FDI) in this sector. The FDI in this sector from August 1991 to December 2005 is US$ 51.84 millions. This is only 0.15% of total FDI inflows and ranked at 30. Today the industry ranks 8th in the export trade in terms of foreign exchange earnings of the country. Leather sector has been included among red categories of industries on account of the potential environmental impact of tannery wastes. Since 1996, the Indian tannery sector has increased its environmental preparedness. Tanneries in Punjab, UP and Tamil Nadu are now connected to pollution control devices. In Calcutta, the problem is being addressed comprehensively with the industry undergoing relocation into a new leather city. A successful lesson has been-learnt in the tannery sector in Tamil Nadu during the last two years.

Waste minimization in tannery sector has benefited significantly. The Ministry of Environment and Forests; Government of India has recognized the need for gaining environmental security of the leather sector. In order to develop a holistic action plan for prevention and control of pollution in tanneries, the Ministry has formed a working group under the chairmanship of Central Pollution Control Board (CPCB) with a directive to-submit the report before 30 September 1999.Need for technological up gradation of the tannery sector on an all India basis has been recognized. Scope for implementing waste minimization circles in Punjab, UP and Calcutta has been identified. Consolidation of outputs in the tannery sector in Tamil Nadu has been felt necessary.

Let us first focus on the sustainable aspects. The leather industry plays a main role in the substantial export earnings. It also provides employment to the marginalized section of the society and gives them the opportunity to participate to the small scale sector. The water pollution due to discharge of untreated effluent from the slaughterhouse, the air pollution due to the foul smell from the slaughterhouse and tannery, unhygienic surroundings due to lack of proper cleaning activities and occupational health hazards to the worker due to the use of chemicals in tanneries are some of the unsustainable aspects of the leather industry. Here we will focus on the current export basket of the leather industry.

CURRENT EXPORT BASKET OF INDIAN LEATHER INDUSTRY

Table 1 and Figure 1 present the export data on Indian leather industry in different product categories.

The Indian leather industry has earned a special status in the national economy as the fourth largest foreign exchange earner with a share of around 7% in the total country's exports. The tanning sector is the basic skeleton on which the entire leather industry depends and it is also one of the largest polluters. The leather processing capacity in India is more than 1900 tanning units out of which 75% are in the small scale sector. The inherent nature of the tanning process is such, that large quantities of water are consumed. Attributed to this factor this industry is chiefly located near river banks: Ganga river system in UP, Bihar and West Bengal and Palar and Cavery river systems in Tamil Nadu .The leather tanning industry in India is made up of a few large export-oriented units and a large number of manual, small-scale units producing mainly for the domestic market. These facilities are mostly rather primitive and do not meet the minimum discharge standards. Release of wastewater from them is seriously compromising groundwater quality, and the problem is compounded by the discharge of heavy metals. Most of the small tanneries are concentrated in clusters which could facilitate common effluent treatment facilities after heavy metals and sulphides have been removed by pre-treatment. But toxic solid

Table 1. Export of leather products in India

Product Category	Exports	US$ Million % on Total Exports
Finished leather	688.05	23%
Leather footwear	950.90	32%
Leather garments	308.98	10%
Footwear goods	212.65	7%
Leather goods	690.66	23%
Saddlers and harness	81.85	3%
Non-leather footwear	48.69	2%

Source: http://leather.webindia.com/exec.htm

Figure 1. Export of leather products in India
Source: http://leather.webindia.com/exec.htm

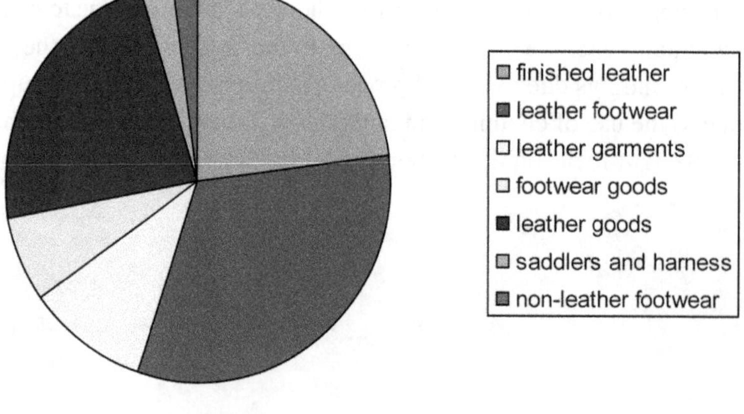

residues and sludge continue to be disposed without treatment, producing noxious gases which cause air pollution. The tanneries cause water pollution problem as well with high BOD and COD values in their discharges, together with chromium, phenols, sulphides, ammonia, dyestuff, heavy metals, detergents and antiseptic agents. Average compliance with national discharge standards is estimated at a meagre 2per cent. Even the largest tanneries remove less than 20 percent of the required pollutants, and 435 tonnes (at least 36times the standard) of highly toxic chromium compounds are discharged annually into rivers. Substantial amounts of solid waste — approximately 73 million tonnes a year — are disposed of similarly. The environmental problems created by industry stem primarily from the use of a strictly linear production process of extracting raw materials and fossil energy, processing the material and energy, and dumping the waste back into natural systems. In response, an innovative new theory termed Sustainable Industrial Network (SINET) is emerging to guide industries towards sustainable production. SINET aims to incorporate the cyclical patterns of ecosystems into designs for industrial production processes that will work in unison with natural systems.

The overall objective of the proposed initiative is to develop and adapt solutions to promote sustainability of the micro regions, specifically through making the Industry network(key economic activity) of the micro region more effective and efficient, thereby making products, processes & services at the micro region more resource efficient and less polluting. The leather industry occupies a prominent place in the Indian economy in view of its substantial export earnings, employment potential and growth. The Indian Leather industry is the third largest export earner in the country. The industry covers a vast spectrum of inputs, activities, skills and products i.e. livestock, hides and skins, tanning, leather products and exports. The industry generates huge amount of waste which is utilized by other allied industries for by-product manufacturing and the remaining amount of waste is then best treated for waste minimization.

These facts and figures states that Indian leather industry uses a horizontally differentiated kind of production process and to perform this with positive profit, this formal sector outsources some part of its production to the so-called informal intermediate sector. This informal sector is neither controlled by the state nor even registered in the accounts of government. Hence, as per the existence of this sector no formal evidence can not display and therefore the potential volume of pollution will be made by this informal sector can not be captured also. Though, its significance can be realized. However, on the basis of these arguments in the section we have tried to fit our within a suitable theoretical framework and try to explain the impact of strict regulation to control pollution on the volume of formal import industry (e.g. leather industry) and also on informal intermediate industry (e.g. outsourcing partner of the leather industry).

THE MODEL

We consider a small open developing economy consisting of four sectors: sector 1, sector 2, sector 3 and sector4. Sector 1 produces exportable products like agricultural commodity (X_1) with labour (L) and capital of type K. Sector 2 produces an importable product (X_2) with the help of labour and non-traded intermediate product (X_3). Sector 3 is a non-traded intermediated sector or informal sector which uses labour and capital of type K. Finally, we considers the existence of another export sector, sector 4 that produces advance exportable product (X_4) with labour and capital of type N. It is to be noted that our exportable sectors are distinguished with respect to the use of type capital. For instance, sector 1 uses capital of type K with L to produce agricultural products and we treat this sector as backward export sector and in similar manner we treat sector 4 as advanced export sector of the economy. On the other hand the import competing sector (sector 2) protected by a tariff[2]. Due to small open economy assumption, the product prices are internationally given. Production function exhibits constant returns to scale with diminishing marginal productivity to each variable input. Capital of type K is perfectly mobile between the sector 1 and sector 3. Wage rate is fixed at $\bar{W}$ in the formal manufacturing sector by the trade union. Wage rate of the workers of rest of the economy is competitive and flexible. All the input output coefficients are variable. The formal import competing sector is made to pay a pollution emission tax for any pollution level higher than the permissible (Ω) level that is determined by the regulatory authority. Since the informal manufacturing sector creates pollution, increase in the use of informal sector output in the formal sector raises the level of pollution and widens the discrepancy between actual and permissible levels of pollution. The efficiency of a representative worker is inversely related to the level of pollution. In this framework, we show that even if the permissible level of pollution is reduced, the polluting informal sector may expand and worsen the environmental standard. Here, we have assumed that pollution is mainly from the informal sector and there is no pollution from the agricultural sector. We have also assumed that the informal manufacturing sector is capital intensive.

The following notations are used to describe the equation structure of the model.

P_i: price of the ith product; i =1,2, 3,4.
X_i: output of the ith sector, i =1,2,3,4.
E: nutritional efficiency of each worker.
LE (Ω): total calories intake of total labour.
a_{Li}: labour-output coefficient in the ith sector, i =1,2,3,4
a_{Ki}: capital-output coefficient in the ith sector, i =1,3
$\bar{W}$: unionized wage of the workers in the formal manufacturing sector.
r: rate of return on capital of type K.
R: rate of return on capital of type N.
Ω: maximum permissible level of pollution.
α_i: emission coefficient.
Z: total level of pollution
K: Stock of capital of type K
N: stock of capital of type N

Here, the maximum permissible level of pollution is denoted by Ω and we can write it as[3]

$$\alpha_4 X_4 + \alpha_2 X_2 + \alpha_1 X_1 \leq \Omega \tag{1}$$

Total level of pollution is denoted by Z and we can express it as

$$Z = \Omega + \alpha_3 X_3 \tag{2}$$

where, α_3 is the emission coefficient of sector 3 .

Production functions exhibits constant returns to scale with diminishing marginal productivity to each factor. Without the loss of generality, we have assumed that, the product of sector '1' as the numeraire. Thus, $P_1=1$.

The general equilibrium is represented by the following set of equations.

$$1 = a_{L1}.W + a_{K1}.r \quad (3)$$

$$P_2^* = P_2\left(1+t\right) = a_{L2}.\bar{W} + a_{32}.P_3 \quad (4)$$

$$P_3 = a_{L3}.W + a_{K3}.r \quad (5)$$

$$P_4 = a_{L4}.W + a_{N4}.R \quad (6)$$

Equations (3-6) are the competitive industry equilibrium conditions in the four sectors.

From the domestic demand-supply equality of the intermediate good we get

$$a_{32}X_2 = X_3 \quad (7)$$

The endowments of the three primary factors in the economy are K, N and L. All the factors of production are fully employed and their full employment conditions are given as

$$a_{K1}X_1 + a_{K3}X_3 = K \quad (8)$$

$$a_{N4}X_4 = N \quad (9)$$

$$a_{L2}X_2 + a_{L1}X_1 + a_{L3}X_3 + a_{L4}X_4 = LE\left(\Omega\right) \quad (10)$$

It should be pointed out that the average efficiency of the workers, E, is considered to be a negative function of the maximum permissible pollution and is given by

$$E = E\left(\Omega\right); E^{/} < 0 \quad (11)$$

The demand for commodity 2 and the volume of import (I) are given by the following equations, respectively.

$$D_2 = D_2\left(P_2, P_3, P_4, Y\right) \tag{12}$$

$$I = D_2\left(P_2, P_3, P_4, Y\right) - X_2 \tag{13}$$

The national income (Y) of the economy at domestic prices is given by

$$Y = X_1 + P_2X_2 + P_4X_4 - rK_F - RN_F + tP_2^{*}I \tag{14.1}$$

Or

$$Y = (\bar{W} - W)a_{L2} + WLE(\Omega) + RN_D + rK_D + tP_2 * I \text{ (14.2)}.$$

Here, we have 11 independent equations (from eqs. 3 to 10 and eqs. 12 to 14) with 10 unknowns namely, W, P_3, r, R, X_2, X_1, X_3, X_4, D_2, I and Y. Thus, the system is consistent. From equation (1), P_1 can be determined, as $\bar{W}$ is fixed and then from equation (2) and (3), w and r can also be determined. Again, from equation (4), R can be determined. So, we can say that, factor prices are independent of factor endowments and hence, *Decomposability Property* holds.

Assumption 1: By assuming the Decomposability Property we want to mean that all the input-output coefficients are independent upon the input returns. Here, $a_{ij} = a_{ij}(W, r, R, P_3)$, where,

$$a_{L1}^{1} = a_{K1}^{2} = a_{L2}^{1} = a_{32}^{4} = a_{L3}^{1} = a_{K3}^{2} = a_{L3}^{1} = a_{N3}^{3} = 0,$$

where $a_{ij}^{\nu} \forall \nu = 1,2,3,4$ is the partial derivative of a_{ij} with respect to the ν th variable.

To complete the working of the above-stated general equilibrium system we have to use following lemmas.

Lemma 1: An increase in the level of output of informal sector, X_3, has a negative effect on the output level of sector 1(X_1) if full employment condition of labour along with the Decomposability Property (Assumption 1) have been satisfied and $\hat{N} = 0$.

Proof of Lemma 1: Let us start with equation (7) and from equation (7),

$$X_2 = X_3 / a_{32} \tag{7.1}$$

Again, from equation (9),

$$X_4 = N / a_{N4} \tag{9.1}$$

Substituting these values in (10), we get,

$$a_{L2}X_3 / a_{32} + a_{L1}X_1 + a_{L4}N / a_{N4} + a_{L3}X_3 = LE(\Omega)$$

or

$$X_3(a_{L2} / a_{32} + a_{L3}) + a_{L1}X_1 + a_{L4}N / a_{N4} = LE(\Omega)$$

or

$$X_3\{(a_{L2} + a_{L3}.a_{32}) / a_{32}\} + a_{L1}X_1 + a_{L4}X_4 = LE(\Omega) \tag{15}$$

Total differentiation of equation (15) gives us,

$$\{(a_{L2} + a_{L3}.a_{32}) / a_{32}\}dX_3 + a_{L1}dX_1 = 0$$

or

$$\left.\frac{dX_1}{dX_3}\right|_{LL} = \{-a_{L1} / (a_{L2} + a_{L3}a_{32})\} / a_{32} < 0$$

Intuitively, we can explain the same in the following manner. Let us start with an increase in X_3. From equation (7) we can say that for maintaining the equilibrium of informal industries X_2 must go up following an increase in X_3. Therefore, for given X_4 and by incorporating the Assumption 1, from equation (10), that is, from the labour market equilibrium we can state that X_1 must go down as both X_2 and X_3 are moving in the upward direction. More precisely, expansion of sector 3 is possible if and only if sector 2 expands. Again, expansion of these sectors claim more demand for labour and hence less labour will be available to sector 1 and sector 1 contract. This completes the proof of Lemma 1.

Remarks 1: From Lemma 1 we get a locus of X_1 and X_3 for which the labour market is in equilibrium and it is negatively sloped. We refer this locus as LL locus.

Lemma 2: An increase in the level of output of informal sector, X_3, has a negative effect on the output level of sector 1(X_1) if full employment condition of capital of type K along with the Decomposability Property (Assumption 1) have been satisfied and $\hat{N} = 0$.

Proof of Lemma 2: Totally differentiating equation (8),we get,

$$a_{KA}dX_1 + a_{KI}dX_3 = 0$$

or

$$\left.\frac{dX_1}{dX_3}\right|_{KK} = -a_{KA} / a_{KI} < 0$$

Intuitively, we can explain the same in the following manner. Let us start with an increase in X_3. From equation (8) we can say that for maintaining the equilibrium of capital market X_1 must go down following an increase in X_3. Actually, expansion of sector 3 needs more capital and following this sector 1 will release capital along with some labour and hence sector 1 may contract.

Remarks 2: From Lemma 2 we get a locus of X_1 and X_3 for which the capital market is in equilibrium and it is negatively sloped. We refer this locus as KK locus.

It is to be noted that both Lemma 1 and Lemma 2 are based on one assumption relate to factor endowment differences and we can express it formally in the following manner.

Assumption 2: Sector 1 and sector 3 form a Heckscher-Ohlin nugget, and the nugget assumes that sector 3 is more capital intensive than sector 1, i.e., $a_{LA} / a_{KA} > \left(a_{LM} / a_{IM} + a_{LI}\right) / a_{KI}$.

Interpretation to Assumption 2: Note,

$$\left\{a_{LA} / \left(a_{LM} + a_{LI}a_{IM}\right)\right\} / a_{IM} > a_{KA} / a_{KI}$$

$$or, a_{LA} / a_{KA} > \left\{\left(a_{LM} + a_{LI}a_{IM}\right) / a_{IM}\right\} / a_{KI}$$

$$or, a_{LA} / a_{KA} > \left(a_{LM} / a_{IM} + a_{LI}\right) / a_{KI}$$

From the above expression, it can be stated that, the agricultural sector is more labour intensive than the informal sector when labour requirement is measured in direct and indirect terms. Thus, we can say that LL is steeper (see figure-2). More interestingly, this assumption (Assumption 2) also judges the stability criteria among the relevant markets.

Hence, from figure 2 we can say that the intersection between KK and LL locus gives us the equilibrium value of $X_1$and X_3. Once we can determine the value of X_3, equation (7) gives us the value of X_2. Again, for given N and a_{N4}, from equation (9) one can determine the value of X_4. For given P_2, P_3, P_4 and X_2, from equation (13) we can express I in terms of Y. Again, from (13) we can express I in terms

Figure 2. Interactions of different markets

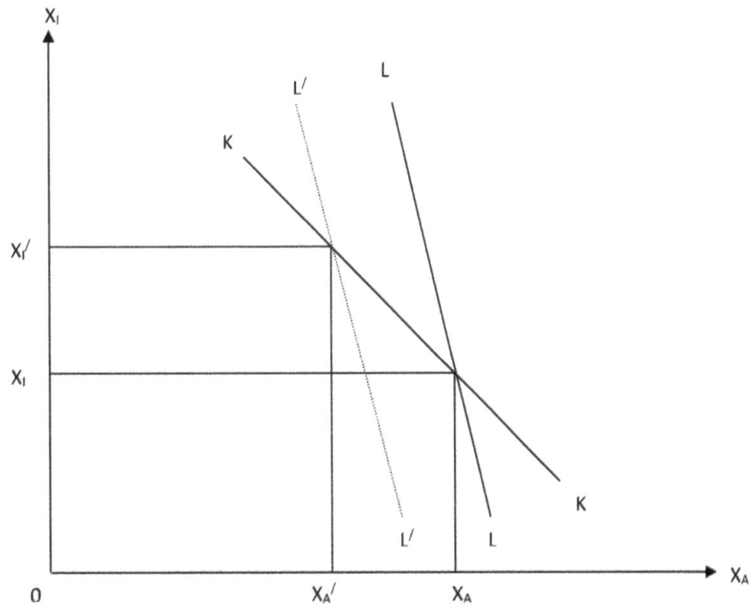

of Y. Hence, from the above two expressions we can solve for I, D_2 and Y. This completes the working of the General equilibrium.

Next we are going to derive the impact of changes in environmental regulations on the output basket of the small open economy. To perform this we have considered two different regimes. One explains the state of weak environmental regulations or legislation and we call it as *Regime of Weak Environmental Regulation* (hereafter RWER). The other is Regime with Strict Environmental Regulation and we refer it as *Regime of Strict Environmental Regulation* (hereafter RSER). Here, we have not used the usual comparative static analysis to capture the impact of changes in environmental related policies on the production system of all the relevant sectors or on the welfare of the small open economy, rather in this study we have considered the mechanism of regime switch to capture the same. By the term regime switch we mean a comparative study of movement of different variables both under the RWER and RSER[4].

DRIVE TOWARDS THE REGIME OF STRICT ENVIRONMENTAL REGULATION (RSER)

Regime With Weak Environmental Regulation (RWER)

Let us start with a situation where our economy is in a state with weak environmental legislation or regulations and it implies an increase in the maximum permissible level of pollution, that is, Ω increases. Formally, we can state this as follow.

Differentiation of equation (7) gives us

$$\lambda_{32}\hat{X}_2 = \hat{X}_3 \quad (7.1)$$

This expression (7.1) tells us that if $\hat{X}_3 > 0$ then $\hat{X}_2 > 0$. Again, $\hat{\Omega} > 0$ implies more freedom to sector 3 to produce more pollution intensive intermediate product for sector 2 and hence we can write $\hat{X}_3 > 0$. This expansion of sector 3 implies sector 2 will also expand and hence, $\hat{X}_2 > 0$.

Again total differentiation of equation (10)

$$\lambda_{L1}\hat{X}_1 + \lambda_{L2}\hat{X}_2 + \lambda_{L3}\hat{X}_3 + \lambda_{L4}\hat{X}_4 = \{(dE(\Omega) / d\Omega)(\Omega / E(\Omega)\}\hat{\Omega} \quad (10.1)$$

or more precisely,

$$\lambda_{L1}\hat{X}_1 + \lambda_{L2}\hat{X}_2 + \lambda_{L3}\hat{X}_3 + \lambda_{L4}\hat{X}_4 = \zeta_{EL}\hat{\Omega} \quad (10.2)$$

where, $\zeta_{EL} = \{(dE(\Omega) / d\Omega)(\Omega / E(\Omega)\}$ is the elasticity of the labour efficiency function, E(Ω), with respect to Ω. Hence, (10.2) tells us that $\hat{\Omega} > 0$ implies a fall in the level of labour supply in terms of efficiency to the rest of the economy. However, we have already claimed that $\hat{X}_3 > 0$ and $\hat{X}_2 > 0$ due to the fact that $\hat{\Omega} > 0$. Therefore, for maintaining the equality of equation (10.2) X_2 should increase, i.e., $\hat{X}_1 < 0$. Moreover, from equation (14.2) we can clearly indicate the loss of welfare due to the increase in maximum permissible level of pollution. REWR implies $\hat{\Omega} > 0$ and we get less labour force available to the economy in terms of efficiency, that is, LE (Ω) will fall. Therefore, the efficiency augmented wage rate may decline under REWR and it will affect the national welfare adversely. We refer this effect as Efficiency Augmented Wage Effect (EAWE). Again, as $\hat{X}_2 > 0$ and $\hat{D}_2 = 0$ (for given Y), and therefore, equation (13) tells us that $\hat{I} < 0$ for $\hat{\Omega} > 0$. Hence, a fall in import leads to a fall in tariff revenue from import and it will again affect Y adversely. We can refer this effect as Tariff Revenue Effect (TRE). As we find that both effects, that is, EAWE and TRE affect Y adversely and hence we can claim that our national welfare may deteriorate in the presence RWER.

Intuitively, from figure 2, we can say that, with the increase in the level of pollution, the maximum permissible level of pollution also increases and the environmental standard gets degraded. Consequently, the health of workers' gets affected and their nutritional efficiency (E) deteriorates. So, total calories intake of total labour falls and eventually, effective labour also gets deteriorated and hence, LL shifts to the left to L′L′. As a result, output of the informal sector, X_3 rises and the output of the agricultural sector, X_1 falls. In other words, pollution emanating mainly from the informal sector, has affected health of the workers' and so, output of the labour intensive agricultural sector falls, whereas, output of the capital intensive informal sector rises. So, it shows the presence of 'Rybczynski type' effect. Again, from equation (7) we can say that, since, output of the informal sector, X_3 rises, hence, output of the formal manufacturing sector, X_2 must also rise. It proves the existence of complementarily in the production between sector 2 and sector 3.

Proposition 1: An increase in the maximum permissible level of pollution or Ω leads to a) an expansion of both sector 2 and sector 3 and a contraction of sector 1; and b) the movement of sector 4 remains undefined.

The following corollary also follows from the above-mentioned economic interpretations.

Corollary 1: In the presence of RWER national welfare deteriorates unambiguously.

Regime of Strict Environmental Regulation (RSER)

Next, we will focus on what happens when a strict environmental control is exercised and it implies $\hat{\Omega} < 0$. The expression (1) can be modified as

$$\alpha_1^1 \hat{X}_1 + \alpha_2^1 \hat{X}_2 + \alpha_4^1 \hat{X}_4 \leq \hat{\Omega} \tag{1.1}$$

Expression (1.1) tells us that if $\hat{\Omega} < 0$, X_2 can't increase too much due to the existence of the inequality and it looks like that sector 2 may contract, that is, $\hat{X}_2 < 0$. We can call it Notional Supply (NS) of sector 2. However, here lies the significance of our paper because in real case sector 2 will shift its burden related to RSER to the informal sector[5] and hence effective demand for X_3 increases, that is, $\hat{X}_3 > 0$. By following this we can say that both sector 2 and 3 will rise and it will happen to cater the balance between effective demand and effective supply (ES) of sector 2[6]. More specifically we can say that here we have to consider two different views to examine the impact of RSER on X_2 and X_3.

i) Inequality regarding Ω. Here, we can say that $\hat{\Omega} < 0, \hat{X}_2^{NS} < 0, \hat{X}_3^{ED} > 0$, and ii) production function view. Here, we get

$$\hat{\Omega} < 0, \hat{X}_2^{ED} > 0, \hat{X}_2^{ES} > 0 \hat{X}_3^{ED} > 0, \hat{X}_3^{ES} > 0 X_2^{ES} = X_2^{ED}.$$

Combining above-mentioned views and maintaining the product market equilibrium conditions, we can say that the demand for sector 2 remains as usual like RWER as changes in Ω will not affect the demand for sector 2. However, it will restrict the production of sector 2 and hence sector 2 can shift some of his production to sector 3 all these happen in such a way that at the final stage of production $X_2 = D_2^{Domestic}$. Therefore, the results regarding sectoral distribution remains unchanged (like under RWER) even under RSER. However, the presence of RSER at least provides some positivity from the welfare aspect. Recalling the effects like EAWE and TRE, here under RSER, we can say that welfare may improve if positive effect of EAWE dominates over TRE.

Intuitively we explain these facts in the given manner. It is to be noted that formal sector's pollution can never exceed the maximum permissible level, Ω, so they subcontract a part of their production to the informal sector. When there is strict environmental control, formal sector subcontracts production to the informal sector and hence, output of the informal sector, that is, X_3 rises. It should be noted that, total pollution can be expressed in terms of equation (1). Therefore, strict environmental control means, maximum permissible level of pollution is restricted to a lower limit. Since, we have just seen that, with strict environmental control, the output of the informal sector rises, it basically implies, total pollution will increase. Note, here, we get a paradoxical result in which, the strict environmental control leads to local outsourcing and hence, leads to more pollution, thereby degrading the environment even more. We can infer from this model, that, it is the Informal sector that plays a major role in increasing the level of environmental pollution. If the informal sector has not been taken into consideration, then, the total level of pollution would have been within the maximum permissible level of pollution.

Proposition 2: A decrease in the maximum permissible level of pollution or Ω leads to a) an expansion of both sector 2 and sector 3 and a contraction of sector 1; and b) the movement of sector 4 remains undefined; c) an increase in the probability of local outsourcing to the pollution intensive informal sector.

The following corollary also follows from the above-mentioned economic interpretations.

Corollary 2: In the presence of RSER national welfare may improves under some reasonable condition.

Drive Towards the Regime of International Mobility of Capital N

International Immobility of Capital N

The model which we use in this section is similar to that of the model of section 4 and hence the working of the general equilibrium is similar to that of section 4.

International Mobility of Capital N

Here we assume that in the presence of international immobility of capital N we have R > R*, where R* is the given return on foreign capital of type N in the international market. In such a situation we have no foreign capital inflow of type N. If R falls to $\tilde{R}$, where, R> $\tilde{R}$ > R*, we find that there is some amount of inflow of foreign health capital (N_F) and at last we will reach at the equilibrium level[7] of N_F where, R = R*.

It is to be noted that here we use the model of the section 3.1. We assume that N_D as an exogenous and N_F as an endogenous variables. Here we also assume that R falls to $\tilde{R}$ where, $R > \tilde{R} > R^*$, and we find an inflow of N_F and ultimately R will reach to R*. In this model again we have 11 endogenous variables with eleven independent equations, therefore the system can be solved and hence we are not going to the detail of the working the model.

We can start with an inflow of N, that is, $\hat{N} = 0$. Now from equation (9) we see that $\hat{X}_4 > 0$ as $\hat{N}_F = \hat{N} > 0$. Again, $\hat{N} > 0$ implies $\hat{R} < 0$. Thus, equation (6) and (5) tell us that $\hat{W} > 0$ and $\hat{r} < 0$ as $\hat{R} < 0$. It is to be noted that sector 3 and sector1 form a H-O nugget and from there one can predict that the unit labour demand for most of the sectors will fall as W increases due to mobility of capital N, that is, all $\hat{a}_{Li} < 0$ as $\hat{W} > 0$. However, by maintaining Assumption 2 we can say that fall in unit labour demand leads to a situation where, sector 1 will get more availability of labour and by maintaining the H-O theorem and Rybczynski theorem we can claim the expansion of sector 1 at the cost of contraction of sector 3 and it also coming from the application of the above-mentioned theories of international trade. Therefore, due the existence of Rybczynski theorem we get $\hat{X}_1 > 0, \hat{X}_3 < 0$ due to $\hat{N} > 0$. We call it *Rybczynski Type effect*. Thus, from equation (7) we can say that $\hat{X}_2 < 0$ as $\hat{N} > 0$.

The economic intuition behind this is very simple to realize. Suppose foreign capital is flowing to sector 4 or to an advanced export sector of a small open economy. Now by using these capital, sector 4 may enhance its infrastructure and suppose these better infrastructural facilities provides better knowledge to our labour whose income has already been increased due to the same. Therefore, high income with better knowledge leads to better standard of living to the said worker. It again implies that people of our small open economy will cut their demand for pollution intensive product (that is, output of sector 2) for better future or for maintaining better standard of living. Thus, the demand of sector 3 to sector 2 will also fall and as result we will see the contraction of sector 3 also. It is to be noted that banned of commodity 2 doesn't imply that our consumer will change their consumption basket, that is, consumers will enjoy the benefits of trade in terms of more import of commodity 2. Thus, overall pollution of our small open economy will also be better-off.

Proposition 3: A shift from international immobility of capital N regime to an international mobility of capital N regime leads to under some reasonable conditions: increase in the levels output of both sector 1 and sector 4 and a reduction in the levels of output of informal sector and manufacturing sector.

Corollary 3: Mobility of capital N to the small open economy leads to (a) decrease in the rate of return to both capital K and capital N and increase in the wage rate of the labour; and (b) an increase in the level of national welfare.

DRIVE TOWARDS THE REGIME OF INTERNATIONAL MOBILITY OF CAPITAL K

International Immobility of Capital K

The model which we use in this section is similar to that of the model of section 4 and hence the working of the general equilibrium is similar to that of section 4.

International Mobility of Capital K

By assuming K_F as an endogenous variable and after using $r = r^*$ in our basic model we will face a problem of uniqueness[8] to solve the general equilibrium. Thus determination of the general equilibrium is not possible. However, from here we can infer that an inflow of K_F leads to a fall in r. From equation (3) and (5) we can argue that a reduction in R leads to an increase in W in both of these equations. If W increases more in equation (5) than in equation (3) we find that sector 1 vanishes. On the other hand if W increases more in equation (3) than in equation (5) we find that sector 3 vanishes. This is the main idea behind vanishing industries argument in pure theory of international trade. This leads to us the following proposition.

Proposition 4: A shift from international immobility of capital N regime to an international mobility of capital K leads to; (i) either only sector 1 survives and the 3 sector vanishes, or (ii) only the sector 3 survives and the sector 1 vanishes.

Case 1: Sector 1 Is the Vanishing Sector

The new equation structure can be written as and the competitive equilibrium condition in the product market are given by the following equations

$$P_2^* = P_2(1+t) = a_{L2}.\bar{W} + a_{32}.P_3 \tag{4}$$

$$P_3 = a_{L3}.W + a_{K3}.r \tag{5}$$

$$P_4 = a_{L4}.W + a_{N4}.R \tag{6}$$

$$a_{32}X_2 = X_3 \tag{7}$$

$$a_{K3}X_3 = K \text{ (8')}$$

$$a_{N4}X_4 = N \tag{9}$$

$$a_{L2}X_2 + a_{L3}X_3 + a_{L4}X_4 = LE(\Omega) \text{ (10')}$$

$$D_2 = D_2(P_2, P_3, P_4, Y) \tag{12}$$

$$I = D_2(P_2, P_3, P_4, Y) - X_2 \tag{13}$$

The national income (Y) of the economy at domestic prices is given by

$$Y = P_2X_2 + P_4X_4 - rK_F - RN_F + tP_2^*I \text{ (14.1')}$$

or

$$Y = (\bar{W} - W)a_{L2} + WLE(\Omega) + RN_D + rK_D + tP_2 * I \text{ (14.2).}$$

There are ten endogenous variables, W, P_3, R, X_2, X_3, X_4, K, D_2, I and Y that can be solved from the above ten equations and hence this completes the working of the General equilibrium. To find out the relationship between X_3 and K we establish the following lemma.

Lemma 3: Under the assumption that $-\frac{\gamma}{\sigma_3}\hat{K}_F < \hat{r} < 0$, where $\gamma = (K_F/K)$; an increase in K_F leads to an increase in X_3.

Proof of Lemma 3: To prove this lemma we have to first of all show that $\hat{X}_3 > 0$, when $\hat{K}_F > 0$. Differentiation of equation (8′) gives us

$$\hat{a}_{K3} + \hat{X}_3 = \gamma \hat{K}_F$$

By definition $\sigma_3 = (\hat{a}_{K3} - \hat{a}_{L3})/(\hat{W} - \hat{r})$ and using the envelop result $W da_{L3} + R da_{K3} = 0$ we can write

$$\hat{a}_{K3} = \sigma_3 \theta_{L3} (\hat{W} - \hat{r})$$

From equation (4) we get $\hat{W} = -(\theta_{K3}/\theta_{L3})\hat{r}$ and inserting it in the expression of $\hat{a}_{K3}$ we can write

$$\hat{a}_{K3} = -\sigma_3$$

Thus $\hat{X}_3$ can be written as $\hat{X}_3 = \gamma \hat{K}_F + \hat{r}\sigma_3$

Hence we can say that $\hat{X}_3 > 0$, when $\hat{K}_F > 0$ *iff* $\hat{r} > -\frac{\gamma}{\sigma_3}\hat{K}_F$.

In fact when $\hat{K}_F > 0$, we have $\hat{r} < 0$.

Thus, $\hat{X}_3 > 0$, *iff* $-\frac{\gamma}{\sigma_3}\hat{K}_F < \hat{r} < 0$.

An increase in K_F implies a fall in r, that is, $\hat{K}_F > 0$ implies $\hat{r} < 0$. From equation (5) we can say that a fall in r (i.e., $\hat{r} < 0$) implies an increase in W (i.e., $\hat{W} > 0$). From equation (8′) we can argue that a fall in r implies an increase in a_{K3} (i.e., $\hat{a}_{K3} > 0$). To maintain full employment condition of the capital market it follows that X_3 must increase[9]. An increase in X_3 ($\hat{X}_3 > 0$) implies an increase in X_2 ($\hat{X}_2 > 0$) also. An increase in W has both positive as well as negative effects on Y. The positive effect is generated due to the EAWE as reflected by the second term on the right hand side of equation (14.2). The negative effect is generated due to the labour reallocation effect (LRE). It is reflected by the first term on the RHS of equation (14.2). A fall in r has a negative effect on Y as reflected by the fourth term on the RHS of equation (14.2). If the sum of LRE and domestic capital income effect dominates over the EAWE we find that there is a fall in Y (i.e. $\hat{Y} < 0$). For given P_3, a fall in Y implies a fall in D_2 ($\hat{D}_2 < 0$). Thus a fall in D_2 and an increase in X_2 lead to fall in I ($\hat{I} < 0$). Again, a fall in I leads to further fall in Y. From equation (6) we can say that an increase in W implies a fall in R ($\hat{R} < 0$). A fall in R implies an increase in a_{N4}, hence from equation (4) we can argue that X_4 must have to fall (i.e., $\hat{X}_4 < 0$) to maintain full employment condition of the N type of capital market of.

Proposition 5: A shift from a regime of international immobility of capital K to mobility of capital K causes;(a) the sector 1 to vanish and rest of the sectors will survive; (b) an increase in the level of output of both import sector and intermediate informal sector and a decrease in the level of output of the advance export sector.

Corollary 5: Mobility of capital K to the small open economy leads to (a) decrease in the rate of return to both capital K and capital N and increase in the wage rate of the labour; and (b) a decrease in the level of national welfare.

Case 2: Sector 3 Is the Vanishing Sector

The new equation structure can be written as and the competitive equilibrium condition in the product market are given by the following equations

$$1 = a_{L1}.W + a_{K1}.r \quad (3)$$

$$P_2^* = P_2(1+t) = a_{L2}.\bar{W} \ (4')$$

$$P_4 = a_{L4}.W + a_{N4}.R \quad (6)$$

$$a_{K1}X_1 = K \ (8'')$$

$$a_{N4}X_4 = N \quad (9)$$

$$a_{L2}X_2 + a_{L1}X_1 + a_{L4}X_4 = LE(\Omega) \ (10'')$$

$$D_2 = D_2(P_2, P_4, Y) \ (12')$$

$$I = D_2(P_2, P_4, Y) - X_2 \ (13')$$

The national income (Y) of the economy at domestic prices is given by

$$Y = P_1X_1 + P_2X_2 + P_4X_4 - rK_F - RN_F + tP_2^*I \quad (14.1)$$

or

$Y = (\bar{W} - W)a_{L2} + WLE(\Omega) + RN_D + rK_D + tP_2 * I$ (14.2).

There are nine endogenous variables, W, R, X_2, X_1, X_4, K, D_2, I and Y that can be solved from the above nine equations and hence the system of equations can be solved. To find out the relationship between X_3 and K we establish the following lemma.

Lemma 4: Under the assumption that - $\frac{\gamma}{\sigma_3} \hat{K}_F < \hat{r} < 0$, where $\gamma = (K_F/K)$; an increase in K_F leads to an increase in X_3.

Proof of Lemma 4: To prove this lemma we have to first of all show that $\hat{X}_1 > 0$, when $\hat{K}_F > 0$. Differentiation of equation (8//) gives us

$$\hat{a}_{K1} + \hat{X}_1 = \gamma \hat{K}_F$$

By definition $\sigma_1 = (\hat{a}_{K1} - \hat{a}_{L1})/(\hat{W} - \hat{r})$ and using the envelop result $Wda_{L1} + Rda_{K1} = 0$ we can write

$$\hat{a}_{K1} = \sigma_1 \theta_{L1} (\hat{W} - \hat{r})$$

From equation (3) we get $\hat{W} = -(\theta_{K1}/\theta_{L1})\hat{r}$ and inserting it in the expression of $\hat{a}_{K1}$ we can write $\hat{a}_{K1}$ = - σ_1

Thus $\hat{X}_1$ can be written as $\hat{X}_1 = \gamma \hat{K}_F + \hat{r}\sigma_1$

Hence we can say that $\hat{X}_1 > 0$, when $\hat{K}_F > 0$ iff $\hat{r} > -\frac{\gamma}{\sigma_1}\hat{K}_F$.

In fact when $\hat{K}_F > 0$, we have $\hat{r} < 0$.

Thus, $\hat{X}_1 > 0$, iff $-\frac{\gamma}{\sigma_1}\hat{K}_F < \hat{r} < 0$.

An increase in K_F implies a fall in r, that is, $\hat{K}_F > 0$ implies $\hat{r} < 0$. From equation (3) we can say that a fall in r (i.e., $\hat{r} < 0$) implies an increase in W (i.e., $\hat{W} > 0$). From equation (8//) we can argue that a fall in r implies an increase in a_{K1} (i.e., $\hat{a}_{K1} > 0$). To maintain full employment condition of the capital market it follows that X_1 must increase[10]. Again, we can say that supply of sector 2 must decline because sector 2 is now using only labour and therefore it is not possible for sector 2 to compete with foreign import. Hence, X_2 should decline (i.e., $\hat{X}_2 < 0$). An increase in W has both positive as well as negative effects on Y. The positive effect is generated due to the EAWE as reflected by the second term on the right hand side of equation (14.2/). The negative effect is generated due to the labour reallocation effect (LRE). It is reflected by the first term on the RHS of equation (14.2). A fall in r has a negative effect on Y as reflected by the fourth term on the RHS of equation (14.2). If the sum of LRE and domestic capital income effect dominates over the EAWE we find that there is a fall in Y (i.e., $\hat{Y} < 0$). A fall in Y implies a fall in D_2 ($\hat{D}_2 > 0$). Thus a fall in D_2 and reduction in X_2 lead to an increase in I (

$\hat{I} > 0$). Again, a rise in I leads to an increase in Y due to TRE. Therefore, finally we can say that if the sum of EAWE and TRE dominates over the sum of LRE and domestic capital income effect, we find a rise in Y (i.e., $\hat{Y} < 0$) and following this an improvement of welfare. From equation (6) we can say that an increase in W implies a fall in R ($\hat{R} < 0$). A fall in R implies an increase in a_{N4}, hence from equation (4) we can argue that X_4 must have to fall (i.e., $\hat{X}_4 < 0$) to maintain full employment condition of the N type of capital market of.

Proposition 6: A shift from a regime of international immobility of capital K to mobility of capital K causes;(a) the sector 3 to vanish and rest of the sectors will survive; (b) a reduction in the level of output of both sector 2 and sector 4 and an increase in the level of output of the sector 1.

Corollary 6: Mobility of capital K to the small open economy leads to (a) decrease in the rate of return to both capital K and capital N and increase in the wage rate of the labour; and (b) an improvement in the level of national welfare.

CONCLUDING REMARKS AND POLICY IMPLICATIONS

The chapter has analyzed the environmental and welfare consequences of foreign capital in a small open economy using a four sector, three factors, full-employment general equilibrium model with tariff and labour market distortions and a non-traded intermediate sector. The non-traded intermediate sector is an informal sector and this sector produces a product by using which formal import competing sector produces a pollution intensive final product. The production system related to pollution intensive product is very much associated with environmental regulations. For instance, strict environmental regulation will permit less pollution and hence less production by the import competing sector and vice-versa. However, to break this shackle import sector may outsource its production subsets to the informal sector and the consequences of environmental degradation will persist. Apart from these, here we consider two types of capital, of which capital of type N is specific to advanced export sector while capital of type K is used by rest of the sectors of the economy. So, FDI of capital K and N may affect the environment either by changing the output of import sector or by changing the same of non-traded informal sector.

The analysis has shown a paradoxical result, that strict environmental control accentuates the total level of pollution. Here a hybrid type of general equilibrium trade model has been used to analyze the problem. From the theoretical framework, it is obvious that one cannot deny the key role played by the informal sector in degrading the environment both under weak and strict environmental regulations. Apart from that in this article we have captured the argument behind the outsourcing of formal sector services to informal sector in the presence of strict environmental regulation and from that we have found that strict environmental regulation raises human capital endowment of the economy, may affect social welfare positively. Similarly, the opposite may occur in the presence of weak environmental regulation. This paper has also found that FDI in the advanced export sector decreases the overall pollution level in the economy and improves the welfare through knowledge explosion and better income distribution. However, the effect of FDI of capital K is very interesting in the sense that such FDI may consequences the possibilities of vanishing industries. This paper claims two different situations, one where such FDI may vanish the usual export sector of the economy or it vanishes the non-trade intermediate sector of the economy. In the former case, where export sector becomes the vanishing sector we find more pollution with loss in welfare. However, the later case, where informal sector becomes the vanishing sector, we find less pollution with more gains from trade in terms of improving welfare.

Finally, it should be mentioned that although the results of the model crucially hinge on the institutional and technological characteristics and the trade pattern of the economy in question, the conditions on which these results depend consist with only parameters of the system and not of any endogenous variables (though in this paper in the regime of international capital mobility we assume endogenous N and K). Hence, the results hold for a wide range of parameter values and these values can show some path to the policymakers to take proper policy measures. From our theoretical framework we have found that even strict environmental regulation alone can't prevent the prosperity of pollution for a small open developing economy. Again, proper implantation of FDI to enhance better infrastructure, better knowledge exposure and obviously with better purchasing power can control the grasp of pollution. Hence, policymakers can adopt a policy in which the interaction between environmental regulation and technological diffusion (in the form of FDI inflow) can take place.

REFERENCES

Antweiler, W., Copeland, B. R., & Taylor, M. S. (2001). Is free trade good for the environment? *The American Economic Review*, *91*(4), 877–908. doi:10.1257/aer.91.4.877

Chatterjee, N., Gupta, K., & Chatterjee, T. (2017). Revisiting the Conflicts between 'Environmental Taxes vs Standard' in the Context of International Trade: The Role of Waste Recycling. *International Journal of Sustainable Economies Management*, *6*(2), 13–29. doi:10.4018/IJSEM.2017040102

Chatterjee, T. (2016). *Environmental Legislation and International Trade: Theory, Policy and Indian experience*. Working paper, MPRA Paper 60583, University Library of Munich, Germany.

Chaudhuri, S., & Gupta, K. (2004). *Inflow of Foreign capital, Environmental Pollution and Welfare in the presence of an Informal sector*. Paper presented at the Indian Statistical Institute, Kolkata conference.

Dasgupta, S., Laplante, B., Wang, H., & Wheeler, D. (2002). Confronting the Environmental Kuznet Kurve. *The Journal of Economic Perspectives*, *16*(1), 147–168. doi:10.1257/0895330027157

Dietzenbacher, E., & Mukhopadhyay, K. (2004). *An empirical examination of the pollution haven hypothesis for India: towards a green Leontief paradox?* Input-Output and General Equilibrium: Data, Modelling and Policy Analysis, held at Free University of Brussels, Brussels, International Conference Jointly Organized by EcoMod Network and IIOA.

Eskeland, G. S., & Harrison, A. (2003). Moving to greener pastures? Multinationals and the pollution haven hypothesis. *Journal of Development Economics, Elsevier*, *70*(1), 1–23. doi:10.1016/S0304-3878(02)00084-6

Gerilla, G. P., Kagawa, S., & Inamura, H. (2002). *International Trade and Carbon Emissions: A Case of China and Japan*. Paper presented at the 14th International conference on Input -Output Techniques held at UQAM, Montreal, Canada.

Grossman, G. M., & Krueger, A. B. (1992). *Environmental impacts of a North American Free Trade Agreement*. Centre for Economic Policy Research Discussion Paper 644.

Haan, M. D. (2002). *Extending the Scope of Environmental Indicators by Taking into Account International Trade Dependencies*. Paper presented at the 14th International conference on Input -Output Techniques held at UQAM, Montreal, Canada.

Hayami, H., & Nakamura, M. (2002). *CO2 emission of an alternative technology and bilateral trade between Japan and Canada: relocating production and an implication for joint implementation*. Keio Economic Observatory Discussion Paper 75, paper presented in the 14th International Conference on Input-Output Techniques, Montreal, Canada.

Hettige, H., Mani, M., & Wheeler, D. (2000). Industrial pollution in economic development: The Environmental Kuznets curve revisited. *Journal of Development Economics*, *62*(2), 445–476. doi:10.1016/S0304-3878(00)00092-4

Jha, S., & Rabindran, S. G. (2004). *Environmental impact of India's trade liberalization*. Paper presented at the "75 years of Development Conference" held at Cornell University, New York, NY.

Lange, G. M., & Hassan, R. (2002). *Trade and the Environment in Southern Africa: The Impact of the 'User Pays' Principle for Water on Exports of Botswana, Namibia, and South Africa*. Paper presented at the 14th International conference on Input –Output Techniques held at UQAM, Montreal, Canada.

Low, P., & Yeats, A. (1992). Do 'dirty' industries migrate? International trade and the environment, The World Bank.

Lucas, R. E., Wheeler, B. D., & Hettige, H. (1992). Economic development, Environmental regulation and the International migration of toxic industrial pollution:1960-1988. International Trade and the Environment, World Bank discussion paper 159, World Bank.

Mani, M., & Wheeler, D. (1998). In search of pollution havens? Dirty industry in the world economy: 1960-1995. *Journal of Environment & Development*, *7*(3), 215–247. doi:10.1177/107049659800700302

Mukhopadhyay, K., & Chakraborty, D. (2004). Environmental Impacts Of Trade Liberalisation in India. In *Econometric Models: theory and applications*. New Delhi: Allied Publishers Limited.

Mukhopadhyay, K., & Chakraborty, D. (2005). Environmental impacts of trade in India. *The International Trade Journal*, *19*(2), 135–163. doi:10.1080/08853900590933116

Mukhopadyhay, K., Chakravorty, D., & Dietzenbacher, E. (2005). *Pollution Haven and factor endowment hypotheses revisited: Evidence from India*. Paper presented in the 5th international input-output conference at Renmin university, Beijing, China.

Wadeskog, A. (2002). *Trade and the Environment in Input-Output Based Environmental Accounts Analysis*. Paper presented at the 14th International conference on Input-Output Techniques held at UQAM, Montreal, Canada.

Wright, D. J. (1974). Goods and services: An input -output analysis. *Energy Policy*, *2*(4), 307–315. doi:10.1016/0301-4215(74)90017-2

KEY TERMS AND DEFINITIONS

Environmental Regulation: Environmental regulations are rules and requirements that consider several aspects of environment. For instance, it includes 1) measures related to pollution control and 2) the way out to reach sustainable development by regulating how much pollution a system releases.

Informal Sector: The informal sector refers to those sectors, where social security of related stakeholders is almost missing, and in this sense, it differs from formal sector. In informal sector labors are self-employed, or who work for those who are self-employed. People who earn a living through self-employment in most cases are not on payrolls, and thus are not taxed. Many informal workers do their businesses in unprotected and unsecured places.

National Output: It is the aggregate of all sectors' output in an economy.

Pollution Haven Hypothesis: Pollution haven hypothesis (PHH) suggests that the developed countries impose tougher environmental policies than do the developing countries, which results in distortion of existing patterns of comparative advantage. So, the polluting industries shift operations from the developed to the developing countries; developing countries thus become "pollution havens."

Trade Liberalization: Trade liberalization is a policy measure in the field of international trade. By implementing this state can control the removal or reduction of restrictions or barriers on the free exchange of goods between nations. In general, we have used trade liberalization either in form foreign capital inflow or in terms of tariff reduction.

Vanishing Industries: This concept has been used frequently in international trade literature. Vanishing industries imply those industries which are fighting for existence in the market due to the implementation of some trade policies. More precisely, a sector which losing its significance in the market can be referred as vanishing sector.

Welfare: It constitutes all aspects of progress of an economy including all the economic, social, environmental, political factors, etc.

ENDNOTES

1 The novelty of the present work has also been mentioned in the literature review section.

2 From the work of Bhagwati (1971), it is well known that in a small open economy the optimal tariff is zero. However, the government in a developing economy like India finds no alternative but to keep some tariff on importable commodities keeping in view the employment preserving effects of tariff and more interestingly the same practice is continuing in the market of electronics goods to protect the home from the Chinese.

3 This level of pollution will be granted by the state for the three well-defined sectors (1, 2 and 4) and that is why we are considering the informal sector. Actually, sector 2 has outsourced some part of its production to sector 3 and in terms of value added there is no role of informal sector and hence government will not insert this sector in the definition of maximum allowable pollution. However, we have to consider this to measure total or actual level of pollution is made by the four sectors.

4 In this case study through regime switch gives us the results under the both regimes (that is, under RWER and also under RSER) but in comparative static we can only refer the impact of increase in Ω on the relevant variables.

5 Here we implicitly assume that there exists sufficient demand for domestic product produced by sector 2 and it is quite acceptable because a fall in Ω leads to an increase in Y due to EAWE and hence $D_2^{Domestic}$ will also increase.

6 Though the NS of sector 2 can decline due to the presence of strict regulations, however, in reality sector 2 will outsorce its some parts of the production process to sector 3 to maintain sector 2's effective demand. Therefore, at the final stage sector 2 get its own product as well as the product will be produced by sector 3 and by adding these we get the ES to sector 2. Therefore, by using this ES sector 2 can fulfill its effective demand.

7 At R=R*, we have the equilibrium level of foreign health capital inflow due to equilibrium in the international health capital market.

8 Inserting R = R* in the variant we can get two different values of W, one from equation (3) and other from equation (5).

9 See lemma 3.

10 See lemma 4.

Chapter 6
Economic Growth and Environmental Impacts of Foreign Direct Investment in Emerging Market Economies

Adem Gök
Kırklareli University, Turkey

ABSTRACT

The chapter investigates the role of FDI on growth, the role of FDI on environmental quality, and the role of environmental quality on FDI in 23 emerging market economies over the period of 1993-2014 by panel VAR analysis. It observes that FDI contributes to economic growth and environmental degradation in emerging market economies. In addition, environmental degradation attracts FDI inflows into host emerging market economies. The results support pollution haven hypothesis and contradict pollution halo hypothesis.

INTRODUCTION

Foreign direct investment (FDI) is an integral part of an open and effective international economic system (OECD, 2002). Emerging market economies have removed many restrictions on financial flows in and out of their countries so that the greater mobility of capital, coupled with extensive privatization and greater globalization in production, has resulted in increase in FDI flows since 1990s (Mabey & McNally, 1999). Also, environmental degradation has accelerated in the forms of greenhouse gas emissions, deforestation and loss of biodiversity since 1990s, which has been driven by increased economic activity, of which FDI has become an increasingly significant contributor (Mabey & McNally, 1999). FDI can fuel economic growth that overwhelms host country regulatory capacity, resulting in inefficient and irreversible environmental destruction (Mabey & McNally, 1999). Hence, it is critical to understand the effects of FDI to identify suitable policy responses.

DOI: 10.4018/978-1-5225-8547-3.ch006

We will analyze whether the economic growth produced by FDI are fueled at the expense of environmental degradation or not. In order to analyze the effect of FDI on both growth and environmental quality simultaneously in 23 emerging market economies, the study employs panel VAR methodology over the period of 1993-2014. The analysis also allows testing pollution heaven hypothesis for emerging market economies. Hence, three relationships will be examined among FDI, environmental quality and growth. First, is the effect of FDI on growth; second, the effect of FDI on environment and last, the effect of environmental quality on FDI.

THE EFFECT OF FDI ON GROWTH

The main benefit of FDI is that it is more conducive to long-run growth than other forms of capital inflows based on the following facts (Walsh and Yu, 2010). FDI is a major source of technology and knowledge. FDI assists human capital formation, contributes to international trade integration and helps to create a more competitive business environment (OECD, 2002). FDI enables knowledge and technology spillover from foreign firms to domestic firms.

There is no universal agreement in the literature about the role of FDI on growth. While, most of the empiricists have found positive significant effect of FDI on growth, others found negative significant or insignificant effect. A brief literature for the effect of FDI on growth is as follows.

Bos et al. (1974) analyzed the effect of US FDI on host countries' growth. They found a negative effect of FDI on growth of host countries based on the finding that the profit outflows back to the US home base exceeded the level of new investment in host countries for the 1965-1969 period. By using 1960 cross-section data for 78 developing countries, Blomström et al. (1994) found that FDI is growth enhancing only if the country is above a certain threshold level of development. Using cross-section data for 46 developing countries, Balasubramanyam et al. (1996) found that FDI as an instrument of international technology transfer has stronger effects on economic growth than domestic investment. In a cross-country analysis of 69 developing countries, Borensztein et al. (1998) found that FDI has positive effect on growth only if the level of education in a host country is higher than a given threshold. In an industrial level panel data analysis of US MNCs in four European countries, Barrell and Pain (1999) concluded that FDI may have positive significant effect on the groth performance of host country if there are transfers of technology and knowledge through FDI. By using data for 11 economies in East Asia and Latin America, Zhang (2001) found that FDI tends to promote economic growth when host countries adopt liberalized trade regime, improve human capital, encourage export-oriented FDI and maintain macroeconomic stability. Reisen and Soto (2001) concluded that developing countries should encourage foreign direct investment and portfolio equity inflows to stimulate long-term growth in a panel data analysis covering 44 countries over the 1986-1997. In a panel GMM analysis of 72 countries over the 1960-1995 periods, Carkovic and Levine (2002) could not find a statistically significant relationship between FDI and host country growth. In a panel data analysis of 18 Latin American countries for the 1970-1999 period, Bengoa and Sanchez-Robles (2003) found that FDI is positively correlated with growth. They concluded that the host country requires adequate human capital, economic stability and liberalized market for growth enhancing FDI. Using cross-country data between 1975 and 1995, Alfaro *et al.* (2004) concluded that FDI promotes economic growth only if the host country has sufficiently developed financial market. Durham (2004) could not find a significant direct relationship between FDI and economic growth in an analysis of 80 countries for the 1979-1998 period. In a Bayesian panel data analysis, Lyroudi et al. (2004) found that FDI does not have any significant effect on the rate of growth in transition economies. In an analysis of 90 countries over the 1980-2002 period, Johnson (2006) concluded that FDI inflows enhance economic growth in developing economies but not in developed economies. Using panel data analysis of 119 developing countries over the 1970-1999 period, Basu and Guariglia (2007) found a positive association between FDI and growth. They concluded that FDI induced growth exacerbates human capital inequality in developing countries. By using panel GMM approach for 23 OECD countries over the 1975-2004 period, Türkcan et al. (2008) found that FDI positively affects growth. Herzer et al. (2008) could not find long-term or short-term effect of FDI on growth. Yang (2008) investigated the effect of FDI inflows on economic growth with a panel data analysis of 110 countries over the period 1973-2002.He concluded that the growth effect of FDI varies by region and over time. Using threshold regression techniques for a panel of 62 countries over the 1975-2000 period, Yi and Chiang (2008) concluded that FDI has positive significant impact on growth when host countries have better levels of initial GDP and human capital. Adams (2009) analyzed the impact of FDI on growth in Sub Saharan Africa for the period 1990–2003 with panel OLS and fixed effect estimations. He found that FDI has positive significant effect on growth only in the OLS estimation. Hence, the study finds that FDI has no significant effect on growth in fixed effect estimation. Azman-Saini et al. (2010) find that FDI has positive significant effect on growth only after financial market development exceeds a threshold level and until the threshold, the benefit of FDI on growth is non-existent. In a panel data analysis of 14 manufacturing sectors for a sample of developed and developing countries over the period 1992–2004, Cipollinna et al. (2012) provided robust evidence on the positive and statistically significant growth effect of FDI in recipient countries. In a panel data analysis of seven southeast European countries in the period 1998-2007, Mehic et al. (2013) found statistically significant positive effect of FDI on economic growth. In a panel data analysis of 54 countries over the period of 1990-2011, Omri et al. (2014) found a bidirectional and positive causality link between FDI inflows and economic growth, which implies that an increase in the stock of FDI contributes to promoting economic growth. In a panel data analysis of 30 OECD countries over the period 1990-2004, Bhattarai (2016) found positive impacts of FDI inflows on economic growth. By using a simultaneous system of equations approach of 124 cross-country data for the period 1971–2010, Iamsiraroj (2016) found that overall effects of FDI are positively associated with growth. In a panel data analysis of 127 countries over the period 1990-2010, Harms and Méon concluded that green field FDI has stronger effect on growth than M&A sales. In a panel GMM estimation of 104 countries over the 1996-2015 period, Hayat (2018) found that FDI inflows has positive significant effect on economic growth and the positive effect of FDI inflows on economic growth declines when the available natural resources expand. Beyond a certain size of natural resources, the positive significant effect of FDI inflows on economic growth turns into negative significant effect. Using panel data analysis of SSA countries over the 1989-2013, Olagbaju and Akinlo (2018) found that FDI does not directly lead to economic growth in SSA, but the financial system through banking sector development enhances the effect of FDI on economic growth in the region.

THE EFFECT OF FDI ON ENVIRONMENT

The costs of FDI inflows are environmental degradation, corrupt act of foreign firms, profit repatriation and exploitation of natural resources. The study concentrates only on the damage given to the environment as main cost of FDI. As the world economy has been growing by increase in investment and trade, the state of the global environment has been rapidly deteriorating (Mabey & McNally, 1999). Most policy makers, dealing with environmental issues, adopt a pollute now, clean up later strategy, ignoring the significant irreversible costs which result from such an approach (Mabey & McNally, 1999).

There are two possible effects of FDI on environmental quality; one is positive and the other is negative.

The positive effect of FDI on environmental quality in the form of lower CO2 emissions is called pollution halo hypothesis. The pollution halo hypothesis posits that foreign firms that are subject to more stringent regulations at home use newer and cleaner technologies and environmental management systems than domestic firms in the production processes (Mabey & McNally, 1999). FDI will raise the emission standard of the host country, resulting in a race-to-the-top phenomenon (Dong et al., 2012).

FDI may also have negative effect on environmental quality. FDI may increase production and consumption of polluting goods, or lead to expanded industrial activity and thus, to increased emissions (OECD, 1997). A company established within a foreign country exerts pressure on the host country government to lower regulations, or to prevent their enforcement, which lead to increase in environmental degradation (Mabey & McNally, 1999).

A brief literature for the effect of FDI on environmental quality is as follows.

In a time-series ARDL analysis of 5 ASEAN countries over the 1970-2001 period, Merican et al. (2007) found that FDI increases pollution in Malaysia, Thailand, and the Philippines and decreases pollution only in Indonesia. They could not find a statistically significant relationship for Singapore. Bello and Abimbola (2010) found a statistically significant negative impact of FDI stock on per capita CO2 emissions in Nigeria over the 1980-2008 period. In a panel data analysis of 164 countries over the period of 1961-2004, Kim and Adilov (2011) found that while lax environmental regulations might attract FDI, the foreign companies utilize less polluting technology as compared to local firms in low-income countries. They concluded that FDI does not necessarily increase pollution levels in the host countries. In a time-series regression analysis of China over the period of 1978-2008, Yan-chun (2011) found that foreign capital penetration has a significantly negative effect on the growth of CO2 emissions due to the spill-over effect and FDI inflows to some extent improve the environmental quality of China. In a time-series analysis for Malaysia over the period of 1965-2010, Hitam and Borhan (2012) found evidence that FDI led to increases environmental degradation. In a panel data analysis of 29 provinces in China over the period of 1996-2006, Lan et al. (2012) found that FDI is negatively associated with pollution emissions in provinces with the higher levels of human capital, whereas FDI is positively related to pollution emissions in provinces with the lower levels of human capital. They concluded that the Chinese government should raise the national level of human capital rather than raising the stringency of environmental regulation if China needs to maintain fast growth and reduce pollution emissions. By using a North–South market share game model in a two-country setting, Dong et al. (2012) concluded that FDI will raise the emission standard of the host country, resulting in a race-to-the-top phenomenon if market sizes of the two countries are small. In a panel Granger causality analysis of 18 Latin American countries over the period of 1980-2007, Blanco et al. (2013) found that causality is running from FDI to CO2 emissions per capita in pollution-intensive industries. They concluded that FDI inflows in pollution-intensive industries can be linked to increases in CO2 emissions per capita and it is relevant for governments in the region to be aware of the detrimental effects that this form of FDI has on the environment. In a panel data analysis of selected MENA countries over the period of 1980-2011, Asghari (2013) found that FDI inflow has a week and statistically significant negative relationship with CO2 emission, which suggests weak support for the pollution halo hypothesis. In a panel data analysis of 54 countries over the period of 1990-2011, Omri et al. (2014) found negative causality running from CO2 emissions to FDI inflows and concluded that except countries in Europe and North Asia, the remaining countries need to implement more environmental regulation policies in order to control CO2 emissions and to prevent FDI capital flights. In a panel cointegration and causality analysis of 99 countries over the 1975-2012 period, Shahbaz et al. (2015) concluded that foreign direct investment increases environmental degradation. In a panel OLS analysis of 12 Asian countries over the period of 1980-2010, Linh and Lin (2015) found the significant role of FDI inflows in reducing CO2 emissions. In a time-series ARDL analysis for Turkey over the 1974-2010 period, Seker et al. (2015) find that FDI has positive significant effect on CO2 emissions and concluded that Turkey should encourage more FDI inflows particularly in technology-intensive and environment-friendly industries to improve environmental quality. In a panel data analysis of 29 Chinese provinces over the 1995-2010 period, Zhang and Zhou (2016) found that FDI contributes to CO2 emissions reductions in China in favor of the pollution halo hypothesis. In a panel data analysis of 17 MENA countries over the period 1990–2012, Abdouli and Hammami (2017) found that FDI increases environmental degradation. In a time-series ARDL analysis for Ghana over the period of 1980-2012, Solarin et al. (2017) found that foreign direct investment has positive significant impact on CO2 emissions. In a spatial autocorrelation analysis of 285 Chinese cities during the period 2003–2014, Liu et al. (2018) found that the effects of FDI to be quite different in relation to different pollutants. They concluded that FDI inflows lead to reduced waste soot and dust pollution and to increased wastewater and sulfur dioxide pollution. Using cross-section analysis of 150 cities in China for 2014, Jiang et al. (2018) concluded that FDI has a positive effect on improving environmental quality in favor of pollution halo hypothesis.

THE EFFECT OF ENVIRONMENTAL QUALITY ON FDI

The negative effect of environmental quality on FDI inflows is called as pollution haven hypothesis, which posits that, the lower environmental quality in the form of higher CO2 emissions lead to higher amount of FDI inflows. According to the pollution haven hypothesis, MNCs would move their operations to developing countries in order to take advantage of less stringent environmental regulations and/or developing countries purposely undervalue their environment (race to the bottom) in order to attract higher amount of foreign investment, which leads to excessive levels of pollution and environmental degradation (Mabey & McNally, 1999). The pollution haven hypothesis is based on the notion that better environmental performance increases costs and reduces competitiveness (OECD, 1997). Low income countries with the ability to tolerate pollution or endowed with extensive resources set environmental standards low and attract pollution intensive and resource seeking FDI (Mabey & McNally, 1999). The reason to blame is the competition for FDI inflows, which cause developing countries to lower or not enforce environmental regulations (Mabey & McNally, 1999; OECD, 1997).This could provide an incentive to use cheaper and more environmentally-damaging technologies in developing countries (OECD, 1997).

In a cross-section analysis of 22 countries over the 1985-1990 period, Xing and Kolstad (2002) found that laxity of environmental regulations in a host country is a significant determinant of FDI from the US for heavily polluting industries and is insignificant for less polluting industries. Hence, they concluded that they confirmed pollution heaven hypothesis. In a Granger causality analysis of 112 countries between 15 to 28 years, Hoffman et al. (2005) found that CO2 emissions Granger cause inward FDI flows in low-income countries, inward FDI Granger cause CO2 emissions in middle-income countries and no Granger causality in high-income countries. They concluded that the pollution haven hypothesis is corroborated only with respect with low-income countries. Based on a panel GMM analysis of 29 provinces in China over 1994-2001 period, He (2006) found supportive evidences for pollution haven hypothesis by concluding that the rise in environmental regulation stringency has modest deterrent effect on FDI inflows. In a bilateral panel data analysis of 25 Western and Eastern European countries, Spatareanu (2007) finds that more stringent environmental regulations in the home country relative to host country is positively correlated with the probability and volume of FDI inflows into host country. In a five-year panel data analysis of 30 provinces in China, Zhang and Fu (2008) found that environmental stringency has a significant and negative effect on FDI, which supports the existence of a pollution haven within China. They concluded that FDI prefers to locate into regions with relatively weak environmental regulations. By using pollution emissions as a proxy for environmental stringency, MacDermott (2009) found evidence in support of the pollution-haven hypothesis in a bilateral panel data analysis of 26 OECD countries over the 1982-1997 period. He concluded that MNCs do seek out countries with weaker environmental regulations for production. In a cointegration analysis for Turkey over the 1987Q1–2009Q4 period, Mutafoglu (2012) found causality running from CO2 emissions to FDI inflows in favor of pollution-haven hypothesis, which predicts lower environmental standards are attracting foreign direct investment inflows. In a Norwegian firm level panel data analysis over the 1999-2005 period, Rezza (2013) confirmed pollution haven hypothesis by providing evidence that the parent companies with the motive of efficiency seeking FDI invest less in affiliates of host countries with more stringent environmental regulations. In a panel data analysis of 12 Asian countries over the period of 1980-2010, Linh and Lin (2015) found long run unidirectional causality relationship running from CO2 emissions to FDI and concluded that less stringent environmental regulations of the host countries have attracted FDI inflows in support of the pollution haven hypothesis. Using US outward FDI data for 50 host countries, Tang (2015) found a significant deterrent effect of local environmental regulations on inward FDI. He concluded that FDI in a host country is not only affected by local environmental regulations but also by environmental regulations in proximate countries. In a panel data analysis of 17 MENA countries, Abdouli and Hammami (2018) found that CO2 emissions have positive significant effect on FDI inflows and FDI inflows have positive significant effect on CO2 emissions. They argued that FDI flows may have resulted in pollution havens and that lowering the environmental regulations may help to attract and retain foreign investments. They concluded that higher level of polluting emissions sends positive signals to prospective foreign investors, hence governments should avoid pollution haven traps through encouraging the coordinated know-how and clean technological transfer with foreign companies.

Inspecting the literature review for the effect of FDI on growth and environment, we see that the results change according to countries analyzed, time period covered and the econometric techniques employed. The literature for the effect of environmental quality on FDI is more robust in favor of pollution haven hypothesis.

The next section presents empirical analysis and last section concludes.

EMPIRICAL ANALYSIS

Data

The chapter aims to study the dynamic and endogenous relationships between FDI, growth and CO2 emissions for 23 emerging market economies over the period of 1993-2014. The variables that are used in the analysis are as follows;

FDI

It consists of Foreign direct investment, net inflows (BoP, current US$) which are taken from World Development Indicators (WDI, 2018). The values are divided by one billion.

GDPPC

It is GDP per capita (current US$), which is taken from WDI (2018). The values are divided by one thousand.

CO2

As a global air pollutant, CO2 emissions (metric tons per capita), which is taken from WDI (2018) is used.

Panel VAR Methodology

Panel VAR is a hybrid econometric methodology combining the traditional VAR approach, which considers all the variables in the structure as endogenous, with the panel-data technique, which allows for explicit inclusion of a fixed effect in the model (Jouida, 2017). Panel VAR model is preferred based on its three features (Quyang & Li, 2018). First, since our three variables are strongly related and interact with each other, panel VAR builds an endogenous system by treating all the variables in an unrestricted way. Second, panel VAR model takes account of cross sectional dynamic heterogeneity when it is compared with time series model. Last, panel VAR model easily captures time variation in the coefficients and in the variance of the shocks, when it is compared with cross-section model.

Since all three variables are strongly related with each other, interacting with each other, hence endogenous, we use panel vector auto regression model for estimation. The optimal lag-length for the panel VAR is tested for maximum lag length of four and it is found that the optimal lag length is one for the model. Hence, we specify a first order panel VAR model as follows;

$$y_{it} = \Gamma_0 + \Gamma_1 y_{it-1} + f_i + d_{c,t} + e_t \tag{1}$$

where y_{it} is a three-variable vector which includes FDI, GDPPC and CO2.

We introduce fixed effects denoted by α_i to allow for individual heterogeneity to each country in the panel in order not to impose the restriction that the underlying structure for each cross-sectional unit is the same. The mean-differencing procedure used to eliminate fixed effects would create biased coefficients since the fixed effects are correlated with the regressors due to lags of the dependent variables (Love & Zicchino, 2006). To tackle this problem, we use forward mean differencing, also known as 'Helmert procedure' (Love and Zicchino, 2006). This procedure removes only the forward mean, i.e. the mean of all the future observations available for each country-year (Love & Zicchino, 2006). This transformation preserves the orthogonality between transformed variables and lags of regressors, so we can use lagged regressors as instruments to estimate the coefficients with System GMM (Love & Zicchino, 2006).

Panel VAR offers two tools as impulse-response functions and variance decomposition.

Impulse-response functions focus on the reaction of one variable to the innovations in another variable in the system, while holding all other shocks equal to zero (Love & Zicchino, 2006). The identifying assumption of the Cholesky decomposition is that the variables that appear earlier in the systems are more exogenous and the ones that appear later are more endogenous. (Love & Zicchino, 2006). In order to analyze impulse-response functions, we estimate their confidence intervals with Monte Carlo simulations.

Finally, we present variance decompositions, which show the magnitude of the total effect. Variance decomposition shows the percent of the variation in one variable that is explained by the shock to another variable, accumulated over time. We report the total effect accumulated over the 10 years by variance decomposition (Love and Zicchino, 2006).

The STATA package developed by Abrigo and Love (2016) is used for the analysis.

Panel VAR Estimation Results

The results from Granger causality test in Table 1 justify using Panel VAR technique in the sense that all variables are endogenous and there exists two-way relationship between any two of them.

According to impulse response functions in Figure 1, one standard deviation shock given to foreign direct investment inflows (FDI) has a positive significant effect on income per capita (GDPPC). Hence

Table 1. Summary statistics

Variable	Obs.	Mean	Std. Dev.	Min	Max
FDI	506	13.484	31.867	-20.933	290.928
GDPPC	506	9.260	12.847	0.298	88.564
CO2	506	7.797	11.568	0.668	70.135

Table 2. Granger Causality test

	FDI	GDPPC	CO2
FDI		0.000	0.000
GDPPC	0.000		0.000
CO2	0.000	0.000	

Source: Author's Own Calculations

Notes: The numbers are the Prob > chi square values. Null hypothesis is that the column variable does not Granger-cause raw variable.

Figure 1. Impulse response function

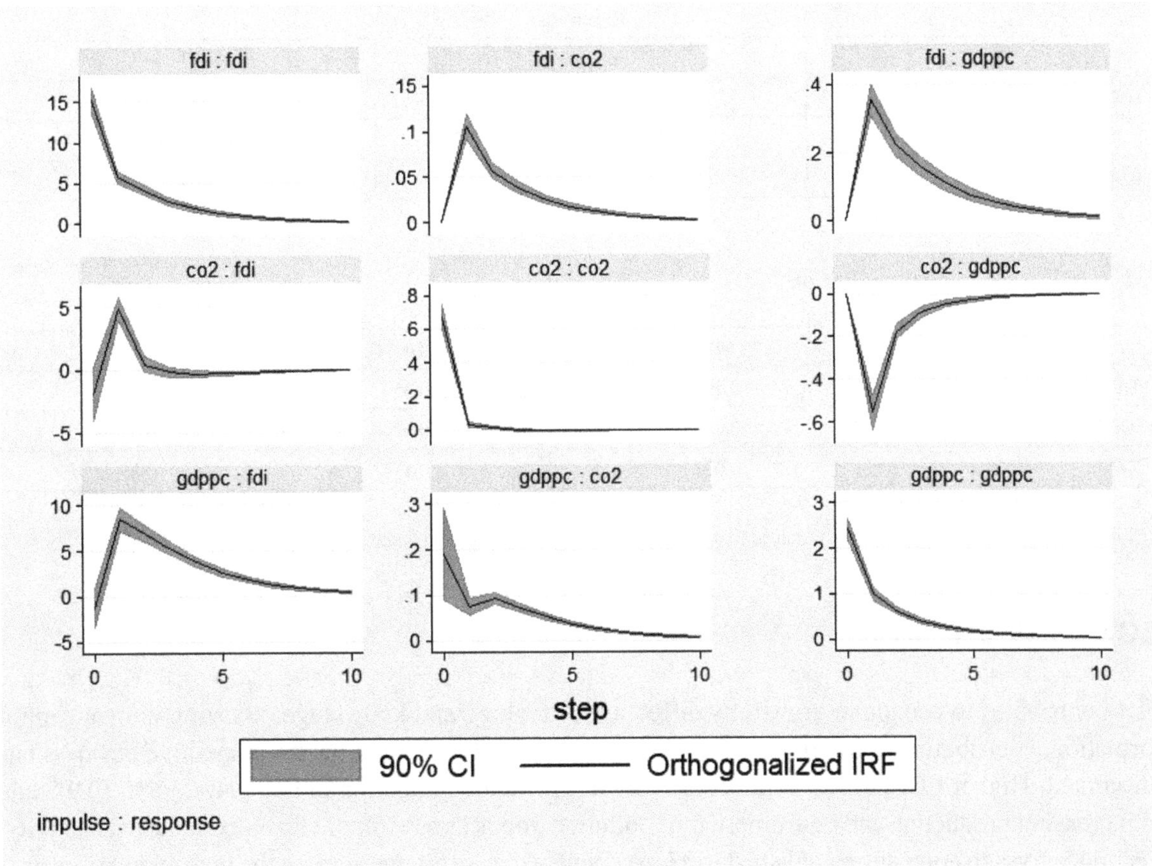

FDI contributes to economic growth by diffusing technology and knowledge, assisting human capital formation, contributing to international trade integration and creating a more competitive business environment (OECD, 2002; Walsh & Yu, 2010).

One standard deviation shock given to foreign direct investment inflows (FDI) has a positive significant effect on CO2 emissions (CO2). Hence, as opposed to pollution halo hypothesis, higher FDI inflows contribute to environmental degradation in two ways. First, FDI leads to increasing production and consumption of polluting goods as a result of expanded industrial activity (OECD, 1997). Second, a foreign company established in a host country may exert pressure on the host country government to lower regulations or to prevent their enforcement (Mabey & McNally, 1999).

One standard deviation shock given to CO2 emissions (CO2) has a positive significant effect on foreign direct investment inflows (FDI). Hence, the lower environmental quality in the form of higher CO2 emissions lead to higher amount of FDI inflows in favor of pollution haven hypothesis based on two reasoning. First, MNCs move their operations to emerging market economies in order to take advantage of less stringent environmental regulations. Second, emerging market economies purposely undervalue their environment in order to attract higher amount of foreign investment. Both reasons lead to excessive levels of pollution and environmental degradation (Mabey & McNally, 1999).

PVAR satisfies the stability condition since all the eigenvalues lie inside the unit circle.

Table 3. Panel VAR stability condition

Eigenvalue		
Real	**Imaginary**	**Modulus**
0.683	0	0.683
0.337	0	0.337
-0.098	0	0.098

Table 4. Variance decomposition

	FDI	GDPPC	CO2
FDI	0.592	0.350	0.057
GDPPC	0.027	0.928	0.043
CO2	0.032	0.114	0.853

Source: Author's Own Calculations

Notes: Percent of variation in the row variable (10 periods ahead) explained by column variable

CONCLUSION

FDI contributes to economic growth by diffusing technology and knowledge, assisting human capital formation, contributing to international trade integration and creating a more competitive business environment. Higher FDI inflows contribute to environmental degradation in two ways. First, FDI leads to increasing production and consumption of polluting goods as a result of expanded industrial activity. Second, a foreign company established in a host country may exert pressure on the host country government to lower regulations or to prevent their enforcement

Lower environmental quality in the form of higher CO2 emissions leads to higher amount of FDI inflows in favor of pollution haven hypothesis based on two reasoning. First, MNCs move their operations to emerging market economies in order to take advantage of less stringent environmental regulations. Second, emerging market economies purposely undervalue their environment in order to attract higher amount of foreign investment. Both reasons lead to excessive levels of pollution and environmental degradation

We found that FDI contributes to economic growth and environmental degradation in emerging market economies. Also, environmental degradation attracts FDI inflows into host emerging market economies. The results support pollution haven hypothesis and contradict pollution halo hypothesis.

The reduction in FDI inflows may not lead to recession, but damage given to the environment by foreign firms and MNCs may be irreversible. Policy makers in emerging market economies should stop adopting and pollute now, clean up later strategy in dealing with environmental issues. They should adopt more stringent environmental policies to dispose of pollution havens. Emerging market economies as a group should coordinate their environmental policies to ensure environmental standards to be raised. The governments of host emerging market economies should combat corrupt acts of MNCs to exert pressure on host country government to lower regulations, or to prevent their enforcement.

REFERENCES

Abdouli, M., & Hammami, S. (2017). Economic growth, FDI inflows and their impact on the environment: An empirical study for the MENA countries. *Quality & Quantity*, *51*(1), 121–146. doi:10.100711135-015-0298-6

Abdouli, M., & Hammami, S. (2018). The dynamic links between environmental quality, foreign direct investment, and economic growth in the Middle Eastern and North African Countries (MENA Region). *Journal of the Knowledge Economy*, *9*(3), 833–853. doi:10.100713132-016-0369-5

Abrigo, M. R., & Love, I. (2016). Estimation of panel vector autoregression in Stata. *The Stata Journal*, *16*(3), 778–804. doi:10.1177/1536867X1601600314

Adams, S. (2009). Foreign direct investment, domestic investment, and economic growth in Sub-Saharan Africa. *Journal of Policy Modeling*, *31*(6), 939–949. doi:10.1016/j.jpolmod.2009.03.003

Alfaro, L., Chanda, A., Kalemli-Ozcan, S., & Sayek, S. (2004). FDI and economic growth: The role of local financial markets. *Journal of International Economics*, *64*(1), 89–112. doi:10.1016/S0022-1996(03)00081-3

Asghari, M. (2013). Does FDI promote MENA region's environment quality? Pollution halo or pollution haven hypothesis. *Int J Sci Res Environ Sci*, *1*(6), 92–100.

Azman-Saini, W. N. W., Law, S. H., & Ahmad, A. H. (2010). FDI and economic growth: New evidence on the role of financial markets. *Economics Letters*, *107*(2), 211–213. doi:10.1016/j.econlet.2010.01.027

Balasubramanyam, V. N., Salisu, M., & Sapsford, D. (1996). Foreign direct investment and growth in EP and IS countries. *Economic Journal (London)*, *106*(434), 92–105. doi:10.2307/2234933

Barrell, R., & Pain, N. (1999). Domestic institutions, agglomerations and foreign direct investment in Europe. *European Economic Review*, *43*(4-6), 925–934. doi:10.1016/S0014-2921(98)00105-6

Basu, P., & Guariglia, A. (2007). Foreign direct investment, inequality, and growth. *Journal of Macroeconomics*, *29*(4), 824–839. doi:10.1016/j.jmacro.2006.02.004

Bello, A. K., & Abimbola, O. M. (2010). Does the level of economic growth influence environmental quality in Nigeria: A test of environmental Kuznets curve (EKC) hypothesis. *Pakistan Journal of Social Sciences*, *7*(4), 325–329. doi:10.3923/pjssci.2010.325.329

Bengoa, M., & Sanchez-Robles, B. (2003). Foreign direct investment, economic freedom and growth: New evidence from Latin America. *European Journal of Political Economy*, *19*(3), 529–545. doi:10.1016/S0176-2680(03)00011-9

Bhattarai, K. (2016). FDI and Growth. *Advances in Management & Applied Economics*, *6*(2), 1–23.

Blanco, L., Gonzalez, F., & Ruiz, I. (2013). The impact of FDI on CO2 emissions in Latin America. *Oxford Development Studies*, *41*(1), 104–121. doi:10.1080/13600818.2012.732055

Blomström, M., Lipsey, R. E., & Zejan, M. (1994). *What Explains Developing Country Growth?* NBER Working Paper, 4132.

Borensztein, E., De Gregorio, J., & Lee, J. W. (1998). How does foreign direct investment affect economic growth? 1. *Journal of International Economics*, *45*(1), 115–135. doi:10.1016/S0022-1996(97)00033-0

Bos, H. C., Sanders, M., & Secchi, C. (1974). *Private Foreign Investment in Developing Countries: A Quantitative Study on the Macroeconomic Effects, Dardrecht*. Reidel. doi:10.1007/978-94-010-2142-5

Carkovic, M., & Levine, R. (2005). Does foreign direct investment accelerate economic growth? *Does foreign direct investment promote development, 195*.

Cipollina, M., Giovannetti, G., Pietrovito, F., & Pozzolo, A. F. (2012). FDI and growth: What cross-country industry data say. *World Economy*, *35*(11), 1599–1629. doi:10.1111/j.1467-9701.2012.01478.x

Dong, B., Gong, J., & Zhao, X. (2012). FDI and environmental regulation: Pollution haven or a race to the top? *Journal of Regulatory Economics*, *41*(2), 216–237. doi:10.100711149-011-9162-3

Durham, J. B. (2004). Absorptive capacity and the effects of foreign direct investment and equity foreign portfolio investment on economic growth. *European Economic Review*, *48*(2), 285–306. doi:10.1016/S0014-2921(02)00264-7

Harms, P., & Méon, P. G. (2018). Good and useless FDI: The growth effects of greenfield investment and mergers and acquisitions. *Review of International Economics*, *26*(1), 37–59. doi:10.1111/roie.12302

Hayat, A. (2018). FDI and economic growth: The role of natural resources? *Journal of Economic Studies (Glasgow, Scotland)*, *45*(2), 283–295. doi:10.1108/JES-05-2015-0082

He, J. (2006). Pollution haven hypothesis and environmental impacts of foreign direct investment: The case of industrial emission of sulfur dioxide (SO2) in Chinese provinces. *Ecological Economics*, *60*(1), 228–245. doi:10.1016/j.ecolecon.2005.12.008

Herzer, D., Klasen, S., & Nowak-Lehmann D, F. (2008). In search of FDI-led growth in developing countries: The way forward. *Economic Modelling*, *25*(5), 793–810. doi:10.1016/j.econmod.2007.11.005

Hitam, M. B., & Borhan, H. B. (2012). FDI, growth and the environment: Impact on quality of life in Malaysia. *Procedia: Social and Behavioral Sciences*, *50*, 333–342. doi:10.1016/j.sbspro.2012.08.038

Hoffmann, R., Lee, C. G., Ramasamy, B., & Yeung, M. (2005). FDI and pollution: A granger causality test using panel data. *Journal of International Development: The Journal of the Development Studies Association*, *17*(3), 311–317. doi:10.1002/jid.1196

Iamsiraroj, S. (2016). The foreign direct investment–economic growth nexus. *International Review of Economics & Finance*, *42*, 116–133. doi:10.1016/j.iref.2015.10.044

Jiang, L., Zhou, H. F., Bai, L., & Zhou, P. (2018). Does foreign direct investment drive environmental degradation in China? An empirical study based on air quality index from a spatial perspective. *Journal of Cleaner Production*, *176*, 864–872. doi:10.1016/j.jclepro.2017.12.048

Johnson, A. (2006). *The effects of FDI inflows on host country economic growth*. The Royal Institute of technology. Centre of Excellence for studies in Science and Innovation.

Jouida, S. (2017). Diversification, capital structure and profitability: A panel VAR approach. *Research in International Business and Finance*.

Jyun-Yi, W., & Chih-Chiang, H. (2008). Does foreign direct investment promote economic growth? Evidence from a threshold regression analysis. *Economic Bulletin, 15*(12), 1–10.

Jyun-Yi, W., & Chih-Chiang, H. (2008). Does foreign direct investment promote economic growth? Evidence from a threshold regression analysis. *Economic Bulletin, 15*(12), 1–10.

Kim, M. H., & Adilov, N. (2012). The lesser of two evils: An empirical investigation of foreign direct investment-pollution tradeoff. *Applied Economics, 44*(20), 2597–2606. doi:10.1080/00036846.2011.566187

Lan, J., Kakinaka, M., & Huang, X. (2012). Foreign direct investment, human capital and environmental pollution in China. *Environmental and Resource Economics, 51*(2), 255–275. doi:10.100710640-011-9498-2

Linh, D., & Lin, S. M. (2015). Dynamic causal relationships among CO2 emissions, energy consumption, economic growth and FDI in the most populous Asian Countries. *Advances in Management and Applied Economics, 5*(1), 69–88.

Liu, Q., Wang, S., Zhang, W., Zhan, D., & Li, J. (2018). Does foreign direct investment affect environmental pollution in China's cities? A spatial econometric perspective. *The Science of the Total Environment, 613*, 521–529. doi:10.1016/j.scitotenv.2017.09.110 PMID:28923755

Love, I., & Zicchino, L. (2006). Financial development and dynamic investment behavior: Evidence from panel VAR. *The Quarterly Review of Economics and Finance, 46*(2), 190–210. doi:10.1016/j.qref.2005.11.007

Lyroudi, K., Papanastasiou, J., & Vamvakidis, A. (2004). Foreign direct investment and economic growth in transition economies. *South-Eastern Europe Journal of Economics, 2*(1), 97–110.

Mabey, N., & McNally, R. (1999). *Foreign direct investment and the environment*. Godalming, UK: WWF-UK.

MacDermott, R. (2009). A panel study of the pollution-haven hypothesis. *Global Economy Journal, 9*(1).

Mehic, E., Silajdzic, S., & Babic-Hodovic, V. (2013). The impact of FDI on economic growth: Some evidence from southeast Europe. *Emerging Markets Finance and Trade, 49*(sup1), 5-20.

Merican, Y., Yusop, Z., Noor, Z. M., & Hook, L. S. (2007). Foreign direct investment and pollution in five Asean nations. *International Journal of Economics & Management, 1*(2), 245–261.

Mutafoglu, T. H. (2012). Foreign direct investment, pollution, and economic growth: Evidence from Turkey. *Journal of Developing Societies, 28*(3), 281–297. doi:10.1177/0169796X12453780

OECD. (1997). *Foreign direct investment and the environment: An overview of the Literature*. Organisation for Economic Co-operation and Development.

OECD. (2002). *Foreign direct investment for development: maximising benefits, minimising costs*. Organisation for Economic Co-operation and Development.

Olagbaju, I. O., & Akinlo, A. E. (2018). FDI And Economic Growth Relationship In Sub-Saharan Africa: Is The Domestic Financial System A Significant Intermediator? *Archives of Business Research, 6*(5). doi:10.14738/abr.65.4540

Omri, A., Nguyen, D. K., & Rault, C. (2014). Causal interactions between CO2 emissions, FDI, and economic growth: Evidence from dynamic simultaneous-equation models. *Economic Modelling, 42*, 382–389. doi:10.1016/j.econmod.2014.07.026

Ouyang, Y., & Li, P. (2018). On the nexus of financial development, economic growth, and energy consumption in China: New perspective from a GMM panel VAR approach. *Energy Economics, 71*, 238–252. doi:10.1016/j.eneco.2018.02.015

Reisen, H., & Soto, M. (2001). Which types of capital inflows foster developing-country growth? *International Finance, 4*(1), 1–14. doi:10.1111/1468-2362.00063

Rezza, A. A. (2013). FDI and pollution havens: Evidence from the Norwegian manufacturing sector. *Ecological Economics, 90*, 140–149. doi:10.1016/j.ecolecon.2013.03.014

Seker, F., Ertugrul, H. M., & Cetin, M. (2015). The impact of foreign direct investment on environmental quality: A bounds testing and causality analysis for Turkey. *Renewable & Sustainable Energy Reviews, 52*, 347–356. doi:10.1016/j.rser.2015.07.118

Shahbaz, M., Nasreen, S., Abbas, F., & Anis, O. (2015). Does foreign direct investment impede environmental quality in high-, middle-, and low-income countries? *Energy Economics, 51*, 275–287. doi:10.1016/j.eneco.2015.06.014

Solarin, S. A., Al-Mulali, U., Musah, I., & Ozturk, I. (2017). Investigating the pollution haven hypothesis in Ghana: An empirical investigation. *Energy, 124*, 706–719. doi:10.1016/j.energy.2017.02.089

Spatareanu, M. (2007). Searching for pollution havens: The impact of environmental regulations on foreign direct investment. *Journal of Environment & Development, 16*(2), 161–182. doi:10.1177/1070496507302873

Tang, J. (2015). Testing the pollution haven effect: Does the type of FDI matter? *Environmental and Resource Economics, 60*(4), 549–578. doi:10.100710640-014-9779-7

Türkcan, B., Duman, A., & Yetkiner, I. H. (2008, May). How does FDI and economic growth affect each other? The OECD case. In *International Conference on Emerging Economic Issues in a Globalizing World* (pp. 21-40). Izmir: Izmir University of Economics and Suny Cortland.

WDI. (2018). *World Development Indicators*. World Bank.

Xing, Y., & Kolstad, C. D. (2002). Do lax environmental regulations attract foreign investment? *Environmental and Resource Economics, 21*(1), 1–22. doi:10.1023/A:1014537013353

Yan-chun, S. D. Y. Y. (2011). FDI and China's Carbon Emissions. *China Population, Resources and Environment, 1*, 10.

Yang, B. (2008). FDI and growth: A varying relationship across regions and over time. *Applied Economics Letters, 15*(2), 105–108. doi:10.1080/13504850600749081

Yu, J., & Walsh, M. J. P. (2010). Determinants of foreign direct investment: A sectoral and institutional approach (No. 10-187). International Monetary Fund.

Zhang, C., & Zhou, X. (2016). Does foreign direct investment lead to lower CO2 emissions? Evidence from a regional analysis in China. *Renewable & Sustainable Energy Reviews, 58*, 943–951. doi:10.1016/j.rser.2015.12.226

Zhang, J., & Fu, X. (2008). FDI and environmental regulations in China. *Journal of the Asia Pacific Economy, 13*(3), 332–353. doi:10.1080/13547860802131326

Zhang, K. H. (2001). Does foreign direct investment promote economic growth? Evidence from East Asia and Latin America. *Contemporary Economic Policy, 19*(2), 175–185. doi:10.1111/j.1465-7287.2001.tb00059.x

KEY TERMS DEFINITIONS

Capital Inflows: It refers to movement of funds from a source country into a host country for the purpose of investment, trade or business production.

Environmental Degradation: It means deterioration of environmental quality by depletion of resources, destruction of ecosystems, the extinction of wildlife, and environmental pollution.

FDI: Foreign direct investment inflows; investment made in a host country by a foreign investor or MNC.

Growth: Economic growth; is the increase in overall production of a country.

Panel VAR: Panel vector autoregressive model; a panel estimation technique which is built with the same logic of standard VAR by adding a cross sectional dimension.

Pollution Halo Hypothesis: It demonstrates that FDI supplies advanced technology to countries and accordingly causes lower carbon emissions.

Pollution Haven Hypothesis: It is the idea that polluting industries will relocate to jurisdictions with less stringent environmental regulations.

APPENDIX: THE LIST OF EMERGING MARKET ECONOMIES

Table 5.

Brazil	India	Poland
Chile	Indonesia	Qatar
China	Korea, Rep.	Russian Federation
Colombia	Malaysia	South Africa
Czech Republic	Mexico	Thailand
Egypt, Arab Rep.	Pakistan	Turkey
Greece	Peru	United Arab Emirates
Hungary	Philippines	

Chapter 7
An Empirical Study on Unique Sustainability Nexus:
Evidence From Developed and Developing Nations

Megha Jain
Daulat Ram College for Women, India

Aishwarya Nagpal
University of Delhi, India

ABSTRACT

In order to understand the role of sustainability in the era of development, the broader purpose of the chapter is to examine the quantitative linkages between HDI and environmental performance for the selected developed and developing nations from 2002 to 2017. To test if the degree of economic expansion and standard of living has a systematic relationship with the level of environmental deterioration (existence of Kuznets curve hypotheses) in a country, the study employs fixed effects panel modeling on the selected country set. Several other macroeconomic and capital flow variables are considered in the extended empirical model development in order to supplement the holistic review of the situation. In addition, the study finds its novelty by considering relevant governance indicators in order to map the umbrella view. The findings of the panel analysis discover HDI to be positively associated with EPI, depicting higher human capital accumulation leading to lower environmental damage and better environmental performance. Additionally, the results confirm the deviation from EKC hypotheses in the context of developing nations while the same is established in case of developed nations.

DOI: 10.4018/978-1-5225-8547-3.ch007

INTRODUCTION

Sustainability is a strategic confrontation in the 21st era for the policy makers and the commercial and professional fraternity on the planet. Undeniably, impending climate change is tangible and the entire world is already facing its unfavorable impacts. Today, development agendas that promote food security, climate change policies and social protection, contributing to sustainable development are all of equal interest for most of the young researchers. Most of the growth strategies that primarily stimulate food insecurity, climate depletion, nation's fragility (refer Table 1 and 2) and social unrest add to unsustainable development. Both developed and developing nations are not untouched by this ongoing climatic sustainable economic growth challenge. Long since, westernized nations have realized that sustainable business growth could not be possible without environmental issues handling simultaneously. Unfortunately, developing nations are yet to realize the same and therefore are found more prone to face the impending unanticipated risk due to the same. With respect to economic growth, it is quite pertinent that emerging nations' planet face arduous challenge that stems from the aggravated third generation's concerns of population growth and reliance on non-fossil fuel based energy sources. Transition towards green growth and sustainability is indispensable. While there is evidence of declining energy consumption accompanying the development process, but for many of these countries, it remains unclear what path economic output will follow or whether it is likely to translate into rising CO_2 emissions over the long term. The climate policy is considered to foreplay for most of the nations to take place in their respective economic policies to ensure long term perpetual economic growth with limited reliance on fossil fuel based energy sources.

Both peace and stability have long been acknowledged as pre-requisites for sustainable advancement. The Fund for Peace, Fragile States Index (FSI)determines state fragility based on twelve factors - migration and displacement, demographic pressures, group grievance, uneven economic development, state legitimacy, human rights and factionalism. Not only does fragility hamper development, but insufficient or uneven development increases fragility.

Table 1 clearly depicts that the World's most fragile states status across the cluster of developed and developing nations. According to the recent scores and rankings, Nepal and Pakistan are found to be the most unbalanced states amongst the developing nations (the higher the ranking, the less stable the country is considered) followed by Bhutan, Sri Lanka, Russia and India. Brazil and South Africa are found to be less fragile among the developing nations (innermost circle in the radar chart, Fig 1A), confirming BRICS as the region's most dense with relatively less fragile states in comparison to South Asian Region. The fragility index for most of the developing nations is found to exceed 70. The radar chart (in the lower panel below the tables) confirms the same where the countries which are at the outermost circle of radar indicate more fragility (refer Fig 1A).

At the same time, developed nations are better off in terms of less fragility and vulnerability, in comparison to the most of the developing nations (refer Table 2). The fragility index for most of the developed nations is found to be less than 50. Amongst the developed nations, the most fragile nations (obtaining the highest FSI) are Italy and Spain, followed by Japan, USA and France. The radar chart (refer Fig 1B) confirms the above where Italy, Spain and Japan remain at the outermost circle of the radar with least fragility for nations like Australia and Canada.

Undoubtedly, implementing the Sustainable Development Goals in fragile framework should be a vital part of the push in order to reunite the global targets. One common concurrence in both the devel-

Table 1. Fragility states index (FSI) for developing nations

Developing Nations	2006	2007	2008	2009	2010	2011	2012	2013	2014	2015	2016	2017
India	70.4	70.8	72.9	77.8	79.2	79.3	78	77.5	76.9	79.3	79.6	77.9
Brazil	63.1	66.9	67.6	69.1	67.4	65.1	64.1	62.1	61.4	62.7	65.3	68.2
China	82.5	81.2	80.3	84.6	83	80.1	78.3	80.9	79	76.5	74.9	74.7
Russia	87.1	81.2	79.7	80.8	79	77.7	77.1	77.1	76.5	80	81	79.2
South Africa	55.7	57.4	62.7	67.4	67.9	67.6	66.8	67.6	66.6	67	69.9	72.3
Bangladesh	96.3	95.9	100.3	98.1	96.1	94.4	92.2	92.5	92.8	91.8	90.7	89.1
Nepal	95.4	93.6	94.2	95.4	95.4	93.7	93	91.8	91	90.5	91.2	**91**
Pakistan	103.1	100.1	103.8	104.1	102.5	102.3	101.6	102.9	103	103	101.7	**98.9**
Sri Lanka	92.4	93.1	95.6	96.7	95.7	93.1	92.2	92.9	92.6	90.7	87.7	86.6

Source: Author's adaptation from the database by the *Fund for Peace*, USA where the higher score indicates greater vulnerability

oped and developing nations is that climate change can essentially thwart the achievement of sustainable development goals in fragile states.

To further examine the climatic change for developed and developing nations in the light of above, it is imperative to understand the Environment Kuznets Curve (EKC) hypothesis. It is often said that economic growth comes at the expense of environmental degradation. The hypothesis that links economic growth with environmental degradation is coined by Simon Kuznets and most popularly known as Environmental Kuznets Curve (EKC) Hypothesis.

It actually encapsulates an essentially dynamic change process. The same establishes direct linkage among growth pairing environmental depletion in early stages of economic development which reverses after reaching a saturation point.

However, the EKC hypothesis doesn't make any explicit indication of time. In this construal, the hypothesis would indicate that the emission's income elasticity declines to zero with increase in income, becomes negative after the threshold level of income (i.e. the income level at which income elasticity become zero). In other words, EKC postulates an inverted U-shaped association between environmental

Table 2. Fragility states index (FSI) for developed nations

Developed Nations	2006	2007	2008	2009	2010	2011	2012	2013	2014	2015	2016	2017
Australia	22	23.2	24.6	25.9	27.3	28.1	29.2	25.4	26.3	24.3	22.5	22.3
Canada	23.1	25.1	26.3	27.7	27.9	27.7	26.8	26	27.4	25.6	23.8	22.6
France	34.3	34.1	34.8	35.3	34.9	34	33.6	32.6	34.8	33.7	34.5	33.5
Germany	39.7	38.4	37.3	36.2	35.4	33.9	31.7	29.7	30.6	28.1	28.6	28.1
Italy	35.1	37.1	39.9	43.9	45.7	45.8	45.8	44.6	43.4	43.2	43.1	**45.2**
Japan	28	28.5	29.7	31.2	31.3	31	43.5	36.1	36.3	36	35.1	37.4
Spain	37.4	39.2	41.6	43.3	43.5	43.1	42.8	44.4	43.1	40.9	39.8	**37.9**
United Kingdom	34.2	34.1	32.9	33.6	33.9	34.1	35.3	33.2	34.3	33.4	32.4	33.2
United States	34.5	33.6	32.8	34	35.3	34.8	34.8	33.5	35.4	35.4	34	35.6

Source: Author's adaptation from the database by the *Fund for Peace*, USA where the higher score indicates greater vulnerability

Figure 1. Time trend of FSI of developing nations

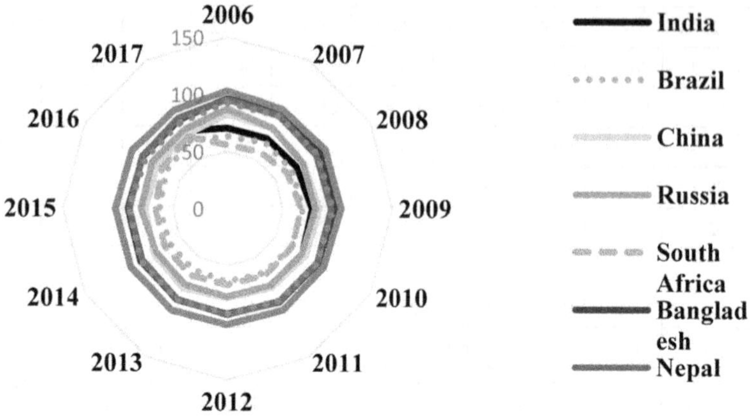

weakening (rising pollution level and inventor of harmful gases emissions) and economic activity level. Most of the literature so far has contemplated EKC as an empirical prodigy and inspected the presence of significant statistical linkage between environmental mortification and the level of economic activity without overtly reviewing the nature of causation among these variables. In general, the same assumes a unidirectional causal linkage – i.e. a change in the level of economic activity or per capita income leads to a resultant change in the ecological quality.

Staring at the tipping point of an environmental crisis, the world is mute and in self-denial. Technologically advanced countries are prepared well for responding to climate change, particularly by developing and establishing suitable sustainable policy, institutional and social capacity for dealing with the consequences. But the poor and developing countries are most affected by climate change, because they are not having enough and sound technologies or scientific development to deal with this impact.

To establish the same, we have used yet another sustainability indicator that focuses on environmental sustainability, given by the Environmental Performance Index[1] (EPI). The initial version of EPI has its roots in the Environmental Sustainability Index (ESI)(1999-2005), developed by a syndicate of Yale Center for Environmental Law and Policy and Columbia University. It ranks 180 nations based on 24 performance parameters across 10 issue groups, enfolding *environmental health*[2] (EH) and *ecosystem vitality* (EV). In general, EH is presumed to progress with economic growth and wealth while EV is assumed to diminish with expanding industrialization and urbanization. Further, EPI highlights how close nations are to the globally targeted environmental policy standards.

Table 3 represents the EPI score in year 2018 (with respect to previous years, 2016 & 2014) of Top 10nations that have persistently outshined over the years due to their adherence to respective environmental sustainability standards. The same hints towards their stable environmental health and ecosystem vitality on air quality, water & sanitation, agriculture, forests, fisheries, biodiversity & habitat, and climate. Most of the developed nations are among the top ten nations that have outshined in terms of their environmental performance.

Figure 3indicates the time trend of the EPI score of developed (2B) and developing Nations (3) from 2002 to 2017.

The environmental performance has improved in the recent years for most of the developing nations (as indicated by country specific points in a year in Fig-2A) specially for Russia, Brazil and Sri Lanka

Table 3. Top 10 Nations EPI Score

EPI	2018	EPI	2016	EPI	2014
Switzerland	87.42	Finland	90.88	Switzerland	87.67
France	83.95	Iceland	90.51	Luxembourg	83.29
Denmark	81.60	Sweden	90.43	Australia	82.40
Malta	80.90	Denmark	89.21	Singapore	81.78
Sweden	80.51	Slovenia	88.98	Czech Republic	81.47
UK	79.89	Spain	88.91	Germany	80.47
Luxembourg	79.12	Portugal	88.63	Spain	79.79
Austria	78.97	Estonia	88.59	Austria	78.09
Ireland	78.77	Malta	88.48	Sweden	78.04
Finland	78.64	France	88.20	Norway	77.75

Source: Adapted from EPI Reports, World Economic Forum database

followed by China and South Africa but stand nowhere in comparison to top few developed nations (refer Fig 2B) that have consistently performed excellent in the recent years. Amongst the developing BRICS nations, Russia and Brazil record high levels of EPI at 73.65 and 69.8 respectively. Whereas in terms of percentage change over the past few years, Russia and India have registered the maximum increase in terms of their EPI scores by 43.59% and 42.02% respectively (on the contrary, South Africa's environmental performance has degraded over years). Amongst the developed nations, France and Spain outperform the other developed countries by taking the EPI score at 86.08 and 83.65 followed by UK and Germany (refer Fig 2B). It is important to note that none of the developed nations considered here are found to EPI score less than 55 whereas the minimum score that the developing nations assume begin from 24 which leaves the tremendous potential for developing nations to work on before they call themselves sustainable in terms of EPI score.

Further to proxy the economic development to test the EKC hypothesis, we have used qualitative composite indicator, Human Development Index (HDI). HDI is one of the significant indices to depict the level of social and economic development (well-being) of a country, coined by UNDP[3] in 1990. It primarily comprises three broad indices – education index, income index and life expectancy index. Alternatively, HDI includes a decent standard of living (given by GNI per capita), knowledge (given by expected years of schooling) and long & healthy life (with a holistic mix of qualitative and quantitative growth parameters). The two fundamental problems in the way of global sustainability entail – 1) Free rider concern where other nations' cooperation towards global public good contribution, remain disproportionate, and 2) escape from the historical responsibility towards global warming.

Just to capture the umbrella view of the probable correlates of environmental performance, we have extended and hence added governance indicators to review the impact of existence of regulatory body and its quality on the environmental performance of an economy. The governance indicators (coined by the World Bank in the 1990s) map the quality of governance broadly in 200 nations, based on the six dimensions including regulatory effectiveness, control of corruption, voice & accountability, rule of law, absence of violence and political stability. These sub-parameters combined score under governance reflect on policy adherence, management style and several broad norms & regulations compliance by a particular nation. Also, these factors are not mutually exclusive rather there could be simultaneity of

Figure 2. Time trend of FSI of developed nations
Source: Authors' representation from EPI Reports, World Economic Forum database

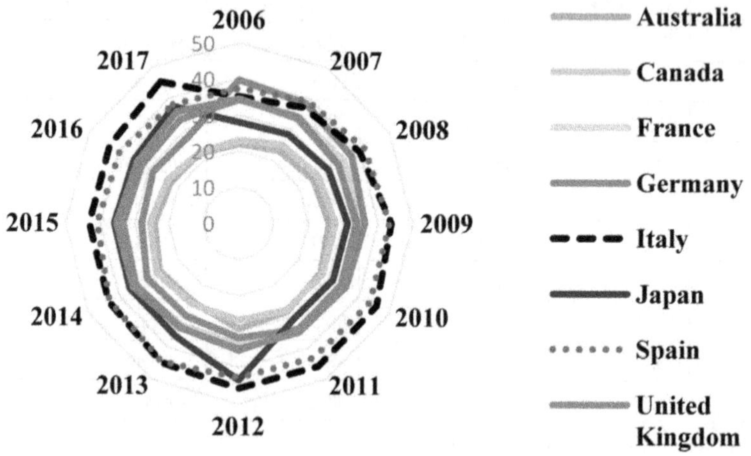

Figure 3. Time trend of EPI of developing nations
Source: Authors' representation based on the data extracted from Yale of EPI Score

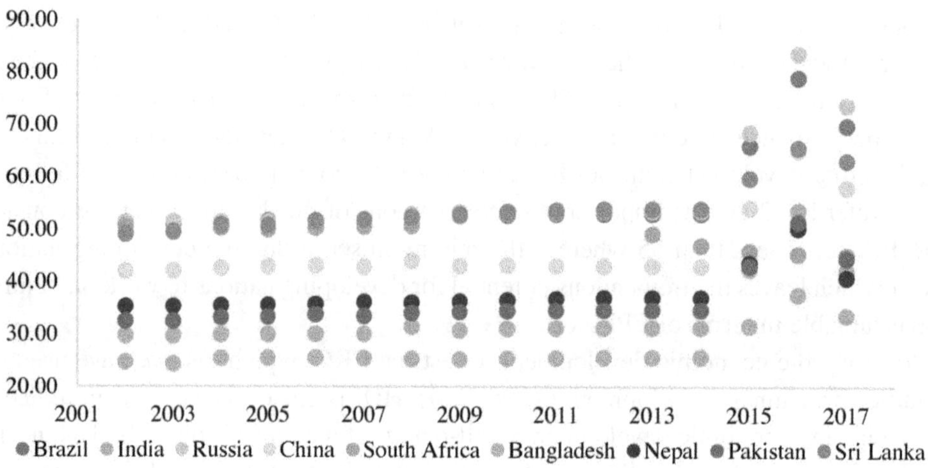

difference sub-parameters reflecting different aspects in a single period for a specific nation. To assimilate governance aspect in EKC hypothesis is quite novel in itself. And to conduct and establish it based on the empirical panel analysis of sample of developed and developing nations is unique and first of this nature so far.

The remaining paper is organized as follows. Section 2 briefly discusses the theoretical and empirical review of literature. Section 3 highlights the underlying objective of the paper, followed by data sources and sample selection in Section 4. Section 5 explains analytical framework, modeling and methodology with preliminary investigation. The empirical strategy and estimation results are presented in Section 6. Section 7 concludes with key policy remarks.

Figure 4. Time trend of EPI of developed nations
Source: Authors' representation based on the data extracted from Yale of EPI Score

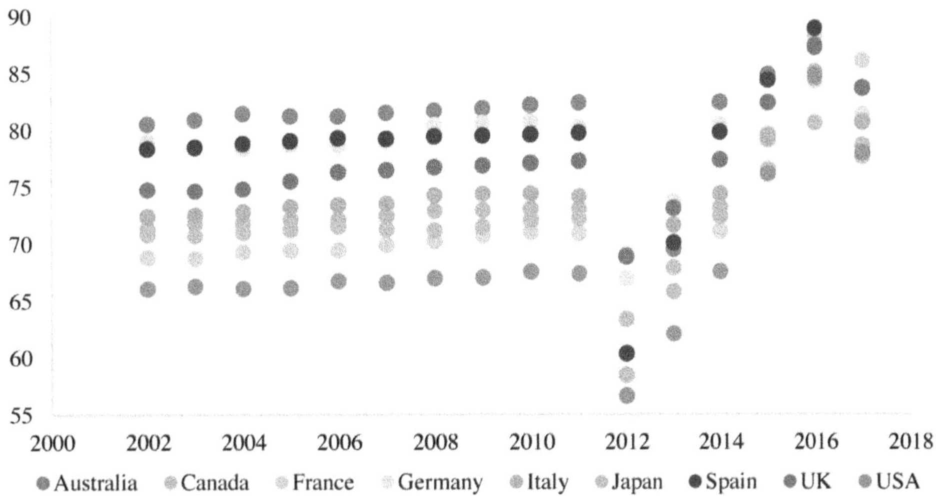

REVIEW OF RELEVANT LITERATURE

There is a paucity of literature in the field that links environmental performance index, HDI, Governance indicators, GDP per capita, urbanization, FDI and other variables.

The existing literature so far has corroborated an inverted 'U-shaped' association either increasing or decreasing, between environmental depletion and a rising per capita income level. Stern and Yandle (2004) have furnished a complete outline and discussions of the empirical literature (Selden & Song, 1994; Ekins, 1997; the special issue of Ecological Economics, 1998; Stern, 1998; Ansuategi & Perrings, 2000; Cavlovic et al. 2000; Anderson and Cavendish, 2001; Antweiler et al. 2001; Bulte and Soest, 2001; Esty, 2001; Dasgupta et al. 2002; Harbaugh et al. 2002; Khanna, 2002; Lieb, 2002; Lindmark, 2002; Stern, 2002; Kelly, 2003; Millimet et al. 2003). Although the uniqueness of the association is still debatable for pollutants mix, over the time period and country dataset. In their assessment of the Kuznets Curve proposition, Stern (1998) and Dasgupta (2002) identified the relevance of inclusion of technological progress, which is directly related to the climate change. At the same time, Andreoni and Levinson (2001) stipulated a theoretical justification of the EKC (assuming economies of scale in pollution abatement).

The well-known Kuznets curve (EKC) envisages emissions' increase until a certain level of income as developing countries "*grow first and clean up later*". The study by Dasgupta (et al. 2006) proves that this contention is incorrect and finds testimony that climatic governance is also doable for developing countries.

Some of the studies have combined governance parameter with social issues like climatic upgradation and poverty alleviation. One of the study by McGillivary (et al. 2005) on a chosen number of developing nations assesses a number of indicators like poverty, inequality, health status, education status, gender bias, empowerment, governance, and subjective well-being (environmental performance). He has obtained that most of the commonly used indicators are highly correlated to income and, as a consequence, they are not able to give any more information than income can.

The existing literature in the HR field on the issue of sustainability recommends that more and more HR executives are keen to modulate their corporation as such to become exclusive environmental champions. A great extent of empirical research emphasizes the effect of environmental management practices on the performance of the organization (Iraldo, Testa, & Frey, 2009; Yang, Lin, Chan, & Sheu, 2010).

The study by Samimi (et al. Kashefi, Salatin & Maryam, 2011) has linked environmental performance to HDI from 2006 to 2010 for 114 countries (comprising both developing and developed nations). The empirical results of the study indicate positive and significant association between HDI and EPI for developed nations only where the same doesn't hold good for developing nations.

Maccari (2014) investigates the relationship between the two components - HDI and EPI for 129 nations for the year 2012. The results indicate a U-shaped association between HDI 2012 and EPI 2012 for the selected nations. At an increasing human development level, the same hints towards the global tendency of nations to depict deteriorating environmental performance only up to a tipping (minimum) point, followed by increasing environmental quality. Overall, nations with medium to low development levels are undergoing the worst environmental conditions in comparison to nations at a lower or a higher human development level.

While Arfanuzzaman (2016) focuses on a specific country study (Bangladesh) over the period 2000-2012. The study discovers that CO_2 emissions, HDI, Income per capita and EPI have a co-integrating relationship in the long run. Whereas transitory effect analysis depicts that no short-run shock of explanatory variables such as CO_2 emissions, HDI, Per Capita Income on the EPI.

Chowdhury & Islam (2017) explore the relationship between EPI and GDP growth rate BRICS nations over the period 2008-2016. The findings suggest a negative linkage between EPI and GDP growth rate. The study empirically establishes existence of no strong correlation for all the BRICS nations except Russia.

All the IPCC reports on climate hint towards the eminent challenge to tackle global warming along with intact economic growth. From all the postulations, economic development determines the health of environmental performance to a significant extent. Yet, the validation behind the unhealthy environmental performance continues to remain debatable both empirically and graphically (due to simultaneous growth of output, energy and foreign investment for developing nations in general).

The current paper finds its niche to investigate empirical dataset till 2017 for both developed and developing nations in order to see any contrasting results in order to benchmark best practices from the developed nations' experience, considering new proxy variables for climate and economic health of these nations with the inclusion of governance and macroeconomic variables to understand the role of regulatory and third generation issues.

OBJECTIVE

In the light of the ongoing sustainability concerns, the broader rationale of the current study is to study the quantitative linkages among Human Development Index (HDI[4], a sustainability measure of standard of living and economic growth indicator), Environmental Performance Index (EPI, measure of environmental health and ecosystem vitality), governance indicators and other macroeconomic variables for developed and developing nations from 2002 to 2017 in order to compare the practices so as to examine the best practices to benchmark for developing nations in order to contain the future footprint of environmental issues due to human intervention and other third generation concerns. There is a paucity of studies on sustainability that have blended qualitative and governance indicators with macroeconomic and financial parameters to depict the umbrella view and that too for developed and developing nations for the period indicated above.

DATA SOURCE AND SAMPLE SELECTION

The data is obtained mainly from World Development Indicators, World Bank. Governance variables are extracted from World Governance Indicators (WGI) by World Bank. EPI data is extracted from the *Yale Center for Environmental Law & Policy (World Economic Forum)*. HDI data is collected from UNDP Human Development reports[5] and reviews on qualitative indicators.

The sample is purposefully considered to be of developing and developed nations[6] in order to examine any pertinent distinction on the association among the studied variables due to differences in the stage of development. The period considered for the study is from *2002 to 2017* so as to investigate the recent reversals (if any) for developing and developed nations for growth pairing with positive impact on the environmental performance.

RESEARCH METHODOLOGY

In order to conduct empirical examination of the linkage among the variables the study has applied *fixed effects panel modeling technique* on the selected developed (nine countries) and developing (BRICS and South Asia mainly) nations. We have tested Breusch and Pagan's Lagrange multiplier (LM) test in order to examine whether the individual effects are present or not in the data set considered in the study. Heterogeneity (longitudinal panel traits) may have its influence, thus making pooled OLS redundant for empirical testing in the current data set in comparison to random effects panel modeling. Further, Hausman test favors the fixed effects over random effects panel modeling for the considered data set (the null hypothesis is rejected). Therefore, we have employed the multiple regression model (panel fixed effects modeling) technique to analyze the data empirically.

So as to have the preliminary investigation of the dataset, it has considered the descriptive statistics in order to understand the measure of central tendency and dispersion (refer Table 4).

Table 4 depicts the broader nature of the panel dataset variables' scattered-ness and variability of developed and developing nations considered in the study.

Table 4 indicates the summary statistics of the variables along with their respective measures of dispersion and ranges. Macroeconomic variables – per capita GDP, GDP growth, population density indicate relative higher mean values and greater range intervals. One could easily notify the vast difference between the developed and developing nations central tendency and measures of dispersion where the average values for developed economies are found to be much higher in comparison to developing nations. Also, the volatility (scattered-ness) identified by standard deviation values is almost at par with greater mean values for governance indicators of developed countries with respect to developing countries.

Table 5 further analyses the sample data of developed nations using correlation (association) technique in order to examine the preliminary linkage among the variables indicated above.

Table 4. Descriptive analysis

Developed Countries						Developing Countries					
Variable	**Obs**	**Mean**	**Std. Dev.**	**Min**	**Max**	**Variable**	**Obs**	**Mean**	**Std. Dev.**	**Min**	**Max**
Sustainability Measure											
EPI	144	74.964	6.444	56.590	88.910	EPI	144	44.040	11.878	24.240	83.500
Qualitative Measure											
HDI	144	0.894	0.025	0.830	0.939	HDI	144	0.637	0.103	0.457	0.816
Financial Measures											
FDI	144	2.257	1.973	-3.623	10.027	FDI	144	1.755	1.229	-0.098	4.554
Fin Mkt Dev	144	131.848	38.609	62.268	206.303	FinMktDev	144	60.735	42.183	15.386	160.125
Macroeconomic Measures											
GDPpc	144	42675.92	6639.446	29008.02	55925.93	GDPpc	144	4331.03	3928.88	465.545	11915.42
Population_g	144	0.646	0.592	-1.854	2.061	Population_g	144	1.058	0.587	-0.460	2.133
Pop_D	144	143.700	117.065	2.558	351.339	Pop_D	144	279.668	339.237	8.716	1265.036
Urbanisation	144	79.785	5.503	67.382	91.535	Urbanisation	144	44.507	22.990	14.263	86.309
Energy usage	144	4614.228	1830.410	2414.484	8441.185	Energy usage	144	1401.94	1435.52	149.733	5167.012
Energy Int	144	4.856	1.516	2.978	8.991	Energy Int	144	6.185	2.650	1.993	11.506
GDPg	144	1.490	1.940	-5.619	4.192	GDPg	144	5.076	3.186	-7.821	14.231
Governance Indicators											
Control of Corruption	144	1.448	0.544	-0.030	2.070	Control of Corruption	144	-0.527	0.432	-1.497	0.568
Government Effectiveness	144	1.447	0.414	0.198	2.007	Government Effectiveness	144	-0.253	0.424	-1.054	0.693
Political Stability and Absence of Violence/ Terrorism	144	0.617	0.390	-0.474	1.275	Political Stability and Absence of Violence/ Terrorism	144	-0.984	0.733	-2.810	0.330
Regulatory Quality	144	1.393	0.333	0.530	1.930	Regulatory Quality	144	-0.313	0.412	-1.127	0.804
Voice and Accountability	144	1.241	0.176	0.912	1.668	Voice and Accountability	144	-0.362	0.725	-1.749	0.716
Rule of Law	144	1.436	0.415	0.275	1.923	Rule of Law	144	-0.414	0.403	-1.048	0.330

Source: Authors' computation using Stata13

Table 5depicts towards key prospective linkages of EPI to HDI and other governance, macroeconomic & financial variables for the considered sample of developed nations used in the study. The following pertinent observations are worth mentioning:

1. EPI is positively and significantly associated with HDI among the developed nations. The same hints towards the healthy position of environmental ecosystem and its vitality with incremental standard of living and per capita income of the people.
2. EPI is found to be negatively and significantly associated to financial market development, energy usage and energy intensity. The same directs towards deteriorating environmental performance with growth of financial markets and expanding inclination towards greater usage of fossil-fuel based energy sources which is cheap and readily available.

3. Also, EPI is found to be positively and significantly associated with regulatory quality governance indicator due to the direct probable aspects of improving environment only with the better regulatory body existence in the developed nations.
4. EPI is found to be insignificantly related to remaining all the other macroeconomic, governance and financial parameters. Since most of the developed nations already have well established urban & rural set-ups to exert least impact on the environmental governance due to the spread and scattered-ness of the citizens.

Indicators like urbanisation, population growth and density are found to have insignificant association with EPI.

Table-4B reflects association of EPI with other macroeconomic, governance and financial indicators for considered sample of developing nations. The results are quite opposite of what we obtained for developed nations. The key results of the association matrix is discussed below:

1. EPI is found to be positively and significantly associated with HDI. The same indicates that even in the case of the developing nations, human development by erased level of income and standard of living would result in better environmental conditions.
2. Other macroeconomic, governance and financial indicators like urbanisation, energy usage, financial market development, control of corruption, regulatory quality, rule of law, government effectiveness and political stability are all found to be positively and significantly affiliated with EPI. The results are quite expected since the developing nations are in their initial phase of development and thus, better governance by bureaucratic system in these nations would prove to incentivise environmental condition. Surprisingly, improvement in the financial markets are conducive in developing nations for the environmental betterment.
3. Population growth and density are found to be negatively and significantly associated with EPI in case of developing nations. Poor urban governance and planning actually leading to depletion of environment in these nations. Additionally, scattered-ness of the urban expanse is also causing deleterious impact for the environment in the considered set of developing countries.
4. Energy intensity and voice & accountability are found to be insignificantly associated with the EPI for the considered sample of emerging (developing) nations.

The study entails estimation of regression equation from the period 2002 to 2017 using panel fixed effects[7] (FE) model.Fixed effectsmodel eliminates the probable impact of time-invariant attributes so astoevaluate the net impact of the explanatory variables on the key (left hand side) outcome variable.Each country is distinct, therefore the country's error term and the constant (that captures discreteproperties) must not be associated with the remaining. In case; the error terms are linked, fixed effectsmodel may not give the true, correct and realistic inferences and the only option left is to probably use random-effects modeling. This is the keyreasoning behind the Hausman[8]specification test (current empirical estimation results mentioned in the explanation section below). We have tested the curvilinear relationship (nonlinear) of environmental performance with HDI over a long period.

Table 5. Correlation table (developed nations)

Developed Nations	EPI	HDI	Urban	Pop_G	FinMktDev	Energy_U	Energy_Int	Pop_D	Corruption	Govt_Eff	Political	Reg_Quality	Rule_Law	Voice
EPI	1													
HDI	0.1835**	1												
sig	0.0277													
Urbanisation	-0.0035	0.45***	1											
sig	0.9672	0												
Population_g	0.0249	0.0756	0.0933	1										
sig	0.7675	0.368	0.2663											
Fin Mkt Dev	-0.2628***	0.175**	0.56***	0.16**	1									
sig	0.0015	0.0358	0	0.0544										
Energy usage	-0.3026***	0.41***	0.27***	0.42***	0.4434***	1								
sig	0.0002	0	0.001	0	0									
Energy Int	-0.2879***	0.25***	0.29***	0.41***	0.3899***	0.9511***	1							
sig	0.0005	0.0025	0.0003	0	0	0								
Pop_D	0.0386	-0.185**	0.0391	-0.65***	-0.0944	-0.6796***	-0.6419***	1						
sig	0.6464	0.026	0.6419	0	0.2602	0	0							
Control of Corruption	0.0451	0.56***	0.61***	0.29***	0.2832***	0.5168***	0.5319***	-0.21***	1					
sig	0.5916	0	0	0.0004	0.0006	0	0	0.0106						
Government Effectiveness	-0.0159	0.48***	0.65***	0.24***	0.3133***	0.539***	0.5581***	-0.23***	0.9127***	1				
sig	0.8502	0	0	0.0029	0.0001	0	0	0.0049	0					
Political Stability and Absence of Violence/ Terrorism	-0.0579	0.43***	0.39***	-0.0619	-0.0033	0.3913***	0.4585***	0.0407	0.4097***	0.3955***	1			
sig	0.4903	0	0	0.4608	0.9686	0	0	0.6281	0	0				
Regulatory Quality	0.1488*	0.64***	0.39***	0.45***	0.2494***	0.5091***	0.4496***	-0.29***	0.8577***	0.7555***	0.310***	1		
sig	0.0752	0	0	0	0.0026	0	0	0.0003	0	0	0.0002			
Rule of Law	0.0376	0.65***	0.63***	0.28***	0.3593***	0.5468***	0.5177***	-0.26***	0.9494***	0.9151***	0.394***	0.8541***	1	
sig	0.6543	0	0	0.0005	0	0	0	0.0015	0	0	0	0		
Voice and Accountability	0.1171	0.41***	0.1297	0.41***	-0.0718	0.4605***	0.5029***	-0.39***	0.7699***	0.6633***	0.275***	0.7804***	0.703***	1
sig	0.1624	0	0.1212	0	0.3924	0	0	0	0	0	0.0008	0	0	

Source: Authors' computation using Stata 13. Parentheses *** depict significant at 1%, ** at 5% and * at 10%.

Table 6. Correlation table (developing nations)

Developing Nations	EPI	HDI	Urban	Pop_G	Fin Mkt Dev	Energy_U	Energy_ Int	Pop_D	Corruption	Govt_Eff	Political	Reg_Quality	Rule_Law	Voice
EPI	1													
HDI	0.82***	1												
sig	0													
Urbanisation	0.56***	0.603***	1											
sig	0	0												
Population_g	-0.54***	-0.76***	-0.401***	1										
sig	0	0	0											
Fin Mkt Dev	0.25***	0.246***	0.300***	-0.195**	1									
Sig	0.002	0.003	0.0003	0.0191										
Energy usage	0.57***	0.65***	0.714***	-0.687***	0.335***	1								
Sig	0	0	0	0	0									
Energy Int	0.131	0.041	0.285***	-0.351***	0.559***	0.623***	1							
Sig	0.117	0.623	0.0005	0	0	0								
Pop_D	-0.63***	-0.45***	-0.500***	0.268***	-0.308***	-0.530***	-0.529***	1						
sig	0	0	0	0.0011	0.0002	0	0							
Control of Corruption	0.419***	0.331***	0.288***	-0.0262	0.547***	0.0607	0.1219	-0.453***	1					
sig	0	0	0.0005	0.7557	0	0.4696	0.1454	0						
Government Effectiveness	0.469***	0.491***	0.432***	-0.1965**	0.683***	0.369***	0.280***	-0.448***	0.793***	1				
sig	0	0	0	0.0183	0	0	0.0007	0	0					
Political Stability and Absence of Violence/Terrorism	0.549***	0.615***	0.532***	-0.432***	0.621***	0.378***	0.196**	-0.325***	0.659***	0.709***	1			
sig	0	0	0	0	0	0	0.0184	0.0001	0	0				
Regulatory Quality	0.572***	0.516***	0.528***	-0.216***	0.555***	0.413***	0.314***	-0.612***	0.866***	0.852***	0.703***	1		
sig	0	0	0	0.0094	0	0	0.0001	0	0	0	0			
Rule of Law	0.311***	0.301***	0.0734	0.0407	0.398***	-0.0665	-0.0921	-0.248***	0.846***	0.747***	0.558***	0.730***	1	
sig	0	0	0.3822	0.6282	0	0.4286	0.2723	0.0027	0	0	0	0		
Voice and Accountability	0.078	0.005	0.221***	0.262***	0.0506	-0.1012	-0.185**	-0.0343	0.575***	0.332***	0.361***	0.492***	0.652***	1
sig	0.353	0.95	0.0077	0.0015	0.5468	0.2277	0.0268	0.6834	0	0	0	0	0	

Source: Authors' computation using Stata 13. Parentheses *** depict significant at 1%, ** at 5% and * at 10%.

Table 7 and 8 includes the panel regression results of empirical testing on developed and developing nations' dataset from 2002 to 2017 as per the trailing regression equation:

$$\begin{aligned} EPI_{it} &= \alpha + \beta_1(Urban_{it}) + \beta_2\left(Pop\_g_{it}\right) + \beta_3\left(FDI_{it}\right) + \beta_4(HDI_{it}) \\ &+\beta_5\left(FinMktDevelop_{it}\right) + \beta_6\left(Energy\,Intensity_{it}\right) + \beta_7\left(HDI_{it}^2\right) \\ &+\beta_8\left(Government\_Effect_{it}\right) + \beta_9\left(Voice\ \&Accountability_{it}\right) \\ &+\beta_{10}\left(Political\,Stability_{it}\right) + \beta_{11}\left(Rule\,of\,Law_{it}\right) + \beta_{12}\left(Regulatory\,Quality_{it}\right) + \varepsilon_{it} \end{aligned} \quad (1)$$

where,

- *EPI* is used to proxy the environmental health of the nations (to represent the climatic uplift).
- *Urban* is used to represent the number of people staying in urban areas as a percentage of total population.
- *Pop_D* is included to estimate the impact due to increasing population density in the urban and non-urban centers in the selected sample dataset of the nations.
- *HDI* represents the social cum economic growth indicator to estimate the magnitude of influence due to improvement in standard of living and per capita income level of the people staying in the selected developed and developing nations group.
- *FDI* captures the financial growth effect in the form of direct foreign investments that have been apportioned to the nations studied here.
- *Energy usage* primarily is considered to investigate the impact due to developed and developing nation's reliance on fossil-fuel based (highly carbon intensive) energy utilization for their 80% of the total requirements.
- *HDI_sq* term is included in the regression equation to find out the reversal in the scenario (direct linkage between growth and climatic depletion), EKC postulation.
- *Fin Mkt Develop* is opted in the equation to basically understand the impact of the strength of financial markets on the environmental governance in emerging and developed nations.
- *Government Effectiveness, Rule of law, Voice and Accountability, Control of Corruption and Regulatory Quality* are taken in the equation to examine the role of governance indicators on the environmental performance. The same are expected to play a vital role to indicate crucial policy implications for developed and selected developing economies (BRICS and South Asia) due to their different stages of economic growth process.

RESULTS AND DISCUSSION

Model 1 to 6 in Table 7 and 8 depict empirical testing results for developed nations (9 countries i.e. Australia, Canada, France, Germany, Italy, Japan, Spain, UK and USA). From Table-5A, the following pertinent observations could be noted:

- EPI is found to be positively and significantly associated with HDI (Model 1 to 6). The relationship holds good for all the models tested. The same confirms the direct strong impact of human development towards better environmental health in the considered set of developed nations. Additionally, these results deviate from the established EKC postulation that corroborates the direct linkage between economic growth and per capita emissions. Since HDI is a vital indicator of human development to include social effects like education and health, this could be contemplated as the desired effect. Because the level of education depends upon the HDI and when a nation's level of education enhances, population growth rate drops and consequently reduces the strain on natural resources, thereby increasing EPI (Samimi et. al. 2011 and Gurluk et. al. 2009).

- As expected, EPI is found to be negatively and significantly impacted by square term of human development in case of developed nations (Model 3). The impact is more pronounced for developed nations given by the reversal of trend over time. The same confirms that developed nations are at advanced stages of development and therefore for them, the relationship between EPI and HDI follows inverted U-shaped linkage over a period of time. The environment is going to get adversely impacted by their continual reliance on the advanced techniques further to improve standard of living and lifestyle after a tipping point.
- Remaining indicators like energy intensity, FDI, population growth, financial market development are all found to obtain insignificant regression coefficient values (Model 2 & 3). The possible reason may be that the developed nations (considered here) have already crossed the stage of development where greater growth would come at the cost of climatic depletion unlike developing nations. These nations' financial markets, urbanisation, population growth, fossil fuel energy resources usage all remain insignificant in the determination of their respective environmental performance.
- Governance indicators depict somewhat expected testing results where government effectiveness is found to be positive but non-significant for developed nations country set
- Out of all the governance indicators, control of corruption and political stability have given significant empirical testing results with EPI in case of selected developed nations mainly because these nations don't need governance on other aspects rather need one umbrella monitoring mechanism to contain any environmental probable deleterious factors.

Table 8 lists the empirical regression results based on FE panel modeling for selected developing nations (9 nations comprising of Brazil, India, Russia, China, South Africa, Sri Lanka, Nepal, Pakistan and Bangladesh). The key observations could be summarized as below:

- EPI is found to be positively and significantly associated with HDI throughout in all the models tested (Model 1 to 6 in Table 8). The results confirm to the direct strong impact of human development towards better environmental governance in developing nations too similar to developed nations. Although the same seems to digress from the main Kuznets curve hypothesis of direct positive linkage between growth and emissions. The same indicates that different strata of the society having higher social development are indeed considered to be more concerned about the environmental perils, thereby leading to higher EPI (Samimi et. al. 2011 and Gurluk et. al. 2009).
- Surprisingly, the empirical regression testing results of developing nations country-set indicate a somewhat contentious relationship of EPI due to increments in foreign direct investment (Model 3) and positive yet significant relationship with financial market strength, contrary to developed nations' testing results (proxied by financial market development, From Model 2 to 6). Since developing nations are in the initial stages of development and hence, improvement in financial

Table 7. Regression results (developed nations)

Developed Nations						
Dependent Variable	EPI	EPI	EPI	EPI	EPI	EPI
	FE Robust	FE Robust	FE Robust	FE Robust	FE Robust	FE Robust
Control Variables	**(1)**	**(2)**	**(3)**	**(4)**	**(5)**	**(6)**
HDI	o.2739***	0.5871*	0.6331**	0.2864***	0.8942***	0.1307***
	(1.2923)	(1.8893)	(1.0694)	(1.8813)	(1.2719)	(1.6025)
Fin Mkt Development		-0.0201				
		(0.0287)				
Energy Intensity		-0.0016				
		(0.0025)				
FDI			0.2193			
			(0.2751)			
HDI_sq			-0.8981*			
			(3.4261)			
Pop_g		0.1288				
		(1.2057)				
Government Effect				0.8966		
				(2.8768)		
Control of Corruption					0.1427**	0.0399*
					(2.1186)	(2.4007)
Political Stability						0.1218**
						(2.9446)
Constant	-24.4961*	36.8123*	31.9923*	-37.6382*	30.0998*	26.3749
	(2.0797)	(1.2811)	(2.7881)	(3.0605)	(2.0559)	(1.3568)
R-square	0.0337	0.2224	0.0547	0.0204	0.0218	0.0517
F-Stats	13.49	23.54	24.89	27.25	24.97	25.07
Probability	0.0003	0.0089	0.003	0.001	0.0027	0.0024
Rho	0.4165	0.225	0.3998	0.4923	0.4496	0.3985
No of Obs.	144	144	144	144	144	144
No of Groups	9	9	9	9	9	9

Source: Author's regression results based on FE Panel Modeling, STATA 13 testing.

Note – 1. *** signifies 1%, ** 5% and * 10% levels of significance (***$p < 0.01$,**$p < 0.05$, *$p < 0.1$).

2. *Z* statistics in parentheses.(Model 4 & 6). The same implies the direct association between regulatory efficiency and environmental performance. As expected, greater political stability would lead to better environmental performance in the developed nations. Further, increased control of corruption will signify better environment in these nations.

markets through institutions would be conducive towards the betterment of prevailing climatic change.

- Energy intensity is found to exert negative and significant impact on environmental performance for developing nations (Model 2). The negative coefficient value are quite expected due to their greater reliance on fossil fuel based energy sources.
- Surprisingly, the square term of HDI remains significant and positive (model 3 & 7). This further confirms the prospective progressive incremental changes in environmental betterment in the long run due to improvement in the human stock of developing economies.
- Governance indicators depict somewhat expected testing results where government effectiveness is found to be positive and significant for developing nations' country-set (Model 4 & 6). The same implies the direct association between regulatory efficiency and environmental performance. Better the quality of legislative/ government in the economies, better would be the environmental condition. Voice & accountability is found to acquire negative and significant values, indicating negative relationship between the environmental performance and voice of citizens. The same is quite logical due to greater power and effectiveness of legislative in these economies. Control of corruption and political stability, contrary to developed nations' testing results remain insignificant for developing nations. For developing nations, governance indicators like government effectiveness and voice & accountability give significant results. The same is due to the need of regulatory interference due to lack of awareness of the citizens on their own to safeguard for future.
- FDI and Population growth are found to be insignificant in all the regression testing results and therefore are not indicated in the final regression table.

CONCLUSION AND POLICY SUGGESTIONS

The current study has endeavored to combine qualitative social factor with environmental performance. Most of the studies so far have drawn inferences based on the quantitative factors inter-linkages with climatic emissions. None of the study has blended both social parameters with financial and macroeconomic variables to investigate the amalgamated impact on the environmental ecosystem for both developed and developing nations. The period consideration is intentionally taken to be more recent so as to have a fair idea of the recent reversals (deviation from the conventional EKC postulation). The empirical results confirm the deviation from EKC hypotheses to link economic growth positively with climatic worsening. A direct inference, that could be drawn based on the empirical panel regression results; is that greater human capital accumulation (through skilled and educated masses) could enable both developed and developing nations to confront growing global warming concern effectively, truly treating it a global phenomenon. Where, some of the macroeconomic and financial control variables like energy usage and financial market development are going to play a crucial role for most of the developing nations towards mitigation of the factors arising due to unfavorable stance in the world. Based on the contrasting empirical results between developed and developing nations, some of the very important policy inferences could be drawn.

It is said that no single policy could work in isolation to correct the situation of global warming in developing nations. There is an immediate need to have multifold policy measures that could merge mitigating and adaptive steps.

Table 8. Regression results (developing nations)

Developing Nations						
Dependent Variable	**EI**	**EI**	**EI**	**EI**	**EI**	**EI**
	FE Robust	**FE Robust**	**FE Robust**	**FE Robust**	**FE Robust**	**FE Robust**
Control Variables	**(1)**	**(2)**	**(3)**	**(4)**	**(5)**	**(6)**
HDI	0.0935***	0.0763***	0.1352***	0.4937***	0.7294***	0.9922***
	(1.7474)	(1.3884)	(1.8745)	(1.2007)	(1.4139)	(1.2280)
Fin Mkt Development		0.1360***		0.1244***	0.1171**	0.1245**
		(0.0518)		(0.0478)	(0.0499)	(0.0554)
Energy Intensity		-0.1787**				
		(1.1529)				
FDI			0.1265			
			(0.0521)			
HDI_sq			0.0016*			
			(0.0034)			
Pop_g		0.0063				
		(2.8013)				
Government Effect				0.8978***	0.7359***	0.1414**
				(1.5858)	(1.6095)	(1.7527)
Control of Corruption				-0.3810	-0.8856	
				(3.0668)	(1.2267)	
Voice & Accountability					-0.2562*	-0.5662**
					(1.3655)	(1.6415)
Political Stability						0.4577
						(1.5347)
Constant	-11.4075*	-15.4295*	1.4525	0.6185	0.9002	2.4821
	(1.7638)	(1.4221)	(1.8269)	(1.4265)	(1.4687)	(1.0271)
R-square	0.6711	0.6833	0.4934	0.4373	0.4437	0.4789
F-Stats	40.14	20.25	16.4	16.82	13.43	29.99
Probability	0	0	0	0	0	0
rho	0.4244	0.4212	0.6554	0.7763	0.7762	0.6647
No of Obs.	144	144	144	144	144	144
No of Groups	9	9	9	9	9	9

Source: Author's regression results based on FE Panel Modeling, STATA 13 testing.
Note – 1. *** signifies 1%, ** 5% and * 10% levels of significance (***p< 0.01,**p< 0.05, *p< 0.1).
2. Z statistics in parentheses.

- **Mitigating Measures:** There shall be macroeconomic strengthening by a persistent pursuit of national and local targets of developing nations in particular towards formulation of climate change policies and bylaws (like endorsement of low emission based techniques, usage of silicon cell based fuel vehicles etc.). Additionally, ETS (environment trading system) could further be promoted in developing nations in particular like in many western developed nations in order to have a greener sustainable future.
- **Adaptive Measures:** There is a requirement to change the entire framework conditions in both developed and developing nations by the policy makers to induce private sector through regulatory government policy interventions that could provide the required stimulus to create positive externalities for the environmental performance.

Some of the developed countries have productively employed "Green Bonds[9]" in the space of projects based on renewable energy sources. Additionally, to foster the renewable energy share; developed countries are moving fairly steadfast from fossil fuels towards the higher share of renewable based energy sources: mainly relying on solar based energy and wind power plus water based energy generation.

Additionally, *Education[10]* to develop *Human Capital* could be instrumental in 'climate change adaptation'. Education does more to reduce deaths from climate-related disasters than economic growth as per one of the recent research findings. It equips youth with the skills to help combat climate change, and be part of a green recovering, and positive future.

Lastly, the foundation of *Tomorrow* shall be laid down *Today.* In order to have a greener sustainable future, greater international coalitions and regional green agreements of developing nations with developed nations could really incentivize and improve the global issue of climate change in entirety.

REFERENCES

Agenor, P. R., & Moreno-Dodson, B. (2006). *Public infrastructure and Growth: New Channels and Policy implications.* World Bank Policy Research Working Paper.

Ahmad, S. (2015). Green human resource management: Policies and practices. *Cogent Business & Management*, *2*(1), 1030817. doi:10.1080/23311975.2015.1030817

Arfanuzzaman, M. (2016). Impact of CO2 emission, per capita income and HDI on Environmental Performance Index: Empirical evidence from Bangladesh. *International Journal of Green Economics*, *10*(3-4), 213–225. doi:10.1504/IJGE.2016.081900

Banister, D., & Berechman, J. (2003). *Transport investment and economic development.* Routledge. doi:10.4324/9780203220870

Banister, D., & Berechman, Y. (2001). Transport investment and the promotion of economic growth. *Journal of Transport Geography*, *9*(3), 209–218.

Bryan, J., Hill, S., Munday, M., & Roberts, A. (1997). Road infrastructure and economic development in the periphery: The case of A55 improvements in North Wales. *Journal of Transport Geography*, *5*(4), 227–237. doi:10.1016/S0966-6923(97)00020-3

Button, K. (1998). Infrastructure investment, endogenous growth and economic convergence. *The Annals of Regional Science*, *32*(1), 145–162. doi:10.1007001680050067

Calderon, C., & Serven, L. (2004). *The effects of infrastructure development on growth and income distribution (No. 270)*. World Bank Publications. doi:10.1596/1813-9450-3400

Canning, D. (1998). *A database of world infrastructure stocks, 1950-95.*World bank policy research working paper, 1929.

Canning, D., & Fay, M. (1993). *The effects of transportation networks on economic growth*. Academic Press.

Canning, D., & Pedroni, P. (1999). *The contribution of infrastructure to aggregate output*. The World Bank Policy Research Working Paper, 2246.

Chowdhury, T., & Islam, S. (2017). Environmental Performance Index and GDP growth rate: Evidence from BRICS countries. *Environment and Ecology*, *8*(4), 31–36.

Clarkson, P. M., Li, Y., Richardson, G. D., & Vasvari, F. P. (2008). Revisiting the relation between environmental performance and environmental disclosure: An empirical analysis. *Accounting, Organizations and Society*, *33*(4), 303–327. doi:10.1016/j.aos.2007.05.003

Copeland, B., & Taylor, R. M. S. (2004). Trade, Growth, and the Environment. *Journal of Economic Literature*, *42*(1), 7–71. doi:10.1257/.42.1.7

Cracolici, M. F., Cuffaro, M., & Nijkamp, P. (2010). The measurement of economic, social and environmental performance of countries: A novel approach. *Social Indicators Research*, *95*(2), 339–356. doi:10.100711205-009-9464-3 PMID:19966915

Demurger, S. (2001). Infrastructure development and economic growth: An explanation for regional disparities in China? *Journal of Comparative Economics*, *29*(1), 95–117. doi:10.1006/jcec.2000.1693

Esfahani, H. S., & Ramirez, M. T. (2003). Institutions, infrastructure, and economic growth. *Journal of Development Economics*, *70*(2), 443–477. doi:10.1016/S0304-3878(02)00105-0

Fay, M., & Yepes, T. (2003). *Investing in Infrastructure: What is needed from 2000 to 2010?* (Vol. 3102). World Bank Publications. doi:10.1596/1813-9450-3102

Grossman, G. M., & Krueger, A. B. (1991). *Environmental impacts of a North American free trade agreement (No. w3914)*. National Bureau of Economic Research. doi:10.3386/w3914

Gurluk, S. (2009). Economic growth, industrial pollution and human development in the Mediterranean Region. *Ecological Economics*, *68*(8-9), 2327–2335. doi:10.1016/j.ecolecon.2009.03.001

Gutierrez, J., Condeço-Melhorado, A., & Martín, J. C. (2010). Using accessibility indicators and GIS to assess spatial spillovers of transport infrastructure investment. *Journal of Transport Geography*, *18*(1), 141–152. doi:10.1016/j.jtrangeo.2008.12.003

Holtz-Eakin, D., & Schwartz, A. E. (1995). Infrastructure in a structural model of economic growth. *Regional Science and Urban Economics*, *25*(2), 131–151. doi:10.1016/0166-0462(94)02080-Z

Hsu, A., & Zomer, A. (2016). *Environmental performance index.* Wiley Stats Ref: Statistics Reference Online.

Hulten, C. R. (1996). *Infrastructure capital and economic growth: How well you use it may be more important than how much you have (No. w5847).* National Bureau of Economic Research. doi:10.3386/w5847

Hulten, C. R., Bennathan, E., & Srinivasan, S. (2006). Infrastructure, externalities, and economic development: A study of the Indian manufacturing industry. *The World Bank Economic Review, 20*(2), 291–308. doi:10.1093/wber/lhj007

Lakshmanan, T. R. (2011). The broader economic consequences of transport infrastructure investments. *Journal of Transport Geography, 19*(1), 1–12. doi:10.1016/j.jtrangeo.2010.01.001

Leggett, J. (1990). *Global warming: the Greenpeace report.* Oxford University Press.

Linneker, B., & Spence, N. (1996). Road transport infrastructure and regional economic development: The regional development effects of the M25 London orbital motorway. *Journal of Transport Geography, 4*(2), 77–92. doi:10.1016/0966-6923(96)00001-4

Maccari, N. (2014). *Environmental Sustainability and Human Development: A Greening of Human Development Index.* Academic Press.

McGillivray, M., & Shorrocks, A. (2005). Inequality and Multidimensional Well-Being. *Review of Income and Wealth, 51*(2), 193–199. doi:10.1111/j.1475-4991.2005.00151.x

Rietveld, P. (1989). Infrastructure and spatial development; a survey of multiregional models. Traffic and transport policy between rural and urban area, to an integral approach on regional level. Transportation planning colloquium 1989, The Hague, November 30-December 1, 1989. Volume ii. In *Publication of: colloquium vervoersplanologisch speurwerk.* Academic Press.

Sachs, G. (2003). *Dreaming With BRICs: The Path to 2050.* Global Economics Paper, 99.

Sahoo, P., & Dash, R. K. (2009). Infrastructure development and economic growth in India. *Journal of the Asia Pacific Economy, 14*(4), 351–365. doi:10.1080/13547860903169340

Samimi, A. J., Kashefi, A., Salatin, P., & Lashkarizadeh, M. (2011). Environmental Performance and HDI: Evidence from countries around the world. *Middle East Journal of Scientific Research, 10*(3), 294–301.

Sanchez-Robles, B. (1998). Infrastructure investment and growth: Some empirical evidence. *Contemporary Economic Policy, 16*(1), 98–108. doi:10.1111/j.1465-7287.1998.tb00504.x

Seitz, H. (1993). A dual economic analysis of the benefits of the public road networks. *The Annals of Regional Science, 27*(3), 223–239. doi:10.1007/BF01581660

Shepherd, B., & Wilson, J. S. (2006). *Road infrastructure in Europe and Central Asia: Does network quality affect trade?* World Bank Policy Research Working Paper, 4104.

Stern, D. I. (2004). The rise and fall of the environmental Kuznets curve. *World Development, 32*(8), 1419–1439. doi:10.1016/j.worlddev.2004.03.004

Stiglitz, J. E. (2000). Capital market liberalization, economic growth, and instability. *World Development, 28*(6), 1075–1086. doi:10.1016/S0305-750X(00)00006-1

Tamazian, A., Chousa, J. P., & Vadlamannati, K. C. (2009). Does higher economic and financial development lead to environmental degradation: Evidence from BRIC countries? *Energy Policy, 37*(1), 246–253. doi:10.1016/j.enpol.2008.08.025

Vickerman, R. (1995). Location, accessibility and regional development: The appraisal of trans-European networks. *Transport Policy, 2*(4), 225–234. doi:10.1016/S0967-070X(95)00013-G

Wang, E. C. (2002). Public infrastructure and economic growth: A new approach applied to East Asian economies. *Journal of Policy Modeling, 24*(5), 411–435. doi:10.1016/S0161-8938(02)00123-0

Yu, N., De Jong, M., Storm, S., & Mi, J. (2012). The growth impact of transport infrastructure investment: A regional analysis for China (1978–2008). *Policy and Society, 31*(1), 25–38. doi:10.1016/j.polsoc.2012.01.004

KEY TERMS AND DEFINITIONS

Environment Kuznets Curve (EKC): The hypothesis that links economic growth with environmental degradation is coined by Simon Kuznets and most popularly known as Environmental Kuznets Curve (EKC) Hypothesis. The same establishes direct linkage among growth pairing environmental depletion in early stages of economic development which reverses after reaching a saturation point.

Governance Indicators: It captures different indicators such as rule of law, regulatory quality, governments' effectiveness, etc., which are helpful to overall economic development.

Human Capital: It is the type of capital generated through education, research and developmental activities. It is the indicator for skilled labor.

Human Development Index (HDI): HDI is one of the significant indices to depict the level of social and economic development (well-being) of a country, coined by United Nations Development Programme in 1990. It primarily comprises three broad indices – education index, income index and life expectancy index.

Panel Model: It is the combination of cross section and time series data. The panel data estimation has more power to explain the variables in place of individual data.

Sustainability: Sustainability is the ability to continue a defined behavior indefinitely. Sustainability focuses on meeting the needs of the present without compromising the ability of future generations to meet their needs. The concept of sustainability is composed of three pillars: economic, environmental, and social – also known informally as profits, planet, and people.

ENDNOTES

1 The Environmental Performance Index (EPI) ranks countries' performance on high-priority environmental issues in two areas: protection of human health and protection of ecosystems. Within these two policy objectives the EPI scores national performance in nine issue areas comprised of more than 20 indicators (et al. EPI 2016 Yale Report).

2 EH comprises air quality, heavy metals and water quality issue groups whereas EV consists of biodiversity & habitat, forest, fisheries, climate & energy, air pollution, water resources and agriculture issue groups.

3 United Nations Development Programme

4 The Human Development Index (HDI) is a summary measure of average achievement in key dimensions of human development: a long and healthy life, being knowledgeable and have a decent standard of living. The HDI is the geometric mean of normalized indices for each of the three dimensions (extracted from http://hdr.undp.org/en/content/human-development-index-hdi).

5 Available at http://data.un.org/ (Accessed on: 9th March 2018).

6 Selected developing nations comprise of Bangladesh, Nepal, India, Pakistan, Sri Lanka, Brazil, Russia, China & South Africa and developed nations consist of Australia, Canada, France, Germany, Spain, Italy, Japan, UK and USA.

7 FE explore the relationship between predictor and outcome variables within an entity (country, person, company, etc.). Each entity has its own individual characteristics that may or may not influence the predictor variables (for example, being a male or female could influence the opinion toward certain issue; or the political system of a particular country could have some effect on trade or GDP). Another important assumption of the FE model is that those time-invariant traits are unique to the individual and should not be correlated with other individual characteristics (Kohler, Ulrich, Frauke Kreuter, Data Analysis Using Stata, 2nd ed., p. 245).

8 Due to the poor properties of Hausman test empirically, it often fails to provide practical results in general.

9 A green bond is a tax-exempt bond issued by federally qualified organizations or by municipalities for the development of brownfield sites. Brownfield sites are areas of land that are underutilized, have abandoned buildings or are underdeveloped, often containing low levels of industrial pollution. Green bonds are short for qualified green building and sustainable design project bonds.

10 Available at https://www.carbonbrief.org/education-is-top-priority-for-climate-change-adaptation-study-shows [Accessed: 10th March 2018].

Chapter 8
Powering the Sustainable Development Goals for Green Growth in Nigeria

Kehinde Adekunle Adetiloye
Covenant University, Nigeria

Abiola Ayopo Babajide
Covenant University, Nigeria

Joseph Niyan Taiwo
Covenant University, Nigeria

ABSTRACT

This chapter is on the use of the Sustainable Development Goals (SDGs) for the achievement of green economy in Nigeria with the specific aim of assessing the performance of key issues in the SDGs. Five goals SDGs 6, 7, 11, 12, and 15 for water and sanitation, safe human settlements, renewable energy, sustainable consumption and production, and ecosystem, respectively, are selected for assessment for the green initiatives and the economy. Budgets on economic and social services follows the pattern theory: that government allocates and reallocates at will without cognizance of the population's interests. The assessment holds the fact that only two of these goals are being met somehow—renewable energy and clean water—and not necessarily because of the need to achieve the goals but as part of private sector and dynamic market initiatives, clearly indicating failures for the others. For the most part, Nigeria failed in the areas of ecosystem, good human settlement, and responsible consumption. The chapter suggests the encouragement of entrepreneurial initiatives, the initiation of new policies on green economy, and the enforcement of regulations already in place to power the economy.

DOI: 10.4018/978-1-5225-8547-3.ch008

INTRODUCTION

The Nigerian economy is one that constantly flounders on the growth path, bedevilled with ever expanding and unsustainable population growth. Several of the United Nations plans and goals designed for growth and meaningful development of countries have failed to record any success for some countries among which is Nigeria. The eight Millennium Development Goals of2015 and seventeen Sustainable Development Goals of 2030 of which very few countries of the emerging and frontier status have achieved any meaningful success in line with the expectation of the United Nations. While the MDGs were to move the countries to a stage of stability for human existence and further development, the SDGs were real human concerns that signposts economic and sustainable environmental and development issues for the entire ecosystem. With the introduction of the SDGs the policy became what countries that missed out of the MDGs could adopt to match up with the others who are strictly following the SDGs. The SDGs can be surmised into three basic areas: the need for participation of all groups on decision making, eradication of inequality and poverty and promotion of environmental protection and ecosystem sustainability. The MDG has come and gone; either partly or fully met, its general assessment was based on two key issues: maternal health and poverty reduction. In each case its measurement data collection from resource poor countries with ineffective polices have been a major setback of the measurement of whatever was achieved (Ahmed, 2014). Measuring the MDGs as it concerns developing countries was circumspectly done in order not to assume over performance especially given that these are areas where there has been underperformance in those goals (Fukuda-Parr, Greenstein, & Stewart How, 2013). Nigeria is one of such developing countries where till date the MDGs remain inconclusive. With the SDGs the countries could make use of the length of time as these goals would be in pursuit up to 2013.

Of the SDGs seventeen goals six directly or indirectly address the issue of green trading and economy. Particularly, SDGs, 6, 7, 11, 12, and 15 deal with the issues of clean sustainable energy in the ecosystem and strong institutions to support human development. While many of the MDGs were baselines for human existence the possibility of jumpstarting to the SDGs with many of the MDGs unfulfilled presents a monumental problem that countries intending to latch to the SGDs must surmount and conquer. Many of the studies conducted on the success of the MDGs blame the social malaise of corruption and insufficient resources on the failure of the Nigerian government to achieve meaningful success (Chandiramani, 2014, Kolawole, Adeigbe, Zaggi, & Owonibi, 2014). The failure many countries experienced is based more on the lack of capacity, inability to be courageous enough to implement and the state fractionalisation and lack of national cohesion such that actual performance was dwarfed in those countries. Asadullah and Savoia (2018) detail that the nationhood experiences on management of the MGDs were very much pivotal to the success recorded by them. This still boils down to country capacity in the management of national affairs. Finally, an official scorecard from the Presidency did not rate the MDGs a success from the Government point of view. Musa (2015) mentioned that only MGD5 was achieved with ease and summarizes the basic issues of concern as culture, attitudinal factors, lack of financial capacity, economic challenges as well insufficient and inadequate supervisory capacity coupled with insufficient data. In spite of all these failures, there comes the superior and more capacity-demanding Sustainable Development Goals for complete achievement by 2030.The larger SDGs showed the understanding of the problems with performance of various capacity-challenged countries and their participation and successful achievement of the current SDGs.

The failures of the MDGs underscore the longer time set for achievement of the SDGs underscoring that some countries may need more time for any achievement. While the MDGs addressed the subsistence matters of living, the SDGs addresses the issues of making human life meaningfully developed on sustainable basis. Kumar, Kumar and Vivekadhish (2016) summarises that the first dealt with hunger, sicknesses and poverty while the latter deals with people-centred development agenda. With the SDGs, countries can now look at the support services that are needed to sustain human development and global progress, given the idea that government services and directed public expenditure would be sufficient to meet the goals with the private sector. With private sector involvement, the idea of business and services provision comes in with profit entrepreneurs and cost to the end-users of such services. These have definitely increased costs to the businesses that would need to align for the achievement of the SDGs. Pedersena (2018) defends the line of thought and establishes the fact that it is a long road to the achievement of these goals because their delivery demands private economic inputs which is a great gift for business.

This chapter reviews the failure of the process to achieve the main goals of the MDGs and assess the performance each of the SGDs which can be used to power the green economy for human development and sustainability in Nigeria. The chapter explores the matters for attention for a successful involvement and participation in the pursuit of the SDGs. The chapter proceeds in the following order. Following after this introduction is the summary if current literature on the SDGs and the green economy with particular reference to Nigeria's inability to successfully prosecute and implement. The next section is an evaluation of success of the reference SDGs. This is followed by the discussion of the implications for trading and industry and the economy while section six concludes and recommends what can be done to ameliorate the issues and challenges identified.

SUMMARIES OF EXTANT LITERATURE ON GREEN GROWTH OF THE SDGS

There is rich literature and studies in the areas of MDGs and what it was meant to eradicate or reduce while the SDGs are still gathering momentum. The green economy is to support an unusually uncommon basic provision for human development. The need for the completion of the MDGs for effecting foundation of the SDGs, and prevention of unsure and reversible successes recorded by some developing countries and the realization of the probability of leaving some countries behind might have prompted the United Nations to extend the period of actualisation of the SDGs, with a much expanded focus. From the previous eight to seventeen goals the UN intended the participation by many more countries and a higher level of success. At the inauguration of the SDGs, it was clear that the goals were to build on what some countries have achieved while it sought to assist others to succeed where they had initially failed with the MDGs (United Nations, 2015).

The SDGs was built on 5 Ps (People, Planet, Prosperity, Peace and Partnership) and has 5 (SDGs 6, 7, 11, 12, and 15) core areas built on the green environment and economy. Basically, the green environment is a response to the abuse the earth has suffered from use of man and the reduction of the greenery of the ecosystem and consequently an attempt to save the ecosystem for the benefit of all with the aim to keep the earth for human development on long term basis. This development Gupta (2009) says is easily distinguished from growth, indicating that development is more qualitatively measured unlike growth that requires management and control for direction. Sustainable development had earlier been defined as a simple idea of making the future healthier and improved compared to the present day (Blewitt, 2008). The UN SDGs with green perspective indicate that there are 46sub-goals in the five identified as of interest to this study.

The SDGs of interest to the green economy in this study are:

- Availability and sustainable management of water and sanitation for all,
- Ensure access to affordable, reliable, sustainable and modern energy for all
- Make cities and human settlements inclusively, safe, resilient and sustainable
- Ensure sustainable consumption and production patterns
- Protect, restore and promote sustainable use of terrestrial ecosystems, sustainably manage forests, combat desertification, and halt and reverse land degradation and halt biodiversity loss

Generally, Nigeria is one cumbered with issues and challenges militating against her development ranging from historical, ethnic, to self-inflicted and man-made. Blessed with natural resources, sustainable development has been a mirage. Environmental sustainability being a key issue has taken a back seat. Odunjo (2013) averred that environmental sustainability is hindered by conservation and sanitation as a result of poor funding with the belief that the issue belongs solely and depends on the government who should ensure adequate funding to combat the neglect and degradation the environment is subjected to. Falebita and Koul (2018) compared India with Nigeria using sustainable development indicators as represented by the SGDs and discovers that there are similarities and differences between the two countries. While Nigeria experimented with various planning models focusing on various issues from macroeconomic to infrastructural, the Indian Planning Commission planned and focused on different things at the different times. Obviously, one achieved a greater results and outcomes than the other. The study recommended and proposed policy drivers for these economies which consisted of a framework that indicates three sub-systems to assist in the pursuit of sustainable development in developing countries. These are dimensions of the economy, present and future manifestation and policy drivers.

Availability and Sustainable Management of Water and Sanitation for All SDG_6,

Public water supply system of most developing countries especially those in Nigeria had since broken down within two decades of the post-colonial era. Public water system was piped into many homes rather than have publicly stationed taps. Alagidede and Alagidede (2016) reported that the MGD6c was lagging behind in fulfilment in six African countries which included Nigeria with grave implications for re-emergence of once overcome tropical and water-borne diseases. There are several sustainable ways of water supply both private and public, which has been in place for the past three decades. Of importance is the boreholes supply that has become common place in many above-average Nigerian homes. Middle class people build water supply for direct home consumption which the electricity supply may render less functional. An interesting part of the water shortage issue is the rise in the number of private suppliers and providers who belong to some communities such as is in Ogun State would not allow public water supply system to function by regularly sabotaging it. This is done to ensure that that the business of private water supplies can continue to thrive. A similar situation is reported in Malawi where the quality of such private water supplies is questioned. The paper recommended that provision of boreholes and shallow wells should be regulated and such provision should be upgraded and recognized for human and health safety (Chidya, Mulwafu & Banda, 2016).Many of the hand-pumps built by donor agencies have either broken down or disused. Klug, Cronk, Shields, and Bartram (2018) discuss the need for categorisation of the faults of the water pumps so attention can be paid for their improved monitoring and effective usage. The case of residents resorting to self-help in the provision of water is actually dangerous in that the conditions of the water as it concerns the chemical constituents cannot be established and Fakere, Folorunso, Omole, Ayoola and Arayela, (2018) recommends the revival of the public water system. Following water shortage and inadequacy, there is the case of open defecation at which the country has been ranked 3rd in the world after India and China. This scourge is mainly influenced by location of residence, wealth factors and others (Abubakar, 2018). This comes with serious implications for public health and environment, implying the need for public latrines and the need for behavioural change by the people. But the public latrines would definitely be maintained neatly and that would not be without cost to the users!

Access to Affordable, Reliable, Sustainable and Modern Energy for All SDG_7

Energy is life! The many different sources of energy production and supply lend them themselves to various implications within the modern economy. Generally, from the SDGs there is a move to reduce the consumption of energy that increases danger to the ecosystem. Deforestation and oil spillage are some ways of depleting the ecosystem especially the challenges that different combustible fuels sources bring. Akuru, Onwkwuobe, Okoro and Obe (2017) document the various sources of renewable clean energy as solar, wind power, hydrogen and fuel cells, biomass and geothermal are abundantly available in Nigeria which can be harnessed. Most of them except nuclear are commonly used in Nigeria. Aliyu, Dada and Adam (2015) document the travails of a country in the energy crisis and expect the discussion and investigation to continue from there. In spite of the less than 50% of the population that are not formally (illegal connections are rife!) connected to the national grid, there are frequent power cuts that have made reliance on it meaningless for business. The review study consisted the various sources and government inertia at changing the status quo leading to stagnancy in total supply which has remained at between 4000 and 6000 megawatts. Akurua, Onukwubeb, Okoro, and Obea (2017) give a current circumstance of electricity in the Nigeria market. The current total installed capacity is 14,380 MW from 27 generation stations nationwide, out of which about7527.5 MW is available and between 3800 and 4700 MW is delivered to consumers (Omonfoman, 2016). The low percentage delivery capacity is due to issues such as lack of investment, gas pipeline vandalism, system losses, poor maintenance culture and limited power evacuation. While efforts at renewable energy gathered momentum, courageous policy and regulatory environment are lagging. With this, market acceptance of payment for what is considered unreliable became an issue. It is arguable if there is not some subsidy for consumption though distribution companies (Discos) have not been fully forthcoming on this. The monetary authorities are enabling better financial conditions for the system through various processes for which they have been unable to fully qualify! The burden of financing their 70% debt and 30% equity capital structure has been is a burden for the banks to bear. The paper concluded that the renewable energy needs to be developed and financially supported so that its full potentials can be realised. The paper encourages Nigerians that renewable energy can be achieved if the government does the needful investment, good policy direction and the private citizens continue their interest in its employment.

The energy situation in Nigeria is chaotic and disorganized, mainly as a result of the bundling of management at the national level. Evidently some areas are prepared to pay for energy if it can be reliably provided while some areas believe it should be exclusive function of the government to provide. Practically unbundling and democratization of the process recommended as by Adhekpukol (2018) has been implemented to some extent. Emodi and Boo (2015) assessed the whole scenario and surmises that there are no government policies to deal with the encouragement of clean renewable energy, the lack of favourable business environment to invite multinationals to develop the sector, direct investment in clean energy technology, renewable portfolio standard development, introduction of tendering schemes, and the introduction of demand side bidding and energy efficient standard law.

Edomah, Foulds and Jones (2017) blamed insufficient or inadequate competence, lack of good vision, improper assessment of expectation, and poor legislation for the lack of capacity to develop the energy sector. The paper recommended chiefly that there is a need to properly define the energy infrastructure and governance nexus in order to limit the unintended consequences on the country's economy. Thus, most of the studies put the buck squarely on the table of the government for lacking initiative, courage and interest to develop clean renewable energy for the country.

Figure 1 indicates the electricity consumption and renewable energy in percentages increase over the years. It is clear that while electricity consumption is coming to a plateau, renewable energy is showing undulating character. Majority of the alternative to electricity in Nigeria is on renewable energy, especially solar. A reason for the spikes of the graph for the renewable energy is that Nigerians resort to it when the main electricity is unavailable. This supports the idea that less than 50% is connected to the national grid.

Sustainable Cities and Human Settlements That Are Inclusive, Safe and ResilientSDG_{11}

The concept of sustainable cities arose from the liveability and the easy maintenance of the dwelling environment. Human settlements are generally evolving to meet the climatic conditions. Settlement in the world is becoming more urban based on the attraction to social amenities and markets. Cities have grown largely out political, economic and social foundations that enable people to decide to reside in particular

Figure 1. Electricity and renewable energy consumed in percentages increase
Source: Data from World Development Indicators

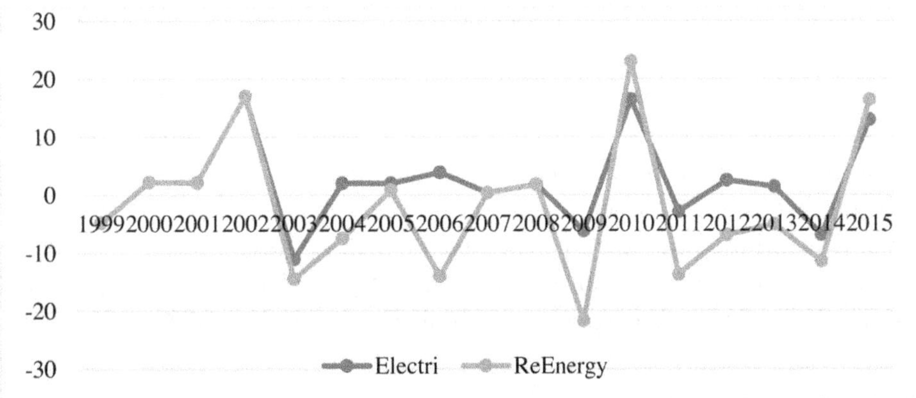

areas and are large generators of waste, voracious consumers of energy and most vulnerable in critical times of disasters. In spite of not having a particular definition, planners and the UN Habitat (2016) believe human settlement refers to a distinct population cluster in which inhabitants live in neighbouring sets of living quarters and has a name and locally recognised status while cities are proper political jurisdiction that contain the historical city centres and urban areas that are heavily populated areas containing the city proper, suburbs and continuously settled commuter areas. The use of environmental planning and management (EPM) to plan and build cities seem seriously lacking in Nigeria. Ugbazi (2013) lists the challenges of planning cities in Nigeria to include poor urban planning and the top down bureaucratic approach. Others are weak legal cultures, foreign philosophies and design and the poor public perception of the role of urban planning in development. Migration is however listed as an important challenge of sustainable cities. The study recommends a stronger commitment of the government and professional groups to achieving a sustainable settlement or cities in the country.

Various names and nomenclature now define cites in the world. Ecocities are environment as a reaction to global climate change issues and rapidly urbanizing cities which is an initiative to promote sustainable development in relation to infrastructure at community, district, town and metropolitan levels (Joss, 2105). Most of Nigerians cities are unplanned in growth but have expanded haphazardly. However, a planned city like Eko Atlantic City, set-upright on the edges of the Atlantic Ocean where serious encroachment has of often been the scourge holds so little concern for disaster management in the future. With five cognate points on project maladaptation Ajibade (2017), intoned how the new planned city is already failing the test of sustainability in its present understanding and suggestion for improvement have not been incorporated. Internal new developments hold unsure promise since planners have failed to control developments of which can be in building for years but already inhabited. The danger in prolonged construction of buildings was aptly brought out by Ismail, Yew and Muhammad (2016) who concluded that the strength of materials used to build fail after 12 years of unfinished work.

Sustainable Consumption and Production PatternsSDG$_{12}$

Sustainable production and consumption refer to responsible use of available resources to meet the needs of the people globally rather than waste so many resources on wants of a few persons that can constitute a global hazard to everyone. Wang, Ghadim, Lim and, Tseng. (2019) in its literature survey documents that engagement in sustainable production and consumption in developing and developed countries have been divergent. The study chronicles that awareness through research have concentrated on developed countries while, the efforts have been mainly on the heavily populated countries of developing countries featuring mainly China India, with Nigerian come a distant 9th. Developing countries often exhibit insufficient resources and changes to established standards are resisted because new practices suggesting collaborative effort might be required to bring disruptive changes. Some factors that have been effective in developed countries might be difficult to adopt in developing countries because of the issues of poverty, corruption and income inequality. For instance, Seng, Kim Hua Tan, Yong Geng, Kannan and Govindan (2016) have documented that different approaches should be adopted in dealing with the issue of sustainable consumption and production (SCP) as conditions are not the same in many economies. In addition, using China as an example, a country like Nigeria, should go green in production and consumption patterns, even green in marketing Zhu and Sarkis (2016).

Protect, Restore and Promote Sustainable Use of Terrestrial Ecosystems SDG_{15}

Nowhere is Nigeria guiltier of abuse of the environment as in the ecosystem, especially in the use of the forest namely, land degradation and unstoppable desertification. While the various governments' encouragements on proper land use for agriculture has been strident, the management of the soil and other forest has been poor. The large population density has forced the management of the ecosystem to be an issue which the academia has focused on but the government do care about. For instance, Arowolo, Deng Olatunji and Obayelu (2018) believe thatthe savannah section of the Nigeria land mass was the most exploited over the period of their study. During this period the ecosystem provided a value of 97.5 of the total ecosystem services value (ESV). In addition, the value of services provision increased while those such as water regulation, gas regulation and climate regulation all decreased. The paper recommended greater attention should be paid to the ecosystem management by the relevant authorities in the future. Fasona, Tadross, Abiodun and Omojola (2013) chronicles the extent of the changes in the ecosystems is determined more by rainfall than any other elements and whatever changes that occur to arable land and human migration can be fully traced to the effect of moisture on the land.

Degradation of land and the natural environment is common not only in the coastal areas but in the upland section of the country. Wang and Dong (2019) chronicle the impact on the environment with the Augmented Mean Group (AMG) estimator which indicates economic growth, non-renewable energy consumption, and urbanization exert positive effects on the ecological footprint (EF) in the sub-Saharan African countries, while renewable energy consumption plays a negative role in the ecological footprint. Adam, Kwameand Klobodu (2018) believe there is a relationship between economic development and land degradation and that the financial impact is differentiated by the type of government in power. These have various policy implications among which the upsurge of developments increase degradation through various emissions, especially CO2, and the requirement to deepen the financial infrastructure to help improve the expected competences from greener environment because of the expected competition.

DATA AND METHODOLOGY AND EVALUATION OF SUCCESSES

The study adopts a process to indicate that the government has neither taken the SDGs seriously nor has a platform for which the green economy can be achieved and even with the MDGs before it. The method adopts the comparison of the budgeting to meet the expected achievement of the SDGs and to measure the goals that can be met without adequate re-allocation of resources and possibly increasing it.

Data is mostly sources from the World Development Index (WDI) on Nigeria. The data covered disparate periods of time, highly irregular and not up-to-date. Data on energy, water, and forest are from the WDI while budget allocation and capital expenditure are form the Statistical Bulletin. The data is managed to bring out some information of the behaviour of allocations for these goals in the past.

The method adopted is analytical and exploratory since the data available precedes the beginning of the SDGs. Data is available from 1960 for some variables none for some. The study adopts the period of 1999 to 2014 as period when data was fully available for the variables that are needed for the study. The variables adopted for the study represent the green economy market for Nigeria. A maximum of 16 series data is available for the study for analysis. The series were extracted from the WDI database. The supporting data is mainly from the Central Bank of Nigeria Statistical Bulletin (2018). Table 1 contains the descriptives of the data available.

Table 1. Descriptive statistics of the percentage increase in each of the green goals for Nigeria

	SOCCOM	CO02EMI	FORESTAR	PTBUDGET	REENERGY	WATER
Mean	21.899	1.53387	11.05109	13.24188	27.64102	57.00398
Median	4.813387	1.222892	11.05109	13.155	27.10033	57.17664
Maximum	137.6131	3.267973	14.42406	23.06	38.21768	67.34497
Minimum	-46.1165	0.51031	7.678119	3.46	17.59131	46.07741
Std. Dev.	56.08494	0.985544	2.14114	4.553165	7.69976	6.763445
Skewness	0.551799	0.484877	8.51E-10	0.148184	0.182205	-0.06387
Kurtosis	2.138128	1.68197	1.790588	3.534946	1.575835	1.789146
JarqueBera	1.307169	1.785084	0.975118	0.249334	1.440694	0.988322
Probablity	0.520178	0.409613	0.614124	0.882791	0.486583	0.610083
Sum	350.384	24.54192	176.8174	211.87	442.2564	912.0637
Sum Sq Devi	47182.81	14.56944	68.76721	310.9696	889.2946	686.1628
Observation	16	16	16	16	16	16

Source: From Data from World Development Indices and Central Bank of Nigeria Statistical Bulletin (2018)

Adopted variables to represent each of the SDGs are Social and Community expenditure (*SOCCOM*), CO02 Emission*CO02EMI*) Afforestation (*FORESTAR*), Budget (*PTBUDGET*): the percentage of the total budget represented in community and social services, Renewable energy(*REENERGY*) and Water provision (*WATER*).

The data above shows that carbon emissions in the country are rather on the increase; from a mean of 1.53 and a minimum of 0.51to a maximum of 3.26. The standard deviation is 0.99 shows that attention has not been paid to the issue of curtailing the emission. This definitely portends some danger in the future if adequate correction is not made now. Nigeria is shopping for heavy industries notwithstanding the environmental hazard some represent at this time while the world is looking out for green industries. The data above also indicate that renewable energy with a mean increase percentage increase annually at 27.64% and minimum of 17%. The increase is evident in the data because Nigerians replace main electricity with renewable sources of power whenever the main electricity is unavailable. Water represents an improving scenario mean of 57.00 and a minimum of 46.08. The standard deviation is 6.73. The Figure 2 shows a plateau.

DISCUSSION OF RESULTS AND OUTPUTS

From the distribution of forest depletion rate is also on the increase as the rate of consumption indicated in Figure 2 shows. The conservation of the fauna is slow and consumption rate is higher than replacement rate. The savannah region is the most affected. Parameters' SD of 2.14% and a maximum of 14.42% while minimum is 7.67% and a mean increase of 13.24%.

The summary statistics of the data reveals that capital budget for social and community services from the Federal Government has been uncoordinated in terms of the increases and decreases it has suffered over the years. The standard deviation this variable is the highest at 56.08. This means there is non-

Figure 2. Percentage increase in water supply and renewable energy social and community capital budget
Source: From Data from World Development Indices and Central Bank of Nigeria Statistical Bulletin (2018)

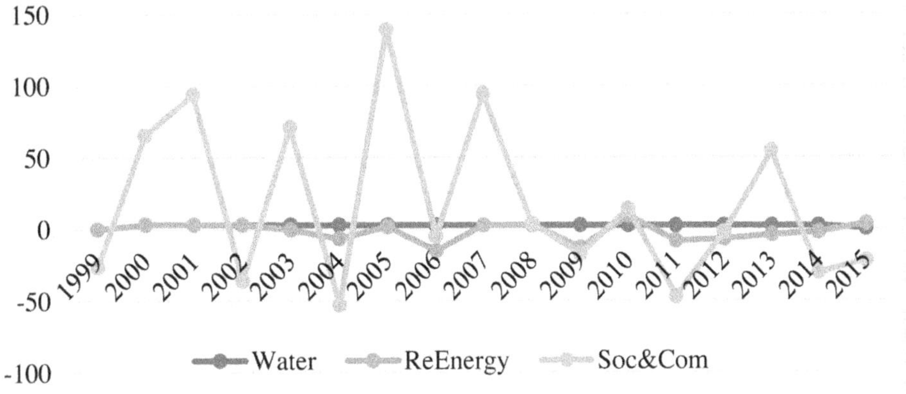

consistency in the amount budgeted yearly percentage. Budgeted amount has oscillated between -46% and 137%. This clearly shows that he amounts expected to be budgeted did not follow any particular pattern. Thus, the budgeted amounts are at whim and caprices of the politicians who decide what they would invest the country's resources on. The allocation of resources to the sector of human development is therefore uncoordinated and lackadaisical. Data for later years of 2015 – 2017 does not show that there would be changes.

Financing the SDGs: Between the Public and Private Sectors

There is no doubt that government finances are very lean in most of African countries including Nigeria. The resources available to invest in human development though scarce are badly prioritized in developing countries. A federal structure for a country like Nigeria hives opportunity to smaller units in the Government such as states and local government to manage resource more prudently for development. The skewed distribution of resources between the three levels of Government is enough source for concern while mal-distribution of resources in favour certain sections and sectors compound issues. Political power is expressed in the process of allocation of resources and elections before a matter of life and death. Politicians and economic managers at every level often re-allocate resources depending on their choices (where totalitarian power is held) or the choice of the local population. Often budgets are neither increased nor are they improved but simply re-allocation when preferences are made. Bunte and Kim (2016) showed clearly that the politician re allocate resources in Nigeria rather than increase spending on a particular line of expenditure when faced with choices among which preferences must be made, given the same level of funding. With SDGs this is not likely to be different. Smarting from the failure of the goals from the government point the choice of directing resources towards achieving the SDGs become a Herculean task.

Business Opportunities in Meeting the SDGs and Recommendation

Government is the main driver of most activities developing economies with the actual enforcement by institutions established to the economic and political institutions to drive the fulfilment and meeting of the enunciated goals are not only weak but very fragile, where they exist. The first challenge is the interest of the government of the day to promote and work with the goals. This seems s to be lacking in the most of the governments of the day. The government of the day would rather pursue two things. Firstly, it would prefer to work with the promises it had made to the people and attempting to fulfil them. Secondly, it would attempt to fulfil those promises from which it can either benefit directly or indirectly. Officials are wont to pursue fulfilment of political campaign promises where there are great benefits for themselves and where self-aggrandisement can be greatly promoted. Most of the benefits that accrue in this way go the list of the community or the environment and not the common people, neither are the fulfilment made for communal benefits. Some of these projects had been seen to fail before the first twelve months after commissioning.

The second is basically institutional. Institutional performance is the foundation for state capacity to function and fulfil its obligations to the people in addition to the being resilient (United Nations Development Programme (2011). Where institutions do not exist or are very weak, then anything can happen. Imbaruddin (2003) had theorised that the most institutions are failing when they are unable to deliver what they were established to do. Part of the failures of the MDGs is reflected in the institutional incapacity as most leaders in government developing countries seek personal and self-fulfilment against national and communal good. Where and when not necessary, agencies of government needlessly compete for attention of the public while failing in their primary constituencies. Abreu and Ceglia (2018) that institutional capacity is created through interactions between a favourable institutional field and the identification of business opportunities by actors. While the actors exist in Nigeria, energy is needlessly spent to dramatize situations anytime they move near their expected ambit of operations. Thus, many of them are less credible for the people to believe in them. This has promoted the continuous lack of cohesion in a very multi-ethnic and multi-religious country and has made it easy for politicians to abuse and use them for selfish ends. Part of the institutional failures is the issue of endemic corruption that has pervaded the system and is affecting financial intermediation (Olokoyo, Adetiloye & Ikpefan, 2016). This is the state of the institutions that would drive the private involvement in the business of fulfilling the SDGs for green economy.

Of the institutional issues to drive the enforcement of the firms and persons to conform to the intention to meet the goals, the country is yet to fully develop. Granted the fact that these would grow and mature to developing resilience overtime, the enablement is clearly infeasible under the current circumstances. For instance, it took the Central Bank of Nigeria (CBN) over eight years to observe the discrepancies in documents submitted for capital exportation from Nigeria by MTN from South Africa. In the capital market, Eke, Adetiloye and Taiwo (2018) documents the failures of the Security and Exchange Commission (SEC) afflict a host of performance indicators which ultimately is inimical to market capitalisation in Nigerian capital market. With the country not recording high in most of the indices of institutional quality, such as ease of doing business, corruption perception index and public integrity index, the possibility of the country beating MNCs at undue exploitation of the country resources becomes difficult. Yet it is sometimes averred that misdemeanours from these firms is practically impossible without some form of collusion from officials.

The remaining two are issues that are being overcome: these are the knowledge base of the economy and the entrepreneurial spirit. Though entrepreneurial development studies are now being taught in universities across Nigeria, commencing from Covenant University in 2002, more is required for graduates bubbling with energy to positively engage their minds in productive entrepreneurial endeavours. The earlier belief that the knowledge base of the economy had increased through foreign direct investment (FDI) has been debunked by Amavilah, Asongu and Andrés (2017) who stated that globalisation through trade rather than through FDI has been more positively impactful to the increase in the knowledge base of the Nigerian economy. The knowledge base to move into this realm is effortlessly and already available. Olokundun *et al* (2018) incisively reports that graduating students of universities now must follow the entrepreneurial path rather than await jobs that are hard to come by. While there is general awareness of the need to become entrepreneurs, it is interesting to see the relative low percentage (22.9%) of graduating students interested in establishing themselves inbusiness once they are finished with school. This is because physical and life sciences seem to dominate future firms today, especially in the technology-based industries. The fact that Nigeria is not ready for this level of development is a source of concern. Ogundeinde and Ejohwomu (2016) intone that there is disequilibrium in the demand and supply of skilled workers especially in the trade sectors - the blue-collar section of the workforce. The paper recommends the establishment of secondary institutions and infrastructure that would provide the breeding ground for practical skill acquisitions for start-ups and town and gown collaborations.

Finally, the goals to be met among the SDGs for green economy in each case can be evaluated as follows.

Water provision has been by both the State governments and the private sector. The private sector has been enduring in the reprocess. A lot more persons are procuring own water for their homes by means of boreholes which would need control later. The State successes has been hampered by the private sector that wanted water consumers to pay for supply. Thus, this is not a challenge and from the data, Nigeria does not suffer the shortages in this area. Energy is one of the most critical issues facing Nigeria.

Many start-ups find it difficult to operate because of the high cost of providing own energy. Electricity for large firms have been provided on ownership basis, but production costs can reduce if the public utility structure is well established to make the provision. The clean renewable energy as being promoted by the SDGs is available among at least five sources of those earlier mentioned. The infrastructure and institutions to drive this is not currently available. The regulators and Government ministry responsible for power have never agreed fully for the benefit of the consumers. In addition, the financial structure of the power firms can cause another series of bank failure if not urgently addressed and many of the banks are overly exposed the power firms. So, this presents a serious challenge. The progress made in this regard is on the privatisation of the sector.

Human settlement presents a challenge that has been around for some time. It has defied solutions proffered over the years. Cities are expanding with constructions that either take long to complete or shell structures being inhabited by people. Planning policies and laws must be enforced if Nigeria will meet the SDG12. The engagement of environmental planning management is key to successful city planning. Finally, the ecosystem needs protection and management as the rate of deforestation alarming in the country. Desertification must be halted with successful tree planting exercises with proper soil and land management.

SUMMARY, CONCLUSION AND RECOMMENDATIONS

The five SDGs were picked out of the seventeen to represent the critically developmental requirements for green economy. From the discussion in this chapter, it is clear that the preparedness of the governments at various levels to meet the SDGs, nay the issues of green economy, is not yet on the front burner as the mature economies of the world have taken the issue. Nigeria is still struggling for the survival and the basic issues of human existence that the MDGs were propelled to establish. Having failed the MDGs, the SDGs are becoming a mirage to achieve. From the theoretical findings, the Nigerian nation has not recorded much success in the adopted SDGs.

From the data available and analysis the country has somehow met one and a second one can be progressively archived. The clean water provision has been met, while renewable energy is generally being up-scaled as the national generation of the electricity has included a number of renewable plants while a growing number of private provisions of electricity on low scale is based on renewable energy – solar. A large number of individual business provision still run on petroleum outputs (fossil) that are injurious to the ecosystem.

Finally the recommendations are based on the performance of the data available. Firstly, the business environment must continue to encourage entrepreneurial efforts at provision of those services that can be so provided, for example borehole water and the use of solar panels for energy must be incentivised which is not the case now. Secondly, new policy directions are needed to bring into the public space new ways to ensure the ecosystem survives for the benefit of humanity in the long run, for example - the housing finance system must be restructured to make funds for construction of wholesome residential buildings within a specified period of time. The green economy that the SDGs envisaged includes responsible production and consumption. Production firms must be censured to ensure their effluents and wastes are not injurious to the environment. A rapid re-afforestation programme must be vigorously pursued to ensure that the greenery of the environment is preserved. Thirdly, the regulators of each of the concerned sectors must strictly enforce performance. The non-availability of policies or rules is not the issue but there adequate and unbiased implementation and enforcement of such rules and policies for the benefit of all that have been lacking in the country.

REFERENCES

Abreu, M. C. S., & Ceglia, D. (2018). On the implementation of a circular economy: The role of institutional capacity-building through industrial symbiosis. *Resources, Conservation and Recycling*, *138*, 99–109. doi:10.1016/j.resconrec.2018.07.001

Abubakar, I. R. (2018). Exploring the determinants of open defecation in Nigeria using demographic and health survey data. *The Science of the Total Environment*, *637-638*, 1455–1465. doi:10.1016/j.scitotenv.2018.05.104 PMID:29801238

Adam S., Kwame E., & Klobodu M. (2018). Financial development and environmental degradation: Does political regime matter? *Journal of Cleaner Production*, *197*(1) 1472-1479

Adhekpukol, E. (2018). The democratization of electricity in Nigeria. *The Electricity Journal*, *31*(2), 1–6. doi:10.1016/j.tej.2018.02.007

Ahmed, S. (2014). *Challenges of achieving and tracking MDG 5*. Available at www.thelancet.com

Ajibade, I. (2017). Can a future city enhance urban resilience and sustainability? A political ecology analysis of Eko Atlantic city, Nigeria. *International Journal of Disaster Risk Reduction*, *26*, 85–92. doi:10.1016/j.ijdrr.2017.09.029

Akuru, U. B., Onwkwuobe, I. E., Okoro, O. I., & Obe, E. S. (2017). Towards 100% renewable energy in Nigeria. *Renewable & Sustainable Energy Reviews*, *71*, 943–953. doi:10.1016/j.rser.2016.12.123

Alagidede, P., & Alagidede, A. N. (2016). The public health effects of water and sanitation in selected West African countries. *Public Health*, *130*, 59–63. doi:10.1016/j.puhe.2015.07.037 PMID:26341551

Aliyu, A. S., Dada, J. O., & Ibrahim Khalil Adam, I. K. (2015). Current status and future prospects of renewable energy in Nigeria. *Renewable & Sustainable Energy Reviews*, *48*, 336–346. doi:10.1016/j.rser.2015.03.098

Amavilah, V., Asongu, S. A., & Andrés, A. R. (2017). Effects of globalization on peace and stability: Implications for governance and the knowledge economy of African countries. *Technological Forecasting and Social Change*, *122*, 91–103. doi:10.1016/j.techfore.2017.04.013

Arowolo, O. A., Deng, X., Olatunji, O. A., & Obayelu, A. E. (2018). Assessing changes in the value of ecosystem services in response to land-use/land-cover dynamics in Nigeria. *The Science of the Total Environment*, *636*(15), 597–609. doi:10.1016/j.scitotenv.2018.04.277 PMID:29723833

Asadullah, M. N., & Savoia, A. (2018). Poverty reduction during 1990–2013: Did millennium development goals adoption and state capacity matter? *World Development*, *105*, 70–82. doi:10.1016/j.worlddev.2017.12.010

Blewitt, J. (2008). *Understanding Sustainable Development*. Earthscan.

Bunte, J. B., & Kim, A. A. (2016). Citizens' Preferences and the Portfolio of Public Goods: Evidence from Nigeria. *World Development*, (92): 28–39. doi:10.1016/j.worlddev.11.008

Chandiramani, J. (2014). Post MDG 2015: The Agenda for Asia and Africa – Are the problems and solutions new? *Procedia: Social and Behavioral Sciences*, *157*, 143–154. doi:10.1016/j.sbspro.2014.11.018

Chidya, R. C. G., Mulwafu, W. O., & Banda, S. C. T. (2016). Water supply dynamics and quality of alternative water sources in low-income areas of Lilongwe City, Malawi. *Physics and Chemistry of the Earth Parts A/B/C*, *93*, 63–75. doi:10.1016/j.pce.2016.03.003

Eke, P.O., Adetiloye, K.A., & Taiwo, J.N. (2018). Regulatory institutional quality and long-run primarycapital market development: the Nigerian case. *Afro-Asian J. Finance and Accounting*, *8*(2), 167–189.

Emodi, N. V., & Boo, K. (2015). Sustainable energy development in Nigeria: Current status and policy options. *Renewable & Sustainable Energy Reviews*, *51*, 356–381. doi:10.1016/j.rser.2015.06.016

Fakere, A. A., Folorunso, C. O., Omole, F. K., Ayoola, H. A., & Arayela, O. (2018). An assessment of self-help water supply in Akure, Nigeria. *Utilities Policy*, *51*, 89–94. doi:10.1016/j.jup.2018.03.004

Falebita, O., & Koul, S. (2018). From developing to sustainable economy: A comparative assessment of India and Nigeria. *Environmental Development*, *25*, 130–137. doi:10.1016/j.envdev.2017.06.007

Fasona, M., Tadross, M., Abiodun, B., & Omojola, A. (2013). Some implications of terrestrial ecosystems response to climate change for adaptation in Nigeria's wooded savannah. *Environmental Development*, *5*(5), 73–95. doi:10.1016/j.envdev.2012.11.003

Fukuda-Parr, S., Greenstein, J., & Stewart, D. (2013). Should MDG Success and Failure be Judged: Faster Progress or Achieving the Targets? *World Development*, *41*, 19–30. doi:10.1016/j.worlddev.2012.06.014

Gupta, K. R. (2009). Economics of Development and Planning: History, Principles, Problems and Practices. Atlantic Publishers & Distributors (P) Ltd.

Imbaruddin, A. (2003). *Understanding the local Government capacities in Indonesia* (PhD thesis). Australian National University, Canberra, Australia.

Ismail M., Yew C. K., & Muhammad B. (2016). Life-span prediction of abandoned reinforced concrete residential buildings *Construction and Building Materials*, *112*(1), 1059-1065.

Klug, T., Cronk, R., Shields, K. F., & Bartram, J. (2018). A categorization of water system breakdowns: Evidence from Liberia, Nigeria, Tanzania, and Uganda. *The Science of the Total Environment*, *619-620*, 1126–1132. doi:10.1016/j.scitotenv.2017.11.183 PMID:29734591

Kolawole. T. O/, Adeigbe, Y. K., Zaggi, Y. H., & Owonibi, E. (2014). Millennium Development Goals (MDGs) in Nigeria: Issues and Problems. *Global Journal of Human-Social Science: C Sociology & Culture, 145*, 42 – 53.

Kumar, S., Kumar, N., & Vivekadhish, S. (2016). Millennium development goals (MDGS) to sustainable development goals (SDGS): Addressing unfinished agenda and strengthening sustainable development and partnership. *Indian Journal of Community Medicine*, *41*(1), 1–4. doi:10.4103/0970-0218.170955 PMID:26917865

Musa, A. (2015). Attainability of Millennium Development Goals (MDGs) in Nigeria. *Current Challenges and Future Prospects Journal of Economics and Sustainable Development*, *6*(19), 45–50.

Nigeria. (2015). *Millennium Development Goals End-Point Report*. Government Press Nigeria.

Odunjo, O. O. (2013). *Why Nigeria is not yet Sustainably Developed. APCBEE Procedia, 5, 383 – 387*. doi:10.1016/j.apcbee

Ogbazi, J. U. (2013). Alternative planning approaches and the sustainable cities programme in Nigeria. *Habitat International*, *40*, 109–118. doi:10.1016/j.habitatint.2013.03.001

Ogundeinde, A., & Ejohwomu, O. (2016). Knowledge Economy: A Panacea for Sustainable Development in Nigeria. *Procedia Engineering*, *145*, 790–795. doi:10.1016/j.proeng.2016.04.103

Olokoyo, F. O., Adetiloye, K. A., & Ikpefan, O. A. (2016). Bank's intermediation role and industrial output in developing economies. *Social Sciences*, *11*(24), 5838–5844.

Olokundun, M., Iyiola, O., Ibidunni, S., Ogbari, M., Falola, H., Salau, O., ... Borishade, T. (2018). Data article on the effectiveness of entrepreneurship curriculum contents on entrepreneurial interest and knowledge of Nigerian university students. *Data in Brief*, *18*, 60–65. doi:10.1016/j.dib.2018.03.011 PMID:29896491

Omonfoman, O. (2016). Getting power generation right in Nigeria! *Premium Times*. Available online: http://blogs.premiumtimesng.com/2016/01/18/getting-power-generation-right-in-nigeria-by-odion-omonfomanaccessed

Pedersena, C.S. (2018). The UN Sustainable Development Goals (SDGs) are a great gift to business! *Procedia CIRP*, (69), 21 – 24.

Tseng, M., Tan, K. H., Geng, Y., & Govindan, K. (2016). Sustainable consumption and production in emerging markets *International Journal of Production Economics*, (181), 257-261.

UN Habitat. (2016). *SDG GOAL 11 Sustainable Cities: Monitoring Framework*. Retrieved from https://unhabitat.org/wp-content/uploads/2016/02/SDG-GoalMonitoring%20Framework%2025-02-16.pdf

United Nations. (2015). *Transforming our world: The 2030 agenda for sustainable development*. A/RES/70/1. Accessed at https://sustainabledevelopment.un.org/content/documents/2125203.pdf

United Nations Development Programme. (2011). *Bureau for Development Policy*. Accessed at www.undp.org/content/dam/undp/library/Poverty Reduction/Inclusive development/Towards Human Resilience/Towards Sustaining MDGProgress_Ch8.pdf

Wang, C., Ghadim, P., Lim, M. K., & Tseng, M. (2019). A literature review of sustainable consumption and production: A comparative analysis in developed and developing economies. *Journal of Cleaner Production*, *206*(1), 741–754. doi:10.1016/j.jclepro.2018.09.172

Wang, J., & Dong, K. (2019). What drives environmental degradation? Evidence from 14 Sub-Saharan African countries. *The Science of the Total Environment*, (656), 15165–15173. PMID:30504018

Zhu, Q., & Sarkis, J. (2016). Green marketing and consumerism as social change in China: analysing the literature. *International Journal of Production Economy*, (181), 289–302.

KEY TERMS AND DEFINITIONS

Clean Water: Provisions of clean potable water for human consumption and use.

Ecosystem: The interrelation of the various groups of fauna and flora in the environment to sustain lives of the various living organisms on a sustainable basis.

Green Economy: An economy that takes cognizance of avoiding the injurious production and consumption and allows the regeneration of the natural products rather than synthetic products.

Housing: The man man-made habitation for human beings that are constructed in taste and style as desired by the owner.

Millennium Development Goals: The eight goals promoted by the United Nations for performance up till 2015. The goals address the issues of poverty and basic human existence.

Renewable Energy: Energy production from sources that can be regenerated and are not wasting fossils. Such energy sources include natural ones like recyclable sources and naturally occurring phenomenon like sunlight and is generally reproducible.

Sustainable Development Goals: The up-scaled goals promoted by the United Nations as a successor to the MDGs. It has 17 goals and is due to end by 2030.

Sustainable Production: One of the goals promoted by the SGDs that encourages the production of consumables that avoids waste and `encourage long term production.

Chapter 9
Changing Patterns of Energy Use and Its Linkage With Some Macroeconomic Variables in India and China

Rajib Bhattacharyya
Goenka College of Commerce and Business Administration, India

ABSTRACT

Over the last decade there has been a gradual change in the global energy landscape, with fast-growing emerging markets overtaking the traditional centers in terms of energy demand. International Energy Outlook 2017 forecasts that energy consumption in non-OECD countries would increase by 41% between 2015 and 2040 in contrast to a 9% increase in OECD countries. The chapter focuses on two major areas: (1) examining the changing pattern of the composition of energy use in the two selected countries of Asia (India and China) and (2) examining the short-run and long-run relationship among energy use, GDP per capita, energy intensity, use of electricity power, extent of urbanization. Using ARDL bound test for the period 1990 to 2014 for the World Development Indicator data 2017-18, it reveals that the powerhouses of global energy demand growth are led by the developing economies of Asia (i.e., China, India, Indonesia, Morocco, Brazil, Singapore, and Thailand). In the case of India, a long-run association has been found between energy use and GDP per capita, energy intensity, use of electricity power, and extent of urbanization, but no instances are for China.

INTRODUCTION

Of late, there has been a gradual change in the global energy landscape, with fast-growing emerging markets overtaking the traditional centres in terms of energy demand. The composition of energy mix is also undergoing a major change which is being guided by technological innovations or inventions and environmental concerns. One of the fundamental characteristics of the energy transition mapped out by this Energy Outlook Survey 2017 is gradual movement towards de-carbonization of the fuel mix. Sig-

DOI: 10.4018/978-1-5225-8547-3.ch009

nificant improvements in the competitiveness of renewable energy have led to the increases in renewable, together with nuclear and hydro energy which expected to provide around half of the increase in global energy till 2035. Natural gas is expected to grow faster than oil or coal, helped by the rapid growth of liquefied natural gas(LNG) increasing the accessibility of gas across the globe. Compared to the growth of vehicles, oil demand continues to increase at a slower pace due to fuel efficiency and technological improvements, such as electric vehicles, battery driven cars etc has been increasingly implemented to keep the environment green. The expansion in the overall demand for energy is expected to continue as increasing prosperity in fast-growing emerging economies lifts billions of people from low incomes. But due to increasing attention in improvements in energy efficiency around the world the extent of this increase is likely to be curbed and making it more sustainable.

Global primary energy consumption grew strongly in 2017, led by natural gas and renewable, with coal's share of the energy mix continuing to decline. Primary energy consumption growth averaged 2.2% in 2017, up from 1.2% in 2016.By fuel, natural gas accounted for the largest increment in energy consumption, followed by renewable and then oil. Energy consumption rose by 3.1% in China. China was the largest growth market for energy for the 17th consecutive year.

Carbon emissions from energy consumption increased by 1.6%, after little or no growth for the three years from 2014 to 2016.Despite the unusually strong growth in the OECD, the vast majority of the increase in global energy consumption came from the developing world, accounting for nearly 80% of the expansion.

LITERATURE REVIEW

Aqeel and Butt (2001) in their paper investigate the causal relationship between energy consumption and economic growth and energy consumption and employment in Pakistan.By applying techniques of co-integration and Hsiao's version of Granger causality, the results infer that economic growth causes total energy consumption. Economic growth also leads to growth in petroleum consumption, while on the other hand, neither economic growth nor gas consumption affect each other. Fatai (2014) in his study reassesses the causal relationships between energy consumption and economic growthin 18 Sub-Saharan Africa countries over the period1980-2011.The results of panel co-integration tests show that energy consumption and economic growth do have a stable long-run equilibrium relationship.Siddique and Majeed (2015) attempted to explore the impact of energy consumption, trade and financial development on growth in five South Asian countries over 1980-2010. The panel co-integration approach is employed to examine the long run association and granger causality analysis for direction.Masuduzzaman (2013) in his paper tries to investigate the relationship between economic growth, electricity consumption and investment for Bangladesh through co-integration and causality analysis over the period 1981 to 2011. The Granger F test results show the existence of unidirectional causality running from electricity consumption to economic growth, electricity consumption to investment and investment to economic growth without feedback in the short run. The source of causation in the long run is also found to be the error correction terms from electricity consumption and economic growth to investment. Khobai, Abel& Roux (2017) investigates the long run relationship and causal relationship between energy consumption and economic growth in the BRICS countries during the period 1990 – 2013. Kabir, Zaku, Tukur & Aikhuele (2013) in their paper tried to examine the causal relationship between energy consumption and National income of Nigeria. The importance of identifying the direction of causality emanates from its relevance in national policy-making issues regarding energy conservation. Noor and Siddiqi (2010) find out a negative long run relationship between energy and GDP in South Asian countries (Pakistan, Bangladesh, Nepal, Sri Lanka and India). Using panel co-integration and fully modified OLS. In the short run, they found unidirectional causality running from energy to GDP. Using a sample of 18 developing countries, Lee (2005) suggests that energy conservation policies are harmful in selected countries and his findings are in support of growth hypothesis. He used panel co-integration technique and panel VECM to check the relationship between energy and GDP over the period 1975-2001. The results supported long run relationship between these two variables after allowing for individual county effects and energy is impetus for GDP growth in these countries. Lee and Chang (2008) confirm a long run relationship between energy consumption, GDP, capital stock and labor using panel co-integration technique for 16 Asian countries over the period of 1971-2002. Their results are in support of growth hypothesis as there is found one way causality running from energy consumption to GDP. Narayan and Popp (2012) argue that there are some countries where energy conservation policies have minimal effects on GDP growth. They found mixed results for the long-run Granger causality relationship between energy and GDP for 93 countries using annual data from 1980 to 2006. They found a long-run relationship between energy and GDP for Asia. The Pedroni panel co-integration method is applied to analyze the co-integration relationship amongthe variables. The causality relationship among the variables is analyzed using Pair-wise Granger-causality technique. The study's results reveal that there is a long run relationship between economic growth, energy consumption, employment and trade openness in BRICS countries.

OBJECTIVE OF THE STUDY AND METHODOLOGY

The fundamental aim of this study is to focus on the region-wise and energy-wise primary energy consumption trend across the globe and mainly the two Asian Tigers viz. India and China. Hence, the present analysis focuses on two major areas- (a) the changing pattern of the composition of energy use in various regions of the world and more particularly the two selected countries of Asia (India and China) and also highlights specifically on the reserves, production and consumption three major components of primary energy- oil, natural gas and coal; (b) to examine the short run and long run relationship between energy use, GDP per capita, energy intensity, use of electricity power, extent of urbanization. The former part is represented in a comparative framework using the time series data for the last decade (2007- 2017) based on BP Statistical Review of World Energy 2018. The latter part has been empirically examined using ARDL bound test for both the short and long run and applying time series data (1990 to 2014) available from the World Development indicator 2017-18 with the help of Statistical software e-views. It also tries to highlight the fundamental policy issues relating to sustainable pattern of energy use.

RELATIONSHIP BETWEEN PRIMARY ENERGY CONSUMPTION, ECONOMIC GROWTH, POPULATION GROWTH AND URBANIZATION

A huge body of existing literature has tried to show the relationship between energy consumption, economic growth, population growth and urbanization. Let us first concentrate on each of these globally as well as from the point of view of India and China. Figure 1 points out the growth of primary energy (here primary energy comprises commercially-traded fuels, including modern renewable used

Figure 1. Primary energy consumption among various regions of the world
[Source: Authors Construction Based on BP Statistical Review of World Energy 2018.]

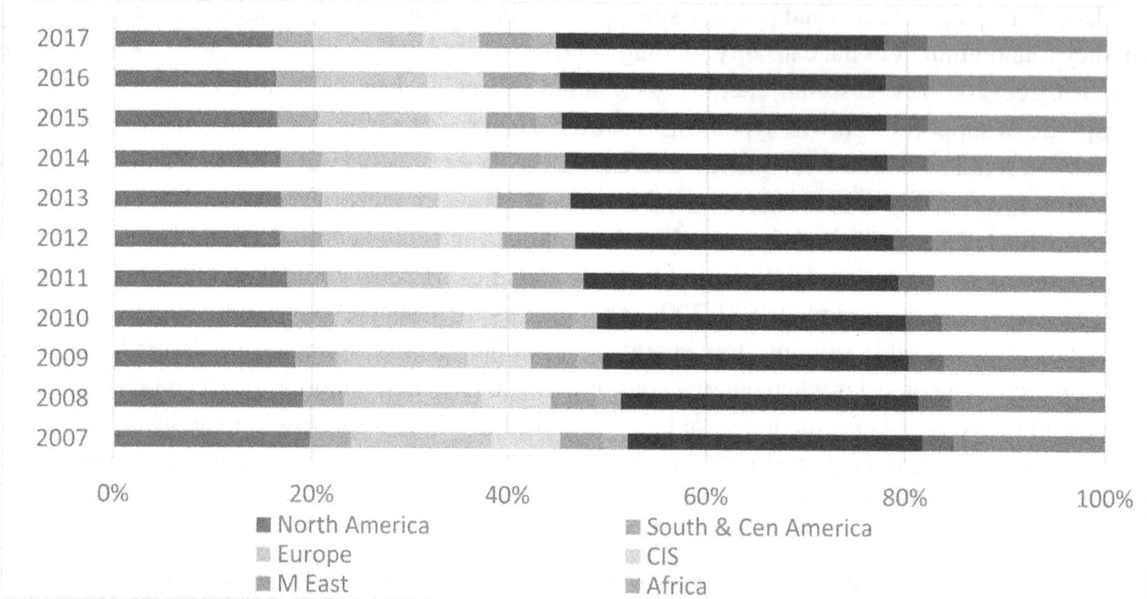

to generate electricity)consumption (million tonnes of oil equivalent) in various regional blocks of the world. It clearly reveals that Asia Pacific region is the highest share in primary energy consumption, which is primarily dominated by India and China. It also clearly demonstrates the energy consumption growth divergence between to fastest growing nations of the world. It emphasizes the fact that China was the largest growth market for energy for the 17th consecutive year. If we consider it from a different regional classification we may state that the non-OECD countries have a higher share (58.5%) compared to OECD countries (41.5%).

Figure 2 shows the composition of regional consumption by energy use in 2017. Coal is the dominant fuel in the Asia Pacific region. In 2017 coal's share of primary energy fell to its lowest level in North America, Europe, CIS and Africa.Oil remains the dominant fuel in Africa, Europe and the Americas, while natural gas dominates in CIS and the Middle East, accounting for more than half of the energy mix in both regions.

Figure 3 shows Composition of Energy Consumption by Various Regions in 2017. Asia is the leading regional consumer of oil, coal, renewable power and hydroelectricity, while North America leads for nuclear power and natural gas. Asia dominates global coal consumption, accounting for almost three quarters of global consumption (74.5%).

Figure 4 shows that in case of China other than coal and hydro-electricity there has been a steady increase in all other components, where as in case of India the increase has been negligible in case of nuclear energy and hydro-electricity.

Now let us briefly review the changes the growth scenario of both India and china over the last two decade as it would provide some insights to whether the rising rates of GDP per capita be supported by the increasing consumption of primary energy.

Figure 2. Composition of regional consumption by energy use in 2017
[Source: Authors Construction Based on BP Statistical Review of World Energy 2018.]

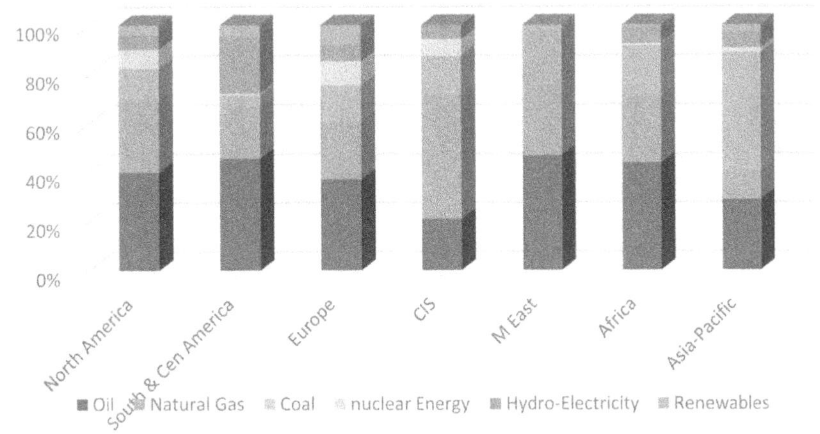

Figure 3. Composition of energy consumption by various regions in 2017
[Source: Authors Construction Based on BP Statistical Review of World Energy 2018.]

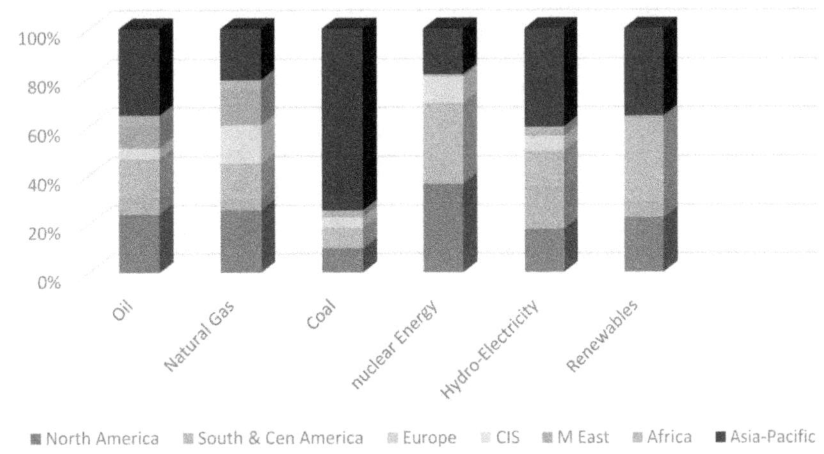

Figure 5a points out the trends in GDP per capita PPP in the two fastest growing nations of Asia (namely China and India). China is way ahead of India in terms of GDP per capita. As China and India are the two fastest growing countries of Asia in terms of growth also and the population growth of these two nations are the fastest in the world it is really alarming whether this pace of growth can be compatible with the pace of energy production and consumption.

Global economic activity is expected to pick up in the coming years, with an anticipated cyclical recovery in investment, manufacturing and trade. From global growth of 3% in 2016, growth rates are expected to rise to around 3.5% in 2018. Figure 5b is drawn on the assumption that in each of the

Figure 4. Changes in the shares of primary energy consumption by fuel in China and India
[Source: Authors Construction Based on BP Statistical Review of World Energy 2018.]

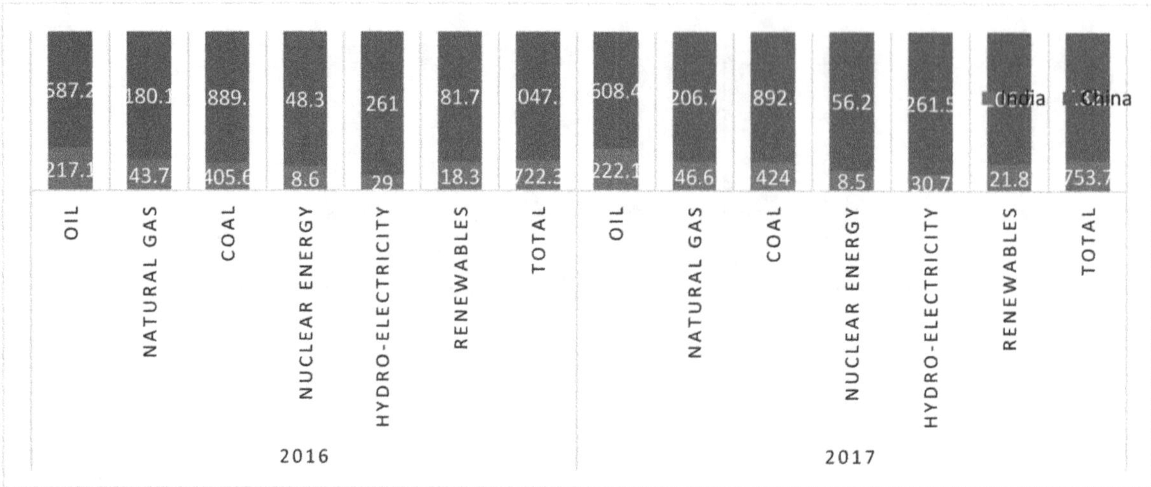

Figure 5a. Comparison of GDP Per capita PPP (constant 2011 International $)
[Source: Authors Construction Based on BP Statistical Review of World Energy 2018.]

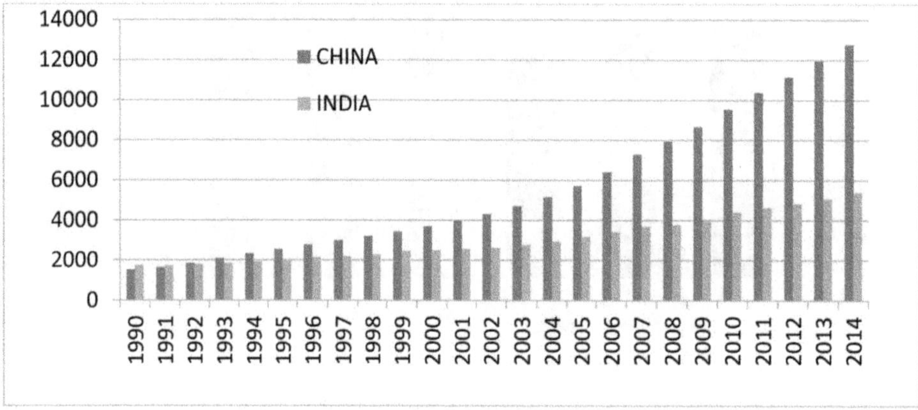

Figure 5b. Real GDP Growth assumption by region (Compounded Av. Annual Growth Rate)
[Source: Authors Construction Based on World Energy Outlook 2017, IMF 2017]

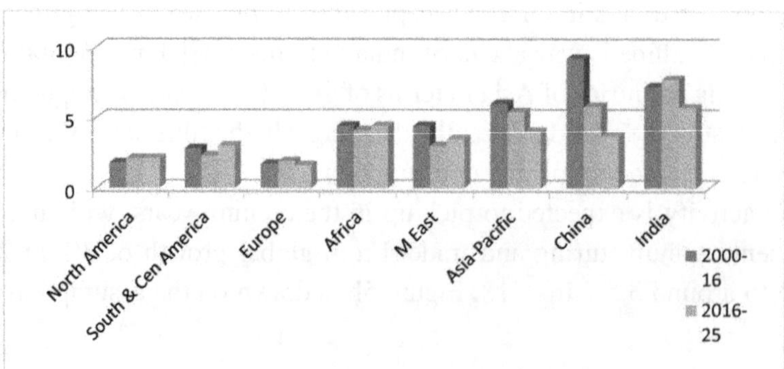

scenarios, the world economy is assumed to grow at a compound average annual rate of 3.4% over the period to 2040 (not shown in Figure 5bexplicitly).

Overall, the global aggregates are quite similar to those of the WEO-2016, although there are some slight downward revisions for medium-term economic growth in some regions, notably for oil-exporting countries in the Middle East and Africa, reflecting the assessment from the International Monetary Fund (IMF, 2017).

The way that economic growth translates into energy demand growth varies substantially by country, depending on each country's economic structures and stages of development, as well as pricing and efficiency policies. In most advanced economies, energy demand is now on a path of gradual structural decline, despite continued growth in national output. Elsewhere, however, economic expansion has much stronger implications for energy demand, particularly in countries where energy-intensive industrial activity accounts for a larger share of GDP. For the global economy as a whole, as of 2016 a 1% rise in GDP is associated with a 0.3% increase in primary energy demand. The level of this demand increase has however reduced: as recently as 2000-05, a 1% increase in GDP meant an average 0.7% rise in energy use. The rate at which the energy intensity of the global economy improves is a critically important indicator.

An increasing share of the global population is living in cities and towns, and the global urbanization rate is projected to rise from 54% in 2016 to 63% in 2040. There are many different avenues for urbanization, i.e. development of new "smart" cities. But overall this transition has major implications for energy consumption: urbanization accelerates the switch to modern fuels, the rise in appliance and vehicle use, and demand for construction materials, including energy-intensive products such as steel and cement. The fastest growth in population is in Africa, underlining the scale of the challenge to provide universal access to modern energy. By 2040, three-out-of-four people in the world are living either in the Asia Pacific region or in Africa (Figure 6a). The global urbanization rate is projected to rise from 54% in 2016 to 63% in 2040, whose region-wise segmentation is shown in figure-6b.

Figure 6a. Population by region
[Source: Authors Construction Based on BP Statistical Review of World Energy 2018.]

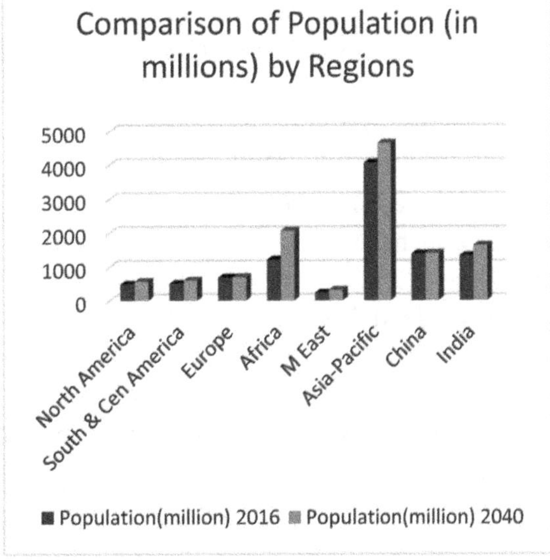

Figure 6b. Urbanization rate by regions
[Source: Authors Construction Based on BP Statistical Review of World Energy 2018.]

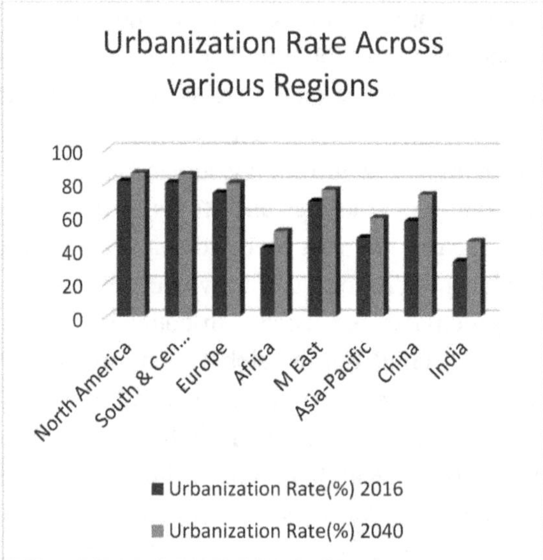

ENERGY-WISE COMPARISON OF PRODUCTION AND CONSUMPTION IN CHINA AND INDIA

Let us now try to focus on three major primary sources of energy- Oil, Natural gas and coal and try to examine their differences in the production and consumption over the last decade (2007 to 2017) in both India and China. Figure-7 points out an important fact that in both China and India the oil production is much below their respective oil consumption and their aggregate production is far below their aggregate consumption for each of the years in the last decade. This puts heavy pressure on oil imports and increases their import bill by a huge amount.

In case of natural gas the changes in the distribution of reserves in various regions of the world is represented in figure-8. In 1997, the share of middle-east was the highest (37.9%), followed by (Common Wealth of Independent States; former Soviet Union) CIS (31.2%) and then Africa (7.9%) and Asia (7.4%). In 2007 the share of middle-east increased to further 45% while the share of CIS declined to 25%. The share of Asia and Africa both increased. But the composition changed again in 2017. The share of the middle-east (though the highest contributor) declined, but that of CIS increased compared to 2007. The Asia Pacific region has also registered an increase in its contribution.

An interesting observation regarding natural gas is that in India its production increased till 2010 but it started to decline thereafter, falling in 2017 to the level of production as it was in 2007, although its consumption has shown an increasing trend. But in case of China both the production and consumption had shown an increasing trend, and since 2009 the growth in consumption has exceeded that of production.

In case of coal Asia Pacific region has been the largest contributor and its share has increased during the last decade or so. It has been closely followed by North-America and CIS region, although their share has remained more or less same.

Figure 7. Comparison of Production and consumption of Oil in China and India
[Source: Authors Construction Based on BP Statistical Review of World Energy 2018.]

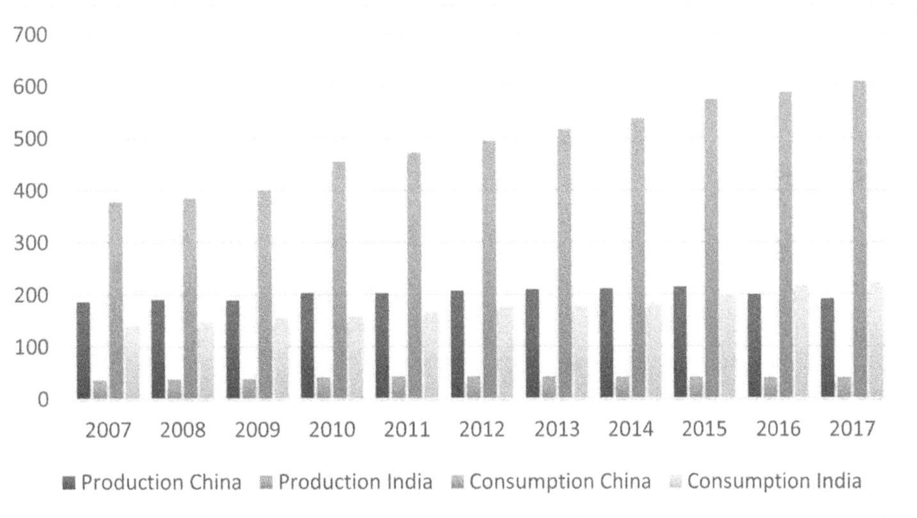

Figure 8. Distribution of Reserves of Natural Gas (1997- 2017)
[Source: Authors Construction Based on BP Statistical Review of World Energy 2018.]

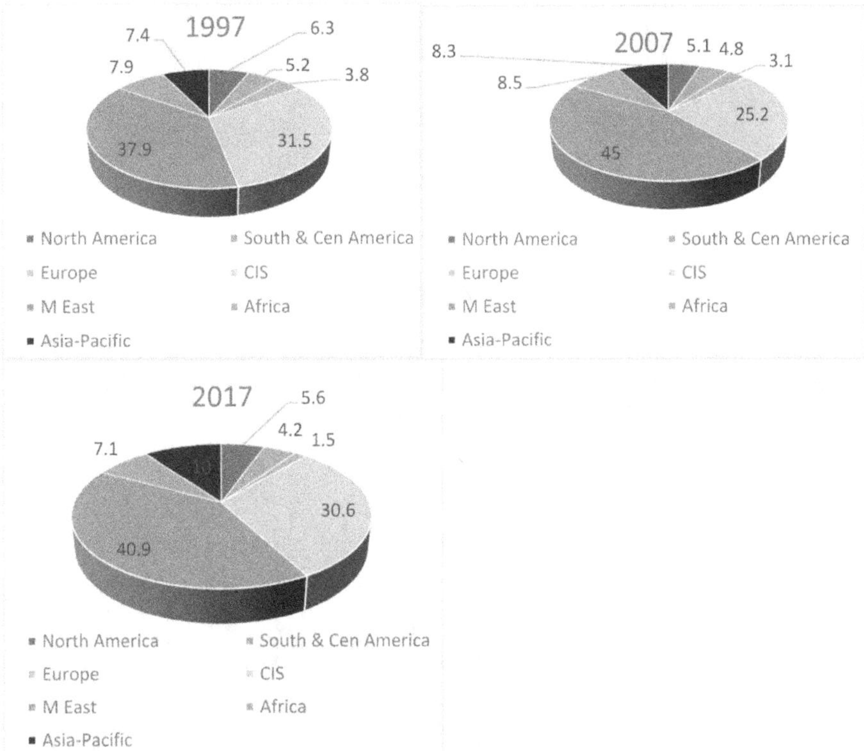

Figure 9. Comparison of Production and consumption of Natural Gas in China and India
[Source: Authors Construction Based on BP Statistical Review of World Energy 2018.]

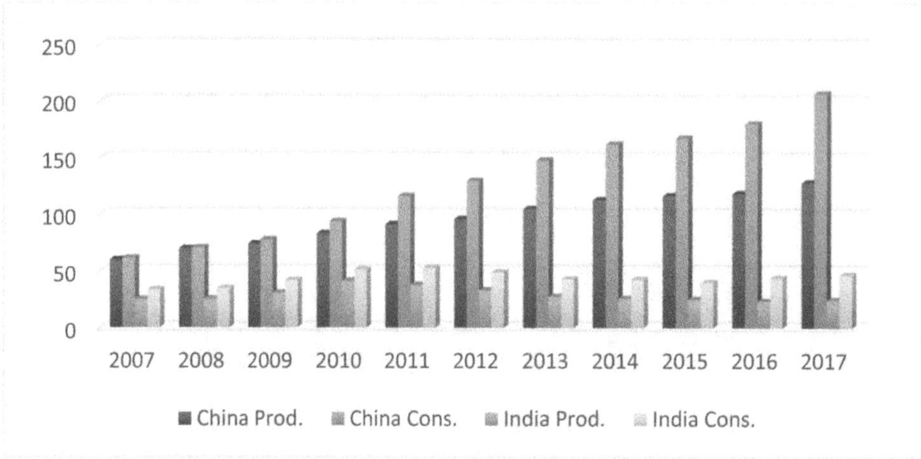

Figure 10. Distribution of Reserves of Coal (1997- 2017)
[Source: Authors Construction Based on BP Statistical Review of World Energy 2018.]

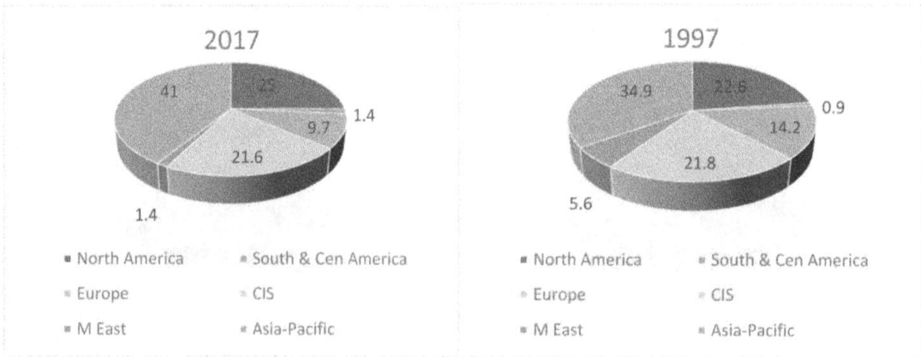

Figure 11. Comparison of Production and consumption of Coal in China and India
[Source: Authors Construction Based on BP Statistical Review of World Energy 2018.]

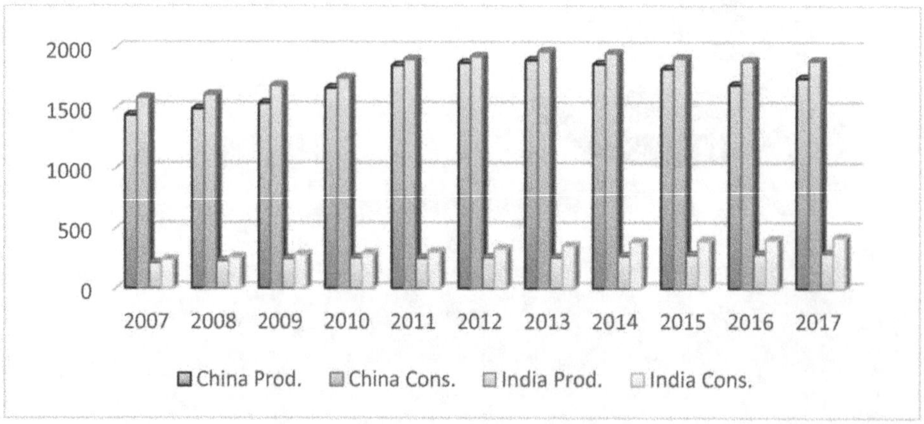

One of the most significant feature of coal is that its production and consumption maintained a close parity with one another in the respective countries during the period 2007 to 2017. Though there has been a huge difference in the level of coal production and consumption between the two countries, but they occupied the highest shares in both production and consumption of coal in the Asia Pacific region. Moreover, though renewable energy and nuclear power are the world's fastest growing forms of energy, fossil fuels are expected to continue to meet much of world's energy demand. There has also been a change in the composition of energy use overtime – coal is increasingly replaced by natural gas, renewables, and nuclear power (in the case of China) in electricity generation. Industrial demand for coal also weakens.

EMPIRICAL ANALYSIS

The background of an empirical analysis has been developed following the ongoing research work which have tried to establish some linkages with energy use (as a dependent variable) and movements in some independent variables like- GDP per capita, energy intensity, use of electricity power, extent of urbanization and such other variables. Here the attempt is to develop an empirical model where the dependent variable is Energy use (kg of oil equivalent per capita) denoted by ENGUSE and the four explanatory variables are GDP per capita, PPP (constant 2011 international $), denoted by GDPPCI; Energy intensity level of primary energy (MJ/$2011 PPP GDP), denoted by ENGINT; Electric power consumption (kWh per capita), denoted by ELECPOW and Urban population (% of total), denoted by URBPOP. All the data are being collected from the World Development Indicator, 2017-18 and it covers a period 1990 to 2014 for both India and China.

Before starting any time series analysis the ADF Unit root test is performed to check whether the series is stationary. The results of the ADF unit root tests are shown in table 1.

Now after checking for unit root we proceed for the testing of co-integration between the variables, based on ARDL framework. Pesaran et al. (2001) suggested, the Autoregressive distributed lag approach (ARDL) to test for co-integration as an alternative to co-integration model for Engle-Granger (1989). The ARDL- ECM model has been developed to check both long run and short run relationship between dependent variable is Energy use (kg of oil equivalent per capita) denoted by ENGUSE and the four explanatory variables are GDP per capita, PPP (constant 2011 international $), denoted by GDPPCI; Energy intensity level of primary energy (MJ/$2011 PPP GDP), denoted by ENGINT; Electric power consumption (kWh per capita), denoted by ELECPOW and Urban population (% of total), denoted by URBPOP. In general the ARDL restricted error correction model (RECM) is shown below. We have taken an unrestricted ARDL model with no trends with 2 lags and estimate the following equation:

$$d\left(ENGUSE\right)=\text{c}+\alpha_0\,\text{d(ENGUSE(-1))}+\alpha_1\text{d(ENGUSE(-2))}+\beta_1\text{d(GDPPCI(-1))}+\beta_2\text{d(GDPPCI(-2))}+\delta_1\text{d(ENGINT(-1))}+\delta_2\text{d(ENGINT(-2))}+\sigma_1\text{d(ELECPOW(-1))}+\sigma_2\text{d(ELECPOW(-2))}+\theta_1\text{d(URBPOP(-1))}+\theta_2\text{d(URBPOP(-2))}$$

$$+\mu_1\text{ENGUSE(-1)}+\mu_2 GDPPCI\text{(-1)}+\mu_3\text{ENGINT(-1)}+\mu_4\text{ELECPOP(-1)}+\mu_5\text{URBPOP(-1)} \tag{1}$$

Table 1. Results of unit test (ADF)

	Variable	t-Statistic	Probability	Critical value	Series Type
INDIA	ENGUSE	3.252742	1.0000	-2.991878	NS
	D(ENGUSE)	-1.860705	0.3416	-3.040391	NS
	D(ENGUSE, 2)	-8.258713	0.0000	-3.004861	S
	GDPPCI	5.940030	1.0000	-2.991878	NS
	D(GDPPCI)	-2.164803	0.2234	-2.998064	NS
	D(GDPPCI, 2)	-4.856760	0.0011	-3.020686	S
	ENGINT	-0.278613	0.9145	-2.991878	NS
	D(ENGINT)	-6.408799	0.0000	-2.998064	S
	ELECPOW	4.840349	1.0000	-2.991878	NS
	D(ELECPOW)	-1.951187	0.3047	-2.998064	NS
	D(ELECPOW, 2)	-6.997651	0.0000	-3.004861	S
	URBPOP	1.623203	0.9991	-3.004861	NS
	D(URBPOP)	-0.174070	0.9290	-2.998064	NS
	D(URBPOP, 2)	-3.550266	0.0161	-3.004861	S
CHINA	ENGUSE	-0.604679	0.8512	-2.998064	NS
	D(ENGUSE)	-2.085752	0.2516	-2.998064	NS
	D(ENGUSE, 2)	-3.858054	0.0082	-3.004861	S
	GDPPCI	0.916126	0.9938	-2.998064	NS
	D(GDPPCI)	-0.766101	0.8099	-2.998064	NS
	D(GDPPCI, 2)	-4.797612	0.0010	-3.004861	S
	ENGINT	-1.995166	0.2866	-3.004861	NS
	D(ENGINT)	-2.886341	0.0631	-3.004861	NS
	D(ENGINT, 2)	-3.599429	0.0150	-3.012363	S
	ELECPOW	5.020705	1.0000	-2.991878	NS
	D(ELECPOW)	-2.033815	0.2714	-2.998064	NS
	D(ELECPOW, T,I)*	-3.365000	0.0411	-3.248592	S
	URBPOP	0.164813	0.9635	-3.004861	NS
	D(URBPOP)	-1.632938	0.4497	-3.004861	NS
	D(URBPOP, 2, None)	-2.455060	0.0167	-1.957204	S

[*, Significant at 10%. All others are significant at 5% level]

where D (ENGUSE) is the dependent variable and GDPPCI, ENGINT, ELECPOW and URBPOP with 1 and 2 lags are taken as independent variable.

Then we check Residual Diagnostics (Serial correlation) using LM Test. Then stability analysis check is being performed using CUSUM Test and finally in order to find whether there exists long-run association between the variables, Wald Test is performed. For checking short run relationship we have incorporated the error term [ECT(-1)] from our basic long run model and gain estimate our model with 2 lags. The error term indicates the speed of adjustment towards long run equilibrium. Again, serial

Table 2. Results for serial correlation (LM Test) and stability analysis (CUSUM Test)

Country	Test Result (Breusch-GodfreySerial Correlation LM Test)				CUSUM Test
India	F-statistic	5.236754	Prob. F(2,4)	0.0764	Stable (Figure-12a)
	Obs*R-squared	15.91993	Prob. Chi-Square(2)	0.0003	
China	F-statistic	38.37184	Prob. F(2,4)	0.0025	Stable (Figure-12b)
	Obs*R-squared	20.91013	Prob. Chi-Square(2)	0.0000	

correlation is tested for short run model using LM test. Then long run causality is checked for each of the four independent variables- GDPPCI, ENGINT, ELECPOW and URBPO Pusing Wald test. These has been done separately for the three countries Bangladesh, China and India. For both the figures (6-8) the blue line lies between the two red lines, signifying stable situation.

Checking Long Run Association Between Variables

Here the author's objective is to determine whether there exists any long run association between ENGUSE, GDPPCI, ENGINT, ELECPOW and URBPOP. This has been tested through Wald Test. The *F* test is used to determine whether the long-run relationship exists between the variables through testing the significance of the lagged levels of the variables. When the long-run relationship exists, the *F* test will show which variable should be normalized. The null hypothesis of no co-integration amongst the variables in the equation (1), i.e. coefficients of ENGUSE(-1), GDPPCI(-1), ENGINT(-1), ELECPOW(-1) and URBPOP(-1)are all zeros. Putting C(12)= C(13)=C(14)=C(15)=C(16)=0. The results of the Wald Test (table 3) are as follows:

Short Run Association Between Variables

In the short run we have incorporated the error term ECT(-1) as one independent variable and again checked for serial correlation using LM test. Here, in order to ensure that there is no serial correlation (table 4) one independent variable D (ENGUSE (-1)) and D (ENGUSE(-2)) was dropped and further stability has been checked using CUSUM test.

In all the three cases the ECT (-1) is negative and statistically significant and the speed of adjustment towards long run equilibrium are 97.22% and 71.31% for India and China respectively.

Finally, Wald test has been applied to check whether there exist short run causality.

From table 5 it is clear that except in case of China (where ENGINT and URBPOP with lag 1 and 2 causes a change in ENGUSE in the short run) there is no short run causality in case of any other country and any other variable.

RESULTS

The empirical analysis provides some linkages with some of the major explanatory macroeconomic variables determining the short run and long run relation with changes in the energy use. The ARDL model incorporating the error correction term also provides the short term causality of these variables.

Figure 12a. CUSUM test result for India

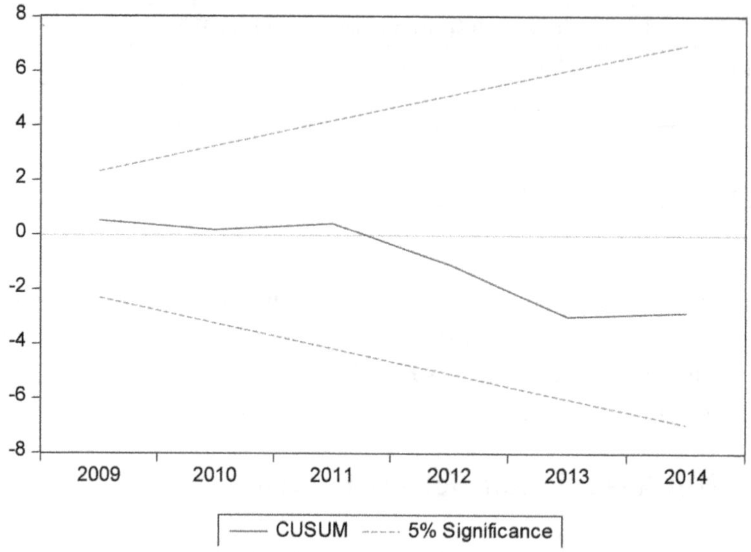

Figure 12b. CUSUM test result for China

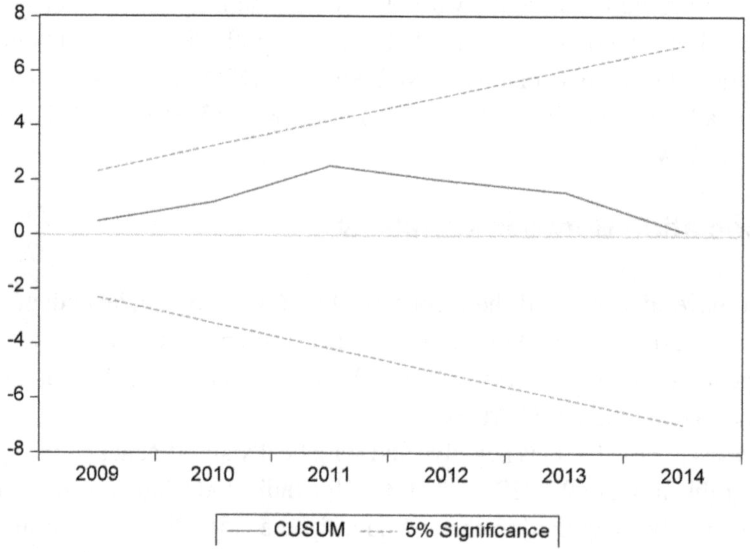

In case of India a long run association has been found between energy use and the four explanatory variables viz. GDP per capita, energy intensity, use of electricity power and extent of urbanization. But in case of China no such long run relation has been revealed. Except in case of China (where ENGINT and URBPOP with lag 1 and 2 causes a change in ENGUSE in the short run i.e. short run causality exists) there is no short run causality in case of any other variables and the other country India.

Table 3. Long run association between variable (Wald Test)

Country	Test Result for Wald Test				Interpretation
India	Test Statistic	Value	df	Probability	*F-Stat* 5.144>*upper Bound 4.85.* ENGUSE, GDPPCI, ENGINT, ELECPOW and URBPOP *has long run association.*
	F-statistic	5.144869	(5, 6)	0.0353	
	Chi-square	25.72435	5	0.0001	
	Null Hypothesis: C(12)=C(13)=C(14)=C(15)=C(16)=0				
China	Test Statistic	Value	df	Probability	*F-Stat* 0.475< *lower Bound 3.79.*ENGUSE, GDPPCI, ENGINT, ELECPOW and URBPOP *has no long run association.*
	F-statistic	0.475536	(5, 6)	0.7840	
	Chi-square	2.377678	5	0.7948	
	Null Hypothesis: C(12)=C(13)=C(14)=C(15)=C(16)=0				

Table 4. Short Run Serial Correlation (Using LM Test)

Country	Prob. Chi-Square(2)	Interpretation
India	0.1404	No serial Correlation
China	0.1152	No serial Correlation

Table 5. Short run causality (Wald test)

Country	Probability	Null Hypothesis	Interpretation
India	0.2459> 0.05	C(2)=C(3)=0	Accept Null. No SR causality. GDPPCI (-1), GDPPCI (-2) cannot cause change in ENGUSE.
	0.3879> 0.05	C(4)=C(5)=0	Accept Null. No SR causality. ENGINT (-1), ENGINT (-2) cannot cause change in ENGUSE.
	0.3865> 0.05	C(6)=C(7)=0	Accept Null. No SR causality. ELECPOW (-1), ELECPOW (-2) cannot cause change in ENGUSE.
	0.7754> 0.05	C(8)=C(9)=0	Accept Null. No SR causality. URBPOP (-1), URBPOP (-2) cannot cause change in ENGUSE.
China	0.0224< 0.05	C(2)=C(3)=0	Reject Null. There exist SR causality. GDPPCI (-1), GDPPCI (-2) can cause change in ENGUSE.
	0.0005< 0.05	C(4)=C(5)=0	Reject Null. There exist SR causality. ENGINT (-1), ENGINT (-2) can cause change in ENGUSE.
	0.3295> 0.05	C(6)=C(7)=0	Accept Null. No SR causality. ELECPOW (-1), ELECPOW (-2) cannot cause change in ENGUSE.
	0.0000< 0.05	C(8)=C(9)=0	Reject Null. There exist SR causality. URBPOP (-1), URBPOP (-2) can cause change in ENGUSE.

CONCLUSION

The above analysis tried to examine the overall economic growth and energy consumption across the globe and in the various regional blocks and attempted to build up a comparative framework to analyze the future growth trends of these two variables. It also focuses on the two fastest growing emerging economies of the world viz. India and China and their growth and energy consumption trend. The global energy system has been steadily- From 60% in 1977, the share of the OECD in global primary energy demand is now 39%. The powerhouses of global energy demand growth are elsewhere, led by the developing economies of Asia viz. China, India, Indonesia, Morocco, Brazil, Singapore and Thailand. The way that economic growth translates into energy demand growth varies substantially by country, depending on each country's economic structures and stages of development, as well as pricing and efficiency policies. In most advanced economies, energy demand is now on a path of gradual structural decline, despite continued growth in national output. Elsewhere, however, economic expansion has much stronger implications for energy demand, particularly in countries where energy-intensive industrial activity accounts for a larger share of GDP. For the global economy as a whole, as of 2016 a 1% rise in GDP is associated with a 0.3% increase in primary energy demand. The rate at which the energy intensity of the global economy improves is a critically important indicator.

An increasing share of the global population is living in cities and towns, and the global urbanization rate is projected to rise from 54% in 2016 to 63% in 2040. There are many different avenues for urbanization, i.e. Development of new "smart" cities. But overall this transition has major implications for energy consumption: urbanization accelerates the switch to modern fuels, the rise in appliance and vehicle use, and demand for construction materials, including energy-intensive products such as steel and cement.

The empirical analysis provides some linkages with some of the major explanatory macroeconomic variables determining the short run and long run relation with changes in the energy use. The ARDL model incorporating the error correction term also provides the short term causality of these variables. In case of India a long run association has been found between energy use and the four explanatory variables viz. GDP per capita, energy intensity, use of electricity power and extent of urbanization. But in case of China no such long run relation has been revealed. Except in case of China (where ENGINT and URBPOP with lag 1 and 2 causes a change in ENGUSE in the short run i.e. short run causality exists) there is no short run causality in case of any other variables and the other country India.

REFERENCES

Aqeel, A., & Butt, M.S. (2001). The Relationship between Energy Consumption and Economic Growth in Pakistan. *Asia-Pacific Development Journal, 8*(2).

Asia/World Energy Outlook 2017. (2016, October). The Institute of Energy Economics, Japan.

Economic Outlook for South East Asia. (2017). OECD.

Fatai, B. O. (2014). Energy Consumption and Economic Growth Nexus: Panel Co-Integration and Causality Tests for Sub-Saharan Africa. *Journal of Energy in Southern Africa, 25*(4).

IEA. (2015). *Energy and Climate Change: World Energy Outlook Special Report.* OECD/IEA.

IEA. (2016). *Energy and Air Pollution: World Energy Outlook Special Report*. OECD/IEA.

IEA. (2017). *The Future of Trucks: Implications for Energy and the Environment*. OECD/IEA.

IMF. (2017). *World Economic Outlook*. Washington, DC: IMF.

Kabir, A., Zaku, S. G., Tukur, A. A., & Aikhuele, J. G. (2013). The relationship between energy consumption and national income of Nigeria. *Journal of Economics and International Finance*, *5*(2), 53–57. doi:10.5897/JEIF12.078

Khobai, H., Abel, S., & Roux, P. L. (2017). *A Review of the Nexus between Energy consumption and Economic growth in the BRICS countries*. Retrieved from https://mpra.ub.uni-muenchen.de/ 82462 /MPRA

Lee, C. C. (2005). Energy consumption and GDP in developing countries: A co-integrated panel analysis. *Energy Economics*, *27*(3), 415–427. doi:10.1016/j.eneco.2005.03.003

Lee, C. C., & Chang, C. P. (2008). Energy consumption and economic growth in Asian economies: A more comprehensive analysis using panel data. *Energy Economics*, *30*(1), 50–65. doi:10.1016/j.reseneeco.2007.03.003

Masuduzzaman, M. (2013). *Electricity Consumption and Economic Growth in Bangladesh: Co-integration and Causality Analysis*. Research Study Series No. – FDRS 02/2013.

Narayan, P. K., & Popp, S. (2012). The energy consumption-real GDP nexus revisited: Empirical evidence from 93 countries. *Economic Modelling*, *29*(2), 303–308. doi:10.1016/j.econmod.2011.10.016

Noor, S., & Siddiqi, M. W. (2010). Energy consumption and economic growth in South Asian countries: A co-intergrated panel analysis. *Journal of the Humanities and Social Sciences*, *5*, 914–921.

Odhiambo, N. M. (2009). Energy consumption and economic growth nexus in Tanzania: An ARDL bounds testing approach. *Energy Policy*, *37*(2), 617–622. doi:10.1016/j.enpol.2008.09.077

Sarkar, M., Rashid, A., & Alam, K. (2010). Nexus between electricity generation and economic growth in Bangladesh. *Asian Social Science*, *6*(12), 16–22.

Siddique, H. M. A., & Majeed, M. T. (2015). Energy Consumption, Economic Growth, Trade and Financial Development Nexus in South Asia. *Pakistan Journal of Commerce and Social Sciences*, *9*(2), 658–682.

World Bank. (2017-18). *World Development Indicators*. Retrieved from http://www.worldbank. org/ data/onlinedatabases/onlinedatabases.html

Yu, E. S. H., & Choi, J. Y. (1985). The Causal Relationship between Energy and GNP: An International Comparison. *Journal of the Energy Division*, *10*, 249–272.

KEY TERMS AND DEFINITIONS

ARDL Bound Test: Autoregressive Distributed Lag Model (ARDL) Bounds testing procedure is a powerful statistical tool in the estimation of level relationships when the underlying property of time series is entirely I(0), entirely I(1) or jointly co-integrated. Bound testing as an extension of ARDL modelling uses F and t-statistics to test the significance of the lagged levels of the variables in a univariate equilibrium correction system when it is unclear if the data generating process underlying a time series is trend or first difference stationary. Here the ARDL model is applied to examine the short and long run association between variables.

Economic Growth: Economic growth basically refer to an increase in the amount of goods and services produced per head of the population over a period of time. It is conventionally measured as the percent rate of increase in real gross domestic product, or real GDP, after taking into account the inflation-adjusted market value of the goods and services produced by an economy over time.

Energy Consumption Pattern: Consumption pattern of energy includes consumption of coal, crude oil and natural gas, petroleum products, electricity. India will overtake China as the largest growth market for energy by late 2020s with the country's energy consumption growing by more than 4.2% per annum, the fastest among all major economies of the world, according to BP Energy Outlook 2018.

Energy Intensity: Energy intensity is a measure of the energy inefficiency of an economy. It is calculated as units of energy per unit of GDP. High energy intensities indicate a high price or cost of converting energy into GDP. Energy efficiency of appliances and buildings, fuel economy of vehicles, better methods and patterns of transportation, capacities and utility of mass transit, energy rationing or conservation efforts may all impact overall energy intensity of a nation.

Energy Use: Energy demand in rural and urban areas is on a steady rise. China and India are amongst the largest energy consumer in the world. The present energy use is mostly in the areas of domestic cooking and lighting, agriculture, transport and industrial sectors. India's energy basket has a mix of all the resources available including renewables. The largest energy source is coal, followed by petroleum and traditional biomass.

Population Growth: Population growth refers to the increase in the number of individuals in a population in a particular year. Many of the world's countries, including many in Sub-Saharan Africa, the Middle East, South Asia and South East Asia, have seen a sharp rise in population in recent times. High population growth puts strain on natural resources, energy use and consumption pattern, food supplies, fuel supplies, employment, housing, etc.

Time-Series Analysis: A set of statistics, usually collected at regular intervals. Secondary time series data for two countries of Asia viz. India and China over the period 1990-2014 has been used to provide an empirical support to the various comparative analysis. Correlation and regression analysis are used to arrive at the results. This has been collected from two main sources: (1) BP Statistical Review of World Energy 2018 and (2) World Development indicator 2017-18.

Chapter 10
The Role of Disaster Regulations and Insurance Regulations on the Development of Disaster Insurance Markets:
Regulatory Models in G-7 Countries

Ashu Tiwari
Indian Institute of Management Rohtak, India

Archana Patro
Indian Institute of Management Rohtak, India

Jahnavi Patky
Indian Institute of Management Rohtak, India

ABSTRACT

Recently, the climate regulations and stop-loss regulations have become a central policy parameter globally. In market-oriented economies, insurers as the biggest stakeholder-industry of natural disaster risk are facing the issue related to industry sustainability. Thus, the policy implications of natural disasters regulation on the insurance industry are enormous. Therefore, this chapter has made an effort to analyze the disaster management in the integrated framework. This integrated framework is based upon the analysis of the role of regulatory actions taken by three actors, namely, disaster regulation, insurance regulations, and firms' actions across the three stages of disaster management, namely, pre-disaster, underwriting, and post-disaster stages in G-7 economies. Based on the outcomes of the current analysis, the chapter found that there are two polar opposite integrated models (i.e., isolated best policy model in the case of Japan and spiral policy model in the case of Italy). Five models fall in between the two.

DOI: 10.4018/978-1-5225-8547-3.ch010

INTRODUCTION

Theoretically, regulations are in general essential for well-functioning of insurance markets. However, the role of regulations is vital for insurance of higher intensity risks. These risks prove costly if appropriate regulatory tools are not employed for aligning objectives of policymakers with that of the insurance firms. Within this class of risks, natural disasters have grabbed significant attention in recent insurance literature. The National Aeronautics and Space Administration/ Goddard Institute for Space Studies NASA/GISS, (2016) reported that the average temperature of the earth has risen by 1.1 degrees Celsius since 1950. As per Cat Perils and Swiss Re (2016), economic losses due to catastrophes have grown to 85% during2015-2016. Other than these, simulation-based studies have highlighted that a mean increase of 2.2 degrees Celsius in temperature increases 5-10% in hurricane wind speed, and doubling of wind speed increases four-fold damage. A 25% increase in 30 min precipitation reduces average flooding period from 100 years to 17 years, and a rise of 1 degree Celsius in temperature will increase 17-28% increase in wildfires (Mills, 2005; Mills 2009). Thus, the insurance industry alone cannot afford the future consequences of insured losses. Therefore, the active and careful efforts by policymakers are vital for managing future consequences of severe nature risks (Herweijer, Ranger & Ward, 2009).

Previously available literature has covered the three stages for the development of disaster insurance. However, in the absence of optimal bridging regulation, the applicability of these regulations for sustainable market development remains questionable. This gap in the academic domain has produced many issues related to nonalignment of policy-and firm objectives (Gutmann, 2011, p. 231). Thus, policy design is critical for the development of disaster insurance market. Therefore, for fulfilling such a policy gap, an integrated analysis of policy regulations is necessary. The current study argues that the risk of natural disaster needs integrated and aligned views with a due focus on positive outcomes. Therefore, the present study has analyzed the interaction of all the three stakeholders in the existing literature across the three stages with the objective of the development of private disaster insurance markets. Therefore, this article is first of its kind which provides a critical assessment of these interactions at all the three stages interdependently. Hence, the outcomes of the current study have implications for the domain as well as for policy formulation.

This study has been carried out in seven parts. Section second surveyed the literature and the gap in the literature. The third section explains the theoretical framework used for hypothesis development. Section fourth discusses data source and collection method. Section five talks about the methodology used for analysis. Section six provides the results of the analysis, and section seven presents conclusion limitation and future research directions.

LITERATURE REVIEW

The context covered in the present chapter is one of the most popular topics in the insurance literature. Therefore numerous studies are available on almost every small aspects of this topic. For example (Andjelkovic, 2001) focused on socio-economic surveys to map the vulnerability of communities against any disaster. Whereas some studies have focused on occupational dependence and vulnerability of people living in high-risk zones (Wang et al., 2013).Out of which some may have an adverse impact on underwriting, risk modeling, and risk transfer techniques (Wang et al., 2013).For example, one common dilemma between policymakers and insurers is post-disaster funding formats. The inappropriate formats may adversely impact the development of natural disaster insurance markets. Whereas small incentives for lower probability risks at the pre-disaster stage, can help in the development of the market. Despite similar other conflicting outcomes, little effort have been made to understand the issue in the integrated framework. The overall literature in the domain on this subject can broadly be classified in three separate stages of disaster management namely, pre-disaster stage, underwriting stage, and post-disaster stage (Outreville, 1992; Andjelkovic, 2001;UNESCO, 2001, UNCTAD, 2007, UNESCO, 2012; Silva, 2009; Dolce, 2012; Schalfer, 2018; Mahito, 2007; Mills, 2009; Kwon, 2010).

Further, some studies are more specific and have covered the perspective of insurance firms and policy perspectives separately, for example, Kunreuther (2015) stressed that the post-disaster participation of insurance firms might improve the adverse consequences of government aid. Insurance firm can participate in evacuation and reporting processes together with government or private agencies to reduce false loss reporting (Poontirakul, Brown, Noy, Seville, & Vargo, 2016; Holzheu & Turner, 2018; Kelly & Kleffner, 2006). However, none of these articles have covered the integrated view of disaster management and disaster insurance. Therefore there are many missing links which this study tries to bridge. The broad question this article is covering is what is the impact of disaster management regulation upon the insurance industry development?

THEORETICAL FRAMEWORK AND HYPOTHESIS DEVELOPMENT

The state has the power to destroy or raise the output of any industry. This is more relevant for industries that require higher regulatory involvement. As per the positive regulatory theories, regulation occurs to reduce information asymmetry among operator, policymakers, and consumers. We can say that regulations align the objectives of the government to that of the operator in order to protect customers as well as the industries from opportunism. Stigler (2018) argued that industries acquire the regulations to design and operate them for their profits. This argument is plausible in the current state of the insurance industry supplying natural disaster cover. In general, industries have particular systems to achieve their goals. These systems are made up of many smaller mechanisms upon which industry depends. Therefore, industries can only mold those regulations which are suitably fit into their smaller mechanisms. In the current state of natural disaster insurance markets, we have identified three stages of disaster management upon which most of the literature has focused namely, pre-disaster stage, disaster stage, and post-disaster stage. At every stage, we identified risk management regulation by government and showed how firms could reap benefits out of each regulation by fitting them into their objectives. Therefore, we proposed three hypotheses;

H1(a): Pre-disaster regulations can promote the insurance industry only if insurance industry can align its objectives in any of the three stages namely, pre-underwriting stage objectives, underwriting stage objectives, and post underwriting stage objectives.

H1(b): Disaster stage regulations can promote the insurance industry only if insurance industry can align its objectives in any of the three stages namely, pre-underwriting stage objectives, underwriting stage objectives, and post underwriting stage objectives.

H1(c): Post-disaster regulations can promote the insurance industry only if insurance industry can align its objectives in any of the three stages namely, pre-underwriting stage objectives, underwriting stage objectives, and post underwriting stage objectives.

$$\partial P(F_i) / \partial R_j \geq P(F_i)$$

where $P(F_i)$ represents profit as a function various activities of the firm, and R_j represents various regulations imposed by government or sectoral regulators to minimize the losses.

DATA SOURCES AND COLLECTION

The outcomes of the present work are based on a total of 60research articles and 28 policy documentsin the domain of Property and Casualty Insurance. Research articles are collectedby coining the various terms such as natural disasters, extreme events, natural disaster insurance, policy for natural disasters, natural disaster policy, systematic risk of natural disasters, role of insurance firms in managing natural disaster risk, policymakers and natural disaster risks, natural catastrophic risk and government regulations, natural catastrophes and regulations.The searched online databases are *Jstor, ProQuest, Science Direct, Scopus, Springer link, Taylor & Francis, Thomson & Reuters, Web of Science, Wiley, Sage, Palgrave Macmillan, Oxford, Emerald Insights and Google Scholar*, for the period of 2000-2016. In addition to the above literature, many policy documents, policy review, research report, and government websites are used for collecting the information.

METHOD FOR ANALYSIS

The author has compiled the literature on the subject and proceeds the following four steps;

1. In the first step, the literature has been collected on the broad theme of extreme events (already took place in the process of data collection).
2. In the second step, actions are identified by two actors and segregated all the possible actions taken by policymakers and insurance firms in three stages.
3. In the third step stage, the current study has identified possible models out of all the actions in the previous step.
4. In the fourth step, the study has tried to identify the model framework used in G-7 economies.

REGULATORY ASPECTS IN VARIOUS STAGES

Pre-Disaster Stage

International Regulators: United Nations structural guidelines under model framework of Sendai Framework 2015-30, Hyogo Framework 2005, and non-structural measure under Kids' ISO 14000 Program (Andjelkovic, 2001, UNICEF, 2012; UNISDR, 2013) and UNCTAD's work towards various

Figure 1. Integrated regulatory framework for disaster insurance
Source: Author
S=Strongly Regulated{R=8-5}
M=Moderately Regulated{R=5-3}
W=Weakly Regulated {Less than 3}

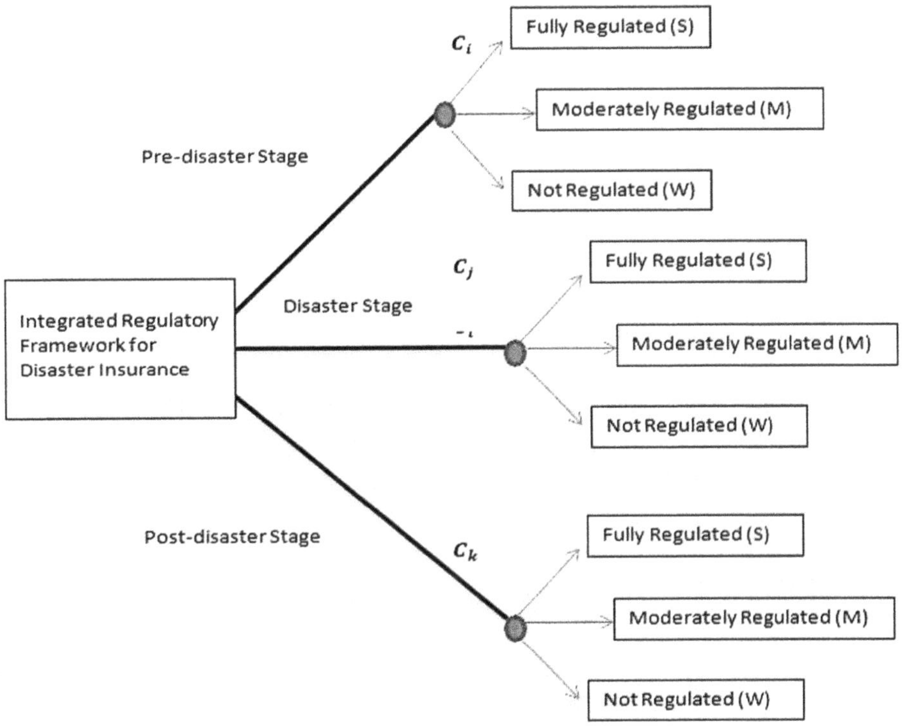

micro-insurance programs and human resource development (Couroux, & Outreville, 1992; UNCTAD, 2007) are few of the efforts to combat natural disaster risk internationally.

National Regulators: Apart from implementing international guidelines and mandates, the paper found seven most critical activities discussed in the literature which can reduce losses. They are building codes (BCR), disaster Zones (DZR) (Silva, 2009) early disaster warning network (INR), town planning with emergency provisions (TPR), disaster resilient infrastructure (DIR), green regulations (green funding, green construction) (GFR), and disaster education (DER) (Andjelkovic, 2001; Mauro, 2012; Kitagawa, Preston, & Chadderton, 2017; Schwarcz & Schwarcz, 2014).

Participation of Insurance Firms: The aftermath of some extreme natural disasters, the insurance firms also started focusing on several activities at the pre-disaster stage that can reduce losses. These activities are funding for green technology (GTF), educating people about the hazards of extreme events (DEF), helping people in constructing disaster-resistant buildings (BCF), and generously funding for green housing projects (Okura, 2007; Mills, 2009; Okura, & Yanase, 2014; Ericson, & Doyle, 2004; Kwon, 2010). Further, if we critically analyze the activity of insurance firms at the pre-underwriting stage, they can broadly be classified into three groups namely *Core Activity, Research Activity, and Participatory Activity.* Like any other industry, the core objective of any insurance firm is to minimize cost and maximize profits. However, unlike other domains, in the insurance industry, most of the aspects related to cost minimization or profit maximization depend on the external environment. Therefore, the insurance firm can only improve risk position by actively participating in allied activities related to risk minimization.

Core Activity: The core activity is risk modeling and policy underwriting. At the pre-disaster stage, the firm can incorporate regulatory actions into policy wordings. From the list of seven critical activities, insurance firm can directly translate some of them into policy wordings. For instance, building codes (BCR), disaster zones codes (ZCR) can be translated into incentive structures. These are not new, and most of the insurance firms are doing that.

Research Activity: Most of the insurance firms are involved in regular research focusing on their core activities such as various formats of co-pays, deductibles, bonus, and discounts. However, research on allied dimensions is still not popular in the domain of insurance. However, research on allied aspects such as the development of codes on town planning with emergency provisions (TPR), disaster resilient infrastructure (DIR), disaster information network (INR) and disaster education (DER)can further benefit industry underwriting efficiency.

Participatory Activity: Some activities, such as disaster education (DER), and Funding for green projects (GFR), do not become part of the insurance activity directly. However, they can improve risk positioning of natural disaster risks—these are the activities where insurance firms can directly participate.

DISASTERS UNDERWRITING STAGE

Based on literature and policy documents, regulators can promote insurance buying by provisions of compulsory insurance (CI), premium subsidy (PS), tax deductions or tax relief (TR), supervision of product design(PDR), and price regulation(PCR). Regulatory checks on capital liquidity and adequacy (CLA), investment pattern (IPR), data safety(DS), and digital authenticity(DA)(Van Schoubroeck, 1997; Gizzi, Potenza, &Zotta, 2015; Grace, Klein, &Kleindorfer, 2004; Hussels, Ward, & Zurbruegg, 2005).

Receptive and Responsive Role of Insurance firms at Underwriting Stage: Atthe underwriting stage, activities of insurance firms can broadly be classified into two main categories namely *risk modeling* and *risk avoidance.*

Risk Modeling: Risk modeling is primarily a stage where firms mainly focus on risk premiums. The firm can easilyminimize the risk premiums by distributing the risk over a large number of people. Thus, regulations which enable firms in achieving such objectives are favorable to industry development. These include regulations related to mandatory insurance buying regulation (CIR), Price Subsidy (PSR), Tax Exemptions (TER), and Tax Rebates (TRR). All three policy tools are favorable for industry development. However, firms cannot directly participate in these activities.

Risk Avoidance: Risk Avoidance can further be classified into three groups namely, policy underwriting, provisioning for possible categories of risks, and investment in less risky projects, by avoiding risky investments.

1. **Policy Underwriting.** The primary function of underwriting is to fulfill two objectives:
   a. To improve risk preventive behavior of insureds
   b. To know the actual risk profile of insureds and avoid adverse selections

2. **Provisioning for Possible Categories of Risks:** Provisioning is to meet the possible future risk contingencies. This can be done by following methods:
    a. To create an appropriate provision for each risk category
    b. Reinsurance
3. Investment in the less risky projects.

Additionally, if a country has appropriate regulations on data safety(DSR), and digital authentication (DAR), the insurance firm can get benefits by appropriately utilizing real-time data based modeling, actual risk profiling. By doing so, preventive behavior can be promoted by insurance firms. Further, technological limitation in terms of reducing the anomalies can be resolved by traditional methods such as deductibles, co-pays, and loading structures clauses (Raviv, 1979). The capital adequacy regulations(CLR), and investment regulations (IPR) can be aligned to objectives of provisions narrated in B-(i). However, product design and price regulation can be aligned with the goals of firms by participating in risk minimizing activity narrated at the pre-disaster stage. Therefore, such regulation creates regulatory friction (Priest, Clark, & Treby 2005).

POST DISASTER STAGE

At this stage, the major focus of policymakers is to provide relief. The relief can be provided in two forms:

1. Monetary Relief
2. Non- monetary relief

Monetary Relief: Monetary relief includes in the following formats:

1. Direct monetary compensations
2. Indirect monetary compensations include tax exemptions, low-interest rates, subsidies

Non-Monetary Relief: Non-monetary relief includes shelter houses, relief camps, food supply, medicines, clothes, and supply of similar items. Generally, non-monetary reliefs are often supplied for short duration. Therefore, they do not hamper the insurance markets. However, direct monetary compensations adversely impact insurance markets. Thus, policymakers cannot promote sound insurance markets without regulating critical aspects of post-disaster relief framework. The extant literature in the domain has discussed the regulatory aspects such as regulation of disaster assistance (FR1), careful post-disaster price regulation (PR), uniform procedures for relief disbursement (CL), charity regulation (FR2), regulation for restoration and reconstruction (IR), Tax Relief (TRR), Interest Rate Relief (IRR), subsidies on construction and restoration materials (SR), and Media Regulation (MR)(Aoki, 2018; Boyle, Cunningham, & Dekens, 2013).

Role of Insurance firms at the Post-Disaster Stage: Insurance firm can participate at post-disaster stage together with government by appropriately aligning their objectives to the existing regulations. For example, existing literature on disaster shows that direct monetary compensation comes from government or non-government agencies. Insurance firms better know the risk behaviors of individuals. Therefore, they can guide policymakers for various formats of direct compensations (FR1, FR2). The relative importance of various types of compensatory regulations also vary. For example, for the insurance industry, formats of direct compensation are more crucial than indirect monetary compensations. The compensation should be designed in such a way to fit in the objectives of insurance firms. One of the insurance principles says that compensation should not raise the economic status of any individual, in other words, it should not be rewarding. Therefore, government ways of designing compensation would be decisive for insurance industry development. Especially, in countries where insurance firms seek higher co-pays and deduction in their policy clauses and policymakers have generous post-disaster funding provisions. (Poontirakul, Brown, Noy, Seville, & Vargo, 2016; Holzheu & Turner, 2018; Kelly & Kleffner, 2006; Kunreuther, 2015).

Additionally, if there are not clear regulatory guidelines for relief disbursements, various media channels highlight the plight of people which in turn pressurize government for an immediate ad-hoc response. This, in turn, creates disbursement of uneven unplanned government assistance. Thus, clear regulatory guidelines for the disbursement of funds, and regulations for media reporting necessary (MR). Post-disaster Tax Relief (TRR), Interest Rate Relief (IRR) and Subsidies (SRR) have not a significant influence on the development of disaster insurance markets. However, regulation on reconstruction and rehabilitation is essential for insurance firms. The insurance firms can offer incentive and can offer funds to build disaster resistance houses during the reconstruction phase.

Based on this agenda we have analyzed the policy models of G-7 countries to understand the viewpoint of an integrated regulatory framework.

FRENCH INTEGRATED REGULATORY FRAMEWORK FOR DISASTER INSURANCE

Pre-Disaster Stage

France has regulations for building codes (BCR), and disaster zones (ZCR). It has also strengthened urban planning codes after a heavy storm in March 2010 (TPR). Additionally, the French government has the provision of the right to information about major risks[1] (INR). This law enforces policymakers to establish efficient disaster information network. Article 13 of the European Directive Seveso II obliged every upper tier site city to maintain information about the local population. The Law promulgated on July 30, 2003, further strengthens provisions for safety-related aspects. At the national level, the Advisory Board on the Prevention of Major Natural Hazards (COPRNM) provides safety advisory for natural disaster risk. Policy makers have also developed curriculum for disaster risk education[2] (DER). France has seismic safety regulations already in place. They have increased spending on risk management in mountain regions aftermath of 2010's Cyclone Xynthia windstorm. However, there is no explicit evidence available on disaster resistant infrastructural regulation. Therefore, at the pre-disaster stage, France has policy provisioning for six regulations out of seven regulations.

Underwriting Stage -France has regulations regarding compulsory insurance buying. But, information regarding subsidies and the tax deduction is not available on insurance buying in France. However, the Solvency II Directive (2009/138/EC) has brought forth many soundness measures such as minimum capital insurers need to hold supervisory structure and transparency guidelines[3].Added to this, in France, there is a uniform price regulation for disaster insurance cover irrespective of the probability of risk[4]. However, there is no provision of compulsory reinsurance for insurance firms (Jametti, & Ungern-Sternberg, 2004).

Post-Disaster Stage

After the 2001 flood, France has put the much regulatory focus on reconstruction work. Policymakers in France have formed the Interministerial Recovery Committee to coordinate with various actors to supply funds for housing projects. In France victims of natural disasters are compensated under 'Cat Net system for which a fixed percentage of premiums from all property and assets, the insurance covers deducted. Out of this fund, compensation is available for all the property owners in the affected area. Such system discourages any preventive action by property owners. However, in France reconstruction work has been done with proper planning and provisions for flood prevention structure (RHR) (Jouannic et al. 2016).

JAPANESE INTEGRATED REGULATORY FRAMEWORK FOR DISASTER INSURANCE

Pre-Disaster Stage

Policymakers in Japan have proactively developed preparedness strategies[5]in terms of having standard housing construction codes (Housing Quality Assurance Act) (BCR), infrastructural resilience adequacies (DIR), and mandatory self-help training for all people (Kitagawa, 2017). It has launched Himawari-9, which is ninth geostationary weather observatory since 1977 for weather surveillance[6].Japan has incorporated weather-related education from the grade fourth (Six years of elementary along with three years of middle education) (DER) (Kimura, 2016). Added to it, Sendai is a first model disaster-resistant city in the world developed in Japan (TPR). Japan government, as well as the insurance industry, has been participating in green funding, for instance, Dai-Ichi Life and Japan Post Insurance have funded solar energy project of cost US$884 million. Japan Ministry of Environment Announced the Finance initiative of developing low carbon society in July 2013(GFR). Recently, Japan has also declared guidelines on disclosure of risk exposure information.

Underwriting Stage

Since Japan is frequently exposed to mega earthquakes, Earthquake Insurance Act was promulgated in 1966. As per this act, earthquake insurance is the part of the fire insurance policy but, it is not mandatory. However, the Japan government has provisions of tax deduction to promote insurance buying against earthquake risk. For instance, national level authority allows a maximum of 50,000-yen tax deduction whereas local authority allows a tax deduction of 25,000 yen from inhabitant's tax liabilities[7].Insurance firms in Japan are engaged in educating customers to reduce losses because there are price regulation and competition in Japan (Sato & Seki, 2010). Japan has mandatory provisions of capital allocation catastrophic risk.

Post-Disaster Stage

In Japan, there are comprehensive post-disaster regulations for disaster aids (Special Financial Aid), relief program, tax moratorium. Most of these laws are implemented by local agencies such as NGOs and local communities work which, in turn. Reduces the chance of charity hazard (Umeda,2013). Japan's integrated insurance model is very close to the concept of Isolated Policy Model described below.

ITALY INTEGRATED REGULATORY FRAMEWORK FOR DISASTER INSURANCE

Pre-Disaster Stage

Contrary to Japan, Italy has low insurance penetration, and there are not regulations and provisions related to ex-ante disaster preparedness (Gizzi et al., 2015). Poor infrastructure and inadequate building codes have worsened the situation of disaster insurance markets in Italy. Though there are significant provisions for disaster risk education on a professional level, there is no primary and secondary curriculum available for disaster risk education[8].

Underwriting Stage

Recently, the Italian government has come up with a set of actions for developing non-life insurance markets particularly for extreme events by allowing 22.5% tax relief on the premiums, tax allowance on the premium with a scaling system, and local tax relief scheme on buying insurance products (Gizzi et al., 2015).

Post-Disaster Stage

In Italy, most of the relief comes from the state-backed limited assistance programs, and the government provides it in an ad hoc way by framing post-disaster provisions. Italy has provision for post-disaster tax exemption and post-disaster PPP in rehabilitation. After huge losses due to disasters, Italy has started focusing on post-disaster town planning and seismic isolation technologies. These are taken into policy design to reduce disaster causalities and preserve cultural heritage. In Italy, there is a visible charity hazard because of high post-disaster government participation (Gizzi et al., 2015).

CANADA INTEGRATED REGULATORY FRAMEWORK FOR DISASTER INSURANCE

Pre-Disaster Stage

In Canada, there has been significant insured damage of $4.9 billion during the year 2016. Therefore, Canadian government has incorporated many disaster mitigation measures such as land zoning (ZCR), implementation of structural codes for buildings (BCR), codes for raising homes in disaster-prone areas, burying of electrical cables to prevent ice build-up, disaster mitigation public awareness programs,

National Alert Aggregation and Dissemination (NAAD) for early-stage disaster warning(INR), tornado safe rooms to minimize the losses due to natural hazard(EMR)(Public Safety Canada, 2015).However, Canada has no nationally adopted disaster risk education curriculum for schools. However, SRI guidelines are applicable in Canada since 2008(GFR).

Under-Writing Stage

Canadian insurance regulations are uniform and do not vary according to the provincial regulations as they follow OSFI guidelines. The provincial role is to implement and supervise the regulations. This, in turn, creates uniformity in the insurance industry. Risk models are based on market forces which creates competition among firms for the price. Regarding regulation on Minimum Capital Adequacy, they have a fixed range of 100% to 150% (Sharara, Hardy, & Saunders, 2010). However, there is not any fixed provision of catastrophic risk reserves. However, among G-7 nations, Canada is the only country where there is no formal risk sharing mechanism. The Canadian insurance industry is capitalized to bear the loss amounted $30 billion which is sufficiently large. However, any disaster loss in excess of$30 billion may cause massive bankruptcies in Canada (CCIR, 2017). Price is not regulated in the Canadian insurance industry. In terms of earthquake insurance, it is available as an "add-on" cover with higher levels of deductibles. Government subsidies against natural disasters for homeowners are not available but, the same is available for farm insurance against weather risk.

Post-Disaster Stage

In terms of post-disaster mitigation efforts, Canada has been working on Emergency Management Framework since 2007, and losses due to disasters are being managed locally by municipalities and communities (Public Safety Canada, 2015). Canada, there are comprehensive post-disaster guidelines available (Public Safety Canada, 2007). Insurance industry invests in consumer awareness programs to mitigate losses. It also participates with local municipalities to bring the Shake Zone earthquake simulator (IBC, 2017). Also, ABC's Community Assistance Mobile Pavilion (CAMP) provides onsite insurance related information to consumers. Insurers in Canada prepares training programs for their employees to deal with the claim related to natural disasters (CCIR, 2017).

GERMANY INTEGRATED REGULATORY FRAMEWORK FOR DISASTER INSURANCE

Pre-Disaster Stage

In Germany, the formal disaster education system is not available (Karutz, 2013). According to Article 30 of Germany's Basic Law and 70ff, in Germany, individual states are responsible for a disaster prevention program. However, in case of big emergency, federal ministries such as Federal Ministry of Food and Agriculture, Federal Ministry of Defence, Federal Ministry of Health, Federal Ministry of Transport and Digital Infrastructure, Federal Ministry of Environment, and Natural Conservation Building and Nuclear Safety also participate in disaster mitigation programs. To coordinate among these ministries, there is an Inter-ministerial (Crisis Management) Coordination Group (IntMinKoGr).

On the other hand, insurers actively participate in the development of disaster-related government policies (Surminski, and Thieken, 2017). In Germany, the government has developed flood zones during 2002-2004(ZCR). The German government has its 'Climate Action Plan' in preparation for COP22 in Marrakesh which, in turn, supports German policy stand on Green Funding (GFR)[9].Early disaster warnings are provide by the Federal Ministry of Transport and Digital Infrastructure, and "Kompass Naturgefahren" is web-based disaster information network(INR). There is no direct information available on regulations for disaster resilient infrastructure. However, there have been mandatory regulatory guidelines for building codes for construction of buildings since 1955(BCR) (Grünthal, Bosse, &Stromeyer, 2014).The provision of compulsory insurance is not implemented in Germany even after a lengthy debate in parliament in 2003.

Underwriting Stage

In Germany, insurance penetration is comparatively low. Therefore, in 2015, the German government has initiated a climate risk reduction program which is made to bring more people under insurance cover. However, even after putting many policy efforts, the role of the insurance industry could not get as much prominence as it got in the case of France and the United States. The federal government has provisions for tax relief for private insurance firms for selling extreme events insurance cover to reduce the economic burden(TRR) (Keskitalo, Carina, Gregor Vulturius, and Peter Scholten, 2014).

Post-Disaster Strategy

No post-disaster federal regulation decides the extent of disaster aid and the definition of disaster victims.

THE UK AND INTEGRATED REGULATORY FRAMEWORK FOR DISASTER INSURANCE

Pre-Disaster Stage

In 2007, two third of overall losses in the UK were occurred due to floods. The structural measures, such as building codes (BCR), Zone codes (ZCR), and structures for preventing water into the house, are important policy parameters. The earlier mitigation plan has largely focused on coastal flooding. However, the new action-plan has focused on surface water and groundwater flooding(TPR). The UK Government allocated £2.3 billion in preventive programs against flood from 2015 to 2021 (HM Government, 2016). In the UK, there are flood monitoring stations which regularly check the water levels of river and sea (INR)[10]. Socially responsible investment- (SRI) legislation has been implemented in the UK since 2000(GFR). The preventive measure such as flood risk monitoring and risk warning programs in the U.K. were taken under the tremendous pressure of insurance companies (HM Government, 2016), disaster education after many flood incidences (Preston, 2012). Insurance industry actively participates in disaster awareness campaigns (INR) (Surminski & Thieken, 2017).

Underwriting Stage

In France and the UK, flood insurance is compulsory (CIR). In the UK, the private insurance market for a natural disaster (particularly for flood risk) is well developed.

Post-Disaster Stage

As per the central government document available on the (website: www.gov.uk, updated on 23 April 2013), the UK policy to respond to emergencies are divided into three levels. Out of which level third is meant for responding to emergencies of catastrophic nature. However, considering the unpredictable nature of the disaster, there is not a well-defined action plan available in this document.

THE US INTEGRATED REGULATORY FRAMEWORK FOR DISASTER INSURANCE

Pre-Disaster Stage

As per the National Association of Insurance Commissioners (NAIC) and CERES, insurance regulators in California, Connecticut, Minnesota, New York, and Washington disclose the climate-related vulnerability to their survey. Though, in the US, there is no provision of disaster education for school curriculum, disaster zones, building construction codes, disaster information network, and green findings have been focused adequately.

Underwriting Stage

In the United States, "9/11" terrorist attack, has changed the landscape of disaster management at large. The US government recognized responsibility and passed the Terrorism Risk Insurance Act of 2002(Michel-Kerjan, 2004). In the US, there is no provision of compulsory insurance for disaster risk. The US government has decided against the background of a sudden surge in prices of extreme events insurance. At the time, insurers were skeptical of providing insurance cover even at higher premiums (Jaffee & Russell, 2003) and thus, the industry was not able to supply coverage at the required level. Before "9/11", Hurricane Andrew has changed the market with the proposition of securitization of extreme event risk. Market-linked securities had grown significantly, except in 2007, when there was a little decline in the cat bonds demand due to the problem of basis risk, and financial crisis in 2008. However, it has restored the growth rate after 2007 (Bouriaux & MacMinn, 2009).

Post-Disaster Stage

In terms of post-disaster recovery, again "9/11" has impacted the recovery and restoration regulation at large in the US. FEMA has struggled a lot while dealing with the losses of Hurricanes Hugo, Andrew, and Katrina, the terrorist attacks of "9/11", and Superstorm Sandy. In March 2003, a cabinet-level Department of Homeland Security was created along with 22 federal agencies to deal the natural disasters. In the US generally, the individual state takes care of the losses, but when the losses surpass a minimum threshold, the losses will come under the purview of federal governments. The Gulf Opportunity Zone Act of 2005 is designated for the areas devastated by Hurricanes. The American Red Cross is recognized by the Congress under Title 36 to have an official relationship with government (it is not a government body). The Red Cross collects charitable public funds at the event of calamities and disburses it as per the requirement.

RESULT AND DISCUSSION

Based on the above assessment, we found following integrated regulatory models for disaster risk insurance. However, the US model of Integrated Insurance Model is mostly driven by market factors with policy intervention at regular intervals.

Isolated Best Policy Model or Type I: In this model, both regulators and insurers separately deal the natural disasters, but regulators at pre and post stages of disasters have state of the art policies. In this model (Figure 2), like all the other industries, the role of regulator for the sector is limited to supervisory activities — for example, Japan.

Sustainable Policy Model or Type II: In this model, policy makers are partially prepared for pre and post stages of a disaster. In this model, the role of insurance firm participation is important for the development of sound insurance markets. Such models are prominently visible in France, the UK, Germany, and Canada.

Spiral Policy Model or Type III: In spiral policy model, the pre-disaster focus of governments is nearly absent. In this model, regulators focus excessively on post-disaster relief. They have poor post-disaster policies. In this model, insurance markets are also poorly developed. Therefore, industry influence on the policy formulation is not profound. In other words, this is a weak coordination model. Such a model is prominently visible in the context of Italy.

As per hypotheses of this chapter, natural disaster insurance markets will develop if all the three stages regulations are favorable for every stage of insurance market development. However, contrary to our hypotheses, we found that except for the Spiral Policy Model, all the other models are favorable for the development of disaster insurance markets.

Figure 2. Isolated best policy model or type I

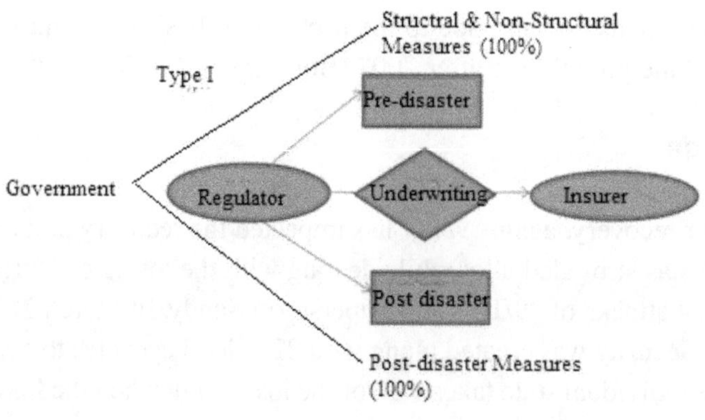

Figure 3. Sustainable policy model or type II

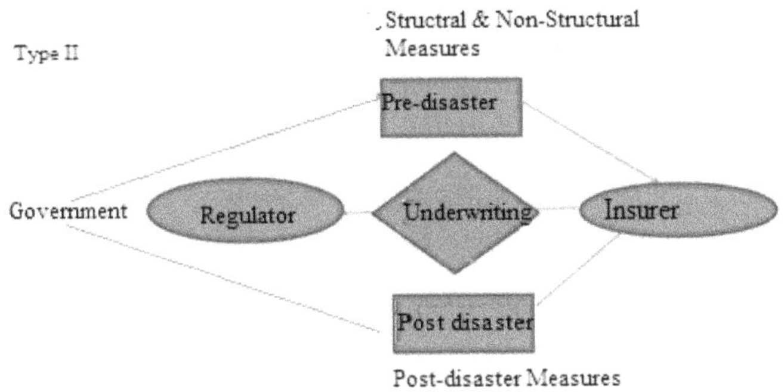

Figure 4. Spiral policy model or type III

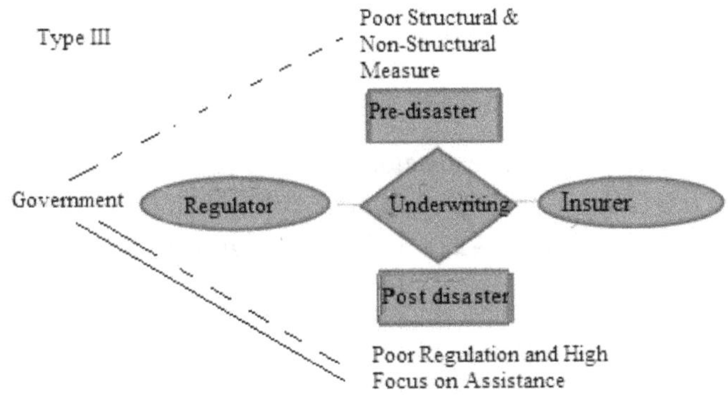

CONCLUSION

We found that there are three types of models based on our result. Based on our analysis if markets are well developed, it is possible to avoid constant regulatory interventions. However, regular supervision of market factors will still be an essential requirement for the well-functioning insurance markets. On the other hand, if markets are underdeveloped, there are two types of models that can work, i.e., isolated best policy models or sustainable policy model. The isolated best policy model is good in the countries where every aspect of the market is strictly controlled, and the effectiveness of law enforcement is quite good. This model is good for those countries where there are proactive laws. Whereas sustainable policy model is good for the countries where there neither fully market oriented economy nor strictly controlled markets exist. In these economies laws are reactive to problems.

REFERENCES

Aloisi, S. (2009). *Italy earthquake exposes poor building standards.* Thomson Reuters.

Andjelkovic, I. (2001). *Guidelines on non-structural measures in urban flood management. International Hydrological Programme (IHP), United Nations Educational, Scientific and Cultural Organization.* UNESCO.

Aoki, N. (2018). Sequencing and combining participation in urban planning: The case of tsunami-ravaged Onagawa Town, Japan. *Cities (London, England)*, *72*, 226–236. doi:10.1016/j.cities.2017.08.020

Baluch, F., Stanley, M., & Chris, P. (2011). Insurance, systemic risk and the financial crisis. *The Geneva Papers on Risk and Insurance. Issues and Practice*, *36*(1), 126–163. doi:10.1057/gpp.2010.40

Birkland, T. A. (1996). Natural disasters as focusing events: Policy communities and political response. *International Journal of Mass Emergencies and Disasters*, *14*(2), 221–243.

Birkland, T. A., & Megan, K. W. (2014). *Focusing events in disasters and development*. Cham: Springer. doi:10.1007/978-3-319-04468-2_3

Bouriaux, S., & Richard, M. (2009). Securitization of Catastrophe Risk: New Developments in Insurance-Linked Securities and Derivatives. *Journal of Insurance Issues*, *32*, 1–34.

Boyle, J., Cunningham, M., & Dekens, J. (2013). *Climate Change Adaptation and Canadian Infrastructure. International Institute for Sustainable Development*. Winnipeg, Canada: IISD.

Canadian Council of Insurance Regulators. (2017). Retrieved from https://www.ccir-ccrra.org/

Couroux, M., & Outreville, J. F. (1992). The development of insurance markets of developing countries: UNCTAD's activities in the field of human resources development. *The Geneva Papers on Risk and Insurance. Issues and Practice*, *17*(2), 232–243. doi:10.1057/gpp.1992.13

Coviello, A. (2008). *The impact of ICT in the insurance industry: The role of Customer Relationship Management*. Academic Press.

Dolce, M. (2012, September). The Italian national seismic prevention program. *15th world conference in earthquake engineering*.

Ericson, R., & Doyle, A. (2004). Catastrophe risk, insurance, and terrorism. *Economy and Society*, *33*(2), 135–173. doi:10.1080/0308514042000225716

Gizzi, F. T., Potenza, M. R., & Zotta, C. (2015). The insurance market of natural hazards for residential properties in Italy. *Open Journal of Earthquake Research*, *5*(01), 35–61. doi:10.4236/ojer.2016.51004

Grace, M. F., Klein, R. W., & Kleindorfer, P. R. (2004). Homeowners insurance with bundled catastrophe coverage. *The Journal of Risk and Insurance*, *71*(3), 351–379. doi:10.1111/j.0022-4367.2004.00094.x

Grünthal, G., Bosse, C., & Stromeyer, D. (2014, May). Building Code Related Seismic Hazard Analyses of Germany and their Relation to SHARE. In *Seismic Hazard Harmonization in Europe (SHARE): DGEB-Workshop* (Vol. 27, pp. 25-41). Academic Press.

Gutmann, A. (2011). *On risk and disaster: Lessons from Hurricane Katrina*. University of Pennsylvania Press.

Herweijer, C., Ranger, N., & Ward, R. E. (2009). Adaptation to climate change: Threats and opportunities for the insurance industry. *The Geneva Papers on Risk and Insurance. Issues and Practice*, *34*(3), 360–380. doi:10.1057/gpp.2009.13

Holzheu, T., & Turner, G. (2018). The Natural Catastrophe Protection Gap: Measurement, root causes and ways of addressing underinsurance for extreme events. *The Geneva Papers on Risk and Insurance. Issues and Practice*, *43*(1), 37–71. doi:10.105741288-017-0075-y

Hussels, S., Ward, D., & Zurbruegg, R. (2005). Stimulating the demand for insurance. *Risk Management & Insurance Review*, *8*(2), 257–278. doi:10.1111/j.1540-6296.2005.00059.x

Insurance Bureau of Canada. (2017). Retrieved from http://www.ibc.ca/on/

Jaffee, D., & Russell, T. (2003). Markets under stress: The case of extreme event insurance. *Economics for an Imperfect World: Essays in Honor of Joseph E. Stiglitz*, 35-52.

Jametti, M., & von Ungern-Sternberg, T. (2004). *Disaster insurance or a disastrous insurance-Natural disaster insurance in France*. Academic Press.

Jouannic, G., Crozier, D., Chloé, T. D. M., Kolli, Z., Arki, F., Matagne, E., & Bomperin, L. (2016). Post-disaster recovery: how to encourage the emergency of economic and social dynamics to improve resilience? In *E3S Web of Conferences* (Vol. 7, p. 17004). EDP Sciences. doi:10.1051/e3sconf/20160717004

Kelly, M., & Kleffner, A. (2006). The distribution of property/liability insurance in Canada: Costs and market structure. *Journal of Insurance Issues*, 51–70.

Keskitalo, E. C. H., Vulturius, G., & Scholten, P. (2014). Adaptation to climate change in the insurance sector: Examples from the UK, Germany and the Netherlands. *Natural Hazards*, *71*(1), 315–334. doi:10.100711069-013-0912-7

Kimura, T. (2016, November 2). School Safety at Scale: Lessons from Japan. *World Bank*. Retrieved from http://www.worldbank.org/en/news/feature/2016/11/02/school-safety-at-scale-lessons-from-japan

Kitagawa, K., Preston, J., & Chadderton, C. (2017). Preparing for disaster: A comparative analysis of education for critical infrastructure collapse. *Journal of Risk Research*, *20*(11), 1450–1465. doi:10.1080/13669877.2016.1178661

Kunreuther, H. (2015). The role of insurance in reducing losses from extreme events: The need for public–private partnerships. *The Geneva Papers on Risk and Insurance. Issues and Practice*, *40*(4), 741–762. doi:10.1057/gpp.2015.14

Kwon, W. J. (2010). An analysis of organizational, market and socio-cultural factors affecting the supply of insurance and other financial services by microfinance institutions in developing economies. *The Geneva Papers on Risk and Insurance. Issues and Practice*, *35*(1), 130–160. doi:10.1057/gpp.2009.32

Lamond, J., & Penning-Rowsell, E. (2014). The robustness of flood insurance regimes given changing risk resulting from climate change. *Climate Risk Management*, *2*, 1–10. doi:10.1016/j.crm.2014.03.001

Linnerooth-Bayer, J., Warner, K., Bals, C., Höppe, P., Burton, I., Loster, T., & Haas, A. (2009). Insurance, developing countries and climate change. *The Geneva Papers on Risk and Insurance. Issues and Practice*, *34*(3), 381–400. doi:10.1057/gpp.2009.15

Mal, S., Singh, R. B., Huggel, C., & Grover, A. (2018). Introducing linkages between climate change, extreme events, and disaster risk reduction. In Climate Change, Extreme Events and Disaster Risk Reduction (pp. 1-14). Springer. doi:10.1007/978-3-319-56469-2_1

Mauro, P. (2012, Dec. 13). Transport and climate change: To curb carbon emissions, focus on the new consumers on the move. *Business Standard*. Retrieved from https://www.business-standard.com/article/opinion/paolo-mauro-transport-and-climate-change-115121200761_1.html

Mills, E. (2005). Insurance in a climate of change. *Science*, *309*(5737), 1040–1044. doi:10.1126cience.1112121 PMID:16099975

Mills, E. (2009). A global review of insurance industry responses to climate change. *The Geneva Papers on Risk and Insurance. Issues and Practice*, *34*(3), 323–359. doi:10.1057/gpp.2009.14

Okura, M. (2007). Coopetitive strategies of Japanese insurance firms a game-theory approach. *International Studies of Management & Organization*, *37*(2), 53–69. doi:10.2753/IMO0020-8825370203

Okura, M., & Yanase, N. (2014). *New Challenges to Broadening Undergraduate Risk Management & Insurance Education in Japan: Effective Use of Seminar Classes on a Nationwide Scale*. Academic Press.

Outreville, J. F. (1992). The relationship between insurance, financial development and market structure in developing countries. *Unctad Review*, *3*, 53–69.

Poontirakul, P., Brown, C., Noy, I., Seville, E., & Vargo, J. (2016). *The role of commercial insurance in post-disaster recovery: Quantitative evidence from the 2011 Christchurch earthquake*. Academic Press.

Priest, S. J., Clark, M. J., & Treby, E. J. (2005). Flood insurance: The challenge of the uninsured. *Area*, *37*(3), 295–302. doi:10.1111/j.1475-4762.2005.00633.x

Public Safety Canada. (2007). *Emergency Management*. Retrieved from https://www.publicsafety.gc.ca/cnt/rsrcs/pblctns/dprtmntl-prfrmnc-rprt-2015-16/index-en.aspx#a07

Public Safety Canada. (2015). *Emergency Management*. Retrieved from https://www.publicsafety.gc.ca/cnt/rsrcs/pblctns/dprtmntl-prfrmnc-rprt-2015-16/index-en.aspx#a17

Raviv, A. (1979). The design of an optimal insurance policy. *The American Economic Review*, *69*(1), 84–96.

Re, S. (2016). *Sustained insurance sector growth in 2017 largely based on demand from emerging markets*. London: Swiss Re.

Sato, M., & Seki, M. (2010). Sustainable business, sustainable planet—A Japanese insurance perspective. *The Geneva Papers on Risk and Insurance. Issues and Practice*, *35*(2), 325–335. doi:10.1057/gpp.2010.7

Sato, T. (2009). Global financial crisis-Japan's experience and policy response. In Remarks at the Asia Economic Policy Conference organized by the Federal Reserve Bank of San Francisco Santa Barbara, CA, United States October (Vol. 20, p. 2009). Academic Press.

Schäfer, H. (2018). Germany: The 'Greenhorn' in the Green Finance Revolution. *Environment*, *60*(1), 18–27. doi:10.1080/00139157.2018.1397472

Schoenmaker, D., & Sass, J. (2016). Cross-border insurance in Europe: Challenges for supervision. *The Geneva Papers on Risk and Insurance. Issues and Practice*, *41*(3), 351–377. doi:10.1057/gpp.2015.35

Schwarcz, D., & Schwarcz, S. L. (2014). Regulating systemic risk in insurance. *The University of Chicago Law Review. University of Chicago. Law School*, 1569–1640.

Schwarze, R., Schwindt, M., Weck-Hannemann, H., Raschky, P., Zahn, F., & Wagner, G. G. (2011). Natural hazard insurance in Europe: Tailored responses to climate change are needed. *Environmental Policy and Governance*, *21*(1), 14–30. doi:10.1002/eet.554

Sharara, I., Hardy, M., & Saunders, D. (2010). *A comparative analysis of US, Canadian and Solvency II capital adequacy requirements in life insurance*. Society of Actuaries.

Silva, K. T. (2009). 'Tsunami Thirdwave' and the politics of disaster management in Sri Lanka. *NorskGeografiskTidsskrift-Norwegian Journal of Geography*, *63*(1), 61–72. doi:10.1080/00291950802712145

Stigler, G. J. (1971). The theory of economic regulation. *The Bell Journal of Economics and Management Science*, *2*(1), 3–21. doi:10.2307/3003160

Surminski, S., & Thieken, A. H. (2017). Promoting flood risk reduction: The role of insurance in Germany and England. *Earth's Future*, *5*(10), 979–1001. doi:10.1002/2017EF000587

Takao, K., Motoyoshi, T., Sato, T., Fukuzondo, T., Seo, K., & Ikeda, S. (2004). Factors determining residents' preparedness for floods in modern megalopolises: The case of the Tokai flood disaster in Japan. *Journal of Risk Research*, *7*(7-8), 775–787. doi:10.1080/1366987031000075996

Tsubota, Y. T., & Yukimasa. (2017). EMS Annual Meeting Abstracts. In *Japan & Bangladesh's Compulsory Education of Weather, Climate and Climate Change*. Yokohama-shi: PADECO Co. Ltd.

Umeda, S. (2013). *Japan: Responses to the Great East Japan Earthquake of 2011*. The Law Library of Congress, Global Legal Research Center.

UNICEF. (2012). *Disaster Risk Reduction in in School Curricula: Case Studies from Thirty Countries*. UNICEF.

UNISDR. (2013). *National progress report on the implementation of the Hyogo Framework for Action (2013-2015)*. UNISDR.

Van Schoubroeck, C. (1997). Legislation and practice concerning natural disasters and insurance in some European countries. *The Geneva Papers on Risk and Insurance. Issues and Practice*, *22*(2), 238–267. doi:10.1057/gpp.1997.19

Wang, W., Shao, Q., Yang, T., Peng, S., Xing, W., Sun, F., & Luo, Y. (2013). Quantitative assessment of the impact of climate variability and human activities on runoff changes: A case study in four catchments of the Haihe River basin, China. *Hydrological Processes*, *27*(8), 1158–1177. doi:10.1002/hyp.9299

KEY TERMS AND DEFINITIONS

Disaster Stage: The state when national regulators and policymakers formulate policy stimulus for the development of the insurance industry. This stage can also be juxtaposed to the underwriting stage of the insurance industry.

G-7 Countries: The world's seven most powerful industrialized countries - the US, Japan, Germany, the UK, France, Italy, and Canada.

National Regulation: In the present context, we are projecting those national level regulations which are either brought to stop the losses of natural disaster or brought to restore the situation after natural disasters.

Post-Disaster Stage: The state when disaster has already occurred, and the government is involved in rescue activities. This stage also involves the period between the occurrence of a disaster to rehabilitation and reconstruction for normalizing the lives of people. At this stage, the insurance industry processes the claims for insured disaster victims.

Pre-Disaster Stage: The preventive state for stopping the losses occurred due to natural disasters. This stage also incorporates regulation regarding stopping the climate change problem.

Sectoral Regulation: By sectoral regulation, we mean the insurance regulations of any kind.

ENDNOTES

1 The law of 22 July 1987/Article L125.2 of the Environmental Code.

2 Ministry of Education, Ministry of Sustainable Development, and Ministry of Research.

3 International Monetary Fund, 2013/https://www.imf.org/external/pubs/ft/scr/2013/cr13181.pdf.

4 http://www.unil.ch/de/files/live/sites/de/files/working-papers/04.12.pdf

5 Disaster Countermeasure Act 1961.

6 Japan Meteorological Agency, 2015.

7 https://www.mof.go.jp/english/financial_system/earthquake_insurance/outline_of_earthquake_insurance.html.

8 National progress report on the implementation of the Hyogo Framework for Action (2013-2015)

9 https://www.bwi.uni-stuttgart.de/abt3/files/forschung/BF7_GreenFinance_Banks_Germany_2017.pdf.

10 https://flood-warning-information.service.gov.uk/river-and-sea-levels.

Chapter 11
Biodiesel Companies and Institutions in Mexico

José G. Vargas-Hernández
University of Guadalajara, Mexico

Juan José Esparza López
University of Guadalajara, Mexico

ABSTRACT

The objective of the chapter is to analyze the role of the institutions in the biodiesel industry in order to know if there is a relationship with the quality and maturity of the same with the ventures. Starting from a literary review, the framework of the current situation is identified, covering aspects related to formal institutions, laws, rules, regulatory bodies, and the theory that supports the relationship between institutions and entrepreneurship. It is thus concluded that the institutions in Mexico have increased their maturity and incentive to increase the number of producers and distributors of biodiesel, thus taking advantage of the growing market.

INTRODUCTION

The current situation of a shortage of natural resources requires the innovations and ventures in production sectors that help to reverse the situation, so the research seeks the stability of markets that achieve competitiveness and preservation of the environment.

The biodiesel market is in constant growth. By 2023 consumption is expected to reach more than 40 million liters around the world. According to OECD (2017) information, the United States, as well as European countries and some countries of South America such as Argentina, Brazil, Colombia and Chile stand out to have quickly added in this new project of an economy with a better vision of the preservation of the environment. This new change in the consumption trends of the people generates new markets that can be exploited by developed country economies as emerging countries that have the necessary resources for the production and supply of biodiesel.

DOI: 10.4018/978-1-5225-8547-3.ch011

Entrepreneurship is given by several factors, some of which may be the best scenarios, such as unique opportunities, innovations that meet specific needs that were not counted in the past. These types of entrepreneurship are what the countries need because they get the most number of benefits, job creation, and sustainable economic growth. The boom in the demand for biodiesel at the global level could be one of those opportunities that must be taken advantage of. However, the opportunity to recognize a growing market alone does not ensure success because the planning and knowledge of the terrain in which entrepreneurs seek to enter, are flaws that could be had. Being a relatively new market few are those who have all the necessary information to say know or be experts in the competitive bioenergy market.

For this reason, formal institutions such as laws or bodies that govern the conduct of industry can be a tool that helps entrepreneurs to have a delimited vision of the actions that are possible to carry out, which can be observed as a knowledge which is transferred from the institutions to the entrepreneurs that helps them to generate success. In addition to the existence of formal institutions with sufficient quality and maturity as can be easy to apply legal frameworks and regulatory bodies with good planning and implementation of actions, such as aid in reducing taxes. This may provide financial support and development on the part of the researchers in a specific line of research, which serves to give rise to a greater degree of entrepreneurship in a specific sector that, has all the incentives.

The background check showed that there was a clear concern about the lack of rules in the game in this sector that made the market in Mexico unable to consolidate. However, there were already bodies that were looking to develop enough regulations to clarify the path of those interested in entering this new market that was emerging at a fast pace. Therefore, in this study, a theoretical analysis will be carried out, comparing the evolution of the biodiesel production companies in Mexico, in order to determine if there is a relationship with the formal institutions and they will solve the inefficiency that was seen in this sector in 2008.

BACKGROUND OF THE PROBLEM

The Mexican government promotes the production in several plants, their distribution and consumption of biofuels and among them biodiesel that promotes the use of clean and renewable energies as alternatives to fossil fuels as a response in a time when climate change has become in priority. Biodiesel is a mixture of monoalkyl esters of fatty acids that is obtained through processes such as the "transesterification" of industrial waste oils and fats. Biodiesel is a mixture of methyl esters of fatty acids that can replace diesel and is obtained from the reaction of vegetable oils or fats with methanol. Glycerin is obtained as a byproduct. Biodiesel is used mainly in Europe and the USA in mixtures with 5% or 20% diesel (B5, B20) or as pure biodiesel (B100). In Brazil and Argentina B5 is used.

In Mexico, in 2003 the Prospective of the use of bioenergy in Mexico was designed, highlighting that the infrastructure that Pemex uses to produce diesel can be used, considering that diesel engines would require minor adjustments to use pure biodiesel. In addition, it is considered that there has been an increase in the cultivation of oil producing plants in tropical and temperate climates and that there are fiscal incentives and subsidies to promote biodiesel. In 2007, a first study was conducted on the possibilities of bioethanol and biodiesel as transportation fuels in Mexico (SENER / BID / GTZ (Edit.), 2007).

The Investment Plan of the Clean Technology Fund (CTF) for Mexico was approved by the fiduciary committee in 2009. On June 18, 2009, the Regulation of the Law of the Federal Government was published in the Official Gazette of the Federation (DOF). Promotion and development of Bioenergetics (LPDB), which entrusts the Inter-Secretarial Commission of Bioenergetics to establish, review and evaluate a strategy to develop the input market ... and promote energy security, food security and sovereignty and environmental sustainability. In 2009 Biotop, which was a project for the evaluation of technical opportunities and research needs for Latin America, mentioned how the Mexican regulatory framework for the promotion of biofuels was at an early stage and was still under development. Limiting for biodiesel companies in Mexico could be due to formal institutions that did not work in the best way.

Among the major limitations of the development of production, distribution and consumption of biodiesel is the performance of formal and informal institutions of the Mexican market, mainly in aspects related to the existence of limited information, energy legislation in transition processes, structures of market, prices, costs, etc.The knowledge of this failure in the Mexican market seeks to be solved as Rembio in 2009 mentions that there were no specific promotion policies for the second generation of biofuels, but these are likely to be included in a new biofuels research program, which will be developed by The National Council and Technology (CONACYT).

The production of biodiesel is a very complex task for companies, which register a high rate of failures. To mention some companies that have failed, is the Plant in Cadereyta, Nuevo León, established in 2005 by GrupoEnergéticos and the Itesm Campus Monterrey, with an annual installed capacity of 18 thousand cubic meters that produced biodiesel from animal fats and vegetable oils and that stopped operating in 2011. In Lázaro Cárdenas, Michoacán, in 2007 a plant attached to a vegetable oil factory was installed, with a capacity of 9 thousand cubic meters of annual production of biodiesel from castor oil, but its shortage caused it to close a year later. The Institute of Bioenergetics of Chiapas installed a biodiesel production plant in 2010 from Jatropha but stopped operating in 2011 due to lack of seed.

In 2013, the Secretariat of Energy developed the Mexican Atlas of Biomass, with information on the production potentials of the different types of biomass that could be used for energy purposes (Riegelhaupt, Odenthal & Janeiro 2016).

The biomass resources used as inputs to produce biodiesel, according to their origin and technology used for processing, are divided into three generations. Riegelhaupt, Odenthal, and Janeiro (2016) develop this characterization considering that the first generation resources are fatty acids, contained in the lipids synthesized by plants and animals, mainly, the vegetable oils of the seeds and oleaginous fruits. The second-generation plants are plant lignocellulosic, residual or cultivated, whose carbohydrates can be transformed to C10 to C12 alkanes by various technological ways, such as Fischer-Tropsch synthesis, hydrolysis followed by reform or isomerization and hydrotreatment.

The third generation is culture of microorganisms selected or modified to produce certain biodiesel precursor molecules, such as lipids and fatty acids. The current degree of uncertainty about the inputs and production processes of 3rd generation biodiesel, its costs and technological viability is very high; for this reason, there are no certain or probable values to perform the necessary calculations and to be able to formulate production scenarios and prices of 3rd generation biodiesel.

The potential for production of first generation biodiesel from oilseed crops is growing. However, the use of animal fats as an input for the production of biodiesel is technically feasible for the production of biofuels (See figure 1).

Figure 1. Production of biodiesel
Source: Tapia (2017). Property of Milenio, S. A. de C. V

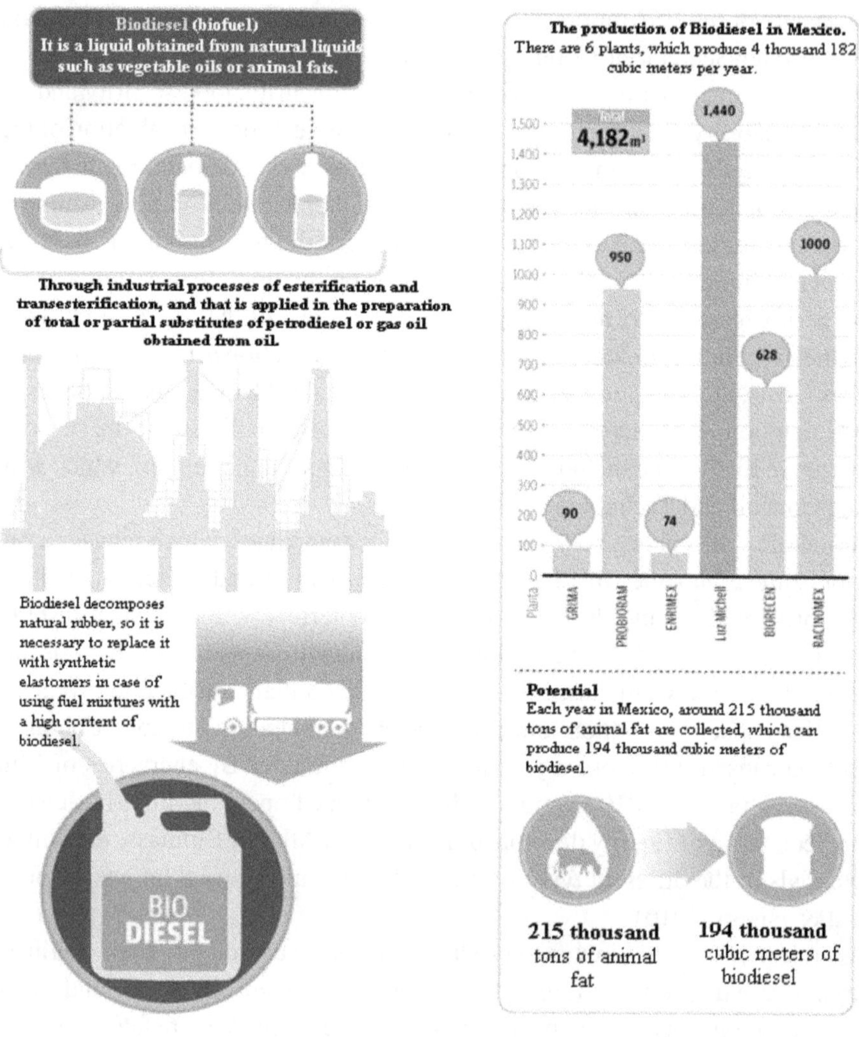

Biodiesel is produced in Mexico with crude vegetable oils whose commercial production has not been able to be sustained due to the lack of competitive costs of the inputs or with used oils and fats that gives rise to a value chain. In this chain of value, according to Riegelhaupt, Odenthal and Janeiro (2016), several agents intervene and participate, such as the producers of the raw material that are the ones that use the oils for the kitchen, such as the traces, greaseries, processors of pork derivatives, etc., whose practices delimit the levels and quality of recovery; harvesters of the cooked oil, such as the fat collectors of butcher shops, who can contribute their efficiency in the organization for the collection to reduce the costs, the collectors and processors that collect and refine the used oils, contribute to the conversion, distribution and sale of biodiesel and finally, the biodiesel processors who convert the oils into biodiesel, co-products and waste such as glycerin that they also distribute commercially.

Currently, in Mexico, the agents of both chains operate for the production of biodiesel, mostly informally. The information related to the capacity, type of inputs and processed volume of the companies that operate in the processing and preparation of biodiesel can be obtained from the same companies, but the information related to their marketing processes, prices and customers is unreliable and limited. Riegelhaupt, Odenthal and Janeiro, (2016) reported four companies to collect used cooking oil as the main input for the production of biodiesel:

1. Reoil Mexico collects Used Residual Cooking Oil and produces "Pre TPO" or Pre-technical plant oil that it exports to the European Union where it is processed in two biodiesel plants.
2. MORECO collects used cooking oil and transforms it into biodiesel in three plants installed in Michoacán, Guanajuato and Querétaro.
3. Biofuels de México collects used cooking oil and produces biodiesel in Puebla, Toluca, Cuernavaca, Tlaquepaque, Zapopan, Tonalá, Veracruz, Cordoba, Xalapa, Boca del Rio, Queretaro, Cancun, Playa del Carmen, Chetumal.
4. SOLBEN, from Monterrey, Nuevo León, collects used cooking oil, produces biodiesel, sells biodiesel plants and provides services such as characterization of seeds and oils, technical support, automation and biodiesel quality analysis.

Although used cooking oils have few alternative uses, some authors maintain that there is an informal collection circuit, with operators that filter, discolor and package the recycled oil to sell it as edible oil.

The technical potential for obtaining cooking oils and animal fats to be used as inputs in the production of biodiesel, is only theoretical because there are currently concurrent uses for many of these sources of fats, and in many cases the capacity and willingness to pay of concurrent users would be higher than that of potential biodiesel users. This is the case of animal fats, which have high demand as inputs for soap, food additives, pet food and other end uses. To determine the production potential of biodiesel from animal fats, the use, among others, of chicken fat, beef tallow (bovine fat) and pork fats can be considered. These fats are obtained in the traces, as co-products of the slaughter of animals, and also in plants that reprocess butcher's fats.

Based on official statistics of SAGARPA (2017, 2010), obtained through consultations with the Agrifood and Fisheries Information Service (SIAP) to determine the potential for biodiesel production from current oilseed crops, they are considered to be the most important sources of fatty acids at the global. Seed to oil conversion factors are an average of industrial performance for pressure extraction technology. For soybean and sunflower, two sequential extractions are carried out, the first by pressure and the second by organic solvent. Riegelhaupt, Odenthal and Janeiro (2016) analyze that for the case of those considered in group 1, as new crops, it is integrated by the Mexican pinion (Jatropha curcas) and the castor bean (Ricinuscommunis). Their contributions to the national production of oils are minimal, and their trends are still undefined.

The minor crops considered in group 2, is composed of canola (Brassica rapa) and sunflower (Heliantusannuus). The canola has low yields, but the sunflower has experienced a significant increase in its cultivation and found a market niche of better prices as a specialty. In the third group, considered as dynamic crops, it is integrated by coconut (Cocos nucifera), oil palm (Elaeisguineensis) and soybean (Glycine max), crops that have had a clear tendency to increase the harvested area and / or the production.

The potential of agricultural residues, esquilmos and stubbles considered as the parts of the vegetables, usually stems and leaves that are not removed from the field during the harvest is estimated at 15 million tMS / year. Riegelhaupt, Odenthal and Janeiro, (2016) assume a conversion rate of 0.25 m3 of biodiesel / tMS based on the average of the values reported for pilot plants and plants projected according to the European Biofuels Technology Platform (EBTP, 2016). Assume a technically sustainable production level of about 3.75 million m3 of biodiesel per year. However, the authors consider that this potential is not economically feasible for the production of biodiesel in the short and medium term, since the conversion technologies known as 2nd generation have not yet reached the degree of technical maturity to be applied on a commercial scale.

The largest potential source of woody forest biomass in Mexico as a raw material for second-generation biodiesel is the native forest vegetation. The estimate of sustainable annual production excludes wood of species and qualities that can be used by the sawmill, cellulose and panel industries, and includes only wood that is useful for energy. The total potential national production calculated by Riegelhaupt, Odenthal and Janeiro (2016), counts forests and jungles located less than 3 km from a road, with land slopes of less than 30%, outside protected natural areas and / or areas of high value for the conservation of biodiversity, is 112 million tMS / a, but some 22 million tMS / a currently used as domestic fuel and 3 million tMS / a destined to manufacture charcoal should be deducted.

The net potential is thus about 87 million tMS / a. This potential is found in almost all the states of the country, and its annual harvestable increase ranges from 2.0 to 4.2 tMS / ha / a. It is therefore similar to the harvesting rates of field residues or agricultural residues, but it has the advantage that the growth can be accumulated in cycles of 10 to 15 years, to harvest from 30 to 50 tMS / ha in an operation at the end of each cycle. As with agricultural wastes, Riegelhaupt, Odenthal and Janeiro (2016) argue that the conversion of woody biomass into biodiesel is technically possible, but there are no economically viable industrial processes so far.

For the development of future scenarios for the introduction of biodiesel in Mexico, several elements have to be analyzed along the biofuel value chain, from the production of inputs to the commercialization of the fuel market and including the conversion infrastructure of biofuels. inputs to biodiesel. The level of future penetration of biodiesel in the Mexican fuel market depends on a large number of economic, technological and institutional factors, as well as political decisions. It has been noted in the empirical review that a problem in Mexico for entrepreneurs interested in the renewable energy markets in specific biodiesel is that the institutions are not clear enough in their actions that helps to understand the market.

The SMEs producers of biofuels to survive in the market have to fight against their main competition, the PEMEX emporium, producer and marketer of fossil fuels. However, the excessive increase in the price of gasoline, alternative fuels, such as biodiesel, are becoming more competitive in the market. However, the biggest challenges for SMEs producing biodiesel are marketing processes.

To analyze the demand of the fuel market, the price that buyers would be willing to pay for biodiesel is determined. Biodiesel is a substitute for diesel of fossil origin, and for this reason the existence of demand for biodiesel depends mainly on the reference price of diesel of fossil origin defined as the price before the application of taxes. If biodiesel can be produced (or imported) and marketed at prices lower than the diesel reference price, there will be demand for biodiesel in the market. If, on the other hand, the reference prices of diesel of fossil origin are lower than those of biodiesel, there will be no demand for alternative renewable fuel. If there is no demand for biodiesel in the market, this can be induced through economic and fiscal support policies to achieve a certain level of penetration of biodiesel in the market or, alternatively, determine the market share that can be obtained and sustain with a certain level of spending on support policies.

There is uncertainty about the supply of bioenergy and biofuels based on renewable resources in the market, as a consequence of the lower price of fossil fuels. This situation means that there are few economic incentives to invest in alternative fuel technologies. To make the production, distribution and consumption of biofuels more efficient and cheaper, institutional aspects such as the legal framework and the supply chain must be resolved. If reached by 2030, the greatest impact will be on the capacity to generate a significant reduction in carbon emissions.

The existence of demand for biodiesel in the fuel market is complemented by the evaluation of the evolution of the installed capacity of infrastructure for the conversion of inputs to biodiesel, to determine that it is sufficient to satisfy the demand at all times. Finally, if there is both demands for biodiesel in the market and conversion capacity, it is required to evaluate the availability of inputs as well as their production costs, or import to produce the biodiesel demanded in the market.

DELIMITATION OF THE PROBLEM

Given the growing market for biodiesel consumption and the fact that there are no companies that monopolize production, a solid production base can be created in Mexico to help the country's economic growth. However, no solid evidence has been found to be advanced at the pace that should be.

Considering that natural factors are conducive to the production of the raw material and there is no monopolizing company of production in Mexico, adding that the demand for biodiesel is increasing, it would be expected that by complying with the theory of resources and capabilities and that the industry is not strong, the biodiesel production sector is increasing. This leads to conclude that there is some other factor inhibiting this growth, and the antecedents of the lack of institutions that help the initiatives of productive companies in biodiesel generate the following question:

How have formal institutions impacted the creation of biodiesel producing companies in Mexico?

JUSTIFICATION

As the biodiesel sector is a growing market that demands more liters' year after year, it is an opportunity for Mexico, to consolidate its productive industry and to be competitive worldwide See figure 2).

As can be seen from 2014 consumption has approached the production with its increase of 1454.6 per year in average consumption compared to the 1436 that increases per year on average the production. It is concluded that, if this trend continues, the demand to consume will be higher than the production, which is why it is a moment for there to be ventures in this sector. The estimators of the variations in the independent variable are good estimators because the coefficient of determination (r^2) is greater than .6 which is a parameter that is used to accept.

However, there is concern that institutions have been able to improve the picture, so that enterprises in this sector have a better direction. The Energy Regulatory Commission in (2014) mentions the regulatory area in which it is in charge of energy, in addition to mentioning the institutions that also help

Figure 2. Projection of biodiesel production and consumption from 2013 to 2023
Source: Prepared by the Organization for Economic Co-operation and Development (OECD Stats, 2017).

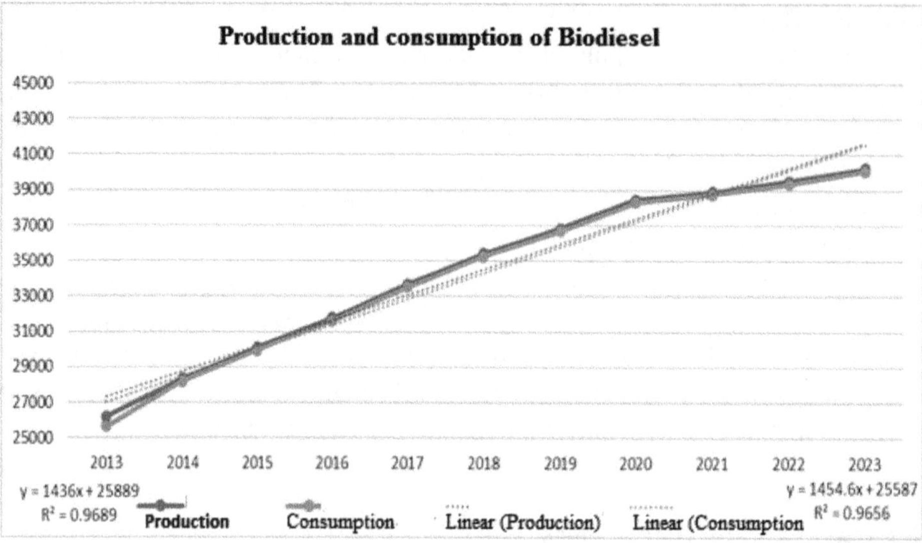

regulate it, such as the National Hydrocarbons Commission (CNH), the Secretary of Energy SENER), the Ministry of Finance and Public Credit (SHCP), the Federal Economic Competition Commission (COFECE) and the Security, Energy and Environment Agency (ASEA).

The objective of the institutions is to create conditions for the efficiency of the energy markets (Energy Regulatory Commission 2015). There is a growth in the regulatory framework of bioenergetics, for which it is necessary to know if the stability in the regulatory framework that has been established has helped in the stability of the market and above all to know if the institutions have favored that there are ventures in biodiesel.

There is a relationship with institutions and entrepreneurs around the world as research in 2015 mentions that "To the extent that the entrepreneur carries out his activity in an environment where the rules of the game are well-defined (i.e. that there is good protection of property rights, that the judicial system functions properly, that governments are stable or that there is no corruption, among other factors), the entrepreneur will enjoy greater security that will positively contribute to the success of his company"(Fuentelzas and Gonzalez, 2015).

THEORETICAL ASSUMPTION

Institutions understood as the limitations to the behavior of an individual or a society, have a very important role in the creation and consolidation of MSME's biodiesel companies concerned. Any entrepreneur or entrepreneur must abide by them for the proper functioning of their organization. Leaving the institutional framework entails tangible and intangible sanctions for the organization. First, the institution is defined as the humanly constructed constraints that structure human interaction (North, 1990). On the other hand, the institutional framework is described by Peng (2012) as the set of formal and informal organizations, which are responsible for regulating the human behavior of people and companies. These are based on three pillars, which are: regulators, normative and cognitive.

As mentioned above, institutions are divided into both formal institutions and informal institutions. Within formal institutions are found the laws, regulations and rules to which every individual who interacts in a society must be subject or otherwise have sanctions, as described in the regulations and laws.As for formal institutions, all MSME's that are established in Mexico will be subject to the Federal Law of mercantile companies. This law is in charge of regulating anonymous companies or not, codes or state laws and municipal regulations on the opening of establishments, which depend on the geographical location where the MSME's biodiesel company is established, as it will change depending on the state or municipality; Income Tax Law (ISR), Single Tax Rate Business Act (IETU), Value Added Tax (VAT), Industrial Property Law, Federal Data Protection Act, Federal Labor Law, Social Security, Law of the Institute of the National Housing Fund for workers. Each law has a particular objective which seeks the regulation of all companies in Mexico.

On the other,side of the institutional framework is informal institutions which include norms, culture and ethics that apply. According to Peng (2012) these formal institutions have two supports: normative and cognitive. The first refers to how it influences the behavior of people and in these case companies, the values, beliefs and actions of relevant actors. On the one hand, of the cognitive pillar, refers to the internal values and beliefs that guide the behavior of individuals and companies. Some of the informal institutions are covered by the culture, beliefs and values of a society and that in some way affects the functioning of MSME's in Mexico.

Culture can be defined as the collective programming of the mind of individuals. This programming or way of thinking distinguishes the members of one group or category of people from another (Hofstede, 2011). Ethics is also part of all informal institutions, defined as "Norms, principles or standards of conduct that govern the individual behavior of organizations" (Vargas, et al. 2005, p.133). Kaushik Basu explains the importance of social norms and culture in the functioning of the economic system, in the first instance it should be understood that all human beings are socially designed to behave in a certain way respecting the social norms that exist (Basu, 2013). All the social norms in which action delimit our behavior and, in this case, delimit the action of the MSME's, each regulation or law limits the possible actions that the companies can carry out.

The central question is what do institutions do? Or why are they so necessary? According to Peng (2012) the role of institutions is to reduce uncertainty because they indicate the legitimate and illegitimate channel, what institutions do is to delimit actions to only acceptable leaving out those outside this range and thus reduce transaction costs. Reducing uncertainty leads to a reduction in transaction costs which are vital for the proper functioning of any economy. The less transaction costs, the economy of a country or a locality function more effectively. Transaction costs were introduced by Coase and defined as the costs of market use (Salgado, 2003). Transaction costs are only the costs of information search, negotiation costs, decision making, formulation costs, and policy implementation. Another definition for transaction costs is the one proposed by Peng (2012) which defines this concept as: the costs associated with economic transactions, or the costs of conducting negotiations.

Institutions, both formal and informal, play a vital role in the reduction of transaction costs, without the existence of these the operation of each transaction in the economy would be much greater. In developed economies transaction costs tend to zero, while in developing economies these costs are much higher. This is explained by the weakness of the institutions, which makes the uncertainty high, which is why it is necessary the signature of contracts between individuals.

In the framework of informal institutions according to Peng (2012) these institutions reduce uncertainty in various ways. The first is related to relationship contracts, known as "personalized exchanges", informal and based mainly on relationships. Robert Putnam's theory of social capital brings much to the subject of reducing transaction costs through informal institutions. Social capital is understood as "the characteristics of social organization, such as networks, norms and trust, which facilitates coordination and cooperation for mutual benefit" (Urteaga, 2013, page 45). These networks of confidence through expected behavior cause confidence among economic agents to be high so that transaction costs will be null because expected behavior.

One concept that helps to understand the importance of informal institutions is "The Culture of Confidence: one can trust the given word because that is the social norm, so people follow it by instinct" (Basu, 2013, p. 167). The main reason why the culture of trust is important is because it is needed to rely on the other's word on multiple occasions it is not feasible to sign any contract at any time and then go to court in if the other party does not comply with the agreement, it is not feasible because of the high costs that the operation will have. That is why the culture of trust between two parties is important.

Another important concept within the theoretical review of formal and informal institutions is institutional transactions, which are defined as major changes that are incorporated into the formal and informal rules of the game that affect organizations as players (Peng, 2012).Property rights are another of the formal institutions that influence business. These rights are social institutions that define the range of privileges granted individuals to specific resources. In other words, it is the right of individuals to direct or indirect power on an object or a good (Mahoney, 2010). The theory of property rights was developed by various theorists including Ronald Cease to explain the social and economic relationships that people should consider when using scarce resources.

From this discussion, it can be developed the following assumption: Formal institutions positively impact the entrepreneurship of biodiesel companies in Mexico.

THEORETICAL AND CONCEPTUAL FRAMEWORK

Emergence of Biodiesel

With the emergence of the industrial revolution by force, the great population growth around the world arises some problems, as Agarwal (2007) mentions humanity faces problems, in which arises the main interest on the environmental deterioration and the crisis of the industry energy. One of the main causes of air pollution is the burning of oil, since the combustion of air produces large amounts of greenhouse gases (carbon dioxide, oxides of nitrogen), sulfur oxides, unburned hydrocarbons and ash thin (Agarwal, 2007). In addition, it needs to be considered that hydrocarbon-based fuel is a non-renewable good, it is finite on the planet and therefore it has been necessary to resort to energies that can be renewable and friendlier to the environment.

Recent studies indicate that there are other sources of energy, which have extremely low emissions and appear to have the potential to become energy sources for automotive propulsion, including alcohols, natural gas, hydrogen and biodiesel. (Medina, Chávez & Jáuregui, 2012, 63)

This leads to the conclusion that an alternative for this destruction that causes economic growth inconsiderate by the environment may be the use of these substitutes for conventional fuels.

The definition of biodiesel used for this work is as follows:

It is a mixture of methyl esters of fatty acids (FAMEs) that is obtained by a process of transesterification, mainly from vegetable oils and animal fats and, more recently from algae. It can be used as a substitute for conventional diesel, as it has similar properties, reducing pollution and extending the life of the vehicle's engine. In its production, glycerin is obtained as a by-product, with multiple industrial applications. (Molina, 2012, 7)

Theories of Entrepreneurship

First, it is necessary to state that it is what is understood as an entrepreneurship. The entrepreneurship is the search for constant change, generation of ideas, speculation of projects that generate beneficial effects for the economy and society (Contreras and González, 2010). In a broader explanation, Sánchez and Pérez (2015) define it as those initiatives of an entrepreneurial nature that relate the way of being an individual where are included the way of thinking, reasoning and acting, with the search for a business opportunity, which give as a result initiative that generate value not only in an economic sense. In addition, concerned with social aspects, where all the actors are involved in the initiative, which go from owners, employees, customers, suppliers and society in general that enjoy this benefit.

However, Baumol (1990) makes a distinction between undertakings that are productive, unproductive and destructive. The productive enterprise is one in which there really is innovation, economic growth and can be associated with the discovery of good business opportunities. There are more distinctions between what are entrepreneurships like the one that is done between entrepreneurship by opportunity and entrepreneurship by necessity. When there is an opportunity venture, there is greater growth in the economy because that innovation has found a new niche market, which is exploitable. What does not happen when individuals are forced to undertake by necessity that the development of jobs and growth of the economy is not with the same acceleration (Reynolds, Bygrave, Autio, Cox and Hay, 2003)

The World Economic Forum also continues to classify high-impact entrepreneurship as one that generates greater benefits for consumers through the use of innovations, which in turn also generate more job opportunities and greater wealth for owners (Economic Forum World, 2014).

For all in their classifications they approach the same point in which they describe the entrepreneur as the one who manages to find opportunities that generate greater benefits and the use of innovations that sustain and exploit the opportunity more time. These entrepreneurs who focus on their clients are the ones who generate the greatest wealth for their owners (Hitt, Ireland, Sirmon & Trahms, 2011). These entrepreneurs tend to plan their actions better and to enter the market early and the most usual is that they undertake in markets with which they have already had interaction, which makes their rate of failure less than in situations in which there is no such planning and market knowledge (Liñán, Fernández, Romero, 2013).

Entrepreneurship is an indispensable mechanism for the development of economies (Schumpeter, 1934), it is necessary for every economy to develop enterprises that foster the generation of valuable jobs and innovations. However, the view was that political rulers should focus on favoring the growth of developed firms with the greatest potential for growth, leaving behind small firms and ventures (Friar and Meyer 2003). The political rulers who are responsible for the development of public policies, which Bazua and Valenti (1993) explains that a public policy is a reference to any social decision, which can be taken by an individual, an organization or the state.

Governments at all levels from federal, state, and local to the importance of firms on the economy, social and political issues have focused on creating the policies needed to support entrepreneurship. But they are faced with the decision whether policies will focus on supporting the nation's leading firms, helping existing firms achieve survival, or focusing on the formation of new enterprises (Stam, Studdle, Hessels & Stel, 2009).

Theories of Formal and Informal Institutions

North (1990) defines institutions as the humanly constructed constraints that structure human interaction, which is understood as the "rules of the game". Companies must take into account the terrain in which they will enter to know how they can act and if it is possible to take advantage. In addition to mentioning that institutions are created to reduce uncertainty. These institutions that are created to reduce uncertainty can encourage investment to increase productivity, but in countries where institutions are not as robust, the effect is the opposite (North 1990).

Peng (2012) have stated that the institutional framework is constituted by both formal and informal organizations, which will mark the actions that can be taken individually and collectively. Formal organizations are institutions that are represented in writing and are usually more rigorous in making them comply with the desired pattern of behavior; these are the laws, the regulations and the rules. However, for the study of this research, the informal institutions that although in many investigations show that it is one of the main factors to consider when entering new markets of which knowledge is lacking, this study only focuses on analyzing how the formal institutions favor or not the ventures.

Undoubtedly, the levels of entrepreneurship in a given country or region are conditioned by the environment in which entrepreneurship is carried out, since such an environment can facilitate or discourage the initiation of new initiatives (Fuentelsaz, González and Macías 2015). Institutions of a formal nature, such as laws or regulations, make it easier to visualize how processes should be carried out, which makes the business easier to manage and if it does not have experience, as is the case of ventures having a well-defined way of acting can achieve success. Proprietary rights, commercial legislation, constitution procedures, ideas, cultural beliefs, gender, attitudes towards the entrepreneur, etc., influence the appearance and development of new companies (Marulanda and Morales, 2016, 18).

Based on the theory of institutions, Urbano and Diaz (2009) affirm that the environment in each country will be decisive in terms of business opportunities that are available in addition to the perception about them and their ability or capability to adaptation to use them in their favor will generate greater incentives for the creation of new companies.

Without the necessary experience, in the new environment in which new start-ups seek to penetrate, they may encounter problems that limit access to financing, make it difficult to hire high-quality personnel and result in higher transaction costs (Aldrich and Auster, 1986). Under the circumstances of uncertainty on the part of those seeking to undertake an initiative, Fuentelzas (2015) mentions how the existence of solid institutions can facilitate the resolution of complications of inexperience, access to resources necessary for its functioning, and stability in the development of its activities. Institutions can facilitate access to resources and provide the necessary stability for the development of the activity, with the consequent effect on levels of business survival.

This demonstrates that the quality of institutions has a strong influence on competitiveness and growth, affects investment decisions, the organization of production and plays a key role in the way societies distribute profits and the costs of developing strategies and policies. However, an unstable institutional environment leads to even more complicated behavior among firms, hinders their cooperation and makes the vision of growth in the short term, which has negative effects on the quality and success of firms (Fuentelzas and González, 2015).

The uncertainty faced by the initiatives means that the number of successful ventures is reduced, however, as Vargas, Guerra, Bojórquez and Bojórquez (2014) mention that institutions have as their main role to reduce uncertainty and distinguish between uncertainty in a) Policy, which refers to ethnic disturbances that can cause problems for firms, and b) economic, which are all transaction costs that can be given by opportunism, to prevent these negative circumstances in the firm refer that firms can make use of contracts.

CONTEXTUAL FRAMEWORK

The main regulatory framework in Mexico is the political constitution of the United Mexican States that establishes the framework of action of the authorities and the governed, through principles, rights and obligations that govern the rest of the national legal framework. Article 4 of the Constitution speaks of "Everyone has the right to a healthy environment for their development and well-being". "The damage and environmental deterioration will generate responsibility for that provokes it in terms of the provisions of the law" which has been added as Decree of the Official Gazette of the Federation on February 08, 2012.In article 25, the constitution mentions that "the State is responsible for national development to ensure that it is comprehensive and sustainable." This demonstrates its concerns about caring for the environment.

The main law in specific terms in renewable energy is the Law on the promotion and development of bioenergetics that in its first article mentions "to promote the production of inputs for bioenergetics from agricultural activities, forestry, algae, biotechnological processes and sovereignty food "its main obligation under this law is to promote the use of bio energies in Mexico. Article 8 of this same law mentions that "the Bioenergetics Committee is created, which will be composed of the members of SAGARPA, SENER, SEMARNAT, the Secretary of Economy and the Secretary of Finance and Public Credit" with which several organizations are involved in the promotion of bioenergy production and research.

Likewise, the energy agency in Mexico, the Secretary of Energy (2017), reports that 7 permits are granted for the production of bioenergetics, 41 bioenergy marketing permits, 5 transport permits and 21 permit exemption notices for Production of bioenergetics.

The National Commission for Science and Technology in February 2017 reports that the Secretary of Energy launches a call for the creation of development projects in sustainable energy technologies that comes with the support of the Bank of Mexico in which the first prizes will be awarded prizes in cash of up to 2 million dollars for the first place, from 500 thousand dollars for the second place and 100 thousand dollars for the third place. There are these types of competitions that encourages the research and development of initiatives in alternative energy with which firms who want to venture but lack financing. This type of competitions can be the solution, these are not isolated situations,it is a way to encourage development that has its opportunity year after year.

The Ministry of Agriculture, Livestock, Rural Development, Fisheries and Food (SAGARPA) (2016) reports that it has promoted from 2013 to date 960 projects for the production of biofuels in Mexico. In the last four years' incentives have been granted around 275 million pesos, which has generated a total investment of 529 million pesos. And on the installation of 7 biofuel plants, six of which are dedicated for the production of biodiesel with 4 plants more than they existed in 2009.

METHOD

This article corresponds to a qualitative research based on a review of the literature on studies applied in Mexico about the characteristics, factors and variables that Mexican biodiesel companies must possesses well as data presented by institutional organisms and comparing with the applied theories of entrepreneurship and institutionalism to appropriate innovation and new forms of administration to the needs of 21st century companies.

The nature of the research is exploratory and descriptive through the analysis of previous research trying to provide quality and flexibility that allows researchers to use multiple data collection methods with the aim to analyze the role of the institutions in the biodiesel industry, to explain and describe the phenomenon under study and to determine if there is a relationship with the quality and maturity of the same with the entrepreneurial ventures.

ANALYSIS OF RESULTS

An attractive market such as biodiesel for its constant growth should have a sufficiently strong regulation to encourage the consolidation of existing companies as well as new entrepreneurs seeking to enter into competition for the market, so that it was imminent that the State should intervene to promote economic growth. The lack of competitiveness in the sale prices of biodiesel with the reference price marked by diesel fuel of fossil origin, the demand for biodiesel can be induced through different formal institutions and support policies.

For example, the analysis of Riegelhaupt, Odenthal and Janeiro (2016) point out, among other options, the establishment of a legal obligation in the form of a quota to certain actors in the market, generally fuel trading companies, to guarantee that a fraction of the total consumption of diesel is replaced with biodiesel. There are different possible designs for the quotas depending on who are the obligated parties, the obligation to mix in the final product or if different mixtures of fossil diesel-diesel are allowed as long as the quota is met globally. An important element in the design of the obligation is the price of the penalty established in case of default to the obligated parties. The price per liter of fuel that the obligated party must pay in case it cannot provide evidence of having marketed the volume established in the obligation. The establishment of a quota guarantees the achievement of a certain penetration of biodiesel in the market. However, the legal obligation by itself does not control the unit cost of support needed per liter of biodiesel introduced in the market,

Another support policy option proposed in the analysis of Riegelhaupt, Odenthal and Janeiro (2016) - which can be implemented independently or in combination with a quota - is to provide economic incentives to improve the competitiveness of biodiesel in the market. In Mexico there are no recent statistics on the production and use of biodiesel, but it is expected to increase due in part to the increase in the price of fossil diesel. Although fiscal incentives would be needed, that was what triggered the development of the biodiesel market in other countries.

The mechanism can be the reduction of production costs (for example through subsidies or tax exemptions to farmers or producers of biodiesel) or the reduction of final marketing prices through monetary support or tax reductions. Whether the economic incentive is established as a subsidy to biodiesel producers or if it is established as a tax exemption, the result sought in both cases is to increase the competitiveness of biodiesel in the market. In this study we refer to this type of political instruments as "economic incentives". The establishment of an economic incentive (e.g. a tax reduction) allows in principle to control the level of support per liter of biodiesel, but does not guarantee by itself the control of the volume of biodiesel introduced in the market.

The two support options described result in additional direct costs to society. These are calculated as the differential between the cost of introducing a certain amount of biodiesel in the market versus that of continuing to use fossil diesel. However, both instruments differ from the point of view of the distribution of said costs among different actors. The establishment of the mandatory quota generally transfers the additional cost of acquisition to suppliers, who in turn transfer the cost to the final consumer. In the case of economic incentives, these usually leave the state budget in the form of tax reductions, tax exemptions or subsidies. To meet a certain demand for biodiesel in the market, not only the necessary inputs must be available, but also sufficient production capacity in the supply chain. A key element of the supply chain is the facilities for converting inputs to biodiesel.

The production of biodiesel requires institutions to consolidate the creation of an agency responsible for regulating and facilitating the development of the biodiesel industry in Mexico. Small producers of biodiesel such as Smart Recycling of Puebla, has the permits from the Ministry of Energy for the production, sale and transportation of biofuel and certification processes for the quality of biofuel, values such as viscosity, density and pH, parts per million glycerin and some waste.

Due to the risks to sustainability that biofuel production could present if not done correctly, several initiatives have been developed to certify liquid biofuels produced in a sustainable manner; among them the RSB3 and the GBEP4, which establish principles and criteria such as: conservation of biodiversity, non-deforestation, GHG mitigation, good use of water resources, respect for human and worker rights, among others. In Mexico, the Ministry of Environment and Natural Resources (SEMARNAT) is developing the voluntary NMX standard for the certification of the production of liquid biofuels of plant origin based on the principles of RSB.

There is the technical possibility of expanding some oil crops more intensively in palm oil, coconut, soy, sunflower, castor and jatropha, to produce biodiesel respecting the principles established in the LPDB and considering that the marginal costs of biodiesel production are increased as the aptitude of the land is reduced. The increase in second-generation biodiesel production can be obtained from the abundant available ligno-cell resources, such as agricultural residues or agro industrial and forestry co-products, when the conversion technologies have reached commercial maturity and become competitive. The conversion infrastructure of crude oils to biodiesel, this is limited for the moment to a small number of demonstration plants of very small scale.

The ventures for companies producing biodiesel in Mexico for the years 2008-2009 that were their beginnings in the Mexican market, there was a confusion and instability, generated uncertainty that caused that the enterprises in this sector were not encouraged, so It was necessary an intervention of formal institutions, and the state who can generate new regulatory frameworks in any sector.

After the review of events on how to change the landscape of institutions in Mexico to be a first-time trial and error, it has been possible to consolidate and strengthen entrepreneurship initiatives in biofuel companies; especially biodiesel has been favored with a growth of twice what existed. So it can be noted that if there is a relationship between the formalization or solids of the institutions with the initiatives and start-up of enterprises, which supports the theoretical basis and study that was carried out by Fuentelzas, who show how institutions are an important factor for successful ventures in their areas.

FUTURE RESEARCH DIRECTION

The future research on entrepreneurship of biodiesel companies in Mexico from a perspective based on the institutions should consider the impact of the institutions in the design and implementation of a program oriented to the promotion of the most economic forms of biodiesel is considered the most reasonable short-term option term. This institutional impact must consider the different combinations of institutional incentives such as economic, fiscal, subsidies, etc. that allow biodiesel to compete in a range of costs similar to that of fossil diesel at current oil prices.

Analyze and evaluate the possibility of introducing a larger-scale program after a detailed analysis of the impact on the Mexican economy as a whole, including the direct cost of support, the positive impacts of the investment, indirect tax revenues, trade balance, and generation of employment, among others.

Another line of relevant research is the analysis, design and implementation of structural programs to strengthen institutional capacities that allow the acquisition of institutional and technical experience for the development of the biofuels and biodiesel market.

Analyze institutional capacities to generate additional income in the agricultural sector and investment in production infrastructure in the industrial sector from investments in the generation of biofuels and biodiesel, with the consequent generation of employment and associated tax revenues.

Analyze the impacts of formal institutions on national and local economies by encouraging the choice of biodiesel against diesel of fossil origin and consider that in addition to the environmental benefits of reducing greenhouse gas emissions, there are other positive economic impacts derived of the introduction of biodiesel.

Evaluate the cost-benefits of adopting an institutional program that stimulates the production, distribution and consumption of technically viable biofuels and biodiesel based on the potential availability of available resources.

Estimate the institutional capacity for the production of biodiesel with national resources with reductions in biodiesel imports, in such a way that they contribute to improve the country's trade balance and to mitigate the negative effect of high oil prices.

CONCLUSION AND RECOMMENDATIONS

There is an incipient industry in biodiesel production in Mexico based on raw materials based on used cooking oils, which are accompanied by processes of processing, collection, distribution and marketing, mainly carried out in institutions that operate informally. However, because the potential for the expansion of biodiesel production is broad based on other types of inputs with increasing production trends, such as fats of animal origin and vegetable and oil-based oils such as soybean, palm and coconut, this implies the establishment of more formal market institutions to carry out the distribution and commercialization of the product. The establishment of market mechanisms in formal institutions will allow reaching higher recovery rates with lower costs, but above all, it will allow covering in greater percentage the current demand for biodiesel.

Because of this one of the concerns that must be had if the economy is to be more competitive compared to countries with a faster growth rate than the Mexican, it is necessary to be clear that formal institutions is a way in which entrepreneurs achieve organizations that exploit available markets and do so in a sustainable manner.

In addition, all those who seek to generate a project in the renewable energy sector as well as any other type of industry need to look for countries with better formal institutions, or in case of entering emerging markets that usually do not have a solid structure in its laws, regulations and regulatory agencies, to anticipate the failures that can be caused and the costs that this would cause to enter the market with proactive strategies and not wait to be in unsustainable situations.

REFERENCES

Agarwal, A. K. (2007). Biofuels (Alcohols And Biodiesel) Applications As Fuels For Internal Combustión Engines. *Progress in Energy And Combustion Science*, *33*(3), 233–271. doi:10.1016/j.pecs.2006.08.003

Aldrich, H., & Auster, E. R. (1986). Even Dwarfs Started Small: Liabilities Of Age And Size And Their Strategic Implications. *Research In Organizational Behavior*, *8*, 165–198.

Basu, K. (2013). *Más allá de la mano invisible*. Fondo de Cultura Económica.

Baumol, W. J. (1990). Entrepreneurship: Productive, Unproductive, And Destructive. *Journal of Political Economy*, *98*(5), 893–921. doi:10.1086/261712

Bazua, F. Y., & Valenti, G. (1993). Hacia Un Enfoque Amplio De Política. *PúblicaRevistaDe Administración Pública*, 84.

Comisión Reguladora De Energía. (2015). *Desarrollo Del Marco Regulatorio MexicanoEn Materia Energética*. Author.

Constitución Política De Los Estados Unidos Mexicanos, Diario Oficial De La Federación. (2017). *Constitución Política De Los Estados Unidos Mexicanos*. Author.

Contreras Comeche, R., & González García, N. (2010). La Medición Del Valor Social Y El Impacto De Los Emprendedores Sociales. In Emprendimiento, Economía Social Y Empleo. IUDESCOOP, Instituto Universitario De Economía Social Y Cooperativa Dela Universidad De Valencia.

Foro Económico Mundial. (2014). *The Bold-Ones High-Impact Entrepreneurs Who Transform Industries*. Foro Económico Mundial.

Friar, J. H., & Meyer, M. H. (2003). Entrepreneurship and start-ups in the Bostonregion: Factors differ- entiating high-growth ventures from micro-ventures. *Small Business Economics*, *21*(2), 145–152. doi:10.1023/A:1025045828202

Fuentelsaz, L., & Gonzáles, C. (2015) El Fracaso Emprendedor A Través De Las Instituciones Y La Calidad Del Emprendimiento. *Universidad Bussiness Review.*

Fuentelsaz, L., González, C., & Maícas, J. P. (2015). ¿Ayudan Las Instituciones A Entender El Emprendimiento*? Economía Industrial.*

Hitt, M. A., Ireland, R. D., Sirmon, D. G., & Trahms, C. A. (2011). Strategic Entrepreneurship: Creating Value For Individuals, Organizations, And Society. *The Academy of Management Perspectives*, *25*(2), 57–75.

Hofstede, G. (2011). *Culture's consequences* (1st ed.). ThousandOaks. SagePubl.

Ley De Promoción Y Desarrollo De Los Bionergéticos. (2008). *Ley De Promoción Y Desarrollo De Los Bionergéticos*. PublicadoEn El Diario Oficial De La Federación El Primero De Febrero De.

Liñán, F., Fernández, J., & Romero, I. (2013). Necessity AndOpportunity Entrepreneurship: The Mediating Effect of Culture. *RevistaDe Economía Mundial*, *33*, 21–47.

Mahoney, J. (2012). Property rights theory. In Economic Foundations of Strategy (pp. 158–199). Champaign, IL: Academic Press.

Marulanda, F., & Morales, S. (2016). Entorno Y Motivaciones Para Emprender. *Revista Escuela De Administración De Negocios,* 8.

Medina, I., Chavez, N. Y., & Jauregui, J. (2012). Biodiesel, Un Combustible Renovable. *InvestigaciónY Ciencia, 20*, 62-70.

Molina, C. (2012). Estudio de la composición y estabilidad de biodiesel obtenido a partir de aceites vegetales limpios y procedentes de aceites de fritura. Servicio de publicaciones de la Universidad de la Laguna.

North, D. (1990). *Institutions, Institutional Change and Economic Performance*. Cambridge, UK: Cambridge University Press. doi:10.1017/CBO9780511808678

OECD. (2017). *OECD Stats FAO Agricultura*. Retrieved from Http://Stats.Oecd.Org/Viewhtml.Aspx?Queryid=58648&Vh=0000&Vf=0&L&Il=&Lang=En#

Peng, M. (2012). *Enfatizando Las Instituciones, La Cultura Y La Ética. Gestión Estratégica*. Editoral Cengage Learning.

Rembio. (2009). *Expert Opinion Based On Delivered Questionnaire*. Author.

Reynolds, P., Bygrave, W. D., Autio, E., Cox, L. W., & Hay, M. (2003). *Global Entrepreneurship Monitor 2002 executive report*. Wellesley, MA: Babson College.

SAGARPA. (2010). *Monografía de cultivos: palma de Aceite*. Subsecretaría de Fomento a los Agronegocios.

SAGARPA. (2016). *Direccion General de Fibras Naturales y Biocombustibles. BIODIÉSEL 06052016. Presentación realizada en el Taller de Biodiésel.* Paquete Tecnológico de Higuerilla y Paquete Tecnológico de Jatropha.

SAGARPA. (2017). *Impulsa SAGARPA Producción De Biocombustibles En México*. Ciudad de México.

Salgado, C. E. (2003). *Teoría de costos de transacción: una breve reseña. Cuadernos de Administración*. Recuperado de http://www.redalyc.org/articulo.oa?id=20502604

Sánchez, L. A., & Pérez, E. (2015). Las Entidades De Economía Social Como Protagonistas De Un Nuevo Modelo De Emprendimiento Y Medidas Legales De Apoyo Al Emprendimiento,CIRIEC-España. *C.I.R.I.E.C. España*, *84*, 35–62.

Schumpeter, J. A. (1934). The Thory Of Economic Development: An Inquiry Into Profits, Capital, Credit, Interest And The Business Cycle. Harvard Economic Studies, 46.

Stam, E., Suddle, K., Hessels, J., & Van Stel, A. J. (2009). High-Growth Entrepreneurs, Public Policies, And Economic Growth. International Studies in Entrepreneurship, 22, 91-110.

Tapia, P. (2017). *Biodiésel, a la espera de brillar en México*. Milenio.

Urbano, D. Y., & Díaz, J. C. (2009). Creación De Empresas E Instituciones: Un Modelo Teórico. In Creación De Empresas. Aproximación Al Estado Del Arte. Lisboa: Juruá.

Urteaga, E. (2013). La teoría del capital social de Robert Putnam: Originalidad y carencias. *Reflexión Política*. Recuperado de http://www.redalyc.org/articulo.oa?id=11028415005

Vargas, J., Guerra, E., Bojórquez, A. Y., & Bojorquez, F. (2014). Gestión Estratégica De Organizaciones. Elaleph, 134.

KEY TERMS AND DEFINITIONS

Biocombustibles: It is a mixture of organic substances that is used as fuel in internal combustion engines. Derived from biomass, organic matter originated in a biological process, spontaneous or provoked, usable as a source of energy.

Biodiesel: Biodiesel is a liquid biofuel that is obtained from lipids of natural origin, such is the case of vegetable oils or animal fats that have had or not previous use, subjected to the transesterification process.

Company: A company is an enterprise or business that has been organized as a business and commercial society including capital and labor and whose main purpose is to obtain an economic benefit.

Entrepreneurship: It is the ability of people to create new businesses. It is the person who knows how to discover, identify a specific business opportunity and then will arrange or get the necessary resources to start it and then take it to fruition.

Formal Institutions: They are the institutions related to constitutions, codes, laws, contracts and other legal elements.

Informal Institutions: Are extensions, interpretations, and modifications of formal rules, rules of behavior, agreements, codes of conduct or conventions and all those aspects that are related to culture.

Institution: Institutions are constraints that arise from human inventiveness to limit political, economic and social interactions. They include informal restrictions, such as sanctions, taboos, customs, traditions, and "codes of conduct," as well as formal rules (constitutions, laws, property rights).

Mexico: A country located in North America.

Chapter 12
Emission Permit Trading:
A Theoretical Analysis

Poulomi Khasnobis
The University of Burdwan, India

Sanjukta Niyogi
The University of Burdwan, India

ABSTRACT

After the Kyoto Protocol, the new concept of carbon trading emerged. The carbon emission can be controlled by cap and tax system. Cap and trade is the permit that determines the maximum amounts of carbon emission. Carbon tax is imposed on amount of carbon emission. Other instruments of carbon emission are border adjustment and cash payment. Carbon permit is determined by market mechanism through demand and supply. Generally, there are two types of markets: regulated and voluntary. The chapter analyzes mechanisms and discusses the mitigating policies like Kyoto Protocol and tries to examine all aspects related to carbon leakage. The developed countries import carbon-intensive goods. Underdeveloped countries produce and export carbon-intensive goods. In this study, the authors show the prospect of carbon trading and various effects of carbon emission reduction policies on a theoretical framework.

INTRODUCTION

Recent years the Global Climate Change is the biggest problem in the world. The Global sea level has risen by amount of 20 cm. It is partly due to melting of mountain ice and partly due to thermal expansion of the oceans. Therefore, the human civilization faces a great crisis.

The Green House Gas (GHG) performs actively for the global warming and climate change. Carbon dioxide (CO2), Chlorofluorocarbon (CFC), and methane (CH4) etc. are the Green House Gases (GHGs). Carbon dioxide is the main culprit of global warming and/or climate change. So, society creates laws and imposes regulation on carbon emission or carbon generating activities. There are many mitigating process to reduce the GHG emission. The effective mitigating process is Cap-system. Every country fixed up a cap of Carbon emission. Cap is a limit of Carbon emission. Countries never cross this limit

DOI: 10.4018/978-1-5225-8547-3.ch012

or cap. Generally, the developing countries have lower level of carbon emission than their approved cap which is set by regulatory authority, while the developed countries generate more carbon emission than their assigned cap. Cap is the constraint of economic activities for most of the countries. Following cap-system new line of trade emerges which is termed as *cap and trade.* In this context, the Multinational Companies (MNCs) gets a huge environmental discount from the developing country. So, the Multinational Companies (MNCs) produces commodity in developing countries and trade with the rest of the world. The developed countries take a protection from the environmental degradation through the cap system. The developed country traded environmental protection instead of economic activities. In this way carbon trade is occurs in the world. So, *cap and trade* is one part of *carbon trade.* Addressing the challenge of climate change has brought about policies and proposals that radically alter emissions from industry, especially from the electricity system. The added costs of climate policies have impacts on different parts of the electricity supply system, ranging from generation to transmission. The magnitude of these added costs resulting from climate policies such as *carbon taxes, cap-and-trade* schemes and mandatory renewable energy targets varies across countries, partly according to the commercial and regulatory structure of their coal based electricity systems(since major emission of carbon-di-oxide occurs from power sector,) and it is difficult to separate the effects of such climate policies from other electricity price drivers such as domestic regulatory regimes, competition, electricity import and export options and historic investments in alternative electricity generation sources. Therefore, in the policy making context, the assessment of carbon leakage risks has recently been embedded in a comparison of electricity prices faced by industry in their country as compared to main trade competitors.

Climate change regulations might only cause firms to relocate their activity to another country with less stringent regulations, whilst reducing economic activity in the initial host country. This is the source of *carbon leakage* (Fischer and Fox 2012). The carbon leakage occurs when there is an increase in carbon-dioxide (CO_2) emission in one country as a result of an emission reduction by a second country with a strict climate policy (Barker,.et.al, 2007). In other words, carbon leakage can be defined as the ratio of emission increasing from a specific sector outside the country over the emission reduction in the sector. *Zmijewski (2011) defines the carbon leakage on the other way. Carbon leakage denotes the allocation of energy intensive and high carbon emitting manufacturing industries from countries with Green House Gas (GHG) emission reduction policies to country without climate regulation in place.*

Most of the literature on carbon leakage is ex-ante and measure the size of positive leakage based on computable general equilibrium models (Burniaux & Martins, 2012; Babiker, 2005; Aichele &Felbermayr, 2013). The estimated leakage depends on the policy scenarios and it varies 2% to 20% (Burniaux &Martins, 2012), one extreme scenario is 130% (Babiker, 2005). Kyoto commitment reduces domestic carbon emissions but not the carbon footprints. Aichele and Felbermayr (2013) find carbon leakage in the gap between domestic consumption and production.

Energy efficiency standards more consistently and significantly caused negative impact on industrial competitiveness than carbon taxes (The World Bank, 2008); in the US, higher electricity price reduced employment both in energy-intensive industries in a county (Kahn and Mansur, 2013) and collectively for a state.

Carbon regulation has intension to reduce global emissions, but there is growing concern that such regulation may simply shift production to unregulated regions and increase global emissions in the process. *Carbon tariffs* have emerged as a possible mechanism to address these concerns by imposing carbon costs on imports at the regulated border. Darke (2012) shows that *carbon leakage* can result despite the implementation of a carbon tariffs when firms choose from discrete production technologies and offshore producers hold a comparative cost advantage. In this context, foreign firms adopt clean technology at a lower emissions price than firms operating in the regulated region, with foreign entry increasing only over emissions price intervals within which foreign firms hold this technology advantage. As a consequence, global emissions decrease when carbon leakage happens under carbon tariffs. Darke (2012) points out the sources of potential welfare improvement, which is realized through carbon tariffs that require both foreign comparative advantage and endogenous choice of technology.

OBJECTIVE

The main objective of this study is to review the literature on carbon trade and more specifically focusing on carbon leakage.

- To calculate how much carbon trading help to mitigate the carbon leakage.
- To know the risk of carbon leakage.
- To explore the concept of carbon emission cap and trade, and carbon leakage in details. The development process will be continuing in developing country through the carbon emission trading hence is it justify for sustainable development.
- To estimate the impact of carbon leakage trade, whether it would beneficial or it seems to be a losing investment.

BACKGROUND HISTORY

1st world climate conference was held in 1979 in Geneva which was sponsored by WMO (World Meteorological Organization). In the year of 1985 Vienna convention was organized for the protection of Ozone layer. After 2 years Montreal protocol was signed. In the year 1988 Intergovernmental Panel on Climate Change (IPCC) was created by WMO.

In 1992, the United Nations Frame work convention on climate change (UNFCCC) was launched during the Earth Summit in Rio De Jan Rio. It sets the legal frame work to negotiate international treaties governing GHG emission reduction. The Kyoto Protocol of 1997 promises of emission cutback was fixed in such an international treaty. 37 industrialized countries and the EU (Europe Union) committed to reduced their emissions in the 2008-2012 period by 5.2% compared to 1990 each nation has country specific emission target ranging from emission cutbacks of 8% (EU and Switzerland) to a maximum emission increase of 10% in Iceland. America has not ratified this agreement (Reinaud, J., 2009). The cap and trade approach to pollution abatement was first demonstrated between 1967 and 1970 for the National Air Pollution Control Administration by Ellission Barton and William Sanjour. The UNFCCC is at little suggests simply a framework; the necessary detail was left to be settled by the Conference of Parties (COP) to the UNFCCC. The COP 17 in Durban (Climate strategy 2012) achieved a time line until 2015 for a new agreement of climate protection to be negotiated and effective in 2020. The negotiating countries are EU, China, and Japan. EU countries move to a 30% unilateral CO2 reduction target by the EU in 2020 remains on the policy agenda. China has announced to introduce the trading in 7 provinces starting in 2015.

BRIEFLY STUDY THE LITERATURE REVIEW

Marcu et al (2014) study carbon leakage related market. This paper builds on the 1st delivery of the project entitled "Carbon Leakage Option for the EU". This paper identified risk of carbon test. The carbon tests apply in the EU, Australia, California, US- Waxman bill and New Zealand. This paper also explains the different mitigating policy of carbon leakage. Kumar (2010) explains the carbon trade mechanism and author discusses a generalised structure of carbon market. The trade mechanism explained here by the graphical presentation. Bhattacharya and Nand (2012) analyse the impact of climate change policy focusing on developing and developed countries. They examine India- US trade as a case study. The US is a very important trade partner for India. Here estimated overall reduction in India export to US under two border adjustment scenarios is 2.3% and 3.5% of India's export to US 2006-07. So, this paper also shows that different impact of climate change policy on developed country like in US per ton carbon effects competitiveness of US manufacturing as a whole, and on developing countries such as in China carbon based border tax creates a positive incentives for industrialized countries but China suffered significantly. This paper addressed different mitigating policies of carbon leakage. Goulder (2013) critical reviews the carbon trade and suggests which system is better for carbon tax and cap and trade system. Reinaud(2009) concentrates on emission trade scheme across the EU, Japan, Australia, Norway, South Korea, New Zealand, Switzerland and the US. Author shows in his paper the impact of uneven climate change policy on competitive loss and job losses. There are different measure addresses to competitive loss and leakage concerns, and highlighted to different mitigating measures. Bulkeley and Newell (2014) explain. Carbon market is not a purely private market since the entire market is created through government policy. Carbon market needs a strong regulation and monitoring policy too. Stram (2014) explains carbon tax can creates a net gain to world society over the long term theoretically since this tax directly encourage to reduced emission, and insists to search new alternative low emits technologies. As through tax Govt. collect revenue which is indirectly come back to all citizens via increasing welfare that makes carbon tax more lucrative to society. But all these gain come to society in long run, in short run some people have to suffer from this technological changes, and they also have to bear some additional cost for these. Therefore carbon tax or emission reduction target creates a trade-off between short term losses to long term gain. Petersen et.al (1998) analyses that the climate treaty negotiated in Kyoto, Japan is required reduce emission of GHG (especially carbon), but the problem is most of the GHG ($CO_{2)}$ emits from energy sector, so this will affect entire country's growth. For these negative sides for implementation of clean technology not only financial incentives are required but also required major effort to gain acceptance of new technology. Policies that could accelerate low emission and fuel efficient technologies include tax incentives for early purchasers of high efficiency vehicles and other means to provide up-front incentives for the purchase of energy-efficient vehicles.

CAUSES OF CARBON LEAKAGE

1. The emissions policy of a country raises the local cost while other country with more relaxed policy may have trading advantage.
2. Since environmental policy adds a premium to certain fuels and commodity price of that fuel increases, that reduces demand. On the other hand that countries which do not impose any premium on that commodity may not control its demand.

Which Sectors Are Responsible for Carbon Leakage?

The responsible sectors of carbon leakage are steel, iron, cement, paper, glass, chemical and sugar industries.

CHANNELS FOR CARBON LEAKAGE

There are two channels

1. **Production Channel:** Is impact on short term competitiveness which is due to difference in cost structure between GHG activities in GHG constraint jurisdiction and less GHG constraint jurisdiction. The former could lose competitiveness which might loss of market share to later. This takes place on international market.
2. **Investment channel**: Investment is long term impact, is result of loss of competitiveness caused by climate policies. That is enough to shifts investment to jurisdiction (Kumar, 2010)

MEASUREMENT ISSUES

There are three types of carbon risk factors like policy and legal factors, technological factors and Market and Economic factors (Fulton and Weber, 2012). Here policy and legal risk factor includes fuel emission capacity of personal vehicles, technological risk factor includes energy storage technology related emission, market and economic risk factor implies changes in consumer preferences due to changes in fossil fuel price. Main measurement issue is the quantification of carbon leakage through carbon trade.

QUALITATIVE RISK TESTS

These risk tests can be used alone or in a combination. When risk test are also used in combination, the threshold level generally made some system lower hence the test regards as stand-alone test the threshold level has higher value. The qualitative risk test has two features (Figure 1), 1) Tiered approach, 2) flexibility of mechanism. The first feature is whether carbon leakage risk test employs tiered approach. An approach determines which sectors are or are not at risk and results in some sectors not receiving any compensation, if the sectors fall below the threshold level. With the tiered approach several risk levels are defined and compensation could be distributed in proportion to the risk levels.

The second feature that needs to be considered is that flexibility of mechanism. Flexibility approach adapts to change the key parameters, including how it is updated. In general mechanism can be up dated.

Figure 1. Risk measurement strategy of carbon leakage
Source: Marcu. A, et.al (2014)

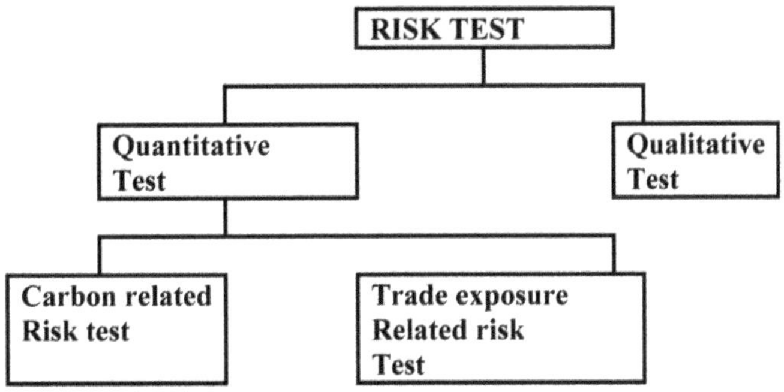

QUANTITATIVE RISK TEST

Under table 1 an overview the quantitative risk test currently used in various operational proposed schemes.

- **Carbon Related Risk Test:** This test checks for the impact of carbon cost relative to a measures of financial performance. Currently two approaches can be identified. 1) Emission intensity, 2) Carbon cost
- **Emissions Intensity Tests:** Are used in California, New Zealand and Australia (see Table 1) and can be looked upon, in a more general way, as an indicator of carbon intensity relative to financial performance. This could also be extrapolated to the carbon intensity of GDP. While emissions-intensity tests can be seen as less targeted than carbon cost tests (discussed below), there remains a relationship between emissions intensity of an installation & its compliance costs.

For these tests, the approach used is that emissions intensity thresholds are defined, which then determined the risk level. It must be emphasized that the data used for these tests are historical, not a forecast.

Carbon Cost impact of carbon cost relative to gross value added. Carbon cost relative to value added is the second approach currently used in the EU, which was also included in the proposed WAXMAN MARKEY BILL (AMERICAN CLEAN ENERGY AND SECURITY ACT) approved by the US House of Representatives in June 2009.This test is currently used as a stand alone or in combination with another test. A price of euro 30/ ton is used in calculating carbon cost. When used as standalone test, the threshold is 30%. When used in conjunction with other quantitative criteria the threshold is 5%. In total 13 sectors qualified based on the combined test covering 36% of total emissions from industrial sectors in EU ETS. The proposed WAXMAN MARKEY Bill also included test for the impact of carbon cost.

TRADE-RELATED RISK TESTS

Trade intensity or trade exposure takes different forms depending on the as outline in Table 1.

In the case of the EU ETS, sectors are considered to be exposed to carbon leakage risk if trade intensity is over 30% (as a stand-alone). A 10% threshold is used if the trade intensity test is combined with another test (carbon cost).

Table 1. The Quantitative risk test used in the EU, ETS, Australia, and California the US Waxman Markey Bill and New Zealand

	FORMULAS	STAND ALONE TEST	COMBINED TEST
EU ETS	**CARBON COST** (Direct emission tCo_2 + Indirect emission tCo_2) * t30/ tCo_2 Gross Value added **TRADE INTENSITY** (Imports + Exports) (Turnover +Imports)	Carbon cost over 30% Trade intensity over 30%	Carbon Cost above 5% Trade intensity above 10%
Australia	**EMISSION INTENSITY** Tones Co_2e Million AUD Revenue **TRADE INTENSITY** Annual value of Imports + Exports Annual value of production		Emission intensity High at least 2000 tCo_2emission per million AUD revenue Moderates: 1000 tCo_2Emission per million AUD revenue Trade Intensity above10%
California	**EMISSION INTENSITY** Tones Co_2e Million USD value added **TRADE INTENSITY** Annual value of Imports + Exports Shipments + Imports		Emission intensity High > 5000 Medium: 1000 – 4999 Low: 100 – 999 Very low < 100 Trade Intensity High: 19% Moderate: 10-19% Low < 10%
US Waxman Markey Bill	**CARBON COST** Cost of Electricity + Fuel cost Shipments **TRADE INTENSITY** Imports + Exports Shipments + Imports	Carbon Cost over 20%	Carbon Cost over 5% Trade Intensity At least 15%
New Zealand	**EMISSION INTENSITY** Tones Co_2e Million NZD revenue **TRADE INTENSITY** All sectors are trade exposed	Emission Intensity High: 1600 Moderate: 800	

(Source: Australian Department of Climate change and Energy efficiency (2007). California Air Resource Board (2006 and 2012) Europe Council and Parliament (2003)

The outcome is that 133 sectors in the EU ETS have trade intensity over 30%, covering a total of 26% of the industrial emissions in the EU ETS (Marcue et al, 2014).California has a similar approach to the EU, but trade exposure is categorized as low, medium and high risk (see Table 1). The trade-intensity test is combined with an emissions-intensity test to assess sectors' carbon leakage risk. Table 4 shows a selection of different sector and their trade intensity in the California ETS.

A slight variation was employed in the Australian ETS where trade intensity is calculated as a ration over domestic production if the ration is higher than 10% in any of the financial years 2004-05, 2005-06 or 2007-08, the sector is considered to be trade exposed. This is then combined with a test on emissions intensity in order to determine the level of compensation. Table 1 gives examples of trade intensity for different activities in Australia. New Zealand has not included any formal measure of trade exposure. Instead it is assumed that all sectors are trade exposed unless it is obvious that they are not, i.e. if it is not a trade commodity.

THE QUANTITATIVE RISK TEST

See Table 1.

TRADE MECHANISM OF CARBON LEAKAGE

From the Kyoto Protocol, defined cap is termed as a limit. This cap is determined by the UNO (United Nation Organisation). Cap is valid for the certain time; cap is fixed (Zimijewski, 2011).

The cap or limit is different for the different country. There are three question arises

1. How cap is determined?
2. Who gets the permit?
3. How do they pay for them?

Boyes (2009) see a market based approach as efficient means to organized exchange. The government started the process by allocating permits. When the govt. allocates the initial set of permit people spend resource lobbying the governments. If this first come, first served, they all race to grab their share.

Boyes (2009) Predicts "Price based allocation" means the business will choose the most efficient way to use their resource. It is less experience for them to buy new equipment and sell their permits. It is less experience to buy permit and improve and not improve their equipment.

As the number of permits goes down and price goes up. It would induce people to use more efficient product technology. Smith (2006) provides the approach to fixation of cap of the carbon emissions. The best approach is that the govt. forum and auction where the different firm has come and it buying permits from the govt. an auction declares a price cap for permit each year. Its bids go over the price cap, sell as many permits as needed that year at the price cap. Apart from that the allocation of permit, it also depends upon the topographical positions, population density and village and urban area of that country. Mainly carbon emitted companies are given permit like sugar, cement, paper industries etc.

So, we can see that different countries have different cap and different firms, have different permit. The Multinationals Companies (MNC's) can make a trade for the different permits for the different country. The developing countries have a less stringent climate policy than the developed country (Reinaud et. al, 2009). So, the MNC that is situated a developed country can buy the permit from the government of developing country. Because developing country has excess permit. The permit is nothing but the permission for carbon emission. The cap of developed country is higher than that of developing country. So, the MNC cannot cross the cap. In developed countries the production of MNCs are disbursed. Since the MNC cannot expand their production in developed countries, MNC can trade with the other developing country by buying the permits and expanding their production in former. (Kumar, 2016) Broadly carbon market can be divided into regulated and voluntary market. These two markets can viewed in two different ways.

Demand Side: When viewed from the demand side of carbon permits, regulated markets refers to countries and companies that have a mandatory on the amount of $CO2$ they can produce. Voluntary market on other hand refers to entities taking action to meet another goal (such as, corporate social responsibility, brand building, product differentiation etc).

Supply Side: When viewed from supply side of carbon permits regulated market refers to carbon instruments that have been certified as Complaint with a Mandatory System. Whereas, Voluntary market refers to carbon instrument that have been developed any mandatory system (e.g. Voluntary carbon standard).

- **AAUs:** Assigned Amounts Units are issued to countries with emission cap under Kyoto protocol (Annex 1 countries).
- **EUAs:** European Union allowances. The allowances in used under EU-ETS. Both AAUs and EUAs represents one metric ton of carbon die oxide equivalent.
- **CERs:** Certified Emission Reduction issued pursuant to the Clean Development Mechanism of Kyoto protocol.
- **ERUs:** Emission Reduction units a unit of GHG issued pursuant to joint implementation of Kyoto protocol. Both CERs and ERUs represents used for compliance with the Chicago Climate Exchange instrument.
- **CCBA:** Climate Community Bio diversity Alliance
- **VCS:** Voluntary Carbon Standard.
- **VER:** Verified Emission Reduction.
- **CN:** Carbon Neutral Protocol.

GAINS FROM CARBON TRADE

From this permit exchange both countries are benefited. As the MNC shifted their production in developing country then the GDP (Gross Domestic Product), NI (National Income) and employment level must be rise. On other hand the developed countries get rid of form the environmental degradation. And for the cap-system new technology has been discovered which protect the environment there are six exchanges trading in UNFCCC.

1. Chicago climate exchange.
2. Europe climate exchange.
3. NA SDAQ OMX commodities Europe.
4. Power Next.
5. Commodity Exchange Bratislava.
6. Europe Energy Exchange.

From the trade mechanism of carbon leakage we can draw the trade pattern between developed and developing country.

Table 2. Trade pattern of developed and developing country

Country	*Export*	*Import*
Developing country	Carbon intensive goods	Non-carbon intensive goods & service
Developed country	Mainly services	Carbon intensive goods

Source: IPCC (2007)

IMPACT OF CLIMATE POLICY ON TRADE

Generally, there are two types of country in the world. One is carbon constrained country and other is unconstrained country. Due to carbon tax, carbon intensive goods are expensive in constraint country than unconstraint country. The firms in carbon intensive industries relocate their investment to environment lower standards. Import of energy intensive goods forms the unconstrained countries can increase while the productions of the same goods in regulate market decreases. Frankel (2009) goes beyond the WTOs argument by expecting leakage to lead even higher level of emission from non-participating countries that would be without leakage. More over successful emission mitigating policy are expected to result in a decrease of fossil fuels price. The panel for climate change (2007) reports leakage rate in a range of 5%-20% due to the possible increases of imports of cheaper carbon intensive goods from non-constraint countries. The industry of constraint countries faces a loss of competitiveness. The affected sector usually creates a more powerful lobby in the trade and environmental negotiations. On other hand lobbyists from these industries demand carbon allowance to counteract carbon limitations, on other hand they make use of the leakage arguments to gain unconstraint countries to constrained countries more protection in the form of border carbon adjustment. EU list of sectors exposed to carbon leakage. EU(2010) defines energy intensive industries that are not able to pass on cost of required allowance in product prices without significant loss of market share to installation outside (community EU), which do not comparable action to reduce emission, as eligible for allowance of carbon emission certificates with a significantly high risk of carbon leakage industries could high amount of free allocation. The mitigating system includes Border Adjustments Measure such as carbon tariffs. Those industries impose tax which emitted higher carbon.

US under the Obama administration pledged to reduce carbon emission by 17% by 2020. Washington legislators had responded to growing concerns about loss in competitiveness in energy intensive industries with the carbon limits and Energy for America's Renewal Act introduced in 2009 by Senator Maria Cantwell. Bill which fails to go be effect starting in 2013. GATT article 2 states that imported product has to be equally taxed and it says that importing country may only apply tariff taxes at border. Article 3 says that "like product" of foreign and domestic origins have to be equal taxes (Messerlin, 2010).

These two articles have to be respected when deciding on the type of Border adjustment measure. For instance, tariffs in contrast to tax are only imposed on a selected group of foreign countries (Table 3).

Therefore they discriminate between imports of different origins and between domestic and foreign products.

Which Industries Are Eligible for the Carbon Policy?

The GREEN HOUSE GAS (GHG) intensive and trade exposed industries are most competitively disadvantage by carbon policy that increases cost. There are three criteria stand for determining the potential eligibility of an industry for the carbon policy.

- Is the sector or product GHG intensive? Under what condition are some sectors viability strongly tied to a GHG process?
- Would the sectors competitive situation be substantially upset by carbon policies through its inability to pass on cost related to them? Would the sectors be exposed to competition from com-

Table 3. Commencement of carbon trading pattern

Region	Participation	Time-Table
EU (2005)	Power Generation and Energy intensive industry	Phase II : 2008 – 2012 Phase III: 2012 – 2020
Japan (2005)	Industry (Food, Pulp, Chemicals)	16 months trading period
New South Wales	Power sector 100 GW	Set to 2012 with commitment to
Norway (2005)	Energy production, refinery, iron and steel, cement, ceramics, lime, glass	Phase II: 2008
Albert (2007)	Electricity, energy, chemicals	Annual target
New Zealand (2008)	Forestry, waste, liquid, fossils, fuel, stationery energy, agriculture, industrial process	Sector in phase Starting with forestry (2008 – 2010)
Switzerland (2008)	Heating process fuels, ceramics, Glass, paper, chemicals, aluminium, lime, food, printing	2008 – 2012
Regional GHG initiative(2009) US north eastern States	Power generation	3 years period from Initiative (2009) 2009-18
South Korea (2008)	Large emitting companies	Late 2008 – 12
Canadas (2010)	Power generation, iron & steel Cement, lime, chemicals	Output based allocation Start in 2010
Australia (2010)	Facilities emitting over a defined threshold per year plus upstream fuel.	Absolute cap starts in 2010

Source: (update from Reinaud and Philibert 2007)

panies? Companies not anticipated responding for some time with significant carbon policies of their own?

- Does sector have only limited ability to cost effectively reduced its emissions or obtain compliance through another means at least in the short term?

The steel products (crude steel) are potential cause of GHG emissions with relatively low value added are potentially most at risk of significant cost increases. High GHG intensive, low value added products are fairly homogeneous and can bought in international markets domestic manufactures of them(raw steel producers) may be price takers on world market with limited price through the carbon related cost. Part of several industries sector may fall into this category (cement, lime, aluminium). So, the GHG intensive and trade exposed industries will not be a straight forward process, as trade exposure, carbon cost, pricing dynamics may differ within a sector (Parker & Boldgett, 2018).

Mitigating Process of Carbon Leakage and Policies

Many techniques should be taken in against to carbon leakage (Marcu et al. 2014)
Like

1. Carbon tax,
2. Cap & trade,

3. Cash payments,
4. Border adjustment. Border taxes are two types -
    a. Countervailing duties.
    b. International reserve allowances
5. The imposition of countervailing duties based on the embedded carbon in imports would raise complex issues of law under the WTO.

IRA requirement essentially cap trade scheme focused on import of GH6 intensive production with each IRA equal to one metric ton of Co_2 equivalent, EPA calculate the IRA, IRA based on GHG emission of generated production.

Apart from that, other process are:

1. Free Allocation,
2. Compensation,
3. ETS in different speed,
4. Targeted access to international offset

The complementary mitigating policy employed to address the carbon emission sources (Sadik, 2005)

1. Vehicle GHG emission regulation.
2. Energy efficiency standards for appliances and equipment on per with the best in class globally.
3. Energy efficient building cost.
4. Increased capital for operating funding for public transit.
5. Increased public investment in renewable energy.
6. Government investment in research and development to help reduced the carbon emission.

Basic Difference Between Montreal and Kyoto Protocol

Kyoto protocol is a treaty but Montreal protocol is an agreement. Objective of Kyoto is reduction of carbon emission by using the eco-friendly technology but Montreal protocol claims for protecting the Ozone layer from Chlorofluorocarbon (CFC).

Montreal Protocol was a success because it was written agreement that include selected gases which are depleting the ozone layer which must be reduced. Multilateral fund for the implementation of Montreal protocol is to assist with developing country parties.

Carbon Trade and Global Policies

Kyoto protocol is introduced in 1997. This is the 1st climate change policy which is held on Rio De Janeiro. It is an internationally treaty which extends 1992 UNFCCC that commits state parties to reduce GHG emission. Kyoto applied on six Gases like carbon di oxide ($CO_{2,}$ CH_4, N_2O, HFCS, PFCS, and $SF6_{)}$. 1ST Commitment period started in 2008 and ended 2012 and 2nd commitment would end by 2020. 37 industrial countries have signed this treaty. But this protocol was failed because member countries cannot reach this commitment.

Next policy was introduced on 31st 2007 at Austria. The attending countries are G8 (Canada, Germany, France, Italy, Japan, Russia, UK, US). Sept 2007, the climate change conference held at Washington. Dec, 2007, climate change conference held at Bali Indonesia. 2008, the climate conference held at Poland. 2009, the climate change summit cop 15, 2011, The climate change conference held at Durban. 2012, the summit held at Qatar. In 2013, climate change conference held at Warsaw Poland. The last climate change conference held at Paris cop 21, 2015.

WHAT IS THE IMPACT OF THE PROTECTION OF CARBON LEAKAGE ON DEVELOPED AND DEVELOPING COUNTRY?

Impact on Developed Country: Recently we tried to estimate the impact of competitiveness effects on domestic industries in developed country with the climate change policy. Few Climate Centre paper under took a study to estimate the potential competitiveness effects of a domestic cap and trade system on US. The manufacturing sector of US emitted Green House Gas. It found that charges at a price of US $ 15 per ton of CO_2.But it does not significantly impact competitiveness of US manufacturing. But a subset of industries that are energy intensive.

The World Bank (2010) finds out that no proof of competitiveness impact on the presence of carbon tax energy intensive industry in US in the presence of carbon taxes. Another study by the World Bank found that many energy-intensive where carbon tax raises export. Gielen and Moriguchi (2002) found that if Japan and Europe introduce carbon taxes on iron and steel of US at $11 per ton of CO2 leakage can be high as 35% by 2020.

Demaily and Quirion (2006), they tried to focus on cap and trade policy system and found that cement has relatively high leakage range between 40% and 70% at a price of euro 20 per ton of CO2. After imposition of carbon tax in US and EU it resulted in the drop of real GDP in the range of 0.6%-0.7%.

Impact on Developing Country: Now we see that the effects of carbon tax on developing country. Since china is not only a newly emerged country but alsoa developing country. After imposition of carbon border tax China would be worse off. China's manufacturing export would be decline one fifth. All developing countries' export declines by 8% corresponding declines in real income would be 3.7% and 2.4%. Firstly, we identified the list of developing countries that large GHG emitters whose share in global emission is more than 0.5%. Based on this the countries export basket for EU. This paper identifies the list of sensitive products. Finding with respect to India suggests that the share of Indian exports to the EU of products could be affected by possible border adjustment could be as high as 24%.

Mattoo(2009) estimated the possible decline of output and export of energy intensive manufactures in the presence of possible border adjustment taxes. A key factor affecting the impact of border taxes is whether they are based on the carbon content of imports or carbon content of domestic production. Example China's manufacturing export would decline by one- fifth while India's major manufacturing export decline by 16%.

Carbon Tax vs. Cap

Carbon tax is imposed on GHG emission. The quantity of pollution reduced depends on the chosen level of tax. If the tax is too low then firms and household continuing to pollute. If tax is too high then to reduced emission and impact on profits of firms, employment level.

A Cap and Trade systems sets a maximum level of pollution. Cap system distributes permits among firms who produce carbon. The trading prices of permit fluctuate becoming more expensive when demand is high relative to supply and vice versa.

CAP v/s Tax: Initially permits are free to the early stage of production of firms. The free permit is known as grand fathering. It helps get firms to accept controls on emission in first place. But with a tax, there is an immediate cost for business to pay on each unit of GHG produced. Therefore, there is bigger initial hit on balanced sheet.

Under the carbon tax the price of emitting a unit of total quantity of pollution is set, but the total quantity of emission is not. So, everyone knows the price being paid for each unit of CO2 emitted but uncertainty about the cost achieving, this reduction.

Cap provides certainty about actual quantity of emission but uncertainty remains about cost of achieving this reduction. The emission is more sensitive than introduction of cap and trade system, because this situation quantity of emission must be control. If the cost of reducing pollution is more sensitive to change in emission, it is better pointing to a tax.

Incentives to reduce emission under the free allocation: Under the cap and trade, allowances can be introduced into the system either by auction or through free allocation. Sometimes levelled against cap and trade is that free allocation eliminates the recipient's incentive to reduce emission. When allowance is received for free, each additional unit of emission carries opportunity cost. Carbon tax and Cap thus offer equivalent incentive to reduce emissions, regardless of whether the allowances are introduced through auction or free provisions.

Volatility of Carbon Emissions Prices: Emission price volatility is a major issue in cap and trade system, though this is not a problem for imposing carbon tax since under carbon tax policy emission price itself is the tax rate. In this policy time profile of tax rate which is imposed by planning authority involves regular changes rather sudden vicissitudes. But in the case of cap and trade henceforth allowances is perfectly inelastic in nature, shift in demand significantly alter the price and may create price volatility through irregular shift in demand.

Emission prices and volatility is not a problem for carbon tax, the carbon tax is volatility. The time profile tax rate imposed by policy maker involves relatively smooth change rather than sudden jumps or ups and downs.

But volatility is an issue for the cap and trade system. Under cap and trade system supply of allowances is perfectly inelastic. Hence shifts in demands can cause significant price changes and irregular shifts in demand can produced price volatility.

Interaction With Other Climate Change Policy: Burtraw and Shobe (2012) have shown that in presence of cap and trade introducing additional GHG reducing policy such as a performance standard might yields no further reduction in overall emission.

Carbon tax leads to a reduction in overall emissions. The price of tax does not change when supplementary policy causes a reduction in emission.

Potential for greater cost effectiveness from broad sector coverage: Stains claims that cap and trade, tax both are very important system. He argues that as a tax moves from initial proposal to implementation various industries will seeks and some will win exclusion from this tax. This would make carbon tax less cost effective.

Under the cap and trade system get define prior to implementation. He points out stake holders struggle less for outright exclusion than for a larger share stock of freely allocated emissions allowances.

CONCLUSION

The trade mechanism of carbon leakage has positive impact upon the two types of countries- developing and developed. According to the Kyoto protocol, we know that the carbon tax, cap etc. are low in the developing countries and high in developed nations. The trade is possible only when the both countries have comparative advantage. Each country has different permits. A MNC produce goods in a country where companies get some cost of advantage. The MNC gets cost of advantage in developing country. So, through the permit traded MNC produced their goods that countries which have excess permit. So, the national income, employment also increases in that country and MNC shifted their product form those countries in which they want to get rid of the environmental degradation.

The developed countries also try to discover advanced technology which is eco-friendly. The technological development is two types. One types of technology which helps to reduce the emission of carbon and other technology which helps to filtering the carbon air and then emitted carbon free air from the factories.

Through the technological progress, the developed country may develop their research and development sector and developed country also uses that technology of their products and further more export it. This paper uses an implication of trade mechanism on the Heckcher-Ohlin (Heckscher, 1919; Ohlin, 1933) model and also shows the impact of climate change policy on trade. I distinguish between developed country and developing country according to the impact of climate change policy. This chapter highlighted carbon leakage test and showed the commencement of trade pattern. There is various mitigating process and policies explained and also highlighted a debate between carbon tax and cap and trade system which is better as a mitigating technique in this chapter.

REFERENCES

Aichele, R. (2013). *Trade Climate policy and Carbon Leakage Theory and Empirical Evidence*. ifo Beitrage Zur Wirtschaftsforschung.

Aichele, R., & Felbermayr, G. (2013). *Climate Change 2014: Mitigation of Climate Change*. Retrieved from https://books.google.co.in/books?isbn=11075821X

Barker, T. (2007). *Technical Summary. In: Climate Change 2007: Mitigation. Contribution of Working Group III to the Fourth Assessment Report of the Intergovernmental Panel on Climate Change*. Cambridge University Press. Retrieved from http://www.mnp.nl/ipcc/pages_media/FAR4docs/final_pdfs_ar4/TS.pdf

Bhattacharya, S., & Nanda, N. (2012). *Potential impact of Carbon Barriers to Trade: The case of India's export to the US under border tax adjustment*. The Energy and Resource Institute TERI-NFA working paper no- 3.

Bulkeley, H., & Newell, P. (2014). *Governing Climate Change*. London: Routledge.

Burniaux, J. M., & Martins, J. O. (2000). *Carbon Emission Leakage: A General Equilibrium View*. Retrieved from https://www.researchgate.net/publication/5204916

Cameron, A., & Mcleod, T. (2015). *Stitching together a Canadian Climate Plan, Patchwork Pollution Solution*. Centre for Natural Resource Policy.

Darke, F. (2012). *Carbon Tariffs: Effects in Settings with Technology Choice and Foreign Production Cost Advantage.* Harvard Business School, Working Paper 13 -021.

Demailly, D., & Quirion, P. (2008a). European Emission Trading Scheme and competitiveness: A case study on the iron and steel industry. *Energy Economics, 30*(4), 2009–2027. doi:10.1016/j.eneco.2007.01.020

Dinda, S. (2004). Environmental Kuznets Curve Hypothesis: A survey. *Ecological Economics, 49*(4), 431–455. doi:10.1016/j.ecolecon.2004.02.011

Fischer, C., & Fox, K. A. (2012). *Climate Policy and Fiscal Constraint: Do tax Interaction Outweigh Carbon Leakage?* SSRN, resource for the future discussion paper no. 12-19.

Frankel, A. J. (2009). *Environmental Effects on International Trade.* Retrieved from https://www.researchgate.net/publication/47408352_Environmental_Effects_of_International_Trade?enrichId=rgreq-4cfa5f7e394b712db54e45a9fd12488b-XXX&enrichSource=Y292ZXJQYWd-lOzQ3NDA4MzUyO0FTOjEzNzY2Mjk1MDI4NTMxOUAxNDA5ODMyODEzNjk1&el=1_x_2&_esc=publicationCoverPdf

Fulto, M., & Weber, C. (2012). *Carbon Asset Risk: Discussion Framework.* World Resource Institute.

Gielen, D. J., & Moriguchi, Y. (2002). CO_2 in the iron and steel industry: An analysis of Japanese emission reduction potentitals. *Energy Economics, 30*, 2009–2027.

Goulder, H. L., & Schein, R. A. (2013). Carbon Tax versus Carbon Trade: A Critical review. *Climate Change Economics (Singapore), 4*(3), 1350010. doi:10.1142/S2010007813500103

Heckscher, E. (1919). The effect of foreign trade on the distribution of income. *Ekonomisk Tidskrift, 21*, 497–512.

Kumar, K. K. S. (2010). *Carbon Trading, Dissemination paper 16, Centre for Excellence Environmental Economics.* Retrieved from http://159.65.137.173/index.php/component/cck/?task=download&file=journal_attachment&id=2615

Mansur, T. E., & Kahn, M. E. (2013). Do Local energy Prices and regulation affect the geographic concentration of employment? Journal of Public Economics, 101, 105–114.

Marcu, A., Egenhofer, C., Roth, S., & Stoefs, W. (2014). *Carbon Leakage: Option for EU, Carbon Market Forum.* Academic Press.

Mattoo, A. (2009). *Reconciling Climate Change and Trade Vulnerabilities to EU Climate Policies.* Peterson Institute of International Economics, Working Paper Series no 09-15.

Messerlin, A. P. (2010). *Climate Change and Trade Policy: From Mutual Destruction to Mutual Support.* SSRN, World Bank Policy Research Working Paper No. 5378.

Ohlin, B. (1933). *Interregional and International Trade.* Cambridge, MA: Harvard University Press.

Paker, L., & Boldgett, J. (2008). *Carbon Leakage and Trade: Issues.* Congressional Research Service.

Petersen, E. (2019). *A Road Map for U.S Carbon Reductions: Science New Series.* American Association for the Advancement of Science Publishing Company.

Reinaud, J. (2009). Trade competitiveness and carbon leakage: challenge and opportunities, Energy. Environment and development programme paper: 09/01. Chatam House.

Sadik, P. (2015). Essential of a carbon tax for Canada, Eco justice. Retrieved from https://www.ecojustice.ca/wp-content/uploads/2015/01/Essentials-of-a-Carbon-Tax-for-Canada.pdf

Shobe, M.W., & Burtraw, D. (2006). *Rethinking Environmental Federalism In A Warming World.* Academic Press.

Smith, S. (2006). *Greenhouse Gas Emission Trading. The Science of Climate Change.* NSW Parliament Library Research Service.

Stram, N. S. (2014). A new strategic plan for a carbon tax. *Energy Policy*, *73*, 519–523. doi:10.1016/j.enpol.2014.05.023

Wheeler, D., & Boyes, M. (2009). *GreenHouse Gas Footprinting Using Overseer-The Whole Picture.* Retrieved from flrc.massey.ac.nz/workshops/11/…./Wheeler_1_2011

Zmijewski, K. (2011). *On the risk of carbon leakage in Poland.* E. Kwiatkowski.

Zotz, A. K. (2012). *Impact of Climate Change mitigating policies in OECD Countries on carbon emission intensive export industry in Latin America.* Inter-American Development Bank. Integration and trade sector policy brief no IDB- PB-195.

KEY TERMS AND DEFINITIONS

Carbon Emission: It is the amount of carbon release due to our daily activities.

Carbon Emission Price: It is the price of trade permits.

Carbon Leakage: It means changes or displacement of carbon emission reduction economic activates due to implementing policies which results increases carbon emission from outside.

Carbon Tax: It refers to imposing taxes on the amount of carbon use.

Climate Change: It means average temperature of earth surface increases to some degree after global warming.

Trade Permit: It is the license of emission limits.

Chapter 13
State-Level Status of Renewable Energy Development in India

Sebak Kumar Jana
Vidyasagar University, India

Moumita Ghosh
Vidyasagar University, India

Asim Kumar Karmakar
Netaji Subhas Open University, India

ABSTRACT

Renewable energy is energy that is collected from renewable resources that are essentially inexhaustible like sunlight, wind, hydropower, and various forms of biomass. India has a huge renewable energy potential, and the availability of renewable energy sources is widely dispersed. The key objectives of the chapter are to assess the state development of renewable energy in India. It is seen that the average percentage users of solar power in India has increased from 0.27% in 2001 to 0.44% in 2011. ANOVA results indicate there is significant difference among the states of India in renewable energy development in comparison to their potential capacities, and there is enough scope for the development of renewable energy like solar energy in India.

INTRODUCTION

Renewable energy is energy that is collected from renewable resources that are essentially inexhaustible. This includes sources like sunlight, wind, hydropower and various forms of biomass. The Indian power sector is one of the most diversified in the world. Sources for power generation range from commercial sources like coal, natural gas, diesel and nuclear power to other non conventional renewable sources like wind, solar, bio-mass, small-hydro. The demand for electricity in the country has been growing at a rapid rate because of huge population in the country and is expected to grow further in the years to come (Bhaskar 2013, Roy and Jana 1998).

DOI: 10.4018/978-1-5225-8547-3.ch013

The major arguments of renewable energy development in India are as follows (Kumar et al 2010, Rathore et al 2019). First, a majority of the population in India still live in rural areas. The sluggish development of the power sector in India has left many rural households with poor quality and unreliable power supply. Secondly, in India the electricity sector occupies the second position in emitting greenhouse gasses. Renewable energy sources (RES) have the potential to provide energy with negligible emissions of air pollutants and green house gases. For generation of 1 KWH for a coal fired power plant, 950 -1000 grams of carbon dioxide is emitted in India. In case of generation solar power, it is only about around 54–60 grams per KWH. During recent years, due to increase in cost of conventional energy and the environmental problems caused by the use of conventional fuels, India is putting emphasis to use renewable energy sources. To meet the increasing demand of power in the country, India has to search for more economical, sustainable, and clean power generation sources. Thirdly, India is a large country with geographical area of 3.287 million square kms including varied regions hills, coastal area, deserts and forests. It is not feasible to connect all the locations through the grid. Decentralized electrification through the development of renewable energy like the rooftop solar power is the best-suited option for providing uninterrupted power supply for the people living in far-flung areas.

India's Intended Nationally Determined Contribution (INDC) to the UNFCCC, outlining the country's post-2020 climate actions builds on its goal of installing 175 gigawatts (GW) of renewable power capacity by 2022 by setting a new target to increase the country's share of non-fossil-based installed electric capacity to 40 percent by 2030. A capacity of 62.84 GW has been set up by December 2017 and this constitutes 18 per cent of the total installed capacity. Now India has 4th and 6th global position in wind and solar power deployment respectively (IBEF 2018).

India has a huge renewable energy potential and availability of renewable energy sources is widely dispersed. In some states, the potential for renewable energy is insignificant (example Delhi) whereas some states have abundant renewable energy sources. Solar energy is concentrated in the northwest region in the country – Gujarat, Rajasthan, Ladakh, Maharashtra and Madhya Pradesh. Wind energy is abundant in some states like Gujarat, Karnataka, Maharashtra, Tamil Nadu and Jammu and Kashmir. and the small hydro potential in the country is concentrated in hilly states of Himachal Pradesh, Uttaranchal, Jammu and Kashmir, Arunachal Pradesh and Chhattisgarh.

As on 31st March, 1990 renewable energy sources capacity was 18 MW. Over the last three decades, the renewable energy has shown an increasing trend. At the initial stage, the capacity addition from renewable energy sources was very slow, but from 2008 onwards the capacity addition was considerable. India accounts for about 4% of the total global electricity generation and its contribution to the global renewable generation capacity is 4.43%. As of July 2018, total installed capacity (grid interactive) of renewable power generation in India stood at 116.82 GW, which is 33.81 per cent of the total installed capacity of 345.49 GW (IBEF, 2018). India's installed capacity during 2010 to 2016 is shown in Table 1. The installed capacity as on 31st March 2016 from renewable energy sources was 42,849 MW. Total installed renewable capacity (MW) during 2006-07 to 2017-18 has been presented in Figure 1. The growth of renewable energy sources like solar power, wind power, small hydro power, biomass and urban & industrial wastages during 2008 to 2016 in India is shown in Figure 1.

In Table 2, we have presented *achievement in grid connected renewable power (as on 31.12.2017).*

Table 1. Year-wise all India installed capacity (in MW) from power stations

	Sources	2010	2011	2012	2013	2014	2015	2016
	Hydro	36863 (23.13%)	37567 (21.64%)	38990 (19.51%)	39491 (17.68%)	40532 (16.53%)	41267 (15.19%).1	42783.42 (14.16%)
Thermal	Coal	84198 (52.82%)	93918 (54.09%)	112022.4 (56.05%)	130221 (58.31%)	145273 (59.23%)	164636 (60.59%)	185172.9 (61.30%)
	Gas	17056 (10.70%)	17706 (10.20%)	18381.1 (9.20%)	20110 (9.00%)	21782 (8.88%)	23062 (8.49%)	24508.6 (8.11%)
	Diesel	1200 (0.75%)	1200 (0.69%)	1200 (0.60%)	1200 (0.54%)	1200 (0.49%)	1200 (0.44%)	99353 (0.33%)
	Sub Total	102454 (64.28%)	112824 (64.98%)	131603.4 (65.84%)	151531 (67.85%)	168255 (68.60%)	188898 (69.52%)	210675.0 (69.74%)
	Nuclear	4560 (2.86%)	4780 (2.75%)	4780 (2.39%)	4780 (2.14%)	4780 (1.95%)	5780 (2.13%)	5780 (1.91%)
	RES (MNRE)	15521 (9.74%)	18455 (10.63%)	24503 (12.26%)	27542 (12.33%)	31692 (12.92%)	35777 (13.17%)	42849.4 (14.18%)
	Total	159398	173626	199877.4	223344	245259	271722	302087.8

Source: Central Electricity Authority (CEA), various years

Figure 1. Total installed renewable capacity (MW) in India
Source: MNRE, 2018

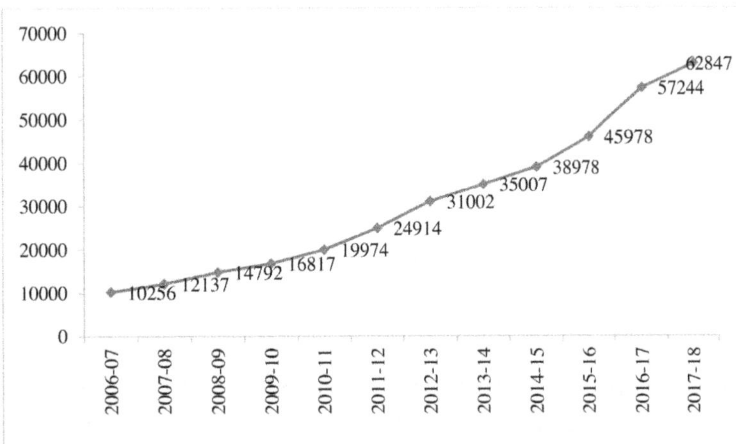

LITERATURE REVIEW

Some studies relevant to our paper are mentioned here. Khare et al (2013) presented the major constraints that are hampering the development of renewable energy in India in spite of India have adequate sunshine and balanced wind speed. Bhattacharya et al (2016) explained the growth process between 1991 and 2012 using the panel estimation techniques and their findings establish cross–sectional dependence and heterogeneity across the countries. Mishra and Behera (2015) found that the renewable energy leads to improvement in overall standard of living of people in rural Odisha. Hrishikesh and Debnath (2017) made a systematic cost benefit analysis with data from selected 12 institutions in Kamrup district of As-

Table 2. Achievement in grid connected renewable power (as on 31.12.2017)

	Cumulative Achievements (MW) (as on 31.12.2017)	% share
Wind Power	32848.5	52.27
Solar Power - Ground Mounted	16070.1	25.57
Solar Power - Roof Top	982.3	1.56
Small Hydro Power	4418.2	7.03
Bio Power (Biomass & Gasification and Bagasse Cogeneration)	8413.8	13.39
Waste to Power	114.1	0.18
Total	62846.9	100.00

Source: MNRE, 2018

Figure 2. Growth of renewable energy installed capacity (MW) in India
Source: MNRE, Various Years

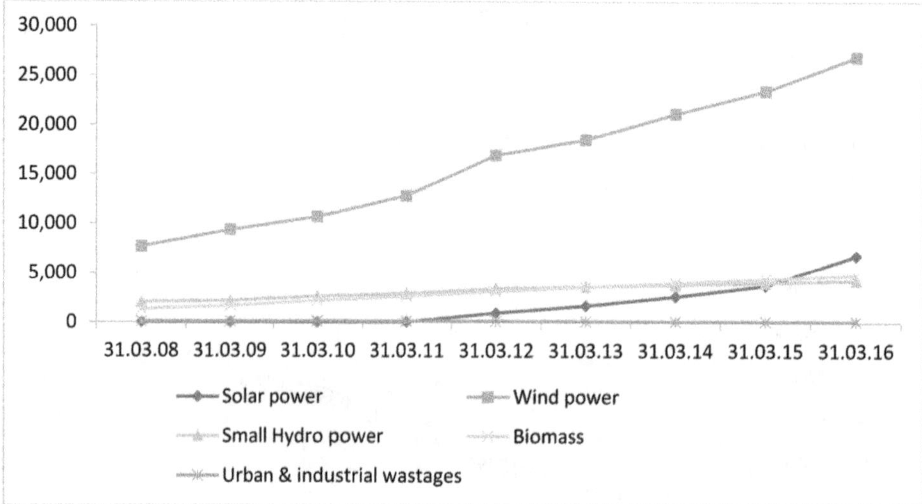

sam to show the economic feasibility of such a project in replacing the existing source of state supplied electricity with a payback period of 5 years. Shruti et al (2016) discussed about the availability, current status, major achievements and future potential of renewable energy in India. Osmani (2014) highlighted the gap between India's energy production and energy consumption. According to Bhattacharya and Jana (2008), India has assumed great importance in recent years due to high growth rate of conventional energy consumption, coal based energy consumption, imports of petroleum fuels and volatility of world oil market. Kanase et al (2010) analysed the off-grid electrification by utilizing Integrated Renewable Energy System (IRES) to satisfy the electrical and cooking needs of the seven unelectrified village in the Almora district of Uttarakhand state, India. Yadav et al (2017) analysed the modelling of system having wind –biomass based hybrid system operating in parallel with limited grid supply system to meet the rural demand. Som and Pathak (2015) highlighted the economical and environmental cost of generating electricity by conventional and non–conventional energy sources. Sangroya and Nayak (2014) find that wind energy has been the fastest growing renewable energy sector in India. Nathan (2015) suggested on the appropriate land procurement and rooftop policies as well as manufacturing strategies and technology. Kasturi (2017) worked on the government's decision to raise solar power generation capacity from the current 8 GW to 100 GW by 2022 and how these massive level of capacity addition decision impact India's electricity distribution companies. Kapoor and Dwivedi (2017) focused on the increasing awareness of existing solar systems and ambitious plan on the solar power generation over the few years. Jain and Patwardhan (2013) attempted to characterise jobs created for renewable energy technologies as a function of multiple attributes to observe the employment effects. Nayar (2016) discussed on the renewable purchase obligation mechanism. To promote investment in renewable energy, the renewable energy purchase obligation mechanism (RPO) and the trade of renewable energy certificate scheme (RECs) should be more emphasised. Nathan (2014) emphasized on solar photovoltaic systems installations for lighting needs in rural areas. Sharma (2012) emphasised on realistic electricity demand projections are necessary for the overall development of the power sector. Kocis and Judit (2014) described the potential relationship between the ratio of renewable consumption in gross energy consumption, GDP per capita, and R&D expenditures. Kar and Gopakumar (2015) envisaged that energy is key important for the economic growth and prosperity in India. In India consumption of energy mainly depends on coal based thermal power and as a result demand for coal has been increasing over the years. Kolhe and Khot (2015) highlighted the merits and demerits of available energy sources and to find the scope of renewable energy sources.

There are a number of studies on the renewable energy development in India. However, there are a limited number of studies on regions status of renewable energy development and potential for states in India. In the present study, we have emphasised on scenario of renewable energy development in various states of India.

OBJECTIVES

The key objectives of the present study are to assess the state-wise development of renewable energy in India. Among many available options for renewable energy, solar photovoltaic is the best alternative for distributed energy generation, because of the rapid decrease in cost along with advancement in technology We have utilised the data of renewable energy (mainly in terms of solar energy) use for different states in India for the years 2001 and 2011. We are also interested to assess state-wise status of renewable energy development in India in terms of potential capacity. The different policies and strategies adopted by the government of India have also been given in brief.

MEHODOLOGY

We have used Analysis of variance (ANOVA) to test whether there is any statistical difference in the use of potential energy across the five regions of India. ANOVA is a technique to test for the significance of the difference between more than two sample means and to make inferences about whether our samples are drawn from the populations having the same mean. The "analysis of variance" procedure or "F-test" is used in such problems where we want to test for the significance o the difference among more than two sample means. The term one-factor analysis of variance refers to the fact that a single variable or factor of interest is controlled and its effect on the elementary units is observed. In other words, in one-way classification, the data is classified according to only one criterion. The basic procedure is to derive two different estimates of population variance from the data, then calculate a statistic from the ratio of these two estimates ('between groups' and 'within groups' variance). The F ratio is the ratio of 'between-groups' variance to 'within-groups' variance. A significant F value indicates that the population means are probably not equal. Before ANOVA was conducted, it was ensured that the necessary assumptions were met. The two assumptions of concern were population normality and homogeneity of variance (Sodhi and Waraich 2016).

We have made the following hypothesis:

H0: There is no significant difference among the five regions of India in percentage of installed capacity to potential capacity of renewable energy.

RENEWABLLE ENERGY POLICIES AND STRATEGIES ADOPTED IN INDIA

Government of India has taken up various policies and strategies over years to promote renewable energy in India (IBEF 2018). National Offshore Wind Energy Policy of GOI: This policy promotes deployment of Offshore Wind Farms up to 12 nautical miles from coast. Under this policy, single window clearance is offered and tax holiday of 10 years for offshore wind energy generation is given.

Renewable Purchase Obligations (RPOs): RPO's are a mechanism by which State Electricity commissions are obliged to purchase certain percentage of power from renewable energy sources. Also, floor prices of the RPO have been set to provide certainty to companies. The floor price has been set at US$ 144 per MW.

Hybrid wind-solar capacity of 10GW by 2022: Hybridization of the two technologies i.e. solar and wing will help in minimizing variability and optimal utilization of infrastructure including land and transmission systems.

Decentralised Power Generation: Electricity to all has become a major thrust area for Government of India. This includes households and villages and slums which are not currently a part of the grid or centralised distribution. Selco Solar Pvt Ltd started installing solar panels in slums which were not connected to the grid as a pilot project in 2008 and has since expanded into other states as well. They have also used standardized financial packages to get the slum people move from kerosene to solar power.

Power Purchase Agreements: With the increasing competition and increasing FDI, players in the solar sector have started bidding at lower prices with solar tariffs reaching record low of Rs 2.44 (US$ 0.04) per unit in May 2017. Power Purchase Agreements with states have become important part of the project cycle for Indian companies. Wind power tariff reached record low of Rs 2.43 (US$ 0.038) in 500 mw reverse auctions by Gujarat Urja Vikas Nigam Limited (GUVNL) in December 2017.

Investment on solar energy: India is one of the best recipients of solar energy with relatively abundant availability for its favourable location in the solar belt. Solar PV emerges as the largest market for new investment with rapidly falling costs. World's largest solar park named 'Shakti Sthala' was launched in Karnataka in March 2018 with an investment of Rs 16,500 crore (US$ 2.55 billion).Solar sector in India received investments of over US$10 billion in CY2017.

National Solar Mission: the National Solar Mission (NSM) was Launched in January 2010, under the National Action Plan on Climate Change (NAPCC). The aim of the mission is to establish India as a global leader in solar energy, through creation of the policy conditions for diffusion of solar technology across the country as fast as possible. The present target of the mission is of installing 100 GW grid-connected solar power plants by the year 2022.

Jawaharlal Nehru National Solar Mission (JNNSM) and Solar Rooftop Policy: The Government of India (GOI), during 2010-2011, launched Jawaharlal Nehru National Solar Mission (JNNSM) under the National Action Plan on Climate Change (NAPCC) to promote the growth of solar power in India. The Mission targets included (i) deployment of 20,000 MW of grid connected solar power by 2022, (ii) 2000 MW of off-grid solar applications including 20 million solar lights by 2022, (iii) 20 million sq. m. Solar thermal collector area, (iv) creating favorable conditions for developing solar manufacturing capability in the country. In 2015, the GOI updated the target of JNNSM from 20,000 MW to 100000 MW. Out of the total 100 GW of solar PV installations, 40 GW will come in the form of the solar rooftop. For achieving the target of 40 GW solar rooftop installation, the Government launched Grid Connected Rooftop and Small Solar Power Plants Program under the umbrella of JNNSM. The main objective of the program is promoting the grid connected SPV rooftop and small SPV power generating plants among residential, community, institutional, industrial, and commercial establishments. In Table 3, state-wise solar rooftop policies in India have been presented with state policies for solar rooftop, system size and grid penetration percentage of distribution transformer capacity. Grid penetration varies from 80% in Karnataka to 15% in the states like Bihar, Haryana and Uttar Pradesh. Currently 20 States of India namely Andhra Pradesh, Chhattisgarh, Delhi, Gujarat, Haryana, Himachal Pradesh, Jammu & Kashmir, Jharkhand, Karnataka, Kerala, Madhya Pradesh, Manipur, Punjab, Puducherry, Rajasthan, Tamil Nadu, Telangana, Uttar Pradesh, Uttarakhand and West Bengal have come out with Solar Policy supporting grid connected rooftop systems (MNRE, 2018).

In Table 4, we have presented the state wise cumulative installation of Solar Photovoltaic (SPV) systems in terms of numbers of lanterns & lamps., home lights, street lights and stand alone power plants as on 31.12.2017 in India.

STATE-WISE PROGRESS OF SOLAR ENERGY CONSUMERS IN INDIA

In this section, we have presented state-wise status of solar energy consumers for the years 2001 and 2011.

State-Wise Status of Solar Energy Consumers in 2001

Table 5 presents state–wise number of consumers using solar energy in India. It has revealed that 0.27% of total electricity consumers in India used solar power as per the census 2001. The state with highest percentage of solar energy consumers in 2001 was Uttaranchal (1.87%) and the state with lowest percentage of solar energy consumers was Delhi (0.09%).

State-Wise Status of Total Solar Energy Consumers in 2011

Table 6 presents state–wise number of consumers using solar energy in India in 2011. It has revealed that 0.44% of total electricity consumers in India use solar power as per the census 2011. The state with highest percentage of solar energy consumers in 2011 was Arunachal Pradesh (2.90) and the state with lowest percentage of solar energy consumers was Delhi (0.05%) Comparing Table 5 and Table 6, we see that the average percentage users of solar power have increased from 0.27% in 2001 to 0.44% in 2011.

Table 3. Solar Rooftop policies in the states of India

Sl. No.	State	State policy for solar Rooftop	System Size	Grid penetration percentage of distribution transformer capacity
1	Andhra Pradesh	Andhra Pradesh Solar Policy 2015	Up to 1 MW_p	-
2	Assam	Assam Solar Policy 2017	1 KW_p to 1 MW_p	-
3	Bihar	-	Up to 1 MW_p	15%
4	Chhattisgarh	Chhattisgarh Solar Energy Policy 2012-2017	50KW_p 1MW_p	-
5	Delhi	Delhi Solar Energy Policy, 2012	1KW_p or more	20%
7	Haryana	Haryana Solar Policy, 2014	Up to 1 MW_p	15%
8	Himachal Pradesh	Himachal Pradesh Solar Power Polcy	Up to 1 MW_p	30%
9	Jharkhand	Jharkhand Solar Power	Up to 1 MW_p	-
9	Karnataka	Karnataka Solar power Policy, 2014-2021	Up to 1 MW_p	80%
10	Kerala	Kerala Solar Policy,2013	1 KW_p to 1 MW_p	50%
11	Madhya Pradesh	Madhya Pradesh Solar Rooftop Policy 2016	0.5-250 KW_p	-
12	Maharashtra	Maharashtra Solar Policy 2016	Up to 1 MW_p	40%
13	North East (Arunachal, Meghalaya,	-	Up to 1 MW_p	15%
14	Odisha	-	≤1MWp	30%
15	Punjab	Punjab Solar Rooftop Policy 2014	1 KW_p to 1 MW_p	30%
16	Rajasthan	Rajasthan Solar Energy Policy,2014	1 KW_p to 1 MW_p	30%
17	Tamil Nadu	Tamil Nadu Solar Energy Policy 2012	-	30%
18	Telangana	Telangana Solar Power Policy,2015	1 KW_p to 1 MW_p	
19	Uttar Pradesh	Uttar Pradesh Rooftop Solar Photovoltaic Power Palnt Policy 2014	1KW_p or more	15%
20	Uttarakhand	Uttarakhand Solar Power Policy,2013	Up to 5000 KW_p	-
21	West Bengal	West Benbgal Solar Power Policy,2013	Higher minimum capacity requirement of 5 KWp	17%
22	Goa and Union Territories	-	1 KW_p to 500 KW_p	30%

Source: Rathore et al (2019)

Table 4. State wise cumulative installation of SPV systems as on 31.12.2017

S. No.	State/UT	Lanterns & Lamps Nos.	Home Lights Nos.	Street Lights Nos.	Pumps Nos.	Stand Alone Power Plants (KWp)
1	Andhra Pradesh	51360	22972	7812	19526	3785.6
2	Arunachal Pradesh	14433	18945	1671	22	650.1
3	Assam	13379	6926	318	45	1605
4	Bihar	210391	12303	955	1882	4168.6
5	Chhattisgarh	3311	7754	2042	26673	28660
6	Delhi	4807	0	301	90	1269
7	Goa	1093	393	707	15	32.72
8	Gujarat	31603	9253	2004	8010	13576.6
9	Haryana	93853	56727	22018	1243	2321.25
10	Himachal Pradesh	33909	29342	58718	6	1905.5
11	Jammu & Kashmir	51224	65319	5806	39	7719.85
12	Jharkhand	138723	9450	787	3598	3639.9
13	Karnataka	7334	52638	2694	4118	7754.01
14	Kerala	54367	41912	1735	818	15825.4
15	Madhya Pradesh	529101	4016	9378	5584	3654
16	Maharashtra	239297	3497	10420	3315	3857.7
17	Manipur	4787	3900	1888	40	1241
18	Meghalaya	24875	7844	4900	19	1084.5
19	Mizoram	9589	6801	5056	37	2019
20	Nagaland	6766	1045	6235	3	1506
21	Odisha	99843	5274	5834	8570	567.515
22	Punjab	17495	8626	42758	1857	2066
23	Rajasthan	225851	166978	6852	41377	10850
24	Sikkim	23300	15059	504	0	850
25	Tamil Nadu	16818	273015	39235	4459	12752.6
26	Telangana	0	0	351	424	6643
27	Tripura	64282	32723	1199	151	667
28	Uttar Pradesh	104791	235909	185091	10877	10041.5
29	Uttarakhand	93927	91595	21905	26	2365.03
30	West Bengal	17662	145332	8726	653	1730
31	Andaman & Nicobar	6296	468	390	5	167
32	Chandigarh	1675	275	898	12	730
33	Lakshadweep	5289	600	2465	0	2190
34	Puducherry	1637	25	417	21	121
35	Others	125797	24047	9150	0	23885
36	NABARD	0	116226	0	4012	0
	Total	**2328865**	**1477189**	**471220**	**147527**	**181901**

Source: MNRE, 2018

Table 5. State-wise status of solar energy consumers in India in 2001

	State	Nos. of electricity Consumers	Nos. of Solar Energy Consumers	% of solar Energy consumers
1	Andhra Pradesh	16849857	37704	0.22
2	Arunachal Pradesh	212615	481	0.23
3	Assam	4935358	10082	0.20
4	Bihar	13982590	40700	0.29
5	Chhattisgarh	4148518	6804	0.16
6	Delhi	2554149	2365	0.09
7	Goa	279216	476	0.17
8	Gujarat	9643989	23115	0.24
9	Haryana	3529642	6874	0.19
10	Himachal Pradesh	1240633	1423	0.11
11	Jammu Kashmir	1551768	10309	0.66
12	Jharkhand	4862590	10333	0.21
13	Karnataka	10232133	21989	0.21
14	Kerala	6595206	33291	0.50
15	Madhya Pradesh	10919653	15130	0.14
16	Maharashtra	19063149	24654	0.13
17	Manipur	397656	918	0.23
18	Meghalaya	420246	1114	0.27
19	Mizoram	160966	849	0.53
20	Nagaland	332050	648	0.20
21	Orissa	7870127	27208	0.35
22	Punjab	4265156	5643	0.13
23	Rajasthan	9342294	31584	0.34
24	Sikkim	104738	149	0.14
25	Tamil Nadu	14173626	34614	0.24
26	Tripura	662023	1268	0.19
27	Uttar Pradesh	25760601	93047	0.36
28	Uttaranchal	1586321	29726	1.87
29	West	15715915	49112	0.31
	India	191392785	521610	0.27

Source: Census of India, GOI, 2001

In Table 7, we have presented state-wise installed capacity and potential energy of solar energy in India. We have classified the states of India by four regions namely Eastern (E), Western (W), Northern (N), Southern(S)) and North-Eastern (N-E).

Table 6. State-wise status of solar energy consumers in India in 2011

	State	Nos. of Consumers	Nos. of Solar Energy Consumers	% of solar Energy consumers
1	Andhra Pradesh	21024534	55005	0.26
2	ArunachalPradesh	261614	7597	2.90
3	Assam	6367295	49218	0.77
4	Bihar	18940629	1,09,389	0.58
5	Chhattisgarh	5622850	49798	0.89
6	Delhi	3340538	1621	0.05
7	Goa	322813	576	0.18
8	Gujarat	12181718	16016	0.13
9	Haryana	4717954	7511	0.16
10	HimachalPradesh	1476581	1834	0.12
11	Jammu Kashmir	2015088	20813	1.03
12	Jharkhand	6181607	44919	0.73
13	Karnataka	13179911	25080	0.19
14	Kerala	7716370	13523	0.18
15	Madhya Pradesh	14967597	40089	0.27
16	Maharashtra	23830580	57589	0.24
17	Manipur	507152	9740	1.92
18	Meghalaya	538299	4302	0.80
19	Mizoram	221077	2936	1.33
20	Nagaland	399965	1257	0.31
21	Orissa	9556431	34216	0.36
22	Punjab	5409699	5754	0.11
23	Rajasthan	12581303	78212	0.62
24	Sikkim	1,28,131	305	0.24
25	Tamil Nadu	18493003	13669	0.07
26	Tripura	842781	15868	1.88
27	Uttar Pradesh	32924266	156837	0.48
28	Uttaranchal	1997068	24267	1.22
29	West Bengal	20067299	238571	1.19
	India	245814153	10,86,512	0.44

Source: Census of India, GOI, 2011

We have used ANOVA to test whether there is no significant difference among the five regions of India in percentage of installed capacity to potential capacity. ANOVA estimation results given in Table 8 show there is significant difference (p = 4%) across regions in % of installed capacity to potential of the states in India among five regions in India. The results clearly reveal that there is enough scope of development of renewable energy like solar power in India.

Table 7. Region-wise % of installed capacity to potential capacity

	State	Region	Installed Capacity of Solar Power (MW)	Solar Potential (MW)	% of Installed Capacity to Potential
1	Andhra Pradesh	S	475.74	38440	1.24
2	Arunachal Pradesh	N-E	0.265	8650	0.00
3	Bihar	E	5	11200	0.04
4	Chhattisgarh	W	73.18	18270	0.40
5	Delhi	N	6.712	2050	0.33
6	Gujarat	W	1024.15	35770	2.86
7	Haryana	N	12.8	4560	0.28
8	Jharkhand	E	16	18180	0.09
9	Karnataka	S	104.22	24700	0.42
10	Kerala	S	12.025	6110	0.20
11	Madhya Pradesh	W	678.58	61660	1.10
12	Maharashtra	W	378.7	64320	0.59
13	Orissa	E	66.92	25780	0.26
14	Punjab	N	342.32	2810	12.18
15	Rajasthan	N	1264.35	142310	0.89
16	Tamil Nadu	S	635.87	17670	3.60
17	Telengana	N	392.39	20410	1.92
18	Tripura	N-E	5	2080	0.24
19	Uttar Pradesh	N	140	22830	0.61
20	Uttarakhand	E	5	16800	0.03
21	West Bengal	E	7.21	6260	0.12

Source: MNRE, Annual Report, 2016-17

Table 8. ANOVA results

ANOVA						
Source of Variation	*SS*	*df*	*MS*	*F*	*P-value*	*F crit*
Between Groups	20.85658	1.00	20.86	4.72	0.04	4.08
Within Groups	176.7441	40.00	4.42			
Total	197.6006	41				

Source: Own Estimation

CONCLUSION

In the future competitive electricity market for India, it becomes very much important to give special consideration for development of renewable energy due to economic, environmental and other social problems related with conventional generation. Solar energy not only be the important source of electricity generation but also to increase energy security and lead the massive market for renewable energy. The major problem with solar power generation is high cost of renewable generation. The Indian government presently is providing subsidy in order to encourage renewable energy generation.

We have presented the status of renewable energy use for different states in India in 2001 and 2011. We have presented state-wise status of renewable energy development in India in terms of potential capacity. We find there is significant difference among the states in renewable energy development in comparison to their potential capacities. To promote renewable energy some policy suggestions are given below. (i) As there is enough scope of energy development in India, more emphasis is needed for the development of renewable energy. (ii) Tax structure including GST should go in favour of renewable energy.(iii) Proper monitoring mechanism should be development so that subsidy given the renewable energy is properly developed.(iv) Proper institutional mechanism should be development so that services for hiring services renewable energy could be developed.(v) Considering the rise in coal prices and oil prices over years, solar energy equipment production should be increased at Government initiative to enjoy the economies of scale. Till now, states have been free to fix their own RPO targets subject to a minimum of 8 per cent for solar. State Electricity Regulatory Commissions may consider notifying the RPO for their respective States in line with the uniform trajectory defined by the Centre, the order noted.

REFERENCES

Bhaskar, B. (2013). *Energy Security and Economic Development in India: a holistic approach.* The Energy and Resources Institute (TERI).

Bhattacharya, M., Paramati, S. R., Ozturk, I., & Bhattacharya, S. (2016). The effect of renewable energy consumption on economic growth: Evidence from top 38 countries. *Applied Energy*, *162*, 733–741.

Bhattacharya, S. C., & Jana, C. (2009). Renewable energy in India: Historical developments and prospects. *Energy*, *34*(8), 981–991.

IBEF. (2018). *Renewable Energy*. IBEF.

Jain, M., & Patwardhan, A. (2013). Employment Outcomes of Renewable Energy Technologies: Implications of Policies in India. *Economic and Political Weekly*, 84–89.

Kanase-Patil, A. B., Saini, R. P., & Sharma, M. P. (2010). Integrated renewable energy systems for off grid rural electrification of remote area. *Renewable Energy*, *35*(6), 1342–1349.

Kannan, K. (2017). Is the Government Overly Aggressive Solar Thrust in Public Interest. *Economic and Political Weekly*, *52*(6).

Kapoor, K. K., & Dwivedi, Y. K. (2017). A take on solar power in India. *Economic and Political Weekly*, *52*(7), 21–24.

Kar, S. K., & Gopakumar, K. (2015). Progress of renewable energy in India. *Adv Energy Res*, *3*(2), 97–115.

Khare, V., Nema, S., & Baredar, P. (2013). Status of solar wind renewable energy in India. *Renewable & Sustainable Energy Reviews*, *27*, 1–10.

Kocsis, I., & Kiss, J. T. (2014). Renewable energy consumption, R&D and GDP in European Union countries. *Environmental Engineering and Management Journal*, *13*(11), 2825–2830.

Kolhe M. R. & Knot, P.G. (2015). Environmental and social issues related to coal and Role of Renewable Energy Sources in India. *International Journal of Advance Research in Computer Science*, *3*(8).

Kumar, A., Kumar, K., Kaushik, N., Sharma, S., & Mishra, S. (2010). Renewable energy in India: Current status and future potentials. *Renewable & Sustainable Energy Reviews*, *14*(8), 2434–2442.

Mishra, P., & Behera, B. (2016). Socio-economic and environmental implications of solar electrification: Experience of rural Odisha. *Renewable & Sustainable Energy Reviews*, *56*, 953–964.

Nathan, H. S. K. (2014). Solar energy for rural electricity in India: A misplaced emphasis. *Economic and Political Weekly*, *49*(50), 60–67.

Nayar, R. (2016). Enforcing Renewable Purchase Obligations. *Economic and Political Weekly*, *51*(40), 21–23.

NRE. (2018). *Annual Report: 2017-18*. Government of India. Retrieved from https://powermin.nic.in/en/content/annual-reports-year-wise-ministry

Osmani, A. R. (2014). Conventional energy to renewable energy: Perspectives for India. *The NEHU Journal*, *12*(2), 41–60.

Rathore, P. K. S., Chauhan, D. S., & Singh, R. P. (2019). Decentralized solar rooftop photovoltaic in India: On the path of sustainable energy security. *Renewable Energy*, *131*, 297–307.

Roy, J., & Jana, S. (1998). Solar lanterns for rural households. *Energy*, *23*(1), 67–68.

Sangroya, D., & Nayak, J. K. (2015). Development of wind energy in India. *International Journal of Renewable Energy Research*, *5*(1), 1–13.

Sharma, S. (2012). True electricity demand and the critical role of renewable energy sources. *Economic and Political Weekly*, *47*(24), 24–27.

Shruti, M. N. K., & Minu, K. (2016). Forecast Analysis of the Potential and Availability of Renewable Energy in India: A Review. *Proceedings of 30th IRF International Conference*.

Som, T., & Pathak, R. (2015). Perspectives and Projections based on the Current Indian Energy Scenario, ER publications. *International Journal of Enhanced Research in Science, Technology & Engineering*, *4*(9).

Yadav, D. K., Bhatti, T. S., & Verma, A. (2017). Study of integrated rural electrification system using wind-biogas based hybrid system and limited grid supply system. *International Journal of Renewable Energy Research*, *7*(1), 1–11.

KEY TERMS AND DEFINITIONS

ANOVA: Analysis of variance (ANOVA) is a statistical technique that is used to check if the means of two or more groups are significantly different from each other.

GST: The full form of GST stands is goods and services tax. GST is a type of tax introduced in India from July 2017. GST is a consumption-based tax ultimately borne by the end consumer of a goods or service.

GW: The gigawatt (GW) is equal to one billion (10^9) watts or 1 gigawatt = 1000 megawatts (MW).

Jawaharlal Nehru National Solar Mission (JNNSM): The Jawaharlal Nehru National Solar Mission is one of the eight key National Missions which comprises India's National Action Plan on Climate Change (NAPCC), which was launched on 30th June 2008 and was approved on January 11, 2010 by the Government of India.

kWp: Solar electricity systems are given a rating in kilowatts peak (kWp). This is essentially the rate at which it generates energy at peak performance for example at noon on a sunny day.

Renewable Energy: Renewable energy is energy that is collected from renewable resources, which are naturally replenished on a human time scale, such as sunlight, wind, rain, tides, waves, and geothermal heat.

RPO: The full form of RPO is renewable purchase obligation. This is a mechanism by which the State Electricity Regulatory Commissions are obliged to purchase a certain percentage of power from renewable energy sources.

Solar Energy: Is radiant light and heat from the Sun that is harnessed using a range of ever-evolving technologies such as solar heating, photovoltaic etc. It is an important form of renewable energy.

Chapter 14
Green Growth and Energy Use in India

Sudhakar Patra
Berhampur University, India

Kabita Kumari Sahu
North Orissa University, India

ABSTRACT

The objective of the chapter is to analyze the trend and pattern of energy use, energy challenges of India, and the sustainability through green growth strategy. The study is based on secondary data collected from energy outlook, integrated energy policy, world development indicators, and RBI database. Energy security and sustainable development are critical issues to ensure India's economic growth and its human development. Transport sector energy demand witnesses a noticeable increase, growing by almost three times, from 125 Mtoe in 2012 to about 360 Mtoe in 2018. India has a vast supply of renewable energy resources, and it has one of the largest programs in the world for deploying renewable energy products and systems. The share of oil has in particular fallen from 36% to 33%, while that of natural gas has increased from 23% to 24%, and that of renewable energy (including nuclear and large hydro) has gone up from 12.5% to 14% in the period 2005-15. There is urgent need to have proper integrated energy policy in India with emphasis more on renewable sources of energy.

INTRODUCTION

Green growth involves rethinking growth strategies with regard to their impact(s) on environmental sustainability and the environmental resources available to poor and vulnerable groups. Green growth and development measures bring positive changes by lifting additional people above poverty, thereby impacting the key education and health indicators as well. These green growth interventions include increased share of renewable energy (RE), sustainable agriculture practices, better natural resource management, and structural changes within industry and infrastructure sector. The income generated from these measures and new investments get distributed, especially across the rural households, thereby reducing the inequality. India, with 17% of the world's population is a homeland of 1.20 billion people

DOI: 10.4018/978-1-5225-8547-3.ch014

and it has a seemingly unquenchable thirst for energy. Energy is acknowledged as a key input towards raising the standard of living of citizens of any country, as is evident from the correlation between per capita electricity (a proxy for all energy forms) consumption and Human Development Index (HDI). Accordingly, energy policies of India have over the years directly aimed to raise per capita energy (and electricity) consumption, even while the main focus of the country's development agenda has been on eradication of poverty. With nearly 304 million Indians without access to electricity, and about 500 million people, still dependent on solid bio-mass for cooking, it may be acknowledged that the country has to still go a long way on securing its energy security objective. While India strives to achieve a double digit growth rate in its national income, making clean energy available to all of its citizens, ought to be included as a key component of the poverty alleviation programmes.

It ranks fifth in the world in terms of primary energy consumption, accounting for about 3.5 per cent of the world's commercial energy demand. The energy consumption of India has gone up manifolds since its independence in 1947. In order to meet its energy needs, the country has tried to harness energy from various natural resources including wood, coal, natural gas, hydro, wind, solar etc. Technological innovation and industrialization has led to the overexploitation of natural resources beyond limits to satisfy the insatiable lust of greed by humans worldwide. One harsh result of its meteoric growth is the widening gap between required energy and actual energy produced. With high economic growth rate and the aspiration of its people to better quality of life, India has a voracious appetite for energy. But the country lacks sufficient domestic energy resources, particularly of petroleum and natural gas, and must import much of its growing requirements. Currently, about 35% of India's commercial energy needs are imported. The future levels and patterns of energy use in India therefore have important implications, at the national level in terms of environmental impacts of energy use, issues of access and equity, and at the global level in terms of geopolitics of energy supply and GHG emissions related to the combustion of fossil fuels. According to World Bank estimates, around 35% of the country's population subsists below the poverty line and does not have access to basic amenities and clean energy forms. Indian economy is characterized by dualism arising from the divide between the rich and the poor in respect of income, energy use and their environmental consequences.(Reddy, 1997).Approximately 40% of house-holds in India do not have access to electricity by the end of 2011 (The India's power sector, World Bank group). The country continues to face electricity shortages, with an overall power shortage of 8.4% and a peaking power shortage of 12.3% in 2010. Despite gradual urbanization, around 72% of the country's population resided in rural areas in 2001. (Ghosh & Mitra, 2015). The rural urban divide in India is manifest not only by the differences in the levels of energy requirement but also in the availability and choice of fuel and technologies to meet the same useful energy needs and services. Energy demands of several households, especially those in the rural areas, continue to be met primarily by inefficient traditional energy forms like fuel wood, crop residue, and animal waste. The poor in India suffer from energy poverty due to lack of access to modern energy services like electricity or clean cooking fuel like LPG (Birol, 2007). In this context, the objective of this paper is to analyze the trend and pattern of energy use, energy challenges of India, the cause and effect relationship between energy and economic development, and the sustainability of its environment for its millions of poor populace. Energy security and sustainable development are critical issues to ensure India's economic growth and its human development objectives.

Table 1. Key development indicators for India and select countries

	GDP in billion (constant 2005 US$)[a]	GDP per capita (constant 2005 US$)[a]	CO_2 emissions (MT)[b]	CO_2 emissions (metric tons per capita)[b]	Energy use (kilograms of oil equivalent per capita)	International Trade Balance in Goods	Cash surplus/ deficit (% of GDP)
Brazil	1206	5853	439.41	2.19	1391.90	–4.13	–1.84
China	5274	3866	9019.52	6.71	2142.81	370.02	–
European Union	15372	30241	3574.10	7.07	3253.82	134.78	–3.63
India	1600	1235	2074.34	1.66	623.72	–139.88	–3.81
Japan	4780	37595	1187.66	9.29	3545.60	–120.64	–7.97
Russian Federation	1000	6844	1808.07	12.65	5283.41	188.04	2.67
United States	14797	46405	5305.57	17.02	6814.82	–727.15	–7.56
South Africa	329	6086	477.24	9.26	2674.82	–18.1	–4.47
World	58055	7996	34649.483	4.94	1897.95	–	–4.94

Source: World Development Indicators (data.worldbank.org)

GREEN GROWTH INTERVENTIONS AND THEIR IMPACT

The objective of green growth interventions is to understand the impact of energy-related green growth interventions on future energy demand, emissions, energy access, energy security, and development indicators. In order to understand these inter-linkages, an integrated modelling framework has been used, combining a bottom-up energy systems model along with a top-down simulation-based dynamic, recursive computable general equilibrium model.

The following green growth interventions are needed in India.

1. Energy efficiency and conservation measures in energy demand sectors (agriculture, transport, industry sector, commercial building, and residential sector)
2. Enhancement of modern energy access
3. Promotion of clean energy supply through renewables and cleaner fossil-fuel–based energy generation technology, and
4. Resource (soil and water) conservation in the agriculture sector.

The three major energy-consuming sectors, namely industry, residential, and transport, continue their dominance of the final energy demand, contributing about 90% over the modelling horizon. Transport sector energy demand witnesses a noticeable increase, growing by almost three times, from 125 million tonne of oil equivalent (Mtoe) in 2012 to about 360 Mtoe in 2018 (BP Statistical Review of World Energy 2018 - India Environment Portal). For understanding the implications of these green growth interventions on energy and development indicators, different indicators and scenarios need to be analysed. The share of renewables in the primary energy supply mix shall increase by 2031.

NATIONAL ENERGY POLICY IN INDIA

The National Energy Policy (NEP) aims to chart the way forward to meet the Government's recent bold announcements in the energy domain. All the Census villages are planned to be electrified by 2018, and universal electrification is to be achieved, with 24x7 electricity by 2022. The share of manufacturing in our GDP is to go up to 25% from the present level of 16%, while the Ministry of Petroleum is targeting reduction of oil imports by 10% from 2014-15 levels, both by 2022. Our NDCs target at reduction of emissions intensity by 33%-35% by 2030 over 2005, achieving a 175 GW renewable energy capacity by 2022, and share of non-fossil fuel based capacity in the electricity mix is aimed at above 40% by 2030. In view of the fact, that energy is handled by different Ministries that have the primary responsibility of setting their own sectoral agenda, an omnibus policy is required to achieve the goal of energy security through coordination between these sources. This is also expected to mainstream emerging energy technologies, and provide consumer energy choices. The NEP builds on the achievements of the earlier omnibus energy policy – the Integrated Energy Policy (IEP), and sets the new agenda consistent with the redefined role of emerging developments in the energy world. A number of far-reaching developments have taken place in the local and global energy space which has to be reflected in our own policy framework. There is a need to support the trends which usher in efficiency by a pro-active policy. While steps have already been taken by the Government to embed many such developments in the sectoral energy policies, however, it is desirable to develop a clear roadmap so that there is clarity amongst all the stakeholders on the Government's long-term energy agenda. Long term investors, both on supply and demand sides, need clarity on stable energy policy outlook. The following global developments call for policy clarity:

Changes in the Energy Mix

The world is moving away from overwhelming dependence on fossil fuel, and within the fossil fuels, away from coal and oil in favour of gas. Against an 88% total share of fossil fuels globally in the primary energy mix in the year 2005, the same fell to 86% in the year 2015. The share of oil has in particular fallen from 36% to 33%, while that of natural gas has increased from 23% to 24%, and that of Renewable Energy (including nuclear and large hydro) has gone up from 12.5% to14% in the period 2005-15 (Draft National Energy Policy - NITI Aayog). The above trends, principally owing to climate change concerns, are expected to be maintained over the medium term.

Abundance in Supply of Natural Gas

The success of horizontal drilling combined with the technology of hydraulic fracture, has come to be established in the US where the production of natural gas went up from 511 BCM in 2005 to 767 BCM in 2015. This has boosted the already rising production of natural gas in the world from 2791 BCM in 2005 to 3539 BCM in the year 2015. As the price of gas is lower than that of oil, and is also one-third lesser as carbon emitting than oil, the ascendency of gas vis-a-vis oil is likely to continue in the near foreseeable future.

Over Supplied Oil and Gas Markets

Due to multiple reasons including the two factors listed above, along with other commodity prices, oil and gas prices have softened, and this is triggering energy policy reforms across the world. The prices of oil and gas have fallen by 50% and 70%, respectively over 2014. Many oil importing countries including India have been able to attempt bold petroleum pricing reforms, and are in a sound fiscal position to attempt larger energy policy reforms.

Maturity of Renewable Energy Technologies

The sharp decline in the prices of wind and solar technologies in the recent years by about 60% and 52% respectively between 2010 and 2015 (in kWh terms), has led to a change in the relative importance of energy sources. Tropical countries, including India, are richly endowed with the above resources, and can harness them in an innovative manner to meet energy requirements at decentralized locations. In the recent auctions, solar and wind energy prices have achieved bus bar grid parity at the generation end.

Climate Change Concerns

The adverse effects of climate change are much more discernible than ever before, with a better understanding of the relationship between energy use and poor environmental outcomes. While the global agenda is of common concern, there is a heightened consciousness of the need to fix poor air quality standards in Indian cities, which is being reflected in tough administrative actions and court mandated orders. In the light of the energy challenges faced by the country, and the global energy related developments, the NEP proposes to set out the national energy objectives and the strategy to meet them. While India strives to attain energy consumption levels equivalent to those of the developed countries, we are also conscious of the present small base. It is proposed that the present policy may be framed for the medium term to be able to guide the investors and the other stakeholders, who are likely to play a major role in the energy sector. During the medium term, we may strengthen the energy infrastructure and aim at scaling up over the longer period. Therefore, the medium term time span of the NEP (2017-2040) will provide clarity to the energy sector actors, and help lay the foundation for India to match the energy consumption parameters of developed countries over the longer period.

TREND AND PATTERN OF COMMERCIAL ENERGY CONSUMPTION IN INDIA

India today happens to be amongst the largest producer and consumers of energy in the world. The energy use is highly intensive and happens to be amongst the highest whereas the per capita consumption of energy is lowest compared to the OECD countries and even most of Asian countries. India today happens to be ranked sixth in terms of energy consumption. The per capita energy consumption of world is 2600, whereas for India it happens to be just over 600 units a year, even much below some of the developing countries. The sad part is that even today about 35% of the population in India lives below 1 dollar per day. India is one of the fastest growing economies in the world with brilliant performance in the 11th Five year plan. The pace of growth unfortunately has not been able to match the supply and demand and as such India is still a net importer of energy. India today imports around 25% of its primary energy.

Table 2. Commercial energy consumption

Source	Unit	2007-08	2008-09	2009-10
Coal	MMT	457.2	493.3	554.4
Petroleum	MMT	140.7	145.3	160.77
Natural Gas(Net)	BCM	31.5	31.8	46.49
Electricity	Billion KWH	813.1	842.8	876.43
Lignite	MMT	34.0	37.3	41.34

Source: Basic Statistics on Indian Petroleum and Natural Gas, 2009-10, Ministry of Petroleum & Natural Gas, New Delhi

India is highly dependent on imports for meeting its petroleum needs and as such 70% of its petroleum products are imported mainly from Middle East countries. The trend of the primary commercial energy consumption in India shows that electricity and coal are the major sources of energy consumed in India. The demand for coal & electricity increased at 8% to 9% during last 3 years. The total consumption of petroleum products was 140.7 MMT in 2007-08 which increased to 145.3 MMT in 2008-09 and to160.77 MMT in 2009-10. The natural gas and Lignite contributes very little to total energy consumption in India.

Total petroleum industry production for 2015-16 as given in table-3 shows that total crude Oil reserve in India is only 770 MMT out of which production is only 33.51 MMT in place of consumption of 160.77MMT. It implies that 80% of cruel Oil requirement is met through imports in India. Coal is essential source of energy in India and three-fourth of electricity is generated from coal in thermal plants (Table 3).

Total recoverable reserve of coal in India is 9930 million tones whereas coal consumption in 2015-16 was 554. 4 million tones (Table 4). United States of America has highest coal reserve of 23470 Million tones out of total World's coal reserve of 82740 Million tones. If the present level of coal consumption continues, the total coal reserve in India will be exhausted very soon.

Table 3. Petroleum Industry Production for 2015-16

Item	Crude Oil(MMT)	Natural Gas(BCM)	Petroleum Products
Reserve	770	1090	----
Production	33.51	-----	152.68
Consumption	160.77	46.49	124.17

Source: Ministry of Petroleum and Natural Gas, Government of India

Table 4. World recoverable coal reserves (in million tones)

Country	Coal	Lignite	Total
India	**9930**	**260**	**10190**
China	8910	2050	10960
Russia	16160	1150	17300
United States	23470	3600	27070
World	82740	17340	100080

Source: Coal Recoverable Reserve, World Energy Council, 2016.

Table 5. Oil and Gas Reserves in India in 2005 and 2009

	Onshore (2005)	Offshore (2005)	Total	Onshore (2009)	Offshore (2009)	Total
Crude Oil (MMT)	376	410	786	405	369	775
Natural Gas(BCM)	340	761	1101	287	787	1074

Sources: Basic Statistics on Indian Petroleum & Natural Gas, 2010-11

The oil and natural gas reserve in India is very low in our country. The annual consumption of natural gas is 46.49BCM as given in table 3 whereas total natural gas reserve in India is only 1074BCM which will be exhausted in 20 years. It can be confidently said that India has energy poverty which will affect sustainable development and energy use by the people. The onshore crude oil has increased from 376MMT in 2005 to 405 MMT in 2009 but offshore crude oil has decreased during same period as shown in table-5. Onshore natural gas reserve has decreased from 340BCM to 287BCM but offshore natural gas has increased marginally from 761BCM to 787BCM from 2005 to 2009.

PROJECTIONS FOR INDIA'S ENERGY REQUIREMENT

Planning Commission, the Government of India predicts that demand increases significantly for coal and oil over the next 20 years. Table 6 shows projections of India's energy requirements in its Integrated Energy Policy (IEP) report published in August 2006. The hydropower requirement will be 12MTOE in 2011-12 which is likely to increase by three times to 35MTOE in 2031-32. Similarly Nuclear Energy requirement will increase from 17MTOEin 2011-12 to 31MTOE in 2016-17 and to 98MTOE in 2031-32. There will be 6 times increase in Nuclear energy requirement in just 20 years. Nuclear energy now contributes more than 4,000 MW of power using a largely indigenous technology, but the nuclear industry's development has been hamstrung by India's refusal to sign the Nuclear Non-Proliferation Treaty, cutting the country off from cooperation and assistance in civil nuclear technology. In 2008, India and the Nuclear Suppliers' Group agreed on a waiver to the embargo on trade in nuclear technology. The waiver has removed most of the obstacles, and India now is planning to have 63,000 MW of nuclear generating capacity by 2032. India's long-range plans, however, foresee coal as the sector with the most growth potential, fueled mostly by demand for power generation. Total coal energy requirement

Table 6. Total energy requirements (MTOE)

Year	Hydro	Nuclear	Coal	Oil	Natural Gas	Total
2011-12	12	17	283	186	48	546
2016-17	18	31	375	241	64	729
2021-22	23	45	521	311	97	997
2026-27	29	71	706	410	135	1351
2031-32	35	98	937	548	197	1815

Source: IEP Report, Page 28, Table 2.10

Table 7. Coal demand projections (million tonnes)

Year	Power	Non Power	Total
2011-12	436	164	627
2016-17	603	221	824
2021-22	832	299	1131

Source: Integrated Energy Policy, Planning Commission
Note: Total Coal Reserve = 10100Million tons, Coal = 9930MT, Lignite = 260MT

is projected to increase from 283MT in 2011-12 to 937 MT in 2031-32 which is four times rise in 20 years. Coal reserves are mainly in the eastern region while the load centers are growing rapidly in the southern, western and northern part of the country. But coal's appeal lies in the facts that coal-fuelled power plants are less costly per installed megawatt than most other designs. Mining of India's large coal deposits can be expanded relatively cheaply, with the product shipped by rail to the power plant. The bulk of India's hydro potential, in contrast, is in the northeastern region and the northern part of the country in the Himalayas. The distribution of energy resources and load centers is consequently much skewed. The medium and long-term plan is to promote pithead stations using domestic coal and coastal stations using imported coal and to strengthen the inter-regional transmission systems.

The projected oil energy requirement increases almost at 20% per year whereas GDP growth rate is only 8% to 9% per year. Natural gas requirement is projected to rise from 48MT in 2011-12 to 197 MT in 2031-32 which is more than four times in 20 years. The projected demand for power and non power coal is shown in table-6. The total demand for power coal will be 832 MT in 2021-22 and for non power coal will be 299MT. During 10 years from 2011-12 to 2021-22, the total coal demand will increase from 627 MT to 1131 MT.

PRIMARY ENERGY CONSUMPTION AND COMPONENTS

The per capita primary energy consumption in India is a low 305 kg against the world average of 1,487 kg. Accordingly, with a total primary energy consumption of 314.7 million metric tones of oil equivalent (MMTOE), India accounts for just 3.4% of the total world primary energy consumption. However, at this stage, the point to note is that while the consumption of primary energy in the world grew at a low compounded annual growth rate (CAGR) of 1.1% during 1991-2001, it experienced a higher growth of 4.3% in India. The world primary energy consumption showed a higher growth rate of 3.1% per annum during the 1970s before declining to the current level. These efficiency gains are apparent in items as diverse as automobiles, airplanes, household electrical goods, power plants and manufacturing equipment. Oil, gas, hydroelectricity, nuclear power and coal are the five constituents of primary energy. Oil and gas account for 62.2% of the total world primary energy consumption. In India, coal is the principal source of energy accounting for over 55% of the total primary energy consumption. However, the share of oil & gas has increased from 34.8% in 1999 to the current level of 38.4%. The reasons for the growing importance of oil and gas are to be found in their multiple, varied and cost-effective applications. As in the case of per capita primary energy consumption, the per capita consumption of oil & gas in India is also a low 117 kg against the world average of 925 kg. Thus, the growth in primary energy consumption, the increasing share of oil & gas in the primary energy consumption, and the low per capita consumption of oil & gas are indicative of an enormous potential for growth in the demand for oil & gas in India.

The commercial energy constitutes a higher proportion of total primary energy compared to non-commercial energy as shown in Table 8. The share of primary energy consumption is projected to increase from 550 MTOE in 2006-07 to 2043MTOE in 2031-32 and the share will increase from 72.2% to 90.4% during the same period. The share of non-commercial energy will significantly reduce to 9.1% in 2031-32. The projected compound annual growth rate of total primary energy requirement from 2006 to 2032 is 5.4% where as it is only 0.76% in case of Non-commercial Energy.

GROWTH RATES AND ELASTICITY OF ENERGY USE IN INDIA

The projections, growth rates and GDP elasticity of total energy requirements are essential for an inclusive growth of Indian economy at the GDP growth rate of 8% per year. During fifteen year period from 1995 to 2010, the compound growth rate of total primary energy is 2.9% and for total primary commercial energy is 4.9%. The compound growth rate of gross generation of electricity is 5.8% and it is for final use of electricity is 4.6% as shown in table - 9. It is clear that electricity is generated at higher rate than its use. The GDP elasticity is an important indicator of energy equity and sustainable development. This elasticity is 0.54 for total primary energy, 0.56 for final energy and 0.99 for gross generation of electricity.

ENERGY AND SUSTAINABLE DEVELOPMENT IN INDIA

India being a growing economy, it's energy and economic development has a cause and effect relationship. Growth in net electricity consumption is expected to be most rapid among the emerging economies of the world, including India. According to the EIA, the annual average increase will be about 4.0 percent from 2002 to 2025. Emerging economies are projected to more than double their net electricity consumption, from 4,645 billion kilowatt hours in 2002 to 11,554 billion in 2025. The projected growth in net electricity consumption for emerging market economies is driven in large part by gross domestic product (GDP) and population growth assumption.

Table 8. Projected total primary energy requirement

Year	Total Primary Energy (MTOE)	Share of Primary Commercial Energy (%)	Share of Non-Commercial Energy (%)
2006-07	550	72.2	27.8
2011-12	715	76.4	23.6
2021-22	1192	84.8	15.2
2031-32	2043	90.4	9.1
Com. Annual Growth Rate	5.4	6.37	0.76

Source: Planning Commission, Government of India, 2012

Table 9. Growth rates and GDP elasticity of energy use in India

Type of Energy	Period	Compound Growth Rate	GDP Elasticity
Total Primary Energy	1995-2010	2.9	0.54
Total Primary Commercial Energy	1995-2010	4.9	0.79
Final Energy	1995-2010	3.4	0.56
Gross generation of Electricity	1995-2010	5.8	0.99
Final use of Electricity	1995-2010	4.6	0.75

Source: Author's calculation based on data

Because of the links between reliable electricity supply, GDP growth, and living standards, many of the nations with emerging economies are attempting to increase access to reliable electricity supply.

There is external resistance for sacrificing economic growth for the sake of protecting environment in the future. But India needs to keep up the pace of economic growth to ensure the good of its masses. India country needs economic growth and development to free itself from the evil clutches of poverty and hunger. It also needs adequate energy either indigenously or by means of import to ensure the desired rate of growth of the economy. India would have to exploit the natural resources in the form of coal, hydro, gas nuclear, and wind in order to maintain the required economic growth. But the challenge is how it can harness the energy resources so as to ensure its energy needs and at the same time make it sustainable for its future generations. In order to deliver a sustained growth of 8%, India would at least need to grow its primary energy supply by 3 to 4 times whereas the electricity supply needs to grow at the rate of 5 to 7 times the present consumption. India has to depend largely upon coal to meet the demand for energy. Coal today accounts for 50% of India's commercial energy consumption and around 78% of the domestic coal production is dedicated to power generation. Coal shall remain the most dominant energy source till 2031-32 and possibly beyond and it will dominate India's energy basket in terms of catering to its present and future needs considering the volatility of crude oil both in terms of price and supply disruptions.

FUTURE RENEWABLE ENERGY DEMAND AND CAPACITY OF INDIA

India is a nation in transition. Considered an "emerging economy," increasing GDP is driving the demand for additional electrical energy, as well as transportation fuels. India is a nation of extremes. Poverty remains in areas with no energy services, while wealth grows in the new business hubs. Coal fired generation currently provides two thirds of the generation capacity, and hydropower supplies the other third. Yet, India is blessed with vast resources of renewable energy in solar, wind, biomass and small hydro. In fact, the technical potential of these renewables exceeds the present installed generation capacity. Unique in the world, India has the only Ministry that is dedicated to the development of renewable energies: the Ministry of New and Renewable Energy. This bodes well for the acceleration of renewable development throughout the nation -- both to meet the underserved needs of millions of rural residents and the growing demand of an energy hungry economy. The estimates of potential capacities of renewable energy sources are given in table 10.

Table 10. Estimates of potential capacities from renewable energy sources (in MWs)

Source	Approx.(In MWs) Potential(In MWS
Biomass energy	19,500
Solar energy	20,000
Wind energy	47,000
Small hydropower	15,000
Ocean energy	50,000

Source: Ministry of Non-Conventional Energy, India.

The sum of these renewable resource potentials, 152,000 MW, is greater than the current total installed energy generating capacity of India. The development and deployment of renewable energy, products, and services in India is driven by the need to

1. Decrease dependence on energy imports
2. Sustain accelerated deployment of renewable energy system and devices
3. Expand cost-effective energy supply
4. Augment energy supply to remote and deficient areas to provide normative consumption levels to all section of the population across the country
5. And finally, switch fuels through new and renewable energy system/device deployment.

India is currently experiencing strong economic growth, while at the same time attempting to extend modern power services to millions still in poverty. Expanding electrical capacity is essential. Renewable energy remains a small fraction of installed capacity, yet India is blessed with over 150,000MW of exploitable renewables. All efforts and investment should consider accelerating these sustainable energy resources before committing to the same fossil fuel path as western nations. The fossil fuel strategy will surely bring price volatility from dwindling supplies and added pollution from carbon combustion. Tapping India's wind, solar, biomass, and hydro could bring high quality jobs from a domestic resource. Extending the electric grid between all states, and ultimately between neighbor nations will expand international trade and co-operation on the subcontinent.

CONCLUSION

There is absence of holistic energy policies as well as the lack of effective leadership and political will. Coal will remain the major source of energy until 2030. Thermal plants that use coal also need to undergo massive technological changes if they are to remain sustainable. Technological change will need regulatory interventions since the capital costs of setting up plants with up-to-date technologies are far higher as compared to subcritical plants. Renovation and modernization measures need a major boost. Research and Development (R&D) for clean coal technology needs a time-bound roadmap. Hence the desired outcomes for India have not been realized as far as energy and sustainable development is concerned. It is essential to supply to the poor people in the form of clean fuel which is our primary concern. More focus should be on supply of subsistence level of energy. India has to grow its primary energy and electricity supply manifold to ensure sustained GDP growth. India must explore and invest in new energy technologies like gas hydrates, coal to liquid, Coal Bed Methane (CBM) etc. India should make use of novel technologies to extract coal efficiently which is economically viable and sustainable. India will also need to seek new and clean coal technologies so as to tap its existing coal reserves which are at present difficult to extract economically using the available conventional technologies. Adequate technologies and allocation of funds for energy related R&D needs to be promoted for developing indigenous solutions which are typical to India. Energy conservation and sustainable energy use can also be directly improved by government policies. Energy loss during transmission can also be brought down by decentralizing energy production and distribution.

REFERENCES

Baldacci, E., Benedict, C., Sanjeev, G., & Qiang, C. (2008). *Social Spending, Human Capital, and Growth in Developing Countries. World Development, 36*. Washington, DC: International Monetary Fund.

Barry, C. (1982). Prologue: Energy Economics and the Environment. In Energy, Economics and the Environment. Lexington Books.

Birol, F. (2007). Energy economics: A place for Energy poverty in the Agenda. *Energy Journal, 28*(3). doi:10.5547/ISSN0195-6574-EJ-Vol28-No3-1

Bloomberg New Energy Finance (BNEF). (2010a). *Clean Energy—Analyst Reaction, February 12, 2010 (London: New Energy Finance).* Bureau of Energy Efficiency. Retrieved from www.bee-india.nic.in

Central Statistical Organisation. (2006). Energy Statistics. Government of India.

Gang, A., Ghosh, D., & Shukla, K. (2001). Integrated modeling system: Energy and Environment Policies. *OPSEARCH.*

Ghosh J. & Mitra, S. (2015). Energy Security Aspects of India. *International Journal of Engineering and Technical Research, 3*(3), 313-319.

Ghosh, S. (2002). Electricity Consumption and Economic Growth in India. *Energy Policy, 30*(2), 125–129. doi:10.1016/S0301-4215(01)00078-7

Global Subsidies Initiative. (2010a). *Relative Subsidies to Energy Sources*. Geneva: GSI Estimates.

Global Subsidies Initiative. (2010b). Biofuel—At What Cost, Government Support for Ethanol and Biodiesel in the European Union—2010 Update. Author.

Grossman, G. M., & Krueger, A. B. (1994). *Economic Growth and the Environment.* NBER Working Paper No. 4634. Washington, DC: International Monetary Fund.

Guerrieri, P., Luciani, M., & Meliciani, V. (2010). The Determinants of Investment in Information and Communication Technologies. *Economics of Innovation and New Technology, 20*(4), 387–403. doi:10.1080/10438599.2010.526313

International Energy Agency. (2008). *World Energy Outlook 2008.* Author.

Johnson, D., & Lybecker, K. (2009). *Challenges to Technology Transfer: A Literature Review of the Constraints on Environmental Technology Dissemination.* Colorado College Working Paper.

Jones, B., & Keen, M. (2009). *Climate Policy and the Recovery, IMF Staff Position Note SPN/09/28.* Washington, DC: International Monetary Fund.

Kao, C. (1999). Spurious Regression and Residual-Based Tests for Cointegration in Panel Data. *Journal of Econometrics, 90*(1), 1–44. doi:10.1016/S0304-4076(98)00023-2

Krupnick, A. J., Parry, I. W. H., Walls, M., Knowles, T., & Hayes, K. (2010). *Toward a New National Energy Policy: Assessing the Options.* Washington, DC: The National Energy Policy Institute, Resources for the Future.

Lamont, O. (1997). Cash Flow and Investment: Evidence from Internal Capital Markets. *The Journal of Finance, 52*(1), 83–109. doi:10.1111/j.1540-6261.1997.tb03809.x

Martin, R., Muûls, M., & Wagner, U. (2011). *Climate Change, Investment and Carbon Markets and Prices—Evidence from Manager Interviews.* San Francisco: Climate Policy Initiative.

McKinsey & Company. (2009). *Pathways to a Low-Carbon Economy.* New York: Author.

Mitchell, D. (2008). *A Note on Rising Food Prices.* World Bank Policy Research Working Paper No. 4682. Washington, DC: World Bank.

Morriss, A. P., Bogart, W. T., Dorchak, A., & Meiners, R. E. (2009). *7 Myths about Green Jobs.* Law & Economics Research Paper No. LE09-001, PERC Policy Series, No. 44. University of Illinois.

Newell, R. G., Jaffee, A. B., & Stavins, R. N. (1999). The Induced Innovation Hypothesis and Energy-Saving Technological Change. *The Quarterly Journal of Economics, 114*(3), 941–975. doi:10.1162/003355399556188

Planning Commission. (2008). Integrated Energy Policy. Government of India.

Reddy, A. K. N., Williams, R. H., & Johansson, T. B. (1997). *Energy after Rio: Prospects and Challenges.* New York: United Nations Development Programme.

KEY TERMS AND DEFINITIONS

Coal: Coal is a hard rock which can be burned as a solid fossil fuel. It is mostly carbon but also contains hydrogen, sulphur, oxygen, and nitrogen. It is a sedimentary rock formed from peat, by the pressure of rocks laid down later on top.

Consumption: Consumption is spending for acquisition of utility as opposed to investing which is spending for goods.

Electricity: Electricity is the set of physical phenomena associated with the presence and motion of matter that has a property of electric charge. In early days, electricity was considered as being not related to magnetism.

Energy: Energy is the quantitative property that must be transferred to an object in order to perform work on, or to heat, the object.

Green Growth: Green growth is the means by which the current economy can make the transition to a sustainable economy while reducing pollution and greenhouse gas emissions, minimizing waste and inefficient use of natural resources, maintaining biodiversity, and strengthening energy security.

Petroleum: Petroleum is a naturally occurring liquid found beneath the Earth's surface that can be refined into fuel. Petroleum is a fossil fuel, meaning that it has been created by the decomposition of organic matter over millions of years.

Sustainability: Sustainability is the process of maintaining change in a balanced environment, in which the exploitation of resources, the direction of investments, the orientation of technological development and institutional change are all in harmony and enhance both current and future potential to meet human needs and aspirations.

Section 2

Green Innovations, Green Urbanization, and Political Aspects for Environmental Protection

Chapter 15
Perception of Indian Consumers Towards Green Products

Prabal Chakraborty
NSHM Knowledge Campus, India

Sidhartha Sankar Laha
Tufanganj Mahavidyalaya, India

Madhabendra Sinha
National Institute of Technology Durgapur, India

ABSTRACT

Both consumers and corporate houses are paying attention to environmental issues, and green products are gaining momentum as a result. This chapter studies the concept of green marketing along with its important aspects influencing the buying decision of consumers in South Kolkata only. Convenience sampling method was adopted to select the total sample of 266 respondents consisting of 103 males and 163 females with the help of structured open- and closed-ended questionnaires. Both primary and secondary data collection methods were adopted here in this research. Independent variables are environment friendly, packaging, innovative, quality, brand value, and dependent variable is purchase intention. A mixed result is observed regarding perceptions towards green products. Thus, based on such findings, no such generalization can be made and have to consider heterogeneity among culture, demographic, geographical variables, which varies from place to place.

INTRODUCTION

During the current period, both consumers as well as corporate houses are focusing on environmental issues and as a result, green products are also accelerating in the market domain. The corporate houses are now taking green marketing as their promotional strategies to reach more customers in the marketing mix coordinator in terms of several things like product, price, place and promotion. Concept of "green marketing" is a trend in various countries and according to Ottoman (1998), Polonsky (1994), Peattie (1992), the "green marketing" concept came from the perspectives of "sustainability".

DOI: 10.4018/978-1-5225-8547-3.ch015

Straughan and Roberts (1999) opined that the concerns for environment have evolved through many phases. From early sixties it began with the "greening concept, concentrating on pollution and energy conservation". After that increased social and political pressure- organizations have to shift the focus on recycling, packaging issues, redesigning the product, and developing alternative products. In nineties, concern for environment has become one of the most burning issues. Organisations from United States and Europe have realised that customers purchase decision will be on the basis of environmental considerations in future – this leads to future opportunity for green marketing. Today, green marketing, is also known as sustainable marketing and environmental marketing involve product or service designing, promoting that, fix up pricing and take care distribution as per the customers' want and the need, with less environmental damage (Jain & Kaur, 2004).

Green marketing is a concept to protect the environment for the future generation and has an impact on the safety of the environmental. Due to growing concern of environmental protection, emergence of a new market is witnessed - which is the green market. Companies interested to cater this market, need to focus on green in all aspect of their business and consumers prefer those companies that have green compliance and are ready to pay higher price for that. Today green marketing is not a simple terminology but also is a marketing strategy with great future potentiality.

As per American Marketing Association green marketing is the marketing of products that are environmentally safe. This may be explained as- "holistic management process responsible for identifying, anticipating and satisfying the requirements of customers and society, in a profitable and sustainable way" (Peattie, 1995). A holistic and responsible strategic management process that identifies, anticipates, satisfies and fulfils stakeholder needs, for a reasonable reward, that does not adversely affect human or natural environmental well-being (Charter, 1992).

Most of the firms have started focusing on sustainable development framework which is regarded as green marketing and are environmentally friendly. Today managers may promote green marketing to earn profits and is able to satisfy customers' needs, which, is now used by many companies to increase their competitive advantage due to concern over environmental issues.

At present the companies have to focus on the consumers' needs and wants and on consumers want to recognize themselves with those companies that are green compliant and are willing to pay more. As result- green marketing is not only an environmental protection tool but also a marketing strategy (Yazdanifard & Mercy, 2011). Marketers need to provide training to their employees, especially their sales representative to give them knowledge regarding promotion of the green product effectively by clearly targeting to the consumers.

Today goal of the organization is to satisfy human needs and wants so that both the buyers are sellers are mutually benefited out of this. Mintu and Lozada (1993) described green marketing as the marketing tool to satisfy both organizational and individual goals through taking care of preservation, protection and conservation of environment. Due to increased media coverage, greater awareness related to environmental issues, incidence of industrial disasters and the rise of activist groups concern for the environment has been rising (Kalafatis et al. 1999). As a result, from early nineties concern for environment are increasing because of the pressure of various stakeholders, governments, environmentalists, non-government organisations (Ghoshal, 2011). This leads to green marketing approach wherein the objective is to preserve environment and satisfy customers for long term profits. Yakup and Sevil (2011) pointed out that global warming, greenhouse effect, pollution, climate changes etc. were areas of concern from the beginning of nineteen eighty. Detrimental impact on environment work as catalyst for green marketing activities and Boztepe (2012) opined that green consumers would refuse any products that may affect their health.

Golkanda (2013) emphasised that organizational focus is to enhance consciousness of consumers related to environmental threats and involve them in social charities to attract for eco-friendly products over conventional products. Corporate using green marketing as promotional tools have to modify, improve design and standardized their products will require innovation and provide competitive advantages also. Green consumers are willing to pay a higher price for environmentally friendly products (Laroche et al., 2001; Peattie, 2001). There are several factors affecting the buying-decision process of consumers. Previous researchers have identified many factors; environmental knowledge (Mostafa, 2006), perceived product price and quality (D'Souza et al., 2007), company's environmental reputation (Schwepker & Cornwell, 1991), environmental concerns (Phau & Ong, 2007), credibility of environmental advertising (Thøgersen, 2000).

The remainder of the paper is structured as follows. The next section documents a brief review of related literature followed by the discussion on the issues of research methodology including hypotheses formation and data collection. The final section concludes the paper after describing the empirical finding in previous section.

LITERATURE REVIEW

Environmentally friendly products based on consumer perspective are the product that are not toxic for the environment, good for health, have a responsibility to the social environment, and good for the earth (Durif et al., 2010). Ottman (2011) stated that firms which are applying green marketing will receive grants and loan from the government, to set up technology for the development. Toyota's Prius offers several benefits to the consumers and natural environment and is one such example (Halbright & Dunn, 2010). Chandra (2009) mentioned that for charging high price, firms need to differentiate its quality, specification and appearance. Eze and Ndubisi, (2013) described that low-price sensitive consumers are willing to pay more and perceive the eco-friendly product more than conventional product in terms of price and quality. According to Chen (2010) consumers prefer green products and will bring positive impact in relation to brand equity. Empirical researches have shown that corporate with higher social responsibility influence the consumers purchasing decision positively (Mohr et al., 2001).

The eco-friendly packaging is an external attribute of the product, as packaging is an external element of product and packaging is an indispensable element for sales (Ampueru and Vila, 2006). Now packaging is a cause of pollution and necessity for eco-friendly packaging is gradually is increasing (Min & Galle, 1997; Rokka & Uusitalo, 2008). Previous studies have shown that today's consumers prefer eco-friendly packaging products over conventional products (Magnier et al., 2016; Rokka & Uusitalo, 2008; Magnier & Schoormans, 2015). Packaging too also play an important role in green marketing as through packaging and its label company has to attract consumers within few seconds and must be eye catching (Danta's et al., 2004). Coca-cola was also another example of innovation with focus to packaging. Almost nearer to two decades they have started about the PET- Bottle. Green product's quality is also a major contributing factor for most of the consumers as green consumers apparently trust on these brands and they do not like to compromise with the product quality which also must be environment friendly (D'Souza et al., 2006). Gan et al. (2008) opined that like conventional product, in case of green product also brand name, quality, price have impact on purchasing decision. Packaging too also play an important here in green marketing as through packaging and label has to attract consumers within few seconds and must be eye catcher (Danta's et al., 2004).

Previous researchers have shown that one of the major elements of green product development is the promotion of eco-labels on the products, which is an effective tool that which can provide quality characteristics of the tangible product and also provide environmental image of the firm (Sammer & Wustenhagen, 2006). In the eyes of consumers, eco-label is an innovation and has an important role in consumers' decision of purchase (Pedersen & Neergaard, 2006). Consumers having environmental knowledge will differentiate the products which are more environmental friendly than the conventional products, in this juncture eco-labels are important (Rashid, 2009). Eco-label also creates a distinctive image to the consumers' cognition and positioning of a product (Purohit, 2012). The market demand for sustainable products is gradually increasing as environmental pollution has also increased and today's consumers' are concerned that it is related to morality (Mazar and Zhong, 2010). Due to these reasons, ethical issues and concerns for health, consumers have changed their behaviour toward purchasing sustainable products. Many previous studies have shown that sustainable products have a competitive advantage over the conventional products (Grankvisit et al., 2004).

Product's sustainability is one type of information about the product, and can be communicated to consumers via certification. Certification gives confidence to the consumers regarding the product's value or safety (Botonaki et al., 2006). Certifications of the sustainable attributes can be divided into two parts (Magnier et al., 2016). According to them one such part is the products' internal sustainability and the second involves the products' external sustainability. Eco-friendly products secure most of the sustainable product at any market place (Chen, 2007). "There are two typical and discrete methods of producing eco-friendly products: one is to make the product with eco-friendly ingredients and the other is to pack the product with eco-friendly packaging" (Soyoung et al., 2016). The eco-friendly ingredient is an internal attribute of a product, and the eco-friendly ingredient is directly related to product itself. Most talked about eco-friendly ingredients are in organic products (Ophuis & Van Trijp, 1995). Today's consumers consider organic products beneficial and gentle for the environment and for health (Hughner et al., 2007; Grankvisit and Beil 2001; Nilkins and Hillers, 1994).

No doubt packaging leads to pollution –previous literatures also support that and minimise that careful packaging is required. Consumers are avoiding excessive packaged products and consider buying organic products nowadays (Tobler et al., 2011). "Packaging is the first element of a product consumer's encounter before making their purchasing decision" as observed by Silayoi and Speece (2004). "The visual signals (e.g., size, color, and shape) of packages primarily affect consumers' product evaluation" opined by (Areas et al., 2011; Rettie and Brewer, 2000). Therefore, we may say that consumers primarily evaluate products' sustainability via the level of packaging. In accordance with World commission on Environmental Development (1978), Sustainable Development is "meeting the needs of the present without compromising the ability of the future generations to meet their own needs". Less pollution, recyclable products, biodegradable packaging, ecologically safe products are the main talking points of green marketing which ultimately leads to sustainable development. No doubt, green marketing is a tool which is dealing with the safety of the environment and at present in India green itself is becoming an identity of eco-consciousness. Environmentally preferable products are generally costlier to purchase than other alternative products. Green consumers are willing to pay a higher price for environmentally friendly products (Laroche et al., 2001; Peattie, 2001).

There are several factors affecting the buying-decision process of consumers. Previous researchers have identified many factors; environmental knowledge (Mostafa, 2006), perceived product price and quality (D'Souza et al., 2007), company's environmental reputation (Schwepker & Cornwell, 1991), environmental concerns (Phau & Ong, 2007), credibility of environmental advertising (Thøgersen,

2000). Several researches also conducted research on consumers green purchasing intentions, among these, many researchers have pointed out that the determinants of consumers' green purchase behaviour, but majority of the research have been conducted in industrialized countries (Bleda & Valente, 2008; Chatterjee, 2009; Chan, 2004; Davis, 1993), but the actual findings often contradict each other (Rahbar & Wahid, 2011). As a result, the findings may only be relevant in certain cultural, demographical and geographical context, and time factor needs to take care of. Complexity in green purchasing behaviour of consumers has been evident, and under different cultural, social and demographical contexts generalization is not often meaningful.

According to Makower's (2011) finding, environmentally friendly products are less attractive in the market. Environmentally friendly products only able to capture 1% market share for each product category, because consumers are reluctant to pay more for environmentally friendly products than conventional products (Gan, et al., 2008). Environmentally friendly products from the consumer perspective are a product that is non-toxic for the environment, "good for health, have a responsibility to the social environment, and good for the earth" (Durif et al., 2010). Coca-cola was also another example of innovation with focus to packaging. Almost nearer to two decades they have started PET-Bottle manufacturing. Green Product's quality is also a major contributing factor for most of the consumers as Green consumers apparently trust on these brands and they do not like to compromise with the product quality, also expect that products must be environment friendly (D'Souza et al., 2006). Gan et al. (2008) opined that like conventional product, in case of green product also brand name, quality, price have impact on purchasing decision.

No doubt green products are costlier than the conventional products (Veloutsou et al., 2013). Customers' willingness to pay with such premium may be because of brand equity. According to Aaker (1991) brand equity is the set of both brand assets and liabilities linked to the brand, its name and symbol that add value or subtracts value from a product or service including brand loyalty, brand awareness, perceived quality and brand associations. Previous studies have shown that eco-centric image of the firm have positive impact on consumers' cognition due to customers' satisfaction and trust. Similarly, previous studies also informed that there is a positive relationship between customer satisfaction and loyalty, which ultimately leads to repeat of purchase. Several researches have been conducted on green purchasing intentions. Among these, many researchers have identified the determinants of consumers' green purchase behaviour, majority of them have been conducted in industrialized countries (Bleda & Valente, 2008; Chatterjee, 2009; Chan, 2004; Davis, 1993) only. However, all these results had showed variances (Rahbar & Wahid, 2011). As a result the results are relevant only to homogeneous cultural, demographical and geographical factors. To study the consumers purchasing behaviour related complexities generalisation will not be at all fruitful and different variables, factors needs to be studied for that reasons.

RESEARCH METHODOLOGY

This research tries to study the concept of green marketing and what are important aspects of it that are influencing the buying decision of consumers. The research objectives are:

- To understand the relationship between different variables affecting consumers' buying decision for green products.

- Factors influencing consumers' buying decisions for green products.

To explore the relationship between consumers' buying decisions and green products, the present research work addressed the following hypotheses:

- **Null Hypothesis:** H_0: There is no such factor in influencing Consumers' buying decision for green products (has no relationship with purchase decisions of green products.)
- **Alternative Hypothesis:** H_1: There is factor in influencing Consumers' buying decision for green products (has a relationship with purchase decisions of green products)

At this research we mainly focused on literature review and quantitative research as literature review gives us direction to understand the basic knowledge of the subject, helps us to identify controversial and neglected areas also which have been discussed. This also helps us to position the study within the context and to construct the empirical research related to theoretical framework. Here the quantitative method is applied to measure the amount and quantity. We used survey as the method to collect and gather data and the questionnaire is built related to the context of the study. In this study, the questionnaire was framed on theoretical knowledge. According to analysed result shown, the final analysis of study was well supported to previous literature review. Moreover, the pilot test was executed after building the questionnaire in order to rectify the mistakes. We selected variables as per extensive literature review.

The population for this research was all consumers of the market who make the purchases of green products. The study was conducted in south Kolkata only and convenience sampling method was adopted to select the total sample size of 266 respondents consisting of 103 males and 163 females. However, primary data was collected from the respondents with the help of structured opened and closed ended questionnaires. Reliability regarding to consistency of this study, the reliability is assessed the homogeneity through using Cronbach's alpha (α) is evaluated as one of the most common measurement tools to test the internal consistency of the instrument. The result of measurement is number fall between 0 and 1; the acceptable range is greater than 0.7 (Heale & Twycross, 2015). Primary data was complemented with secondary data as well through publications on the said topic from different journals, magazines, and internet. The responses of the measurement were scored using a 5- point Likert scale and have response answer –Strongly disagree to strongly agree. Here, in this research independent variables are environment friendly, packaging, innovative, quality, brand value and dependent variable is purchase intention. We did multiple linear regressions as statistical tool.

FINDINGS AND DISCUSSIONS

The Regression Coefficient R = 0.83 or 83% means that correlation between dependent variable and independent variables is positive. The coefficient of determination $R^2 = 0.70$, which indicates that 70% of variation in dependent variable is explained by independent variables. The F-test value of 121.23 is significant because the significance level is = 0.00, 0.00 is less than 0.05 means correlation between dependable variable and independent variable is statistically significant and the regression model is

Table 1. Details of demographic characteristics of the respondents

Gender	**Male** **Female**	**103** **163**
Age	21-30 31-40 41-50 51-60 61-70	109 71 47 35 4
Educational Qualification	Higher Secondary Graduate Post Graduate	41 147 88
Monthly Income	15,000-25,000 25,001-35,000 35,001-45,000 45,001-55,000 55,001-65,000	78 50 67 39 32

Source: Authors' own calculation using primary survey data

Table 2. ANOVA results

Model	Sum of Squares	df	Mean Square	F-Statistic	Sig
Regression	217.88	5	43.57	121.23	0.00
Residual	93.45	262	0.35		
Total	311.33	265			

Source: Authors' own calculation using primary survey data

Table 3. Model summary

Model	R	R-Square	Adjusted R-Square	Std. Error of the Estimate
1	0.84	0.7	0.69	0.59

Source: Authors' own calculation using primary survey data

Table 4. Regression coefficients

Model	Unstandardized Coefficients		Standardized Coefficients	t	Sig.	Collinearity Statistics	
	Beta	Std. Error	Beta			Tolerance	VIF
(Constant)	-0.74	0.17		-4.29	0.00		
envfriendly	0.29	0.04	0.26	6.06	0.00	0.61	1.63
innovative	-0.20	0.04	-0.21	-4.52	0.00	0.52	1.92
quality	0.90	0.06	0.67	14.26	0.00	0.51	1.93
packaging	-0.12	0.03	-0.14	-3.62	0.00	0.72	1.38
brandvalue	0.33	0.04	0.31	7.18	0.00	0.58	1.70

Source: Authors' own calculation using primary survey data

valid. Again, all the independent variables brand value, environment friendly, packaging, innovative, quality all are significant as per our study results. According to the results of regression analysis, we have discarded Null hypothesis and accepting the alternative hypothesis. As per our study more the products will be environmentally friendly more will be the purchase intention.

Consumers prefer innovative products but not at the cost of health and environment. Innovation should be backed by certification or authenticity otherwise it will have no meaning. Mostly innovation is related to cost curtailment and for the direct benefits of the organization. Quality is definitely related with the purchase intention. Packaging is important but consumers do not prefer excessive packaging –more the packaging less will be the purchase. Consumers generally prefer appropriate packaging and it should be environment friendly also. Again, brand value like conventional products has positive impact on consumers' willingness to buy green products. Similarly, multicollineraity aspects we also checked here and it is well below 2.

CONCLUDING REMARKS

Because of green movement and its popularity consumer's consumer awareness and motivation are one of the driving forces that bring changes in the market place and we are witnessing more eco friendly products as a result. However, in comparison with consumers in the developed countries, the Indian consumers are much less aware of global warming issues. Successful marketing always try to recognize current trends of the market and position their products in such a way that supports buyer intentions. Green colour is slowly becoming the symbol of eco-consciousness of present generation people of India.

Today, many organizations have realized their responsibility to protect the environment and focusing on products and production processes "go green", as it reduce pollution and increase profits (Hart & Ahuja, 1997). Green marketing- today is a creative opportunity for the organizations to innovate in such a manner that invites difference and achieve business success. Because of lifestyle modification and change of consumption habits of the consumers- particularly in industrial world is happening due to focus on marketing –we have witnessed environmental damages also. As a result marketing is not above all the criticisms particularly for the satisfaction of the customer need and want with short term objective with environmental degradation.

Today, marketing can be used as an important instrument to attract consumers who have a concern for environment friendly product and can contribute to more sustainable forms of society.

India's rapid GDP growth rate, highly negative environmental impact - demand for eco-friendly products may ensure a cleaner environment. Consumers usually prefer, trust the performance of well known established brands, this may be an opportunity for green products also.

Green products are gaining importance today and green marketing is an important tool for the protection of environment for future generation no doubt. As a result, we have witnessed a new market totally with high prospect. Coca-cola was an example of innovation with proper focus to packaging. Almost nearer to two decades they have started about PET- Bottle. Green Product's quality is also a major contributing factor for most of the consumers as Green consumers apparently trust these brands and they do not like to compromise with the product quality, also these products must be environment friendly (D'Souza et al.,2006). Gan et al., 2008 opined that like conventional product, in case of green product also brand name, quality, price have impact on purchasing decision. Packaging too also play an important here in green marketing as through packaging and label it has to attract consumers within few seconds only and it must be eye catching (Danta's et al., 2004). No doubt green products are costlier than the conventional products (Veloutsou et al., 2013) and customers' willingness to pay with such premium may be because of brand equity. The findings of our study are also echoing on these lines and explained as well.

This research was conducted to study the relationship between the variables that actually affect the consumers buying decision related to green products and the factors responsible for that. The research has clearly identified a positive relationship and green it may be beneficial for the green marketers to develop marketing mix strategies. According to Makower's (2011), environmentally friendly products are less attractive in the market even today. Environmentally friendly products only have secured 1% market share for each product category as consumers are really reluctant to pay premium price for environmentally friendly products than conventional products (Gan et al., 2008). Future research could have been done based on this aspect also.

The convenience sampling technique was used because of time and cost constraints. Further research is required with a greater number of sample and geographical coverage. Several researches have been conducted on green purchasing intentions and among these, many researchers have identified the determinants of consumers' green purchase behavior but majority of them have been conducted the research in industrialized countries only (Bleda & Valente, 2008; Chatterjee, 2009; Chan, 2004; Davis, 1993). Most interesting aspect is -the results of those studies differ from each other (Rahbar & Wahid, 2011). Thus based on such findings no such generalization can be made and have to consider heterogeneity among culture, demographic, geographical variables-which varies from place to place. Also we need to study the role of government of different countries regarding their contributions for green products. Another important aspect could be the role of government of the country to develop the platform for green products. Another important area we need focus-the role of media - particularly their role to aware the general people towards green products.

REFERENCES

Ampuero, O., & Vila, N. (2006). Consumer perceptions of product packaging. *Journal of Consumer Marketing*, *23*(2), 100–112. doi:10.1108/07363760610655032

Ares, G., Piqueras-Fiszman, B., Varela, P., Marco, R. M., López, A. M., & Fiszman, S. (2011). Food labels: Do consumers perceive what semiotics want to convey? *Food Quality and Preference*, *22*(7), 689–698. doi:10.1016/j.foodqual.2011.05.006

Bleda, M., & Valente, M. (2009). Graded eco-labels: A demand-oriented approach to reduce pollution. *Technological Forecasting and Social Change*, *76*(4), 512–524. doi:10.1016/j.techfore.2008.05.003

Botonaki, A., Polymeros, K., Tsakiridou, E., & Mattas, K. (2006). The role of food quality certification on consumers' food choices. *British Food Journal*, *108*(2), 77–90. doi:10.1108/00070700610644906

Boztepe, A. (2012). Green marketing and its impact on consumer buying behavior. *European Journal of Economic & Political Studies*, *5*(1).

Chan, R. Y. (2004). Consumer responses to environmental advertising in China. *Marketing Intelligence & Planning*, *22*(4), 427–437. doi:10.1108/02634500410542789

Chandra, M. (2009). *Green marketing: A new dimension in the marketing field*. Economic Challenger.

Charter, M. (1992). *Green marketing –A responsible approach to business*. Greenleaf Publishing.

Chatterjee, P. (2009). Green brand extension strategy and online communities. *Journal of Systems and Information Technology*, *11*(4), 367–384. doi:10.1108/13287260911002503

Chen, M. F. (2007). Consumer attitudes and purchase intentions in relation to organic foods in Taiwan: Moderating effects of food-related personality traits. *Food Quality and Preference*, *18*(7), 1008–1021. doi:10.1016/j.foodqual.2007.04.004

Chen, Y. S. (2010). The drivers of green brand equity: Green brand image, green satisfaction, and green trust. *Journal of Business Ethics*, *93*(2), 307–319. doi:10.100710551-009-0223-9

D'Souza, C., Taghian, M., & Khosla, R. (2007). Examination of environmental beliefs and its impact on the influence of price, quality and demographic characteristics with respect to green purchase intention. *Journal of Targeting. Measurement and Analysis for Marketing*, *15*(2), 69–78. doi:10.1057/palgrave.jt.5750039

Dantas, M. I., Minim, V. P., Deliza, R., & Puschmann, R. (2004). The effect of packaging on the perception of minimally processed products. *Journal of International Food & Agribusiness Marketing*, *16*(2), 71–83. doi:10.1300/J047v16n02_05

Davis, J. J. (1993). Strategies for environmental advertising. *Journal of Consumer Marketing*, *10*(2), 19–36. doi:10.1108/07363769310039102

Durif, F., Boivin, C., & Julien, C. (2010). In search of a green product definition. *Innovative Marketing*, *6*(1), 25–33.

Eze, U. C., & Ndubisi, N. O. (2013). Green buyer behavior: Evidence from Asia consumers. *Journal of Asian and African Studies*, *48*(4), 413–426. doi:10.1177/0021909613493602

Gan, C., Wee, H. Y., Ozanne, L., & Kao, T. H. (2008). Consumers' purchasing behavior towards green products in New Zealand. *Innovative Marketing*, *4*(1), 93–102.

Ghoshal, M. (2008). Green Marketing A Changing Concept in Changing Time. *Journal of IMR-Mgt*, *2*(1), 1–24.

Golkonda, S. B. (2013). *Bioproducts: Consumers' perception and buying behavior* (Doctoral dissertation). Tennessee State University.

Grankvist, G., & Biel, A. (2001). The importance of beliefs and purchase criteria in the choice of eco-labeled food products. *Journal of Environmental Psychology*, *21*(4), 405–410. doi:10.1006/jevp.2001.0234

Grankvist, G., Dahlstrand, U., & Biel, A. (2004). The impact of environmental labelling on consumer preference: Negative vs. positive labels. *Journal of Consumer Policy*, *27*(2), 213–230. doi:10.1023/B:COPO.0000028167.54739.94

Halbright, R., & Dunn, M. (2010). *Case Study: The Toyota Prius*. Managerial Marketing.

Hart, S. L., & Ahuja, G. (1997). Does it pay to be green? *Business Strategy and the Environment*, *5*, 31–37.

Heale, R., & Twycross, A. (2015). Validity and reliability in quantitative studies. *Evidence-Based Nursing*. PMID:25979629

Hughner, R. S., McDonagh, P., Prothero, A., Shultz, C. J., & Stanton, J. (2007). Who are organic food consumers? A compilation and review of why people purchase organic food. *Journal of Consumer Behaviour: An International Research Review*, *6*(2-3), 94–110. doi:10.1002/cb.210

Jain, S. K., & Kaur, G. (2004). Green Marketing: An Indian Perspective. *Decision, 31*(2).

Kalafatis, S. P., Pollard, M., East, R., & Tsogas, M. H. (1999). Green marketing and Ajzen's theory of planned behaviour: A cross-market examination. *Journal of Consumer Marketing*, *16*(5), 441–460. doi:10.1108/07363769910289550

Laroche, M., Bergeron, J., & Barbaro-Forleo, G. (2001). Targeting consumers who are willing to pay more for environmentally friendly products. *Journal of Consumer Marketing*, *18*(6), 503–520. doi:10.1108/EUM0000000006155

Magnier, L., & Schoormans, J. (2015). Consumer reactions to sustainable packaging: The interplay of visual appearance, verbal claim and environmental concern. *Journal of Environmental Psychology*, *44*, 53–62. doi:10.1016/j.jenvp.2015.09.005

Magnier, L., & Schoormans, J. (2015). Consumer reactions to sustainable packaging: The interplay of visual appearance, verbal claim and environmental concern. *Journal of Environmental Psychology*, *44*, 53–62. doi:10.1016/j.jenvp.2015.09.005

Magnier, L., Schoormans, J., & Mugge, R. (2016). Judging a product by its cover: Packaging sustainability and perceptions of quality in food products. *Food Quality and Preference*, *53*, 132–142. doi:10.1016/j.foodqual.2016.06.006

Makower, J. (2011). *Green marketing is over. Let's move on.* Green Biz.

Mazar, N., & Zhong, C. B. (2010). Do green products make us better people? *Psychological Science*, *21*(4), 494–498. doi:10.1177/0956797610363538 PMID:20424089

Min, H., & Galle, W. P. (1997). Green purchasing strategies: Trends and implications. *International Journal of Purchasing and Materials Management*, *33*(2), 10–17. doi:10.1111/j.1745-493X.1997.tb00026.x

Mintu, A. T., & Lozada, H. R. (1993). Green Marketing Education: A call for action. *Marketing Education Review*, *3*(3), 17–23. doi:10.1080/10528008.1993.11488420

Mohr, L. A., Webb, D. J., & Harris, K. E. (2001). Do consumers expect companies to be socially responsible? The impact of corporate social responsibility on buying behavior. *The Journal of Consumer Affairs*, *35*(1), 45–72. doi:10.1111/j.1745-6606.2001.tb00102.x

Mostafa, M. M. (2007). A hierarchical analysis of the green consciousness of the Egyptian consumer. *Psychology and Marketing*, *24*(5), 445–473. doi:10.1002/mar.20168

Ophuis, P. A. O., & Van Trijp, H. C. (1995). Perceived quality: A market driven and consumer oriented approach. *Food Quality and Preference*, *6*(3), 177–183. doi:10.1016/0950-3293(94)00028-T

Ottman, J. (1993). *Green Marketing: Challenges and Opportunities for the New Marketing Age*. New York: McGraw-Hill.

Ottman, J. (2017). *The new rules of green marketing: Strategies, tools, and inspiration for sustainable branding*. Routledge. doi:10.4324/9781351278683

PeattieK. (1995). Retrieved from www.wikipedia.org

Peattie, K. (2001). Golden goose or wild goose? The hunt for the green consumer. *Business Strategy and the Environment*, *10*(4), 187–199. doi:10.1002/bse.292

Pedersen, E. R., & Neergaard, P. (2006). Caveat emptor–let the buyer beware! Environmental labelling and the limitations of 'green'consumerism. *Business Strategy and the Environment*, *15*(1), 15–29. doi:10.1002/bse.434

Phau, I., & Ong, D. (2007). An investigation of the effects of environmental claims in promotional messages for clothing brands. *Marketing Intelligence & Planning*, *25*(7), 772–788. doi:10.1108/02634500710834214

Polonsky, M. J. (1994). An Introduction to Green Marketing. *Electronic Green Journal*, *1*(2).

Purohit, H. C. (2012). Product positioning and consumer attitude towards eco-friendly labeling and advertisement: An analytical study. *Journal of Management Research*, *12*(3), 153.

Rahbar, E., & Abdul Wahid, N. (2011). Investigation of green marketing tools' effect on consumers' purchase behavior. *Business Strategy Series*, *12*(2), 73–83. doi:10.1108/17515631111114877

Rashid, N. R. N. A. (2009). Awareness of eco-label in Malaysia's green marketing initiative. *International Journal of Business and Management*, *4*(8), 132. doi:10.5539/ijbm.v4n8p132

Rettie, R., & Brewer, C. (2000). The verbal and visual components of package design. *Journal of Product and Brand Management*, *9*(1), 56–70. doi:10.1108/10610420010316339

Rokka, J., & Uusitalo, L. (2008). Preference for green packaging in consumer product choices–do consumers care? *International Journal of Consumer Studies*, *32*(5), 516–525. doi:10.1111/j.1470-6431.2008.00710.x

Sammer, K., & Wüstenhagen, R. (2006). The influence of eco-labelling on consumer behaviour–Results of a discrete choice analysis for washing machines. *Business Strategy and the Environment*, *15*(3), 185–199. doi:10.1002/bse.522

Schwepker, C. H. Jr, & Cornwell, T. B. (1991). An examination of ecologically concerned consumers and their intention to purchase ecologically packaged products. *Journal of Public Policy & Marketing*, *10*(2), 77–101. doi:10.1177/074391569101000205

Silayoi, M. P. (2003). *The Effects of Packaging Elements on Consumer Choice, Satisfaction, and Loyalty* (Doctoral dissertation). Bangkok University Bangkok, Thailand.

Silayoi, P., & Speece, M. (2004). Packaging and purchase decisions: An exploratory study on the impact of involvement level and time pressure. *British Food Journal*, *106*(8), 607–628. doi:10.1108/00070700410553602

Straughan, R. D., & Roberts, J. A. (1999). Environmental segmentation alternatives: A look at green consumer behavior in the new millennium. *Journal of Consumer Marketing*, *16*(6), 558–575. doi:10.1108/07363769910297506

Thøgersen, J. (2000). Psychological determinants of paying attention to eco-labels in purchase decisions: Model development and multinational validation. *Journal of Consumer Policy*, *23*(3), 285–313. doi:10.1023/A:1007122319675

Thøgersen, J., & Zhou, Y. (2012). Chinese consumers' adoption of a 'green' innovation - The case of organic food. *Journal of Marketing Management*, *28*(3-4), 313–333. doi:10.1080/0267257X.2012.658834

Tobler, C., Visschers, V. H., & Siegrist, M. (2011). Eating green. Consumers' willingness to adopt ecological food consumption behaviours. *Appetite*, *57*(3), 674–682. doi:10.1016/j.appet.2011.08.010 PMID:21896294

Veloutsou, C., Christodoulides, G., & de Chernatony, L. (2013). A taxonomy of measures for consumer-based brand equity: Drawing on the views of managers in Europe. *Journal of Product and Brand Management*, *22*(3), 238–248. doi:10.1108/JPBM-02-2013-0256

Wilkins, J. L., & Hillers, V. N. (1994). Influences of pesticide residue and environmental concerns on organic food preference among food cooperative members and non-members in Washington State. *Journal of Nutrition Education*, *26*(1), 26–33. doi:10.1016/S0022-3182(12)80831-4

Yakup, A. D., & Sevil, Z. (2012). A theoretical approach to the concept of the costs of quality. *International Journal of Business and Social Science*, *3*(11).

Yazdanifard, R., & Mercy, I. E. (2011).The impact of green marketing on customer satisfaction and environmental safety. *International Conference on Computer Communication and Management*, *5*, 637-641.

KEY TERMS AND DEFINITIONS

Convenience Sampling: Convenience Sampling is a type of non-probability sampling method. The sample is taken from a group of people easy to contact or to reach.

Correlation: It is a statistical measure that captures the degree of associations between two variables. Positive correlation means the relation between the variables is direct and negative correlation means inverse relation between the two.

Environmentally Friendly: The term *environmentally friendly* is related to product sustainability and marketing, and referred to goods and services and follow guidelines and policies that claims minimal, or no harm on the environment.

Green Products: Green products are denoted as those products that are less detrimental to environment and human health than conventional products. Green products may be developed from recycled components or be manufactured through more energy-conservation, and will have less packaging. Green, environmental and eco-marketing are parts of the new marketing approaches today.

Kolkata: It is one of the four metropolitan cities in India.

Packaging: Packaging is the blending of science, art and technology to protect products for distribution, storage, sale, and is used for government, business, institutional, industrial, and personal use.

Chapter 16
An Empirical Study on Green Initiatives by S&P BSE SENSEX Companies in India at the Outlet of Companies Act, 2013

Dipayan Singha
Lalbaba College, India

Megnath Routh
Sonarpur Mahavidyalaya, India

Amit Majumdar
Bijoy Krishna Girls' College, India

ABSTRACT

Considering the necessity to build up corporate social responsibility (CSR) activities in general and sustainability in particular under statutory obligations, Ministry of Corporate Affairs, Government of India had notified in Companies Act 2013 (section 135) that every public limited company and private limited company having net worth of more than 500 crore or turnover more than 1000 crore or net profit more than 5 crore needs to comply with CSR rules (i.e., contributing 2% or more for the welfare of society following the prescribed guidelines under Schedule VII). The chapter focuses on CSR activities of companies registered under BSE SENSEX and evaluating their current status in CSR activities from the perspective of the broad heading of planet and people. A detailed analysis is done to highlight the current situation of the companies towards sustainable development through corporate sustainability index and statistical tools like Kruskal-Wallis test and Mann-Whitney U test to represent the contributions of these companies towards the environmental responsibilities. The study of CSR reveals the endeavors of surveyed companies towards the holistic development covering the noteworthy issue of environmental protection and sustainability; however, a continuous vigil from the regulatory bodies is the need of the hour to ensure that adherence to CSR practices should not only be in mere form but in true spirits.

DOI: 10.4018/978-1-5225-8547-3.ch016

INTRODUCTION

Corporate social responsibility under the new Companies Act 2013 has brought a bundle of changes in Indian corporate business. CSR introduction in Section 135 is referred as a give and take policy, as the companies are taking resources from the society it needs to reduce the gap by providing something back the society. The concept goes way back in 1994 when John Elkington coined the need or Triple Bottom Line which was based on 3 pillars namely people, planet and profit. Ministry of corporate affairs notified Section 135 and schedule VII and the provisions regarding Companies (Corporate Social Responsibility Policy) Rules, 2014 or generally known as CSR rules which came into effect from 1st April 2014. Companies now need to share a part of their profit on CSR activities as a contribution to the society, and these expenses cannot be claimed as business expenses. The guidelines issued by MCA on social, environmental and economic responsibilities of business mandated adaptation of CSR by the companies having the following yardsticks during any financial year.

1. Companies with a net worth of Rs. 500 crore or more, or
2. Companies having turnover of Rs.1000 crore or more, or
3. Companies achieving a profit of Rs. 5 crore or more

And these companies shall constitute a CSR committee on the board. Composition of corporate social responsibility committee is subjected to disclosure under sub section (3) of section 134. These companies must constitute of minimum 3 directors containing an independent director. SEBI also mandated a top hundred listed companies at BSE and NSE on the basis of market capitalization for proper inclusion and disclosure of business responsibility report in their annual report. The CSR committee formulates and recommends about the CSR policy to the board and the amount of expenditure to be incurred in these activities. Monitoring these activities and policies are also another important function of CSR committee.

With great powers come great responsibility that is why CSR committee is bound to some responsibilities which are:

- Recommendations of the CSR committee are approved by the board which eventually becomes the CSR policy and disclosure of the contents of such policy in company report and website is required. Rule 9 of the CSR rules clarifies that a company qualifying under section 135 shall include a CSR report along with board report.
- The company must spend at least 2% of the average net profits of three years immediately preceding financial year. Computation of net profit is as per section 198 of the companies act, MCA clarifies that profit means profit before tax.

Companies may engage in various activities notified are: (I) In Schedule VII, for items (i) to (x), the following items and entries shall be substituted, namely:

1. Eradicating hunger, poverty and malnutrition, promoting preventive health care and sanitation and making available safe drinking water:
2. Promoting education, including special education and employment enhancing vocation skills especially among children, women, elderly, and the differently abled and livelihood enhancement projects;

3. Promoting gender equality, empowering women, setting up homes and hostels for women and orphans; setting up old age homes, day care centers and such other facilities for senior citizens and measures for reducing inequalities faced by socially and economically backward groups;
4. Ensuring environmental sustainability, ecological balance, protection of flora and fauna, animal welfare, agroforestry, conservation of natural resources and maintaining quality of soil, air and water;
5. Protection of national heritage, alt and culture including restoration of buildings and sites of historical importance and works of art; setting up public libraries; promotion and development of traditional and handicrafts:
6. Measures for the benefit of armed forces veterans, war widows and their dependents;
7. Training to promote rural sports, nationally recognized sports, Paralympic sports and Olympic sports;
8. Contribution to the Prime Minister's National Relief Fund or any other fund set up by the Central Government for socio-economic development and relief and welfare of the Scheduled Caste, the Scheduled Tribes, other backward classes, minorities and women;
9. Contributions or funds provided to technology incubators located within academic institutions which are approved by the Central Government
10. Rural development projects.

Activities that will not qualify as CSR activities are:

- Projects that only benefit employees of the company are not to be qualified as CSR projects
- One off events- things that are done once and not repeated.
- Expenses made for the sake of complying with the regulations of an act.
- Contribution to political parties
- Activities to pursue or profit own business.
- Projects outside India

The concept of Triple Bottom Line was coined by John Elkington in his 1999 book," Cannibals with Forks: The Triple Bottom Line of 21st Century Business". The introduction of these bottom lines helped to recognise profits along with organisations impact on people and planet. TBL can be referred as an impact study of the company on local and global scale via sustainability.

The idea of triple P also known as Triple Bottom Line stands on the base of three pillars namely people, planet and profit. But nowadays it's extended to four pillars including future oriented approach and known as Quadruple Bottom Line. As there is no universal method of valuing people and planet so a collaborative effort is made to represent all the values is terms of Indian rupees. Many oppose the measurement of people and environment in terms of rupees as this creates a value only but the need for preservation and development is ignored. And it is also true that what is measured is given importance. Measuring the input that is being taken from the society will give the requirement to return to the society as the ministry of corporate affairs have mentioned the ten areas of investments to be made in respect of CSR activities in their Schedule VII (Table 1). Ministry of Corporate Affairs have indulged the most required sections for a sustainable development of environment and people. Out of the three P's profit was the only part that was focused till date, with next to nil contribution towards people and planet. But mandating of CSR companies are bound to contribute at least 2% of profit before tax.

Table 1. Classification of Schedule VII I respect of TBL

PEOPLE	PLANET
Eradicating hunger, poverty and malnutrition, promoting preventive health care and sanitation.	Ensuring environmental sustainability, ecological balance, etc.
Promoting education, employment enhancing vocation skills and livelihood enhancement projects;	Protection of national heritage, art and culture.
Promoting gender equality, empowering women, senior citizens and measures for reducing inequalities faced by socially and economically backward groups;	Training to promote rural sports, nationally recognized sports, Paralympic sports and Olympic sports
Measures for the benefit of armed forces veterans, war widows and their dependents;	Contribution to the Prime Minister's National Relief Fund or any other fund set up by the Central Government
	Contributions or funds provided to technology incubators located within academic institutions which are approved by the Central Government
	Rural development projects.

Area of CSR activities as mentioned by Ministry Of Corporate Affairs in Schedule VII under the head People and Planet which represents the pillars of TBL.

Bombay Stock Exchange (BSE) consists of more than 5200 listed companies and is one of the largest Exchanges in the world and also the oldest Indian stock exchange. S&P BSE SENSEX 30 which is also referred as "Standard and Poor Bombay Stock Exchange's Sensitivity Index" or Sensex is the first and most popular index from the house of India's oldest stock exchange. The S&P BSE SENSEX 30 measures its index through a free float market capitalization weighted index. Free-float market capitalization is determined as the market value of total shares of the company which are readily available for trading in the market. Now by readily available share it means those shares which are tradable in the market and excludes promoters' holding, government holding, strategic holding and other locked-in shares, which will not be available in the market for trading in normal course of action. It was first published in 1986 considering the base value 100 in the year 1978-79. BSE has taken various initiatives in the nature of sustainability and corporate social responsibility. BSE via its theme based indices portraits the present carbon and green initiatives taken up by different companies, like S&P BSE CARBONEX and S&P BSE GREENEX. BSE and Indian Institute of Corporate Affairs (IICA) which is established by ministry of corporate affairs has signed a memorandum of understanding (MoU) on September 23, 2013 to work collaboratively in the realm of business sustainability, investor education, Corporate Social Responsibilities and other united areas. Corporate Social Responsibility Index will be launched as a gesture to represent the most valuable CSR contributing companies. An advisory committee consisting of officials from IICA and BSE was formed to formulate the CSR index construction, design and roll out procedure.

BSE GREENEX or green index is India's first carbon efficient live index which was developed in 2012 by BSE in collaboration with IIM Ahmadabad for the green purpose of measuring carbon emission by companies. This index provides its benefits to socially concern and profit concerned investors, industries and government by encouraging energy efficient practise. The index is calculated considering top ranking companies of different sectors like power, steel, cement etc. which is directly related to BSE SENSEX. If a company is removed from BSE 100 list then that company automatically gets delisted from BSE GREENEX. The index calculation is focused on energy efficiency which is measured by gradual decrease in energy consumption, waste reduction, adaptation of renewable energy and costs incurred on energy. The index provides significance to business as well as investors also. On the other hand, BSE CARBONEX which was launched in 2012 is a carbon based thematic index that values an organisations commitment to climate change.

Environmental sustainability under corporate social responsibility act is a major game changer in green initiatives. Sustainability is the need of the hour as the concentration of Greenhouse Gases has increased day by day and industries are specifically responsible for carbon dioxide emission which leads to the path of global warming. Major initiatives under environmental sustainability are waste management, emission control, maximising energy efficiency and productivity. An emphasis on sustainability today will contribute to a better future tomorrow.

REVIEW OF RELEVANT LITERATURE

Corporate Social Responsibility being a diversified compulsion mandated by the government of India under the Companies Act 2013. Ensuring environmental sustainability, ecological balance, protection of flora and fauna, animal welfare, agro-forestry, conservation of natural resources and maintaining quality of soil, air and water can benefit the future generation by initiatives of companies to focus on environmental sustainability. Windsor (2001) in his article attempted to figure out whether CSR activities results in positive relationship between society and business in long run. The researcher also studied about the changing phase of CSR. Looking to the past trends of CSR and Caroll's model, researcher found the emerging alternatives of CSR i.e. global corporate citizenship, stakeholder management practices and conception of responsibility. According to Henriques and Richardson (2004) progress has been achieved in understanding the triple bottom line of sustainable development since the early 1990s. Understanding the economic bottom line, as opposed to the purely financial, is an essential pre-condition to achieving sustainability. However, understanding and measuring the interactions between the economic and the social and between the economic and the environmental bottom lines remain the key challenges. Elkington (2004) considered TBL agenda as most people would currently understand it is only the beginning. A much more comprehensive approach will be needed that involves a wide range of stakeholders and coordinates across many areas of government policy, including tax policy, technology policy, economic development policy, labour policy, security policy, corporate reporting policy and so on. Developing this comprehensive approach to sustainable development and environmental protection will be a central governance challenge – and, even more critically, a market challenge – in the 21st century. Da Piedade and Thomas (2006) on stakeholder demands and the introduction of the 'Triple Bottom Line' as a means of reporting corporate performance, make it critical that South African companies assess why they should undertake corporate responsibility initiatives. The findings indicate the need for corporate responsibility action in the areas of ecology, the environment, health and well-being, building human capital and in the encouragement of economic development. Oba et al. (2012) studies a positive relationship between quality of environmental disclosure and financial performance using environmental Disclosure Index Score using 12 checklist items and a rating scale of 0-1. Ameer and Othman (2012) in their study created four sustainability indices based on sustainability report disclosed by companies and rated them from 0-4. The study concluded that an existence of bi-directional relationship between sustainability practices and financial performance was found. Montiel and Delgado Ceballos (2014) referred as corporate sustainability (CS) and corporate social responsibility (CSR) as simultaneous concepts in which CS satisfies environmental, social and economical standards rather CSR satisfies part of the holistic sustainability.

The list of studies had a diversified focus on CSR in accordance to TBL and corporate sustainability. The present study focuses on creating Corporate Sustainability Index of listed BSE SENSEX companies based on their performance on various sustainability issues as laid down in the Companies Act, 2013.

OBJECTIVE OF THE CHAPTER

The study revolves around companies that are listed in BSE SENSEX and their role in CSR activities particularly related to the welfare of environment. Contribution made by these companies to give back some benefit to the society is evaluated in terms of their green initiatives only as laid down in the Act.

- The companies listed in BSE SENSEX and their contributions towards environment.
- Computing Corporate Sustainability Index for a better understanding of contributions.
- To study the variations of focus of Sustainability parameters among public and private BSE listed companies in India.

DATA AND METHODOLOGY

The study is totally based on data collected from various sources of corporate disclosure in general and corporate social responsibility report in particular primarily including company website and other corporate communications. Data collected are regarding the financial year 2016-17 to represent the current status of companies registered under BSE SENSEX. Further the study revolves around these companies and their contributions to environmental issues. An attempt is made to evaluate the concurrent situation of companies under section 135 and their responsibilities towards the noteworthy pillar of environment.

As per NGOBOX report the prescribed CSR of big 500 companies which consist of major listed companies in Bombay Stock Exchange and National Stock Exchange for the last five years i.e. 2014-15, 2015-16, 2016-17, 2017-18, 2018-19 these companies had to spend a total of 8188 crore rupees in 2014-15, 8899 crore rupees in 2015-16, 9610 crore rupees in 2016-17, 11,215 crore rupees in 2017-18, 11,625 crore rupees in 2018-19.Projected CSR fund distribution from the year 2014-15 to the year 2018-19 represents that most of the funds have been primarily spend towards education and skill development with a percentage of 32.3% and secondarily on poverty alleviation with a percentage of 29.4%, healthcare and WASH. the 3rd position of funds priority is given to protection of heritage and art with a percentage of 12.3% and on the 4th priority comes environmental sustainability with an accumulated percentage of 10.1% through these five years (Figure 1).

The NGOBOX report also provides a clear understanding of CSR spend towards environmental sustainability during the last five years from 2014-15 to 2018-19. These big 500 companies had a total spending of 595 crore rupees in 2014-15, 651 crore rupees in 2015-16, 1181 crore rupees in 2016-17, 1075 crore rupees in 2017-18, 1117 crore rupees in 2018-19. The above chart represents an increasing trend over the last five years but when the total scenario is justified only 10.1% of total spending has been made so far.

After collecting the data about the surveyed S&P BSE SENSEX companies an attempt is envisaged towards preparation of indices based on practice of corporates towards sustainability issue known as Corporate Sustainability Index (CSI John Elkington-1994). The index is prepared based on their per-

Figure 1. CSR spending towards environment
Source: NGOBOX report 2018-19

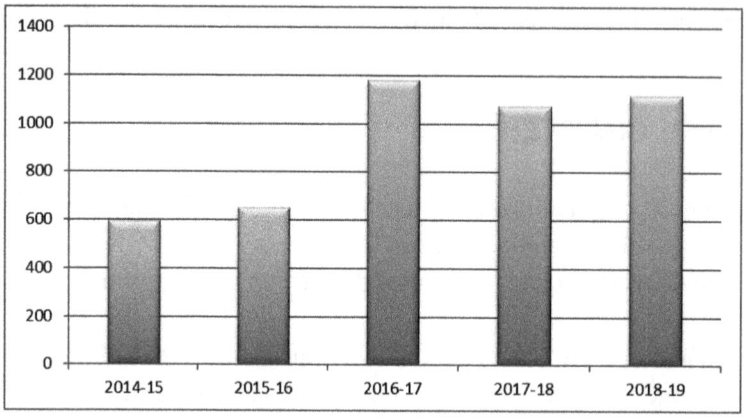

formance on various sustainability issues as laid down in the Companies Act, 2013 and United Nations Sustainable Development Goals (SDGs). The compliance of the surveyed companies in accordance to Water Conservation, Sanitation, Sustainability, Plantation, Ecological Balance, Renewable Energy, Emission Control, Conservation and Waste Management is measured by assigning score '1' for compliance of each sustainable parameter and '0' for non-compliance of the parameters. Finally, the total score obtained from these sectoral parameters is converted into percentage to have the idea of surveyed company's performance towards sustainability in terms of corporate sustainability index.

Increasing global warming, air pollution, lack of preservation and management, biodiversity loss and soil degradation have concerned human beings in recent time. The blame of environmental degradation is to be boned by human beings whereas the duty to protect the environment is also in the hands of human beings. The study is primly focused on the contributions made by BSE listed companies as they are the ones responsible for degrading the environment to a great extent. These companies merely work for profits only and are now contributing for the society and environment through the instrument of CSR as mandated by law. To comply with the compulsions of CSR in India these listed companies provide two percentage of their profit after tax. According to schedule vii, companies need to invest in different sectors mentioned by the law. But the study unfolds the truth of sector imbalances made by the company while contributing in different sectors. Environment is mostly ignored or given minimum importance while compared to education, poverty, hunger and gender inequality. Few companies promote environmental development and honestly support the need irrespective of mandated laws.

Table 2 represents the BSE Sensex companies and their Corporate Sustainability Index on the basis of diversified investments made by these companies in sectors like water conservation, Sanitation, Sustainability, Plantation, Ecological balance, Renewable energy, Emission control, Conservation and Waste management. Companies like Adani Ports & SEZ, Axis Bank, Bharti Airtel, Coal India, Dr. Reddys Laboratories, HDFC Bank, Hero Motocorp, Hindustan Unilever, HDFC, Indusind Bank, Infosys, ITC, Mahindra &Mahindra, ONGC, PGCIL, Reliance Industries, SBI, Sun Pharmaceutical, TCS, Tata Motors, Tata Steel, Wipro, Yes Bank are having CSI of 40 percentage and above which indicates that these companies promote more than four sectors mentioned in schedule VII of the Companies Act, 2013. Whereas companies like Asian Paints, Bajaj Auto, ICICI Bank, Kotak Mahindra Bank, Larsen & Tou-

Table 2. Corporate Sustainability Index(CSI) of S&P BSE SENSEX Companies

SL. NO.	COMPANY NAME	CSI
1	ADANI PORTS & SEZ	40
2	ASIAN PAINTS	20
3	AXIS BANK	50
4	BAJAJ AUTO	20
5	BHARTI AIRTEL	30
6	COAL INDIA	40
7	DR. REDDYS LABORATORIES	50
8	HDFC BANK	50
9	HERO MOTOCORP	30
10	HINDUSTAN UNILEVER	60
11	HDFC	40
12	ICICI BANK	20
13	INDUSIND BANK	50
14	INFOSYS	30
15	ITC	40
16	KOTAK MAHINDRA BANK	20
17	LARSEN & TOUBRO	20
18	MAHINDRA & MAHINDRA	30
19	MARUTI SUZUKI	20
20	NTPC	20
21	ONGC	50
22	PGCIL	60
23	RELIANCE INDUSTRIES	50
24	SBI	30
25	SUN PHARMACEUTICAL	10
26	TCS	40
27	TATA MOTORS	30
28	TATA STEEL	40
29	WIPRO	40
30	YES BANK	50

Source: Authors Computation based on Corporate disclosure towards environmental issues

bro, Maruti Suzuki, NTPC contribute to only two sectors and results in 20% of CSI. Further the study comprises of non-parametric tests for ordinal data like Kruskal-Wallis test and Mann-Whitney U test.

Hypothesis is a predictive supposition to be proved or disproved by statistical means. It is helpful where population parameters are not available, hypothesis testing is used in that case to decide whether the sample data supports the problem or not. Hypothesis testing is helpful to guide highly probable established facts (Table 3 and 4). When the establishment is based on the assumption that two or more

Table 3. Hypothesis test summary

	Null Hypothesis	Test	Sig.	Decision
1	The distribution of CSI is the same across categories of COMPANY.	Independent-Samples Kruskal-Wallis Test	.465	Retain the null hypothesis.

Asymptotic significances are displayed. The significance level is .05.

Table 4. Independent sample test

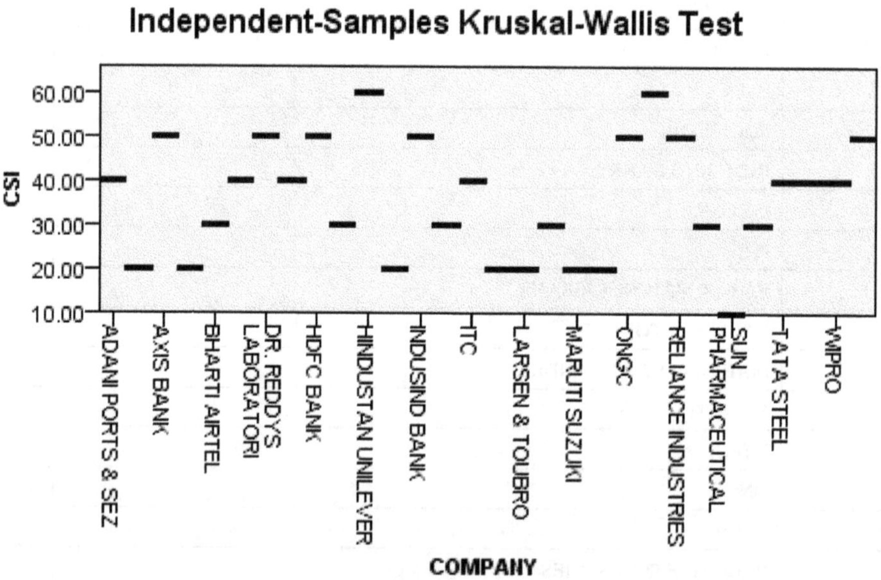

Total N	30
Test Statistic	29.000
Degrees of Freedom	29
Asymptotic Sig. (2-sided test)	.465

1. The test statistic is adjusted for ties.
2. Multiple comparisons are not performed because the overall test does not show significant differences across samples.

sample data is based from different population are equal, then the assumption is considered to be null hypothesis. But when the sample attributes do not support the null hypothesis i.e. they are not equal to each other, then the assumption is called alternative hypothesis. Hypothesis testing can generally lead to two types of error. Rejecting the null hypothesis when it is true is referred to be type one error whereas accepting the null hypothesis when it is false is type two error. Type-I error is represented by α (alpha) which is the test level of significance and type two error is represented by β(beta) and can be called β error. The null hypothesis is generally rejected if the statistically calculated standardised value of a research study falls in the rejection region and the null hypothesis is will be accepted if the statistically calculated standardised value of a research study falls in the acceptance region.

The Kruskal-Wallis test is performed considering the null hypothesis assumes that all distribution functions are equal and obtained from identical population. While the alternate hypothesis that at least one of the sample is of different population. The first test results in retaining the null hypothesis with a significance level of 0.05.

Mann-Whitney (Table 5) is a non-parametric test that resembles t-test which compares two independent population means. Further Mann-Whitney U test is conducted by dividing the BSE listed companies into two groups of Public Sector Unit and Non-Public Sector Unit.

Mann-Whitney U test is used to compare differences between Public Sector Unit and Non-Public Sector Unit considering Corporate Sustainability index to be dependent variable. In which the null hypothesis considers that two samples come from identical population and the alternative hypothesis assumes that these two samples are from different populations. BSE listed companies consist of 5 PSU companies and 25 Non-PSU companies having mean rank of 17.8 and 15.04. The null hypothesis is to be accepted as there is low significance of difference in private and public companies while considering corporate sustainability (Table 6).

CONCLUSION

Corporate Social Responsibility as mandated by the law is being followed by all the companies to the extent it requires while few companies participate voluntarily by contributing more than prescribed 2 percentage. Environment being a noteworthy issue at the outset of growing concerns from all quarters in general and United Nations Sustainability Development Goals in particular, an ample amount of focus is required to be given in protection and conservation of the environment. The study reveals the current involvement of BSE SENSEX companies in environmental works like water conservation, sanitation,

Table 5. Hypothesis test summary

	Null Hypothesis	Test	Sig.	Decision
1	The distribution of CSI is the same across categories of VALUES.	Independent-Samples Mann-Whitney U Test	.552[1]	Retain the null hypothesis.

Asymptotic significances are displayed. The significance level is .05.

[1]Exact significance is displayed for this test.

Table 6. Independent sample Mann-Whitney U test

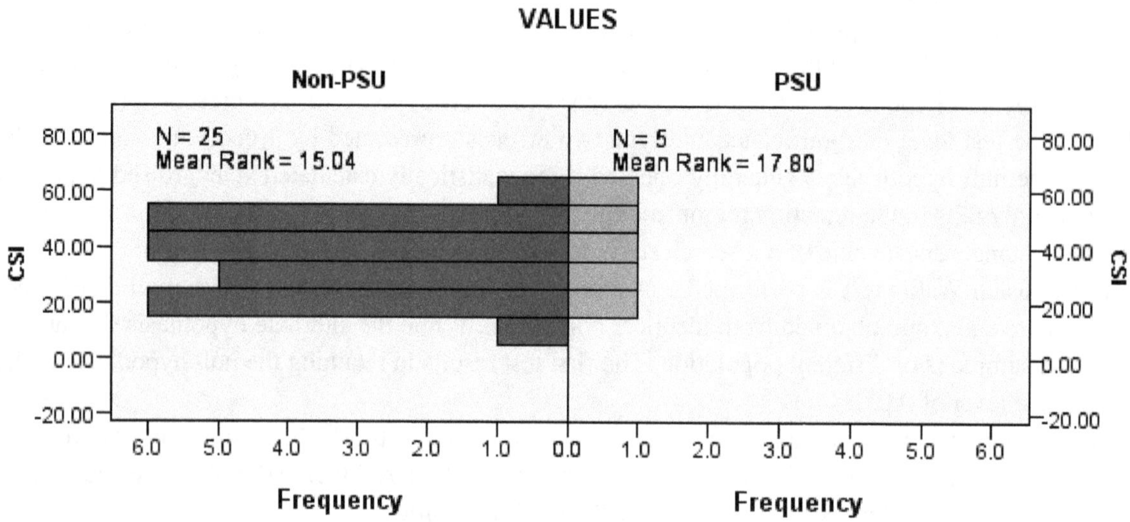

Total N	30
Mann-Whitney U	51.000
Wilcoxon W	376.000
Test Statistic	51.000
Standard Error	17.557
Standardized Test Statistic	-.655
Asymptotic Sig. (2-sided test)	.512
Exact Sig. (2-sided test)	.552

sustainability, plantation, ecological balance, renewable energy, emission control, conservation and waste management as an initiative towards protection of 'Planet'. Bombay Stock Exchange has already taken its initiatives via representation of BSE GREENEX and BSE CARBONEX which mutually benefit the investors and company with remembrance of the environment at large. Although parameters are provided, companies like Asian Paints, Bajaj Auto, ICICI Bank, Kotak Mahindra Bank, Larsen & Toubro, Maruti Suzuki and Sun Pharmaceutical tend to neglect the importance of environment. Mann-Whitney U test was implemented to compare differences between Public Sector Unit and Non-Public Sector Unit considering Corporate Sustainability index to be dependent variable but the results revealed low significance of difference in private and public companies while considering corporate sustainability was noticed. But this does not reflect that these companies are not contributing for 'People', these companies are involved in providing education, eradicating hunger and poverty etc. However, the broader perspective of the responsibility of big corporate house towards the sustainability issue in general and protection of environment in particular under the aegis of new regulatory mechanism in India is a noteworthy, laudable and unique one, the impact study towards this direction may be a future prospective research work.

REFERENCES

Ameer, R., & Othman, R. (2012). Sustainability Practices and Corporate Financial Performance: A Study Based on Top Global Corporations. *Journal of Business Ethics*, *108*(1), 61–79. doi:10.100710551-011-1063-y

Da Piedade, L., & Thomas, A. (2006). The case for corporate responsibility: An exploratory study. *SA Journal of Human Resource Management*, *4*(2), 65–74.

Elkington, J. (2004). *Enter the Triple Bottom Line*. Retrieved from http://www.johnelkington.com/TBL-elkington-chapter.pdf

Henriques, A., & Richardson, J. (2004). *The Triple Bottom Line: Does It All Add Up? Assessing the Sustainability of Business and CSR*. London: Earthscan Publications Limited. Available http://issuu.com/irothko/docs/henriques.the-triple-bottom-line---does-it-all-add

Montiel, I., & Delgado-Ceballos, J. (2014). Defining and Measuring Corporate Sustainability: Are We There Yet? *Organization & Environment*, *27*(2), 113–139. doi:10.1177/1086026614526413

Oba, V. C., Fodio, M. I., & Soje, B. (2012). The Value Relevance of Environmental Responsibility Information Disclosure in Nigeria. *Acta Universitatis Danubius Economica*, *8*(6), 100–113.

Windsor, D. (2001). The future of corporate social responsibility. *The International Journal of Organizational Analysis*, *9*(3), 225–256. doi:10.1108/eb028934

KEY TERMS AND DEFINITIONS

BSE CARBONEX: BSE CARBONEX was launched in 2012, is a carbon-based thematic index that values an organization's commitment to climate change. That aims at providing a benchmark as well as awareness to the dangers imposed by climate change. The assessment of these companies is made on the basis of carbon emission and carbon efficiency.

BSE GREENEX: BSE GREENEX or green index is India's first carbon efficient live index which was developed in 2012 by BSE in collaboration with IIM Ahmedabad for the green purpose of measuring carbon emission by companies. This index provides its benefits to socially concern and profit concerned investors, industries and government by encouraging energy efficient practice. The index is calculated considering top ranking companies of different sectors like power, steel, cement etc. The index is measured on the terms of energy efficiency by gradual decrease in energy consumption, waste reduction, adaptation of renewable energy and costs incurred on energy. The index provides significance to business as well as investors also.

Corporate Social Responsibility (CSR): Corporate social responsibility is the responsibility of a business towards its environment and people. As these businesses operate on the base of environmental resources, sustainability must be maintained for long term success. Companies now need to share a part of their profit on CSR activities as a contribution to the society, and these expenses cannot be claimed as business expenses.

Corporate Sustainability (CS): CS is referred as the corporate management paradigm which subordinates traditional profit maximization and aims in achieving social goals for sustainable development. Corporate sustainability includes sustainable development, corporate social responsibility, stakeholders theory, and corporate accountability.

Corporate Sustainability Index (CSI): Corporate sustainability index is the index prepared based on their performance on various sustainability issues as laid down in the Companies Act, 2013 and United Nations Sustainable Development Goals (SDGs). this index is created with a view for sustainable development through environment compatible investment and to encourage corporations to be ethically responsible.

Kruskal-Wallis Test: Kruskal-Wallis Test is a nonparametric test that assesses for significant differences on a continuous dependent variable by a categorical independent variable. In which the null hypothesis is considers that the samples are from identical population whereas the alternate hypothesis assumes that the samples are from different populations.

Mann-Whitney U Test: Mann-Whitney is a non-parametric test that resembles t-test which compares two independent population means. In the study Mann-Whitney U test is conducted compare the public sector unit and non-public sector unit of BSE SENSEX companies considering corporate sustainable index as dependent variable.

New Companies Act: Companies Act 2013 has brought a bundle of changes in Indian corporate business. It is basically the rules and guidelines that every company needs to follow to operate in India. Section 135 and schedule VII and the provisions regarding companies (corporate social responsibility policy) rules, 2014 or generally known as CSR rules which came into effect from 1st April 2014.

Standard and Poor Bombay Stock Exchange's Sensitivity Index (S&P BSE SENSEX): Standard and Poor Bombay Stock Exchange's Sensitivity Index or Sensex is the first and most popular index from the house of India's oldest stock exchange. The S&P BSE SENSEX 30 measures its index through a free float market capitalization weighted index. Free-float market capitalization is determined as the market value of total shares of the company which are readily available for trading in the market. Sensex simply defines the current market position of major listed companies.

Sustainability: Sustainability is the efficient use of resources to meet the present needs without compromising the future. Environmental sustainability under corporate social responsibility act is a major game changer in green initiatives. Major initiatives under environmental sustainability are waste management, emission control, maximizing energy efficiency and productivity. An emphasis on sustainability today will contribute to a better future tomorrow.

Triple Bottom Line (TBL): The idea of triple P also known as triple bottom line stands on the base of three pillars namely people, planet and profit which measures the impact of the company on local and global scale via sustainability. Measuring the input that these companies take from the society will give the requirement to return to the society.

Chapter 17
Marketing of Greener Products: Trends and Practices

Subhasis Sen
Symbiosis International University (Deemed), India

Kannan Rajagopal
Symbiosis International University (Deemed), India

Kinkini Bhattacharjee
Katwa College, India

ABSTRACT

The objective of the chapter is to discuss different aspects of marketing of greener products with some secondary source information. The theoretical analysis and the data reveal that there have been increasing implications of different generations towards greener or ecological products. More specifically, the younger generations prefer the greener products more as compared to older population.

INTRODUCTION TO GREEN MARKETING

Marketing can be defined as a business philosophy or management techniques aimed towards providing better service to a customer, organization or a society. Marketing field has more scope for development as compared to any other fields of management like sales, advertising etc. According to the Chartered Institute of Marketing, Marketing is the management process for identifying, anticipating and satisfying customer requirement profitably. On the other hand, management consultants like Peter Drucker would like to believe that Marketing is the whole business seen from its final result that is from the customers' point of view. Customer is the main focus of this field.

According to the American Marketing Association, *green marketing* is the marketing of products that are presumed to be environmentally safe. Thus green marketing incorporates a broad range of activities, including product modification, changes to the production process, packaging changes, as well as

DOI: 10.4018/978-1-5225-8547-3.ch017

modifying advertising. Yet defining green marketing is not a simple task where several meanings intersect and contradict each other; an example of this will be the existence of varying social, environmental and retail definitions attached to this term. Other similar terms used are *Environmental Marketing* and *Ecological Marketing*.

Green Marketing is defined as "A holistic and responsible management process that identifies, anticipates, satisfies and fulfils stakeholder requirements, for a reasonable reward, that does not adversely affect human or natural environment wellbeing". Modifying the previous definition, Peattie went ahead to redefine green marketing in 1995 as the holistic management process responsible for satisfying the requirements of customer and society, in a profitable and sustainable way.

Green Marketing aims to address the environmental issues related with marketing. Going green not only makes a firm good but also pays rich dividends. It is the job of the stakeholders and the institution to enforce green marketing. Lai and Wen, in 2006, found that green marketing and process innovations have a positive impact on corporate competitive advantage. Green Marketing is using claims about a product's environmental "friendliness" in order to promote the product.

"I'll go out for a breath of fresh air" is an often-heard phrase. But how many of us realize that this has become irrelevant in today's world, because the quality of air in our cities is anything but fresh. The moment you step out of the house and are on the road you can actually see the air getting polluted; a cloud of smoke from the exhaust of a bus, car, or a scooter; smoke billowing from a factory chimney, fly ash generated by thermal power plants, and speeding cars causing dust to rise from the roads. Natural phenomena such as the eruption of a volcano and even someone smoking a cigarette can also cause air pollution One business area where environmental issues have received a great deal of discussion in the popular and professional press is marketing. Terms like "Green Marketing" and "Environmental marketing" appear frequently in the popular press. Many governments around the world have become so concerned about green marketing activities that they have attempted to regulate them.

According to American Marketing Association, Green Marketing is the marketing of products that are presumed to be environmentally safe. Thus green marketing incorporates a broad range of activities, including product modification, changes to the production process, packaging changes, as well as modifying advertising. Yet defining green marketing is not a simple task. Other similar terms used are Environmental Marketing and Ecological Marketing. The term green marketing came into prominence in the late 1980s and early 1990s. The American Marketing Association (AMA) held the first workshop on "Ecological Marketing" in 1975. The proceedings of this workshop resulted in one of the first books on green marketing entitled "Ecological Marketing" Thus green marketing incorporates a broad range of activities, including product modification, changes to the production process, packaging changes, as well as modifying advertising. Yet defining green marketing is not a simple task. Indeed the terminology used in this area has varied, it includes: Green Marketing, Environmental Marketing and Ecological Marketing.

WHY IS GREEN MARKETING IMPORTANT?

The question of why green marketing has increased in importance is quite simple and relies on the basic definition of Economics: Economics is the study of how people use their limited resources to try to satisfy unlimited wants.

Thus mankind has limited resources on the earth, with which she/he must attempt to provide for the worlds' unlimited wants. In market societies where there is "freedom of choice", it has generally been accepted that individuals and organizations have the right to attempt to have their wants satisfied. As firms face limited natural resources, they must develop new or alternative ways of satisfying these unlimited wants. Ultimately green marketing looks at how marketing activities utilize these limited resources, while satisfying consumers wants, both of individuals and industry.

THE GREEN CONSUMER

The green consumers are the driving forces behind the green marketing process. It is they who drive consumer demand, which in turn encourages improvements in the environmental performance of many products and companies. Thus, for a marketer it is important to identify the types of green consumers. Many organizations have found that two out of every three consumer is green in developed country but country like Bangladesh and its organization has found that one out of every six consumer is green, but their environmental commitments vary because of their different standards, expectation from producers, demand and buying power. It is thus not efficient to say that the green consumer is one who engages in green consumption, specifically, consumes in a more sustainable and socially responsible way. A consumer acquires bundle of wants and needs and this is also true for the green consumer. To satisfy those needs businesses have to break down the market into different groups of consumers that differ in their responses to the firm's marketing mix program. The segments (Kotabe & Helsen (1998), p.184) arrived at should preferably have the following features: 1) Measurable 2) Sizeable 3) Accessible 4) Actionable 5) Competitive intensity 6) Growth potential A great deal of market research has been concerned with identifying the green consumer. A clear picture has not yet been established and it differs a lot between markets. But some generalizations about the green consumer can be made on the basis of the research done so far. The green consumer:

- Is inconsistent
- Is confused
- Is generally a woman
- Is adults who are likely to be more concerned about the environment
- Is sophisticated in wants and needs (Peattie, 1992, p. 118)

BENEFITS OF GREEN MARKETING

Green marketing offers business bottom line incentives and top line growth possibilities. While modification of business or production processes may involve start-up costs; it will save money in the long term. For example the cost of installing solar energy is an investment in future energy cost savings. Companies that develop new and improved products and services with environmental impacts in mind give themselves access to new markets, substantially increase profits and enjoy competitive advantages over those marketing non-environmentally responsible alternatives.

WHY ARE FIRMS USING GREEN MARKETING?

When looking through the literature there are several suggested reasons for firms increased use of Green Marketing. Five possible reasons cited are:

1. Organizations perceive environmental marketing to be an opportunity that can be used to achieve its objectives.
2. Organizations believe they have a moral obligation to be more socially responsible.
3. Governmental bodies are forcing firms to become more responsible.
4. Competitors' environmental activities pressure firms to change their environmental marketing activities.
5. Cost factors associated with waste disposal, or reductions in material usage forces firms to modify their behavior.

There are numerous examples of firms who have strived to become more environmentally responsible, in an attempt to better satisfy their consumer needs. McDonald's replaced its clam shell packaging with waxed paper because of increased consumer concern relating to polystyrene production and Ozone depletion.

Tuna manufacturers modified their fishing techniques because of the increased concern over driftnet fishing, and the resulting death of dolphins.

Xerox introduced a "high quality" recycled photocopier paper in an attempt to satisfy the demands of firms for less environmentally harmful products. This is not to imply that all firms who have undertaken environmental marketing activities actually improve their behavior. In some cases firms have misled consumers in an attempt to gain market share. In other cases firms have jumped on the green bandwagon without considering the accuracy of their behavior, their claims, or the effectiveness of their products. This lack of consideration of the true "greenness" of activities may result in firms making false or misleading green marketing claims.

GREEN MARKETING AND SOCIAL RESPONSIBILITY

Many firms are beginning to realize that they are members of the wider community and therefore must behave in an environmentally responsible fashion. This translates into firms that believe they must achieve environmental objectives as well as profit related objectives. This results in environmental issues being integrated into the firm's corporate culture. There are examples of firms adopting both strategies. Organizations like the Body Shop heavily promote the fact that they are environmentally responsible. While this behaviour is a competitive advantage, the firm was established specifically to offer consumers environmentally responsible alternatives to conventional cosmetic products. This philosophy is directly tied to the overall corporate culture, rather than simply being a competitive tool.

Fund managers and corporate developers too, are taking into account the environmental viability of the company they invest in Venture Capitalists are investing in green business because they believe it's a growth opportunity.

Britain based HSBC became the world's first bank to go carbon neutral late last year and is now turning its 11000 buildings in 76 countries worldwide into models of energy efficiency.

"Our customers have told us that they decide where they shop based on whether the business is a good neighbor" - says David North, Tesco's community director.

An example of a firm that does not promote its environmental initiatives is Coca-Cola. They have invested large sums of money in various recycling activities, as well as having modified their packaging to minimize its environmental impact. While being concerned about the environment, Coke has not used this concern as a marketing tool. Thus many consumers may not realize that Coke is a very environmentally committed organization. Another firm who is very environmentally responsible but does not promote this fact, at least outside the organization, is Walt Disney World (WDW). WDW has an extensive waste management program and infrastructure in place, yet these facilities are not highlighted in their general tourist promotional activities.

GOVERNMENTAL PRESSURE

As with all marketing related activities, governments want to "protect" consumers and society; this protection has significant green marketing implications. Governmental regulations relating to environmental marketing are designed to protect consumers in several ways,

1. Reduce production of harmful goods or by-products;
2. Modify consumer and industry's use and/or consumption of harmful goods; or
3. Ensure that all types of consumers have the ability to evaluate the environmental composition of goods.

Governments establish regulations designed to control the amount of hazardous wastes produced by firms. Many by-products of production are controlled through the issuing of various environmental licenses, thus modifying organizational behavior.

In some cases governments try to "induce" final consumers to become more responsible. For example, some governments have introduced voluntary curb-side recycling programs, making it easier for consumers to act responsibly. In other cases governments tax individuals who act in an irresponsible fashion. For example in Australia there is a higher gas tax associated with leaded petrol. New Delhi, the India's capital was getting polluted gradually at a very fast pace till Supreme Court of India forced a change of fuel on it. In 2002, a directive was issued to completely adopt CNG in all public transport systems to curb pollution. One of the more recent publicized environmental regulations undertaken by governments has been the establishment of guidelines designed to "control" green marketing claims. These regulations include the Australian Trade Practices Commission's (TPC)" Environmental Claims in Marketing- A Guideline, the US Federal Trade Commission's (FTC) "Guides for the Use of Environmental Marketing Claims" and the regulations suggested by the National Association of Attorneys-General .These regulations are all designed to ensure consumers have the appropriate information which would enable them to evaluate firm's environmental claims. In addition to these guidelines many States in the US have introduced legislation to control various environmental marketing activities. Investment analysts are starting to see the environmental awareness of managers as a barometer of the likely long term success of their companies. Green policies, they say, tend to indicate hands on management, high consumer confidence and good corporate governance.

HSBC won't deals with companies on projects like oil pipelines through Russia, that don't measure up to their environmental, social and governance standards

COMPETITIVE PRESSURE

Another major force in the environmental and Green marketing area has been firms' desire to maintain their competitive position. In many cases firms observe competitors promoting their environmental behaviors and attempt to emulate this behavior. In some instances this competitive pressure has caused an entire industry to modify and thus reduce its detrimental environmental behavior. For example, it could be argued that Xerox's "Revive 100% Recycled paper" was introduced a few years ago in an attempt to address the introduction of recycled photocopier paper by other manufacturers.

COST OR PROFIT ISSUES

Firms may also use green marketing in an attempt to address cost or profit related issues. Disposing of environmentally harmful by-products, such as polychlorinated biphenyl (PCB)contaminated oil are becoming increasingly costly and in some cases difficult. Therefore firms that can reduce harmful wastes may incur substantial cost savings. When attempting to minimize waste, firms are often forced to re-examine their production processes. In these cases they often develop more effective production processes that not only reduce waste, but reduce the need for some raw materials. This serves as a double cost savings, since both waste and raw material are reduced. In other cases firms attempt to find end-of-pipe solutions, instead of minimizing waste. In these situations firms try to find markets or uses for their waste materials, where one firm's waste becomes another firm's input of production. One Australian example of this is a firm who produces acidic waste water as a by-product of production and sells it to a firm involved in neutralizing base materials.

GREEN MARKETING DOES LEAD TO SUCCESS

Green marketing is not a theoretical concept only. A lot of firms are using this concept to consolidate their market positions. A few examples are-

- Tesco is pumping $200 mn into environmental technologies to reduce the amount of energy they use by 50% compared with 2000 levels, by 2010. In addition to building 80new eco stores across Britain over the next year –the greenest of which will be constructed of recycled materials and will burn food waste for electricity-they are also making small changes that could have big results. They are paying customers not to use plastic bags which they expect would cut consumption by 25% in two years. Goldman Sachs has invested $30 mn in Canadian alternative-fuels Company

Logen. It was one of the several green ventures for ex-Goldman and Nature Conservancy head Henry Paulson, US Treasury secy.

- According to a recent report from the climate group, an international environmental charity, and 43 multinationals –including Bayer, DuPont –saved a combined $11.6 bn by improving energy efficiency, reducing waste output and harnessing solar power.
- The World's two largest insurance companies Swiss Re and Munich Re are now taking strict company policies on climate change into consideration when determining risks. Similarly in Japan about 800 companies annually publish reports explaining how they plan to cut carbon emissions and make their products and factories greener. GE last month signed a deal of $10 billion with British Petroleum to develop hydrogen power plants that will capture carbon and bury it underground so it doesn't lead to global warming.

Goldman Sachs has invested more than $ 1bn in renewable energy sources, including biofuels.

Markets are also beginning to recognize that companies that do not do right by Mother Nature may have more volatile stock prices.

Goldman Sachs

ESG (Environmental, Social and Governance) Index now ranks the world's largest companies based on how environmentally friendly their operations are.

SOME PROBLEMS WITH GOING GREEN

No Matter why a firm uses green marketing there are a number of potential problems that they must overcome. One of the main problems is that firms using green marketing must ensure that their activities are not misleading to consumers or industry, and do not reach any of the regulations or laws dealing with environmental marketing. For example marketers in the US must ensure their green marketing claims can meet the following set of criteria, in order to comply with the FTC's guidelines. Green marketing claims must;* clearly state environmental benefits;* Explain environmental characteristics;* Explain how benefits are achieved;* Ensure comparative differences are justified;* Ensure negative factors are taken into consideration; and* only use meaningful terms and pictures. Another problem firm's face is that those who modify their products due to increased consumer concern must contend with the fact that consumers' perceptions are sometimes not correct. Take for example the McDonald's case where it has replaced its clam shells with plastic coated paper. There is ongoing scientific debate which is more environmentally friendly. Some scientific evidence suggests that when taking a cradle-to-grave approach, polystyrene is less environmentally harmful. If this is the case McDonald's bowed to consumer pressure, yet has chosen the more environmentally harmful option. When firms attempt to become socially responsible, they may face the risk that the environmentally responsible action of today will be found to be harmful in the future. Take for example the aerosol industry which has switched from CFCs (chlorofluorocarbons) to HFCs (hydro fluorocarbons) only to be told HFCs are also a greenhouse gas. Some firms now use DME (dimethyl ether) as an aerosol propellant, which may also harm the ozone layer .Given the limited scientific knowledge at any point in time, it may be impossible for a firm to be certain they have made the correct environmental decision. This may explain why some firms, like Coca-Cola and Walt Disney World, are becoming socially responsible without publicizing the point. They may be protecting themselves from potential future negative backlash; if it is determined they made the wrong decision in the past. While governmental regulation is designed to give consumers the opportunity to make better decisions or to motivate them to be more environmentally responsible, there are difficulties in establishing policies that will address all environmental issues. For example, guidelines developed to control environmental marketing address only a very narrow set of issues, i.e., the truth fullness of environmental marketing claims. If governments want to modify consumer behavior they need to establish a different set of regulations. Thus governmental attempts to protect the environment may result in a proliferation of regulations and guidelines, with no one central controlling body. Reacting to competitive pressures can cause all "followers" to make the same mistake as the "leader." A costly example of this was the Mobil Corporation who followed the competition and introduced "bio degradable" plastic garbage bags. While technically these bags were biodegradable, the conditions under which they were disposed did not allow biodegradation to occur. Mobil was sued by several US states for using misleading advertising claims. Thus blindly following the competition can have costly ramifications. The push to reduce costs or increase profits may not force firms to address the important issue of environmental degradation. End-of-pipe solutions may not actually reduce the waste but rather shift it around. While this may be beneficial, it does not necessarily address the larger environmental problem, though it may minimize its short term affects. Ultimately most waste produced will enter the waste stream, therefore to be environmentally responsible organizations should attempt to minimize their waste, rather than find "appropriate" uses for it.

Green marketing covers more than a firm's marketing claims. While firms must bear much of the responsibility for environmental degradation, ultimately it is consumers who demand goods, and thus create environmental problems. One example of this is where McDonald 'sis often blamed for polluting the environment because much of their packaging finishes up as roadside waste. It must be remembered that it is the uncaring consumer who chooses to disposes of their waste in an inappropriate fashion. Ultimately green marketing requires that consumers want a cleaner environment and are willing to "pay" for it, possibly through higher priced goods, modified individual lifestyles, or even governmental intervention. Until this occurs it will be difficult for firms alone to lead the green marketing revolution. Having said this, it must not be forgotten that the industrial buyer also has the ability to pressure suppliers to modify their activities. Thus an environmental committed organization may not only produce goods that have reduced their detrimental impact on the environment, they may also be able to pressure their suppliers to behave in a more environmentally "responsible" fashion. Final consumers and industrial buyers also have the ability to pressure organizations to integrate the environment into their corporate culture and thus ensure all organizations minimize the detrimental environmental impact of their activities.

ECOLABELS

ECOLABELS establishes a means for customers to make a choice which has less environmental consequences and thus bring about a change in the process of manufacturing of these products. The problem associated is to advertise the environmental qualities of products and make the people aware by spreading information regarding via eco labeling schemes. A body of research has already been set up to study the use and effectiveness of ecolabels.

Ecolabels can be either voluntary or mandatory. For example, EU has come up with mandatory energy labels from A to F where A refers to least energy consumption and F to maximum energy usage. Also various voluntary labels, classified based on ISO standards, are available which can be categorized into three major classes namely TYPE I, TYPE II and TYPE III.TYPE I basically belongs to the category of ecolabels and is a well researched category. TYPE II is self claimed environmental labels while TYPE III is quantified environmental data provided in a standardized way.

The major issues with these environmental labels and emblems is that consumers firstly need to understand the meanings of the various standard labels in order to make a judgment and also have trust on the label specifications. Also another major concern is that these labels will influence the buying behavior of consumers only if they are interested in environmental friendly products. Thus, although labels may satisfy all required criteria it may not directly influence the green purchasing decisions.

SUCCESS OR FAILURE

We have looked into various statistics to understand whether green marketing is a success or failure. Improvements have been seen in specific product segments as a result of use of ecolabels. For example, the Food retail Coop Sweden, declared that due to the consumers involving more and more in ecological food products there was a downfall in the use of pesticides by 14,000 kg and artificial fertilizers by 1,000,000 kg. In Sweden, consumers going for alternative detergents that had ecolabels have lead to a 15% decrease in chemical products and thus use of more biodegradable surfactants.

Conclusion can be drawn that use of ecolabelled products does affect sales but it is altered by parameters such as country and the type of product. For example, the market share of ecolabelled printing paper in Nordic countries is 70% while the market share of ecolabelled laundry products is around 90% in Sweden. Other examples include ecological food products like organic products which has very low percentage sales as compared to total food sales varying from almost 4% in Denmark to less than 1% in England. Such statistics cannot be considered as a success for green products and for that matter this sector has seen a further decrease in sales.

GREEN MARKET SATURATED OR NON EXISTENT

The big question that still needs to be answered is whether the market for green products is over saturated or is it not existent at all. Awareness about green products is a pre-condition for green product sales. Also the fact that the number of truly interested consumers in green products is not rising leads to the small market share. Statistics show that only 10-15% of the consumers are true green product loyal.

Another hindrance in the success of green products is the unavailability of green alternatives for all kinds of products and hence it is impractical to achieve high market share until and unless there is an expansion in the green product line. Since there are very limited options for the consumer, he/she rarely compares environmental qualities of products before making purchase decisions and therefore marketers do not show keen interest in launching such substitutes. We cannot identify a consumer as green since the decision of a consumer changes according to the situation. The same green product consumer may choose to go for a non-green one in case of a different situation or type of product. Thus we cannot consider green behavior to be a fixed attitude.

MORE EFFICIENT

It is very important to lay emphasis on consumer awareness and understanding and trust on ecolabels. Improved consumer tools that are transparent and which are non misleading need to be introduced. It has been proved that consumers that are environmentally inclined are appealed more to such ecolabels while those individuals who are less interested tend to look for negatives in these ecological friendly products.

MORE WAYS TO INCREASE APPEAL OF GREEN PRODUCTS

The main strategy to be employed is to make the environmentally inclined consumers aware of the environmental qualities of the green products. Though ecolabelling is successful in providing competitive edge, it has now become a policy tool.

It is the responsibility of the marketers and market researchers to understand the reasons behind the poor performance of the ecolabel led products.

STEPS

It is important to have a comprehensive understanding of the green market for us to improve its market status and to adopt various aspects of conventional marketing for the same.

Demand Analysis is not the study of identifying the number of green consumer at present but also takes into account the current and future opportunities for the product. The market of these products is not only restricted to the existing consumers. We can increase the size of green product consumers by attracting individuals who are currently unaware of the benefits or are resistant to the use of these green products by communicating to them the advantages of these and stimulating increased use.

Examples of "green" advertising claims includes the following

- Biodegradable
- Compostable
- Recyclable/recycled
- Environmentally safe
- Ozone friendly

Reasons for the Company to Use Green Marketing

The Marketing Research shows that consumers prefer and are even willing to spend more money on the products they perceive as environmentally safe. More than half of American consumers have purchased a product because of a label that said it was environmentally safe or biodegradable. Consumers generally can't tell whether a product will do what the advertiser claims-degrade in a landfill, and not deplete the ozone layer. Even if the claims are true, it may not be evident for five, ten, fifty or more years. There are claims of deception with "green" claims. For example if we consider the company manufacturing the Fibers claims for disposable tableware

- Biodegradable
- Compostable in municipal solid waste composting facilities
- Recyclable

In fact, according to the experts of bio degradable products verdicts states that it

- Won't degrade in landfill
- Especially it would not degraded in few conventional municipal composting facilities
- More importantly no facilities accepts it for recycling

As a result of concerns about growing use of such claims, there has been Guidelines issued for the Use of Environmental Marketing Claims. Any way, in which a message can be received in the labeling, advertising, and promotional materials, any form a message can take words, symbols, emblems, logos, depictions and product brand names.

The Guiding principle states the following:

Any qualifications or disclosures should be sufficiently clear, prominent and understandable to prevent deception

1. Claim should make clear whether it applies to the product or the package
2. Claims should not overstate the environmental attribute or benefit

When it comes to Environmental Marketing claims, General claims (e.g., "eco-safe") must be not misleading, substantiated in advance of the claim, and burden of proof on advertiser.

Claims of degradability, biodegradability, and photo degradability are considered deceptive unless there is scientific evidence that the entire product or package will *completely* break down and return to nature (i.e. decompose) within a reasonably short period of time.

Claims of compostability (of the product or package) are deceptive unless all the materials in the product or package will break down into usable compost in a safe and timely manner in an appropriate composting facility; or a home compost pile. It is considered to be deceptive if the item is not compostable in a home compost pile; and there are no institutional or municipal composting facilities in the community where the item is sold.

Claims of recyclability are deceptive unless the product or package can be collected, separated or otherwise recovered from the solid waste stream for reuse; or in the manufacture or assembly of another package or product through an established recycling program. If only part of a package or item is recyclable, any claim of recyclability must be adequately qualified to avoid consumer deception. A claim of recyclability is not deceptive if only minor, incidental components are non-recyclable. Claims of recyclability have unique potential for deception because not all communities have recycling facilities and not all facilities recycle the same products and packages.

As a general rule, use of the term "recyclable" and/or use of symbols that imply recyclability are deceptive unless collection sites for recycling the material are available to a *substantial majority of consumers or communities* even if collection sites are established in a significant percentage of communities or available to a significant percentage of the population unless the claim is qualified to indicate the limited availability of recycling programs.

Symbols that imply recyclability include three chasing arrows, *the* Guide lines says that, unless qualified, it means product or package is made of *recycled* materials as well as being recyclable.

When it comes to specific materials like Plastics, SPI symbol code developed by the Society of the Plastics Industry to indicate the type of plastic from which product is made numbers run from 1 to 7.

Claims relating to the preservation of the ozone layer

For example:

- Ozone safe
- Ozone friendly
- Contains no CFCs

are considered to be deceptive if the product contains any ozone-depleting substance. Problem: all ozone is not alike: ozone layer in upper atmosphere is necessary to prevent sun's harmful radiation from reaching earth ozone at ground level forms smog can cause serious breathing problems. "ozone safe" products should not harm the atmosphere at either level.

The Concept of Green Power

Green marketing is heavily used in electricity generation. The Green power is the electric power that is generated by renewable resources and which is of less polluting than fossil fuels and nuclear power. The types of Green Power includes Wind, Bio-Energy, Geothermal energy, Solar power, Hydroelectric power.

The Green Power Point of Attraction to the Customer

Electricity generation is largest industrial polluter in US; currently produces:

- The emissions of sulfur dioxide (main cause of acid rain)
- 30 percent of the nitrogen oxide emissions (stress forest ecosystems; combine with organic compounds in sunlight to form smog)
- 40 percent of carbon dioxide emissions
- Toxic-metal emissions (mercury and lead)
- Nuclear waste.

Consumers do not have to change their electricity provider. Customers choose to pay a premium on their electricity bill to cover the extra cost of purchasing clean, sustainable energy. Marketing strategies and messages especially in the B2B marketplace still need to make legitimate and credible claims about their products and services. While it may be in vogue to suggest a green attribute of your product, it is essential to avoid trivializing the subject with marginal or inconsequential claims. Instead, there should be an obvious green benefit. Major companies (such as PepsiCo), government agencies, and educational institutions (such as Duke) have expressed their commitment to buying green products for infrastructure and other processes. For these companies, agencies, and institutions whom are mandating the purchase of green products, green has become a fundamental part of the decision making process. Where appropriate the variables have become cheaper, faster, better, and greener.

Consider the case of Miura Boiler — a global leader in the manufacture of industrial steam boilers — and their effort to become a market leader in the North American market. Steam remains a primary source of energy in manufacturing and processing food, textiles, pharmaceuticals, automotive products, and others. It also is drives critical systems for large educational institutions and hospitals by supplying steam for not only heat, but hot water, sterilization, and other important systems.

The typical industrial steam boiler manufacturer uses oil and gas to boil large amounts of water and turn them into steam in about two hours. Miura, a Japanese company with experience working under strict water conservation and emissions regulations in the Japanese market, developed a technology that could actually turn water to steam in about five minutes prior to entering the North American market.

This technology, developed before being "green" meant something other than money or a popular frog on a children's TV show, boils the same amount of water as its counterparts. However, instead of using "one large pot," these boilers distribute a similar amount of water boiled in several smaller pots enabling faster boiling times and increased water usage efficiency. In turn, this reduced the amount of fuel (oil and gas) required to run these systems — an advantage that, as the cost of oil and gas began to climb, increasingly caught the attention of North American industrial boiler buyers.

Similarly ITC has been 'Carbon Positive' three years in a row (storing twice the amount of CO2 than the Company emits).'Water Positive' six years in a row (creating three times more Rainwater Harvesting potential than ITC's net consumption).Close to 100% solid waste recycling. ITC's Social and Farm Forestry initiative has greened over 80,000 hectares creating an estimated 35 million person days of employment among the disadvantaged. ITC's Watershed Development Initiative brings precious water to nearly 35,000 hectares of dry lands and moisture stressed areas. ITC's Sustainable Community Development initiatives include women empowerment, supplementary education, integrated animal husbandry programmes.

The reality is that while many businesses and institutions place a value on environmental responsibility, green products that come with a higher price tag, like hybrid cars, can sometimes face marketing obstacles. While green marketing is an increasingly important way to attract B2B customers and deliver your message, cheaper, faster, and better remain cornerstones of attracting customers. For Miura however, fuel savings, of an estimated at 18 to 20 percent, was another compelling reason to buy a product that conserves resources, reduces the facility's carbon footprint, and was a socially responsible choice.

Things to consider while implementing a green marketing strategy:

- Green is not just the color of money; it is the color of social-responsibility.
- More and more companies and institutions want to be socially responsible and perceived as buying green.
- Don't trivialize the subject with unsubstantiated or marginal claims.
- While there are no strict guidelines for green claims, energy savings, resource conservation, and reduced emissions are benchmarks of green B2B products. Other valid platforms include: biodegradable and/or easily recycled, reduced toxins, and engineering for increased efficiency and reduced maintenance.
- Price will always be a factor considered in purchasing decisions.

- Selling green products at price points higher than competitors can dampen sales, unless the cost of consumables, such as energy, is predicted to dramatically increase in the near-term. If you plan to sell an energy-consuming green product at a higher price than less-efficient competitors, you may want to provide customers with information about applicable utility rebate programs, and government incentives.
- Present your green message proudly and boldly.
- Don't hide your green message. It deserves more than a simple bullet point.
- Keep your message focused and answer the question: "Why would someone buy your product?"
- A focused message that answers this question is preferable to generalities that require the buyer to search for meaning.
- Green marketing is an evolving discipline, but uses similar marketing tools to more established marketing areas.

Campaigns that leverage user commentary, case studies, thought leadership initiatives and other means attract potential buyers and establish a comfort level with your company.

GREEN PRODUCT

Green product stresses the straight and tangible benefits provided by greener design, such as energy efficiency or recycled content, rather than stressing the environmental attributes them. Reducing the environmental impact of a product improves the product's overall performance and quality in ways that are important, not just the most dedicated and loyal green consumer, but to all consumers. For example, CNG (Converted Natural Gas) use in the vehicles, superconcentrated laundry detergents not only save energy and packaging, they save end space, money and effort. Organically grown food not only better preserves soil and reduces the amount of toxins in the water supply; they have superior taste and health benefits compared to their counterparts. Therefore green product means any product, which is not hazardous for environment and customer as well, and it also work as a future remedy of negative impact of a product.

GREEN MARKETING PROCESS

Green marketing process comprises with external and internal Ps. After integrating external and internal Ps, green success will automatically come through four Ss. Here external 7 Ps consists of Paying customers, Providers, Politicians, Pressure groups, Problems, Predictions and Partners; internal 7Ps consists of Products, Promotion, Price, Place, Providing information, Processes and Policies. After integrating external and internal 7Ps, we can find out the green successes through 4 Ss such as Satisfaction – of stakeholder needs, Safety – of products and processes, Social acceptability –of the company and Sustainability – of its activities.

IMPORTANCE OF GREEN MARKETING

Green marketing offers business bottom line incentives and top line growth possibilities. While modification of business or production processes may involve start-up costs, it will save money in the long term. For example the cost of installing solar energy is an investment in future energy cost savings. Companies that develop new and improved products and services with environmental impacts in mind give themselves access to new markets, substantially increase profits and enjoy competitive advantages over those marketing non environmentally responsible alternatives. When looking through the literature there are several suggested reasons for firms increased use of Green Marketing.

Five possible reasons are as follows:

1. Organizations perceives environmental marketing to be an opportunity that can be used to achieve its objectives
2. Organizations believe they have a moral obligation to be more socially responsible
3. Governmental bodies are forcing firms to become more responsible
4. Competitors' environmental activities pressure firms to change their environmental marketing activities
5. Cost factors associated with waste disposal, or reductions in material usage forces firms to modify their behavior

THE FOUR Ps OF GREEN MARKETING like conventional marketers, green marketers must address the four Ps in innovative ways.

The Product: Entrepreneurs wanting to exploit emerging green market either: identify customers 'environmental needs and develop products to address these needs; or develop environmentally responsible products to have less impact than competitors. The increasingly wide varieties of products on the market that support sustainable development and are good for the triple bottom line include products made from recycled goods, such as Quik'N Tuff housing materials made from recycled broccoli boxes. Efficient products, which save water, energy or gasoline, save money and reduce environmental impact. Queensland's only waterless printer, Print point, reduces operating costs by using less water than conventional printers and is able to pass the savings on to customers. McDonalds, for example, changed their packaging from polystyrene clamshells to paper. Organic products — many consumers are prepared to pay a premium for organic products, which offer promise of quality. Organic butchers, for example, promote the added qualities such as taste and tenderness. A service that rents or loans products – such as toy libraries. Certified products may meet or exceed environmentally responsible criteria. Whatever the product or service, it is vital to ensure that products meet or exceed the quality expectations of customers and is thoroughly tested.

Price: Pricing is a critical element of the marketing mix. Most customers are prepared to pay a premium if there is a perception of additional product value. This value may be improved performance, function, design, visual appeal or taste. Environmental benefits are usually an added bonus but will often be the deciding factor between products of equal value and quality. Environmentally responsible products, however, are often less expensive when product life cycle costs are taken into consideration. For example, fuel-efficient vehicles, water-efficient printing and non-hazardous products.

Place: The choice of where and when to make a product available has a significant impact on the customers being attracted. Very few customers go out of their way to buy green products merely for the sake of it. Marketers looking to successfully introduce new green products should, in most cases, position them broadly in the market place so they are not just appealing to a small green niche market. The location must also be consistent with the image which a company wants to project. The location must differentiate a company from its competitors. This can be achieved by in-store promotions and visually appealing displays or using recycled materials to emphasize the environmental and other benefits.

Promotion: Promoting products and services to target markets includes paid advertising, public relations, sales promotions, direct marketing and on-site promotions. Smart green marketers will be able to reinforce environmental credibility by using sustainable marketing and communications tools and practices. For example, many companies in the financial industry are providing electronic statements by email, e-marketing is rapidly replacing more traditional marketing methods, and printed materials can be produced using recycled materials and efficient processes, such as waterless printing. Retailers, for example, are recognizing the value of alliances with other companies, environmental groups and research organizations when promoting their environmental commitment. To reduce the use of plastic bags and promote their green commitment, some retailers sell shopping bags, under the banner of the Go Green Environment Fund. The key to successful green marketing is credibility. Never overstate environmental claims or establish unrealistic expectations, and communicate simply and through sources that people trust. Promote your green credentials and achievements. Publicize stories of the company and employee green initiatives. Enter environmental awards programs to profile environmental credentials to customers and stakeholders.

CHALLENGES IN GREEN MARKETING NEED FORSTANDARDIZATION

It is found that only 5% of the marketing messages from ——Green campaigns are entirely true and there is a lack of standardization to authenticate these claims. There is no standardization to authenticate these claims. There is no standardization currently in place to certify a product as organic. Unless some regulatory bodies are involved in providing the certifications there will not be any verifiable means. A standard quality control board needs to be in place for such labeling and licensing. NEW CONCEPT Indian literate and urban consumer is getting more aware about the merits of Green products. But it is still a new concept for the masses. The consumer needs to be educated and made aware of the environmental threats. The new green movements need to reach the masses and that will take a lot of time and effort. By India's ayurvedic heritage, Indian consumers do appreciate the importance of using natural and herbal beauty products. Indian consumer is exposed to healthy living lifestyles such as yoga and natural food consumption. In those aspects the consumer is already aware and will be inclined to accept the green products.

PATIENCE AND PERSEVERANCE

The investors and corporate need to view the environment as a major long-term investment opportunity, the marketers need to look at the long-term benefits from this new green movement. It will require a lot of patience and no immediate results. Since it is a new concept and idea, it will have its own acceptance period.

AVOIDING GREEN MYOPIA

The first rule of green marketing is focusing on customer benefits i.e. the primary reason why consumers buy certain products in the first place. Do this right, and motivate consumers to switch brands or even pay a premium for the greener alternative. It is not going to help if a product is developed which is absolutely green in various aspects but does not pass the customer satisfaction criteria. This will lead to green myopia. Also if the green products are priced very high then again it will lose its market acceptability.

GOLDEN RULES OF GREEN MARKETING

1. **Know Your Customer:** Make sure that the consumer is aware of and concerned about the issues that your product attempts to address. Whirlpool learned the hard way that consumers wouldn't pay a premium for a CFC-free refrigerator because consumers didn't know what CFCs were.
2. **Educating Your Customers:** Isn't just a matter of letting people know you're doing whatever you're doing to protect the environment, but also a matter of letting them know why it matters. Otherwise, for a significant portion of your target market, it's a case of "So what?" and your green marketing campaign goes nowhere.
3. **Being Genuine and Transparent:** Means that a) you are actually doing what you claim to be doing in your green marketing campaign and b) the rest of your business policies are consistent with whatever you are doing that's environmentally friendly. Both these conditions have to be met for your business to establish the kind of environmental credentials that will allow a green marketing campaign to succeed.
4. **Reassure the Buyer:** Consumers must be made to believe that the product performs the job it's supposed to do-they won't forego product quality in the name of the environment.
5. **Consider Your Pricing:** If you're charging a premium for your product-and many environmentally preferable products cost more due to economies of scale and use of higher quality ingredients-make sure those consumers can afford the premium and feel it's worth it.
6. **Giving Your Customers an Opportunity to Participate:** Means personalizing the benefits of your environmentally friendly actions, normally through letting the customer take part in positive environmental action.
7. **Thus Leading Brands Should Recognize that Consumer Expectations have Changed:** It is not enough for a company to green its products; consumers expect the products that they purchase pocket friendly and also to help reduce the environmental impact in their own lives too.

Adopting Green Marketing Strategy and Its Relation to Production Cost in Industries

- Green Marketing is seen world over as an important ingredient for sustainable development and an advanced model for manufacturing enterprises. This concept takes into account principles of environmental protection and conservation in the production and service sector by minimizing waste and pollution to the environment, saving energy and other resources while establishing a production economy. There are two types of measures responsible for green sustainable development: a) conservation of resources such as energy, natural gas, oil, fossil fuels, water, electricity etc. b)pollution and environmental emissions. An improvement in these two aspects enhances the entire production and distribution process, including product design, process planning, material supply, production planning, manufacturing, distribution and post scale technical support.With alarming rise in global warming, there will be a subsequent increase in awareness created amongst society and new stricter laws enforced by the government in order to encourage GREEN PRODUCTION and relatively higher taxes imposed to improve the situation. For example, Department of Environment, Food and Rural Affairs discusses about industrial manufacturing and pollution issues associated with it. Also it informs about plans of government in increasing taxes related to such issues as land filling, air and water pollution.

Various types of changes in system and operation may be required to move over to the manufacture of green products, some of which are discussed below:

- **Change of Process Input:** Change in raw materials and parts will be required to manufacture eco-friendly substitutes.
- **Change of Process Parameters:** There might be a need to change parameters like voltage, coolant rate, feeding speed to bring down energy consumption and waste.
- **Change of Processing Method (Single Operation):** A change in equipments or process logic will be required in order to lower energy consumption and waste.
- **Change of Entire Processing Method Involving Multiple Operations:** There might arise a need to change the entire manufacturing set-up and introduce a green tech based manufacturing paradigm.

GREEN MARKETING: WHAT DOES THE EXISTING DATA SAY?

Green Marketing is the marketing of products and services based on environmental awareness. Companies involved in green marketing makes decisions relating to the entire process of the company's product such as processing, packaging and distribution. Green marketing concept comprised of six factors such as green segmentation, green band equity, green brand image, green satisfaction, green trust and green awareness.

Our global data shows a strong evidence for paying more for eco-friendly products. In Table 1 we have found that Millennials aged 22-35 are more than any other generation to pay extra for eco-friendly or sustainable products. On the other hand 58% of Gen Z, 55% of Gen X and 46% of Baby Boomers are

Table 1. Percentage of who agree that they would pay more for ecofriendly products

Generation	% of who agree
Gen Z (16-21)	58%
Millennials (23-25)	61%
Gen X (36-54)	55%
Baby Boomers (55-64)	46%

Source: Global Web Index Q2 2018

likely to pay more for that product. It is important to note that if Millennials are more conscious about their purchases that will be reflected on their believes and values and Gen Z is close of trials. The Millennials control future of the consumer market. New data shows that Americans especially Millennials do not want to consume any product which harms the planet. Millennials named Patagonia, Whole Foods, Tesla and the Honest Company with their most trusted bands have notable social and environmental practices. Walmart made the list for its recent sustainability initiatives.

Many U.S consumers have desire for more sustainable products. The sales data shows that consumer's spending power affect the change that they want to see in the world. The sustainability of market has climb up in recent years. So, corporations are more do well to understand the attributes of sustainability and meet the sustainable traits to the consumers (Figure 1).

48% of US consumer says that they would probably change their consumption habit to reduce their impact on the environment (Figure 2). These consumers are putting their dollars ($128.5 billion) on sustainable fast moving consumer goods (FMCG) products. Since 2014, these shoppers have grown sustainable product sales by nearly 20%. The data expect that by 2021, the influential shoppers spend on sustainable product up to $150 billion where sustainable FMCG goods have increased from $14 billion to $22 billion.

Today the sales of sustainable products are 22% of the total store sale. The growth of sustainable category mainly driven by organic, sustainable and clean attributes of that goods. It is to be notes that between 2014 and 2017, the sales of conventional products dropped by almost four percent while the sales of sustainable product grew by 3 percent. By 2021, the data expect that the sales of sustainable products will be 25% of total store sales.

There is a significantly large gap between generations in the U.S to sustainable purchase goal. The survey says that Millennials are twice than Baby Boomers (75% vs 34%) to changing their consumption habits towards sustainable products. They are more willing to pay for environmentally friendly or

Figure 1. Sustainable product sales in the US market. Sustainability combines free from, clean, simple, sustainable and organic labels.
Source: Nielsen Product Insider, Powered by label insight

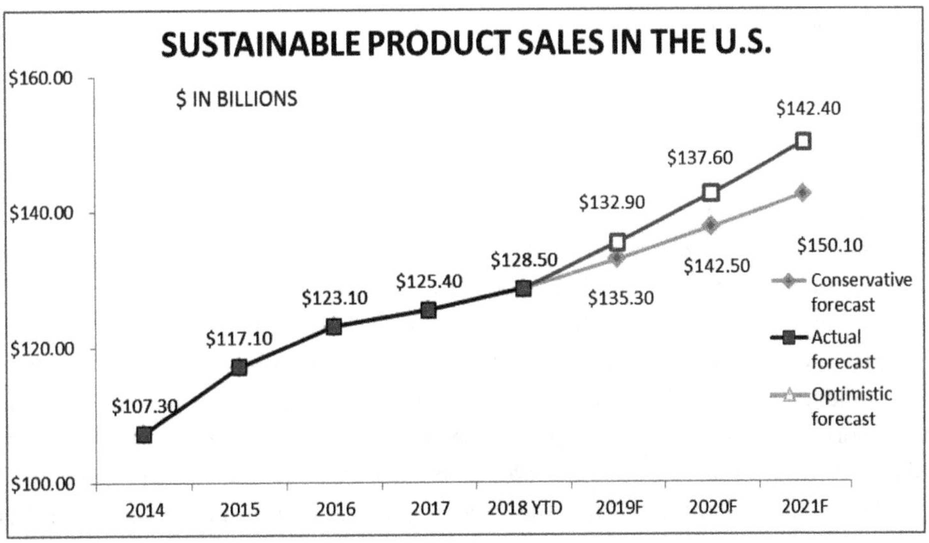

Figure 2. Share of sales of sustainable products
Source: Nielsen Product Insider, Powered by label insight

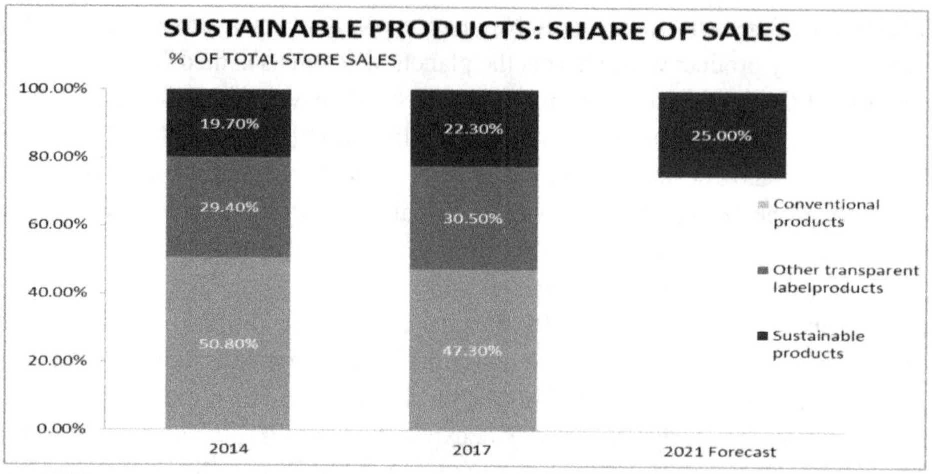

sustainable ingredients (90% vs 61%), organic ingredients (86% vs 59%) or products that have socially responsibility claims (80% vs 48%).

According to Sarah Schmansky it is also observed that sustainability divides the generation by technology. We have found that 67% of Sustainable shoppers in U.S are more likely to be digitally engaged. The device is playing a significant role about their purchasing decisions. According to Nielson, age is not only factor for looking sustainable consumers. 60% of Americans fall into the "Sustainable Mainstream" category who want to be more sustainable.

2018 is the year of the influential sustainable consumer. But very soon it is to be decade of the sustainable shopper. With a limited store, U.S consumers continue to choose sustainable products over conventional options. Companies need to evaluate their product and the impact of ingredients on the product. The nature of consumer is shifted towards "Healthy for me and healthy for the world" and this will increase the sales of FMCG products. Technology will help consumers to match the right ingredients to their needs. Companies will need to clearly communicate and they have the data to prove how their sustainable factors help consumers.

CONCLUSION

Now this is the right time to select——Green marketing globally. It will come with drastic change in the world of business if all nations will make strict roles because green marketing is essential to save world from pollution. From the business point of view because a clever marketer is one who not only convinces the consumer, but also involves the consumer in marketing his product. Green marketing should not be considered as just one more approach to marketing, but has to be pursued with much greater vigor, as it has an environmental and social dimension to it. With the threat of global warming looming large, it is extremely important that green marketing becomes the norm rather than an exception or just a fad. Recycling of paper, metals, plastics, etc., in a safe and environmentally harmless manner should become much more systematized and universal. It has to become the general norm to use energy-efficient lamps and other electrical goods. Marketers also have the responsibility to make the consumers understand the need for and benefits of green products as compared to non-green ones. In green marketing, consumers are willing to pay more to maintain a cleaner and greener environment. Finally, consumers, industrial buyers and suppliers need to pressurize to minimize the negative effects on the environment-friendly. Green marketing assumes even more importance and relevance in developing countries like India. Thus an environmental committed organization may not only produce goods that have reduced their detrimental impact on the environment, they may also be able to pressure their suppliers to behave in a more environmentally "responsible" fashion. Final consumers and industrial buyers also have the ability to pressure organizations to integrate the environment into their corporate culture and thus ensure all organizations minimize the detrimental environmental impact of their activities.

REFERENCES

Alsmadi, S. (2007). Green Marketing and the Concern over the Environment: Measuring Environmental Consciousness of Jordanian Consumers. *Journal of Promotion Management, 13*(3–4).

Donaldson, R. H. (2005). Green brands. *NZ Marketing Magazine, 24*(8), 14–17.

Jain, S. K., & Kaur, G. (2004). Green Marketing: An Attitudinal and Behavioural Analysis of Indian Consumers. *Global Business Review, 5*(2), 187–205. doi:10.1177/097215090400500203

Karna, J., Hansen, E., & Juslin, H. (2003). Social Responsibility in Environmental Marketing Planning. *European Journal of Marketing, 37*(5/6), 848–873. doi:10.1108/03090560310465170

Kilbourne, W. E. (1998). Green Marketing: A Theoretical Perspective. *Journal of Marketing Management, 14*(6), 641–656. doi:10.1362/026725798784867743

Kotler, P. (1999). Marketing Management. Prentice Hall of India Private Limited.

Mathur, L. K., & Mathur, I. (2000). An Analysis of the wealth effect of green marketing strategies. *Journal of Business Research, 50*(2), 193–200. doi:10.1016/S0148-2963(99)00032-6

Ottman, J. (1993). *Green Marketing: Challenges and Opportunities for the New Marketing Age*. Lincolnwood, IL: NTC Business Books.

Ottman, J. A. (2006). Avoiding Green Marketing Myopia. *Environment*, 48.

Oyewole, P. (2001). Social Costs of Environmental Justice Associated with the Practice of Green Marketing. *Journal of Business Ethics, 29*(3), 239–252. doi:10.1023/A:1026592805470

Prothero, A. (1998). Green Marketing: The 'Fad' That Won't Slip Slide Away. *Journal of Marketing Management, 14*(6), 507–513. doi:10.1362/026725798784867680

Prothero, A., & Fitchett, J. A. (2000). Greening Capitalism: Opportunities for Green Community. *Journal of Macromarketing, 20*(1), 46–56. doi:10.1177/0276146700201005

KEY TERMS AND DEFINITIONS

Ecolabels: It establishes a means for customers to make a choice which has less environmental consequences.

Environmental Product: The products which are environment friendly.

FMCG: Fast-moving consumer goods (FMCG) are products that are sold quickly and at a relatively low cost. Examples include non-durable goods such as packaged foods, beverages, toiletries, over-the-counter drugs, and other consumables.

Green Consumer: It refers to the consumers who opt for greener products.

Green Marketing: It is related to buying and selling of environment friendly products.

Millennial: This is the range of population lying in the young generations.

Sustainability: It refers to the process of production and consumption maintaining the health of environment.

Chapter 18
Major Components of Green Urbanization and Their Relative Importance:
A Study on Some Districts of West Bengal (India)

Subikash Mookherjee
Mahishadal Raj College, India

Debasish Mondal
Vidyasagar University, India

ABSTRACT

Aspirations for being urban in character are considered as a significant phenomenon of socio-economic development in developing countries. Urbanization, in economic sense only, means intensive economic activities by a large number of people in a relatively small plot of land, where secondary and tertiary sectors play a dominant role and where certain amenities are bound to be available for general citizens, though it doesn't seem complete without addressing the issue of nature. Though urbanization of an area is tried to be measured by some academicians through applying the method of indexing with available indicators and their data-driven weights, environmental issues are not incorporated there for any kind of factor analysis to identify their individual relative importance. This chapter intervenes at this juncture and focuses on construction of an urbanization index for some selected "town area units" belonging to some selected districts of West Bengal and run a factor analysis of it on some identified environmental factors. It observes negative relationship between QVSE and IGU, positive association between IGU and PR, and positive relation between IWDS and IGU.

DOI: 10.4018/978-1-5225-8547-3.ch018

INTRODUCTION

It is undoubtedly considered as a historical fact that, urban primacy has been a feature of urbanization of West Bengal in India and there was a continuous increase of population in highly urbanized districts around Kolkata, one of the four metropolitan cities of the country. This feature of mono-centric urbanization subsequently led to slowing down the process of urbanization in the peripheral parts of West Bengal from 1951 onwards and quite a different trend has been noticed very recently during the first decade of the new millennium (i.e., 2001-2011). The Census data of 2011 has vehemently revealed that the urbanization process of the state exhibits a growing trend and begins to spread, taking into account the environmental factors in it. These have been accompanied by a noticeable decline in the percentage share of the population in the Class I towns and substantial population growth in small towns. Simultaneously with a substantial increment in the number of census towns with some added environmental facilities, the traditional rural fabric of most of the villages has changed and majority of the rural people has started to think for a better living with a better access to available amenities. Of course previously designated and statutory towns are there and will be there over the course of time but the changing drives of the rural area-units towards green urbanization both from the demand side and supply side is the major concern and this study makes an attempt to explore this changing pattern of urbanization towards more eco-friendly kind of nature and find out some policy implications.

Under this background, the present study has decided to pursue a research work about the ongoing 'green urbanization' process in the rural areas of West Bengal which are primarily classified under statutorily structured community development blocks (i.e., C. D. Blocks or only blocks). For the purpose of our study, we have strategically designed a systematic stratified sampling method to choose six districts of West Bengal and further we have chosen two blocks from each of the six selected districts following another method which is also based on certain arguments. The study is pursued covering a time period of three census decades (1991, 2001 and 2011) and we aim to see whether there are adequate measures for green urbanization acting actively to keep pace with developmental aspirations of the people in different parts of West Bengal.

This article intends to propose a new concept the *'Index for Green Urbanization' (IGU)* to be applied for all the census-units (i.e., villages and census-towns lying within a block) of the state which is obtained by adopting coherent methodologies on the basis of selected indicators for available environmental amenities and other criteria which are very much likely to indicate the gravity and degree of green urbanization in a particular area-unit. In constructing the *IGU* we have tried to incorporate various factor indices which are specifically based on selected item-wise parameters of different types of environmental amenities available, the underlying dimension indices of both the *town criteria index (TCI)* and the *environmental criteria index (ECI)* and finally to determine actual weights for those factor-indices and dimension indices by applying a new method, namely the *Iterative Average Correlation Method (IACM)* as proposed by Mondal, Mookherjee and Pattanayek (2017).

A BRIEF PROFILE OF WEST BENGAL AND ITS GENERAL URBANIZATION

The Indian state of West Bengal is located in the eastern part of India on the north of Bay of Bengal. It is India's fourth most populous state, with over 91 million inhabitants (as of 2011 census) and it has an area of 88,752 square kilometer (i.e., 34,267 square miles). This state is actually a part of the earlier ethno-linguistic Bengal region, and now it is bordered by Bangladesh in the east, Nepal in the north-west and Bhutan in the north; it shares borders with five Indian states - Odisha, Jharkhand, Bihar, Sikkim and Assam. The state capital is Kolkata (formerly, Calcutta), the third-largest city in India. In terms of physical geography, West Bengal includes the Darjeeling Himalayan hill region, the Gangetic plains, the Rurh region, and the delta region of coastal Sundarbans. The main ethnic group is the Bengalis, with Bengali Hindus forming the demographic majority. On politico-administrative front, there are twenty three districts at present (as of December 31, 2017) classified under five administrative divisions (namely, the Presidency division, the Burdwan division, the Jalpaiguri division, the Medinipur division and the Maldah division), in which four districts are relatively new – the districts of Alipurduar, Kalimpong, Jhargram and Paschim Barddhaman. Moreover there are 341 community development blocks at present in the entire state spread over the districts.

A considerable section of West Bengal's population is seemed to increasingly opting for the non-agricultural way of life, which supposedly results in rapid urbanization in most of the districts of the state and this fact is substantiated by the census data published in 2011. The data shows that since 2001 there has been a huge increase in the number of urban centers across the state against a decline in the number of villages. The decadal growth of urban population in West Bengal has been found to be little higher than the national average. While the national average is 31.16 per cent, the decadal growth rate in the state is 31.89 per cent. 'A sharp rise of the number of census towns since 2001 is a clear indication that people from rural backgrounds are increasingly discarding agriculture as a livelihood option and opting for more urban alternatives. A 'census town' is defined as a semi-urban centre with a minimum population of 5000 people; a population density of 400 persons pr square kilometer and where over 75 per cent of the male main working population is engaged in non-agricultural activities' (Ghosh, 2011). The number of such census towns in West Bengal has gone up from 255 in 2001 to 780 in 2011 and the number of total towns (both statutory and non-statutory) has increased from 378 to 909 during the period. Meanwhile, the number of villages has come down from 40782 in 2001 to 40203 in 2011. Interestingly the number of census towns had come down from 266 in 1991 to 255 in 2001 as a fair number of census towns were declassified due to various reasons (Censuses 1991, 2001 & 2011; DGCO, Government of India).

A SUMMARIZED REVIEW OF LITERATURE

The Indian Census, since the very beginning, besides giving the basic count of population of various towns and cities in the country, produces and presents data on various demographic, social and economic characteristics separately for rural and urban areas. No statistical study of urbanization is possible unless adequate note is taken of the Census definition of 'town' which varies from country to country and from one census year to another. In the case of India, we find that, the Census definition of 'town' remained more or less the same for the period 1901 – 1951 and it was only in 1961 that several modifications were introduced to make the definition more satisfying from the statistical point of view. But an interesting feature of the Indian Census has been the latitude given to Census Superintendents in regard to the classification of places on the border-line of 'rural' and 'urban'. We shall deal with this aspect here and also refer briefly to the impact on urbanization of the new definition of 'town' adopted in 1961. The definition of a 'town' as given in the *first general report* of the Census of India, 1901 is as follows: Town includes: (a) Every municipality of whatever size, (b) All civil lines not included within municipal limits and (c)

Every other continuous collection of houses, permanently resided by not less than 5000 persons, which the Provincial Superintendent may decide to treat as a 'town' for census purposes.

Thus, the primary consideration, for deciding whether a particular place is a town or not lied at the hands of administrative set-up and not on the size of its population. Not all municipalities, civil lines areas and cantonments had a population of over 5000 and yet these were classified as towns. At the same time, all places over a population of 5000 were not necessarily towns. These were over-grown villages and the Census Superintendents had the discretionary power to call them as such. The Census Superintendents even had the discretion to treat as a town, any place irrespective of its administrative set-up or population size for special reasons.

The Census of 1961 adopted a two-fold categorization to identify urban centers and till date this continues. *Firstly,* the settlements that were given urban civic status like Corporation, Municipality and Cantonment, by the state governments were identified as Statutory Towns. As urban development is a state subject (and so is the responsibility of assigning civic status), there is a wide variation in the criteria adopted in assigning civic status across the states. Whichever settlements were assigned such a status by the state governments were included in the urban frame by the census and listed as statutory towns. Keeping these in view, and to make the data on urbanization spatially comparable, the census added a category of non-statutory or Census Towns. *Secondly,* three demographic criteria were applied to identify these Census Towns. These were (a) population size of 5000 or more, (b) density of at least 400 persons per square kilometer and (c) at least 75% of the male main workers to be engaged outside agriculture. The adoption of such a theory, based on two-fold categorization of 'statutory' and 'census' towns, were expected to rationalize the base of the urban frame at that time. The definition of 'town' therefore is not totally objective in as much as it is not based on a rigid statistical test. The census authorities however were aware of these limitations but they preferred administrative expediency to statistical precision.

It is observed that the study of urbanization is not seemed to be done under any kind of statistical precision on the basis of available data. Which place is urbanized and which is not cannot be unambiguously settled unless one goes for common statistical applications and certain norms. Therefore, along with the existing literature this article intends to enquire about the methodological issues which can be used and applied in obtaining some fruitful conclusions regarding declaring a place as urban or not. This ongoing article is clearly based on the available literature, studied so far and indebted to the fields of both Urban Economic Studies and Statistics.

OBJECTIVES OF THE STUDY, DATA SOURCES AND METHODOLOGIES APPLIED

As we have gone through the available literature on urbanization of area units (villages or census towns, as may be classified) in West Bengal, we have found that even if urbanization is defined as an index of transformation; however no indexing (i.e., a sort of quantification) is there in the literature by comprising the indicators of urbanization with justifiable weights. In other words, the level or degree of urbanization or green urbanization of any place has not been attempted to be properly measured (through quantification) or evaluated till date.

Undoubtedly, environmental indicators play a crucial role in determining eco-friendly urbanization of a place. The census authority and some other private bodies collect and publish data regarding availability of eco-friendly elements in a place; however these data are not considered to determine the level of green urbanization of a place. In this study, we are to address the above mentioned problem and we shall try to construct a true urbanization index, based on certain well-accepted indicators, on which urbanization (or, green urbanization) of a place can be measured and compared with that of others. Basically a normal yard-stick for measurement of urbanization of all places is to be obtained from our adopted methodology.

We want to deal with the following objectives here -

1. Identification of urban characteristics and indicators, both in the spheres of town criteria and environmental amenities, which are prevalent in villages and census towns (i.e., census units) in the sample blocks of the selected sample districts of West Bengal.
2. To develop a suitable methodology for construction of a Town Criteria Index (i.e., TCI) for a census unit on the basis of census town criteria, put forward by the Census authority,
3. To construct two Dimension Indices encompassing gross available environmental amenities in a place and these will help us to construct the Environmental Criteria Index (i.e., ECI).
4. To construct the *Index for Green Urbanization (IGU)* for a place (i.e., census unit) on the basis of its TCI and ECI by applying a suitable methodology, for having an idea about the pattern of green urbanization for all the sample census-units of West Bengal.
5. To determine appropriate weights for the underlying components of all the above mentioned TCI and ECI and finally the 'Index for Green Urbanization' by applying the *Iterative Average Correlation Method (IACM)* as proposed by Mondal, Mookherjee and Pattanayek (2017) and to make a comparison of these values with those obtained by applying the conventional *Principal Component Analysis (PCA)*.
6. To perform a *pooled data analysis* in examining the respective simple, partial and ortho-partial (Mondal, 2008) correlation values and to apply the *concept of average correlation* in determining the relative importance of some identified factors in explaining the *variation in IGU* across the census units and over the study-period.

Data Sources

For this analysis, we have extensively used secondary data provided by the Director General of Census Operations (DGCO), Ministry of Home Affairs, Government of India. The required data which have supplied information regarding total population, population density, workers' profile, environmental amenities available etc are collected through visiting their websites or through visiting their offices personally. The books which are consulted for this purpose are (i) Primary Census Abstracts (PCA) of West Bengal for the years 2011, 2001 and 1991; (ii) Census Village Directories of West Bengal for the years 2011, 2001 and 1991 and (iii) Different Issues of District Census Handbooks, published for six sample districts of West Bengal over the decades of 1991, 2001 and 2011 (see References).

Methods on Index Construction

We have constructed criterion indices for the above three point criteria for all the census-units by applying the standard formula: $\{(Xa - Xmin) / (Xmax - Xmin)\}$. In fact, this is the ideal form of constructing an index and this method has vast applicability in the field of research. The elements of *Xmax* and *Xmin* are selected on the basis of observed method of goalposts selection through rationalization of these observations by forward projection and backward projection of the data-set for all criteria, each by ten years and thereby extending the range of study area concerned (Mondal, 2005).

Generally, we are having two types of indexing methods in which the first one suggests that the variables are to be normalized by their respective observed maxima and the observed minima values, following the UNDP methodology of index-construction. After the required normalization of all the variables the index for any dimension is to be constructed by following the principle of arithmetic mean with appropriate weights. At this juncture, it can be mentioned that the principle of normative goalposts are applied in specific cases. In a series of X, if normative goalposts are adopted, then *Xa* is the actual value of a particular criterion for a village, *Xmin* is the minimum justifiable value for that criterion i.e., normative minimum and *Xmax* is the maximum justifiable value i.e., normative maximum.

It can be argued that inter-unit comparison of any dimension for a particular year is made possible by this kind of indexing, but inter-temporal comparison of the units is not possible by this kind of indexing. Both types of comparisons are made possible only when we will assume the normative maximum as 100 and the normative minimum as 0 (zero), but some over-estimated and some under-estimated results may arise due to incorporation of these two normative extremes. We should therefore be searching those rational maximum and minimum values which are supposed to lie inside our working data set for this kind of index formation.

On the other hand, the method of observed extremes to normalize variables also creates problem. Firstly, we cannot know properly whether the changes in the final index values of a state take place because of its improved performance or because of the shifting of goalposts. Secondly, since the values of observed maximum and minimum do alter from year to year, representing changes in the goalposts themselves, meaningful inter-temporal comparisons are not possible. Thus, fixation of goalposts for variables by using appropriate methodology is very much required to carry out meaningful trend analysis of any index. To find a way-out for this problem, we have done a backward projection of the given data-set for a particular criterion by ten years and a forward projection of same kind to obtain an extended range of the data-set so that the rationalized goalposts are conveniently selected for the construction of required indices.

At the next step, when the criterion indices are found, we need to construct the *Town Criteria Index (TCI)* by taking a linear combination of all the three criterion-indices, in which three coefficients are to be associated with the indices, acting as their respective weights. Thus, the simple method of weighted arithmetic mean of the individual criterion (or, dimension) indices is used to determine the TCI (or, any final index value) at this study. However, the question regarding the choice of appropriate weights for the criteria might arise and in response to this query, we have used the *Principal Components Analysis* (PCA) to obtain respective weights for the same criteria and found the required TCI. However, our main contribution through this research lies in introducing the concept of *Iterative Average Correlation Method* (IACM) to determine the actual weights of the concerned dimensions of an index as advancement over the other two methods as there exist some limitations in their applicability. Therefore, we have used three methods simultaneously to determine weights for the individual criterion, made a comparison among those three and obtain three likely different values of Town Criteria Index for the stipulated 1033 census-units under the selected 12 sample blocks belonging to 6 sample districts and finally accepted those values of TCI, which are computed by applying IACM, for further analysis.

To construct the *Environmental Criteria Index (ECI)* for all the census-units, under the purview of a particular block, we have identified 2 dimensions of different types of environmental amenities which are likely to be available and these could be named as the Dimension of Health (DIH) and the Dimension of Socio-environmental Infrastructure (DISEI) respectively. Moreover, each dimension is comprised of some factors which are essentially related to different types of environmental amenities and these factors are based on various elementary parameters, for which village level data are provided by the census authority. In this study we have selected 6 elementary parameters of different types of environment related amenities and classified these parameters in 2 dimensions. In detail, the factors belonging to *Dimension of Health (DIH)* are: (i) Availability of waste disposal system in a census-unit (i.e., F1) (ii) Quantified volume of smoke emission per thousand persons (F2) and (iii) Quantified volume of solid waste dumping per thousand persons (F3). The factors belonging to the *Dimension of Socio-environmental Infrastructure (DISEI)* can be listed as: (i) Availability of sufficient greenery and water bodies in an area, if any (F4), (ii) Availability of sufficient roadways in an area, if any (F5) (iii) and available sources for water supply and availability of sufficient water usage in an area, if any (F6).

We have used the same formula of Index construction, mentioned above, to obtain the respective factor indices with actual values, respective rationalized maximum and minimum values for each parameter. Next we have applied the method of arithmetic mean as usual to combine the factor indices and obtained the concurrent Dimension Index with relative weights. Later, we have constructed the ECI with two of its underlying dimension indices, applying arithmetic mean, and here also, we have identified the weights by applying the above mentioned methods -, the PCA and the IACM. Lastly, the *Index for Green Urbanization (IGU)* is constructed from the linear combination of both *Town Criteria Index (TCI)* and *Environmental Criteria Index (ECI)* with their respective shares as weights which have helped us in preparing the ranks of the listed census-units of a selected block in the scale of green urbanization and a comparison amongst those area-units in terms of IGU can be made possible.

REVIEW OF LITERATURE ON CHOICE OF WEIGHTS FOR THE INDICATORS AND DIMENSIONS

It is already mentioned that the crucial part of this article is to focus on determination of actual weights to the indicators and dimensions of the relevant interim indices and the final index, a few issues and methods are to be raised here. Weights to indicators can be assigned in a number of ways. One can simply judge the significance of an indicator on the basis of value-judgment and accordingly can assign a weight to it. In technical terms, one can assign equal weights to all indicators or assign different weights to different indicators according to their merit on the basis of acceptable reasoning. Side by side, there are a few available statistical methods like the PCA, which are not supposedly based on individual decision, rather coming-out from the data-base itself to determine actual weights for the concerned indicators.

Attaching equal weights (i.e., EWP) to all concerned parameters in explaining a particular final index can be done through subjective value judgment and there might be some sort of arbitrariness in it. The famous UNDP methodology for construction of HDI is based on such principle in which all the dimension indices are given same weight (i.e., 1/3 each), and this methodology of 'homogeneous weight principle' is accepted and applied by the majority of the researchers in the field of Social Sciences (UNDP, 1990). But this phenomenon of attaching uniform weight cannot be possible in all cases, where the independent indicators are of different nature and are having different degrees of explanatory power in them and thereby, this weighting principle has been criticized as arbitrary. Hopkins (1991) mentioned that there might not be perfect substitutability among the DIs and that's why the concept of attaching equal weights is unjust. Desai (1991) and Ravallion (1997) also opined in favour of flexible weights as equal weights might not reflect the reality.

Thus we need a deviation to go away beyond UNDP principle of attaching same weight to all variables and try another mechanism to obtain actual weights which may be different from one another and which are supposed to explain the relative different importance of each dimension index in explaining one particular final index. Noorbaksh (1998) and others claimed that the weights to individual indices should also be obtained from the data and this kind of data-driven weights should make the analysis more trustworthy. Many of them suggested that the coefficients of the first principal component of the individual indices could be used as their weights. Biswas and Caliendo (2002) have also suggested in favour of Principal Component Analysis (PCA). Even if PCA has gained significant importance in the arena of weight determination over time, in this paper we are going to raise a point against it and proceed further to introduce the new method of IACM for the said purpose.

The theory of Principal Component Analysis, as developed by Pearson (1901), Hotelling (1933) and Anderson (1963), with all its modifications afterwards, is accepted by a large number of social scientists as a way out from the complex problem of actual weight determination. The principal components are constructed as a linear combination of the available variables in such a manner that the variance of the linear combination is maximized subject to the constraint that the sum of the squared coefficients must be equal to unity. The Principal Component Analysis suggests that if the variances of the dimension indices and the respective co-variances amongst themselves are found almost equal, the weights of those dimensions, obtained through the co-efficient of the first principal component will almost be equal (Noorbaksh, 1998), (Biswas & Caliendo, 2002). On the other hand, if the respective variances and pair-wise co-variances of the dimension indices are found unequal, the principal component analysis would supposedly provide unequal weights and the method would probably be considered as more relevant (Biswas & Caliendo, 2002). However, the major difficulty of PCA is that it pays much attention to the variability of available data for a particular dimension (indicator) and does not take into account the actual explanatory power of that dimension (indicator). Thus for PCA, more the variability, more would be the assigned weight to a dimension.

The analysis of principal components is very much based upon variations of the individual dimensions. If variability of a particular DI is found to be very high, in PCA, this DI is supposed to have higher weight in contrast to others in determining the FI value. However, even if a particular DI has highest degree of variability amongst all, it does not ensure that it has highest explanatory power in explaining the dependent variable (e.g. the final index). As weights are meant to reveal degree of explanatory power, dealing with variability of a DI through PCA would not suffice to meet the requirement of explanatory power. Moreover, variability of a particular set of variables can be significantly different for different reasons.

This study is trying to offer an alternative measure in determining actual weights of an index and its comprising dimension indices which is based on correlation method. It proposes that the weights of individual dimensions (or indicators) are actually the proportion of their respective 'average squared correlation' values with that of the final index and this methodology of obtaining actual weights through 'average squared correlation' values might be named as the Iterative Average Correlation Method

(IACM). In accordance with statistical texts, we may define 'average squared correlation' or simply the 'average correlation' (AvCor) of a particular variable (or dimension) as the average value of its all sorts of correlations, i.e., its squared simple correlation (i.e., r^2), its squared ortho-partial correlation (Mondal, 2008) and its squared semi ortho-partial correlation(s), if any (Mondal, Mookherjee & Pattanayek, 2017).

A graphical analysis, based on Venn Diagrams of two and three mutually related variable-sets is presented in Section 5 for better understanding of the definition of average correlation.

The detailed methodology for advocating 'average correlation principle' and its significance as a tool for weights-determination is given below. Let DI1, DI2 and DI3 are three underlying dimension indices of a composite final index. If it is assumed that the dimension-indices are mutually uncorrelated (i.e., there is no overlapping region among them), their exclusive correlation values with the final index will unambiguously be treated as their true explanatory power and therefore their respective weights. However, if those dimension-indices are mutually interrelated, then their variances [i.e., V(DI1), V(DI2) and V(DI3)] and their pair-wise co-variances [i.e., COV(DI1, DI2), COV(DI1,DI3) and COV(DI2,DI3)] must have some effective role in determining their respective weights. Among these three dimension indices DI1 will have higher weight than DI2, and DI2 will have higher weight than DI3 if the correlation between DI1 and DI2 is greater than that between DI1 and DI3, and the correlation between DI1 and DI3 is greater than that between DI2 and DI3. Larger the difference between these correlations, larger will be the difference of the weights of the dimensions. This weighting principle is based on the assumption that the correlation between any two indices is due to their interdependence and we may not have any specific (and prior) knowledge about the nature of this dependence. Thus, a high degree of correlation between DI1 and DI2 is supposed to lead towards higher weights for both of DI1 and DI2. To eliminate this problem, simple correlations between the respective dimension indices and the final index cannot be used and the average correlation of them with the final index, as mentioned earlier, can be used to determine their proper weights.

As the final index cannot be calculated unless the weights are determined and as the weights (or the average correlations) cannot be calculated unless the final index is determined, they are to be calculated simultaneously through an iterative process. The process starts with some arbitrarily fixed weights of the individual indices. On the basis of these weights a development index is determined. In the third step average correlations of the individual indices with the development index are obtained and these are used as weights to arrive at the new development index. In the next step we are to have new average correlations and new weights and thereby, another new development index is to be obtained. The process is to be repeated until the values of average correlations do converge to their earlier values and the final weights along with the final development index are to be calculated. All these calculations, in relation to this method proposed, can be obtained only through the application of specific computer programming. We have developed such a programming and on the basis of that, we have performed the empirical analyses which are presented in the following chapters.

AN UNDERSTANDING ON AVERAGE CORRELATION (AVCOR)

Let us suppose there are two interdependent explanatory variables X_1 and X_2 (depicted by two circles X_1 and X_2 respectively in Figure 1) explaining the variability of an explained variable Y (depicted by the rectangle in Figure 1) in a three-variable (one explained and two explanatory) regression model. The explanatory power of variable X_1 is decomposed into two areas denoted by (1) and (1.2). The proportion

Figure 1. Venn Diagram of Two Variables X_1 & X_2 (in Sets) showing the corresponding Regions of Simple Correlation, Ortho-partial Correlation and the Average Correlation

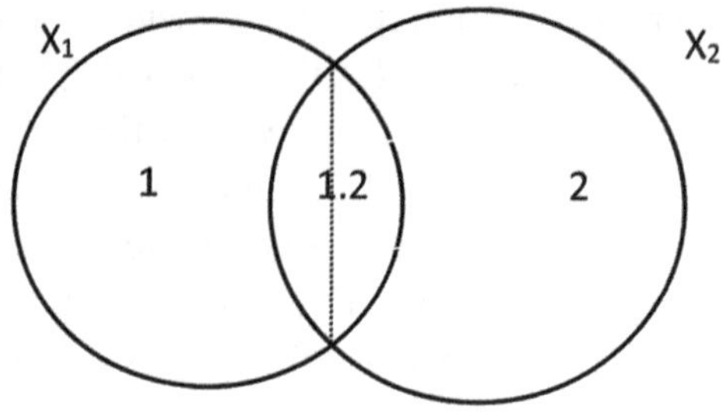

of the area (1+1.2) in the whole rectangle explains the squared simple correlation of X_1 with Y, denoted by r_1^2. Similarly, the explanatory power of variable X_2 is decomposed into two areas denoted by (2) and (1.2). The proportion of the area (2+1.2) in the whole rectangle explains the squared simple correlation of X_2 with Y, denoted by r_2^2.

The proportion of area (1) only in the whole rectangle explains the squared ortho-partial correlation (Mondal, 2008) of X_1 with Y, denoted by $r_{(OP)1}^2$. This part explains to what extent the variability of Y is explained by X_1 alone independent of X_2. Thus, if we regress X_1 on X_2 and take the residue (denoted by $e_{1.2}$) that will give us that part of X_1 which is not linearly explained by X_2. Now if Y is regressed on this $e_{1.2}$, we have this correlation $r_{(OP)1}^2$. Therefore, for variable X_1, we have squared ortho-partial correlation on the one hand, and squared simple correlation on the other explaining the variability of Y. The average explanatory power of the variable X_1 is just the average of these two squared correlations. Symbolically, average squared correlation (or, simply average correlation) values of variable X_1 is given by

$$\frac{(1)+(1+1.2)}{2}=(1)+\frac{(1.2)}{2}$$

And for variable X_2, in a similar manner, average explanatory power of it is just the average of its ortho-partial correlation and simple correlation, both in squared forms. Symbolically, average squared correlation (or, simply average correlation) values of variable X_2 is given by

$$\frac{(2)+(2+1.2)}{2}=(2)+\frac{(1.2)}{2}$$

Let us suppose there are three interdependent explanatory variables X_1, X_2 and X_3 (depicted by circles and oval-shapes in Figure 2) explaining the variability of an explained variable Y (depicted by the rectangle in Figure 2) in a four-variable (one explained and three explanatory) regression model.

We can have the squared simple correlation values of these three variables of X_1, X_2 and X_3 in regions covered in the diagram as r_1^2 = (1)+(1.2)+(1.3)+(1.2.3), r_2^2 = (2)+(1.2)+(2.3)+(1.2.3) and r_3^2 = (3)+(1.3)+(2.3)+(1.2.3).

Where, the region of (1) is purely the non-intersecting exclusive squared correlation part of X_1, which is the 'squared ortho-partial correlation' of X_1 with Y, denoted by $r_{(OP)1}^2$.

Figure 2. Venn Diagram of Three Variables X_1, X_2 & X_3 (in Sets) - showing the Corresponding Regions of Simple Correlation, Ortho-partial Correlation, Semi Ortho-partial Correlation and the Average Correlation

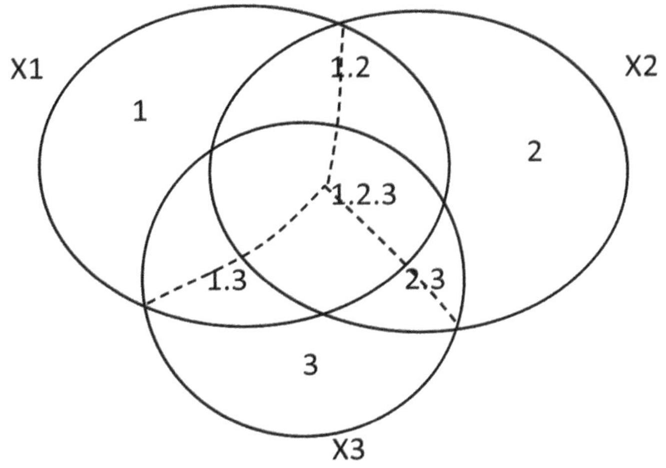

This part explains to what extent the variability of Y is explained by X_1 alone independent of both X_2 and X_3. Thus, if we regress X_1 on X_2 and X_3 and take the residue (denoted by $e_{1.23}$) that will give us that part of X_1 which is not linearly explained by either X_2 or X_3. Now if Y is regressed on this $e_{1.23}$, we can have this type of correlation $r_{(OP)1}^2$. Thus, for variable X_1, the 'squared ortho-partial correlation' is obtained.

On the other hand, if we regress X_1 on X_3 and obtain the residue (denoted by $e_{1.3}$), that will give us that part of X_1 which is not linearly explained by X_3. Now if Y is regressed on this $e_{1.3}$, we can have the correlation of Y with that part of X_1 which is not linearly explained by X_3, the squared of which can be called 'squared semi ortho-partial correlation', identified by the region (1+1.2) and can be denoted by $r_{(SOP)1.2}^2$. Thus, for variable X_1, we may have one squared semi ortho-partial correlation.

Similarly, if we regress X_1 on X_2 and obtain the residue (denoted by $e_{1.2}$), that will give us that part of X_1 which is not linearly explained by X_2. Now if Y is regressed on this $e_{1.2}$, we can have the correlation of Y with that part of X_1 which is not linearly explained by X_2, the squared of which can be called 'squared semi ortho-partial correlation', identified by the region (1+1.3) and can be denoted by $r_{(SOP)1.3}^2$. Thus, for variable X_1, we may have another squared semi ortho-partial correlation.

Therefore, for variable X_1, we are having two 'squared semi ortho-partial correlations' separately and these are identified by the regions (1+1.2) and (1+1.3).

As argued earlier, the region of (1+1.2+1.3+1.2.3) is identified as the 'squared simple correlation' of X_1 and so for X_2 and X_3 respectively.

We are having three two-joint regions and one three-joint region for this three explanatory variable model and these areas can be accommodated to define semi ortho-partial correlation values. For instance, for the variable of X_1, there are two semi ortho-partial correlation regions, {1+(1.2)} and {1+(1.3)}; for X_2, the semi ortho-partial correlation regions are {2+(1.2)} and {2+(2.3)}, and for X3, the semi ortho-partial correlation regions are {3+(1.3)} and {3+(2.3)}.

To compute the value of Average Correlation (AvCor) for a particular variable, firstly, one has to take average of all its 'two-joint squared semi ortho-partial correlation' values and obtain the 'average two-joint squared semi ortho-partial correlation'. Next, the average of all three components i.e., the 'squared ortho-partial correlation', the 'average two-joint squared semi ortho-partial correlation' and the 'squared simple correlation' is to be computed and this value is to be considered as 'average squared correlation' value or simply the 'average correlation' value of the concerned variable.

For variable X_1, the 'squared ortho-partial correlation' of X_1 is: (1),

The 'average two-joint squared semi ortho-partial correlation' of X_1 is:

$$\frac{\left\{1+\left(1.2\right)+1+\left(1.3\right)\right\}}{2}=1+\frac{1.2}{2}+\frac{1.3}{2}$$

and The 'squared simple correlation' of X_1 is: [1+(1.2)+(1.3)+(1.2.3)]

Therefore, the '**Average Squared Correlation' of X_1** can be determined as:

$$\text{AvCor}(X_1)=\frac{1+\left\{1+\left(1.2\right)/2+\left(1.3\right)/2\right\}+\left\{1+\left(1.2\right)+\left(1.3\right)+\left(1.2.3\right)\right\}}{3}$$

Or, $\text{AvCor}(X_1)$ =1+(1.2)/2+(1.3)/2+(1.2.3)/3

Similarly, the '**Average Squared Correlation' of X_2** can be obtained as

$\text{AvCor}(X_2)$ = 2+(1.2)/2+(2.3)/2+(1.2.3)/3,

and **that of X_3** as

$\text{AvCor}(X_3)$ =3+(1.3)/2+(2.3)/2+(1.2.3)/3

If we extend the system to a **five-variable regression model**, with four interdependent explanatory variables (X_1, X_2, X_3 and X_4) and one explained variable (Y), the method of determining 'average correlation' for an individual variable will become little more complicated, as in this case we are to deal with not only with 'two-joint' intersection regions, but also with the 'three-joint' intersection regions, adding more types of 'squared semi ortho-partial correlations' in the system. Diagrammatic representation of four mutually related variable-set is not possible in a two-dimensional space.

In this model, for X_1, the '**squared ortho-partial correlation**' (i.e., OPC) is (1).

The '**squared simple correlation'** of X_1(i.e., SC) is:

[1+(1.2)+(1.3)+(1.4)+(1.2.3)+(1.3.4)+(1.2.4)+(1.2.3.4)].

and the 'squared semi ortho-partial correlations' for the '**two-joint region**'s are

SOPC(2j): [1+(1.2)], [1+(1.3)] and [1+(1.4)]

and that of for the **'three-joint regions'** are

SOPC(3j): [1+ 1.2+1.3+(1.2.3)], [1+1.2+1.4+(1.2.4) and [1+1.3+1.4+(1.3.4)]

Now, the **average of'two-joint squared semi ortho-partial correlations'** Av[SOPC(2j)] is

$$\frac{\left[1+(1.2)\right]+\left[1+(1.3)\right]+\left[1+(1.4)\right]}{3}$$

Or, Av[SOPC(2j)] $= 1+\frac{1}{3}(1.2)+\frac{1}{3}(1.3)+\frac{1}{3}(1.4)$

Secondly, the **average of 'three-joint squared semi ortho-partial correlations'** Av[SOPC(3j)] is

$$\frac{\left[1+1.2+1.3+(1.2.3)\right]+[1+1.2+1.4+(1.2.4)+\left[1+1.3+1.4+(1.3.4)\right]}{3}$$

Or, Av[SOPC(3j)] $=1+\frac{2}{3}(1.2)+\frac{2}{3}(1.3)+\frac{2}{3}(1.4)+\frac{1}{3}(1.2.3)+\frac{1}{3}(1.2.4)+\frac{1}{3}(1.3.4)$

Therefore, the **'SquaredAverage Correlation' of X_1**(AvCor) can be determined as: AvCor(X_1) = ¼[OPC+SOPC(2j)+SOPC(3j)+SC] =

$$\frac{\left[\begin{array}{l}1+\left\{1+\frac{1.2}{3}+\frac{1.3}{3}+\frac{1.4}{3}\right]+\\ \left\{1+\frac{2}{3}(1.2)+\frac{2}{3}(1.3)+\frac{2}{3}(1.4)+\frac{1}{3}(1.2.3)+\frac{1}{3}(1.2.4)+\frac{1}{3}(1.3.4)\right]+\\ \left\{1+(1.2)+(1.3)+(1.4)+(1.2.3)+(1.3.4)+(1.2.4)+(1.2.3.4)\right\}\end{array}\right]}{4}$$

$$=\frac{1}{2}(1.2)+\frac{1}{2}(1.3)+\frac{1}{2}(1.4)+\frac{1}{3}(1.2.3)+\frac{1}{3}(1.2.4)+\frac{1}{3}(1.3.4)+\frac{1}{4}(1.2.3.4)$$

Similarly, AvCor(X_2), AvCor(X_3) and AvCor(X_4) can be determined by using the same techniques as mentioned below

AvCor(X_2) =

$$2+\frac{1}{2}(1.2)+\frac{1}{2}(2.3)+\frac{1}{2}(2.4)+\frac{1}{3}(1.2.3)+\frac{1}{3}(1.2.4)+\frac{1}{3}(2.3.4)+\frac{1}{4}(1.2.3.4)$$

AvCor(X_3)=

$$3+\frac{1}{2}(1.3)+\frac{1}{2}(2.3)+\frac{1}{2}(3.4)+\frac{1}{3}(1.2.3)+\frac{1}{3}(1.3.4)+\frac{1}{3}(2.3.4)+\frac{1}{4}(1.2.3.4).$$

And, AvCor(X_4) =

$$4+\frac{1}{2}(1.4)+\frac{1}{2}(2.4)+\frac{1}{2}(3.4)+\frac{1}{3}(1.2.4)+\frac{1}{3}(1.3.4)+\frac{1}{3}(2.3.4)+\frac{1}{4}(1.2.3.4)$$

For a general formula, if there are 4 explanatory variables (viz., $X_{j_1}, X_{j_2}, X_{j_3}$ *and* X_{j_4}) in a system, the 'average correlation' of a representative variable X_{j_1} [i.e., AvCor(X_{j_1})] can be determined as:

AvCor(X_{j_1}) =

$$j_1+\frac{1}{2}\sum_{j_2=2}^{4}(j_1.j_2)+\frac{1}{3}\sum_{\substack{j_2=2\\ j_2<j_3}}^{3}\sum_{j_3=3}^{4}(j_1.j_2.j_3)+\frac{1}{4}(j_1.j_2.j_3)$$

If there are (k+1) variables in the system with k number of explanatory variables, then the average correlation of the first representative variable Xj_1 can be expressed as

AvCor(Xj_1) =

$$j_1+\frac{1}{2}\sum_{j_2=2}^{k}(j_1.j_2)+\frac{1}{3}\sum_{\substack{j_2=2\\ j_2<j_3}}^{k-1}\sum_{j_3=3}^{k}(j_1.j_2.j_3)+$$

$$\frac{1}{4}\sum_{\substack{j_2=2\\ j_2<j_3}}^{k-2}\sum_{\substack{j_3=3\\ j_2<j_3<j_4}}^{k-1}\sum_{j_4=4}^{k}(j_1.j_2.j_3.j_4)+\ldots+\frac{1}{k}(j_1.j_2.j_3\ldots j_k)$$

In this formula we are endowed with the individual *ortho-partial correlation* of Xj_1, the *simple correlation* of Xj_1 and *(k-1) types of semi ortho-partial correlations* implied for overlapping regions of varied number of variables ranging between two-joints to (k-1) joints, related to Xj_1.

In a similar fashion, the 'average correlation' values of other variables X_{j2}, X_{j3}, ..., X_{jk} can very well be calculated.

Through this method, we can have a generalized definition of Average Correlation of any explanatory variable and using this technique, exclusive relative importance of that variable in explaining the dependent variable can be identified.

RESULTS: WEIGHTS TO THE INDICATORS OBTAINED

To compute the index-values, as specified, we have used respective weights for the stage-wise indicators (or the dimensions) as obtained through the application of two different methods - the PCA and the IACM which are already discussed. In Table 1, the calculated weights for the respective stage-wise indicators and dimensions, obtained through the application of PCA are presented and in Table 2, the same, obtained through the application of IACM are presented.

The data-driven weights for the TCI components like index of total population (TP), index of population density (PD) and index for proportion of male main workers employed in non-agricultural sector (MMWNA) as determined under PCA are 0.1614, 0.2466 and 0.5920 respectively. The weights for the dimensions of ECI, as revealed by PCA are 0.3494 and 0.6506, for DIH and DISEI respectively. The weights of other concerned components and sub-components like F1, F2, F3 etc. are also presented in the table.

If we have a look at Table 2, we see that the data-driven weights for the components and sub-components of every index, related to our study are determined through the application of Iterative Average Correlation Method (IACM). This time the obtained weights are evolving out as different from those obtained under PCA for different components, even though both methods are providing data-driven weights. For example, in IACM, the weights of the IGU components TCI and ECI are 0.5451 and 0.4549 respectively and these values clearly differ from those obtained from PCA (i.e., 0.4825 and 0.5175 in order). Similarly, weights for the same three TCI components are found as 0.2268, 0.3205 and 0.4527 in IACM which are different for the same components obtained from the other method. Also, the weights for the two dimensions of ECI (i.e., DIH and DISEI), as revealed by IACM are 0.4550 and 0.5450 respectively. The weights of other concerned components and sub-components like F1, F2, F3 etc are computed likewise. It can be mentioned in this context that, computation of weights under IACM needs serious applica-

Table 1. Computation of weights for various factors, criteria and dimensions by applying principal component analysis (PCA)

Under Principal Component Analysis			
DIH for ECI	F1	F2	F3
Weights	0.2719	0.3266	0.4015
DISEI for ECI	F4	F5	F6
Weights	0.6593	0.1039	0.2368
ECI	DIH	DISEI	
Weights	0.3494	0.6506	
TCI	TP	PD	MMWNA
Weights	0.1614	0.2466	0.5920
IGU	TCI	ECI	
Weights	0.4825	0.5175	

Source: Calculated by the Author by applying statistical technique and software package STATA

Table 2. Computation of weights for various indicators, factors, criteria and dimensions by applying IACM

Under Iterative Average Correlation Method			
DIH for ECI	F1	F2	F3
Weights	0.3487	0.2290	0.4223
DISEI for ECI	F4	F5	F6
Weights	0.5214	0.1537	0.3249
ECI	DIH	DISEI	
Weights	0.4550	0.5450	
TCI	TP	PD	MMWNA
Weights	0.2268	0.3205	0.4527
IGU	TCI	AI	
Weights	0.5451	0.4049	

Source: Calculated by the Author by applying statistical technique and computer programming

tion of computer programming and for this purpose we have developed a special type of such software programming following which the values of average correlations for selected variables are obtained and iterations of the same are applied till the non-changing nature of the values are arrived. Moreover it is already analyzed that the IACM weights seem to be more acceptable than the PCA weights as the former principle is based on purely explanatory power of an individual variable and thereby carrying more significance in statistical sense than the other.

FINDINGS OF THE STUDY AND INTERPRETATION FOR CENSUS-UNITS

The major findings drawn from the study are presented here and further analysis is carried out only by using those weights which are obtained through the application of IACM. The IGU of all the concerned census-units (more specifically, 1033) taken from selected 12 blocks of 6 sample districts of West Bengal are computed. For all the census-units, the TCI values under the application of PCA appear larger as the variability(s) of the underlying criteria were seemed significantly high, rather than their actual explanatory power. Same computation technique is applied to all other census-units covered for three census decades to obtain desired results but due to its vastness the results obtained for the census-units in different aspects are not shown here. Moreover, the computed values of ECI, in two different applications, are shown for the same census-units for the same study-period. As observed, Babanpur obtained 0.682 ECI value in IACM and 0.843 in PCA; whereas Teleni Para got 0.487 ECI value in IACM and 0.452 in PCA. As argued earlier, we are to take away those weights and thereby those index-values, which are based on explanatory power of an individual component (i.e., which are determined through the application of IACM). We have observed that, Babanpur obtained 0.364 IGU value in 1991, 0.493 IGU in 2001 and 0.722 in 2011 implying a steady increase in its 'green urbanization' status, as measured through IGU. Similarly, Teleni Para obtained 0.289 IGU value in 1991, 0.470 IGU in 2001 and 0.597 in

2011 implying an increase in its IGU values over the decades. Almost all of the units have experienced similar upward movement in IGU values over the study period.

Side by side, a *block level study on green urbanization* is carried out for the selected blocks (i.e., 12) on the basis of our data sources and methodology adopted and it reveals that, amongst the selected twelve blocks of West Bengal, the block of Barrackpore 2 belonging to the district of North 24 Parganas comes first in 2011 (BIGU = 0.598), followed by the block of Chinsurah-Magra (BIGU = 0.488) under Hooghly district and Suti 2 (BIGU = 0.409) of Murshidabad district. However, the urbane characteristics for the block of Sainthia under Birbhum district is found dismal over the decades (BIGU = 0.204 in 2011, 0.165 in 2001 and 0.112 in 1991) as it comes at the bottom in BIGU value in every census studied. The detailed tabular presentation of the results of BIGU (as an average of all the IGU values of all the census units of a block) is given in Table 3 and it appears that Barrackpore 2 maintains its top position in green urbanization index over the three decades of census and Sainthia the lowest for the same period; both however are showing an upward trend though. A radar presentation of this study is given in Figure 3 and this allows us to have a look about the variations in BIGU across the selected blocks over the decades.

At the next stage, a *district level study on green urbanization of West Bengal* is carried from the available data for the mentioned period and it reveals that the general perception about the nature and extent of district level urbanization is true. From our study it appears that, the district of North 24 Parganas comes first (DIGU = 0.468) in 2011, followed by Hooghly (DIGU = 0.394) and Purba Medinipur (DIGU = 0.345) and moreover, North 24 Parganas and Hooghly maintain the first and second positions respectively all along and all these findings are shown in Table 4. This table clearly narrates that, the rate of growth in DIGU for the districts of Purba Medinipur (36%) and Hooghly (30%) are found very high during the period 2001 - 2011 and that for Birbhum (47%) and North 24 Parganas (43%) were relatively higher during 1991 - 2001. Moreover, the district level trend-lines show that, even if we are having upward movement along the trend-lines for all the selected districts, in terms of DIGU, there

Table 3. Pattern of urbanization in 12 selected sample blocks, belonging to 6 sample districts of West Bengal in terms of BIGU for the Study period

SERIAL	DISTRICTS	BLOCKS	1991	2001	2011
1	North 24 Parganas	**Barrackpore 2**	0.357	0.483	**0.598**
2	North 24 Parganas	Basirhat 1	0.182	0.289	0.337
3	Birbhum	Murarai 1	0.151	0.219	0.250
4	Birbhum	Sainthia	0.112	0.165	0.204
5	Hooghly	**Chinsurah-Magra**	0.286	0.378	**0.488**
6	Hooghly	Jangipara	0.166	0.226	0.300
7	Murshidabad	**Suti 2**	0.267	0.357	**0.409**
8	Murshidabad	Bharatpur 2	0.164	0.225	0.278
9	Purba Medinipur	Kolaghat	0.219	0.289	0.384
10	Purba Medinipur	Chandipur	0.151	0.219	0.306
11	Cooch Behar	Cooch Behar 2	0.153	0.230	0.233
12	Cooch Behar	Tufanganj 2	0.156	0.188	0.260

Source: Calculation by the Author on the basis of selected Census Data

Figure 3. A Radar presentation of the block level urbanization of West Bengal in terms of BIGU over the census-years
Source: Drawn on the basis of Table 3

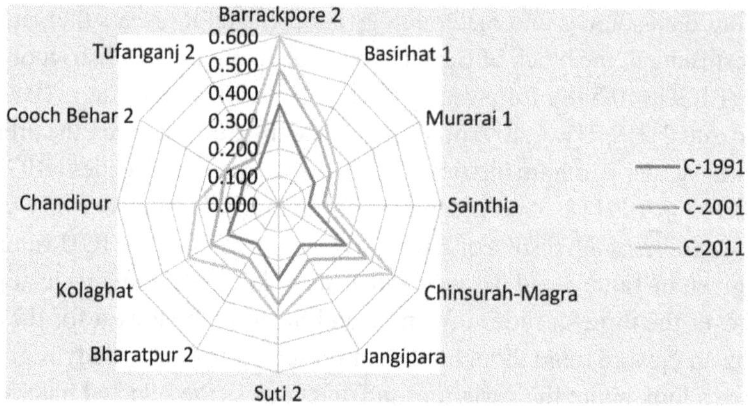

Table 4. Pattern of urbanization in 6 sample districts of West Bengal in terms of their DIGU values over the study period of three decades

SERIAL	DISTRICTS	1991	2001	2011
1	**North 24 Parganas**	0.269	0.386 (**43%**)	**0.468 (21%)**
2	**Birbhum**	0.131	0.192 (**47%**)	0.227 (18%)
3	**Hooghly**	0.226	0.302 (34%)	**0.394 (30%)**
4	**Murshidabad**	0.216	0.291 (35%)	0.344 (18%)
5	**Purba Medinipur**	0.185	0.254 (37%)	**0.345 (36%)**
6	**Cooch Behar**	0.155	0.209 (35%)	0.247 (18%)

Source: Calculation by the Author on the basis of selected Census Data
Note: Figures in the parentheses indicate per cent increase in the value over previous census year

are notable variations in slopes of the respective trends among the districts. In actual sense, the rates of growth of DIGU have come down for all the districts concerned from 2001 to 2011; however in the districts of Purba Medinipur and Hooghly this fall is marginal. This feature clearly indicates that the urbanization syndrome in the districts of Purba Medinipur and Hooghly look much promising than the rest four in terms of our selected parameters.

Moreover, we have tried to show the pattern of district level urbanization, measured in terms of DIGU values, as obtained through simple average of BIGU values of the selected blocks of a district, in radar presentation (Figure 4). The illustration of Figure 4 states that the districts of Birbhum and Cooch Behar are still lagging behind in contrast to others. The case of Birbhum district has appeared as interesting with very high rate of growth of DIGU in 2001 (47%) and a very low rate of growth for the same in 2001 (18%). For other districts, the rate of growth of DIGU varies in between 34% to 47% in 2001 and in between 18% to 36% in 2011 implying moderately low level of expansion in urbane characteristics.

Figure 4. Pattern of district level green urbanization presented through radar
Source: Drawn on the basis of Table 4

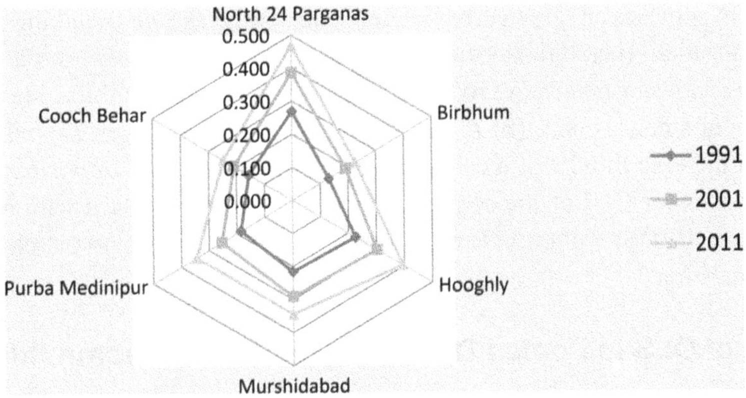

General Interpretation

On the basis of our methodological application, we have found out the IGU of West Bengal, with the values of its components - the TCI and the ECI, for the three census-years 1991, 2001 and 2011 and these are shown in Table 5. It is found that the value of IGU has increased significantly from 1991 to 2001 (i.e., almost 40 per cent) and further to 2011 (i.e., almost 24 per cent), but the drastic improvement is noticed in the sphere of environmental criteria as its index-value is increased by 52 per cent (i.e., from 0.128 to 0.194) during 1991 to 2001 and further by 67 per cent (i.e., from 0.194 to 0.324) during 2001 to 2011.

One point is to be noted here that the *Index for Green Urbanization (IGU)* for *West Bengal* is constructed by taking into account only the six sample districts, the selected sample blocks lying within these districts and their corresponding TCI and ECI values on average. However, the results obtained from these analyses can very well reflect the true picture and it is matched with the census outcomes. Moreover, there is a tendency of it in upward direction indicating higher levels of urbanization in future decades also.

Table 5. Pattern of West Bengal urbanization over three decades of census in terms of TCI, AI and UI values (in aggregates)

W.B.	1991	2001	2011
TCI	0.204	0.276 (35%)	0.288 (4%)
ECI	0.128	0.194 (52%)	0.324 (67%)
IGU	**0.173**	**0.243 (40%)**	**0.302 (24%)**

Source: Calculation by the Author on the basis of selected Census Data
Note: Figures in the parentheses indicate per cent increase in the value over previous census year

FACTOR ANALYSIS OF GREEN URBANIZATION WITH HYPOTHESIS TESTING

We are to test a few hypotheses on 'green urbanization' and in this case we are taking the obtained 'index value of green urbanization' (i.e., IGU) as the dependent variable. The *hypotheses* are (a) an increase in *volume of greenery and water bodies* (VGWB) will lead to an increase in the value of Index for Green Urbanization (IGU) of a census unit, (b) A fall in *quantified volume of smoke emission* (QVSE) will certainly lead to an increase in IGU of a census unit, (c) An increase in *proportion of roadways* (PR) will bring higher values for GUI of the concerned places and (d) any place with relatively *improved waste disposal system* (IWDS) will provide relatively higher IGU values and thereby indicating higher level of green urbanization.

An Application of OLS in Pooled Data Analysis for the Factors Identified

The OLS analysis in pooled data framework on the basis of available data (sources mentioned) is performed and it is presented in Table 6 in a summarized manner. This table is showing the results of pooled regression of Y (IGU) on X_1 (VGWB), X_2 (QVSE), X_3 (PR) and X_4 (IWDS) respectively. We do observe that the coefficient of determination, i.e., R^2 is 0.3033, which is statistically significant (level of significance 7.74E-241). Here, the coefficients of all four factors, viz., VGWB, QVSE, PR and IWDS are statistically significant, as obtained from their 't'-values and 'P'-values through multiple regressions. In a nutshell, VGWB, PR and IWDS are found directly related to IGU whereas QVSE is found inversely related to IGU.

These 't'-values indicate squared correlations of the factors with IGU ($r^2 = t^2/(t^2 + \text{degree of freedom})$) and in the existing literature these are known as partial correlation of the factors. Here we observe that QVSE is the most significant factor which explains partially 13.73% of the variability of Y followed by

Table 6. Results from pooled regression of IGU on its determinants

Variables	**Coeffs**	**'t' Value**	**'P' Value**	**Sq. Partial Correlation**	**Coeffs**	**'t' Value**	**'P' Value**	**Sq. Simple Correlation**
VGWB	0.2869	10.78	1.23E-26	**0.0362**	-0.13952	-4.99	6.29E-07	**0.008**
QVSE	-0.7458	-22.19	2.13E-101	**0.1373**	-0.81969	-28.48	1.27E-158	**0.2075**
PR	0.187	16.81	9.05E-61	**0.0837**	0.27026	23.97	1.18E-116	**0.1565**
IWDS	-0.0358	-4.65	3.45E-06	**0.0069**	-0.13415	-16.92	1.67E-61	**0.0846**
R^2	**Adj R^2**	**F-Value**	**P-Value**					
0.3033	0.3024	337	7.74E-241					
Variable	**Coeffs**	**'t' Value**	**'P' Value**	**Sq. Ortho-partial Correlation**		**Variable**	**Relative Importance (AvCor)**	**'t' Value of Relative Importance**
VGWB	0.2869	9.13	1.26E-19	0.0262		**VGWB**	**0.0142**	2.03
QVSE	-0.7458	-19.66	3.66E-81	0.1109		**QVSE**	**0.1505**	-7.14
PR	0.187	14.51	3.33E-46	0.0637		**PR**	**0.1013**	5.7
IWDS	-0.0358	-3.89	1.01E-04	0.0049		**IWDS**	**0.0373**	3.34

Source: Own calculation using Census data and statistical techniques

PR which explains about 08.37% of the variability of Y. VGWB is the third significant variable which explains about 03.62% of the variability of Y. IWDS is the least significant variable and it explains only about 0.69% which is less than 1, of the variability of Y. However, these are not true partial correlations as explained by Mondal (2008). Thus, partial correlation (henceforth, we shall call it pseudo partial correlation) of any variable actually overestimates true partial correlation or ortho-partial correlation of the variable. Ortho-partial correlations of four factors, i.e., X_1, X_2, X_3 and X_4 are obtained as 0.0262, 0.1109, 0.0637 and 0.0049 respectively.

Economic Interpretation

Ortho-partial correlations differ from their respective simple correlation due to overlapping nature among the variables or due to multi-collinearity. In our case we have observed that for variables X_1 (VGWB), X_2 (QVSE), X_3 (PR) and X_4 (IWDS), simple correlations are greater than their ortho-partial correlations and this is due to existence of multi-collinearity with no enhancement-synergism or due to positive overlapping. For all four variables, ortho-partial correlations underestimate whereas simple correlations overestimate the relative importance of the respective variables. Thus, neither the simple correlations nor the ortho-partial correlations can properly estimate the relative importance of the explanatory factors. Partial correlations are always greater than the ortho-partial correlations, so these values overestimate the true partial correlations and may either underestimate or overestimate the relative importance of the explanatory factors. Several attempts are made in the literature to evaluate the relative importance of the explanatory factors and we, in reference to one such attempt, shall try to evaluate the relative importance of explanatory factors explaining the variability of IGU.

Methodologically, *true relative importance* of an explanatory variable can be obtained by *averaging squared simple correlation and squared ortho-partial correlation*, in case of a model of two explanatory variables. For a model of more than two explanatory variables, it is computed individually by averaging the squared simple correlation, a series of squared semi ortho-partial correlations (as available) and the squared ortho-partial correlation. Here we observe that the squared simple correlations of X_1 (VGWB), X_2 (QVSE), X_3 (PR) and X_4 (IWDS) with GUI (Y) are respectively $r_1^2 = 0.0080$, $r_2^2 = 0.2075$, $r_3^2 = 0.1565$ and $r_4^2 = 0.0846$. Moreover, VGWB, QVSE, PR and IWDS are statistically significant at less than 1% level of significance.

As we have already said the relative importance of an explanatory variable lies between the squared ortho-partial correlation and the squared simple correlation, the relative importance of the variable can be calculated by averaging of these two through a series of squared semi ortho-partial correlations. For example, for the second variable, i.e., QVSE has the squared ortho-partial correlation of 0.1109 which is less than squared simple correlation of 0.2075; the relative importance of the variable is calculated to be 0.1505 with a significant negative t-value.

In fact, relative importance is considered as the real contribution of a particular factor in explaining the dependent variable (i.e., the final index). There might be some sort of overlapping in the values of simple correlation, whereas ortho-partial correlation indicates typical segmented non-overlapping value of a factor, leaving aside the conjoint areas of explanation. Hence, the average of all three forms of correlation (i.e., the simple, the ortho-partial and the semi ortho-partial, if any) is needed for a particular factor to establish its relative importance amongst all in explaining the dependent variable.

In this way relative importance of other three explanatory variables, VGWB, PR and IWDS are calculated as 0.0142, 0.1013 and 0.0373 respectively. Thus the multiple R^2 of 0.3033 that implies an explanatory power of 30.33% is decomposed among the explanatory factors in the following way: 01.42% of the variability of IGU is explained by VGWB, 15.05% by QVSE, 10.13% by PR and the remaining 3.73% by IWDS and all of them have t-values statistically significant at less than 1% level of significance.

CONCLUSION

It goes beyond saying that lesser volume of smoke emission is bound to increase the relative hygiene of the urbane households and thereby enhances their attitude towards better living. This phenomenon is supposed to bring gradual green urbanization in the concerned place through better living appliances. Hence the negative relationship between QVSE and IGU is conceived in this analysis. Secondly, the positive association between IGU and PR (i.e., proportion of available roadways), as we have found, might be due to increased awareness against road congestion, traffic jam and excessive carbon emission in the society about a better and improved kind of living. Thirdly the positive relation between IWDS and IGU, as we have established here, is obvious as IWDS is considered as the boosting factor to clean environment. Finally, we have found positive relationship between the VGWB and IGUI in our study and this can also be supported for obvious reasons. It goes beyond saying that green urbanization of any place depends significantly on the available volume of water bodies and greenery there as these areas are considered as natural sources of pure oxygen.

REFERENCES

Anderson, T. W. (1963). Asymptotic Theory for Principal Component Analysis. *Annals of Mathematical Statistics, 34*(1), 122–148. doi:10.1214/aoms/1177704248

Bilbao-Ubillos, J. (2013). Another Approach to Measuring Human Development - The Composite Dynamic Human Development Index. *Social Indicators Research, 111*(2), 473–484. doi:10.100711205-012-0015-y

Biswas, B. & Caliendo, F. (2002). *A Multivariate Analysis of the Human Development Index.* Economic Research Institute Study Papers, Paper 244. Utah State University.

Bose, A. (1978). *India's Urbanization 1901 - 2001* (2nd ed.). New Delhi, India: Tata McGraw Hill.

Carrino, L. (2015). *The Weighting Role of Normalization in a Multidimensional Analysis of Social Inclusion.* Working Paper 32/2015, Department of Economics, Ca'Foscari University of Venice.

Census Village Directory of West Bengal. (2011). Director General of Census Operations, Ministry of Home Affairs, Government of India.

Chakravarty, S. R. (2003). A Generalized Human Development Index. *Review of Development Economics, 7*(1), 99–114. doi:10.1111/1467-9361.00178

Chakravarty, S. R. (2011). A Reconsideration of the Tradeoffs in the New Human Development Index. *The Journal of Economic Inequality, 9*(3), 471–474. doi:10.100710888-011-9190-3

Chatterjee, M. (2013). *A Preliminary Discussion on the Census 2011 Results. Urban India, 33(1).*

Dasgupta, B., Giri, P., Bhattacharya, A., Bhattacharya, B., & Basak, N. (1988). Measure of Urban Concentration in West Bengal. In Urbanization, Migration and Rural Change – A Study of West Bengal. A. Mukherjee & Co. Pvt. Ltd.

Denis, E., & Zerah, M. H. (2017). *Subaltern Urbanization in India - An Introduction to the Dynamics of Ordinary Towns. Springer India.*

Desai, M. (1991). Human Development: Concepts and Measurement. *European Economic Review, 35*(2-3), 350–357. doi:10.1016/0014-2921(91)90136-7

Dreze, J., & Sen, A. K. (1995). *India - Economic Development and Social Opportunity*. New Delhi, India: Oxford University Press.

Ghosh, D. (2011). *Provisional Population Totals – West Bengal, Census of India, 2011, MHA*. New Delhi: Government of India.

Giri, P. (1988). Growth of Small and Medium Towns in West Bengal. In Urbanization, Migration and Rural Change: A Study of West Bengal. A Mukherjee & Co. Pvt. Ltd.

Giri, P. (1998). Urbanization in West Bengal, 1951 – 1991. *Economic and Political Weekly*, (21), 3033-3038.

Hopkins, M. (1991). Human Development Revisited - A New UNDP Report. *World Development, 19*(10), pp1469–pp1473. doi:10.1016/0305-750X(91)90089-Z

Hotelling, H. (1933). Analysis of a Complex of Statistical Variables into Principal Components. *Journal of Educational Psychology, 24*(6), 417–441, 498–520. doi:10.1037/h0071325

Ivanova, I., Arcelus, F., & Srinivasan, G. (2005). An Assessment of the Measurement Properties of the Human Development Index. *Social Indicators Research, 46*(2), 157–179. doi:10.1023/A:1006839208067

Kundu, A. (2011). Politics and Economics of Urban Growth [New Delhi, India]. *Economic and Political Weekly, 46*(20), 10–13.

Mondal, D. (2004). *District Development Index of West Bengal 1991 and 2001*. Occasional Paper No.16, Department of Economics with Rural Development (under DRS), Vidyasagar University.

Mondal, D. (2005). *Human Development Index - An Essay on Methodology and Implication*. Kolkata, India: FIRMA KLM Private Limited.

Mondal, D. (2008). On the Test of Significance of Linear Multiple Regression Coefficients. *Communication in Statistics- Simulation and Computation, 37*(4), 713–730.

Mondal, D., Mookherjee, S., & Pattanayek, S. K. (2017). Does the analysis of principal components effectively help in determining actual weights for dimensions of an index? An appraisal in Indian context. *International Journal of Management and Development Studies, 6*(10), 28–36.

Mookherjee, S., Pattanayek, S. K., & Mondal, D. (2017). An Appraisal of Urbanization Status of Villages in A Particular Block of West Bengal: An Exploration through Construction of A Generalized Urbanization Index. *ZENITH International Journal of Business Economics & Management Research*, *7*(12), 97–110.

Noorbakhsh, F. (1998). The Human Development Index: Some Technical Issues and Alternative Indices. *Journal of International Development*, *10*(5), 589–605. doi:10.1002/(SICI)1099-1328(199807/08)10:5<589::AID-JID484>3.0.CO;2-S

Palazzi, P., & Lauri, A. (1998). The Human Development Index: Suggested Corrections. *Quarterly Review. Indexes - Banca Nazionale del Lavoro*, *51*(205), 193–221.

Pattanayek, S. K., & Mondal, D. (2016). Educational Development in Blocks of Paschim Medinipur District (West Bengal) between 2005-06 and 2012-13: Panel Data Analysis through Education Index. *Artha Vijnana*, *58*(1), 71–93. doi:10.21648/arthavij/2016/v58/i1/121274

Pattanayek, S. K., & Mondal, D. (2016). Nature of Development in Health through Health Index in the Blocks of Paschim Medinipur District in West Bengal during 2005-06 to 2014-15. *International Research Journal of Basic and Applied Sciences*, *2*(1), 1-6.

Pearson, K. (1901). On Lines and Planes of Closest Fit to Systems of Points in Space. *Philosophical Magazine, Series 6*, *12*(11), 559–572. doi:10.1080/14786440109462720

Primary Census Abstract of West Bengal. (2011). Director General of Census Operations, Ministry of Home Affairs, Government of India.

Ramachandran, R. (2012). *Urbanization and Urban Systems in India*. Oxford, UK: Oxford University Press.

Ravallion, M. (1997). Good and Bad Growth: The Human Development Reports. *World Development*, *25*(5), 631–638. doi:10.1016/S0305-750X(96)00141-6

Ravallion, M. (2012). Mash-up Indices of Development. *The World Bank Research Observer*, *27*(1), 1–32. doi:10.1093/wbro/lkr009

Ravallion, M. (2016). The World Bank - Why It Is Still Needed and Why It Still Disappoints. *The Journal of Economic Perspectives*, *30*(1), 77–94. doi:10.1257/jep.30.1.77

Sivaramakrishnan, K. C., Kundu, A., & Singh, B. N. (2011). Handbook of Urbanization in India (2nd ed.). Oxford University Press.

Srinivasan, T. N. (1994). Human Development - A New Paradigm or a Reinvention of the Wheel. *The American Economic Review*, *84*(2), 238–243.

KEY TERMS AND DEFINITIONS

Average Correlation: In statistics, *correlation* is defined as a measure of relationship between the statistical dispersion within individual categories and the dispersion across the whole population or sample. The measure is defined as the ratio of two standard deviations representing these types of variations. 'Average Correlation' of a particular variable (or dimension) is defined as the average value of its all sorts of correlations, i.e., its squared simple correlation (i.e., r^2), its squared ortho-partial correlation and its squared semi ortho-partial correlation(s), if any.

Factor Analysis: It is a statistical process in which the values of observed data are expressed as functions of a number of possible causes in order to find which are the most important. Factor analysis is a technique that is used to reduce a large number of variables into fewer numbers of factors. This technique extracts maximum common variance from all variables and puts them into a common platform.

Green Urbanization: It is defined as the practice of creating some sort of balances between urbanization and ecology which is supposedly to be beneficial to both human and the environment. It can be considered as an attempt to shape more sustainable places, communities and lifestyles, and consume less of the world's resources. It is interdisciplinary, combining the collaboration of landscape architects, engineers, urban planners, ecologists, transport planners, sociologists and economists.

Index: In economics, an index is defined as a statistical measure of changes in a representative group of individual data points. These data may be derived from any number of sources, including company performance, prices, productivity, employment, etc. Economic indices generally track economic health of an identified geographical area from different perspectives.

Principal Components: Principal component analysis (PCA) is a statistical procedure that uses an orthogonal transformation to convert a set of observations of possibly correlated variables (entities each of which takes on various numerical values) into a set of values of linearly uncorrelated variables called principal components. Principal component analysis is an approach to factor analysis that considers the total variance in the data, which is unlike common factor analysis, and transforms the original variables into a smaller set of linear combinations.

Relative Importance: The relative importance of a factor represents its basic value-weight, including any imputations. It is nothing but the true (i.e., actual) contribution of an individual factor in explaining the dependent variable excluding the overlapping (i.e., joint) contributions as appeared from other factors.

Weights: In statistics, imputing weights is known as a technique in which a data item (such as an average) is emphasized more than other data items comprising a group or summary. A number (weight) is assigned to each data item that reflects its relative importance based on the objective of the data collection.

Chapter 19
Urbanization and Ownership of Polluting Vehicles:
A Study From Urban India

Asish Kumar Pal
Rabindra Mahavidyalaya, India

Atanu Sengupta
The University of Burdwan, India

ABSTRACT

Most Indian cities are experiencing rapid urbanization, and a majority of the country's population is expected to live in cities within a span of the next two decades. The rapid development in urban India has also resulted in a tremendous increase in the number of motor vehicles, and in some cities, this has doubled in the last decade. This is the main source of air pollution and poor ambient air quality impacting millions of dwellers. This chapter presents a review of the vehicular population in urban Indian cities with its pattern and determinants. The transport system is shared by two parts such as public transport as well as private transport system. To reduce the vehicular pollution, we have to emphasize on public transport system rather than private transport. In an underdeveloped country, it is very tough to use public transport. Due to lack of government fund, new technology, proper checking, etc., private cars, buses, and tracks are increased rapidly. We use these randomly for transport purposes. This causes pollution.

INTRODUCTION

It is said that there is no free lunch in this universe. Development and the concomitant urbanization cannot be an exception to this. Pollution is a staple problem of today's world. Rich or poor, planed or market oriented, democratic or autocratic, modern or traditional —— nation all over are steeped in pollution. While the facets of pollution changes from country to country or region to region, it is undeniable that we cannot live without it. In a way, it is the price of the riches that the science and technology bestowed upon us. Like a thrown of a rose or the catered pillar from which the butterfly is brown, pollution is embedded if we are to enjoy the magnificence of human triumph in science and technology. Air pollution is

DOI: 10.4018/978-1-5225-8547-3.ch019

one of the very important sources of pollution. It is more prevalent in the cities and urban conglomerates of the developed and developing world. A major source of air pollution in the city proper is the spurt of vehicles. Development is almost synonymous with a movement from mechanical vehicles (such as bicycles or rickshaws) to the fuel consuming two wheelers and four wheelers. Vehicles are necessary for transit of both man and goods across the length and breadth of a city.

However, the vehicular population could have been checked if there would have been an emphasis on efficient public transit system (such as light-railways, metro-railways etc.). However, the problem is accentuated both by and increasing inefficiency of public transport (use of backdated fuel consumption technology) and also the rise in the privately own two wheelers and four wheelers. Added to this inadequate road space, dilapidated and ill- maintained road ways, the increase in number of vehicles per kilometer of roads and the slow average movement of vehicles flare up the problem. In Delhi, the data shows that of the total 3,000 metric tons of pollutants belched out every day, close to two third (66%) is from vehicles. Similarly the contribution of vehicles to urban air pollution is 52% in Bombay and close to one-third in Kolkata.

As the country is rapidly changing to a path of growth and development, increasing urbanization is a necessary outcome. There will be an expansion and development of existing centres with a popping up of a large number of new centre. Actually urbanization is a fact of life in underdeveloped countries. With urbanization comes the problem of urban transport. Urbanization increases the demand for urban transport. This transport system is shared by two parts such as public transport as well as private transport system. People flock to the urban centres to take the advantages of new possibilities emerging there (Lucas 2002). With this increased urbanization, an expansion of ownership of petro-fuel consuming vehicles is almost warranted. City life requires rapid and smooth transit. It saves both time and reduces the exertion resulting from using traditional vehicles. In essence, it expands the efficiency at the workplace. However, this is the main source of air pollution and poor ambient air quality impacting millions of dwellers. These issues of vehicular emission are wide and variegated. There is no meaningful way to undertake a coherent analysis across this mesh of issues. Ecological economics is a melting point of several issues of science. In the name rigour most of the papers over simplified the issues by trying to cut Gordian Knot in a rather abstruse (if not Vulgar way). Such 'rigouras' papers are over simplified and miss the flavor of problems at hand. These papers do not fall into the trap. We deliberately disdain ourselves from empirical analysis. In the present paper, we concentrate on some issues that are relevant to deal this important aspect of developmental dilemma.

REVIEW AND RELEVANT LITERATURE

Different studies have been done in the field of motor vehicular emissions in the different regions of the world, especially to establish the level of air pollution from the operation of motor vehicles and the general urban air quality as a whole. Three of such studies which have relevance to this study are: the vehicle activity study in Nairobi, Kenya, conducted in March 2001 by the U.S. EPA, CE-CERT5, and GSSR6 the evaluation of evaporative emissions from gasoline powered motor vehicles under South African conditions, conducted in 2003 by Van des Westhuisena *et al.* (2004); and the impact of automobile emissions on the level of platinum and lead in Accra, Ghana conducted in 2001 by Kylander *et al.* (2003). All of these find strong correlates between air pollution and vehicular efficiency (in the fuel use).

Ambient temperature and local meteorology influences the concentration and location of vehicle-emitted pollutants. For example, elevated sulphur dioxide levels are typically reported in the winter and elevated ground-ozone levels in the summer (Goldberg et al. 2001; Rainham et al. 2005).

Traffic wardens, part of the Federal Capital Territory Area Command (FCTAC), were included in the study to link measured pollutant concentrations with health impacts. Wardens are the highest exposure group because they stand in intersections and direct traffic, so they are directly and frequently exposed to vehicle emissions. Thus, it is reasonable to expect their health status to directly reflect that level of exposure. There are roughly 300 active traffic wardens in Abuja who work on average 8 hours per day between the hours of 7am and 8pm, 5-7 days per week, with 2 weeks of vacation per year (Akoni 2008). Different studies have been done in the field of motor vehicular emissions in the different regions of the world, especially to establish the level of air pollution from the operation of motor vehicles and the general urban air quality as a whole. Three of such studies which have relevance to this study are: the vehicle activity study in Nairobi, Kenya, conducted in March 2001 by the U.S. EPA, CE-CERT5, and GSSR6 the evaluation of evaporative emissions from gasoline powered motor vehicles under South African conditions, conducted in 2003 by Van des Westhuisena *et al.* (2004); and the impact of automobile emissions on the level of platinum and lead in Accra, Ghana conducted in 2001 by Kylander *et al.* (2003). All of these find strong correlates between air pollution and vehicular efficiency (in the fuel use).

A Case Study on Beijing is done by Hao and Wang (2005) urban air pollution is one of the major environmental issues. Air pollution problems are induced by high-speed urbanization, rapid economic growth, and explosive motorization. Chinese cities pose a direct threat to long-term economic sustainability and social benefit. Air pollution problems in Chinese cities are serious, especially in large cities.

From the CPCB report of 2010, air pollution is one of the serious environmental concerns of the urban Asian cities including India where majority of the population is exposed to poor air quality. Most of the Indian Cities are also experiencing rapid urbanization and the majority of the country's population is expected to be living in cities within a span of next two decades. Since poor ambient air quality is largely an urban problem this will directly affect millions of the dwellers in the cities. The rapid urbanization in India has also resulted in a tremendous increase the number of motor vehicles. The vehicle fleets have even doubled in some cities in the last one decade. This increased mobility, however, come with a high price. As the number of vehicles continues to grow and the consequent congestion increases, vehicles are now becoming the main source of air pollution in urban India.

The developing countries suffer more than the developed countries from air pollution which happens from vehicle emissions. High levels of lead, primarily from vehicle emissions, have been identified as the greatest environmental danger in a number of large cities in the developing world. For them the problem is becoming more acute as the numbers of motor vehicles are growing rapidly. Delhi's inhabitants inhale the most polluted air in the country and vehicular pollution is responsible for 64 percent of the pollutants which make it so (Bhattacharyya et. al. 2002).

Transport is a vital component of any vibrant city. With the case study of Ahmadabad, the primary reasons for pollution and lack of management in respect of transport are lack of integration between land use and transport planning, concentration of economic and other activities in the core of the city, lack of scientific design of road networks, high rate of growth of vehicles, mixed traffic on roads, and low quality and adulterated fuels (Brar 2004).

The pressures on transport systems are increasing in most developing countries, as part of the process of growth. It is even worst in urban areas where population densities are higher Motor vehicle ownership and use are growing even faster than population, with vehicle ownership growth rates of 15 to 20% per year common in some developing countries (World Bank 1995).

Shariff (2012) expressed his concern that private vehicles today have become the main means of travel of urban living in developing countries. Consistent economic growth, rising incomes, and urbanization have led to rapid growth in vehicle ownership and usage. Private vehicle ownership is also associated with externalities such as traffic congestions, accidents, inadequate parking spaces and pollutions. Rising vehicle congestion and slower travel speeds are the most obvious impact of rapid motorization. With the increase in vehicle ownership, it has been emphasized that the demand for travel to central city areas would grow far beyond the capacity of the road network. Hence air pollution and other environmental hazards are another important concern. According to WHO report published in 1994 the Indian capital is the fourth most polluted city in the world. And no wonder, the amount of pollutants the transport sector pumps into Delhi more than the sum of vehicular pollutants emitted in Mumbai, Bangalore, and Kolkata. However, the Delhi has taken stringent steps recently that brought down the vehicular pollution to a considerable extent. India is moving on a fast track with the increase in GDP by 2.5 times, industrial pollution by 8 times over the last two decades (Pattanaik & Pattanaik 2002).

Noise, air and water pollution are all serious problems in Indian cities, and transport sources contribute all three kinds. Heavy transportation in metropolitan cities is a major contributor to environmental pollution in addition to industrial and commercial activities. Indian cities face a transport crisis characterized by levels of congestion, noise pollution, traffic facilities and injuries, and inequality far exceeding those in most European and North American cities. India's transport crisis has been exacerbated by the extremely rapid growth of India's largest cities in a context of low incomes, limited and outdated transport infrastructure, rampant suburban sprawl, sharply rising motor vehicle ownership and use, deteriorating bus services, a wide range of motorized and non-motorized transport modes sharing roadways, and inadequate as well as uncoordinated land use and transport planning (Pucher et. al. 2004).

According to India Development Report of 1997 the reasons for deterioration of urban air quality throughout the Indian cities are growing industrialization without any priority for pollution abatement, and rising number of motor vehicles especially of poorly maintained vehicles that used leaded fuel. The rate of generation of solid waste in urban centers has outpaced population growth in recent years with the wastes normally disposed in low-lying areas of the city's outskirts (India: State of the Environment 2001). The total pollution load from transport sector has increased from 0.15 million tones in 1947 to 10.3 million tones in 1997 (TERI 1997). Like many other parts of the world, air pollution from motor vehicles is one of the most serious and rapidly growing problems in urban centers of India (UNEP/WHO, 1992). In India, the number of motor vehicles has grown from 0.3 million in 1951 to approximately 50 million in 2000, of which, two wheelers (mainly driven by two stroke engines) accounts for 70% of the total vehicular population.

According to UNEP-WHO report, 1992 and the World Development Report 1992 vehicles are nowhere the principal cause but its relative importance is growing rapidly over time. In World Bank's report of 1992 the Bank expressed the premonition that such economic growth will be associated with applying environmental damage. Degraded air quality would be one of such impending damage that may cripple the developing country.

According to the report of CPCB in 2010, air pollution is a major environmental risk to health and is estimated to cause approximately 2 million premature deaths worldwide per year. The high level of pollutants are mainly responsible for respiratory and other air pollution related ailments including lung cancer, asthma etc., which is significantly higher than the national average (CSE, 2001 and CPCB, 2002).

Now coming to Kolkata, condition is not at all better. Traffic problem in Kolkata seems to be on its way to accruing the dimension of cities like Bangkok, where commuters more or less live in their vehicles, bathing and getting dressed for works while inching their way through nightmarish traffic jams. Kolkata's citizens already spend hours gulping down fumes while stuck in traffic jams. During the last decade the road length has not increased significantly in Kolkata. So Traffic jam occurs. As Traffic moves slowly, slow moving vehicles emit more carbon monoxide, the problem is more surmounted for the kolkata by the lack of adequate data availabity. The vehicular pollution is severe in the Kolkata Municipality Corporation. Due to the huge population growth, the estimated energy demand (both diesel and petrol) increases from 352 thousand tones in 1990-91 to 1603 thousand tones in 2000-01, nearly five times increase, It is also estimated to be 30 percent of the total pollution (Agarwal 1996).

According to NEERI study in 1973-34, 176.7millions tones of CO emitted in Kolkata's atmosphere every day and transports sector contributes 138.7metric tones. Most of the emission flows from four wheelers (approx. 78%) and two & three wheelers 22% of the total emission. A huge number of motor vehicles in Kolkata have been increased over the recent years. From the CPCB report we know the pollution in Kolkata raises due to large number of vehicles, the inadequate and narrow road network. In Kolkata, we see a fair number of rickshaws and bicycles, which reduce the average traffic speed and as a result emission increases (Chakraborty 1997). According to a report of the National Commission on urbanization 1988, the increase in projected travel demand per day in Kolkata in 2001 will be 63% compared to the 1981 base (Haldar 1997).

URBANIZATION AND VEHICULAR POPULATION

Urban Population

Between 1951 and 2011, the urban population has quadrupled, from 62.4 million to 377.1 million, and its proportion has increased from 17.3% to 31.16% (1). In 1991, there were 18 cities with a population of over 1 million; in 2012 this is estimated to extend to 46 cities (2). This rapid increase in unplanned urban population has resulted in an increase in consumption patterns and a higher demand for transport, energy and other infrastructure, thereby putting a load on the pollution problem.

Vehicular Population

Number of vehicles sold in India is increasing at a rapid pace. In 2005-06 there were 8.9M vehicles sold and in five years this number has scaled to 15M (in 2010-11) (3). While accelerated growth in number of vehicles aids growth and development, the problem stems from their concentration in a few selected cities. It is alarming to note that 32 percent of these vehicles are plying in metropolitan cities alone which constitute about 11 percent of the total population. Delhi, which contains 1.4 percent of the Indian population, accounts for nearly 7 percent of all motor vehicles in India. Two-wheelers and cars account for more than 80 percent of the vehicle population in most large cities (3). Analysis of data presented in Table 1 reveals that, during the year 2000, personalized vehicle population share was more than 90 percent of the total vehicle population.

URBANIZATION AND VEHICULAR OWNERSHIP IN WEST BENGAL PERSPECTIVE

It is argued that urbanization leads to a rise in the middle classes and the concomitant rise in the ownership of vehicles. We now consider this argument using the West Bengal data. We have divided state by two sectors as rural and urban and analysed the several vehicles holdings households. There is a clear dichotomy in the ownership pattern among the rural and urban households. Though the total number of vehicle owning households is far higher in the rural sector as compared to the urban sector, most of the Vehicle owners in the rural area owns bicycle. In fact, though bicycle owners in the rural area are much higher, for the other two categories urban owners far exceed the rural owners. Since bicycle are non-fuel consuming and hence (at least directly) less polluting than the other two categories, it is clear that urbanization leads to a higher ownership of polluting vehicles.

From table 1, we realize that the total percentage of polluting vehicles in urban area is greater than rural area in West Bengal. But in case of non polluting vehicles it is lower in the urban area. Obviously it is clear that the pollution in the urban area is higher than the rural area. In percentage term, the ownership of fuel consuming vehicles is more than three times higher in the urban areas.

To fix the idea we consider the district wise distribution of vehicles both in rural and urban areas of West Bengal. An analysis of the Census data reveals that in the rural area of Hooghly (rural) we get the highest percentage of polluting vehicles (8.35%) and Dakshindinajpur is the lowest percentage of polluting vehicles (2.05%) district. Undoubtedly rural Hooghly is well linked to the urban sector and shows a high degree of semi-urban or pre-urban features. As for urban areas, we get the highest percentage of two wheeler & four wheeler vehicles in the district of Barddhaman (21.44%) - and the least percentage of two wheeler & four wheeler vehicles holding district is Nadia (7.78%). Here Kolkata is pulled down to the second position. However, the composition of polluting vehicles clears this dilemma. It is in the ownership of fuel consuming two-wheelers that Burdwan (18.44%) outstrips Kolkata (8.70%). In terms of ownership of fuel consuming four wheelers that Kolkata (6.87%) surpasses Burdwan (3%). In fact Darjeeling (4.59%) and 24-Parganas (North) (3.5%) also overwhelm Barddhaman in this matter.

Table 1. Ownership of vehicles (% of total)-West Bengal 2011

West Bengal	% of bi-cycle holding	% of Scoter, Motor cycle, Moped	% Car, Jeep, Van
Total	52.59	5.03	1.89
Rural	54.28	3.06	1.21
Urban	48.43	9.86	3.57

(Source: Census data 2011)

URBANIZATION AND VEHICULAR OWNERSHIP: ALL INDIA PERSPECTIVE

An important aspect of urban transport system is the possession of vehicles. We have two indices to understand this feature: (i) proportion of household ownership of fuel consuming vehicles as a proportion of such vehicles in the state (intensity of ownership) and (iii) Proportion of household owning of fuel consuming vehicles (ownership index). The former relates to the intensity of household ownership of vehicles. The latter denotes the inequality of ownership pattern.

From table 2 we see for all the states, in the intensity index, urban sector dominate the corresponding rural areas. Here we see in urban India, the state where intensity of ownership of polluting vehicles is the largest in Haryana (83.24%) and lowest in West Bengal (21.72%). In the rural sector, this is lowest in Bihar and highest in Goa. Again rural Goa is more closely knitted to the outward world than rural Bihar. It is probably more "urbanized" than rural Bihar. Considering rural-urban divide, the lowest is Goa, followed by Kerala. The divide is highest in Jharkhand, followed by Assam. Clearly development, growth and urbanization reduce the rural-urban divide.

Here we see this is the highest in Chandigarh (62.79%) and the lowest position in the state of Jharkhand (3.49%) in the urban area of India. In fact, Jharkhand show a strange picture. For urban Jharkhand, the intensity is high but ownership index is low. It is so low that it falls below the rural level.

We now consider the situation at the more disaggregated level. The Census 2011 allows us to move at the district level. It also allows us to understand the state level variability of the possession of fuel consuming vehicles. . For lack of space, we consider only the intensity index in this paper. We have considered three parameters-the district with maximum intensity, the one with minimum and the coefficient of variation.

The district with the greatest vehicle intensity is Kurukshetra of Haryana while the lowest is Dhubri of Assam. In the rural area, the highest is in Delhi East while the lowest in urban area is Lakshisarai in Bihar. If we consider variability in terms of C.V., it is lowest in Goa both for rural and urban area. This implies that intensity of fuel consuming vehicles is, more or less, similarly high in all the districts of Goa. In general, however, variability is lowest in urban area as compared to rural area.

In essence, it is seen that both intensity and ownership index of fuel consuming vehicles is strongly related with urbanization. Not only, it is high in the urban area, it is also higher in the rural areas that have strong leaks with the growth centres that are in, most cases, urban in nature. However to delve in the matter deeply, we consider an exploratory analysis.

EXPLORATORY ANALYSIS

Now we have discussed the key parameters (total, rural, and urban) all over India. We have considered the various key parameters as the dependent variables as well as independent variable. We have considered the proportion of percentage of polluting vehicle household to test the relationship with this variable and a set of explanatory variables. Banks often provide easy loans to purchase cars. An important variable that might affect this is the proportion of households having bank accounts. An index for income level is used and households above them are treated as rich. The proportion of "rich" people is a good explanatory variable for explaining the ownership of fuel consuming vehicles. Literacy rate might signal as an indicator of pollution awareness. It may be argued that literacy might be linked with higher standard of living that gives rise to a mixed effect on owning fuel consuming vehicles. However since

Table 2. State-Wise distribution of intensity of ownership of polluting vehicles all over India

State	Intensity of ownership of rural polluting vehicles	Intensity of ownership of urban polluting vehicles	Index of urban dominance
(1)	(2)	(3)	=((3)-(2))/(3)
Andhra Pradesh	15.90	40.61	0.61
Assam	8.68	35.79	0.76
Bihar	7.18	28.77	0.75
Chandigarh	23.05	48.30	0.52
Chhattisgarh	9.97	35.25	0.72
Delhi	36.50	53.25	0.31
Goa	56.66	64.49	0.12
Gujarat	31.77	45.49	0.3
Haryana	25.33	83.24	0.7
Himachal	46.81	73.14	0.36
Jharkhand	8.46	73.14	0.88
J & K	36.62	54.12	0.32
Karnataka	23.69	49.78	0.52
Kerala	39.47	48.56	0.19
Madhya Pradesh	15.26	37.85	0.6
Maharashtra	25.33	44.50	0.43
Orissa	9.43	32.49	0.71
Punjab	29.28	42.55	0.31
Rajasthan	22.02	42.30	0.48
Tamil Nadu	22.85	37.27	0.39
Uttar Pradesh	10.30	32.55	0.68
Uttaranchal	22.26	43.26	0.49
West Bengal	7.29	21.72	0.66
North East	13.67	40.80	0.66
Group of UT	12.83	42.39	0.7

(Source: Census data, 2011)
(Note: Intensity of ownership of polluting vehicles is calculated as all polluting vehicles/total vehicles)

these effects are already captured by separate dummies, we are left with the "pure" effect of literacy only in our analysis. Another variable is capturing rural –urban residence. The last variable is dummy.

For our analysis, we have considered three types of analysis: OLS, Hetcov estimators and finally Tobit regression. The analysis shows that the ownership of fuel consuming vehicles is positively related with all these variables. Our education system provides no awareness to combat this phenomenon. When people are poor they are forced to use traditional vehicles (such as bicycles), move on foot or use public mode of transport. When income of a person sufficiently rises, he opts for vehicles that are fuel consuming and pollute. There is no alternative strong value system to combat the brunt of this tendency. In short, it

Table 3. State-Wise distribution of ownership per household polluting vehicles all over India

State	Ownership of rural polluting vehicles/household	Ownership of urban polluting vehicles/household	Index of urban dominance
(1)	(2)	(3)	=((3)-(2))/(3)
Andhra Pradesh	5.66	28.40	0.8
Assam	4.47	23.70	0.81
Bihar	3.10	18.43	0.83
Chandigarh	23.33	62.79	0.63
Chhattisgarh	6.44	36.41	0.82
Delhi	27.99	41.91	0.33
Goa	40.03	58.78	0.32
Gujarat	13.66	41.57	0.67
Haryana	15.68	41.93	0.63
Himachal	7.96	25.88	0.69
Jharkhand	4.55	3.49	-0.3
J & K	5.32	27.64	0.81
Karnatak	8.65	34.14	0.75
Kerala	10.25	25.14	0.59
Madhya Pradesh	6.89	34.13	0.8
Maharashtra	9.61	26.02	0.63
Orissa	5.14	32.64	0.84
Punjab	30.69	49.89	0.38
Rajasthan	8.94	37.50	0.76
Tamil Nadu	11.81	27.35	0.57
Uttar Pradesh	8.17	30.32	0.73
Uttaranchal	7.41	40.30	0.82
West Bengal	4.27	13.43	0.68
North East	8.74	18.74	0.53
Group of UT	8.36	37.79	0.78

(Source: Census data, 2011)

appears that development adds to vehicular pollution –the so-called Environmental Catch-up Hypothesis (Brock and Taylor 2003). This is shown in the following regression analysis (Table 5).

Besides, in table 4 we have seen the three positions from the three aspects- maximum, minimum and coefficient of variation in both rural and urban. In rural India Dhubri district of Assam Own intensity polluting vehicle holding households is the minimum and maximum in Delhi East. If we see from the urban side in Kurukshetra district of Haryana it is the maximum and minimum in Lakhisarai of Bihar. So from the above discussion we see in urban area the vehicular pollution is higher possible than rural area.

Table 4. Distribution of own intensity polluting vehicle holding households of the maximum, minimum and coefficient of variation

Rural						Urban				
state	district	max	district	min	CV	district	max	district	min	CV
Andhra Pradesh	Rangareddi	10.45	Vizianagaram	2.81	37.88	Hyderabad	50.18	Prakasam	13.78	36.19
Assam	Sibsagar	12.14	Dhubri	1.04	65.90	Sibsagar	46.41	Dhubri	6.68	49.38
Bihar	Vaishali	5.70	Kishanganj	1.39	33.71	Patna	32.41	Lakhisarai *	4.58	45.14
Chandigarh	Chandigarh	23.33	Chandigarh	23.33		Chandigarh	62.79	Chandigarh	62.79	
Chhattisgarh	Durg	10.24	Dantewada*	2.99	32.12	Korba *	45.96	Kawardha *	19.38	42.13
Delhi	East *	62.07	North *	15.07	52.72	West *	51.91	North East *	26.25	18.88
Goa	South Goa	43.20	North Goa	37.96	9.13	North Goa	62.08	South Goa	55.35	8.10
Gujarat	Rajkot	27.68	Dohad *	3.49	47.69	Vadodara	57.02	Patan *	21.78	21.34
Haryana	Ambala	25.38	Jind	9.17	30.49	Kurukshetra	79.94	Gurgaon	25.58	37.32
Himachal	Una	15.61	Chamba	3.72	48.02	Una	39.50	Shimla	15.16	25.18
Jharkhand	Dhanbad	11.56	Sahibganj	1.52	54.07	Purbi Singhbhum	52.48	Sahibganj	7.10	44.12
J & K	Jammu	12.88	Doda	1.66	58.22	Jammu	40.46	Kupwara	7.74	49.84
Karnataka	Bangalore	19.28	Gulbarga	3.57	42.65	Bangalore	44.92	Gadag *	17.15	27.03
Kerala	Ernakulam	18.26	Kannur	5.04	40.43	Ernakulam	34.50	Kasaragod	12.04	33.30
Madhya Pradesh	Indore	21.83	Dindori *	2.64	47.42	Indore	51.16	Sheopur *	16.35	26.09
Maharashtra	Pune	19.57	Parbhani	3.15	52.59	Pune	47.38	Hingoli *	15.24	28.95
Orissa	Khordha *	9.93	Malkangiri *	2.05	43.72	Anugul *	51.06	Gajapati *	12.76	36.32
Punjab	Fatehgarh Sahib *	45.39	Mansa *	14.82	26.93	Rupnagar	74.10	Muktsar *	35.32	19.90
Rajasthan	Kota	14.13	Churu	2.91	34.21	Udaipur	60.98	Churu	10.78	37.25
Tamil Nadu	Namakkal	26.28	The Nilgiris	4.77	53.62	Chennai	39.04	The Nilgiris	8.96	31.12
Uttar Pradesh	Gautam Buddha Nagar *	19.97	Banda	3.40	37.92	Gautam Buddha Nagar *	53.18	Shrawasti *	11.81	40.05
Uttaranchal	Dehradun	21.18	Bageshwar	1.63	629.88	Dehradun	55.60	Bageshwar	10.61	53.87
West Bengal	Hugli	8.35	Dakshin Dinajpur *	2.05	40.93	Barddhaman	21.43	Nadia	7.77	30.27
North East	Imphal West	21.96	Tuensang	1.30	84.11	Daman	55.37	Yanam	15.97	56.88
Group of UT	Diu	26.38	Nicobar	9.93	34.96	Imphal West	42.72	Chandel	2.47	38.05

Table 5. Result of Regression Analysis

Ols			Tobit			hetcov		
Variable	coefficient	t-ratio	Variable	coefficient	t-ratio	Variable	coefficient	t-ratio
bhh	0.50361	4.380	bhh	0.15015	4.4201	bhh	0.50361	3.581
lit	0.31944	2.235	lit	0.10300	2.4293	lit	0.31944	2.599
rich	1.7288	1.806	rich	0.45737	1.6165	rich	1.7288	3.225
urbn	0.80844	1.387	urbn	0.23339	1.3665	urbn	0.80844	1.614
dummy	0.40033	2.314	dummy	0.11862	2.3358	dummy	0.40033	1.693

Notes: Ppvh-percentage of polluting vehicle household
Bhh- banking facility having household
Lit- literacy rate
Rich – not poor (high income level)
Dummy- proxy variable or numerical variable i.e qualitative
Urbn-urban

INADEQUATE PUBLIC TRANSPORT SYSTEM

Public transport systems in India are not generally efficient, thanks to outdated technology, incompetent management, corruption, overstaffing, and low worker productivity (Pucher, Mittal & Ittyerah, 2005). Pucher et al (2005) expressed their opinion in "urban Transport Policy" in 2004 that the huge improvements are required in India's public transport system for insufficient fund. Due to small road space the vehicles face on traffic problem at causes emission and spread pollution in many large cities of India and towns of West Bengal. In India most of the buses and trains are overcrowded. For this problem most of the passengers who earn middle income they are forced to purchase two-wheelers and four-wheelers. Actually the inadequacy of public transport pressurizes the private transport mechanism. However, the security of government funds and the inefficiency of the public system lend its support to the issue of privatization The Indian cities are varied considerably in terms of the population, are urban form, topography and economic activities, thus the requirement of public transport mechanism vary from one city to another.

Priority to the Use of Public Transport

From the national urban transport policy (2014) it is well known that public transport occupies less road space and causes less pollution per passenger-km than personal vehicles. As such, public transport is a more sustainable form of transport. Therefore the central government would promote investments in public transport as well as measures that make its use more attractive than in the past. The central government would encourage all state capitals as well as other cities with a population of more than one million to start planning for high capacity public transport systems. In doing so, Form the "Better Traffic Management" is recommended by T. Krisno Prasad (IPS, DGP and Chairman, Road Safety Authority, Telengana state, Hyderabad) on 2nd conference on 'National Security Strategy' (09.05. 2018), they should look at various proven technologies around the world, including the use of available waterways. They should adopt a technology that would best suit the city requirements in the next 30 years. Comprehensive city wide plans should be drawn up comprising trunk and feeder corridors as well as good integration with personal modes, suburban traffic, etc. High cost trunk root systems should, through appropriate hub-spoke arrangements be integrated with feeder system that enable higher ridership on such trunk systems. However, this system is also inefficient with waste of resources. An urban transport planner has a tough task. He has to balance between equity, efficiency and sustainability of transit system. This requires long run planning by the urban planners.

CONCLUSION

In this chapter we have shown the relationship between urbanization and vehicular population using the West Bengal as well as India data. For our analysis we concentrated on various secondary sources. We see urbanization raises the possession of fuel consuming vehicles. From our above discussion we also understand that the Probability of polluting Vehicles holding is higher in the urban area than the rural area. To reduce the vehicular pollution we have to emphasize on public transport system rather than private transport. In an underdeveloped country it is very tough to use public transport. Due to lack of government fund, new technology, proper checking etc. private cars, buses and tracks are increased rapidly. We use these randomly for transport purposes. This causes huge pollution.

REFERENCES

Badami, M., Tiwari, G., & Mohan, D. (2004). *Access and Mobility for the urban poor in India: bridging the gap between policy and needs.* Urban Land Reforms.

Bose, R. K. (1996). Energy Demand and Environmental Implications in Urban Transport - Case of Delhi. *Atmospheric Environment, 30*, 403-412.

Bose, R. K. (1998, December). Automobiles and environmental sustainability: issues and options for developing countries. Asian Transport Journal, 13.1-13.16.

Breese, G. (1969). *Urbanisation in Newly Developing Countries*. New Delhi: Prentice Hall.

Brockerhoff, M. (1999). Urban Growth in Developing Countries: A review of Projections and Predictions. *Population and Development Review, 25*(4), 757-77.

Brown, C. (1980). Equalising differences in the labour market. *The Quarterly Journal of Economics, 94*(1), 113–134. doi:10.2307/1884607

Case, A., & Deaton, A. (2005). Broken Down by Work and Sex: How our Health Declines (A. David, Ed.). Academic Press. doi:10.7208/chicago/9780226903217.003.0007

Chakraborty, D. (1997). Kolkata in pollution perspective. World Transport Policy and Practice, 3(3).

Clean Air Initiative. (2004). *CNG Buses in Delhi. Clean Technologies Information Pool.* Author.

Davis, K. (1962). Urbanisation in India – Past and Future. In India's Urban Future. University of California Press.

Davis, K. (1965). The urbanization of the human population. *Scientific American, 213*(3), 41–53. doi: 10.1038cientificamerican0965-40

Davis, K., & Golden, H. H. (1954). Urbanisation and development in pre- Industrial. Areas. *Economic Development and Cultural Change, 3*(1), 6–26. doi:10.1086/449673

Delhi Metro Rail Corporation Ltd. (2003b). Project Update. Delhi Metro Rail Corporation.

Delhi Metro Railway Corporation Ltd. (2003a). History of the Delhi Metro. Delhi Metro Rail Corporation.

Environment News India. (2001, September 10). *India may pull old vehicles off roads*. Author.

Gakenheimer, R. (1999). Urban mobility in the developing world. *Transportation Research, 33A*, 671–690.

Gakenheimer, R. (2002). *Planning Transportation and Land Use for Cities in India*. Cambridge, MA: Massachusetts Institute of Technology.

Gakenheimer, R., & Zegras, C. (2003). *Travel Demand Drivers: Mumbai and Chennai, India*. Geneva, Switzerland: World Business Council for Sustainable Development.

Government of Ghana. (1995). *Ghana - Vision 2020. Presidential Report to Parliament on Coordinated Programme of Economic and Social Development Policies*. Accra: Government of Ghana.

Goyal, Ghatge, Nema, & Tamhane. (2005). Understanding Urban Vehicular Pollution Problem Vis-a-Vis Ambient Air Quality - Case Study of a Megacity. *Environmental Monitoring and Assessment, 119*, 557-569.

Goyal, P. (2003). Present Scenario of Air Quality in Delhi: A Case Study of CNG Implementation. *Atmospheric Environment, 37*(38), 5423–5431. doi:10.1016/j.atmosenv.2003.09.005

Gwillian, K. (2003). Urban transport in Developing countries. *Transport Reviews, 23*(2), 197–216. doi:10.1080/01441640309893

Hao, J., & Wang, L. (2005). Improving Urban Air Quality in China: Beijing Case Study. *Journal of the Air & Waste Management Association, 55*(9), 1298–1305. doi:10.1080/10473289.2005.10464726 PMID:16259425

Kandlikar, M., & Ramchandran, G. (2000). The causes and consequences of particulate air pollution in urban India: A synthesis of the science. *Annual Review of Energy and the Environment, 25*(1), 629–694. doi:10.1146/annurev.energy.25.1.629

Kathuria, V. (2006). Vehicular Pollution Control in Delhi. *Transport and Environment*, 373-387.

Krupnic, A. J. (1997). Urban Air Pollution in developing countries: Problem & Policies. In P. Dasgupta & G. Maler (Eds.), *The Environment and development issue* (Vol. 2). Oxford University Press.

Kundu, A. (1983). Theories of City Size Distribution and Indian Urban Structure–A Reappraisal. *Economic and Political Weekly, 18*(3).

Kundu, A. (1994). Pattern of Urbanisation with Special Reference to Small and Medium Towns in India. In Sectoral Issues in the Indian Economy. Har – Anand Publications.

Low, N., & Banerjee-Guha, S. (2003). The global tyranny of roads: Observations from Mumbai and Melbourne. *World Transport Policy and Practice*, *9*(2), 5–17.

Lucas, R. E. (2002). *Lectures in Growth theory*. Oxford University Press.

Marwah, B. R., Sibal, V. K., & Sawant, S. (2001). Bus transport in Delhi. In S. Morris (Ed.), *India Infrastructure Report 2001*. New Delhi, India: Oxford University Press.

Ministry of Road Transport and Highways. (2003). Handbook on Transport Statistics in India Transport Research Office. Ministry of Road Transport and Highways.

Mumbai Metropolitan Region development Authority. (2003). *Mumbai Urban Transport Project*. Mumbai, India: MMRDA.

Padam, S., & Singh, S. K. (2001). Urbanisation and Urban Transport in India: The Sketch for a Policy. *Transport Asia Project Workshop*, Pune, India.

Pucher, J., Korattyswaroopam, N., & Ittyerah, N. (2004). The crisis of public transport in India: Overwhelming needs but limited resources. *Journal of Public Transportation*, *7*(3), 95–113. doi:10.5038/2375-0901.7.3.5

Pucher, J., & Lefevre, C. (1996). *Urban Transport Crisis in Europe and North America*. London: Macmillan Press. doi:10.1057/9780230371835

Raj, D. (2001). *Ban on old Vehicles hurt autorickshaw drivers*. Environmental Bulletin India.

Ramachandran, R. (1989). *Urbanisation and Urban System in India*. Oxford, UK: Oxford University Press.

Shariff. (2012). Private Vehicle Ownership and Transportation Planning in Malaysia. *IPCSIT, 26*.

Sibal, V., & Sachdeva, Y. (2001). Urban transport scenarios in India and its linkages with energy and environment. *Urban Transport Journal*, *2*(1), 12–20.

Sreedharan, E. (2003). *Need for Urban Mass Transport System for our cities*. New Delhi, India: Press Information Bureau, Government of India.

Tata Energy Research Institute. (1997). *Environmental Aspects of Energy use in Large Indian Metropolises*. Delhi, India: Tata Energy Research Institute.

Times of India. (2002). *Delhi roads have reached saturation point*. Author.

Tiwari, G. (2001). Pedestrian infrastructure in the city transport system: Delhi case study. *World Transport Policy and Practice*, *7*(4), 13–18.

Tiwari, G., & Mohan, D. (1999). Sustainable transport systems: Linkages between environmental issues, public transport, non-motorised transport, and safety. *Economic and Political Weekly*, *34*(25), 1589–1596.

U.S Bureau of Labour Statistics. (1972). *Handbook of Labour Statistics*. Washington, DC: U.S Government Printing Office.

Van der Westhuisen, H. (1998). *Evaporative emissions and fuel loss in South Africa, Unpublished B.Eng. Project Report*. Centre for Automotive Engineering, University of Stellenbosch.

Vasconcellos, E. (2001). *Urban Transport, Environment and Equity: The case for Developing*. Earthscan Press.

Weaver, C. (2004). Challenges and Success of Delhi's CNG Program: Lessons for other Cities. Presented at the Leap Frog factor: Towards Clean Air in Asian Cities, New Delhi, India.

Whitelegg, J., & Williams, N. (2000). Non-motorised transport and sustainable development: Evidence from Calcutta. *Local Environment*, *5*(1), 7–18. doi:10.1080/135498300113237

WHO-UNEP Report. (1988). *Urban Air Pollution in the Megacities of the World.* Author.

Wise. (Ed.). (2005). *Analyse in the Economics of Aging*. The University of Chicago Press.

World Bank. (2002). *India's Transport Sector. The Challenges Ahead.* Washington, DC: The World Bank.

Wynne, G. (2005). *Bogota's BRT achieves firebox coverage of operating costs. Passenger Transport, Nov. 5, 2001*. Washington, DC: American Public Transportation Association.

KEY TERMS AND DEFINITIONS

Developed Countries: Developed economies are the countries that enjoy certain high standards. Such countries generally have a good infrastructure, stable economy with very high per capita income. The degree of development, industrialization, and general standard of living for its citizens is very high.

Developing Countries: A developing country also called a less developed economy or underdeveloped country is a nation with an underdeveloped industrial base, and a low human development index (HDI) relative to other countries.

Pollution: Pollution is something introduced into the environment that is dirty, unclean, or has a harmful effect.

Population: The whole number of people or inhabitants in a country or region.

Private Transport: Private transport (as opposed to public transport) is transportation service which is not available for use by the general public. Private transport is the dominant form of transportation in most of the world.

Public Transport: Public Transport is transport of passengers by group travel systems available for use by the general public, typically managed on a schedule, operated on established routes, and that charge a posted fee for each trip.

Urban: An urban area or urban agglomeration is a human settlement with high population density and infrastructure of built environment. Urban areas are created through urbanization and are categorized by urban morphology as cities, towns, conurbations, or suburbs.

Vehicle: A vehicle is a machine such as a car, bus, or truck which has an engine ad is used to carry people from place to place.

Chapter 20
Political Economy of the Green Innovations in the Construction Industry

Begum Sertyesilisik
Istanbul Technical University, Turkey

ABSTRACT

Green innovations are important in enhancing sustainability performance of the industries and of their outputs. They can influence the carbon emissions, energy efficiency of the industries affecting global green trade, and energy policies. Construction industry is one of the main industries contributing to the global economy and sustainable development. It has, however, bigger environmental footprint than majority of the other industries. Green innovations can contribute to the reduction in the environmental footprint of the construction industry. For this reason, green innovation in the construction industry needs to be supported by the effective policies. This chapter aims to introduce and investigate the political economy of the green innovations in the construction industry. This chapter emphasizes that the effectiveness of the green innovations in the construction industry can be fostered by effective political economy and strategies.

INTRODUCTION

Climate change and humanity's environmental footprints challenge survival and welfare of the earth. Humanity's environmental footprint needs to be reduced to enable the nature to restore and regenerate itself. Human-beings tend to consider themselves to be superior to other living creatures failing to observe the ethical behaviour of animals. Animals do not exploit resources beyond their needs. For example, they stop hunting in case they have hunted to feed themselves. Human-beings, on the other hand, tend to exploit resources without respecting nature, and future generations. Ethics is respecting each other, the nature and the next generations of all species. It can be defined as "... *a system of moral principles and a branch of philosophy which defines what is good for individuals and society...*" (BBC website,

DOI: 10.4018/978-1-5225-8547-3.ch020

2018). Sustainability ethics needs to be integrated in the production and consumption processes in all industries. All industries need to respect nature, future generations and biodiversity in their investment strategies and in their supply.

Global construction industry contributes to the global economy. Global construction industry contributes to the social sustainability through employment opportunities, even for less educated workforce, increasing the welfare of the people as well as through supplying the sheltering and accommodation needs of the people. Construction industry, however, has adverse environmental impacts throughout the construction/production processes as well as the entire lifecycle of their outputs (e.g. constructions, buildings). Construction industry is material, water, and energy intensive. The magnitude and size of its environmental footprint can be better understood considering its outputs' embodied water, embodied carbon and embodied energy. Construction process, starting from raw material extraction, is energy and water intensive. Construction processes and lifecycle of its outputs have carbon footprint especially due to the energy required for the material production and construction processes as well as due to the transportation and mismanaged construction phase (e.g. due to errors in construction causing wasted materials). Furthermore, operation phase of the buildings has environmental footprint especially due to heating and cooling needs of the occupants as well as water consumed by the occupants. Even in the post-occupation phase, in the demolition phase, the buildings have their environmental footprint especially due to the landfill wastes. Sustainability performance of the construction industry needs to be enhanced as it influences global welfare, living conditions, and climate adversely. There have been various efforts (e.g. green or sustainable building assessment tools) in reducing environmental footprint of the construction industry. These efforts have not been effective to cope with the climate change problem which is being observed in an accelerated way. For this reason, effective strategies and efficient technologies for reducing environmental footprint of the construction industry are needed.

Innovation is an important pillar of the effective strategies and efficient technologies needed for reducing the environmental footstep of the construction industry. All innovation processes start with inventions. Innovations are inventions especially at the product, material and production levels that have been reached to the market and customer. Innovation can be at different levels. As Schumpeter ([1911] 1934: 66) identified, the innovations can be related with production process, product, materials/resources, markets and organization forms (Ziemnowicz, 2013: 1172). Innovation can result in introduction of a new product and/or a new process to the market. All innovation processes start with an invention process. Innovation can be achieved through successful inventions which can reach to their customers. Not all inventions can be transformed into innovations. Feasibility and investment return rates are among the main factors influencing inventions' success. Inventions can be transformed into innovations if they are feasible and if the investment return rate is fast. Invention and innovation capability is what differentiates humanity from the animals and what makes human-beings superior to other living creatures. Innovation can change humanity's perception of the degree of limitedness of the resources as well as increase in the effectiveness and efficiency of resource usage (Sertyesilisik, 2018b). Innovation can lead to dematerialization which can enable reduction in perceived limitedness of the resources. For example, even if people living 3000 years ago were experiencing resource scarcity problem, if they could have a chance for using today's technology, they would probably not have experienced this problem (Sertyesilisik, 2018b). Hence, the main problem with respect to the scarcity of the resources is the technology level (Sertyesilisik, 2018b). For this reason, innovation plays an important role for enhancing sustainability performance of the humanity and for reducing humanity's environmental footprint (Sertyesilisik, 2016a).

Not all innovations are green. Green innovations are innovations especially at the product, material and production process levels that respect sustainability of the nature and of the future generations as well as contribute to the sustainable development and to the regeneration of the nature. Green innovations differ from other innovations with respect to their potential contribution to the reduction in the environmental footprint of products or production processes as well as with respect to their main aim. Both of the innovation types (green and non-green innovations) can be performed for enhancing competitiveness of the companies and for enabling the companies to have competitive advantage through differentiated products. Green innovations, however, have the potential to enable the companies to gain competitive advantage through enhanced sustainability performance of the product or processes as well as through introducing new substitutes to the market replacing or eliminating non-green product or processes. Saunila et al. (2018: 631) have emphasized that green innovations are mainly concerned with environmental problems (Rennings, 2000; Li et al., 2017) whereas the main driver for non-green innovations is about their impact on the competitive advantage of the companies (Baregheh et al., 2009). Companies' main motivation towards sustainable innovation can be "to sustain, improve and renew the environmental, social and societal quality of its business processes…" (Bossink, 2013: 1; Mousavi & Bossink, 2017: 1264). Furthermore, green innovations can contribute to the competitiveness of the companies through their reduced environmental footprint which can reduce the companies' costs with respect to reduced production costs (dematerialization, carbon tax, etc.) as well as through enhanced value created.

Political economy of the innovations covers two-way interaction of political economy and innovations. Political and economic decisions and factors affect innovation rate and innovations' effectiveness. Furthermore, innovations can affect policies and economies. Political economy of the green innovation is about the interactions among political economy, environment and green innovations. Political and economic decisions as well as factors can affect green innovation rate, its effectiveness, sustainability of the nature and of the future generations. Furthermore, green innovations can affect policies, economy, nature and future generations. Similarly, political economy of the green innovation in the construction industry deals with interactions among green innovations in the construction industry, political economy, and environment. Political and economic decisions and factors can have impact on the green innovation rate in the construction industry, the effectiveness of green innovations as well as on the sustainability of the nature and of the future generations. Additionally, green innovations in the construction industry can have influence on the policies, economy, nature and future generations. For this reason, political economy of the green innovations can contribute to the reduction of the environmental footprint of the construction industry as well as of the built environment. This chapter aims to introduce and investigate the political economy of the green innovations in the construction industry.

BACKGROUND

Innovations can be the key tools for enhancing sustainability performance of the humanity as well as of the supply and demand sides. Sustainability problem of the world is becoming more and more severe due to reluctance and ineffectiveness of the precautions taken (Sertyesilisik, 2016a). More disruptive innovations might be needed to deal with the challenges of the humanity in the future. Exponential innovation has been stated to be observed in all industries. The rate of innovation has increased and is being increased in an accelerated way. Exponential technology leads to exponential innovation (Hagel, Brown, Samoylova, & Lui, 2013). Technological improvements can increase the synergy and rate of innovation.

Hagel et al. (2013) have prepared the Shift Index and have identified three main forces affecting the shift in the global business environment which reveal the importance of political and economic factors as well as their interactions. These three forces reveal the importance of political and economic factors as well as their interactions. In other words, they emphasize the importance and role of the political economy in fostering innovation.

Green innovation acts as an enabler for reducing environmental footprint of the construction industry. Green innovation is an emerging tool for reducing humanity's environmental footprint. "...According to Kemp and Pearson (2007), green innovation can effectively reduce environmental pollution ... leading to sustainable development." (Saunila, et al., 2018: 631). Green innovations can improve leanness and sustainability of the production processes as well as of the outputs (e.g. construction materials; buildings). They can result in dematerialization enabling usage of relatively fewer materials. Innovations can contribute to the reduction in the construction cost. Furthermore, green innovations can enable emergence of the opportunities in restoring the nature and in supporting regeneration of the nature (e.g. carbon capturing technologies).

Green innovation process can be challenging. It can be a complex process especially due to the participation of various stakeholders having different priorities (Alkemade & Suurs, 2012; Mousavi & Bossink, 2017: 1264).Furthermore, transformation of inventions into innovations is a critical point for green innovations. Successful green inventions can bring both tangible and intangible benefits. Examples for these potential benefits include depreciation of the nature, enhanced welfare, wellbeing and happiness of the humanity, eliminated opportunity cost of being non-sustainable. Green inventions, however, might not always be feasible if their feasibility is solely assessed by their monetary point of view. Green inventions feasibility can be more accurately assessed considering their impacts in the short and long runs. Green inventions need to be transformed into green innovations as they have lower environmental impact even if they might not be feasible. The feasibility of these green innovations can be supported by the subsidies, incentives and policies. For example, there are initiatives supporting sustainable built environment which can encourage green innovation directly or indirectly. The "Financing Climate Futures: Rethinking Infrastructure" initiative has been launched by the UN Environment, OECD, and the World Bank Group (OECD website, 2018). "Financing Climate Futures: Rethinking Infrastructure" report emphasized the importance of innovation, finance and infrastructure for achieving the targets set in the Paris Agreement and the 2030 Agenda for Sustainable Development (OECD website, 2018a). Furthermore, carbon tax is another factor affecting the cost of non-sustainable products and production processes. OECD (2008)'s report "Effective Carbon Rates 2018 - Pricing Carbon Emissions Through Taxes and Emissions Trading" has been prepared with the main aimof establishing carbon-neutral growth/development and decarbonizing the economy as a result of pricing CO_2 emissions. This report focused on 42 OECD and G20 countries with respect to the carbon pricing mechanisms used in each of these countries (OECD website, 2018b). The report revealed the carbon pricing levels incapability in achieving decarbonisation levels needed (OECD website, 2018b). In addition to these financial supports, feasibility of the green innovations can be more accurately calculated in case opportunity cost of the deprived nature is considered. Remedying deprived nature is costly. Furthermore, damages cannot always be irreversible despite of the money spent. Trying to repair the parts of the damaged nature which has been deprived beyond its self healing capacity is like trying to replace the nature by the man-made environment which is nearly impossible. Green innovation has great potential for reducing environmental footprint of the production processes and of the products. Policies need to encourage green innovation. As policies need to ensure welfare and wellbeing of the people, in the short and long runs which can be supported by enhanced sustainability. Construction industry's environmental footprint reveals the importance of reducing its environmental footprint through green innovations. Furthermore, construction industry's role in the sustainable development indicates its potential for enhancing sustainability policies. For this reason, political economy of the sustainability (Sertyesilisik, 2018) and of the construction industry (Sertyesilisik & Sertyesilisik, 2018) emphasise the importance of effective political economy in the field of green innovations in the construction industry.

GREEN INNOVATION IN THE CONSTRUCTION INDUSTRY

Drivers for Green Innovation in the Construction Industry

Construction industry is relatively less innovation intensive compared to majority of the other industries. One of the main reasons for this is the tendency of using tested technologies due to the safety concerns of all stakeholders in the construction industry. There are, however, various drivers for or pull and push factors contributing to the acceleration of the innovation rate in the construction industry. These drivers can be grouped into economic, political and legal, and environmental factors as well as the interactions of these factors which can foster the need for innovation and green innovation in the construction industry.

- **Economic Factors:** Intensified competition in the global construction market as well as changes in the purchasing power of the people/potential customers enforce the companies to become more competitive and value focused. Companies' investment on the research and development activities is a strategic decision which can influence their survival in the competitive market. Innovation can act as a tool for competitive advantage as well as for reducing the cost of the product and of the production process. For this reason, successful innovations can support the companies' competitiveness and their capability of supplying high quality outputs at the lowest possible price. Furthermore, green innovations can encourage sustainability performance and competitiveness of the companiesMousavi & Bossink (2017: 1263) have emphasised this fact stating the change in the competition in the industries as companies' innovation capabilities and sustainability have started to have more and more influence in their competitiveness. Companies' investment in the green invention and innovation activities can be supported by their strategic management decisions and culture in favour of environment. Furthermore, reducing environmental footprint of the companies as well as of their outputs is also related with their corporate social responsibility understanding and their corporate culture. Companies' strategic decisions on how to compete in the market depend on the characteristics of the competition. Their decisions can be influenced by the game theory principles and Nash equilibrium principles considering competitive companies' strategies, interests and capabilities.
- **Political and Legal Factors:** Governments can be motivated in fostering innovation and particularly green innovation to enhance competitiveness of the construction industry due to its role in the economy, employment and in the sustainable development. Enhanced competitiveness of the construction industry can contribute to the countries' economies and people's welfare. In this way, globally competitive construction industry can contribute to the GDP and GNP due to its companies' ability to win bids in the global market as well as through their enhanced capacity to get the value-added jobs and to perform highly asset specific tasks. Furthermore, global policies can

play an important role for enhancing the sustainability of the production processes. For example, carbon taxing, as a political economy tool, can encourage the companies to reduce their carbon footprint. In addition to taxing policies, effectively and accurately established and designed incentives and subsidies can motivate the reduction in the environmental footprint of the companies as well as their research and development activities and investments in this field. Political and legal factors can trigger each other and they can give authority to each other. Climate justice and climate law can be examples for interaction between political and legal factors. Policies and laws need to comply with humanity's contemporary and future needs. They need to be designed and prepared in a way to enhance creation of synergy as a result of the interaction of policies and legal factors.

- **Environmental Factors:** Construction industry needs to become more climate resilient and more environmental friendly due to the current situation of the climate change and of the world. Green innovations can play an important role for supporting construction industries and its outputs' ability and capacity to cope with the challenges of the climate change, deterioration of the world and relative scarcity of the resources. They can result in enhanced dematerialization, enhanced climate resilience as well as reduced environmental footprint of the construction processes and of the built environment. Furthermore, green innovations can lead to new ways of energy generations and to the emergence of the alternative materials. Companies' characteristics and environmental priorities can influence their willingness for investing in green innovation. Companies giving priority to the 'economic, institutional, and social sustainability', tend to give more and more importance to the green innovation which can further contribute to the social sustainability (Saunila et al., 2018: 631). Economic and institutional factors can foster green innovation (Saunila et al., 2018: 631). Furthermore, green innovations substituting and reducing energy demand can contribute to the budget of the peopleGreen innovations having capacity to enhance resilience of the built environment can enable saving humanity's lives in case of disasters. Green innovations' role in improving built environment's disaster resilience is becoming important due to disasters caused by the climate change. All these reveal the potential impacts of green innovations to the creation of the tangible and intangible benefits.
- **Interactions of Economic, Political and Legal as well as Environmental Factors**: Economic, political and legal as well as environmental factors are interrelated and their interactions can result either in synergy or in entropy. For this reason, interactions of these factors need to be carefully examined and monitored to ensure creation of synergy in favour of green innovations in the construction industry. Furthermore, it is important to analyse their interactions to prevent entropy in the green innovation field. Global collaboration regarding these factors can further contribute to the creation of synergy in the green innovation in the construction industry. This can be achieved not only due to the shared resources in a cost effective way but also through the economies of scale of the green innovations.

Contemporary Green Innovations in the Construction Industry

Green innovations in the construction industry can be observed in the fields of construction project management and output (either materials or constructions).Innovations can enable emergence of new perspectives, technologies and technics to the solution of the problems experienced in the construction industry. Innovations and green innovations in other industries can foster the speed of the innovation and of the green innovation in the construction industry in addition to the economic, political, and environmental drivers for innovation.

Green innovations in the field of construction project management: Innovations in other industries are being benchmarked to the construction project management to solve the problems encountered. For example, lean approach has been benchmarked from automobile industry, whereas agile approach has been benchmarked from the aviation industry to the construction project management. Recently, IoT has started to transform the construction industry and the construction project management processes. Furthermore, as construction industry is not isolated from the changes, innovations and developments in other industries, the 4th industrial development has the potential to be adopted to the construction industry in the near future. The 4th industrial development's adaptation to the construction project management can cause changes in the construction industry. For example, it can influence the way human resources are employed and integrated to the managerial and production processes as well as the skills they need to possess. Construction project management processes are becoming more IT based and smarter. For example, Building Information Modelling has been started to be used widespread in the construction industry. It can influence all processes of the construction project management and entire lifecycle of the constructions. Furthermore, construction project management can be improved by the biomimicry which can be described as benchmarking either shape or function as well as both shape and function from the nature (Sertyesilisik, 2016a). Nature can be a source for solutions to the managerial and technical issues (Sertyesilisik, 2016a) enhancing competitiveness of the companies. All these changes and trends have great potential to influence green innovation practices and their success.

Green innovations in the field of the construction industry's outputs (e.g. construction materials, buildings, and constructions): Construction materials are becoming more smart, resilient, sustainable with the help of green innovations. Smart materials (e.g. thermo- or electro-chromic materials, piezoelectric materials, etc.) have at least one characteristics (e.g. color, shape, volume etc.) which can be altered reversibly by outside factors (e.g. change in the pressure, temperature, moisture, or Ph levels, light level, electric or magnetic fields) (Choudhary, n.d.; Das, n.d.; Quora website, n.d.; GCSE Bitesize website, n.d.). Furthermore, construction materials are becoming more IT based (e.g. smart bricks) enhancing smartness and sustainability of the constructions. Construction materials' sustainability performance can be improved with the help of successful green innovations. Sustainable materials are the materials which have lower embodied water, embodied carbon, and embodied energy compared to non-sustainable materials. They are environmental friendly due to their low carbon and environmental footprint. Furthermore, sustainable construction materials can be available in the nature. For example, they can be either rapidly replenishable materials (e.g. bamboo), recyclable and locally available (Sustainable Materials website, 2018). They can environmental friendly throughout their lifecycle (Metroplan Ltd. website, 2011). Their integration to the production and construction processes as inputs can be enhanced through green innovations. Green innovations in the field of resilient materials has been intensified due to the unpreventable climate change and the need for adapting the built environment to the extreme weather conditions which are expected to be observed more frequently. Research centers have been established in the field of enhancing resilience of the constructions and materials. For example, CaliBaja Center for Resilient Materials & Systems in UC San Diego Jacobs School of Engineering carries out researches in the field of designing, testing and manufacturing materials and systems for extreme conditions (e.g.

extreme temperatures, deformations, etc.) (CaliBaja Center for Resilient Materials & Systems website, 2017). Furthermore, green innovations are performed to reduce embodied water and embodied energy of the construction materials and of the buildings as well as to integrate renewable energy technologies and alternative energy sources to the built environment.

Political Economy of the Green Innovation in the Construction Industry

Innovation has impact on the economy. It can contribute to the productivity growth (Jahns, 2010: vi). Schumpeter (1934) has identified entrepreneur as *'the agent of innovation'* whereas entrepreneurial innovation as the main cause of and as a strategic pull and push factor to the economic change and development (Ziemnowicz, 2013: 1171-1174). Furthermore, Schumpeter emphasized that economic development can be achieved in case innovation is diffused (Brouwer, 1991: 58) as innovation diffusion is related with the innovations acceptance within the economic system (Ziemnowicz, 2013: 1172). The accurate impacts of the innovations can be assessed once diffusion of innovation is achieved.

Sustainable development and green economy rely on sustainable technologies and green innovation. Green innovation can act as one of the enablers of the green economy which can support sustainable development. *"…'green growth' will require structural transformation and technological innovation"* (Criscuolo & Menon, 2015: 38). Furthermore, green innovation can support the countries to overcome the shortcomings of the "environmental Kuznets curve" while they are being developed. The Simon Kuznets hypothesis explains the "U" type of relationship between the economic development level and social inequality (Sahli & Rejeb, 2015: 1649). The "environmental Kuznets curve" is adaptation of the Simon Kuznets hypothesis to the sustainability topic to explain the relationship between development of a country and deterioration of its nature (Sahli & Rejeb, 2015: 1650).

Green innovation in the construction industry can shift the production possibility frontier (PPF) curve enhancing efficiency of the resource usage. "…The PPF assumes that all inputs are used efficiently." (Investopedia website, n.d.). As there is relationship between "frontier production functions and technical efficiency" (Battese, 1992), innovations can enable increase in the production efficiency. Green innovations can result in enhanced compliance of the production and of the products to the 3R principles and to the circular economy principles as well as in the emergence of substitutes of non-sustainable products and production processes. Green and lean innovations can contribute to the sustainability and dematerialization performances of the production processes, innovation processes, and of the innovations complying with the Adolf Loose's *'less is more'* principle.

Construction industry's contribution to the sustainable development and to the economy can be enhanced through green innovations. Innovation can play an important role in supporting companies' role in the sustainable development (Mousavi & Bossink, 2017: 1263). For this reason, the success in the innovation strategies is vital for sustainable development (Xu et al., 2018: 618). Complying with the sustainable development goals, innovation strategies' success depends on the creation of values with respect to the environmental, economic and social aspects (Adams et al., 2016). Green innovations can help the construction companies become integrated with the circular economy principles. Furthermore, green innovations can adapt these circular economy and 3R (reuse, recycle, reduce) principles to the constructions in the design, construction, maintenance and repair as well as in the demolition phase.

Innovations can improve the purchasing power of the people in two ways. They can enable availability of new jobs as well as to the reduction in the price through improved leanness and agility of the production processes and dematerialization. In this way, they can have potential for contributing to the purchasing power of the people through reduced prices enabled by reduced costs. Furthermore, they can support the social sustainability through creation of new jobs. Green innovations can result in new employment opportunities and new fields of employment. For example, in the European Union, green innovations have provided new job opportunities and they have contributed to the reduction in the unemployment rate.

Successful innovations can contribute to the competitiveness of the companies as they can produce in a more cost effective, fast, sustainable and lean way. Green innovations can result in the emergence of new ways of production enabling creation of synergy, reduced or no idle workforce, enhanced efficiency and effectiveness in the production process. For this reason, successful innovations can act as a competitive advantage tool.

Political economy plays an important role in fostering the green innovation. Economic situations, decisions, and policies can enable emergence and establishment of innovation climate in the industry. Political economy decisions on the policies with respect to the environmental footprint of the companies and their outputs as well as with respect to innovation supports provided to the companies have the potential for fostering green innovation. Furthermore, policy makers can support green innovation (Criscuolo & Menon, 2015: 52For example, policy makers and governments in the United States and China have fostered green innovation in the 'green energy' field through: programmes (e.g. the National Basic Research Programme in China); laboratory facilities provided; policies and regulations (e.g. VAT reduction mechanisms) as well as through direct supports (e.g. loan guarantees, feed-in-tariffs, renewable energy certificates) (Criscuolo & Menon, 2015: 52-53). Political economy of the green innovations in the construction industry needs to encourage innovation to be based on and supported by the lean, agile, and sustainability principles in order to foster the innovation rate and effectiveness. Adhering to these principles can support the sustainability performance of the construction companies encouraging them to invest in green innovation practices which can further improve their lean and agility performances. Furthermore, big companies can influence the innovation policies and their effectiveness. They can provide feedback on the difficulties and challenges they are experiencing and they can suggest solutions for enhancing green innovation in the construction industry. Their feedback and solutions can be considered by the policy makers as lessons learned and as the level of effectiveness of the current policies in the field of green innovation so that they can enhance effectiveness of their policies.

SOLUTIONS AND RECOMMENDATIONS

Political Economy and Strategies for Fostering Green Innovation in the Construction Industry

Effective and successful political economy and strategies can foster green innovation in the construction industry. These strategies need to encourage global and interdisciplinary collaboration in the policy making and in the education arena at all levels. Global collaboration in policy making for green innovation and environmental issues can enhance effectiveness of the policies. These policies need to cover policies for integrating construction industry and universities. They need to enable establishment of global policies encouraging green trade as well as green energy usage in the construction industry. Furthermore, as these strategies can be achieved with the help of the education pillar, they need to cover changes in the universities' curriculum. Political economy capable of fostering the green innovation and of strengthening green innovation climate in the construction industry can be established addressing the drivers, policies as well as by the capability and capacity levels of the construction industry, universities and pre-university education. These constructs of the political economy for fostering green innovation have been presented in the Figure 1.

Drivers: Market driven and environmental factors can promote green innovation. Market driven factors can act as drivers for green innovation as they have direct impact to the supply and demand sides. Intensified competition and scarcity in the resources can foster innovation with respect to dematerialization as well as enhanced effectiveness and efficiency of the production processes. Furthermore, environmental factors (e.g. availability and scarcity of the raw materials and minerals, climate change, etc.) force humanity to reduce its environmental footprint and they can act as a driver for green innovation. The magnitude of both of these factors can be affected by the effectiveness of the policies and their impact on the economy.

Policies: Policies with respect to the incentives, education, investment, art and collaboration can affect the emergence of and strengthening of the innovation culture and climate which are needed for fostering green innovation in the construction industry. Furthermore, policies can influence innovation culture, innovation capability and capacity levels of the construction industry, universities and pre-university education. Enhanced innovation capability and capacity of the universities can further contribute to the success rate and effectiveness of the green innovations. Policies contributing to the innovation infrastructure of the construction industry and of the universities as well as collaboration between university and industry can foster innovation capacity of the construction industry (Figure 2). For example, Burritt, Guthrie, Evans & Christ (2017) have emphasized the role and support of the research and development activities carried out in collaboration between universities and industries in enhancing success of these activities as well as in enhancing companies' competitiveness (Walker et al., 2008; Hughes et al., 2008) contributing to the knowledge economies (Nielsen, 2017). The collaboration among universities and construction industry can be interdisciplinary and it can be encouraged at the

Figure 1. Constructs of the political economy for fostering green innovation in the construction industry

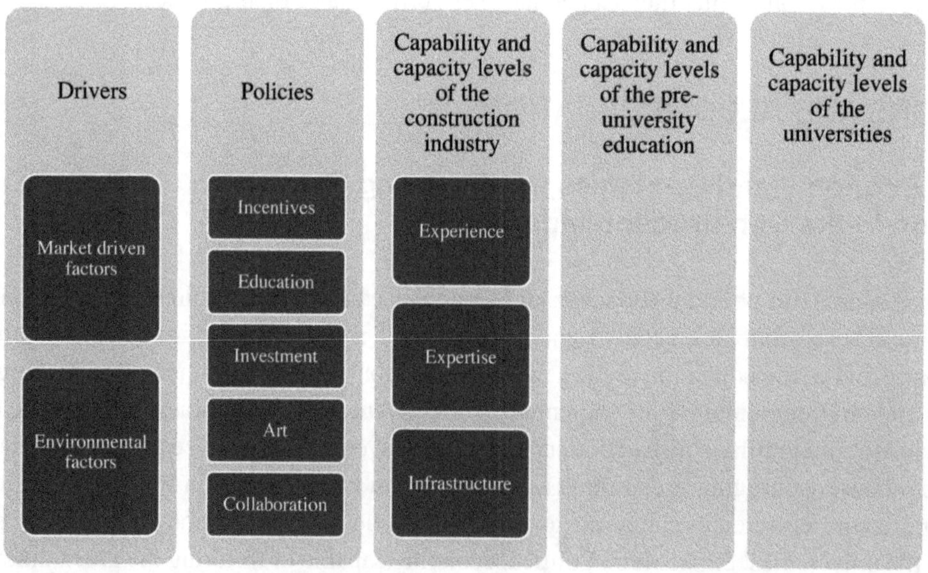

global level to enable them to get benefit from synergy which can emerge due to the shared experience as well as joint usage of research facilities and infrastructure. This type of collaboration enabling share of tangible and intangible resources can further enhance research and innovation capacity of the universities and of the companies. Incentives and funds supporting collaboration between industry and universities can be established considering the current situation of the construction industry and of the universities with respect to their capabilities and capacity levels in order to enhance effectiveness of these incentives and funds in fostering the creation of innovation synergy and the innovation climate in the construction industry. Encouraging the construction companies to carry out green innovations can further encourage collaboration between universities and companies. Construction companies can be motivated in green innovations through some changes in the insurances and public tenders. Insurances can be established for invention and innovation processes and their failure so that companies can cover their costs in case of failed inventions and innovations. Furthermore, laws and regulations arranging the public tenders can be improved in a way to support innovation activities. Especially in the public tenders, construction companies can get additional points for their green invention and innovations to encourage the construction companies to perform relevant research and development activities. These additional points can be provided at different levels even for failed innovations and inventions in order not to discourage the companies in case of their failed innovations activities. Furthermore, the policies enhancing innovation capacity of the universities and of the pre-university education can support the innovation capacity of the future professionals. Green policies for fostering green trade, energy and innovation have been summarized in the Figure 2. Subsidies for innovative activities and internships provided can encourage construction companies to collaborate with the university students. This collaboration can further contribute to the green innovation capacity of the future construction professionals. These policies can be complemented with the education policies aiming to enhance university students' green innovation capacity. Furthermore, global internship programmes can be encouraged by relevant policies enabling to experience green innovation practices in different countries.

Green policies can encourage green innovation encouraging green trade (e.g. tax exemptions, tariff regulations). Construction companies and material manufacturers operating globally or internationally tend to have geographically dispersed supply chains. Their activities, production processes, outputs, as well as their green innovation capacities have impact on the sustainability of the world. Policies can encourage improvement of the construction supply chains' lean and sustainability performance at the global level. For example, carbon tax policies can influence the supply chain decisions of the construction companies and they can have global impact on sustainability due to the globalization of the construction companies. Tsai, Yang, Huang, & Wu (2017: 1412)'s research has emphasised the importance of "...activity-based costing decision model incorporating carbon tax costs and construction resources..." This can be achieved through embedding sustainability and lean principles to the supply chains (Sertyesilisik, 2016b) as well as through green trade policies. Green trade in the construction industry can be encouraged by the global policies as environmental footprint and green innovation capacity have impact on the globe. Globally effective policies can be established with the help of global commitment and global collaboration (Sertyesilisik, 2018b). Global collaboration for sustainability and for fostering green innovation in the construction can be achieved through policies based on sustainable collaboration as sustainable collaboration is a collaboration which is peaceful, fair and reliable economic collaboration. For this reason, commitment of the supply and demand sides as well as of the politics is vital for the effectiveness of the policies. Global collaboration towards solution of the problems is more effective than fighting each other for the so-called "scarce" resources. There is relativity in the degree of scarcity

Figure 2. Green policies for fostering green trade, energy and innovation in the construction industry

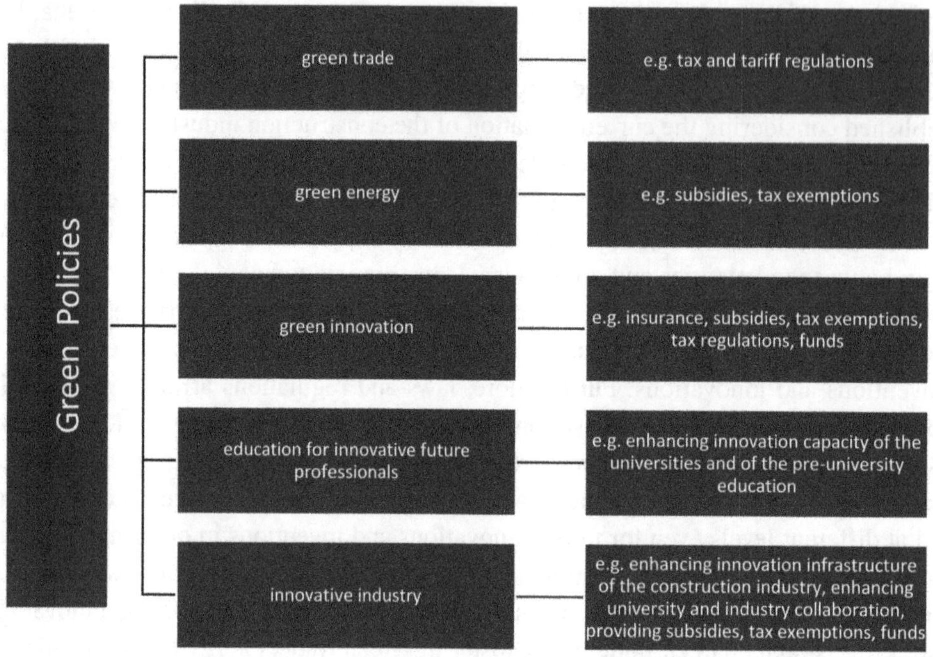

of the resources due to its dependence on the technology used (Sertyesilisik, 2018b). Humanity should collaborate for integration of their tangible and intangible resources (e.g. experience, know-how, etc.) as well as for directing their efforts with the aim of creating synergy in the establishment of a sustainable future through respecting each other. Policies can be effective in encouraging green energy usage in the construction industry both in the production/construction processes and in the built environment (e.g. subsidies, tax exemptions). Feasibility of the green energy innovations can be increased with the help of these subsidies and tax exemptions. Furthermore, green innovations contribution to the sustainability performance of the construction industry and to reducing its environmental footprint reveals green innovations' intangible benefits. These intangible benefits can have tangible benefits indirectly. For example, these intangible benefits can be related with the enhanced well-being and welfare of the people as well as reduced health expenses.

Capability and Capacity Levels of the Construction Industry: Innovation capability and capacity levels of the industry are affected by the quality of the pre- and university education, the experience and expertise as well as by the infrastructure of the industry. Construction professionals' experience can foster their ability to recognise the production/construction problems, their ability to identify potential problem areas and areas which need to be improved. Their experience can contribute to the effectiveness of the research and development activities enabling them to focus on the problems identified based on their first-hand experience. Green innovation capability and capacity of the companies can be enhanced, sustained and improved with the help of innovation culture. Companies' culture needs to be transformed and innovation culture. In other words, green innovation culture is recommended to be integrated to the companies' culture. Companies in the construction industry need to be able to achieve continuous innovation and continuous improvement. They can learn from companies capable of doing continuous innovation and they can benchmark from them. For example, Google is one of the companies which has achieved continuous innovation thanks to its organizational characteristics (Steiber & Alänge, 2013: 243-261). Similarly, Ahmed (1998: 30)'s research emphasised the importance of the innovation culture and climate. Companies' innovation culture can contribute to its competitive advantage (Dobni, 2008: 555). Their innovation culture can influence companies' transformation into learning organizations to enhance their innovation capacities. Furthermore, companies' capability for green innovation can be enhanced through improvements with regard to their sensing capability through activities for enabling the company to become alert to innovation opportunities (e.g. proactive sustainability strategy and procedures); seizing capability through activities for getting benefit from the sustainable innovation (e.g. strategy formation, advertisement, business model); and reconfiguring capabilities for enhancing innovation (e.g. changes in the organization of the work responsibilities, business practices, etc.) (Mousavi & Bossink, 2017: 1274). Similary, Jahns (2010: vi) has emphasised the importance of innovation culture, infrastructure as well as efficient and effective processes.

Capability and Capacity Levels of the Universities: Future construction professionals' capabilities and capacities depend on the quality of their higher education. Professionals are change agents for sustainability (Sertyesilisik & Sertyesilisik, 2014) as well as for the green innovations. Investments need to be carried out to adopt the future human resources to the changing working conditions in the future as well as to keep the education at the universities up-to-date (Sertyesilisik, 2017b, 2017c). The university curriculum needs to enable them to perform deep learning approach. This approach can be effective for enhancing sustainability in the construction industry (Al-Khaddar, Wooder, Sertyesilisik & Tunstall, 2012). Future professionals need to be equipped with the requirements of the contemporary and future construction industry (Sertyesilisik, 2017b, 2017c). Their capability to innovate especially to carry out green innovation can help them to find jobs. World Economic Forum (2016)' s report revealed that 'new energy supplies and technologies' as well as 'climate change, natural resources' are two of the main fields where the employment is being and expected to be increased for the period of 2015-2020.Furthermore, green innovation capability and capacity of the universities can contribute to the students' innovation capacity. International research and development programmes (e.g. Horizon 2020) play vital role in establishing and enhancing international and interdisciplinary collaboration which can create synergy through experience and infrastructure (e.g. laboratories) shared. Furthermore, benchmarking from companies the corporate social responsibility concept, universities can have university social responsibility. In this way, the universities can contribute not only to the supply side's sustainability performance and innovation capacity but also to the demand characteristics in favour of environmental friendly industry. Universities can play important role in enhancing communities' consciousness with respect to the sustainability ethics. They can enable the students to have sustainability culture.

Capability and Capacity Levels of the Pre-University Education: Future construction professionals' capacity to innovate depends on their education starting from their Kindergartenages. Policies need to enable budgets to be allocated for transformation of the education starting from kindergarten to foster innovation and green innovation. This transformation can foster innovation and green innovation. Furthermore, it can encourage change in the universities' curriculum. Especially, STEM (Science, Technology, Engineering, and Mathematics) or STEAM (Science, Technology, Engineering, Arts and Mathematics) education at the pre-university education has high potential for contributing to the innovation capacity of the future generations. Furthermore, STEM or STEAM education can foster the change in the universities' curriculums so that universities can comply with the students changing background, capacity, and requirements. For this reason, STEM or STEAM education can trigger the increase in the quality of the university education (Sertyesilisik, 2017c) as well as the innovation capacity and competitiveness of the university. Enhanced capacity of the graduates can foster the construction industry's progress, and innovation contributing to the countries' development and GDP. Furthermore, education needs to equip everyone with environment consciousness and sustainability ethics. In this way, green innovation culture can be established with the integration of the enhanced research and development capacities and capabilities of potential future professionals with their enhanced level of environment consciousness and sustainability ethics. Transformation in the education necessitates political commitment and industries' support. Figure 3 presents the impact of the education in enhancing green innovation capacity of the construction industry.

FUTURE RESEARCH DIRECTIONS

This chapter focused on and emphasised the importance of the political economy of the green innovations in the construction industry. Green innovations and construction industry play important role in the sustainable development. For this reason, effectiveness of the green innovations need to be enhanced. Future research is recommended to be carried out on the ways of:

- Enhancing interdisciplinary collaboration among universities and construction industry globally: Success of green innovations can be enhanced through interdisciplinary collaboration as well as through benchmarking from other industries' technologies and solutions. Furthermore, collaboration among universities and industries complement each other. The developed and competitive construction industry can demand and invest for green innovation enabling the universities to improve their research and development infrastructure, capacity and capability. For this reason, successful and effective strategies for enhancing interdisciplinary collaboration among universities and construction industry globally can contribute to the green innovation success rate.
- Enhancing research and development infrastructure of the universities and of the industries: Research and development capacity and capability of the universities and of the industries can be directly influenced by their research and development related infrastructure affecting accomplishment of the green inventions and green innovations. Furthermore, infrastructure of the universi-

Figure 3. Impact of the education in enhancing green innovation capacity of the construction industry

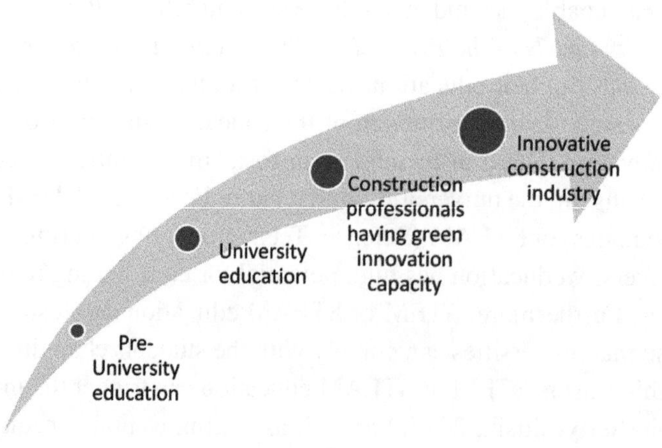

ties and of the industries can support each other through collaboration between universities and industries. For this reason, effective policies and strategies need to be used and established for enhancing research and development infrastructure, capacity and capabilities of the universities as well as of the industries.

- Identifying effectiveness of the policies for fostering green innovation in the construction industry: Identification of each policy's impact on fostering green innovation can be useful for policy makers in focusing on the most effective policies. In this way, they can allocate the resources in an efficient and effective way adhering to the Pareto principle.
- Identifying failures of the policies for fostering green innovation in the construction industry: Identification of the policies failed is important for policy makers to take the remedy action revising the relevant policies in the field of green innovation in the construction industry. Learning from the failed policies can reduce the risk of repeating the same failures and it can result in enhancing effectiveness of the policies to be followed in the future.
- Establishment of the insurance for failed inventions and innovations: Invention and innovation processes can be costly requiring money to be invested. Each invention and innovation process, however, has its risk of failure. This risk can discourage the companies to invest for research and development activities. For this reason, establishment of the insurance for failed inventions and innovations can be an effective tool for motivating the companies in investing in green inventions and innovations.

CONCLUSION

This chapter introduced and investigated the political economy of the green innovations in the construction industry. Despite of the construction industry's contribution to the global economy, its environmental footprint is big. Green innovations can result in the reduction in the environmental footprint of the construction industry. They can act as key tools for enhancing sustainability performance and competitiveness of the industry enabling construction industry to build not only for humanity living today but also for humanity of the future while creating value for the next generations. Successful green innovations can contribute to the corporate social responsibility in the construction industry due to their potential impact on the economy, nature, welfare and wellbeing of the humanity. In other words, contribution of the green innovations to the corporate social responsibility can be enabled through humanity's self-respect, as well as through respecting the nature, and future generations. For this reason, sustainability ethics, green innovations, and corporate social responsibility are interrelated.

Economic, political and legal, and environmental factors as well as their interaction drive the need for green innovation in the construction industry. All these factors' interactions need to be carefully observed and managed so that their interactions can create synergy. Threat of the climate change and its adverse consequences further act as push factors for green innovations. Humanity has started to gain first-hand experience in the field of climate change caused disasters. Impact of the climate change threat in acting as driver for green innovations depends on the humanity's perception and understanding of the severity of the adverse consequences of the climate change. The climate change threat and its adverse consequences as well as the way it is perceived can contribute to increase in the inelasticity of demand for green innovations. Humanity's consciousness for the importance of the green innovations can be enhanced through education.

Contemporary green innovations in the construction industry are mainly in the fields of construction project management, material and constructions. The effectiveness and success of these innovations can be fostered by effective political economy and strategies based on the following constructs: drivers (e.g. market driven and environmental factors), policies (e.g. incentives, education, investment, art, and collaboration); capability and capacity levels of the construction industry (e.g. experience, expertise, and infrastructure); capability and capacity levels of the universities as well as capability and capacity levels of the pre-university education. For this reason, political economy of and strategies for enhancing green innovation can be prepared and established considering these constructs in addition to other subjects which are perceived to be effective and efficient. These policies need to be kept updated with the needs of the construction industry and changes in the industries. Furthermore, their effectiveness need to be monitored so that failed policies can be replaced with the more effective and successful solutions for enhancing green innovation in the construction industry. Green innovations contributions to the welfare and wellbeing of the society needs to be highlighted to enhance the awareness of the people. Policies need to consider incentives and subsidies as well as insurances for green inventions and green innovations to encourage and support green innovation climate.

Political economy for fostering green innovation in the construction industry needs to enable and encourage interdisciplinary and global collaboration among the universities and construction industry as well as integration of the construction industry and universities. Effective political economy for green innovation needs to encourage companies and the universities to invest in their research and development infrastructure. Furthermore, innovation culture needs to be integrated to the companies' culture. Political economy for green innovation can encourage global green trade and green energy usage in the construction industry. Green innovation can be fostered through policies updating pre-university, university and post-graduate education in a way to enhance innovation capability, capacity, and culture of the future construction professionals. Professionals, politicians, researchers and academics are expected to get benefit from this chapter.

REFERENCES

Adams, R., Jeanrenaud, S., Bessant, J., Denyer, D., & Overy, P. (2016). Sustainability oriented innovation: A systematic review. *International Journal of Management Reviews*, *18*(2), 180–205. doi:10.1111/ijmr.12068

Ahmed, P. K. (1998). Culture and climate for innovation. *European Journal of Innovation Management*, *1*(1), 30–43. doi:10.1108/14601069810199131

Al-Khaddar, R., Wooder, T., Sertyesilisik, B., & Tunstall, A. (2012). Deep Learning Approach's Effectiveness on Sustainability Improvement in the UK Construction Industry. *Management of Environmental Quality*, *23*(2), 126–139. doi:10.1108/14777831211204886

BBC website. (2018). *Ethics guide*. Retrieved from http://www.bbc.co.uk/ethics/introduction/intro_1.shtml

Burritt, R., Guthrie, J., Evans, E., & Christ, K. (2017). Expanding Collaboration Between Industry and Business Faculties in Australia. In Improving Collaboration Between Industry and Business Schools. RMIT University.

CaliBaja Center for Resilient Materials & Systems website. (2017). *Home: CaliBaja Center for Resilient Materials & Systems*. Retrieved from http://jacobsschool.ucsd.edu/resilientmaterials/

Chen, Y. S., Lai, S. B., & Wen, C. T. (2006). The influence of green innovation performance on corporate advantage in Taiwan. *Journal of Business Ethics*, *67*(4), 331–339. doi:10.100710551-006-9025-5

Choudhary, R. (n.d.). *What is meant by smart materials?* Retrieved from https://www.quora.com/What-is-meant-by-smart-materials

Criscuolo, C., & Menon, C. (2015). Environmental policies and risk finance in the green sector: Cross-country evidence. *Energy Policy*, *83*, 38–56. doi:10.1016/j.enpol.2015.03.023

Das, A. (n.d.). *What is meant by smart materials?* Retrieved from https://www.quora.com/What-is-meant-by-smart-materials

Dobni, C.B. (2008). Measuring innovation culture in organizations: The development of a generalized innovation culture construct using exploratory factor analysis. *European Journal of Innovation Management, 11*(4), 539-559. doi:10.1108/14601060810911156

GCSE Bitesize website. (n.d.). *Smart materials*. Retrieved from http://www.bbc.co.uk/schools/gcsebitesize/design/electronics/materialsrev5.shtml

Hagel, J., Brown, J. S., Samoylova, T., & Lui, M. (2013). *From exponential technologies to exponential innovation Report 2 of the 2013 Shift Index series*. Retrieved from https://www2.deloitte.com/insights/us/en/industry/technology/from-exponential-technologies-to-exponential-innovation.html

Hughes, T., O'Regan, N., & Wornham, D. (2008). The credibility issue: Closing the academic/practitioner gap. *Strategic Change*, *17*(7-8), 215–233. doi:10.1002/jsc.828

Investopedia website. (n.d.). *Production possibility frontier*. Retrieved from https://www.investopedia.com/terms/p/productionpossibilityfrontier.asp

Jahns, C. (2010). Preface. In A. Lopez-Claros (Ed.), *The innovation for development report 2009-2010: Strengthening innovation for the prosperity of nations. European Business School.* Palgrave MacMillan.

Kaklauskas, A., Banaitis, A., Ferreira, F. A. F., Ferreira, J. J. M.. Amaratunga, D., … Banaitiene, N. (2018). *An Evaluation System for University–Industry Partnership Sustainability: Enhancing Options for Entrepreneurial Universities*. Academic Press.

Kemp, R., & Pearson, P. (2007). *Final Report MEI Project about Measuring Eco-innovation*. Maastricht: UM Merit.

Li, D., Zheng, M., Cao, C., Chen, X., Ren, S., & Huang, M. (2017). The impact of legitimacy pressure and corporate profitability on green innovation: Evidence from China top 100. *Journal of Cleaner Production, 141*, 41–49. doi:10.1016/j.jclepro.2016.08.123

Metroplan Ltd. Website. (2011). *Eco-friendly a range of products that won't cost the earth.* Retrieved from http://www.metroplan-ecofriendly.co.uk/sustainable-material

Mousavi, S., & Bossink, B. A. G. (2017). Firms' capabilities for sustainable innovation: The case of biofuel for aviation. *Journal of Cleaner Production*, *167*, 1263–1275. doi:10.1016/j.jclepro.2017.07.146

Nielsen, C. (2017). A personal reflection: European experiences on value exchange in university–industry collaborations. *Academic Leadership Series*, *8*, 53–61.

OECD website. (2018a). *Financing Climate Futures: Rethinking Infrastructure*. Retrieved from http://www.oecd.org/environment/cc/climate-futures/?utm_source=Adestra&utm_medium=email&utm_content=Financing%20Climate%20Futures%3A%20Rethinking%20Infrastructure&utm_campaign=Climate%20change%20%282nd%20edition%29&utm_term=demo

OECD website. (2018b). *Effective Carbon Rates 2018 - Pricing Carbon Emissions Through Taxes and Emissions Trading*. Retrieved from http://www.oecd.org/tax/effective-carbon-rates-2018-9789264305304-en.htm?utm_source=Adestra&utm_medium=email&utm_content=&utm_campaign=Financing%20Climate%20Futures%20%28DRAFT%29&utm_term=demo

Porter, M. E., & Van der Linde, C. (1995). Toward a new conception of the environment-competitiveness relationship. *The Journal of Economic Perspectives*, *9*(4), 97–118. doi:10.1257/jep.9.4.97

Rennings, K. (2000). Redefining innovation – eco-innovation research and the contribution from ecological economics. *Ecological Economics*, *32*(2), 319–332. doi:10.1016/S0921-8009(99)00112-3

Sahli, I., & Rejeb, J. B. (2015). The Environmental Kuznets Curve and Corruption in the Mena Region. World Conference on Technology, Innovation and Entrepreneurship. *Procedia: Social and Behavioral Sciences*, *195*, 1648–1657. doi:10.1016/j.sbspro.2015.06.231

Saunila, M., Ukko, J., & Rantala, T. (2018). Sustainability as a driver of green innovation investment and exploitation. *Journal of Cleaner Production*, *179*, 631–641. doi:10.1016/j.jclepro.2017.11.211

Sertyesilisik, B. (2014). Lean and Agile Construction Project Management: As a Way of Reducing Environmental Footprint of the Construction Industry. In H. Xu, & X. Wang (Eds.), Optimization and Control Methods in Industrial Engineering and Construction Intelligent Systems, Control and Automation: Science and Engineering. Springer Verlag.

Sertyesilisik, B. (2016a). A preliminary study on the regenerative construction project management concept for enhancing sustainability performance of the construction industry. *International Journal of Construction Management*, 1-17. doi:10.1080/15623599.2016.1222665

Sertyesilisik, B. (2016b). Embedding sustainability dynamics in the lean construction supply chain management. *YBL Journal of Built Environment.*, *4*(1), 60–78. doi:10.1515/jbe-2016-0006

Sertyesilisik, B. (2017a). Building Information Modelling as a tool for enhancing disaster resilience of the construction industry. *Transactions of the VSB – Technical University of Ostrava, 12*(1), 9-18.

Sertyesilisik, B. (2017b). Global Trends in the Construction Industry: Challenges of Employment. In F. Yenilmez & E. Kılıç (Eds.), *Handbook of Research on Unemployment and Labor Market Sustainability in the Era of Globalization* (pp. 255–274). IGI Global Publishing. doi:10.4018/978-1-5225-2008-5.ch015

Sertyesilisik, B. (2017c). Enhancing Global Competency of Future Construction Professionals. In L. Leavitt, S. Wisdom, & K. Leavitt (Eds.), *Cultural Awareness and Competency Development in Higher Education*. IGI Global Publishing. doi:10.4018/978-1-5225-2145-7.ch016

Sertyesilisik, B. (2017d). Green Marketing as a Tool for Reducing Environmental Footprint of the Construction Industry. In *Green Marketing and Environmental Responsibility in Modern Corporations* (pp. 1–30). IGI Global Publishing. doi:10.4018/978-1-5225-2331-4.ch001

Sertyesilisik, B. (2018a). Ways for Achieving Sustainable Development and Enhancing Welfare of the Urban Poor. In S. N. Zubairu & O. F. Adedayo (Eds.), *Inclusive City Growth and the Poor: Policies, Challenges and Prospects*. Community Participation Research Group Publisher.

Sertyesilisik, B. (2018b). Global Sustainability Leadership: A Key for the Peace in the World. In Global Leadership Initiatives for Conflict Resolution and Peace building. IGI Global Publishing. doi:10.4018/978-1-5225-4993-2.ch003

Sertyesilisik, B. (2018c). Potential Changes in the Demand and Supply Sides in the Construction Industry: Emerging Concepts for the Sustainable and Innovative Economy. In B. Christiansen (Ed.), *Emerging Economic Models for Global Sustainability and Social Development*. IGI Global Publishing.

Sertyesilisik, B., & Kivircik, I. (2017). Integrated BIM Usage in Construction Project: As a Way of Enhancing Sustainability and Lean Performance of Construction Industry. In P. Wu (Ed.), *Integrated Building Information Modelling*. Bentham Science Publication. doi:10.2174/9781681084572117010011

Sertyesilisik, B., Remiszewski, B., & Al-Khaddar, R. (2012). Sustainable waste management in the UK construction industry. *International Journal of Construction Project Management.*, *4*(2), 173–188.

Sertyesilisik, B., & Sertyesilisik, E. (2015). Sustainability Leaders for Sustainable Cities. In Leadership and Sustainability in the Built Environment. Spon Research, Routledge.

Sertyesilisik, B., & Sertyesilisik, E. (2016). Ways of Fostering Green Economy and Green Growth. In W. Filho, D.M. Pociovalisteanu, & A. Q. Al-Amin (Eds.), Sustainable Economic Development: Green Economy and Green Growth. Springer.

Sertyesilisik, B., & Sertyesilisik, E. (2016). Eco industrial Development: As a Way of Enhancing Sustainable Development. *Journal of Economic Development Environment and People.*, *5*(1), 6–27. doi:10.26458/jedep.v5i1.133

Steiber, A., & Alänge, S. (2013). A corporate system for continuous innovation: The case of Google Inc. *European Journal of Innovation Management*, *16*(2), 243–264. doi:10.1108/14601061311324566

Sustainable Materials website. (2018). *How Sustainable Materials Should be Used in Construction.* Retrieved from http://www.sustainablematerials.org.uk/

Tsai, W. H., Yang, C. H., Huang, C. T., & Wu, Y. Y. (2017). The impact of the carbon tax policy on green building strategy. *Journal of Environmental Planning and Management*, *60*(8), 1412–1438. doi: 10.1080/09640568.2016.1221800

Walker, D. H. T., Anbari, F. T., Bredillet, C., Söderlund, J., Cicmil, S., & Thomas, J. (2008). Collaborative academic/practitioner research in project management: Examples and applications. *International Journal of Managing Projects in Business*, *1*(2), 168–192. doi:10.1108/17538370810866313

World Economic Forum. (2016). *The Future Jobs Employment, Skills and Workforce Strategy for the Fourth Industrial Revolution*. Retrieved from http://www3.weforum.org/docs/WEF_Future_of_Jobs.pdf

Xu, Y., Zhang, L., Yeh, C. H., & Liu, Y. (2018). Evaluating WEEE recycling innovation strategies with interacting sustainability-related criteria. *Journal of Cleaner Production, 190*, 618–629. doi:10.1016/j.jclepro.2018.04.078

Ziemnowicz, C. (2013). Joseph A. Schumpeter and Innovation. In Encyclopedia of Creativity, Invention, Innovation and Entrepreneurship. Springer. doi:10.1007/978-1-4614-3858-8

KEY TERMS AND DEFINITIONS

Circular Economy: Economy that is based on reduced or eliminated waste both from lean and sustainability point of views. Circular economy can be supported by green innovations, eco-industrial development zones, and effective political economy.

Construction Industry: Industry that supplies infrastructure and superstructure constructions as well as their inputs (e.g., construction materials).

Global Green Innovation: Green innovation that has impact at the global level.

Green Energy: Energy that is generated in an environmentally friendly way with the help of renewable energy sources.

Green Innovation: Innovation especially at the product, material and production process levels, that respects sustainability of the nature and of the future generations as well as contributes to the sustainable development and to the regeneration of the nature.

Green Policies: Policies enhancing and contributing to the sustainability performance of the demand and supply sides.

Innovation: Invention especially at the product, material and production levels that has been reached to the market and customer.

Policies: Guiding rules at the country level.

Political Economy: Effects of the policies on the economy and effects of the economy on the policies.

Political Economy of the Green Innovation: Interactions among political economy, environment and green innovations. Politic and economic decisions and factors affect green innovation rate, its effectiveness, sustainability of the nature and of the future generations as well as green innovations affecting policies, economy, nature and future generations.

Political Economy of the Green Innovation in the Construction Industry: Interactions among green innovations in the construction industry, political economy, and environment.

Political Economy of the Innovation: Two-way interaction of political economy and innovations. Political and economic decisions and factors affect innovation rate and effectiveness as well as innovations affecting policies and economy.

Chapter 21
Ecological Vision of Mahatma Gandhi in Contemporary World

Anandita Biswas
Diamond Harbour Women's University, India

ABSTRACT

Environmental degradation and concern for environmental protection and maintaining ecological balance in the last few decades has become the subject of serious political contention and public outcry. Human activity in the name of development has adversely affected the global biodiversity in an unprecedented manner. Eco-development demands structural and moral transformation of the current social, political, and value system. It presupposes a participatory political structure that allows maximum devolution of power to the local communities. And such a coordination and cooperation between development discourse and survival of nature can be found in the works and ideas of Mahatma Gandhi.

INTRODUCTION

Life has existed on earth for millions of years in a highly diverse form with millions of species. But roughly during the last couple of decades, 'life providing conditions' on our planet have changed in such a drastic way as to create a crisis of survival. It is the need of the hour to replace the modernist version of development agenda by a model that respects the real, basic needs of all human beings and all forms of life of this generation as well as the generations to come. It is feasible only if diversity and equality, human rights and love for life, respect and compassion for every form of life-existence are accepted as founding principles of public policy, social organizations and governmental initiative. The present-day development model is driven by competition and greed rather than self-restraint and need. The apathy of the modern economy towards the extent and manner of resource use has been criticized by the environmentalists. In the words of Edward O. Wilson, one of the world's leading experts on bio-diversity, biologists generally agree that "on the land at least and on a worldwide basis, species are vanishing 100 times faster than before the arrival of Homo sapiens" (Dogra, 2010, p.7).

DOI: 10.4018/978-1-5225-8547-3.ch021

This chapter quite logically and pertinently resonates to the theme of the book by highlighting the detailed analysis of the current crisis human civilization is going through. The chapter in a vivid manner emphasizes the major political and economic implication of Green trading on basing the argument from an environment-friendly perspective with philosophical conjecture. Case studies related to particular environmental issues and movements can further substantiate the philosophical standpoint of the arguments the chapter has dealt with. The purpose of my paper is to examine the ways in which environmental issues affect human lives and other life forms and how the existing policies and programmes address this vital aspect of existence. The structure of the chapter will begin by elucidating the basic concepts of development, ecology and sustainable development and the relationship among them. Thereafter, the chapter will proceed to discuss in detail the Gandhian perspectives on environment and ecology corroborating it with Gandhian philosophy. The third section of the chapter will deal with the feasibility of implementation of Gandhian principles. It will highlight the environmental movement in India focusing on *Narmada Bachao Andolan* and *Chipko* movement which were living examples of Gandhian environmentalism that portrayed him as a 'man with deep ecological view of life'. The books referred to are sufficient to build an ideological base. However, upcoming research works on Green trading and environmental issues can definitely substantiate the present theme of the work. The following chapter is primarily based on philosophical insights rather than statistical or numerical data analysis. As environmental issues demand graver attention and prompt action coupled with immediate implementation of policies and programmes, philosophical or hypothetical re-questioning of the environmental crisis is generally regarded as redundant. That is the reason there happens to be literature void and adequate background information to the theme I dealt with in this chapter.

More *a priori* debate and value-oriented research of environmental issues needs to be inculcated by scholars and academicians. Case studies related to particular environmental issues and moments can substantiate the philosophical standpoint of the arguments the chapter has dealt with. The chapter has made an attempt to deal with the current issues of industrialism along with the modernization drive that dictate the present political establishment with its natural fall out on environmental balance. However, statistical analysis and field surveys are missing in this chapter which can, though be taken up by the researchers in future. Thus, the future scope to further the analytical framework related to this theme remains open.

Major weaknesses of the work are

- Lack of adequate historical analysis.
- Data and statistical frameworks have been totally ignored.
- References primarily dealt with value-oriented knowledge and less on policy research.

However, the major strength of this chapter lies in the fact that

- Serious issues that deal with particularly the 'vulnerable' and 'marginalized' section of the populace should make a starting point basing on value oriented research instead of relying on a value neutral one.
- Moreover, environmental issues are such that it touches the 'core' and the 'periphery', biotic and the abiotic existence, present and the future of a civilization. Therefore a superb agglomeration between philosophical insights and quantitative research is the need of the time, which has holistically been dealt with in the present paper.

The conflict between the ecological and economic imperatives is institutionalized in a kind of 'ideological schizophrenia', while economic growth is sacrosanct, so is the 'environment' and there exist a tacit battle for mastery between them. The post-industrial revolution era witnessed spectacular advancement in science and technology that sought to make people's life comfortable but at the cost of environment. The natural fall-out of industrialization and urbanization was destruction of forests and wetlands, exhaustion of fossil fuels, minerals and underground water. The ozone layer at the stratosphere is getting depleted making way for almost uninterrupted entry of harmful ultraviolet rays from the sun. Tropical rain forest, once considered as the lungs of the planet, generating over 20 per cent of oxygen, is being rapidly destroyed by the wood and paper-pulp traders. Air and water are being heavily polluted. The research journal *Science* recently warned that the Earth's forests, deserts, landscapes and vital ecosystems risk a "major transformation" in the next century due to climate change "if we allow climate change to go unchecked, the vegetation of this planet is going to look completely different than it does today, and that means a huge risk to the diversity of the planet" says the co-author Jonathan Overpeck, dean of the School for Environment and Sustainability at the University of Michigan (The Statesman, 2018, p. 12).

The rampant and corrosive usage of natural resources has made development unsustainable and destructive in nature. However, the broader question that remains is, if growth-oriented development leads to destruction of nature what is the way out? Should development stop in order to protect environment? The consensus is that neither should development stop nor nature be annihilated. Therefore, the probable reconcilement between the two is sustainable development or eco-development.

ENVIRONMENT, ECOLOGY AND THE POLITICS OF DEVELOPMENT

Twenty centuries of 'progress' have brought the average citizen a vote, a national anthem, a Ford, a bank account, and a high opinion of himself, but not the capacity to live in high density without befouling and denuding his environment, nor a conviction that such capacity, rather than such density, is the true test of whether he is civilized.

A thing is right when it tends to preserve the integrity, stability, and beauty of the biotic community. (Leopold, 1993, Game Management)

Environment is the basis of an organism's sustenance. Without an environment, conducive to it, no organism can survive. The environment consists of both the biotic world- the flora and fauna, and also the physical world- soil, water, air, etc. Each and every organism shares a complex relationship with its environment. Both the organism and its environment are dependent on each other. The sustenance of one broadly defines the development of the other. Any disruption of this inter-dependent cycle breaks the entire cycle of 'eco-balance.' What we call the eco-system is the superb maintenance of inter-dependent relationship of each units of the family of environment.

Human habitations have evolved within certain environmental structure and life supporting conditions. It is impossible for a human being to live in another planet where there is no air to breathe, no water to drink or no suitable temperature to survive. Thus, survival is based on certain conditions that make it possible for lives to live. Soil, water, flora and fauna, etc, constitute 'the ecological infrastructure of society.' The term 'ecology' is derived from two Greek words, 'oikos'- meaning household or dwelling, and 'logos', meaning science. Ernst Haeckel, a German biologist in 1866 defined ecology as 'the science of relations between organisms and their environment'. He coined the word *Oecologie*, that later changed as *ecology* in 1893 (Ball, 2003, p. 535). Initially, it evolved as a sub-field of biology. J.L. Chapman and M.J. Reiss defined ecology as the study of organisms in relations to the surroundings in which they live. These surroundings are called the environment of the organism. Environment comprises of two basic components – physical or abiotic and living or biotic. Ecology interrogates the basic reality that why an organism lives in a particular atmosphere and physical surrounding and not in another, why a particular type of environment is best suited to the survival and reproduction of particular species. These are the questions that demands relentless investigation and sincere contemplation- for ecology "is like an enormous jigsaw puzzle" (Chakraborty, 2001, p. 417).

The term 'ecology' has three aspects – a discipline, a system and a perception. Ecology as a discipline and as a system is the domain of the scientists. The political application of the term is concerned with the third dimension, i.e. ecological perspective with its moral and ethical foundation (Vinod & Deshpande, 2013, pp. 429-444). Andrew Dobson attempts to differentiate between environmentalism and ecologism (Dobson, 1995, pp. 2-3). Environmentalism is primarily a managerial approach to environmental problems. The intrinsic assumption of environmentalism is that the current predicaments and dilemmas are caused by the prevalent patterns of production and distribution and thus it confirms that by transforming them and co-opting new patterns can lead to solution to environmental problem. This is rather a technocratic approach to 'save the planet', to use O'Riordan's terminology. On the other hand, ecologism holds that a sustainable and fulfilling existence presupposes radical changes in our relationship with the non-human natural world and in our mode of social and political life (Luke, 2009, pp. 487-498). Thus, ecologism examines the anthropocentric worldview of environmentalism. As Dobson states, "Ecologism can properly take its place alongside other political ideologies; in common with other political ideologies it has things to say across the whole range of political, social and economic life" (Dobson, 1990, p. 3). According to Dobson "ecologism seeks radically to call into question a whole series of political, economic and social practices; it envisages a postindustrial future that is quite distinct from that which we are most generally acquainted" (Dobson, 1995, pp. 2-3). Ecologism as an ideology motivates a new perspective towards- a) society-nature relationship and b) traditional-economic logic. Ecology as a discipline within the broader circumference of social science deals with four primary issues – environmental pollution, depletion of natural resources, population growth and the destruction of the survival economy by the economy driven by market compulsion. The emergence of a new, non- conventional, anti-mainstream ideology thus came to be known as ecologism or ecocentrism (Chattopadhyay, 2006, pp. 83-92).

Ecologism as an ideology is opposed to 'technocentrism'. David Pepper states, "Technocentrism recognizes environmental problems but believes either unrestrainedly that our current form of society will always solve them and achieve unlimited growth… or more cautiously, that by careful economic and environmental management they can be negotiated…In either case considerable faith is placed in the usefulness of classical science, technology, conventional economic reasoning…Technocratics envisage no radical alteration of social, economic or political structures" (Pepper, 1993, pp.3-4).

Ecologism, on the other hand, considers human kind a part of the macro global ecosystem and should be or subjected to the ecological laws. Pepper argues that these ecological laws constrain human action, particularly through imposing limits to economic and population growth…Ecocentrics lack faith in modern large-scale technology and the technical and bureaucratic elites, and they abhor centralization and materialism (Pepper, 1993). Even ecocentrism is not free of extremism. There are certain ideologues within the doctrine who prefer a 'deep' ecology and favour an agrarian economy within the system having no industry at all (Chattopadhyay, 2006, p. 84).

Ecocentrism gives primacy to ecology while anthropocentrism deals with man-centric project. The discourse on anthropocentrism in environment study has a history of five-six decades. In 1967, Lynn White introduced the issue of anthropocentrism to a significant focus as the cardinal issue in environmental discussion.

Anthropocentrism is an understanding that deduces man to be at the centre of the universe and located him at the apex order. He is the possessor and the controller of the entire abode and the nature was there to satiate his thirst and lust. The whole gamut of existence and environmental cycle is man-centric and therefore what he does for self-gratification even at the cost of the environment is justifiable. Anthropocentrism is such an extreme doctrine that justifies endless and ruthless usage of nature and natural variant to satiate human need and beastly greed. No measurement of sustainable usage or balancing nature on ethical ground was taken into consideration. Thus, nature exists for man and human-need becomes the measure of all things: man with his special faculty of rationality has every right to use nature for his purpose. This extreme position has come to be known as *strong anthropocentrism*. On the other hand, there is yet another understanding which suggests on rational consideration checks on human actions can be justified. This position gradually came to be known as *weak anthropocentrism*. This is yet a man-centric ideology, though moderate in its disposition. It, at least, attempts to bind human action to a certain extent on the ground that nature has to be preserved in order to meet human needs in the long run. It also argued that unbridled usage of nature and uncontrolled use of resources is irrational as it will affect human interest in future. If nature is exploited injudiciously even human survival will be at stake. Therefore, restriction on reckless exploitation of nature is a necessary prerequisite for the sustainability of the human race. It is from this perspective, the notion of 'sustainable development' gained momentum (Vinod and Deshpande, 2013, p. 436).

DEEP ECOLOGY

The origin of Deep Ecology dates back to an essay published by the Norwegian Arne Naess in 1972 that initiated the project for the environmentalists to embrace an ethic called the biospheric egalitarianism that would locate humans on a more or less equal echelon with other species. Biospheric egalitarianism would be a truly 'deep' ecology, in contrast to the 'shallow' ecology which concerned itself entirely on pollution or resource depletion without penetrating deep into issues of serious ecological crisis. Therefore, as Ramchandra Guha asserts, in philosophical term, Deep Ecology can be stated as distinctive from anthropocentrism. The belief that humans stand apart and above the rest of creation is the clear message of anthropocentrism whereas biocentrism rejects a human-centered perspective by perceiving history from the perspective of other species and nature as a whole (Guha, 2014, p. 116). Anne Naess, the pioneer of Deep Ecology outlines eight principles for uniting Deep Ecologists:

- The flourishing of human and nonhuman beings has intrinsic worth. The worth of nonhuman beings is independent of their usefulness for human purposes.
- Richness and diversity of life forms on earth, including forms of human cultures, have intrinsic worth.
- Humans have no right to reduce this richness and diversity, except to satisfy vital needs.
- The flourishing of human life and cultures is compatible with a substantially smaller human population.

- Present human interference with the nonhuman world is excessive, and the situation is worsening.
- The foregoing points indicates that changes are necessary in the dominant way humans until now have behaved in their relation to the earth as a whole. The changes will, in a fundamental manner, affect political, social, technological, economic, and ideological structures.
- The ideological change in the rich countries will mainly be that of increased appreciation of life quality rather than high material standard of living, in this way preparing [the way for] a global state of ecologically sustainable development.
- Those who subscribe to the foregoing points have an obligation, directly or indirectly, to try to implement the necessary changes by nonviolent means (Rothenberg, 1993, pp. 127-128, cited in Guha, 2014, p. 117).

The significance of Deep Ecology was reflected in many debates and discussion, in and outside the academic world. It gradually came to be accepted that the presence and activities of humans have been and will be the greatest threat to the survival of other species. Deep Ecology finds anthropocentrism as problematic. Deep Ecologists argue that human being should live nonchalantly and judiciously and should not try to transform the nature or its natural balance. Nature possesses an intrinsic value and it will be endangered if we do not maintain the natural law of balance. Deep Ecologism highlights the immanence of mystification and engages in deification of nature. However, it is also true that neither extreme anthropocentrism nor extreme anti-anthropocentrism is a prudent proposition in real world. What is feasible is a moderate Ecologism that dismisses absolute anthropocentrism while accepting moderate anthropocentrism that highlights the necessity and urgency of protection of nature for the interest of the humans. It needs to be remembered that nature has to be protected not only for nature's sake but more importantly for sake of survival of human civilization.

For Ecologism, a sustainable society needs to be based on three corresponding ideologies of bio-regionalism, biodiversity and biocentrism. These principles demand a far-reaching metamorphosis not only in our social habits and practices but also mental set-up and psychological dispensation.

These transformation needs to be founded on the belief that the Earth as a physical object is not extensive but limited in its purpose and ambit. Given this finitude, Ecologism contends that it is most essential to remember that 'the Earth itself has a limited carrying capacity (for population), productive capacity (for resources of all types) and absorbent capacity (for pollution)' (Dobson, 1990, p. 117).

Therefore, the Earth is finite in its manifestation. The finitude of the Earth thus puts three limits to human habits and practices,

- Limits to economic growth,
- Limits to consumption and
- Limits to population growth

Unlimited productions exhaust natural resources and subvert the stability of the economy of the entire ecosystem. The ideology of Ecologism vehemently protests against the consumerist ideology of the modern market economy. The doctrine of Ecologism is founded on certain ethical values, restrained habits and rational practices, which are pathetically absent in the conventional market economy (Chattopadhyay, 2006, pp. 90-91).

At present it is the workings of the economic system that is the major challenge to the resource base of the planet. Currently, the ecological crisis portrays a situation where the 'raw materials' or in other words the natural world is in revolt against an industrial system. This scenario threatens to return the planet to Chapter One of the Genesis, when 'the earth was waste and void, and darkness was the face of the deep'. Since the collapse of Communism and 'end of ideology', one idea that has preoccupied the mind of the people and soul of the states is relentless competition and prodigious consumption, rampant destruction of nature and natural habitant and erosion of moral values and ethics. Intensified resource-use, contamination by million chemicals in the global environment, the effect on climate resulting in climate change and global warming, the consequences of the uninhibited extension of global capital, now threaten the world beyond anything previously wrought by human activity upon earth. That the beneficiaries of this process have become addicted to its continuation into perpetuity only intensifies the danger (Seabrook, 2006, p. 7).

Scholars and academicians expressed their reservations to the economic perspective of development. The vehement opposition however, came from the Latin American countries. An alternative approach was looked for that would challenge the single focused economic-growth approach and would concentrate upon social justice. Therefore, in response to the lacuna of economic development model, there emerged the concept of human development that involved studies of human condition focusing on capability approach. The concept of human development was first put forward by Amartya Sen and elaborated by Martha Nussbaum, Sabina Alkire, Ingrid Robeyns. According to them, the primary concern of development should be the expansion of the choices of people so that they can lead lives that value and consequently improve the human condition in order to make people live full lives. Therefore, human development is not simply about economic growth. It is much more than that. Here, economic growth is simply a means that will expand peoples' choices to achieve the end that is living full life with human dignity and honour. These choices will be enlarged once human capabilities are building up. Capabilities are "the substantive freedoms [a person] enjoys to lead the kind of life [they have] reason to value" (Sen, 1999, p. 87). The primary capabilities for human development are: to lead long and healthy lives, to be knowledgeable (to be educated), to have access to the resources and social services needed for a decent standard of living and to be able to participate in the life of the community. Without these, many choices are simply not available and many opportunities in life remain inaccessible. Undoubtedly, philosophers, theoreticians, economists and political leaders have always been emphasizing the humanitarian aspect of development.

A path breaking event happened in 1990 when a new concept of development emerged. The UNDP defined development from altogether a different perspective. The First Report on Human Development tried to define it "as a process of enlarging the range of people's choices increasing their opportunities for education, health care, income and employment and covering the full range of human choices from a sound physical environment to economic and political freedom". The Report further stated, "this report is about people and about how development enlarges their choices. It is about more than GNP growth, more than income and wealth and more than producing commodities and accumulating capital. A person's access to income may be one of the choices, but it is not the sum total of human behavior". It viewed human development as "a process of enlarging people's choices. The most critical of these wide-ranging choices are to live a long and healthy life, to be educated and to have access to resources needed for a decent standard of living. Additional choices include political freedom, guaranteed human rights and personal self-respect". The 1990 report introduced the Human Development Index (HDI) and identified three essential elements as primary to human life: life, expectancy, knowledge and decent standard of living (Ghosh, 2009, p. 322).

But how will a life survive decently in a 'gas chamber'? Delhi High Court in a verdict regarding the pollution level in Delhi identified the capital city as nothing short of a gas chamber. The holy Ganges, once the pride of our country is now a breeding ground of *Coliforms. E. Coli*, *streptococci* and *Clostridium perferingens* bacteria. It is now the dumping ground of human excreta, waste and industrial waste. Unrestricted and illegal constructions, deforestation, soil erosion, automobile and other chemical as well as biological pollution in every possible way are threatening the survival of life on earth. And, unfortunately, it is human being who is responsible for his own annihilation.

Claude Alvares rightly says, the "logic of industrialization demands ample space, geographical space, colonies. The industrialization effort of the South (after independence) has to interiorize the concept of the colonies- colonizing its own hinterlands, mostly settled with subsistent and ecologically harmonious communities, and subordinating these to the requirements of the industrial programme" (Alvares, 1992, p. 6).

Thus, on one count, at least, the Rio Conference of 1992 was a watershed in modern environmental history. We do not talk anymore of development; we are talking of 'sustainable development.' This change is truly defining as now at least an attempt would be made to make development aim at respecting the threshold of nature. Population is rising and with it pollution and waste is piling up too. Modern civilization along with technological innovation and superfast lifestyle is 'gifting the earth chemical and e-waste. Natural resources have become scarce and random disposal of waste has brought the gates of inferno closer to mankind.

SUSTAINABLE DEVELOPMENT

The obvious question that comes to our mind is if growth-oriented development is destructive in nature, what is the option available? Should development come to a halt in order to protect environment? One section of the environmentalist preferred to implement the prescription of zero-growth as it is the only way to safeguard environment. The other section though preferred to go back to the 'golden days' of harmonious relation between man and nature. But for many environmentalists, neither should development stop nor nature be annihilated or destroyed to pursue development agenda. A reconcilement between the two can be achieved through the project and policy of 'sustainable development'.

The 1960s witnessed the emergence, particularly in the western industrialized world, of the 'modern environmentalism'. Rachel Carson's *Silent Spring* (1962) on the ecological repercussion of use of pesticides, is often considered to be an epoch-making venture in the history of environmentalism. It is considered to be the first environmental critique of industrial agriculture and modern urbanization. *Silent Spring* expeditiously set the context for other writings on the issue of environment. With this, a range of critiques aimed against development practices, started to gather considerable political and social traction. Challenges to developmental practices, moreover, found expression in two sharply voiced and contending ideological frames- namely the unsettling of the idea of development as orthodoxy by popular ecological struggles, alongside perspectives that pressed for managerial strategies aimed at greening development outcomes. Sustainable development had its birth from such ideological and technical warp and woof (D'Souza, 2012, p. 181).

A sustainable society, as projected by ecologists is founded on three inter-related, mutually-inclusive values- bioregionalism, biodiversity and biocentrism.

A bioregion is a geographical entity that is nourished by and flourished with flora and fauna, minerals and diverse kinds of metals. A bioregion survives in tune with its own rhythm - we must get to know the land around us, learn its lore and its potential, and live with it and not against it (Dobson, 1990, p. 117). Ecologism deplores the obliteration of bioregional spirit in a world overloaded with an insane spree of industrialization and craving for sumptuousness. It demands that one should be aware of the source of the food one get to eat.

Bioregionalism signifies biodiversity that stresses the coexistence and mutuality of variant flora and fauna. The production syndrome of mainstream development pattern refutes the essence of biodiversity. This complex state has been superbly elucidated by the well-known environmentalist Vandana Shiva: 'The spread of monocultures of "fast-growing species" in forestry and "high-yielding varieties" in agriculture has been justified on grounds of increased productivity. All technological transformation of biodiversity is justified in the language of "improvement" and increase of "economic value". However, "improvement" and "value" are not neutral terms. They are contextual and value-laden. Improvement of tree species means one thing for a paper corporation which needs pulping wood and an entirely different thing for a peasant who needs fodder and green manure. Improvement of crop species means one thing for a self-provisioning farmer…The argument used most frequently in favour of eucalyptus monocultures is that it is fast growing. However, the only fast growth that eucalyptus contributes to its pulp wood. It is not fast growing in terms of yield of wood for other purposes. In terms of yields of non-wood biomass for fodder, eucalyptus has zero yield since its leaves are not eaten by cattle' (Shiva, 1991, p. 48). The present system of plant and animal procreation tends to destroy diverse varieties of species. Monocultures have wiped out diversity. As Professor Chattopadhyay contends "diversity can be preserved only when uniformity and homogenization no longer remain the logic of production" (Chattopadhyay, 2006, p. 88).

Biocentrism, the third founding ideology of Ecologism eulogizes a strong sense of respect for nature in its own right. Biocentrism states that the biotic atmosphere of the earth has an intrinsic value. It logically contends that every living being (both human and non-human) has the potentiality to improve its own life provided no harm or destruction is committed against it. It vociferously repudiates the anthropocentric standpoint of unilinear dependency of non-human world on human lives and rejects the proposition that non-human living beings cannot have a good of their own because 'a being must have conscious feelings, desires or purposes in order to have a good of its own' (Hayward, 1994, p. 64). Robin Attfield points out by citing the examples of trees that they 'grow, blossom and decay; they can thrive and wither, be endangered by fire, and be protected from commercial pillage. Now what can thrive, reach maturity, be endangered and be protected itself, … has a good' (Quoted in Hayward 1994, 64). Therefore, the well-being of non-human organisms comprises of the entire growth and nourishment of their biological powers.

By the late 1960s and early 1970s there emerged some vocal platforms at the international level that not only aimed at dealing with ecological degradation and pollution but instituted the journey to probe prospect as well as feasibility for greening the concept and aspect of development. These platforms found expressions in organizations like the *International Union for Conservation of Nature (IUCN), International Biological Programme (IBP)* and the *Man and the Biosphere Programme (MAB)* (D'Souza, 2012, p. 184). The World Conservation Strategy (WCS) document, published in 1980 not only chalked out various strands of managerial environmentalism, but at the same time proposed one of the first sincere attempt at 'imbuing' the idea of development with environmental ideas and principles. It openly advocated the term 'eco-development.' The term eco-development was, in fact, first coined by Maurice Strong, the then secretary-general of the Stockholm Conference. As D'Souza points out that WCS stands out prominently for being one of eth first documents to 'codify' the idea of sustainable development. The WCS exercise was significant in examining the subsequent report of the World Commission on Environment and Development (WCED) titled '*Our Common Future*'- commonly referred to as the Brundtland report published in 1987. This document was later on considered to be one of the most bona fide codifications of the widely popular and compelling definition for the term sustainable development.

Sustainable development means 'development that meets the needs of the present without compromising the needs of the future generations to meet their own needs.' In simple terms, the quality of the earth we will leave for our future generations must be, if not better, as inherited. The definition offered by the Brundtland made us re-think about the present crisis in development agenda with regard to the environmental policies and mechanisms without making any attempt to fully overhaul the existing economic development system. The main thrust of the WCED report, in fact, seemed to have successfully managed to straddle both worlds- connecting the challenge of development with social, political and environmental aspects, without advocating the complete upsetting of the 'business-as-usual' model (D'Souza, 2013, p. 186). According to Steven Bernstein, the Brundtland report was the first major attempt to not only synchronize the complex relationship between environment and development through the mechanism of 'sustainable development' but it remarkably and categorically enthused a Keynesian adaptation of 'command-and-control regulation and economic/market based incentives for environmental management' (Bernstein, 2001, p. 69).

Professor Satyabrata Chakraborty raises some valid questions regarding the efficacy of the environment-development debate. According to him, every production utilizes natural resources and creates waste. Sustainability would mean that utilization of renewable resources must not exceed the regenerative capacity of nature. Similarly, creation of waste from production and consumption must be equal to or below the assimilative capacity of the earth. Economist Herman E. Daly terms this as 'steady-state economy'. The problem is that the regenerative and assimilative capacities are not defined. They differ with human activity. A constant examination between economic activities and environmental response is thus important. But difficulty arises when the question of non-renewable resources come up. If we are to leave behind the same physical stock of such resources, there can be no further utilization of them. This implies an extremely conservationist stance of neglecting 'the needs of the present'. Therefore, Chakraborty suggests that some amount of exhaustible resources has to be expended with relentless efforts for efficiency and search for substitute (Chakraborty, 2001, p. 424).

Talks and deliberations among policy-makers, government officials, academicians and even industrialists are held in a fashionable way regarding sustainable development, but the question is how sincere they are when it comes to implementation of such theme? Chakraborty, therefore, remarks, that "devoid of any ethical imperative, environmentalism thus is reduced to a 'technological fix'." As Rajni Kothari aptly says, "sustainability has been adopted as rhetoric, not as an ethical principle which restructures our relationship with the earth and its creatures in the realm of knowledge and arenas of action…The environmentalist label and the sustainability slogan have become deceptive jargon that is used as convenient cover for conducting business as usual" (Kothari, 1993, cited in Chakraborty, 2001).

A consensus was reached at least at the theoretical, perceptional and ideological level among some in the third world and the west that sustainable development cannot afford to be congruous with 'growth-oriented', 'profit-maximizing' and 'inegalitarian economic course of action'. Thus, they arrived at a conclusion that in place of harbouring for luxurious and fussy lifestyle and wasteful consumption of the rich, production should aim at meting the basic needs of the population like food, shelter, health, education and cultural recreations (Chakraborty, 2001, p. 425).

The emergence of human society and its progress is intertwined intensely around the concept of 'sustainable development' that has assumed significance for the sake of sustenance of human civilization and Mother Earth. From Gandhian perspective, sustainable development is economic development founded on the basic premise of ecological principles like environmental harmony, economic-efficiency, resource (including energy), conservation, local self-reliance and equity with social justice. Implicitly, Gandhian approach to sustainable development is "environmentally sustainable" (Jana, 2018, p. 6). Economic stability and social cohesion cannot be attained in the absence of environmental sustainability. Both twentieth and twenty-first centuries are marked by frustration, insecurity, competition accompanied by the silent killer of depression. Modern lifestyle, technological innovation, economic boom and industrial explosion contain within itself the seeds of destruction. Growth, estimated in terms of Gross Domestic Product (GDP), is surprisingly and inaccurately equated with the development index. Pragmatically though, the rise of the GDP in no way guarantees rise in the well-being of the masses.

GDP-driven economy utterly ignores the social costs such as the devaluation of human labour in the workplace by placing them in an unsafe and precarious work environment, unhealthy residential complex (often slums) and infectious sanitary conditions. Nobel Laureate Simon Kuznets thus warns that the brain behind the modern apparatus of measuring the GDP, had warned that over simplification of GDP calculation could be deceptive and subject to 'illusion and resulting abuse'. 'Profit-business-profit cycle' is basically leading human civilization towards a vortex of inequality and unsustainability. In the words of the former UN Secretary- General Ban-Ki-Moon, "Sustainable development is the central challenge of our times. Our world is under strain. Poverty continued to plague communities and families. Climate change threatens livelihoods. Conflicts are raging. Inequalities are deepening. These crises will only worsen unless we change our course" (Jana, 2018, p. 6).

MAHATMA ON ECOLOGY

Mahatma Gandhi was not an environmentalist. Yet his works and life-philosophy made him one of the greatest environmentalists of all times. During his lifetime, environmentalism was not an issue. But his farsightedness aided him to send a note of caution to the world about the detrimental effects of industrialism and consumerism, which he expressed in his book '*Hind Swaraj*'. Modern economy is driven by a frenzy of greed and competition, frustration and self-aggrandizement that silently and surreptitiously control and transform human soul into a materialistic-alienated machine. Gandhi asserted that true economics stands for social justice; it promotes the good of all equally, including the weakest and is indispensable for decent life. Dr. J.C. Kumarappa termed Gandhian economy as "economy of permanence". In fact, concern for 'green' broadly defined Gandhian vision to strike a harmonious chord between nature and the requirements of the people. Gandhi's deep ecological view of life was not confined to human beings alone. He was inspired with the thought of 'unity of life'. He strongly believed that every creature had the right to live as much as human beings and stressed the necessity of a living-harmonious bond between humans and rest of the animate world. His conviction that human being should live in coordination to the surrounding made him an apostle of modern environmentalism.

The ethical principle of ecology is a basic facet of Gandhian philosophy. Gandhi was neither an environmentalist nor a systematic thinker, neither a politician nor a policy-maker. A philosopher per se, he invented his idea which he conceptualized through his own life situation. His life transmitted his philosophy. His life was the best example of his teachings. His views on ecology can be discerned from his scattered speeches and writings. From many of such sources, it became clear that he admonished Eurocentric growth-oriented development policy. According to Gandhi, the Eurocentric model of development is the brainchild of Europe which has been imported to India and imposed on Indian civilization. Gandhi made a scathing criticism of modern civilization in *Hind Swaraj* which was first written in Gujarati in 1908 and then published in English in 1909. This book in subtle way defined the personality of this great Indian spiritual leader. In this work, as noted scholar Ramchandra Guha notes, "Gandhi decisively rejects industrialization as an option for India, then a colony struggling to free itself from British rule. For industrial society, as Gandhi had observed it in the West-in person and through the writings of Ruskin and company-was selfish, competitive, and grossly destructive of nature. He thought that 'the distinguishing characteristic of modern civilization is an indefinite multiplication of wants,' to satisfy which one had to forage far and wide for raw materials and commodities. Gandhi believed that by contrast preindustrial civilizations were marked by an 'imperative restriction upon, and a strict regulating of, these wants.' In uncharacteristically intemperate tones, he spoke of 'wholeheartedly detest[ing]this mad desire to destroy distance and time, to increase animal appetites, and go to the end of the earth in search of their satisfaction. If modern civilization stands for all this, and I have understood it to do so, I call it satanic'" (Guha, 2014, pp. 29-30).

Mahatma, all throughout his life had despised wasteful production, large-scale industrialization, and technological automation. In *Hind Swaraj* he clarified "instead of welcoming machinery as a boon, we should look upon it as an evil" (Gandhi 1938, 97). For him, "it is machinery that has impoverished India. It is difficult to measure the harm that Manchester has done to us. It is due to Manchester that Indian handicraft has all but disappeared" (Gandhi, 1938, p. 93).

Renowned scholar Partha Chatterjee offered a synoptic view of Gandhian criticism of the western scheme of social production "Gandhi attacks the notions of modernity and progress and subverts the central claim made on behalf of those notions, namely their correspondence with a new organization of society in which the productive capacities of human labour are multiplied several times, creating increased wealth and prosperity for all, and hence increased leisure, comfort, health and happiness. Gandhi argues that far from achieving these objectives, modern civilization makes man a prisoner of his craving for luxury and self-indulgence, releases the forces of unbridled competition and thereby brings upon society the evils of poverty, disease, war and suffering. It is precisely because modern civilization looks at man as a limitless consumer and thus sets out to open the floodgates of industrial production that it also becomes the source of inequity, oppression and violence on a scale hitherto unknown in human history" (Chaterjee, 1984, pp. 157-58).

Gandhi in his initial phase abhorred industrialism. In course of time a change of perception was noticeable. He reiterated that industrialization and or mechanization per se is not evil though what is dangerous is the obsession for machinery and industrialism. "Mechanization is good when the hands are too few for the work intended to be accomplished. It is an evil when there are more hands than required for the work, as is the case in India. The problem is how to utilize their idle hours, which are equal to the working days of six months in the year. Strange as it may appear, every mill generally is a menace to the villagers. I have not worked out the figures, but I am quite safe in saying that every mill-hand does the work of at least ten labourers doing the same work in their villages. In other words, he earns more than he did in his village at the expense of ten fellow-villagers. Thus spinning and weaving mills have deprived the villagers of a substantial means of livelihood. It is no answer to reply to say that they turn out cheaper, better cloth, if they do so at all. For, if they have displaced thousands of workers, the cheapest mill cloth is dearer than the dearest khadi woven in the villages" (Harijan, 1934, cited in Gandhi, 1947, pp. 102-103).

Gandhi further noted that "Machinery has its place; it has come to stay. But it must not be allowed to displace necessary human labour. I would welcome every improvement in the cottage machine, but I know that it is criminal to displace hand labour by the introduction of power-driven spindles unless one is at the same time ready to give millions of farmers some other occupation in their houses" (Young India, 1925, cited in Gandhi, 1947, p.30). On September 14th Gandhi wrote in the *Harijan:* "Dead machinery must not be pitted against the millions of living machines represented by the villagers scattered in her seven hundred thousand villages of India. Machinery to be well used has to help and ease human effort. The present use of machinery tends more and more to concentrate wealth in the hands of a few in total disregard of millions of men and women whose bread is snatched by it out of their mouths" (Young India, 1925, cited in Gandhi, 1947, p.31). These excerpts are basically documents that explains quite clearly Gandhi's stand on the modern day growth oriented development. For Gandhi, 'production by the masses' appealed more than 'mass production' (Pyarelal, 1959, pp. 28-29).

When confronted with the question whether he was against all machinery, Gandhi said: "How can I be when I know that even this body is a most delicate piece of machinery? The spinning wheel is a machine: a little tooth pick is a machine. What I object to is the craze for machine and not machinery as such. The craze is for what they call labour saving machinery. Men go on 'saving labour' till thousand and without work and thrown to open street to die of starvation. I want to save time and labour not for a fraction of mankind but for all. I want concentration of wealth, not in the hands of a few, but in the hands of all. Today, machinery merely helps a few to ride on the back of millions. The impetus behind it all is not philanthropy to save labour but greed. It is against this constitution of things that I am fighting with all might" (Bandyopadhyay, 2009, p. 7).

Gandhian viewpoint on industrialization was not simply driven by moral and ethical consideration but he was much more convinced about protection of the nature and environmental ambience that led him to launch the alternative mode of economic thinking based on ecological jurisprudence. In *Hind Swaraj* he said, "Formerly men worked in the open air only as much as they liked. Now thousands of workmen meet together and for the sake of maintenance work in factories or mines. Their condition is worse than that of the beasts. They are obliged to work, at the risk of their lives, at the most dangerous occupations, for the sake of millionaires. There are now diseases of which people never dreamt before…"(Gandhi, 1938, p. 36). Gandhi was therefore, critical about the environmental degradation and pollution caused by the modern factory system.

Gandhi was opposed to the modern version of industrialism as it encouraged violence in its subtlest form. Exploitation of natural resources, destruction and acquisition of fertile land and soil for large-scale industrialization are blatant form of extortion depriving both the tribal and the local habitants of their survival and also demolishing the natural balance of the environment. "The natural resources of the countryside have been increasingly channelized to meet the needs of the urban-industrial sector; the diversion of forests, water, etc. to the elite having accelerated processes of environmental degradation… it has deprived rural and tribal communities of their traditional rights of access and use" (Guha, 1993, p.6). Gandhi was aware of the centre-periphery dilemma and thus he said, the blood of the villages is the cement with which the edifice of the cities is built.

Gandhi proposed an unorthodox and simple alternative of economics to be practiced as a voluntary action by both the individual and the state. His economics was based on minimization of wants and use of recycled resources. He just did not propose it, he practiced it as well. He often wrote letters on the backside of the used paper. Gandhi's concept of an independent model of development was based on village model- a decentralized, agriculture and labour intensive, eco-friendly and tune with the nature. Instead of making the city powerful he concentrated on villages to make them independent, self sufficient, eco-friendly and morally defensible. His ideal village was "It will have cottages with sufficient light and ventilation, built of a material obtainable within a radius of five miles of it. The cottages will have courtyards enabling householders to plant vegetables for domestic use and to house their cattle. The village lanes and streets will be free of all avoidable dust. It will have wells according to its needs and accessible to all. It will have houses of worship for all, also a common meeting place, a village common for grazing its cattle, a co-operative dairy, primary and secondary schools in which industrial [i.e. vocational] education will be the central fact, and it will have Panchayats [village councils] for settling disputes. It will produce its own grains, vegetables and fruit, and its own Khadi [hand-spun cotton]. This is roughly my idea of a model village" (Collected Works, Vol. 64).

Though in 21st century, standing in the midst of technological revolution and Wi-Fi world, Gandhian imagery sounds absurd, obdurate and out of the fashion. To a person of this century this kind of visualization is simply an attempt to take us at least two hundred years back ignoring the significance of innovation of science, technology and communication. But a calm and prudent thought on Gandhian way of things would lead us to clearing the mirror and indulge in self introspection. Why there is Stockholm, Rio de Janeiro, Hague and Copenhagen conference on climate change? Why the world thinks about Paris agreement? Why we still consider Brundtland a milestone? Why the Supreme Court of India needs to interfere frequently in environmental cases? Why there are so many bodies and organizations working day and night to combat man-made disaster and engaging in relentless effort to protect the earth from further deterioration? All because we did not pay heed to the voices of the Mahatma. His idolization of the village was not a proposition but a symbol. His village was actually a miniature of the bioregion that could survive on its own in tuning with the natural rhythm. His bioregionalism emphasized self sufficient economy that grew on its own resources and labour power with an eco-friendly production. Self-reliance in economy based on Khadi industry and swadeshi products was a remarkable achievement India had during the colonial era. In fact, the present Indian government, basing some of its programmes on Gandhian values has brought back the concept of self-reliance with its 'Make in India' epithet. Decentralization of production with the essential village industries according to Gandhi could make small units self reliant and independent of outside vagaries. Gandhi even put equal importance on conservation of forest and afforestation programmes which according to him could not be taken merely through state action but through popular initiative and popular awareness.

Inspired by Gandhi, the Government of India launched its "*Swach Bharat Abhiyan*" or the *Swach Bharat Mission* that aimed to clean up the roads and alleys, streets and other infrastructure of various cities, towns and villages of India. It proceeds with the aim to eradicate the menace of open defecation by taking initiatives to construct household-owned and community owned toilets. Government targeted to achieve an "open-defecation free India" by 2nd October 2019 to dedicate a clean Bharat to the Mahatma. Gandhi wrote in *Harijan*, "The things to attend to in the villages are cleansing tanks and wells and keeping them clean, getting rid of dump-heaps…Lanes and streets have to be cleansed of all rubbish, which should be classified. There are portions which can be turned into manure, portions which simply to be buried and portions which can be directly turned into wealth. Every bone picked up is valuable raw material from which useful articles can be made or which can be crushed into rich manure. Rags and waste-paper can be turned into paper, and excreta picked up are golden manure for village fields" (Harijan, 1947, p. 135). Gandhi not only thought about village sanitation, he was equally concerned with urban sanitation as well. In September 1929 he wrote, "I have seen thousands of men and women dirtying the banks of the Ganga at Hardwar. Pilgrims defecate at the very spot where people sit, wash their faces, etc. in the Ganga and then again fill their pots at the very same spot. I have come across pilgrims defiling lakes in the same manner at places of pilgrimage…Such recklessness leads to pollution of air and water. Is it surprising then that cholera, typhoid and other infectious diseases follow as a result of this? It is no exaggeration to say that almost 75 per cent of diseases are caused by our insanitary habits" (Collected Works, vol. 62, p. 452).

Gandhi's ideal society was a 'sustainable society' from the ecological point of view. His prescription for limiting economic growth, population, pollution and environmental degradation by a self reliant economy and self restraint individual living in harmony with the nature driven by the doctrine of *sarvodaya, non-violence and truthfulness* became the founding tenets of a sustainable society nurtured and nourished by mutual respect and cohabitation. Gandhi' life is enriched with a very clear set of principles, ideas and convictions which offer compelling evidence that we are still in a position to shape our destiny, rather than be shaped by circumstances.

GANDHIAN APPROACH TO ECOLOGICAL MOVEMENT IN INDIA

Swaraj means a continuous attempt to free ourselves from the government regulations. It does not matter whether the government is an alien government or our own. If, after the coming of swaraj the people of India will keep on looking to the government for regulating every detail of this lives, then that swaraj will be meaningless. (Mahatma Gandhi in Young India)

In such situations well organized, democratically structured and socially responsible people's movements can play an important role in checking dangerous and arbitrary misuse of power. There are several indications that in most part of our country there is a greater need for more democratic people's movements. This is primarily because the government is intoxicated by the development syndrome. One reason for such addictive proclivity towards market oriented development strategy is the current pattern of the global economy. India has to compete with other developing countries in most areas of exports, it has to keep the wages low, compromise with the norms of healthy environment and put more than bearable pressure on natural resources. Progress in the name of development, in the ultimate analysis is depriving the lives of their basic amenities and facilities and in course driving them towards a doomed future. In such a scenario, protests and movements against injustice and unlawful acts are the natural consequence a democracy can expect. And Gandhi had showed the way. As a leader of the movement launched for India's independence, Gandhi always gave primacy to involvement of the people. He had tremendous faith on the people and suspicion on the apparatus of the government. His love for people's power helped him mobilize people for sustained action on a voluntary basis. After independence, India has witnessed a huge number of development projects in different parts of the country but no project has stirred up such widespread controversy as the grandiose Sardar Sarovar Project on Narmada River and the endearing *Chipko Andolan*. Noted environmentalist Vandana Shiva considered *Narmada Bachao Andolan* to have become a bigger issue than displacement. It is the issue that is concerned with wastage of water for entertainment complexes along Sabarmati in Ahmedabad. It has become a issue of valuable water being used for genocidal agricultural practices. The broader question related not just to the Sadar Sarovar Dam but with regard to all development projects is that whether the people of India would be able to live in their own land or will their land and water become assets for the globally profitable corporate. The Narmada Bachao Andolan (NBA) as a mass movement reached its zenith with the massive Sangharsh Yatra of December 1990-January 1991. This was aimed at halting the work on the dam with thousands of participants. One fascinating aspect of this movement was its supreme commitment to nonviolence and people's participation. NBA lost its tempo on many quarters. But it has not its dynamism. The central question that remains though is for whose development? 'Chipko', more sophisticated movement with a superb human touch exemplified unconditional love and dependence for the nature. 'Chipko' is a Hindi word that connotes "to hug". The significance of the Chipko movement lies in the fact that when some men approached to bring down trees with axes for business and other industrial purposes, manifesting highest form of violence against nature they confronted unarmed and defenseless women who charged with their belief in non-violence clung to the trees and told the perpetrators: "We will not let you cut the trees; first cut us down, then you can cut the trees". These women were defended by their faith in interconnectedness with the nature were ready to risk injury and death. The Chipko movement grew out of such daring and resolute action of the illiterate, poor, weak women armoured with Gandhian weapon of Satyagraha, ahimsa and sarvodaya. The Chipko and Narmada movements constitute the refrain of contemporary India's conscientious objection to the invasion of modernity in the Gandhian non-violent mode.

The traditional attitude of awe and reverence for Nature resulted in a spontaneous balance between human consumption and conservation. The two maxims of rational ecology, namely 'maximum diversity' and 'minimum interference' are in tune with traditional ecological awareness.

To soothe our strained nerves we love to go to forests, mountains and villages to enjoy a quiet life and a moonlit night away from the hustle-bustle and humdrum of the city life. In Santiniketan, the lights used to be turned off on full moon nights to serve the dual purpose of saving power and enjoying nature, rejuvenating the soul. Unfortunately, this tradition was discontinued to serve the demands of modernity.

Today's Hip Hop culture protruding the lustful tongue is in rapid velocity gobbling up finer sensibilities and rational responsiveness. The beauty of nature is sought even today, though not in the extensive jungle or the fathomless sea but in the artificial, luxurious resorts. Too much light sometimes make us think about the beauty of darkness, too much noise compel us to value the rhythm of silence. Too much abundance forces us to appreciate the significance of necessity. Before the earth sinks into the abyss and punishes us for our greed, let us appreciate the beauty of darkness, the serenity of silence and regality in frugality. Respect for nature and simple lifestyle can only save us from imminent ecological disaster. How do we do it is now the question.

REFERENCES

Alvares, C. (1992). *Science, Development and Violence: The Revolt Against Modernity*. New Delhi: Oxford University Press.

Ball, T. (2003). Green Political Theory. In T. Ball & R. Bellamy (Eds.), *The Canbridge History of Twentieth Century Political Thought*. Cambridge, UK: Cambridge University Press. doi:10.1017/CHOL9780521563543.027

Bandyopadhyay, D. (2009. March 3). Mahatma's profound thoughts. *The Statesman*.

Bernstein, S. (2001). *The Compromise of Liberal Environmentalism*. New York: Columbia Press University. doi:10.7312/bern12036

Chakraborty, S. (2001). Environment and Politics in India. In R. Chatterji (Ed.), *Politics India: The State-Society Interface*. New Delhi: South Asian Publishers.

Chatterjee, P. (1984). Gandhi and the Critique of Civil Society. In R. Guha (Ed.), *Subaltern Studies III: Writings on South Asian History and Society*. New Delhi: Oxford University Press.

Chattopadhyay, T. (2006). *'Man' and 'Ecology' in Marx and Gandhi*. Kolkata: Mitram.

D'Souza, R. (2012). Sustainable Development. In B. S. Chimni & S. Mallavarapu (Eds.), *International Relations: Perspectives for the Global South*. Delhi: Pearson.

Dobson, A. (1990). *Green Political Thought: An Introduction*. London: Unwin Hymen.

Dogra, B. (2010, June 10). Development model needs to change. *The Statesman*.

Gadgil, M., & Guha, R. (1995). *Ecology and Equity: the use and abuse of nature in contemporary India*. New Delhi: Penguin.

Gandhi, M. (1976). *The Collected Works of Mahatma Gandhi* (Vol. 62-64). New Delhi: The Publications Division, Government of India.

Ghosh, P. (2009). *International Relations*. New Delhi: PHI.

Guha, R. (2014). *Environmentalism: A Global History*. Gurgaon: Penguin Random House.

Hayword, T. (1994). *Ecological Thought: An Introduction*. Cambridge, UK: Polity Press.

Hinduism According to Gandhi. (2014). New Delhi: Orient Publishing.

Jana, J. (2018, October 2). Gandhian Development. *The Statesman*.

Luke, T. W. (2009). An Apparatus of Answers? *New Political Science*, *31*(4), 487–498. doi:10.1080/07393140903322562

Major changes ahead for ecosystems. (2018, September 1). *The Statesman*.

Norton, B. G. (1987). *Why Preserve Natural Variety?* Princeton, NJ: Princeton University Press.

Parekh, B. (1989). *Gandhi's Political Philosophy: A Critical Examination*. London: Macmillan.

Parekh, B. (2008). Gandhi and Interreligious Dialogue. In D. Allen (Ed.), *The Philosophy of Mahatma Gandhi for the Twenty First Century*. Lexington: Lanhan.

Pepper, D. (1993). *Eco-socialism: from Deep Ecology to Social Justice*. London: Routledge.

Pyarelal. (1959). *Towards New Horizons*. Ahmedabad: Navajivan.

Seabrook, J. (2006, November 5). Ecology versus Economics. *The Statesman*.

Shiva, V. (1991). Biodiversity, Biotechnology and Profits. In *Biodiversity, Social and Ecological Perspectives*. Penang, Malaysia: World Rainforest Movement.

Vinod, M. J., & Deshpande, M. (2013). *Contemporary Political Theory*. Delhi: PHI.

KEY TERMS AND DEFINITIONS

Development: It signifies a process of evolution.

Non-Violence: It refers to Gandhian prescription to the use of peaceful means to bring about political and social transformation.

Sarvodaya: It is the Gandhian view of social and economic development of a community from a holistic perspective.

Sustainable: Development: It refers to a policy towards a reconcilement between economic development and natural balance.

Chapter 22
Energy Security and Economic Growth in South Asia:
An Alternative Policy Option

Debasish Nandy
Kazi Nazrul University, India

ABSTRACT

Energy security and economic growth are interrelated. South Asia is at a critical juncture today. Development is the overriding priority for the region because of the high incidence of poverty, but energy is proving to be a critical constraint. The entire region is suffering from an acute energy crisis. Firstly, South Asian countries are confronted with the huge challenge of securing energy to sustain rapid economic growth and meeting the rising aspirations of the people. Secondly, the region is home to a huge population that lacks access to clean forms of energy. A large section of the population, particularly in rural areas lacks access to electricity and relies on the traditional use of biomass for cooking. With limited domestic energy sources, most South Asian countries are also highly dependent on energy imports, particularly crude oil, from other regions. Thirdly, on the issue of energy security SAARC, countries need to establish a platform of common interest. There are three objectives of this chapter: exploring new alternatives of energy sources of South Asian States, searching for relationship between energy security and economic growth, and re-thinking about an alternative policy options regarding energy security in South Asia.

INTRODUCTION

Energy security has been a major concern to South Asian states in the 21st century due to the overwhelming effect of globalization. So to maintain a secured future different initiatives are being taken in the energy sector in this region. It is therefore essential to take steps to ensure necessary energy supplies and their proper distribution in this region to support steady socio-economic development. The main objective of this chapter is to illustrate the forthcoming steps and activities for the effective development in the energy sector of South Asian states. The policy makers of SAARC countries often make statements desiring to increase the economic level of the country to that of the middle-income countries by 2020 without men-

DOI: 10.4018/978-1-5225-8547-3.ch022

tioning increasing needs of energy, whereas growing size of the economy and rising energy demand go hand in hand. So attention towards the energy sector has to be a top-notch in order to get the best out of this sector. Along with energy development, the concern of energy security comes with modernization, as the use of energy is increasing day by day and people's life and economy are becoming dependent on the usage of energy. This chapter attempts to present a broad overview of energy scenario and energy security of South Asian region. It will further try to explore the complex relationship between energy security and economic growth in South Asia.

REVIEW OF LITERATURE

Much has been written on energy security of South Asian States, but there are a small number of writing on South Asian energy security in a broad-spectrum. It is very difficult to make a comparative study of energy security of South Asian States. There is a research gap between county-wise energy security and Regional energy security. I have tried to make a bridge between the two. Mistry (2011) on "Domestic and International Influences on India's Energy Policy, 1947-2008" is very relevant literature to understand the India's energy security. Khan (2013) on "India's Middle-East Energy Strategy'' has indicated India's energy dependency on Middle-East. The study of Dhakal and Jenkins (1991) is one of the very interesting literatures to understand the Bhutan's energy sources. The article of Jamtsho (2015) is very relevant to research on Bhutan's energy efficiency. The related studies to add are Ahmad et al (2001), Mahmood and Muhammed (2018) etc. Zadzorova (2015) on "How has China been Safeguarding Its Oil Imports from Middle East and Africa" aims to delineate the Chinese strategies to import fuels from Middle-East countries.

OBJECTIVES OF THE RESEARCH

There are three objectives of this chapter-

1. To explore new alternatives of energy sources of South Asian States.
2. In search of relationship between energy security and economic growth.
3. To re-think about an alternative policy options regarding energy security in South Asia.

RESEARCH METHODOLOGY

The present book chapter is based on two research methodologies—(1) Content analysis method & (2) observation method. It has been written on the basis primary & secondary data.

CONTEXTUALIZING THE ENERGY SECURITY

Energy is one of the basic needs to sustain social development. In the present world, electricity is the backbone of all industrialized countries (World Bank, 2013). The United Nations Sustainable Development Goals (SDGs) (United Nations, 2016), scheduled to be achieved over the next 15 years, aim to end poverty, protect the planet, and ensure the prosperity of all. Presently 1.2 billion people in the world are without access to modern electricity, while 2.9 billion people have to cook using inefficient and polluting fuels such as firewood or kerosene. Majority of these people are concentrated in about a dozen countries in Africa and Asia. The energy security in least developed countries (LDCs) is a major challenge that needs to be addressed urgently. At the same time, it is important to be aware that energy is the dominant contributor to a climate change, accounting for about 60% of the total greenhouse gas (GHG) emissions (International Energy Agency, 2015).

The world is facing an enormous challenge to provide sufficient quantity of clean energy to its burgeoning population. Energy is a fundamental asset for enabling socio economic development and poverty eradication in any country. There is a close relationship between energy security and development. Most of the South Asian states are facing tremendous energy security threat due uncontrolled demands of fuel. The concept of modernization often clashes with sustainable development. South Asian states always clamor for sustainable development, but they are less concerned about the inept handling of the modernization process. Absence of indigenous technology and shortage of own sources of conventional energy collectively compel these states to implement the wrong energy policy in a wrong way. The notion of sustainable development is not a new phenomenon. Green energy has a friendly link with sustainable development. Nevertheless, green energy is not sufficient to mitigate the demands of the domestic consumption in this region. Over populous South Asian states have been continuously importing the conventional fuels without securing the alternative sources. As a regional organization the role of SAARC is questionable. Whether the spirit of regionalism has been successful in arriving at a consensus regarding the future of energy security or not, is doubtful. Indeed, SAARC has not been able to do so. It implies two things–(1) absence of consensus & (2) question of capability. The use of large-scale pollution creating fuel in South Asian states is a matter of grave concern. If supply of energy is not proliferated adequately, there will be serious adverse implications for the nation's economic and social development.

Relations between energy consumption and Human Development Index, energy consumption and economic growth, biomass fuel consumption and economic growth on the one hand and different energy sources that are trapped to meet the World Energy Demand have been presented. Energy is a strategic input for socio-economic development. Energy has direct linkages with economic security, food security and environmental sustainability. For a developing country, the energy security issue needs to be considered in the context of sustainable human development. In order to ensure energy security for sustainable development it would be necessary to consider the energy needs of the country under long term perspectives. For a developing country like Bangladesh, energy development program should be so conceived as would ensure energy security under long term perspective not only to meet the demand according to the present requirement but also to ensure energy security for future generation. A conceptual framework for energy policy is to be outlined in the SAARC manifesto.

The Indian Experience

In the 21st century, oil issue has been the key issue in India's foreign policy. Regarding overseas oil, India has initiated high-level diplomacy. According to Dinshaw Mistry, "India's oil policy for two decades after its independence was shaped by a historical –international factor—the colonial legacy. Its oil industry was largely controlled by the British –owned Burmah and American companies Standard –Vacuum and Caltex. These firms imported oil from their fields in the Middle-East; thus from 1940s to 1960s, most of India's imported oil came from Iran, Saudi Arabia, with smaller amounts coming from Kuwait and Indonesia" (Mistry, 2011:326). During 1977-1982 period, New Delhi was dependent on Moscow and approximately 5-15% of total India's imported crude oil came from USSR. India's quest for energy security leads to the strengthening the oil diplomacy. India imported 23% of its total oil from USSR in 1984-85, 17% in 1985-86 and 17% in 1989-90 respectively. After the collapse of USSR India has stopped oil import from Moscow and started to extend its dependency on other destinations. With the collapse USSR Russian oil supply to India has almost ended. To augment commercial purchases from the world market, Indian government and oil firms sought to secure oilfields abroad. These assets added 3 to 5 million tons annually to India's oil supply in the mid-and late 1990s (Energy Tribune, 2008)

The un-impeded force of globalization implied three things, such as *first,* rapid growth of FDI based industries, *second,* rapid change of society, *third,* the growing tendency for modern amenities. Presently India is facing energy insecurity due to the aforesaid uncontrolled demand. India's main sources of energy are coal, oil and gas. We have a confirmed discovery of gas in Krishna-Godavari (KG) basin D-6 by Reliance Industries but that is from over 9 years back. Since then, not even the private sector has discovered any new find. If our own exploration is going to stagger in both oil and gas and if we do not put in enormous resources that are required in research and development to deal with the peculiar geographical problems found only in India, then the future seems insecure.

India's Energy Security and Diplomacy

India is the seventh largest country in the world in terms of geographic landmass, and the second largest in terms of population – with 1.2 billion people. The country enjoys an abundance of traditional and non-traditional energy sources, but these sources are insufficient to meet India's growing needs. It therefore resorts to importing most of its energy from abroad, especially from Middle East crude oil and natural gas exporters. Meeting the growing demand for energy is a major challenge that is constantly confronting Indian leaders. The country has crude oil imports from around 40% in 1990 to 70% in 2011. In 2012, over 64% of these imports came from the Middle East, a trend that is expected to continue. By 2032, over 91% of the country's energy needs will to be imported. Thus, in an effort to secure both best prices and energy security, the country has concluded a number of short- and long-term contracts at government level and, to a lesser extent, through private companies (Khan, 2013) .Saudi Arabia and Iran are two major sources of India's energy sources. Over the decades, India has been exporting fuel despite of many challenges.

In middle of 2004, UPA –I government led by the Congress did not link the Iran-India pipeline with the MFN issue, and this resulted in a positive response from Pakistan (Maralinga, 2005: 74-85) . In March 2006, Pakistan, India and Iran held their first tripartite governmental talks in Tehran. Still other political factors delayed the project. There was a dilemma to India, whether it would continue its friendly relationship with Iran and continue the process of tri-national gas pipeline project or not; because, during that time India was moving towards "Civil Nuclear Deal" with the US for mitigating its energy deficiency. Then South Block argued that, for adapting the realist foreign policy India was silent about Iran. Then strong allegation was raised against the Manmohan Singh led UPA –I government whether India's foreign policy will be directed by USA or its own decision. However, by this pipeline Indo-Pak relations might be on a better footing. Although some groups in the US noted that the gas pipeline could advance the India-Pakistan peace process----it could bind the two countries in economic linkages that would be hard to cut off for political reasons (Krepon & Haider, 2005: 307-20).

Qatar holds the 9th largest reserves in OPEC and 13th largest in the world. Qatar's crude oil production ranks 17th in the world, with most of the country's production sent abroad as exports. Due to some technical shortcomings Iran is not able to produce LNG. Indian firms are also less interested to setup LNG facilities in Iran due to American sanctions on it. However, there is shows a light of hope that in mid of 2015, the administration has partly withdrawn its embargo from Iran. Hopefully, India would like to use this opportunity to revitalize the India-Iran oil diplomacy with a new outlook.

Kuwait has been a reliable and fourth largest supplier of crude oil to India. During 2014-15, Kuwait was the fourth largest oil supplier to India after Saudi Arabia, Iraq and Venezuela and it meets about 10% of India's energy needs. Total bilateral trade with Kuwait during 2014-15 was US$ 14.58 billion (Rs.88, 843.72core). India's imports from Kuwait during 2014-15 were US$ 13.38billion of which POL accounted for US$ 12.28 billion (Crude oil import was worth US$ 11.47 billion). The reduction in Kuwait's exports to India, compared to 2013-14, was due to the sharp fall in crude oil price in the last two quarters of 2014-15 and reduced purchase of crude oil from Kuwait by Indian oil PSUs. In Rupee terms, the total imports from Kuwait were at 81,510.69 cores during 2014-15(Source: Embassy of India, Kuwait, November, 2015, Report).

Oman is one of old diplomatic and trading partners of India with which India concluded a Treaty of Friendship, Commerce and Navigation on May 13, 1953. Since then Indo-Oman friendship has been extended in many ways especially in the field of petroleum goods. Through bilateral reciprocal relationship both have enhanced strategic partnership also. Due to Oman's strategic location, India may use it in a multipurpose direction. Due to Oman's strategic location at the straits of Dormouse and its proximity to the Bab-el- Mandeb, both are willing to cooperate in relation to Gulf security and maritime security near the Somalia coast. Both countries are increasing their joint air and naval exercises.

However, due to Arab spring and thereafter political disturbances in several parts of Wes Asia, India's policy outlook towards this region has been changed. India's orientation towards this region is to be revised. It is obvious, that, some Arab regimes are going through severe loss of sovereignty and some even threat of disintegration, civil wars and identity crisis. An independent Indian approach has much greater chance to broaden and deepen our relationship with the three states. India has started to give emphasized on African nations for its oil import. But geographically and strategically, Arab states are more significant to India. If India takes slow policy towards West Asia, then, China may impose its dominance on various oilfields. So, India should rethink over it.

In Search of Energy: India's New Destination

India's two immediate neighbours--- Myanmar and Bangladesh have good volume of natural gas reservation. According to India's Act Look (previously known as look east policy), these two countries are strategically important for direct access to South-East Asian countries. Moreover India aims to import natural gas from both Bangladesh and Myanmar and hence long-term negotiations are going on. Due to the Chinese factor Myanmar project has been stagnant .On the other hand, due to domestic political equations Bangladesh project is also the same. The then Minister of External Affairs, Jaswant Singh talked to Myanmar government during his visit to Myanmar in 2001(Hindustan Times, 2001). This project has a political aspect. While the Iran- Pakistan –India pipeline project stopped due to American intervention, then this project, nonetheless, could not be successful due to the interference of China.

Although, in 2005, the leaders of these three countries discussed the proposed project, but it failed to make any progress. Bangladesh has taken a bargaining method in dealing with this project. It demands for removal of non-tariff barriers; a trade and transport corridor linking Nepal and Bangladesh through Indian Territory (Energy Politics, 2007).

Extended Oil Diplomacy Towards African Nations

India's oil dependency on African nations has been increased for the last few years. Since India's economic liberalization was launched in the early-nineties, India's foreign policy has been driven towards the African continent. The huge stock of natural sources, especially oil and gas in African states attracted India. Indian policy makers were also conscious about African market. Actually, Africa's growing strategic importance and India's growing energy needs have forced it to diversify its oil imports. In the past, India has depended on West Asian countries for its oil imports (Alam, 2012:44). Like other super powers (UK, China etc.), India also started to explore the potentiality of petroleum stock in African states. ManmohanSingh and NarendraModi both have paid their attention on Africa. Through the previous Afro-Asian sentiment Modihas been trying to revive the bi-lateral relations. China has already aimed to Africa. A tuff completion has been started between USA and China for reserving of oil from AU states. India also lately started its race in this occasion.

Oil diplomacy was one of the key agenda of the India-Africa Summit, which held from October 26 to 29, 2016 in New Delhi. To secure its energy security, through more investment in the African oil and gas sector, a senior official engaged in organising the event has said. India currently sourced about 16% of its $125-billion worth of oil imports from African nations and the government was keen to step up its oil diplomacy and increase the share to between 20% and 25% in the short term, the official pointed out. One of the subjects of engagement of the oil diplomacy would be to explore opportunities for India to access larger energy imports through long-term contracts rather than the current predominant spot contracts. For example, in the case of Nigeria, diplomatic facilitations would broach larger investments by Indian Oil Corporation (IOC), the country's largest oil refiner-marketer, in upgrading and modernising Nigerian oil refineries in lieu of long-term contracts for energy imports from the African nation. In Mozambique, Oil India Limited, Bharat Petroleum Corporation Limited and ONGC had already committed investments to the tune of $7-billion in developing oil and gas assets and the target was to double this investment over the next five years (http://www.engineeringnews.co.za).

India and Central Asia Energy Cooperation

In 2000 Indian government published its 'Hydrocarbon vision 2025', where the question of energy crisis has been clearly manifested. Whereas in 2006-07, the demand of gas was 49 billion cubic meters, then by 2024-25 it would reach to 125 billion cubic meters. The central Asian countries may be a significant destination for India. India already made a close ties with Kazakhstan, Uzbekistan, Turkmenistan, Tajikistan, Kyrgyzstan for getting gas and oil. This region is rich in hydrocarbon. Kazakhstan is one of the major oil producing countries. It is expected that by 2019 Kazakhstan will be one of the largest (among best 5) oil producing country. Turkmenistan may be the 6th largest oil producing country by 2019. Uzbekistan has 655 trillion cubic feet, in Kazakhstan 85 trillion cubic feet and Turkmenistan 100 trillion cubic feet.

Actually, Central Asian region has reservation of 2.7% of world's total oil stock and 7% of total gas reservation. Against this backdrop, India aimed to close linkage with this region. There are mainly three problems to import oil and gas from the Central Asian countries **(1)** Geographical constrains .It is very difficult to carry oil and gas through pipeline via Afghanistan for its location.**(2)** There is a proposed pipeline project from Turkmenistan. In 2005, ADB submitted a feasibility study to the petroleum ministers Turkmenistan, Afghanistan, Pakistan and India. In May, 2007, India joined a four-party agreement with the ADB on this proposed pipeline (Mistry, 2011:333). But due to Afghanistan's political and security problem it has been materialised even today. **(3)** The Central Asian states are partly controlled by China. China is trying to stop India's initiatives regarding the pipeline project .India's energy pipeline diplomacy is back into play with the National Democratic Alliance government working on simultaneous plans for constructing transnational crude oil and gas pipelines to India from Turkmenistan, Russia and Kazakhstan. The International North-South Transport Corridor was first agreed upon between India, Iran and Russia in 2000. The route connects Mumbai in India to Bandar Abbas port in Iran and then Bandar-e Anzali in northern Iran on the Caspian Sea coast. From there, goods are expected to be transported to Astrakhan in Russia and then to Central Asia. After establishing the Chabahar Port in Iran, India has started to extend its energy security relations with the Central Asian states.

Latin America: A Far Destination of Energy Security for India

South America rose 10 per cent each as Indian refineries bought heavier but cheaper grade oil. Indian refineries have consistently reduced imports from traditional markets like Saudi Arabia and stepped up purchases from newer geographical entities like Mexico and Venezuela as imports have become viable due to availability of cheaper variants and softening of shipping cost. India imported 189.44 MT of crude oil in 2014-15, almost unchanged from the previous fiscal, to meet over 80 per cent of its oil needs. Venezuela was a very close third with 24.40 MT of oil supplies, 13 per cent higher than 2013-14.

Mexico supplied 5.06 MT of crude oil in 2014-15, marginally higher than 4.94 MT a year ago. A bilateral Agreement on cooperation in the hydrocarbons sector was signed during President Chavez's visit in March 2005, along with a MoU offering ONGC Videsh Ltd. (OVL) opportunities for oil and gas exploration in Venezuela, including a heavy oil field in the Orinoco belt, following which OVL opened its office in Venezuela. An agreement between OVL and CVP (subsidiary of PDVSA, Venezuela's national oil company) was signed for the creation of a Joint Venture called "Petrolera Indo-Venezuela SA" for production and exploration of oil in the San Cristobal field in which OVL has a 40% stake while PDVSA has the remaining 60% share.

China's Aggressive Oil Diplomacy: Threat to India's Energy Security

Vast oil consumption of China requires policies that ensure that 1.3 billion people and tremendous Chinese market will not be affected by the lack of oil. With this in mind, this essay's main aim is to examine how China has been achieving oil deals and ensuring oil supplies from two significant regions – the Middle East and Africa. The first part of the essay gives an overview of history of China's increasing oil consumption, its oil policy, and involvement of African and Middle Eastern states in it. Second part is concerned with the pre-import preparation, presenting Chinese financial contribution to foreign states, selling of weapons and political support as methods that can be identified as used by China to ensure flow of oil from the two regions. And the final part examines shipping lanes from Africa and the Middle East, their possible dangers and China's attention to it (Zadzorova, 2015).

The oil suppliers from Africa and the Middle East since the 2000s, countries such as Iraq, Angola, Sudan or Congo are among those which have supplied oil to the Chinese market as it has been highlighted by Shinn's article, the flow of oil from Angola, Sudan or Equatorial Guinea to China demonstrates the fact that China cooperates with these states despite "violation of human rights and serious abuses committed by their governments." The oil represents almost one fifth of the China's energy demand, meaning that yet in 2009 China needed almost 120 million tons of oil equivalent to cover its domestic oil needs. There is number of states in the Middle East as well as in Africa in which the latter applies. China does not only neglect internal situation, but it has even pursued steps that have worsened domestic situation in particular states in Africa and the Middle East. These actions may be considered as a component of the Chinese foreign oil policy.

Pakistan

Energy is a crucial input in the process of economic growth. Sustainable economic growth necessitates the sufficient and continuous availability of energy. Pakistan is confronting energy insecurity which is seriously hindering the economic development and this study is an attempt to investigate the relationship between energy security and economic growth. The major concern of energy security is associated with the availability of suitable energy supply in cheap and consistent way to fulfill energy demand in the future. In this study, the demand and supply gap of energy is used as a proxy variable for energy security. Tahir Mahmood and MuhammedTayyab have mentioned in their research that the Error Correction Model (ECM) is used to analyze the short-run and long-run causality between energy gap and the economic growth. The results show that unidirectional causality runs from energy demand and supply gap to economic growth in short-run as well as in the long-run. This relationship is negative and statistically significant in both the short- run and the long run which indicates that low energy security (i.e., increasing energy gap) halts the economic growth of Pakistan. Consequently, the study concludes that government should focus on better management of energy demand and energy supply. (Mahmmod&Tayyab, 2018: 47-64).

In Pakistan, there is a good reservation of Gas in Baluchistan province. This province is least developed and industrially backward. Here energy could not enhance the industrial development. Pakistan's dependency on Iran for Oil and Gas due to geographical proximity could not make it self-dependent. Economic growth and development are two inter-related parameters of a country's advancement. Due to lack of balanced economic policy and wrong policy implementation on the basis of natural resources, Pakistan has been suffering from lot of social, political and economic crisis. In Pakistan, there is no substantial energy policy which could be viable for economic growth. It's over dependency on Middle-East for energy import and absence of indigenous alternative energy -generation technology jointly failed to achieve fastest economic growth. In domestic level the equal distributive policy of energy has not been reflected.

Energy security largely depends upon a country's political economy. Since its emergence Pakistan has braced itself for a 'political economy of defence' by according a very high priority to defence. Pakistan has been spending a major portion of its revenues to modernize its military apparatus. In nuclear power completion, Pakistan is very much competitive to India. The Pakistani political leaders' sense of aggressive insecurity vis-à-vis India, its identity crisis and border tensions with Afghanistan have all helped to boost the military expenditure disproportionally, at the cost of development projects (Kukreja, 2005:140).Its nuclear power has been used primarily in defence rather than for the benefit of society. The internal energy deficiency could be mitigated by using imported uranium in generation of electricity.

Bangladesh

The primary concern of energy production in Bangladesh is the protracted effects of energy demand and this requirement of energy will be more than double by 2020. With commercial energy increasing by 400%, 53% of the present supply of energy comes from traditional fuels and the remaining from commercial sources. Therefore traditional energy supplies have been transferred away towards commercial energy which has been the characteristic of Bangladesh's energy development since 1980's. Energy consumption of the country in 2000 and projected demands of commercial energy estimated by Gas Demand and Reserve Committee for business as usual GDP growth rate (4.55) and cumulative natural gas demand for different GDP growth scenarios (3%, 4.55%,6% & 7%) up to 2050 have been presented. Availability of indigenous commercial, non-commercial and non-renewable energy sources have been assessed.

For a developing country like Bangladesh the energy development strategies are dependent on the sustaining relations between energy consumption and economic growth, energy consumption and Human Development index, biomass fuels consumption and economic growth and different energy sources providing world energy demand. A long term comprehensive and integrated energy policy along with appropriate strategies should be formulated to ensure energy security over short, medium and long terms for the country. The policy should ensure tapping of all possible sources of energy, adequate supply of energy to its various uses and equitable access of renewable energy to all segments of society (Ahmad et al, 2011). Due emphasis must be given on the usage of the renewable energy sources and extensive research and development programs should be conducted for the further development of renewable technologies.

As the domestic energy sources of Bangladesh are extremely limited, the option for importing hydropower from Nepal, perhaps also from Bhutan and India, should be pursued by promoting mutually beneficial GBM regional co-operation on energy .The co-operation regime may include the establishment of a Regional Electricity Grid. Energy sector must be made sufficient through the improvement of management and operational aspects relating to generation, transmission and distribution. In this context, it is essential to curb the system loss, improve transparency and accountability, remove financial constraints and introduce proper billing system and collection procedures. In Bangladesh the sources of energy consumption are Bio-mass (wood, animal and agricultural residues, municipal waste etc.) which contributes about 65% of the total energy consumption and the remaining 35% stands for commercial sources which are natural gas, oil, coal and hydroelectricity.

In Bangladesh's perspective there are the probable strategies for the development of energy sector ---Political Consensus on energy policyand long term energy policy for the development of energy sector. For that reason political consensus of opinion is necessary among the political parties, so that with the change of political government the decisions are not frequently changed. In the political manifesto the parties should declare their policy on energy with reference to short-marginal financial gain that must fit the national contexts. Political consensus should also be reached on issues related to energy sector reforms and equitable distribution of energy among different geographical areas and socio-economic groups. Energy conservation "Energy Conservation" means reduction in energy consumption by any deliberate action, including improved technology, fuel switching, maintenance and operation of existing technology and other change in behaviour of end users. Although there is Energy conservation law and also good potential to compensate energy demand through energy conservation, no success has been achieved in the past due to the lack of serious actions. Bangladesh has different energy sources. Bangladesh has moderate reserves and resources of natural gas. With the latest gas field found in Narayanganj, now there are 26 discovered gas fields in Bangladesh. By ensuring local demand export of natural gas from reserved gas fields may facilitate medium to long term energy security. Traditional energy sources (e.g. coal, LPG) should be substituted with commercial energy. Bangladesh is moving towards renewable energy sources, like solar power, wind power, bio-gas, bio-diesel etc. Apart from these, it has established a nuclear power plant in order to generate electricity.

Maldives

The South Asian tiny republic Maldives is a vulnerable state in all terms. It is a dependent country. The tourism based economy of Maldives depends upon uninterrupted energy supply. It has no own conventional energy sources. The Maldivian economy continues to be plagued by large budget deficits. The budget deficit was about 16% of GDP in 2010 and dropped to 10% in 2011. Government expenditure was 41% of GDP and revenue was about 28% of GDP. Recent large budget deficits have led to a sharp build-up of public debt, prompting the World Bank and the International Monetary Fund (IMF) to classify Maldives as being at moderate risk of debt distress. In December 2009, the IMF approved a $93 million loan for the country. After the first two disbursements, the IMF withheld subsequent disbursements due to concerns that the budget deficit must be further reduced. Maldives is facing a foreign exchange shortage. The official exchange rate against the U.S. dollar was rufiyaa 12.8 in 2012. It is dependent for its fuel on the Middle-East countries. It has no own sources of conventional energy. Maldives is moving towards renewal-green energy. Due to its geographical position, solar and wind power have been popularised in domestic purposes in a number of islands.

Sri Lanka

The combination of rising oil prices and increasing domestic demand for energy in middle-income Sri Lanka places a higher premium on achieving energy security. The concept of energy security involves the association of national security and the availability of natural resources for energy consumption. In particular, it entails the provision of affordable power to the population while reducing dependence on volatile global oil markets. Sri Lanka will experience considerable demand-side pressures for energy. The demand for fuel for transport will grow two and a half times by 2020 (75% of fuel is used for transport). In addition, the demand for power is expected to grow by 5.2% per annum (20% of imported oil is used for power generation).

In a context of rapidly increasing demand, the challenge for energy policy is to reduce the dependence on imported energy by developing supplies within the country. In 2013, oil imports amounted to $4.3 billion and accounted for 24% of all imports. In 2012, the corresponding figures were $5 billion and 26% respectively. (Thermal generation was higher due to less recourse to hydro power as a result of lower rainfall.) As the economy becomes more complex and income rises, demand for fuel (both transport and power) will rise. On the transport front, higher levels of economic activity will result in more haulage and rising incomes will lead to more private vehicles. In the power sector, demand will increase from both industries, fuelled by a more complex economy and households driven by rising incomes. At present, biomass accounts for about 40% of energy consumption. This figure will decline due to both higher incomes and increased urbanization. It is noteworthy that while the CEB has a plan to meet increasing demand for power, there is no such plan for the transport sector which accounts for 75% of fuel consumption. This is the current state of affairs despite the fact that fuel consumption is expected to increase much faster than power-250% as supposed to 50% from a much higher base, by 2020.There is need, therefore, for an integrated multimodal transport plan which attaches high priority to fuel conservation/efficiency and balancing the Supply and Demand to increase energy security .

The key challenge for strengthening energy security is to increase supplies to meet rising demand, while reducing the dependence on imported oil in a global context where its price is expected to increase steadily. At present, thermal generation (diesel, heavy oil, naphtha & coal) accounts for 70% of the energy supply; and hydro: 30% (includes other renewables). The whole thrust of future energy management should be to reduce the dependence on thermal generation, which not only absorbs valuable foreign exchange, involving very high opportunity costs, but also results in high unit costs. The way ahead needs to encompass the following: (1) exploring potential hydro capacity in the non-Maheweli river networks; (2) increasing renewables; (3) examining the role of coal, taking into account both direct as well as the indirect costs (externalities associated with the carbon footprint); and (4) maximizing the benefits of the discovery of commercial quantities of natural gas in the Manner basin. The challenge is to develop the optimal generation mix to maximize energy security at the lowest possible unit cost. The PF will publish shortly a follow-up note which will seek to examine these issues, particularly in the light of the natural gas discovery which is a potential game-changer for Sri Lanka's energy security. The uncertainty regarding power supplies/costs being created by the current drought only adds greater urgency to the need for decisive policy action.

Afghanistan

Afghanistan is a war-torn country. Over the decades, it has witnessed a number of wars and terrorist attacks. Being a vulnerable country it is facing lot of problems. The process of industrialization has not been started yet. Modernization and development depends upon a countries political economy. Energy security ensures a country to move towards economic growth. Due to energy deficiency Afghanistan could not be an industrial hub. It is a big territory without any significant production. The essence of energy security was lately realized by the Afghan leaders. It has no adequate indigenous technology to extract the own fuel. On the other hand, due to vexed relationship between politics and development the issue of energy security could not be processed properly. The thinking about alternative sources still has not been properly materialized. The shadow of Taliban regime had badly affected the country's economic structure and energy outlook.

Afghanistan has made great strides in improving electricity access for its people since 2001. However, it is still a long way from achieving energy security as it suffers from inconsistent energy supply and lack of development of indigenous sources of power. The findings reveal significant political, security and technical challenges in all three areas. First, the state of bilateral relations between Afghanistan and some Central Asian states, in addition to capacity issues within their borders, raise questions about reliability of these countries as suppliers in the long run. Furthermore, Afghanistan's efforts to develop its hydro power potential to achieve self-sufficiency could also draw it into conflicts with the Central Asian countries as it would undermine the supply of water to Afghanistan's neighbours from these trans-boundary rivers. To minimise the risk of such conflicts, it is important that Kabul promotes dialogues with its neighbouring countries over water-sharing. Finally, the potential of Afghanistan as a transit hub remains contingent on the prevailing geopolitical and security situation on the ground. The countries involved in trans-national energy projects should explore possibilities of co-opting insurgents into the system incentivising them to keep these projects running. The publication is part of a joint collaboration of the FES Regional Peace and Security Programme, FES Kazakhstan and the FES Afghanistan office (https://www.fes-asia.org/news/afghanistans-energy-security-tracing-central-asian-countries-contribution).

Besides the vast potential in renewable sources of energy, Afghanistan has also substantial hydrocarbon resources that may bolster Afghanistan's energy security and, in turn, economic growth. The December 2011 study by the US Geological Survey (USGS) estimated that Afghanistan is endowed with potentially exploitable reserves of 1.596 billion barrels of oil and 36.462 trillion cubic feet of natural gas, with the Amu Darya Basin and the Afghan-Tajik Basin holding "18 times the oil and triple the natural gas resources previously thought." Afghanistan could, for instance, utilize its domestic gas supplies for electricity generation to lower its import dependence on gas-generated electricity from Uzbekistan and Turkmenistan and use its own domestic oil supplies to lower its dependence on imported diesel fuel. To harness its potential, Afghanistan's energy sector requires investment. Investment, however, requires security which is as scarce as access to electricity in Afghanistan.

Nepal

Nepal has been suffering from the chaotic energy crisis for about a decade now despite having a potential for generating 43,000 MW of hydroelectricity, 2,100 MW of solar power, and 3,000 MW of wind power. The normal life of its citizens is being crippled with long hours of load shedding and never ending queues in front of the gas stations reflecting the state of the energy-hungry country. The strategic advantages to potential investors are explored that encourage investments into national priority projects facilitated by the progressive policies of the Government of Nepal (Understanding Energy Crisis in Nepal, 2016).

Generally, developing an electricity power system is extremely capital intensive, and hence, it requires substantial financial capital as well as adequate technical expertise contributed both from the private and public sectors. In Nepal, the electricity imported from India accounted for 27% of the total energy supply in 2014/15 while growing steadily year after year (Nepal Electricity Authority, 2016). The never-ending power shortages also gravely affect the Nepal's industrial sector. On the other hand and importantly, a large unfulfilled domestic demand for energy represents a great opportunity for potential investors, with or without export prospects. In addition, the Government of Nepal (GoN) has been very proactive recently in formulating the long-term economic visions with the aim of removing Nepal out of the LDC status by 2022 to a Middle Income Country by 2030(Ministry of Finance, 2016). The vision 2030 will require the transformation of subsistence-based farming into a large-scale commercial agriculture, and also a massive upgrading of the currently dismal industrial base. The GoN has made a crucial step towards the country industrialization by adopting Special Economic Zone Act which offers attractive facilities and privileges to the export-oriented industries. However, all these initiatives will create huge additional demands for the electricity. It is therefore critical that Nepal starts implementing its energy policies and effectively manage the deficits of its electricity supplies.

Bhutan

Bhutan does not have any act or legislation that addresses energy efficiency, and given the low energy costs, end users can have little motivation to implement energy efficiency. The Royal Government of Bhutan (RGoB) recognizing the need to promote Energy Efficiency to enhance energy security had initiated studies like BEEBS and energy efficiency in buildings sector. Furthermore, the Alternative Renewable Energy Policy (AREP) states that a separate Energy Efficiency Policy shall be developed (DRE 2013). India has a regulatory authority set up by the Government of India called Bureau of Energy Efficiency, whose sole responsibility is to enhance energy efficiency in India. There is a need of a similar champion or legal regulatory body in Bhutan which is dedicated to enhance Energy Efficiency (Jamtsho, Sherab2015:96).

Bhutan is a small Himalayan kingdom with nearly 0.8 million population. Being one of the poorest nations in the world, Bhutan has achieved a significant economic progress in recent years. Export of hydropower contributes most of its foreign exchange (over 85%). It has one of the largest hydropower potentials in the world. Only 5% of the total hydropower potential is currently being utilized. The government of Bhutan has developed a master plan to tap this green energy resource to generate power not only for domestic use but also for export to surrounding countries. Bhutan has no fossil fuel (liquid fuel or gas) reserves except 1.3 million tonnes of coal reserves in the south-western region from which it extracts approximately 1,000 tonnes per year for domestic consumption. It imports liquid fuel over 1,000 barrels per day for automobile and other essential uses Nevertheless, Bhutan's energy mix consists West Bengal (India) Assam (India) Wang Chhu River system Tibet (China) Amo (Torsa) Chhu River system Puna Tsang Chhu River system Drangme Chhu River system Tibet (China) 588 FirozAlam et al. / Energy Procedia 110 (2017) 586 – 591 primarily of hydro resources. At present, overall, 99.5% of power is generated from hydropower. It is one of the main drivers of Bhutan's US$1.91 billion economy, accounting for a fifth of GDP in 2016 .Bhutan has vast hydropower resources. Its first hydropower plant was established in 1967 to supply power to the capital, Thimphu (Jenkins, 1991).

COLLECTIVE INITIATIVE FOR ENERGY SECURITY: THE SOUTH ASIAN DILEMMA

South Asian States are immensely realizing the hard-core fact of energy crisis. There is a sea-gap between demand and supply. SAARC can be a common platform to mitigate the energy crisis. But there are lot of problems to materialize this. The economy and politics of member countries are different. It is very difficult to convergence of interests of member countries. The relational equations among the member countries are very complex, for instance Indo-Pak, Indo-Sri Lanka, Indo-Bangladesh, Indo-Nepal relations. India is the core state in South Asia. Pakistan is periphery and rest are periphery. Nevertheless, India has tried to secure energy for Nepal and Bhutan by providing its own technology and fund. Now, the influence of extra regional power has been determinant factor for energy security programme in South Asia. However, there are some factors in energy cooperation in South Asia---(1) the technical strains that near double-digit economic growth are putting on India's dilapidated power infrastructure, (2) the economic costs the country is incurring by increasing reliance on the Middle East for oil and gas resources; (3) the prospects for expanded wind, solar, energy efficiency and nuclear power generation in India to help reduce the nation's growing carbon footprint as it accelerates the use of coal; (4) the implications of Pakistan's expanded use of coal; (5) an analysis of how poor energy pricing systems are bringing about an energy shortage throughout the region (6) an examination of how strains in Indo-Bangladesh relations threaten the construction of vital regional energy infrastructure projects; (7) a discussion of how continued political . There is a dilemma in securing energy security among the SAARC countries due to aforesaid factors.

Alternative Policy Option

It is clear that all of the South Asian states are suffering from acute energy deficiency. No states has its own energy reserves sufficiently. The major threatening issue for this region is to arrange alternative sources of energy. Few states have initiated to generate energy through alternative channels. They are hiring technologies from developed countries. Solar power, wind-mill, bio-gas, bio-diesel have been marked as alternative sources of energy. Is it possible to supply energy for a vast populated country through the alternative sources? In recent years, a number of SAARC Summits held in different cities of South Asia. Security issue got priority in discussion. But that is only terrorism issue. Energy security issue partially discussed by the members. Energy security could not be a key issue in SAARC summits due to divergence policy orientation of the member countries. Due to absence of mutual trust and lack of confidence building measures SAARC could not be a platform to mitigate the energy crisis.

Hence, some countries are importing electricity from other neighbours. Bangladesh is importing electricity from Bhutan and India. On the other hand, due to the geographical isolation Sri Lanka and Maldives are not able to import surplus electricity from other South Asian neighbours. As I have mentioned in earlier that Sri Lanka and Maldives are not in a position to explore the alternative sources of energy through their indigenous technology. As far as alternative sources are concerned, same thing is applicable for Nepal, Bhutan and Bangladesh. If SAARC countries are connected with a common grid, then it would be very helpful for the member countries. SAARC is to be formed an energy taskforce immediately, as it can start to invent alternative energy sources within a common platform. The reserve of conventional energy is limited. Energy supply is also matter of diplomacy and compulsion. Any time it can be restricted. The thinking of green energy has been popularized among the South Asian states. This is the high time to materialise the green energy projects in SAARC. Without it the notion of sustainable development can't not be implemented.

CONCLUSION

South Asia has witnessed a growing imbalance between energy demand and its supply from indigenous sources resulting in increased import dependence. Energy endowments differ among the South Asian countries. However, access to the significant energy resources in the neighbouring countries is denied, which increases the cost of energy supply and reduces energy security of the individual countries and of the region as a whole. The countries in the region could benefit significantly only by strengthening the mechanism of energy trade through improved connectivity. Therefore, greater cooperation within South Asia could be one of the most effective ways to deal with this Regional Energy deficit and ensure Energy Security of the Region. A common policy is to be implemented immediately in South Asia in order to continue the process of sustainable development.

REFERENCES

Ahmad, Q. K. B., Asit, K., Rangachari, R., & Sainju, M. M. (Eds.). (2001). Ganges-Brahmaputra-Meghna Region: A Framework for Sustainable Development. University Press Limited.

Alam, M. B. (2012, December). Significance of Africa in India's Foreign Policy. *World Focus*.

Delegation to Visit Myanmar for Oil Deal. (2001, February 8). *Hindustan Times*.

Dhakal, D. N. S., & Jenkins, G. P. (1991). *International Trade in Energy: The Chukha Hydroelectric Project in Bhutan*. Harvard Institute for International Development.

Energy Politics: India –Bangladesh –Myanmar Relations. (2007). IPCS Special Report, Institute of Peace and Conflict Studies.

Gas Utilization Report. (2002). *Committee Report on Utilization of Natural Gas in Bangladesh*. Author.

International Energy Agency. (2015). *Energy and Climate Change*. World Energy Outlook Special Briefing for COP21. IEA.

Jamtsho, S. (2015). Sustainable Energy in Bhutan: Opportunities for Energy Efficiency. *The International Journal on Green Growth and Development, 1*(2), 75–102.

Khan, Z-u-I. (2013). *India's Middle-East Energy Strategy*. Aljazeera Center for Studies.

Krepon, M., & Haider, Z. (2005, April 19). A Pipeline for Peace? *The Indian Express*.

Kukreja, V. (2005). Pakistan's Political Economy: Misplaced Priorities and Economic Uncertainties. In Pakistan: Democracy, Development and Security Issues. Sage Publications.

Mahalingam, S. (2005). Politics of the Iran-Pakistan –India Gas Pipeline Project. In I. P. Khosla (Ed.), *Energy and Diplomacy*. New Delhi: Konark.

Mahmood, T., & Muhammed, T. A. (2008). Energy Security And Economic Growth In Pakistan. *Pakistan Journal of Applied Economics, 28*(1).

Ministry of Finance. (2016). Final Economic Survey. Government of Nepal.

Mistry, D. (2011). Domestic and International Influences on India's Energy Policy, 1947-2008. In India's Foreign Policy: Retrospect and Prospect. Oxford University Press.

Nepal Electricity Authority. (2016). A Year in Review 2015-16. Author.

United Nations. (2016). *The Sustainable Development Goals Report 2016*. New York: United Nations.

World Bank. (2013). *End Excrement Poverty - Promote Shared Prosperity*. Author.

Zadzorova, N. (2015, October 4). How has China been Safeguarding Its Oil Imports from Middle East and Africa. *E-International Relations Studies*.

KEY TERMS AND DEFINITIONS

Alternative Policy: When existing policy failed to resolve the crisis then policymakers think other options in order to mitigate the problem. It is called alternative policy.

Economic Growth: Economic growth has also been driven by productivity gains. That measures how much each hour of worker time produces in output. Its free market economy encourages technological innovations.

Energy Security: Energy security as the uninterrupted availability of energy sources at an affordable price. Energy security has many aspects: long-term energy security mainly deals with timely investments to supply energy in line with economic developments and environmental needs.

Least Developed: Least developed countries are those countries which are facing economic challenges, low rate of human development index, unemployment, illiteracy, etc.

Middle-Income: Middle-income indicates the status in between lower-income and high-income group.

SAARC: South Asian Association for Regional Cooperation (SAARC) was formed in 1985 looking at greater regional cooperation among the South Asian States. Primarily there were seven states, namely, India, Bangladesh, Pakistan, Nepal, Sri Lanka, Bhutan, and Maldives. Afghanistan is the new member of SAARC. Now total number of members is eight.

Sustainable Development: Sustainable development is development that meets the needs of the present without compromising the ability of future generations to meet their own needs.

About the Contributors

Ramesh Chandra Das is currently Associate Professor of Economics at Vidyasagar University, West Bengal, India with twenty years of teaching and research experience in undergraduate and post graduate levels. He has obtained Masters, M. Phil and Ph. D Degree in Economics from the University of Calcutta. Dr. Das has contributed several research papers to national and international journals with reputations along with completions of three minor research projects sponsored by UGC, India. He has written one text book on Microeconomics and one Macroeconomics (coauthored) for different fields of students and academicians and edited a list of handbooks on Globalization, Investment and Growth, Global Indicators of Economic and Political Convergence, Infrastructure Development and Social, Health, and Environmental Infrastructures for Economic Growth, Military Expenditure and Microfinance, etc. all published by IGI Global, USA. He has been acting as editor-in-chief in Asian Journal of Research in Business Economics and Management and one of the editorial advisory board members of Society for the Study on Business and Finance.

* * *

Henry Thomas Asogwa was born on 2nd September, 1982 at Otukpo, Benue State, Nigeria. He has M.Sc in Economics from University of Nigeria, and is currently a Ph.D Student at Nnamdi Azikiwe University, Awka in Anambra State, Nigeria.

Abiola Ayopo Babajide is an Associate Professor (Development Finance) in Department of Banking & Finance, College of Business & Social Sciences, Covenant University, Ota, Nigeria. She holds a Ph. D degree in Finance, obtained in 2011. She is an associate member of the Institute of Chartered Accountant of Nigeria (ICAN), and a member of American Finance Association. She writes and present widely on Development Finance – Microfinance, Entrepreneurship/Small Business Finance and Capital Market Development. She has published in reputable local and international outlet.

Kinkini Bhattacharjee has obtained her bachelor and master degree in Economics from the University of Burdwan with good marks. She is presently working as guest lecturer in the Department of Economics, Katwa College, West Bengal, India. She has research interests on quantitative economics. Besides, she is doing bachelor degree in education.

Mainak Bhattacharjee is presently an Assistant Professor in Economics at Loreto College, Kolkata, India. He has also worked in the same post in The Heritage College, Kolkata, India. He has obtained masters in Economics respectively from the Jadavpur University. He has been working in the areas of Macroeconomics and International Trade. He has produced many research articles published in reputed journals.

Rajib Bhattacharyya, Ph.D (Economics), is at present an Associate Professor in Economics at Goenka College of Commerce & B.A, Kolkata, India. He has 18 years of teaching experience at UG and 9 years at P.G. level. His fields of interests are International Trade and Finance, Development Economics, Women and Development. He has contributed a good number of articles in national and international journals/books in different areas of international economics and women entrepreneurship development.

Anandita Biswas is currently Assistant Professor in the Department of Political Science at Diamond Harbour Women's University, West Bengal, India. She has obtained her BA, MA and M. Phil degree from the Calcutta University. She has about eight years of teaching and research experience. Her areas of research lie in Contemporary Indian Politics with special interest on Religion, Language and Caste Politics. She has a number of articles published in recognized books and journals.

Zehra Nur Canbolat is a Research Assistant of finance at Istanbul Medipol University, Faculty of Economics and Administrative Sciences, Istanbul-Turkey. She received her master degree from Marmara University from quantitative methods. She is a PhD candidate in Management and Strategy program in Istanbul Medipol University. Her research interests lie in quantitative methods, data science, web mining, text mining.

Prabal Chakraborty is presently working as Assistant Professor in Management at NSHM Knowledge Campus, Durgapur, India. He is pursuing PhD from JIS University, Kolkata, India. He successfully completed MBA from Institute of engineering & Management. He is doing research on - various fields of Marketing, Healthcare Management, and Healthcare Economics. He has presented his papers in 15 conferences and has published 5 research papers in reputed journals. Prior to join in academics he worked in different reputed organisations- SRL Ranbaxy, Novartis, Gland Pharma and more than fifteen years of working experience in corporate sector. He also worked as Area Manager, Regional Manager, and Marketing Manager with a good number of team members.

Tonmoy Chatterjee, PhD, is an Assistant Professor in Economics at Ananda Chandra College, West Bengal, India. He has also served as faculty member in the Department of Economics of Sidho-Kanho-Birsha University, West Bengal. He has worked as Research Assistant in Centre for Studies in Social Sciences, Calcutta, for World Bank project (under CTRPFP). Dr. Chatterjee has obtained Prof. M. J. Manohar Rao Award from the Indian Econometric Society for the best research paper in 2012. He has published a number research articles in several international and national journals of economics including Review of Economics, International Journal of Sustainable Economies Management, Economic Affairs, Foreign Trade Review, The Pakistan Development Review etc., and also in various international edited volumes.

Kanchan Datta is an Associate Professor of Economics in the University of North Bengal. He obtained his Ph.D degree in the year 2010 from the University of North Bengal. Dr. Datta has published many research papers in various journals and also has participated in many national and international conferences. His special interest is in Time series Econometrics. In the University he teaches Basic plus Advanced Econometrics and Advanced International Economics. He was the Head of the Department during the time period 8th July 2015 - 7th July 2017. He is an editorial board member of UGC affiliated Journal 'Economic Affairs'.

Hasan Dinçer is an Associate Professor of Finance at Istanbul Medipol University, Faculty of Economics and Administrative Sciences, Turkey. Dr. Dincer has BAs in Financial Markets and Investment Management at Marmara University. He received PhD in Finance and Banking with his thesis entitled "The Effect of Changes on the Competitive Strategies of New Service Development in the Banking Sector". He has work experience in the finance sector as a portfolio specialist and his major academic studies focuses on financial instruments, performance evaluation, and economics. He is the executive editor of the International Journal of Finance and Banking Studies (IJFBS) and the founder member of the Society for the Study of Business and Finance (SSBF).

Moumita Ghosh passed M.Sc. in Economics from the Kalyani University, West Bengal, India in the year 2013. She was awarded the M. Phil degree in Economics from Vidyasagar University, West Bengal, India, in the year 2017. The title of her M.Phil dissertation was "Renewable Energy Development in India with Special Reference to West Bengal."

Adem Gök is currently employed in Department of Economics at Kırklareli University, Turkey since 2016. He received his bachelor degree from Boğaziçi University, Turkey. He holds a Ph.D in Economics from Marmara University since 2016. His main research areas include economic growth, economics of governance and foreign direct investment.

Deniz Güvercin earned the doctorate degree from Bilgi University (2015), and Master of Science degree from Istanbul Technical University and Iowa State University. He is an Assistant Professor in Economics at the Istanbul Arel University, Turkey. He delivers classes on Macroeconomics, International Economics, and Financial Economics. He has published several papers and book chapters on issues in macroeconomics, international economics and development economics.

Megha Jain is currently teaching as an Assistant Professor at Daulat Ram College, New Delhi and is under pursual of her research in Management (Economics) from Faculty of Management Studies, University of Delhi, India. She is a columnist in Financial Express and presented her various papers and research proposals at IIMs, IITs and University level international conferences.

Sebak Kumar Jana is currently Professor of Economics in the Department of Economics with Rural Development, Vidyasagar University, West Bengal, India. Dr. Jana was graduated from Presidency College, Kolkata in 1989 and did his post graduation in Economics from University of Calcutta in 1991. He obtained M. Phil. and Ph.D. degree in Economics from Jadavpur University, Kolkata. His major area of academic interest includes environmental and resource economics, rural development and economics of education. He has about seventy publications in Journals and in edited books. He, as Principal Investigator, has completed a few research projects funded by ICSSR, UGC and NABARD and IWMI.

Asim Kumar Karmakar is currently Assistant Professor in Economics, School of Professional Studies, Netaji Subhas Open University, Kalyani, West Bengal, India (Formerly Assistant Professor Department of Economics, Jadavpur University, India) . He obtained his Ph. D degree in Economics from Jadavpur University, Kolkata in 1998. He has contributed more than 100 research papers in reputed journals and edited books viz Springer, IGI Global at home and abroad, and written books on different fields of economics. Dr. Karmakar has co-authored 9 text books. His areas of research interest are Indian Economy, International Trade, Finance and Environmental Economics.

Adekunle Adetiloye Kehinde teaches International Finance at Covenant University, Ota Nigeria where he obtained his PhD. Before venturing into academics, he was a banker in the mortgage industry in Nigeria where he spent considerable time. He teaches other finance courses such as International Finance and Financial Systems, Real Estate Finance and Investments and others. He also performs other functions in the Department of Banking and Finance at Covenant University. He has published a number of articles in both national and international journals. He is the winner of the Best Paper Award of IAABD conference in 2012.

Poulomi Khasnobis has completed Masters Degree and M. Phil in Economics from Burdwan University, India. Currently she is working on a ICSSR project, titled 'Is Internal Migration and Inclusive Development?' Also she is pursuing her Ph.D on crime and economics in University of Burdwan.

Sidhartha Sankar Laha is Assistant Professor of Economics at Tufanganj College, Cooch Behar, West Bengal. He did M.A in Economics and Ph.D. on International Economics in the North Bengal University, India. He has published number of articles in the reputed research journals and also contributed few edited books and has completed few research projects of University Grants Commission and Indian Council of Social Science Research. Dr. Laha has presented papers in national and international seminars and workshops. He is specialised in the area of international economics, rural development, research methodology and health economics and a member in the editorial board of UGC approved journal East- India Journal of Social Sciences. Currently, he is working as a Coordinator, Department of Economics, Cooch Behar Panchanan Barma University.

Sudhansu Sekhar Mahapatra is presently functioning as Associate Professor in the Department of Commerce, Sikkim University, Gangtok, India. Prior to his joining Sikkim University in 2014, he was working as Associate Professor and Head, Department of Commerce in Sikkim Government College. For a brief period, he was Principal of Sikkim Government College, West Sikkim. A doctorate in Commerce, Dr. Mahapatra has 28 years of teaching experience at College and University level. He has published a number of articles in reputed journals. He was a member of Academic Council of Sikkim University.

Amit Majumder is presently working as Assistant Professor & Head of the Department of Commerce (UG &PG), Bijoy Krishna Girls' College, Howrah since. He is also a visiting Faculty, Department of Commerce, University of Calcutta. Dr. Majumder had sole authored 2 books from international publisher from Germany and contributed in 52 edited volumes, 32 nationally and internationally acclaimed peer-reviewed and referred journals. He is successfully supervising the Ph.D. Scholars of University of Calcutta and other national Universities and institutions. His areas of interests are Strategic Management, Corporate Governance, Corporate Social Responsibility, etc.

Debashis Mazumdar has done his MA in Economics from Jadavpur University, Kolkata; M.Phil in Economics from Calcutta University, and Ph. D in Economics from Rabindra Bharati University, Kolkata, India. At present, he is working as Professor of Economics at The Heritage College, Kolkata. Dr. Mazumder was Associate Professor in Bangabasi College under Calcutta University. He is also acting as visiting faculty in the Post Graduate Department of Commerce at Nababullygunge Mahavidyalaya Kolkata, and in the PG (Economics) Section of Indira Gandhi National Open University (IGNOU), Muralidhar Girs' College Center, Kolkata. He has written a good number of text books on Managerial Economics and contributed articles in many national and international journals.

Debasish Mondal is presently Professor at the Department of Economics with Rural Development of Vidyasagar University, West Bengal, India. He has been teaching Economics at the post-graduate level and onwards for over thirty years and supervised a fair number of doctoral works. His areas of work include economic and econometric analysis with focus on methodologies. He has published several articles in some reputed journals on game theory, consumer behaviour, economic inequality and regression techniques and has written two books titled, 'Rural Development: Theory and Experience' and 'Human Development Index: An Essay on Methodology and Implications'.

Subikash Mookherjee is presently Associate Professor as well as Head of the Department of Economics at Mahishadal Raj College, West Bengal, India. He has been teaching Economics and Environmental Studies at the undergraduate level (regular mode) and Environmental Science and Business Economics at the post-graduate level (distance learning education mode) since 2000 AD. He has obtained his M.Sc. and M. Phil degrees from University of Calcutta. His M. Phil dissertation work was in the field of 'Environmental Economics'. Mr. Mookherjee has already successfully defended his doctoral thesis on 'Urbanization of West Bengal' and he has a few good publications on this topic.

Sovik Mukherjee is presently an Assistant Professor in Department of Economics under the Faculty of Commerce and Management Studies, St. Xavier's University, Kolkata, India and a Doctoral Research Scholar in the Department of Economics, Jadavpur University, Kolkata, India. His educational qualifications comprises of a B.A. (Honours Distinction), an M.A. and an M. Phil in Economics from Jadavpur University, India. His areas of interest lie in Environmental Economics, Applied Growth Econometrics, Economics of Financial Crises and Applications of Game Theoretic Models in Industrial Organization. He was awarded with the Ujjayini Memorial University Gold Medal Award by Jadavpur University in 2013 for academic excellence. The Mother Teresa Gold Medal Award 2017 was awarded to him for his contributions in the field of Economic Growth Research by the Global Economic Progress and Research Association, New Delhi. Also, he is a Visiting Research Fellow at NISPAcee, Slovakia for 2019-2020. Besides, he is an Author-Affiliate at Information Resources Management Association, USA and has to his credit research papers published in journals of international repute, viz. Springer, IGI Global, etc.

Aishwarya Nagpal is currently a research scholar at FMS, Delhi University. She is pursuing her research in the area of International Finance. She has teaching experience with Daulat Ram College, New Delhi. She has presented her papers at various forums and many international publications in her credits.

Debasish Nandy (M.A., M. Phil, PhD) is currently working as an Associate Professor and Head in the Department of Political Science at Kazi Nazrul University, West Bengal, India. He has published many research articles in national and international journals and books. Dr. Nandy has done two research projects on South Asian Politics. He is the editor of "International Journal of South & South-East Asian Research". He also appeared on Bengali TV channels as a political analyst. His research interests include South Asian Politics and India's Foreign Policy.

Sanjukta Niyogi has completed M.Sc degree from Burdwan University (India) in Economics. Presently she is doing Ph.D in Burdwan University on the area of environmental economics.

Asish Kumar Pal has been teaching as a Government Approved Part time Lecturer at the Department of Economics, Rabindra Mahavidyalaya, Champadanga, Hooghly, West Bengal. His areas of interests lie in Microeconomics, Development Economics, and Environment Economics.

Jahnavi Patky is FPM Scholar in Human Resource management area at IIM Rohtak. She has completed her Bachelors of Engineering in Electronics and Telecommunication. She belongs to Maharashtra, India. She is currently enrolled in the FPM program of Indian Institute of Management Rohtak. She represented India in BRICS Youth Summit 2018 hosted by South Africa.

Sudhakar Patra received his graduation degree in Economics from Ravenshaw College, Odisha in 1985, Master's degree from Utkal University, Odisha in 1987, M.Phil from Jawahar Lal Nehru University, New Delhi in 1990 and Ph.D from Utkal University in 1993. DrPatra is presently working as Professor of Economics at Berhampur University, Odisha. Dr. Patra has published research papers in International Journals and National Journals and in Edited books. DrPatra has completed four major research projects and has participated in workshops at Asian Institute of Technology, Bangkok, Thailand and Kathmandu. He has visited foreign countries several times to present research papers in International Conferences and chair technical sessions at Bangladesh, Sri Lanka, Thailand and Nepal.

Archana Patro is an Assistant Professor in the Finance& Accounting area at IIM Rohtak. She has done her Ph.D. from Indian Institute of Management Indore. Beforethat, she has completed her MBA in Finance specialization and did her Bachelors in Physics Honours with distinction. Apart from this, she has done her Diploma in IFRS from KPMG. She is Member and student of CIMA – Chartered Institute of Management Accountants.

Kannan Rajagopal earned his B.Sc., MSW, M. Phil., PGDHRM, MBA, PhD in Marketing and PhD in HR from Bharathiar University (Coimbatore) and is associated with SCMHRD, Symbiosis International (Deemed University) Pune. His professional interests include Brand Management and Business Marketing. He has presented research papers in reputed International Conferences in India and abroad. He has 2 decades of work experience in automotive marketing.

Anjan Ray Chaudhury is presently Assistant Professor in Economics at Durgapur Government College, West Bengal, India. He obtained his Master Degree in Economics from the University of Calcutta. He got the Research Fellowship offered by University Grants Commission and worked as a full-time Research Fellow at the Institute of Development Studies, Kolkata. His PhD work was on 'Horizontal Inequality: The Concept, Measurement and Determinants', later on the completion of his Ph.D. work, he has been continuously working on Welfare Economics and International Economics. Dr. Ray Chaudhury has published research articles in some reputed international and national journals.

Meghnath Routh, M.com, is presently working as a guest lecturer in the department of commerce, Sonarpur Mahavidyalaya under the University of Calcutta. Meghnath Routh has presented papers in 4 National and International seminars along with four publications including books and journal. Areas of interest are Corporate Social Responsibility, Goods and Service Tax, Financial Inclusion, Cryptocurrency, etc.

Jayeeta Roy Chowdhury is currently pursuing Ph. D in Economics from Jadavpur University. She has been associated with Loreto College, Kolkata and later on The Heritage College, Kolkata as the Guest Faculty of Economics. Her areas of interest are International Trade and Econometrics.

Kabita Kumari Sahu, PhD, is working as Assistant Professor in P. G. Department of Economics in North Orissa University, Odisha. Dr. Sahu has published about hundred numbers of research articles in reputed National and International Conferences and Journals. She has about 10 years of teaching and research experience to teach Economics to post graduate students of North Orissa Universities of Odisha. She has guided three Ph. D. scholars and 20 M. Phil students of the university.

Subhasis Sen earned his B.Com. (Hons.), MBA, M.Phil., and PhD in Business Management from University of Calcutta and is associated with SCMHRD, Symbiosis International (Deemed University) Pune. His professional interests include Sales & Distribution Management, Services Marketing, Sports Marketing and Strategic Marketing Decisions. He has published research papers in prestigious journals of national and global repute. He has around 2 decades of experience in academics, finance and IT services.

Atanu Sengupta is presently Professor of Economics at Burdwan University, India. He has successfully supervised many scholars in M. Phil. and Ph.D level research works. He has published about 50 papers in various refereed national and international journals such as *Economic and Political Weekly, Sankhya,* and also in various edited volumes. He has also published 8 books in his credit. His areas of interests are in Econometrics, Financial Economics, Development Economics, Microeconomics and Growth Theory. Dr. Sengupta has also authored chapters in several District Human Development Reports of West Bengal.

Partha Pratim Sengupta is Professor of Economics and Head, Department of Humanities and Social Sciences, National Institute of Technology Durgapur, India. He has been teaching at the institute since thirty-five years, out of which twenty years of teaching at PG level and Research. Till now more than twenty students have been awarded Doctorate degree under the supervision of Professor Sengupta. He published more than one hundred research papers in national and international level peer reviewed journals. He has been invited to present papers at several conferences in India and abroad. His areas of research interest include International Economics, Business Economics, Development Economics, and Entrepreneurship Management.

Begum Sertyesilisik is currently Associate Professor at Istanbul Technical University. She has been awarded a PhD at the Middle East Technical University; an MSc at the Istanbul Technical University; a MBA at the Istanbul Technical University; and a BSc in Architecture at the Istanbul Technical University. She has specialized in the areas of sustainable construction project management, construction contracts, project management, sustainability, sustainable built environment, as well as contract and dispute management.

Dipayan Singha, M.com, is presently working as a college contractual in the department of commerce, Lalbaba College and also as a guest lecturer in Ramsaday College under the University of Calcutta. Dipayan Singha has presented papers in 7 National and International seminars along with seven publications including books and journal. Areas of interest are Corporate Social Responsibility, Goods and Service Tax, National Rural Employment Guarantee Act, Women Empowerment, Financial Inclusion, Cryptocurrency etc.

Madhabendra Sinha is currently a Senior Research Fellow in Economics at the Department of Humanities and Social Sciences, National Institute of Technology Durgapur, India. He has obtained the degree of MSc and MPhil in Economics from the University of Calcutta, India. His research interests include International Economics, Time Series Econometrics, Open Economy Macroeconomics, Development Economics and Applied Econometrics etc. He has published and presented more than thirty-five research papers in national and international level journals, seminars, workshops and conferences in India and abroad also.

Joseph Niyan Taiwo is a Senior Lecturer with the department of Banking and Finance, Covenant University, Ota, Nigeria. He holds a Ph.D degree in Banking and Finance, obtained from Covenant University, Ota. His research interest includes Microfinancing, Small and Medium Scale Enterprises, Entrepreneurial Development, Bank Inspection and Practice. He has over fifty journal articles published in reputable local and international outlet. He is a member of the Institute of bankers, London.

Ashu Tiwari has completed her MBA and has four years of working experience in the field of insurance underwriting and claims. She is currently enrolled Ph.D. program of Indian Institute of Management Rohtak in the area of economics and public policy. Before joining IIMR, she has also worked for a project funded by the Norway government at Centre for Economic Studies and Planning in JNU, New Delhi.

José G. Vargas-Hernández, M.B.A, Ph.D, is a member of the National System of Researchers of Mexico and a research professor at University Center for Economic and Managerial Sciences, University of Guadalajara. Professor Vargas-Hernández has a Ph. D. in Public Administration and a Ph.D. in Organizational Economics. He has undertaken studies in Organizational Behavior and has a Master of Business Administration, published four books and more than 200 papers in international journals and reviews (some translated to English, French, German, Portuguese, Farsi, Chinese, etc.) and more than 300 essays in national journals and reviews. He has obtained several international Awards and recognition.

Serhat Yüksel is Assistant Professor of Finance at İstanbul Medipol University, Turkey. Before this position, he worked as a senior internal auditor for seven years in Finansbank, Istanbul, and one year in Konya Food and Agriculture University as an assistant professor. Dr. Yüksel has a BS in Business Administration (in English) from Yeditepe University (2006) with full scholarship. He got his master degree from the economics in Boğaziçi University (2008). He also has a PhD in Banking from Marmara University (2015). His research interests lie in banking, finance and financial crisis.

Index

T

U

V

W

www.ingramcontent.com/pod-product-compliance
Lightning Source LLC
LaVergne TN
LVHW062110300926
849161LV00010B/2424
* 9 7 8 1 5 2 2 5 8 5 4 7 3 *